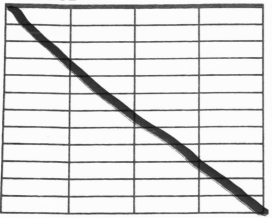

THE AMERICAN DOCTRINE
OF JUDICIAL SUPREMACY

Da Capo Press Reprints in

AMERICAN CONSTITUTIONAL AND LEGAL HISTORY

GENERAL EDITOR: LEONARD W. LEVY

Claremont Graduate School

THE
AMERICAN DOCTRINE
OF
JUDICIAL SUPREMACY

By

CHARLES GROVE HAINES

DA CAPO PRESS • NEW YORK • 1973

Library of Congress Cataloging in Publication Data

Haines, Charles Grove, 1879-1948.
   The American doctrine of judicial supremacy.

   (Da Capo Press reprints in American constitutional
and legal history)
   Reprint of the 2d ed., 1932, which was issued as v. 1
of Publications of the University of California at
Los Angeles in social sciences.
   Bibliography: p.
   1. Judicial review — United States. I. Title.
II. Series: California. University. University at
Los Angeles. Publications . . . in social sciences, v. 1.
KF4575.H29 1973   347'.73   73-250
ISBN 0-306-70569-9

This Da Capo Press edition of *The American Doctrine of Judicial Supremacy* is an
unabridged republication of the second edition, revised and enlarged, published
in Berkeley, California in 1932 as Volume I of the *Publications of The University
of California at Los Angeles in Social Sciences*. It is reprinted by special arrangement with the University of California Press and reproduced by permission from
a copy in the Alderman Library, University of Virginia.

Published by Da Capo Press, Inc.
A Subsidiary of Plenum Publishing Corporation
227 West 17th Street, New York, New York 10011

PUBLICATIONS OF THE
UNIVERSITY OF CALIFORNIA AT LOS ANGELES

IN

SOCIAL SCIENCES

VOLUME I

1932

EDITORS

C. G. HAINES   G. M. McBRIDE
J. B. LOCKEY   L. A. MAVERICK
W. C. WESTERGAARD

THE AMERICAN DOCTRINE
OF JUDICIAL SUPREMACY

BY

CHARLES GROVE HAINES, Ph.D.

Author of *The Revival of Natural Law Concepts, etc.*

SECOND EDITION

Revised and Enlarged

UNIVERSITY OF CALIFORNIA PRESS

BERKELEY, CALIFORNIA

1932

Publications of the
University of California at Los Angeles
in Social Sciences
Volume I, xviii + 705 pages
Issued November 10, 1932

Sales Representatives:

University of California Press
Berkeley, California

———

Cambridge University Press
London, England

(Orders originating in Great Britain only)

Printed in the United States of America

To my Mother

CONTENTS

[ix]

[xi]

APPENDICES

PREFACE

SINCE THE PUBLICATION of the first edition of this work in 1914 a number of special studies have been issued which clarify and explain hitherto unexplored phases of the origin and development of the practice of review of legislation by American courts. Judicial review as the central issue of a national political campaign (1924) led to frequent and thorough public discussions of the controversial matters in relation to this feature of the government of the United States. Economic tendencies and political developments since the Peace of Versailles have brought to the forefront the consideration of the theory and practice of judicial review in foreign countries, its recent adoption in Austria, Czechoslovakia, and Germany, and agitation for its acceptance in other countries. These and other factors have made the principle of judicial supremacy in the interpretation of constitutional terms and principles one of the foremost features of modern constitutionalism.

Few works deal with this interesting and important phase of the American government, hence revision of the volume was deemed advisable in the light of recent contributions. A number of the original chapters were largely rewritten. New chapters were included dealing with English procedure in relation to the review of colonial acts, the theories and ideas involved in the establishment of the American doctrine of judicial review, the

[xiii]

interrelations of politics and federal constitutional law, and some of the postulates and principles on which thinking in relation to judicial review has been based.

Though the main purpose of the volume is to consider the origin and significance of the American doctrine of judicial review of legislation, particularly in relation to federal law and jurisprudence, an introductory chapter treats of the types of judicial review and the peculiarities and limitations which affect its adoption in foreign countries. Supplementary data relative to the review of acts of Congress by the federal courts and judicial review of legislation in foreign countries, together with a selected bibliography, have been presented in appendices.

CHARLES GROVE HAINES

Los Angeles, January, 1932.

PREFACE TO THE FIRST EDITION

IN A PRELIMINARY ESSAY published a few years ago in the Columbia *Studies in History, Economics and Public Law*, I attempted to describe some of the important conflicts which arose over the assertion of the right of the courts in the United States to declare legislative acts invalid. Since the appearance of this essay the authority of the judiciary over legislation has received much attention and the effort to restrict this power has become one of the foremost political issues of the day. Persistent objections to judicial interference with social and economic reform, increasing agitation for the recall of judges and the recall of judicial decisions, and renewed endeavors to limit the range of judicial legislation are tending to bring about some important modifications in the constitutional law of the United States. Notwithstanding the absorbing interest in this feature of American public law, only a few attempts have been made to present an account of its origin and development.

The only works which deal fully with the history and precedents for the American practice of judicial review are the essay on Judicial Power and Unconstitutional Legislation, by Brinton Coxe, published in 1893, and Professor Thayer's account in his article on the "Origin and Scope of the American Doctrine of Constitutional Law," and in his collection of Cases on Constitutional Law, prepared in 1893 and 1895, respectively. These authors have given an authoritative survey of precedents and an analysis of the nature and scope of this practice in

American law, which still present the best treatment of certain phases of the subject. I have used these works freely and have profited by the great contributions made in them. Since 1893 some interesting facts have come to light and the developments of recent years have made it seem advisable to undertake the present volume.

It is the intention of this study to present in brief compass the history, scope, and results of judicial control over legislation in the United States. The aim throughout the volume has been to bring together for consideration the principles which have developed in connection with judicial review and to suggest some of the results which these principles have had upon governmental practice rather than to deal exhaustively with any single phase of the subject. In order to present an accurate survey of the development of the practice of declaring legislative acts void it was regarded necessary to quote fully from early precedents as well as from the opinions which were either favorable or unfavorable to the American doctrine. It is hoped that the many quotations used throughout the volume will not detract seriously from the interest in the account but will tend to show more clearly why this practice was adopted in the United States and may aid in understanding the significance of the doctrine.

Among many authors of recent articles and monographs whose contributions have been invaluable to me, I wish to mention Professor Roscoe Pound. His articles on "Common Law and Legislation," "The Spirit of the Common Law," "The Need of a Sociological Jurisprudence," "The Scope and Purpose of Sociological Jurisprudence" and many other recent papers have presented the matter of the relation of courts to legislation, in historical development and present-day applications, in such a clear and illuminating manner that all investigators in legal history are, indeed, greatly indebted to him. Other articles and treatises have been used freely in particular parts of the study, but my obligations in this respect must be evidenced, so far as is possible, through footnote references.

Professor McLaughlin's excellent essay on "The Power of a Court to Declare a Law Unconstitutional" appeared when this study was almost completed. It was possible, therefore, to use but little this very valuable contribution. The relation of courts to legislation in England has been so exhaustively covered by Professor C. H. McIlwain in his volume, *The High Court of Parliament and its Supremacy*, that it seemed unnecessary to do more than give a sketch of English precedents. Although I have been obliged to disagree with some of the conclusions of Professor McIlwain relative to the importance of precedents favorable to the superiority of common law courts prior to the time of Sir Edward Coke, I have found his thorough examination of the relation of courts to legislation in the English system of government exceedingly helpful.

Professor J. Lynn Barnard, of the School of Pedagogy of Philadelphia, and Professor Thomas Reed Powell, of Columbia University, have been kind enough to read portions of the manuscript and have made important suggestions and corrections. To Professor Charles A. Beard of Columbia University I owe a deep debt of gratitude for his judgment on the general plan of the volume. Dr. S. B. L. Penrose and Professor William R. Davis, of Whitman College, along with Professors Beard and Barnard, have read the proof and have made many improvements in style and content. In the preparation of the manuscript and the reading of proof I have had the constant assistance of my wife, whose helpful suggestions have aided me greatly in putting the material into its present form.

Some of the material offered in this study was published originally in the *Political Science Review* for February, 1908, and the *Michigan Law Review* for November, 1912. Through the kindness of the editor of the Columbia *Studies in History, Economics and Public Law*, I have been granted the privilege of reprinting some of the pages of my essay on "The Conflict over Judicial Powers." The major portion of the earlier accounts has been entirely revised and rewritten so as to furnish a continuous treatment of the development of judicial control over legislation in the United States.

THE AMERICAN DOCTRINE OF
JUDICIAL SUPREMACY

CHAPTER I

TYPES AND CHARACTERISTICS OF GOVERN-MENTS IN RELATION TO JUDICIAL REVIEW OF LEGISLATION

THE PRACTICE of the courts in reviewing legislative enactments and in determining whether or not they are in accord with the expressed or implied provisions of a written fundamental law or constitution evolved as one of the products of political thinking which was characteristic of the late eighteenth and early nineteenth centuries. Political developments of the last century have made this practice a foremost feature of popular or representative government organized under a written constitution. With the adoption of the practice of judicial review by a score or more of nations and with a persistent effort to extend its application to the governments of peoples where it has so far not been recognized, there has developed an increasing interest in this feature of the political system of the United States.[1]

Where judicial review of legislation has been adopted as a feature of the government the actual practice varies greatly—the result of different theories, postulates, and legal customs. It is interesting to compare the operation of this practice under divergent national customs and traditions. And it is suggestive to contrast the results

---

[1] Among the countries which have recently adopted judicial review of legislation are Austria, Chile, Czechoslovakia, Rumania, and Germany.

The problem of "constitutional justice," as Hans Kelsen calls it, is considered of extreme political importance. See Preface to Charles Eisenmann, *La justice constitutionnelle et la haute cour constitutionnelle d'autriche* (Paris, 1928).

which follow from the adoption of the review of legislation by the courts with the actual effects of legislative control over written constitutions.[2]

I. LEGAL CUSTOMS AND PRACTICES WHICH AFFECT JUDICIAL REVIEW OF LEGISLATION

Among the features which modify provisions for judicial review of legislation, is the fact that in continental European systems of government or those whose legal foundations have evolved under the influences and traditions of the Roman law, governmental authority emanates from the executive[3] and is guided by him to a greater extent than is the custom in Anglo-American countries; while the legislature within its narrower scope is conceded to have at least a limited authority to interpret as well as to make laws.[4]   Certain conditions natu-

---

[2] See my "Judicial Review of Legislation in the United States and of Implied Limitations on Legislatures," 2 *Texas Law Rev.* (April 1924), from which portions of this chapter are taken with the permission of the editors.

[3] For the European practice of executive control and domination of the legislature, consult R. C. Brooks, *Government and Politics of Switzerland* (New York, 1920) 94–95.

[4] Consult Léon de Courtois du Manoir, *L'interprétation des lois par le législateur et le principe de la separation des pouvoirs législatif et judiciare* (Paris, 1909), on the interpretation of laws by the legislature in France and in Belgium.

A recent instance of the interpretation of a law by the French legislature occurred when a special act was passed [April 14, 1908] reversing the judicial interpretation of the law relating to the separation of church and state, art. 9, sec. 2, of the law of December 9, 1905. Apropos of this interpretative act which it is claimed terminated twenty thousand suits against the administration of state property J. Barthélemy observes that the right of the legislature to interpret laws has frequently been affirmed as an axiom for which it is superfluous to furnish demonstration. The term interpretative act appears to be used first in the law of April 14, 1908. Authority to enact interpretative laws with retroactive effect, it is claimed, does not violate the theory of the separation of powers and does not encroach on the powers of the judiciary. In French law there does not seem to be a clear distinction between interpretative acts and new laws, though the tendency seems to be to enact fewer interpretative acts. J. Barthélemy, "De l'interprétation des lois par le législateur," 25 *Revue du Droit Public* (1908) 456;

rally result from these facts, namely: the larger part of the rules and regulations relating to individual rights are prescribed by executive officials and frequently separate courts or councils are established to deal with controversies between individuals and public officers; the courts, as a rule, are not permitted to, or in practice do not, follow in an authoritative manner earlier precedents or decisions;[5] the natural deference to executive officers and a traditional non-contentious habit of mind resulting therefrom lead to the acceptance of the authority of administrative officers rather than to a frequent contesting of their authority;[6] and finally, provision is frequently made for "a state of siege" to be declared by the execu-

Gaston Jèze, "Le principe de la non-retroactivité des lois et les lois interprétatives," 41 *Revue du Droit Public* (1924) 167; and Léon Duguit, *Traité de droit constitutionnel* (ed. 2; Paris, 1923) 2:219 ff.

Constitutions frequently contain provisions authorizing the legislature to interpret laws and it is not uncommon for such a clause to be inserted in a constitution which charges the courts with the duty of preserving the written fundamental law. Cf. constitutions of Colombia, 1886, art. 76, sec. 1; Costa Rica, 1871, art. 73, sec. 13; Belgium, 1830, art. 28; Greece, 1911, art. 26; Guatemala, 1879, art. 54, sec. 1; Portugal, 1911, art. 26, sec. 1; Rumania, 1923, art. 36.

[5] In Brazil where the federal courts follow the practice of holding acts of Congress invalid, "the continental European system has in general been followed, which is more inclined to go anew into each case on its own merits, even though the exact point may have been settled in a relatively recent decision. This system avoids the rigidity which characterizes our public law, especially in view of the relative difficulty of amending our constitutions when a judicial decision has interpreted them in such a way as to make amendment desirable. On the other hand, it has the obvious defect of making the law uncertain even with regard to the most fundamental matters of constitutional relations. So frequent have been the instances of conflicting decisions and reversals by the Supreme Court of Brazil that many Brazilian jurists have commented on it adversely."—H. G. James, *The Constitutional System of Brazil* (Washington, 1923) 108. The French Civil Code, art. 5, provides that "judges may not in the cases brought before them, render judgment in the form of general or regulative decrees." It is well known that this provision is not strictly followed in practice.

[6] Referring to the reluctance of the citizen in Argentine to institute proceedings involving a declaration of the unconstitutionality of a legislative act, Dr. Rowe says, "the respect for authority inherited from Spain is so strong that the citizen prefers to abide by the law rather than to test its constitutionality."—*The Federal System of the Argentine Republic* (Washington, 1921) 112.

tive at his discretion or subject to the consent of Congress, during which individual rights and guaranties may, to a considerable degree, be subordinated to the executive power. The frequency of the establishment of the "state of siege" particularly in Latin-American countries militates against the establishment of well defined checks upon executive or administrative powers.[7] Martial law, which in Anglo-American countries is the only thing comparable to the "state of siege," is seldom resorted to and then only when the civil authorities judge that the public necessity requires extreme military measures.[8]

The practice of the review of legislative acts by the courts is affected to no small degree by the control which legislatures exercise over the courts and over the constitution. If the constitution can readily be amended by the legislative chambers with a procedure differing slightly or not at all from that followed in the enactment of laws, the judicial veto of a law, when there is a well formulated popular sentiment on the issue,[9] has the effect merely of delaying action. But if legislative amendment

---

[7] Cf. James, op. cit., chap. 12, on the frequent recourse to the "state of siege" in Brazil and its result in narrowing the scope of protection accorded to individual rights guaranteed by the constitution. In Argentine, says Dr. Rowe, "one is impressed with the frequent use of the power to suspend the constitutional guaranties, and especially the numerous instances in which the circumstances in no way justified such extreme measures."—Cf. Rowe, op. cit., 120 ff. The results of the "state of siege," according to an Argentine jurist, are as follows: "The residence, correspondence, and private papers of the citizen may be seized and searched without previous judicial order; the right of public meeting, of association, the right to carry arms, the freedom of speech and of the press, all these liberties may be denied by the public authority to the extent and according to the standards which it may deem necessary for the preservation or the reestablishment of the public peace." 3 S. C. N. 405.

[8] For the limitations on the application of the rule of law in England during the great war, see W. W. Willoughby and Lindsay Rogers, An Introduction to the Problem of Government (New York, 1921) 95 ff.

[9] The present German constitution permits amendment by legislation with the requirement of a two-thirds vote of both chambers. The constitution may also be amended by a referendum vote (art. 76). Cf. Constitutions of Czechoslovakia, arts. 1 and 2, and of Austria, art. 44.

of the constitution can be made effective only after a new election of members and a second vote in the chambers, there is a possibility that an unfavorable judicial opinion may become a factor in the election and may so influence the popular judgment as to defeat the will of the legislature. In such instances the courts are in a strong position to resist what they may deem a legislative violation of the fundamental law. Furthermore, where the amendment of the constitution requires a popular referendum or action by states in a federal union and the procedure is purposely designed to restrict the amending process, judicial nullification of laws may have a high degree of finality. In the United States the method of amending the federal Constitution was intentionally made difficult. In only three instances have interpretations of the Constitution by the courts been changed by amendments, and in only two of these cases was a veto of a Congressional act reversed by such action.[10]

In countries that adopt written constitutions and either do not insert extensive bills of individual rights or guaranties,[11] or do not include general safeguards— such as the inhibition against the impairment of the obligation of contracts, the prohibition of the denial of due process of law or of the equal protection of the laws

---

[10] The decision in Chisholm v. Georgia, 2 Dall. 419 (1793) that a state might be sued by a citizen of another state was reversed by the adoption of the eleventh amendment. The judgment in Dred Scott v. Sandford, 19 Howard, 393 (1857) that Congress may not prohibit slavery in the territories was set aside by the thirteenth amendment and the decision in Pollock v. Farmers Loan Trust Co., 157 U. S. 429 and 158 U. S. 601 (1895), that an income tax was a direct tax and subject to apportionment to the states on the basis of population was reversed by the sixteenth amendment.

[11] The constitutions of Canada and of France have no provisions guaranteeing individual rights. Frequently where bills of rights are included the enforcement of the guaranties is ultimately controlled by the executive and legislative departments and only to a limited degree by the courts.

—by which legislation is to be controlled, judicial review
has comparatively little opportunity for growth, for
there is practically no basis upon which the courts may
construe implied limitations on legislative and executive
powers. A combination of these and other differences
renders unreliable as between governments any comparison of judicial review of legislation, unless due weight
is given to the variations in legal traditions and political
habits upon which the respective governmental systems
are based.

II. CLASSIFICATION OF GOVERNMENTS IN RELATION TO JUDICIAL REVIEW OF LEGISLATION

Due allowance being made for these and other differences in legal rules and traditions, the governments of
the world may, with respect to judicial review of legislation, be roughly grouped into three main classes:

(a) *Governments in which the legislature interprets
finally the fundamental law.*[12]

---

[12] To this class belong many of the governments of the world. Only
some representative examples may be given. For the constitutional provisions relating to judicial review of legislation, see Appendix II.

Ecuador, 1906. Congress is entrusted with the function of interpreting
the constitution, in an authoritative manner (art. 7).

Belgium, 1830. Following the French theory of the separation of
powers the courts of Belgium are denied the authority to declare legislative acts void.

England. There is no formal written constitution and no authority in
the courts to invalidate legislative acts.

France, 1874–5. Chamber of Deputies and Senate interpret the constitution by ordinary legislative enactments. They must meet in joint
assembly to amend the constitution. The laws prevent the courts from
examining acts to test their constitutionality. Arts. 11 and 12 of the law
of August 5, 1790, Title II and Constitution of September 3, 1790, Title
III, chapter 5, article 3. These provisions are considered in force today.

Italy, 1848. There is no provision for amending the written constitution. The legislative bodies in practice both interpret finally and amend
the constitution.   (*Continued on page 7*)

(*b*) *Governments in which the authority of the courts to interpret finally provisions of the constitution, and, as a consequence, to invalidate legislative acts in conflict therewith, is implied as a necessary requirement to maintain the equilibrium between federal and state governments.*[13]

Japan, 1889. Courts are subject to regulation by the emperor and the legislative chambers, and are subject to these powers in the interpretation of the constitution.

Paraguay, 1870. Congress is authorized to settle doubts which may arise regarding the equilibrium of the three high powers of the state (art. 103).

Peru, 1920. Congress is entrusted with the power of examination of violations of the constitution and the taking of proper measures for fixing responsibility therefor (art. 83).

Poland, 1921. The courts are denied the power to examine into the validity of laws (art. 81).

Spain, 1876. There is no provision for amending the constitution. The legislative bodies interpret and amend the constitution.

Sweden, 1809. Interpretations and amendments of the constitution alike are to be made by the king and the two legislative chambers combined (art. 83).

Switzerland, 1874. The federal legislature has final authority to interpret the constitution (art. 113). Federal and cantonal courts may review cantonal or state acts which are regarded as conflicting with the federal constitution and laws.

In countries such as Belgium and Holland the legislature both interprets and amends the constitution. The amending process, however, requires, after the proposal to amend is offered, a dissolution of the chambers and an adoption of the amendment by the newly elected houses, either by a majority or an extraordinary majority vote.

[13] Argentine, 1860. Acts deemed contrary to the written constitution may be invalidated by state and federal courts. Article 100 authorizes the federal courts to decide all cases which arise under the provisions of the constitution, the laws of the nation or treaties with foreign powers. This provision is interpreted in accordance with the American practice to imply the right to hold void acts deemed contrary to the constitution.

Australia, 1900. Acts may be invalidated by state and commonwealth or national courts. By article 74 appeal to the Judicial Committee of the Privy Council of England is prohibited, unless the High Court of Australia agrees to refer a case to the committee.

Brazil, 1891. Acts may be invalidated by state and federal courts (arts. 59 and 60). Following the reasoning of American judges the federal courts are authorized to try all cases based on provisions of the constitution, or on laws and regulations of the executive.

(c) Governments in which the constitution grants authority to the courts to interpret the constitution and to prevent violations of its provisions.[14]

1. English system of legislative supremacy—

The English system of guaranteeing individual rights is unique. After the great charters of liberty such as Magna Carta, the Bill of Rights, and the Petition of Rights were issued and a body of fundamental law had developed in England, which served to check the royal

---

Canada, 1867. Acts may be invalidated by provincial or state courts, by the Dominion Supreme Court, or by the Judicial Committee of the Privy Council in England. This authority is not expressly granted, but is implied as necessary to define the relations between the Provinces and the Dominion.

Germany, 1919. The highest court is not granted the authority to interpret finally the constitution but may pass on the validity of state acts which are in conflict with the constitution and national laws. The courts have asserted the right to declare acts of the national legislature void.

Mexico, 1917. The federal supreme court is regarded as authorized to invalidate acts which interfere with the individual rights guaranteed by the federal constitution (art. 103).

United States, 1787. Provisions in relation to the grant of authority to declare acts void will be considered in detail later.

[14] Austria, 1920. The supreme constitutional court at the instance of the government may pass on the validity of state and federal laws, on the validity of executive ordinances, and on jurisdictional conflicts. Other courts may not examine the validity of laws duly proclaimed (arts. 89, 137–139).

Bolivia, 1880. The courts are authorized to decide on the constitutionality of laws or decrees (arts. 110, 138, and 139).

Colombia, 1886. The constitution gives the supreme court power to pass on the validity of any legislative act, objected to by the government as unconstitutional (art. 151, sec. 4).

If the president vetoes a bill on the ground that it is contrary to the constitution and the legislative chambers repass it by a two-thirds vote, it may not become a law unless it is approved as constitutional by the supreme court (art. 90).

Cuba, 1901. The supreme court is authorized to decide as to the constitutionality of laws, decrees, and regulations whenever this question is raised by a party to a suit (art. 83, sec. 4).

Czechoslovakia, 1920. The constitutional court shall decide whether laws confrom to the constitution (arts. 1 and 2).

Haiti, 1918. The Court of Cassation shall decide upon the constitutionality of laws. The courts are expected to refuse to apply those laws which have been declared unconstitutional (art. 99).

powers and prerogatives, a revolution occurred by which Parliament became supreme and the king subordinate. After this change Coke's theory, proposed in the great conflict with James I, that reason and the common law as interpreted by the courts must be looked upon as superior to both the king and Parliament, was discarded and by a gradual process parliamentary supremacy was established.

English law then is comprised of fundamental enactments, customs, conventions, administrative orders, and statutes, all of which are equally subject to change by

Honduras, 1894. The courts are expected to refuse to apply laws when they are contrary to the constitution (art. 125).

Irish Free State, 1921. The highest court is authorized to pass on the validity of any law which may be regarded in conflict with the constitution (art. 65).

Nicaragua, 1911. The courts are to apply preferably, first, the constitution and constitutive laws, second, the laws and legislative decrees, and third, the executive decrees and resolutions (art. 122).

Portugal, 1911. The courts in the settlement of cases between private parties are authorized to pass on the validity of laws and to determine whether they are in accordance with the constitution and the principles laid down therein (art. 63). But by article 26 Congress is granted the exclusive power to see to the observance of the constitution and the laws and also to interpret the laws.

Rumania, 1923. The Court of Appeals is to declare inapplicable the laws contrary to the constitution (art. 102). Other provisions seem to qualify seriously this grant of authority (see arts. 36 and 107).

Venezuela, 1928. The federal Court of Cassation is granted the power to declare void the laws of the nation and of the states which are contrary to the constitution (art. 120, secs. 9–13).

The fact that such provisions as the above are in the constitutions does not mean that the courts in practice hold legislative acts void, and in certain instances the power is rarely exercised. There are a few governments in which the power is considered as belonging to the courts to review the acts of coordinate departments, but in which the power has been exercised so infrequently as to have little significance, such as Greece and Norway. In Rumania, prior to 1914, and in South Africa, prior to the establishment of the Union in 1910, the courts asserted the right to hold acts void, but few laws were not applied.

For an account of the practice in Norway, see Mikael H. Lie, *Domstolene og Grunloven* (Oslo, 1923); in Rumania, Gaston Jèze, "L'inconstitutionnalité des lois en Roumanie," 29 *Revue du Droit Public* (1912) 138, 365. A notable decision in South Africa is Brown v. Leyds 4 *Off. Reports*, High Court, South African Republic 17 ff. and 14 *Cape Law Jour.* 71, 2 and 97–106.

the supreme legislative department.[15]   In England the
executive and the legislature, under the designation King,
Lords, and Commons, combine to legislate and to administer the laws; the judiciary and all other public authorities are bound to obey the mandates of Parliament as the
highest power of the state. According to Lord Shaw the
British legislature is supreme and the judiciary is bound.
The power which formulates and enacts laws can choose
its own road; the power which interprets and applies
them follows the path prescribed. The corrective of the
action of Parliament as a human and fallible institution
is not "a legal corrective, lies not with the judiciary, but
lies with Parliament itself, acted upon by a fresh wave
of public opinion, a higher sense of duty, a wider range
of experience or a broader perspective in the regions of
applied justice."[16] In a distinct and well defined sense
the English legislature is supreme and the judiciary is
subordinate.

The judges hold that they cannot act "as regents over
what is done by Parliament with the consent of the King,
Lords and Commons."[17]   There is in England no written
fundamental law and no distinct line of demarcation
between constitutional law and statutory law. Although
the courts determine the nature and trend of law to a
very large extent, it is nevertheless true that the English
nation is governed under a legislative supremacy.[18]

---

[15] See Lowell, *Government of England* (New York, 1910), Introduction,
1–15.

[16] Lord Shaw, Member of Judicial Committee of Privy Council, 45 *Am.
Law Rev.* (April 1911) 275, note, "Where the legislature is free and the
judiciary bound."

[17] Lee v. Bude and Torrington June. Ry. Co., L. R. 6 C. P. 576, 582
(1871).

[18] See Webb v. Outtrim, in which the English Privy Council noted that
whereas the American Union has erected a tribunal which possesses jurisdiction to annul a statute upon the ground of unconstitutionality, "in the
British Constitution, though sometimes the phrase 'unconstitutional' is used

Parliamentary supremacy in England is modified to a considerable extent by what is known as the "rule of law."[19] All officers are held strictly within the law as laid down by Parliament, and the courts of England exercise an extensive review of the acts of public functionaries to see that they keep within the powers granted by law.[20] This, according to Professor Dicey, means, "the absolute supremacy or predominance of regular law as opposed to the influence of arbitrary power. . . . . Englishmen are ruled by the law, and by the law alone; a man may be punished for a breach of law, but he can be punished for nothing else."[21] Under this rule English courts recently held that the King in Council by executive order could not take the property of a citizen during war time for military purposes without awarding just compensation for losses incurred.[22] This practice of the courts,

---

to describe a statute which though within the legal power of the legislature to enact, is contrary to the tone and spirit of our institutions and law, still, notwithstanding such condemnation, the statute in question is law and must be obeyed," (1907) Appeal Cases, 89. On the meaning of the term "unconstitutional" in England, see A. V. Dicey, *The Law of the Constitution* (ed. 7; London, 1908), 516, and Appendix K. Dicey states that "the one fundamental dogma of English constitutional law is the absolute legislative sovereignty or despotism of the King in Parliament," *ibid.* 141. For a discussion and criticism of the modern theory of parliamentary sovereignty, cf., C. H. McIlwain, *The High Court of Parliament and Its Supremacy* (New Haven, 1910), chap. 5 and notes. The use of the term "unconstitutional" is replacing the designation "*ultra vires*" for acts which are regarded as contrary to the British North America Act and the former word is in common use in Australia.

[19] Cf. Dicey, *op. cit.*, chap. 12, where the English rule of law is contrasted with the French *Droit Administratif*. For modification of Dicey's views, see "The Development of Administrative Law in England," 31 *Law Quart. Rev.* (April, 1915) 148; also W. W. Willoughby and Lindsay Rogers, *An Introduction to the Problem of Government* (New York, 1921) 95 ff.

[20] According to a principle of the common law not even the king himself could excuse an illegal act. Sands v. Child, etc., 3 Lev. 352 (1693) and Raleigh v. Goschen, 1 Ch. 73 (1898).

[21] *The Law of the Constitution*, 198.

[22] Re *Petition of Right* (1915) 3 K. B. 649 and Attorney General v. De Keyser's Hotel (1920) A. C. 508; see Leslie Scott and Alfred Hildesley, *The Case of Requisition* (London, 1920).

however, stops short whenever Parliament expresses a clear and unequivocal mandate. For example, the courts of England decided that labor unions were corporations in the sense that they might be sued before the English courts. After an active campaign before the people and in Parliament, an act was passed in effect reversing this decision; the courts thereafter were bound to follow and accept the act of Parliament.[23] In recent years the "rule of law" has been limited by the Defense of the Realm Act during war time and the Emergency Powers Act, 1920, which accorded executive officers summary powers to deal with certain emergencies and also by the wide discretionary powers granted to administrative officers in the making and the enforcement of rules which have the force of laws.[24] But England has no written constitution, and it is generally believed that parliamentary supremacy with corresponding unlimited powers in administrative officers is a natural result where no definite fundamental law has been formulated.

2. *French system of legislative supremacy—*

A different plan of securing individual guaranties was developed in France, where a form of government and of legal principles was adopted, based, in large part, upon Roman law, principles, and practices. Though a declaration of rights was framed in 1789, including most of the individual guaranties of the English charters, the method of securing these individual rights was placed on an altogether different basis. The same theory of the sep-

---

23 Taff Vale Ry. v. Amalgamated Society of Railway Servants (1901) A. C. 426 and Trades Dispute Act of 1906, which reversed this decision.

24 See William A. Robson, *Justice and Administrative Law* (London, 1928), chap. 3.

aration of powers which was thought in America to require judicial review of legislative acts to preserve written constitutions and to protect individual rights was interpreted in France to forbid the judges from interfering in the exercise of legislative powers and to prevent them from suspending the execution of laws.[25] Owing to the resistance of the courts to executive orders and decrees prior to 1789, it was made an offense for a judge to interfere in the affairs of public administration. The result of these provisions and their interpretation is that France and certain other governments which are based to a large extent upon a system of law similar to the French expressly prohibit the courts from refusing to execute laws duly made and promulgated.

While in France the constitution, unlike the situation in England, is a definite written document, it nevertheless gives wide latitude to the legislature and provides only in part for the general organization and distribution of public powers. No bill of rights is included, though certain French commentators claim that the Declaration of Rights of 1789 is a part of the present public law.[26] The French constitution is dependent for its ultimate interpretation on the judgment and will of the legislature. The same bodies that make or amend the constitution, meeting for this purpose in joint session, may interpret its provisions in the form of a legislative act. As a matter of fact few amendments have been added to the

---

[25] See Gaston Jèze, "Le contrôle juridictionnel des lois," 41 *Revue du Droit Public* (1924) 399–401.

Express restrictions on the judges relative to the review of legislative acts were adopted in France because the judges in the old régime in their efforts to check the royal prerogatives claimed the supreme authority in the state.

[26] Léon Duguit, *Traité de droit constitutionnel* (ed. 2; Paris, 1921–1925) 2:161.

constitution and the legislative body seldom passes interpretative acts. There are not many provisions which involve issues of interpretation such as frequently arise in American public law.

To the French, then, the constitutionality of an act has no other purport than that the legislature does not regard the measure contrary to the articles of the constitution. Constitutional law has an insignificant place in the government of France. There is considerable discussion and agitation in France to have the courts declare legislative acts invalid and thereby to place the constitution and certain provisions declaratory of individual rights in a category superior to ordinary legislative enactments. Most Frenchmen who favor the adoption of the principle of judicial review of legislation emphatically declare that they do not wish to adopt the American theory of the separation of powers, the American doctrine of affording protection to vested rights, the broad rule of reason as a requirement for legislative acts under the due process of law clause, and other implied limitations which American judges have interpreted as restrictions upon the exercise of legislative powers.[27]

This does not mean that private rights are without protection in France. The courts, enforcing the rules of law exercise, as in England, an extensive review of the acts of public officers in that they possess the authority of holding executive ordinances illegal and of restraining administrative action either for an excess or misuse of power. Ordinary courts exercise a limited control over administrative action through what is known as *l'exception d'illégalité* whereby they refuse to impose fines for

---

[27] Cf. my article on ''Some Phases of the Theory and Practice of Judicial Review of Legislation in Foreign Countries,'' 24 *Am. Pol. Sci. Rev.* (Aug. 1930) 583 ff.

the violation of illegal ordinances.[28] More effective remedies have been devised by the administrative courts through the *recours pour excès de pouvoir* by which administrative ordinances may be reviewed and declared invalid.[29]

Unlike England, France has a written constitution and she regards it as a rigid document, whereas the Constitution of the United States is thought to be flexible owing to the many changes through legislation and interpretation. France is one of the chief examples of a government with a written constitution and legislative supremacy; that is, where the protection and guaranties of the constitution have their ultimate sanction in the legislature itself, guided and tempered by public opinion—the source of legislative power and authority.

Italy and Poland have followed France in denying to the courts the power to examine into the validity of laws. To this list belong other countries with written constitutions, such as Japan,[30] Spain, and Sweden, in which it is taken for granted that the normal functions of courts do not include the power of examining into the validity of legislative acts. So common is this impression that unless such power is expressly granted to the courts, or

---

[28] See Marc Réglade, ''L'exception d'illégalité en France,'' 40 *Revue du Droit Public* (1923) 393 ff. and James W. Garner, ''French Administrative Law,'' 33 *Yale Law Jour.* (April 1924) 600 ff.

[29] Garner, *op. cit.*, 602 ff.; see also du Clos, *Le recours pour excès de pouvoir* (1906), Jean Appleton, *Les progres recents du recours pour excès du pouvoir* (1917), and Raphaël Alibert, *Le Contrôle juridictionnel de l'administration au moyen du recours pour excès de pouvoir* (Paris, 1926).

[30] In Japan the judiciary can refuse to apply invalid ordinances. As for laws which have been passed by the Diet and sanctioned by the emperor, the courts of law have no power of judicial review, even when they are unconstitutional. The legislative power is supreme and the executive and the judicial powers are under the legislative power. The legislative power has the supreme power to interpret the constitution, and the judicial must be subject to the interpretation by the legislative power.—Naokichi Kitazawa, *The Government of Japan* (Princeton, 1929) 86. See also Tatsukichi Minobe, *Essentials of Japanese Constitutional Law*, 494 ff.

is regarded as necessary to adjust federal relations, it is assumed that the functions of the courts are confined to the interpretation and application of the laws, and this does not include an examination of their validity. The interpretation of constitutional provisions is deemed in the nature of a political act, and by its very nature outside of the authority and jurisdiction of the courts.

3. *Federal Systems of Switzerland, Canada, and Australia—*

A modification of the English and French systems was adopted in Switzerland, where since the Middle Ages some form of federal government has prevailed. In Switzerland the legislature has been regarded as supreme, and has been granted the final interpretation of the constitution. But in order to render a federal system effective and to adjust the relations between the nation and the cantons, the courts were given the authority to review the acts of the cantonal legislatures. The ultimate guaranty, then, of individual rights in Switzerland, as in France, rests with the legislative body as influenced and guided by the public sentiment of the nation. The legislature of Switzerland is the final interpreter of the constitution, subject only to a referendum by which such a decision may be changed. It is worthy of note that Switzerland with a federal form of government and a written constitution deliberately rejected the main feature of the American plan of judicial review, after a careful study and report on the plan by a group of experts.[31]

---

[31] See Georges Solyom, *La juridiction constitutionnelle aux états-unis et en suisse* (Paris, 1923) and Georges Begue, *Étude sur le tribunal federal suisse et specialment sur le recours pour violation de droits individuels* (Paris, 1903).

The federal systems of Canada and Australia, among the governments in group two, carry the principle of judicial review of legislation one step farther than is done in Switzerland. The courts of these countries are regarded as having the right to review all legislative acts both of the states and of the central governments in order to maintain the balance of powers as defined in the constitutions. But judicial review of legislation in such countries as Canada and Australia has a narrow and limited application, for their constitutions contain few provisions for the protection of individual rights and no general phrases such as due process of law or equal protection of the laws, from which implied limitations may readily be interpreted.[32]

Citizens of Canada also take pride in the fact that their courts do not, as they say, meddle with matters of economic or social policy, as did the Supreme Court of the United States in the *Lochner Case*,[33] or the *Minimum Wage Case*.[34] Having no special provisions in the constitution for the protection of acquired or vested rights, corporations or citizens cannot appeal to the Canadian courts for the protection of such rights, unless a branch of the government attempts to assert authority clearly beyond the scope of its jurisdiction. Rate-making, the

[32] William R. Riddell, *The Constitution of Canada in its History and Practical Working* (New Haven, 1917) ; also C. G. Haines, ''Judicial Review of Legislation in Canada,'' 28 *Harv. Law Rev.* (April 1915) 565 and ''Judicial Review of Legislation in Australia,'' 30 *Harv. Law Rev.* (April 1916) 595.

Justice Clark of Australia argues in favor of the implied right of the courts to declare laws void when deemed in conflict with a written constitution. He defends the supremacy of the judiciary whether it exists under a federal or a unitary constitution which ''finds its ultimate logical foundation in the conception of the supremacy of law as distinguished from the possession and exercise of governmental power.''—A. Inglis Clark, ''The Supremacy of the Judiciary, etc.,'' 17 *Harv. Law Rev.* (Nov. 1903) 18.

[33] Lochner v. New York, 198 U. S. 45 (1905).

[34] Adkins v. Children's Hospital, 261 U. S. 525 (1923).

control of public-service corporations, and most other
economic or social affairs are regulated by Canadian
legislatures or commissions established by these bodies,
which operate subject only to review by the legislative
bodies themselves or to an ultimate appeal to the electorate. The primary question is under which jurisdiction,
Provincial or Dominion, a matter of public regulation lies.

4. *Judicial review in Latin American nations—*

Certain South American countries, such as Brazil and
Argentina, not only provide for the review by the courts
of acts of the states, which may be in conflict with national
powers, but also have accepted the American practice of
declaring void the acts of coordinate branches of the government. The Brazilian courts, following the general
purpose to adopt the American system of judicial review,
as defined by Chief Justice Marshall, do not hesitate to
declare void acts of the national congress.[35]   Similar
authority is exercised by the courts of Argentine.[36]

A somewhat limited form of judicial review of legislation has been devised in the writ of *amparo* used in
the Republic of Mexico and in other Latin American
countries. The writ of *amparo* as established in Mexico
was originally designed to authorize the federal courts to
aid every citizen in the preservation of the rights conceded by the constitution. In practice the application of
the writ has been narrowed to the twenty-nine enumerated guaranties in the constitution, and laws will not be
declared void unless one of these guaranties has been
violated. The writ lies only against laws, or acts done by

---

[35] Joao Barbalho, *Constituiçao Federal Brazileira: Commentarios* (Rio
Janeiro, 1902) and Pedro Lessa, *Do Poder Judiciario: Direito Constitucional
Brasilerio* (Rio Janeiro, 1915).

[36] Juan A. González Calderón, *Derecho Constitucional Argentino* (ed. 2,
3 vols.; Buenos Aires, 1923).

public officers. Suit may be brought originally in a district court but the decisions of these courts must be reviewed by the supreme court. Very few complaints arise which involve the constitutionality of laws. Owing to the difficulties which have militated against orderly judicial procedure in the determination of private rights in Mexico, and the limited scope of the writ of *amparo*, it is obvious that legislative acts can seldom be held void under such a restricted form of judicial review.[37]

Judicial review of legislative acts is often confused with or not properly distinguished from other forms of review of governmental acts by the courts. Certain types of review of official acts approach in effect review of legislation, while others have a different significance. It will clarify the ensuing consideration of the peculiarities of the American system of review of legislation by the courts to define briefly some of the more important forms of court review of the validity of official action.

III. TYPES OF JUDICIAL REVIEW

1. *Customary methods of review of official action by courts—*

It is customary in most countries for the courts to exercise a limited control over the acts of subordinate corporations and units of government, such as municipalities and other public organizations, bodies which usually exercise delegated legislative and administrative powers. This form of judicial control is usually referred

---

[37] Judge Benito Flores, "The Writ of *Amparo* under Mexican Law," 7 *Am. Bar Assoc. Jour.* (Aug. 1921) 388.

S. Moreno, *Tratado del Juicio de Amparo* (Mexico, 1902), and Ignacio L. Vallarta, *El Juicio de Amparo y el writ of Habeas Corpus* (Mexico, 1881). See Appendix II, 631 ff.

to as declaring acts *ultra vires,* meaning that the acts of these subordinate corporations or public governmental bodies are void if they attempt to exercise powers beyond those which are expressly or by necessary implication granted to them. Furthermore, it is not uncommon for the courts to require that the acts of these subordinate bodies must be reasonable and to hold certain acts invalid if regarded as unfair or unreasonable. This doctrine of *ultra vires* was familiar to the American colonists since the acts of their legislative bodies might be declared void by the courts as contrary to the terms of their charters. English colonial governments frequently were founded on charters and the practice of the English courts in preventing *ultra vires* acts of colonial authorities resembles the modern system of review of legislative acts. It was this experience which accounted for the use of the phrase *ultra vires* by Canadian and Australian justices when passing on the validity of the acts of their legislative bodies.

Misunderstandings have resulted from the failure to distinguish between review of legislation and judicial review of ordinances and of the acts of subordinate administrative and executive officers, which is a common practice throughout the world. An extensive review of this character is exercised by the English courts under what is known as the "rule of law," and by review in France and other countries with similar political systems of all acts of executive and administrative officers. In Germany where the main body of rules and regulations applicable to the individual is composed of executive ordinances or administrative orders, judicial review of legislation will be greatly limited in its scope.

Another basis for misunderstanding has arisen over the failure to distinguish between review by the courts, as a coordinate department, over the acts of the legislative and executive departments of the same government and the review by national or local courts over the acts of states or provinces in federal systems of government. Where a federal government is established some agency must delimit the powers between the central and local governments. Since the establishment of effective federal systems, common practice has placed this delimitation of powers upon the courts, and the judiciary tests the validity of laws of the states or provinces in order to discover whether they are in accord with the limitations defined in the fundamental written law. This is the practice in Switzerland, where the national courts exercise such powers but are denied the greater authority of passing on the acts of the coordinate departments. Judicial review of subordinate divisions, corresponding to the American states, is established in Australia, in Canada, and in the new German and Austrian constitutions, and comprises the most important part of judicial review in the latter countries. A similar review has been established in the federal systems of Brazil, Argentina, and Venezuela. This type of judicial review needs to be distinguished carefully from the attempt of the courts to pass on the acts of coordinate legislative bodies. It is in the latter field that the courts exercise their most important function in the review of legislation in the United States. A number of federal systems of government like that of the United States provide for review of legislative acts of the states by the state courts—another type of review by a coordinate department over the acts of bodies with a similar status.

2. *American system of judicial review*—

In the government of the United States the courts exercise, first, an extensive surveillance over the acts of subordinate units of government, such as cities and counties, both to keep local authorities within their jurisdiction and to test their acts as to fairness and reasonableness, and this surveillance is often considered a regular part of judicial review; second, all acts, orders, or rules of administrative and executive officers are subject to review by courts to see that they keep within the law and that their powers are not abused to the detriment of the lives, liberties, and property of individual citizens —a type of review which is much more extensive in countries with a civil-law background, such as France and Germany; third, another phase of judicial review in the United States inheres in the control exercised by the courts over acts of the states, which are regarded as in conflict with the federal Constitution, treaties, laws, and regulations (this authority is exercised frequently both by state and federal courts); fourth, the most important part of judicial review in this country is the practice of the courts, federal and state, of declaring void the acts of coordinate departments; for example, the federal courts, in invalidating acts of Congress, and the state courts, in invalidating acts of the state legislatures.

Of even greater significance than the adoption of all four of the above phases of judicial review of legislation in the United States is the fact that a large part of the powers now exercised by the courts in reviewing legislation has resulted from the application to executive and legislative acts of judge-made concepts and restrictions. A considerable part of these restrictions has grown up in connection with the doctrines of according judicial protection to vested rights and of construing implied limitations on legislative powers, developed from such phrases as due process of law and equal protection of the laws, and conceived as inherent in the American concept of free government. It is the extensive authority wielded through these judge-made restrictions which in the latter half of the nineteenth century changed the nature of judicial review of legislation and resulted in the establishment of a broad judicial censorship over all legislation—a censorship which not infrequently led to the charge that the government of the United States was a government by judges.

The distinguishing characteristic of the American system of government is the extraordinary power and position of the judiciary. The people, it is maintained, established in the constitution written limitations upon the legislature; these limitations and the constitutions are superior to any legislative act; it is the function of the judiciary to say what the law is, and if legislative acts are found to be in conflict with the constitution, to declare such laws invalid. Thus the judiciary, a coordinate branch of the government, becomes the particular guardian of the terms of the written constitution. The legislative and executive departments are held within the bounds of authority as understood and interpreted by the judicial power and there is a well marked distinction between constitutional laws and ordinary statutes. Not only does the written constitution require an extraordinary process for its amendment, but there also has developed an elaborate series of precedents and judicial determinations which, with the sanction of the highest court, have the force and effect of the original provisions of the constitution. The constitution and the rules deduced from it are held to be a paramount law before which all statutes and public acts that are not in accord with its provisions must give way. The judiciary has the sole right to place an authoritative interpretation upon the fundamental written law.

The practice of all departments of government to defer to the courts and abide by their decisions, when in a suit between private parties the majority of justices hold that in their opinion a statute or executive order is unconstitutional and therefore null and void, is the most significant feature of constitutional law in the United States.[38] As a result of this rule of interpretation and the customary understandings developing therefrom it is coming to be held that in many respects the judiciary exercises supreme power in the United States.

The authority can be used only in a negative way to prohibit certain lines of governmental activity, and there are well defined limitations and restrictions on the exercise of supreme authority by courts. But after making due allowance for all limitations, it is nevertheless true that the supremacy of the courts extends to a wide field of government activities and that this supremacy is the most significant feature of the government of the United States.[39] The control of courts over legislation, combined

---

[38] See Gaston Jèze, ''Le contrôle juridictionnel des lois,'' 41 *Revue du Droit Public* (1924) 399 ff. in which he attempts to distinguish between the direct control over the constitutionality of laws and the indirect control under what he terms *l'exception d'inconstitutionnalité* similar to the American model.—*Ibid.*, 413.

[39] Sir Henry Maine referred to this peculiar practice of American courts as ''not only a most interesting but a virtually unique creation of the founders of the Constitution. . . . . The success of this experiment has blinded men to its novelty. There is no precedent for it, either in the ancient or in the modern world.''—*Popular Government* (New York, 1886) 217. This statement exaggerates the degree of originality which may be accorded to the founders of the American Government.

with the notion of the supremacy of law as embodied in Anglo-Saxon jurisprudence, constitutes the basis of *the American doctrine of judicial supremacy.*[40]

3. *Supremacy of law in Anglo-Saxon jurisprudence—*

The impression commonly prevails that legislatures make laws, while courts interpret them and determine individual rights in accordance with settled rules laid down, in the main, by legislation. One of the fundamental facts of political organization, namely, that a great portion of the law is made by courts of justice, has rarely received due consideration.

The greater portion of the English law is made by judges and not by legislatures. ''A large part, and as many would add, the best part, of the law of England is judge-made law'' observes Professor Dicey:

that is to say, consists of rules, to be collected from the judgments of the Courts. This portion of the law has not been created by Act of Parliament, and is not recorded in the statute-book. It is the work of the Courts; it is recorded in the Reports; it is, in short, the fruit of judicial legislation. The amount of

---

[40] ''No feature in the government of the United States'' wrote Lord Bryce, ''has awakened so much curiosity in the European mind, caused so much discussion, received so much admiration, and been more frequently misunderstood, than the duties assigned to the Supreme Court and the functions which it discharges in guarding the ark of the Constitution. . . . . There is no part of the American system which reflects more credit on its authors or has worked better in practice.''—*The American Commonwealth* (London and New York, 1888) 1:237, 250. It will be noted that Bryce followed in his treatment the reasoning of Hamilton and Marshall as amplified by American judges, and formed his judgment at a time when judicial review was a relatively unimportant phase of the American government.

''The political power which the Americans have intrusted to their courts of justice is therefore immense. . . . . I am inclined to believe this practice of the American courts to be at once the most favorable to liberty as well as to the public order . . . . the power vested in the American courts of justice of pronouncing a statute to be unconstitutional, forms one of the most powerful barriers which has ever been devised against the tyranny of political assemblies.''—Alexis de Tocqueville, *Democracy in America* (trans. by Henry Reeve; London, 1835) 1:142–144.

such judge-made law is in England far more extensive than a student easily realizes. Nine-tenths, at least, of the law of torts are not to be discovered in any volume of statutes. Many Acts of Parliament, again such as the Sale of Goods Act, 1893, or the Bill of Exchange Act, 1882, are little else than the reproduction in a statutory shape of the rules originally established by the courts.[41]

Enactments like the statute of frauds, it is noted, "have been the subject of so much judicial interpretation as to derive nearly all their real significance from the sense put upon them by the Courts."[42] In the judgment of Professor Dicey, whole branches of modern law are deduced from judicial decisions, or from the doctrines of writers such as Coke, whose dicta are accepted by the courts as law.[43] Law means to the English-speaking people a body of rules enforced by the courts; what they approve and enforce is law, what they refuse to recognize is not law.[44]

The great bulk of the law in this country as well as in England is to be found in the form of case-made law as distinguished from statutory or codified law. Various estimates have been made of the relative proportions of judge-made to statute law. It has been maintained that on a conservative basis three-fourths of all law in Anglo-Saxon countries is made by the courts. An eminent member of the bar in the United States asserted that "the great bulk of our jurisprudence in this country and

---

[41] A. V. Dicey, *Lectures on the Relation between Law and Public Opinion in England during the Nineteenth Century* (New York, 1905) 361, 362.

[42] Dicey, *op. cit.*, 362 and 483, Appendix.

[43] *Ibid.*, 363 and Appendix, 486.

[44] A. Lawrence Lowell, *Government of England*, 2:473. Sir Frederick Pollock believes that, "the best and most rational portion of the English law is in the main judge-made law. Our judges have always shown and still show a really marvelous capacity for developing principles of the unwritten law, and in applying them to questions raised by novel circumstances."— Note, 9 *Law Quart. Rev.* (April 1893) 106.

in England still remains in the shape of case-made law, as distinguished from statutory or codified law."[45] The ruling principle of Anglo-Saxon jurisprudence, is the supremacy of the law as made, interpreted, and applied by courts of justice.

4. *American doctrine of judicial supremacy*—

In addition to the doctrine of the supremacy of law in Anglo-Saxon jurisprudence, the peculiar principle to be found in the law of the United States, which makes the judiciary the special guardian of constitutions and invests the courts with the authority to declare invalid any laws deemed in conflict therewith, establishes in the United States a supremacy of the courts in a sense not recognized in English law. For the supremacy of law in England does not involve to so great a degree a supremacy of the judiciary, since the decisions of the courts are always subject to the superior power of Parliament. While the courts may determine the great bulk of legal relations, the authority of Parliament may be invoked at any time either to correct a judicial procedure or, if need be, to reverse a judicial decision. In practice this high authority is seldom exercised.

The principles of law and political practice which place the guardianship of the expressed and implied terms of written constitutions primarily in courts of justice, and the dominance of judge-made law in accordance with common-law standards and principles, constitute the bases of what may appropriately be termed *the American doctrine of judicial supremacy.* Recognizing

---

[45] William B. Hornblower, "A Century of 'Judge-Made' Law," 7 *Col. Law Rev.* (June 1907) 453, 454.

[46] For use of other phrases to designate this power consult J. B. Thayer, "The Origin and Scope of The American Doctrine of Constitutional Law," 7 *Harv. Law Rev.* (October 1893) 129; Edward S. Corwin, *The Doctrine of*

the limitations placed upon judicial authority by the process of amendment, by the discretion allowed the executive and legislative departments of government with regard to acts which do not permit of judicial control, and making due allowance for the fact that the judicial power may be called into operation only by means of a case involving the interests of private parties, the final word on so many matters of government and law rests with the courts as expositors of the common law and as guardians of written constitutions, that the term judicial supremacy may well be used to designate the peculiar powers entrusted to the federal and state courts in the United States.[47] To present the nature of the American doctrine of judicial supremacy, to trace its development in the law of the United States, and to indicate its importance in the American political system, constitute the purpose of the following pages. The significance of the American practice will be explained and clarified by supplementary notes and comments on the provisions and the legal practices of other countries, relative to the efforts to limit executive and legislative powers, by means of fundamental enactments and superior law doctrines.

Judicial Review (Princeton, 1914); Walter F. Dodd, *Revision and Amendment of State Constitutions* (Baltimore, 1910), 209–253, wherein the power is described as judicial control and judicial veto power with respect to amendment; Horace A. Davis, *The Judicial Veto* (Boston, 1914); William Trickett, "The Great Usurpation," 40 *Am. Law Rev.* (May-June 1906) 356, and "Judicial Nullification of Acts of Congress," *North Am. Rev.*, 185–848 (August 1907); Gilbert E. Roe, *Our Judicial Oligarchy* (New York, 1912).

[47] "The doctrine of the supremacy of law which was evolved to check the usurpations of a king ruling by paramount title has thus been turned into an instrument to control the action of popularly chosen officials and legislators by the supposedly fixed and absolute standards of an abstract Law."—John Dickinson, *Administrative Justice and the Supremacy of Law in the United States* (Cambridge, 1927) 98–99.

CHAPTER II

THE LEGAL AND POLITICAL BACKGROUND FOR THE IDEAS LEADING TO THE REVIEW OF LEGISLATIVE ACTS BY THE COURTS

THE PRIMARY principles formulated as a basis for the American doctrine of judicial review of legislation were: first, that a written constitution is a fundamental law and as such superior to common and statutory law; second, that the powers of the legislature and of the other departments of government are limited by the terms of the constitution—the constitution being in the nature of a commission to the legislature and to other departments of government by which powers are delegated and limitations defined; third, that the judges are expected to enforce the provisions of the written constitutions as the superior laws, and to refuse to enforce any legislative act or executive order in conflict therewith. These principles were supplemented and modified by other theories and postulates which account for their effective application in American law. They acquired their significance in American legal thinking because of a background of ideas inherited from Europe relating to superior fundamental laws and to the origin of such laws in concepts of natural laws or natural rights.

1. *Doctrines of natural laws or fundamental laws*—

The belief that there are superior laws, fundamental and immutable, which guide human conduct, and to which the ordinary rules and regulations made by man must conform, is one of the most important ideas in the evolution of legal thought. A brief account of the history of natural-law ideas and of the significance of their application in the development of constitutional law has been given elsewhere,[1] and it is not necessary to review in detail this history.[2]

The Greeks perceived rather vaguely the idea of fundamental laws as now understood and they instituted a unique plan for their guardianship.[3] In their efforts to establish a rule of law based on the ancient customary rules the Greeks regarded certain laws of such permanence that it was a matter of serious public concern to change them. One of the fundamental principles of Greek thought was the idea of the sovereignty of law;[4] it prevailed widely during the Middle Ages; and it was transmitted to modern times in the form of theories of the *supremacy of law* or of the *reign of law.*

Greek concepts of natural law developed in the Stoic philosophy into what were regarded as guiding principles of reason which were held to be immanent in the

---

[1] See my article "The Law of Nature in State and Federal Judicial Decisions," 25 *Yale Law Jour.* (June 1916) 617, and my treatise, *The Revival of Natural Law Concepts* (Cambridge, 1930), for an account of the growth and influence of natural-law ideas in public law. With the permission of the editors of the Harvard University Press several extracts from *The Revival of Natural Law Concepts* are used in this chapter. Cf. also Edward S. Corwin, "The Higher Law Background of American Constitutional Law," 42 *Harv. Law Rev.* (Dec. 1928 and Jan. 1929) 149, 365, and John Dickinson, "The Law Behind the Law," 29 *Col. Law Rev.* (Feb. and March 1929) 113, 285.

[2] On the history of the law of nature see John W. Salmond, "The Law of Nature," 11 *Law Quart. Rev.* (April 1895) 121; James Bryce, "The Law of Nature," *Studies in History and Jurisprudence* (New York, 1901) 2:556, and Sir Frederick Pollock, "The History of the Law of Nature," *Jour. Soc. of Comp. Legis.,* 2 (1900) 418–433, and *Essays in the Law* (London, 1922) chap. 2.

[3] Sir Paul Vinogradoff, *Jurisprudence of the Greek City* (London, 1923) 138; cf. also G. M. Calhoun "Greek Law and Modern Jurisprudence," 11 *Cal. Law Rev.* (July 1923) 308 and D. Goodell, "An Athenian Parallel to a function of our Supreme Court," *Yale Review,* 2 (May 1893) 64.

[4] See Plato, *The Laws;* also, Ernest Barker, *Greek Political Theory: Plato and His Predecessors* (London, 1918) chap. 15.

universe. Natural laws were an expression of these principles.[5]

Cicero thought civil laws were merely the application of this eternal natural law.[6] Eventually the Roman jurists identified the *jus naturale,* or natural law, and the *jus gentium,* or law of nations, which was recognized through reason as a body of principles, universal and equitable in its applications.

The Graeco-Roman concepts of natural law were molded by the Church Fathers so as to conform to Christian thinking. Natural law became equivalent to the law of God. In this form the natural law doctrine was made a part of the canon law. To the canonists the *jus naturale,* representing the general moral principles which God had implanted in human nature became the norm by which the justice of all civil laws must be tested.[7]

Medieval legal doctrines were based essentially on superior legal concepts which regarded law in its origin as of equal rank with the state and as not depending on the state for its existence. The idea persisted for centuries that the end of the state is the attainment of justice and that civil authorities act legitimately only when they follow the principles of justice.[8]

There was prevalent at this time a conception of an inflexible code, emanating from the divine will and interpreted and applied through the light of reason, and from this conception came the doctrine that the higher laws of reason or of nature controlled the lower laws or enactments of man. Sometimes a distinction was made between

---

[5] Cf. *The Revival of Natural Law Concepts,* 4 ff.

[6] *De Legibus,* ii. 4. 10; R. W. and A. J. Carlyle, *A History of Medieval Political Theory in the West* (New York, 1903) 1:3 ff.; Cf. Salmond, *op. cit.,* 127 ff., and Bryce, *op. cit.,* 568 ff.

[7] R. W. and A. J. Carlyle, *op. cit.,* 1:106 ff. and 2:28, 98, 102, 105, 113.

[8] See *The Revival of Natural Law Concepts,* 14 ff.

certain immutable principles and rules derived therefrom which were subject to change. In practice natural law might be referred to as a guide to the interpretation of laws, or in certain instances it might be appealed to where no rule of law had been declared. All laws in conflict with natural law must be considered void.

Building on the concept of natural law, medieval jurists developed ideas of *inborn and indestructible rights belonging to the individual as such*—a philosophical foundation for the later declarations of rights.

Medievalists agreed on the existence of natural law; they differed merely as to its force and effectiveness. To some a statute or an executive act which violated natural law was void; to others interested either in the claims of kings and princes to be sovereign in the civil domain or in the idea of popular sovereignty, natural law comprised guiding principles, directive only in the processes of lawmaking.

2. *English concepts of fundamental law*[9]—

There is considerable doubt regarding the significance of ideas of a fundamental law in early English law. Some authorities maintain that the notion of a fundamental law has persisted throughout the growth of the system of the common law.[10] Other legal scholars insist that there is no substantial evidence in the medieval period to support the doctrine of a supreme fundamental law in England.[11] At times Magna Carta was referred to as a fundamental law or as supporting the view that there

---

[9] Cf. *The Revival of Natural Law Concepts*, 28 ff.

[10] C. H. McIlwain, *The High Court of Parliament and its Supremacy* (New Haven, 1910) 57, 63. Cf. also Sir Paul Vinogradoff, ''Magna Carta C. 39,'' *Magna Carta Commemoration Essays* (London, 1927) 79.

[11] Theodore F. T. Plucknett, *Statutes and their Interpretation in the First Half of the Fourteenth Century* (Cambridge, 1922) 26–31, 35, 36.

was a definitely formulated body of rights which the king was bound to observe;[12] or the law may have been regarded, as expressed by Bracton, as being supreme and hence limiting the authority of the king. But the theory that there was a supreme or fundamental law which limited both the king and Parliament received only occasional support prior to the time of Sir Edward Coke.

The doctrine that there were superior principles of right and justice which acts of Parliament might not contravene was asserted and vigorously defended by Lord Coke in his controversy with the Stuart kings. In the well-known case of Dr. Bonham, wherein the Royal College of Physicians attempted to impose a fine for the illegal practice of medicine, Coke asserted that it was an established maxim of the common law that no man can be judge in his own case. And he continued:

it appears in our books that in many cases the common law will control acts of parliament and sometimes adjudge them to be utterly void; for when an act of parliament is against common right or reason, or repugnant or impossible to be performed, the common law will control it and adjudge such act to be void.[13]

A number of cases were cited in support of this dictum.[14] Concerning this opinion there have been many disputes. Supporters of Coke have tried to show that the opinion,

---

[12] G. B. Adams, *The Origin of the English Constitution* (New Haven, 1920).

[13] 8 Co. 118a (1610) and 2 Brownl. (C. P. 1610) 255, 265. In a similar opinion the Chief Justice said: "Fortescue and Littleton and all others agree that the law consists of three parts: First, common law; secondly, Statute law, which corrects, abridges and explains the common law; third, custom, which takes away the common law. But the common law corrects, allows and disallows both statute law and custom, for if there be repugnancy in statute or unreasonableness in custom, the common law disallows and rejects it."—Rowles v. Mason, 2 Brownl. 197.

[14] Tregor's Case Y. B. Pasch. 8 Edw. III, 26; Fitzherbert, Cessavit 42; Fitzherbert, Annuities 41. For an analysis of these cases, consult Plucknett, *Statutes and their Interpretation in the First Half of the 14th Century*, 66–70, and "Bonham's Case and Judicial Review," 40 *Harv. Law Rev.* (Nov. 1926) 35 ff.

with the precedents upon which it is based, is an essentially accurate reflection of the situation in England at the time when the principle of the supremacy of law was winning its way over the tendencies toward the establishment of an absolute monarchy.[15] On the other hand, historians have endeavored to prove that the cases on which Coke based his theory of the supremacy of common law courts do not bear the construction which he gave to them. Most English legal authorities agree that there is no specific case on record in which an English court of justice has directly overruled or disregarded the plain meaning of an act of Parliament.[16] In England the medieval doctrine that law is above the state, which meant that there was a fundamental law which could not be changed, came to mean primarily the supremacy of law which parliament could change at will.

Coke is held responsible for formulating the "myth of Magna Carta" and to a certain extent the corresponding fiction of the supremacy of the common law courts, when he pledged himself to the popular side of the conflict with the king, and "cast into it all the weight of his profound if somewhat undigested learning and his powerful if somewhat unscrupulous intellect."[17]

---

[15] Cf. views of Sir Henry Hobart in Day v. Savadge, Hobart, 85 (K. B. 1614) and Lord Holt in City of London v. Wood, Modern 669, 687 (Mayor's Court, 1701).

[16] Roscoe Pound, "Common Law and Legislation," 21 *Harv. Law Rev.* (April 1908) 391. Sir Frederick Pollock, *First Book of Jurisprudence* (ed. 3; 1911) 264 and *Essays in the Law*, 41. J. G. Holland, *Elements of Jurisprudence* (ed. 10, London, 1908) 36.

[17] Cf. Edward Jenks, "The Myth of Magna Carta," *Independent Review*, 4:260, for comments on what is termed the unhistorical and vicious method of Coke, "It is a tribute to Coke's character and ability, that he imposed his ingenious but unsound historical doctrines not only on an uncritical age, but on succeeding ages which deem themselves critical. It is not, perhaps, altogether a testimony to the industry and acumen of a generation which might well be impartial in such matters that the legend invented by Coke has been so long allowed to pass current as the gospel of history."

After a period of comparative neglect the Charter was rendered popular by its use as a weapon to check the extensive prerogatives claimed by James and by Charles. Coke, Hampden, Eliot, and Pym gave an interpretation to long forgotten clauses of Magna Carta that supported their partisan views of constitutional reform. So great was this creative effort of Coke and his followers that a contrast may well be made between two charters—one, the original feudal charter; the other, the seventeenth century charter, as it came to be accepted by the political leaders, the judges and lawyers, and the majority of the people of England.[18]

According to Coke's theory the common law courts were superior in authority to the king and to Parliament. This theory found advocates among the justices of England prior to 1688, was regularly repeated in the law texts until the middle of the eighteenth century, and appears to have been frequently cited in arguments in English and colonial courts. After 1688 English courts gradually restricted the principle to acts which were impossible to be performed and acts wherein absurd consequences might arise.[19] Whatever effects Coke's attempt to set up a superior and fundamental law may have had, the Revolution of 1688 marked the abandonment of his doctrine as a practical principle of English politics.

A middle ground between the pretensions of Coke, that both the king and Parliament were limited by a common reason and superior principles of justice of

[18] W. S. McKechnie, ''Magna Carta (1215-1915)'' in Malden, *Magna Carta Commemoration Essays* (London, 1927) 12. McKechnie thinks that the inaccurate eulogies of Coke and Hampden rendered a great service to the cause of constitutional government.—*Ibid.*, 19.

[19] See Blackstone, later editions, and Stewart v. Lawton, where Coke's doctrine in Bonham's case was held to apply ''only where a statute requires something impossible to be done.''—1 Bing. (C. P. 1823) 374.

which the common law courts were the ultimate interpreters, and that of Pollock, Holland, and Holdsworth,
to the effect that no cases are on record in which the will
of the king or of Parliament was thwarted by the courts,
resting their opinions on a higher law basis, probably
comes nearer to stating the actual situation in England.
Even if it be true, as is claimed, that there is no case on
record in which the clearly expressed will of the king or
of Parliament was really checked by the courts there were
instances in which the courts interpreting the common
law changed the meaning of statutes, refused to give
them the effect intended, or to apply a rule of his majesty
in council until the King, Lords, and Commons joined in
an unmistakable mandate, which the courts reluctantly
at times conceded it was their duty to obey. Short of
such mandates clearly and unequivocally expressed there
was a wide realm in which the courts applied the basic
principles of reason of the common law and were seldom
interfered with by either the king or Parliament.[20] Moreover, the frequent confirmations or reaffirmations of
Magna Carta served to impress upon the public mind
that here were enshrined fundamental principles upon
which the superstructure of the English constitution
might arise. Coke's reiteration of these principles served
to strengthen the basic doctrine of the supremacy of
the law.

It was Coke's version of the supremacy of the common law principles as exemplification of rules of reason
and of justice, that served as a convenient precedent
when American justices were confronted with the demand
that limits must be placed on legislative powers in order
to safeguard individual rights and privileges.

---

[20]Plucknett, *Statutes and Their Interpretation in the First Half of the
14th Century* (Cambridge, 1922), Part II.

3. French ideas of fundamental law[21]—

In France doctrines of natural rights and of superior laws were inherited from medieval legal thought. Exponents of the philosophy of the Catholic church accepted and applied the natural law principles of the canon law. And prior to the French Revolution the Physiocrats expounded a doctrine of rights based upon the laws of nature. But the increasing tendency to accord unlimited powers to the king restricted the efficiency of natural laws as ruling principles for the affairs of men. The concentration of power in the hands of the king and the frequent arbitrary exercise of this power brought a reaction which led to an attempt on the part of the parliaments to limit his authority by an appeal to higher laws. In fact, the idea of a fundamental law or constitution sharply differentiated from ordinary legislation has been attributed primarily to the French.[22] Whether this claim can be substantiated or not, it is certain that prior to the period of the French Revolution a notion was developing in France that certain laws were of such superior sanctity that they could not be changed by imperial edicts even though sovereign power was recognized as located in the king.[23]

A convenient vagueness in the term fundamental laws encouraged the members of the parliaments to intervene on behalf of the people whenever a favorable opportunity occurred. The king could in the end secure his way, by arresting and banishing the leaders of the parliaments, but these bodies regarded themselves as mediators be-

---

[21] Cf. *The Revival of Natural Law Concepts*, 59 ff.

[22] Charles Borgeaud, *Amendment and Adoption of Constitutions* (New York, 1895) 3.

[23] A. Esmein, *Cours élémentaire histoire du droit français*, 582 ff. and V. Marcaggi, *Les origines de la declaration des droits de l'homme de 1789* (ed. 2; Paris, 1912) 85.

tween the king and the people and served to keep before
the public a belief in fundamental laws which the king
could not change.[24] Some of the *cahiers* issued preceding
the French Revolution, in resisting certain decrees frankly
based their protests on the doctrine of fundamental and
superior laws. These mild protests accomplished little
toward checking the tendencies in the direction of royal
absolutism. But they strengthened the insistence on
higher law ideas which were soon to find expression in
the Declaration of the Rights of Man and of the Citizen.

4. *American fundamental law concepts*[25]—

In the American colonies conditions were favorable
not only to the reception of higher law theories but also
to their adoption as primary principles of private and
public law. With a scarcity of law books and an increasing disrespect for English legal precedents administra-
trators of the law were compelled to fall back on the
Bible or on popular conceptions of natural law. Judges
and commentators in the colonies frequently indicated
their belief in natural laws which were considered true
laws and legislation was deemed binding only in so far
as it was an expression of these laws.

The popularity of the concepts of natural rights and
of natural law was greatly increased when they were
espoused by the leaders of the American and French
revolutions. The American Revolution not only came
first but also resulted in a more specific formulation of
the natural rights as inherent in the individual. James
Otis, Samuel Adams, John Adams, Thomas Paine, Patrick Henry, and Thomas Jefferson made frequent use of

---

[24] Consult André Blondel, *Le contrôle juridictionnel de la constitutionnalité des lois* (Paris, 1928) 133 ff.

[25] American ideas of natural law and of fundamental law will be considered in more detail in subsequent chapters.

the natural rights' doctrine to support the right of rebellion against the arbitrary exercise of governmental powers. The Declaration of Independence gave a standard formula for the use of advocates of the doctrine in the dictum that men are "endowed by their creator with certain unalienable rights, that among these are Life, Liberty, and the pursuit of Happiness."[26]

The doctrine of freedom and equality of men in the natural state, such as that described by Seneca and formulated into a dogma of medieval thought, was translated into a principle of political action. Governments in order to justify their existence were to be measured by the security they furnished for the natural principles of freedom and equality.

John Locke, the apologist for the English Revolution, regarded the law of nature as a body of rules for the conduct of men in their natural condition. Reason, Locke considered as the interpreter of this law; equality, its

---

[26] For a detailed account of colonial and revolutionary ideas of natural rights consult my treatise on *The Revival of Natural Law Concepts*, 52 ff., and two articles by B. F. Wright, Jr., "Natural Law in American Political Theory," 4 *Southwestern Pol. and Soc. Sci. Quart.* (Dec. 1923) 202 and "American Interpretations of Natural Law," 20 *Am. Pol. Sci. Rev.* (Aug. 1926) 624 ff.

A few representative extracts from the writings of Samuel Adams may well be quoted:

"Your Excellency will acknowledge that there are certain original inherent rights belonging to the people, which Parliament itself cannot divest them of, consistent with their own constitution."

"That there are certain essential rights of the British Constitution of Government, which are founded in the law of God and nature, and are the common rights of mankind . . . . and that no law of society can, consistent with the law of God and nature, divest them of those rights."

"That in all free states the constitution is fixed; and as the supreme legislative derives its power and authority from the constitution, it cannot overleap the bounds of it without destroying its own foundation, ... That it is an essential unalterable right in nature, ingrafted into the British Constitution, as a fundamental law and ever held sacred and irrevocable by the subjects within the realm, that what a man has honestly acquired is absolutely his own, which he may freely give, but cannot be taken from him without his consent."—Samuel Adams, *Writings* (Cushing's ed.) 16, 17, 23, 185, 186.

fundamental condition. Conceiving men as existing in a state of nature Locke constructed his doctrine of *natural rights which belong to man in the pre-political state.* These rights were life, liberty, and property.[27] Legislatures were bound to rule, in his judgment, according to the law of nature and to carry on their functions by fixed and general laws rather than by arbitrary decrees; and laws which transgressed certain fundamental principles were not laws "properly so called."[28] There seems to be a warrant here for the opinions of American justices that acts of legislatures though not expressly prohibited by written constitutions may nevertheless be void because not "legislative in character."

Legislative enactments contrary to natural law or natural justice were regarded as *ipso facto* void and it was declared to be the duty of all persons to resist their enforcement. The view of the English philosopher that "that which is not just is not law and that which is not law ought not to be obeyed," was not infrequently taken as the starting point in the application of legal rules. Moreover, the belief in natural law and in inalienable rights aided materially in giving support to the courts when they were asserting the right to declare void enactments which interfered with these natural rights or contravened the express terms of written constitutions.

5. *Doctrines of Vattel—*

The formulation of ideas relating to fundamental laws was aided by Vattel, whose work on the *Law of Nations* was extensively used in France, England, and the United States. Vattel attempted to put into popular form the

---

[27] John Locke, *Second Treatise of Civil Government*, Book 2, sec. 6.

[28] Locke, *op. cit.*, chap. 11, sec. 87; cf. *The Revival of Natural Law Concepts*, 22, 23.

theories of natural law as developed by Wolff.[29] A law of nature which was founded on the nature of things and on the nature of man was regarded as the basis of all law, public and private.[30]

Vattel also gave encouragement to the movement to establish written constitutions as the foundations of public authority. He maintained that the fundamental laws enacted by the nation itself are not subject to change by the legislature. The distinction between fundamental and ordinary laws was clearly drawn and American legal authorities soon began to make practical applications of the distinction. Some extracts from his chapter on "the constitution of a state" to which reference was frequently made during the revolutionary period are as follows:

It has been seen already that every political society must necessarily establish a public authority which regulates common affairs, prescribes the conduct of each in view of the public good, and possesses the means of compelling obedience. This authority belongs essentially to the whole body of the society, but it can be exercised in many ways, and it is for each society to determine and adopt the way which suits it best.

The fundamental law which determines the manner in which the public authority is to be exercised, is what forms the *constitution of the State*. In it can be seen the organization of which the Nation acts as a political body; how and by whom the people are to be governed, and what are the rights and duties of those who govern. This constitution is nothing else at bottom than the establishment of the system according to which a Nation proposes to work in common to obtain the advantages for which a political society is formed.

---

[29] Cf. Frederick von Wolff's *Jus naturae methodo scientifica pertractatum* (1740–48).

[30] E. de Vattel, *The Law of Nations or the Principles of Natural Law applied to the Conduct and to the Affairs of Nations and of Sovereigns* (trans. from edition of 1758 by Charles G. Fenwick in "The Classics of International Law," Washington, 1916).

Laws are rules laid down by the public authority to be observed in society. They ought all to have in view the welfare of the State and of its citizens. Laws which are passed directly in view of the public welfare are *public laws;* and in this class those which relate to the body itself and the very nature of the society, to the form of government and the manner in which the public authority is to be exercised, those laws, in a word, which together form the constitution of the State, are the *fundamental laws.* . . . .

The constitution of a State and its laws are the foundation of public peace and the firm support of political authority, and the security for the liberty of the citizens. But this constitution is a mere dead letter, and the best laws are useless if they be not sacredly observed. It is therefore the duty of the nation to be ever on the watch that the laws be equally respected both by those who govern and by the people who are to be ruled by them. To attack the constitution of the State and to violate its laws is a capital crime against society; and if the persons who are guilty of it are those in authority, they add to this crime a perfidious abuse of the power confided to them. A Nation must uniformly put down such violations with all the vigor and vigilance which the importance of the case demands. . . . .

The constitution and laws of a State are rarely attacked from the front, it is against secret and gradual attacks that a Nation must chiefly guard. Sudden revolutions strike the imaginations of men; their history is written, and their secret sources are made known; but changes are overlooked when they come about insensibly by a series of steps which are scarcely noted. . . . .

Still another important question is here presented. It belongs essentially to the social body to make laws concerning the manner in which it is to be governed and the conduct of its citizens. This function is called the *legislative power*. The exercise of it may be confided by the Nation to the Prince, or to an assembly, or to both conjointly; and they are thereby empowered to make new laws and to repeal old ones. The question arises whether their power extends to the fundamental laws, whether they can change the constitution of the State. The principles we have laid down lead us to decide definitely that the authority of these legislators does not get that far, and that the fundamental laws must be sacred to them, unless they are expressly empowered by the Nation to change them; for the constitution of a State should possess stability; and since the Nation established it in the first place and afterwards confided the *power* to certain persons, the fundamental laws are excepted from their authority. It is clear that the society had only in view to provide that the state should be furnished with laws enacted for special occasions, and with that object it gave to the legislators the power to repeal existing civil laws and such public ones as were not fundamental, and to make new ones. Nothing leads us to think that it wished to subject the constitution itself to their will. In a word, it is from the constitution that those legislators derive their power: how, then, could they change it without destroying the source of their authority? . . . .

We infer from what has been said that if there arise in the State disputes over the fundamental laws, over the public administration, or over the rights of the various powers which have a share in it, it belongs to the Nation alone to decide them, and settle them according to its political constitution.[31]

It is interesting to observe how the advocates of the American doctrine of judicial review made frequent use of the argument of Vattel that the constitution limited the legislative authority, but neglected to note that to Vattel the constitution was in the nature of political laws, whose preservation was not entrusted to any department of government but rested primarily with the people. The acceptance by the leaders of the American Revolution of the doctrine of natural rights and of ideas of fundamental laws limiting public authority will be described in the next chapter.

---

[31] Vattel, *op. cit.*, 3:17–19.

Chapter III

DEVELOPMENT OF THE PRACTICE OF JUDICIAL REVIEW OF LEGISLATIVE ACTS IN THE COLONIAL AND REVOLUTIONARY PERIODS

I. ENGLISH PROCEDURE IN ADMINISTRATIVE AND JUDICIAL REVIEW OF COLONIAL ACTS

1. *Administrative review and disallowance of acts by the Privy Council—*

IMPORTANT precedents and principles which aided in the acceptance of the American doctrine of judicial review of legislation were formulated and announced on the continent of Europe and in England prior to the time of the American Revolution. It was, however, in the exercise of authority by the English government over the colonies in America that a unique form of review by the Privy Council of the acts of the colonial legislatures was developed as a means of controlling colonial action.

The distinction between the authority of courts to hold void the acts of subordinate agencies of government and the power to invalidate an act of a coordinate legislative department has been previously noted. Exercise of the authority in the case of a superior government over an inferior government furnishes an analogy, and suggests the possibility of such authority for courts in dealing with the acts of a coordinate legislature. In this respect the practice of English colonial administrative agencies and of the assertion of authority by the Privy

Council influenced the colonists in that they realized the possibility of having their judgments reviewed and in certain instances their statutes invalidated by a superior tribunal.

Through the charters granted to the colonies and by means of parliamentary acts provisions were made that colonial laws, usages, or customs which were repugnant to acts relating to the colonies or were contrary to English laws were void.[1] In the royal colonies the English government exercised a double check upon colonial laws. By instructions to the governors undesirable measures might be vetoed, and by requiring that all acts be transmitted to England, there was an opportunity for disallowance by the Privy Council. No systematic review of colonial legislation was provided until 1660. And conditions in the charters made such review difficult for certain of the charter and proprietary colonies. The authority and the procedure to place a check upon undesirable acts after 1696 were delegated primarily to the Board of Trade and to the colonial governors. In the exercise of administrative review over legislative acts, ideas and principles were developed which in many respects prepared the way for the adoption of the doctrine of judicial review of legislative acts when the colonial governments were molded to suit the conditions of the American states.

---

[1] "And itt is further enacted and declared by the Authority aforesaid That all Lawes By-lawes Usages or Customs att this tyme or which hereafter shall bee in practice or endeavoured or pretended to bee in force or practice in any of the said Plantations which are in any wise repugnant to the before mentioned Lawes or any of them soe far as they doe relate to the said Plantations or any of them or which are wayes repugnant to this present Act or to any other Law hereafter to bee made in this Kingdome soe farr as such Law shall relate to and mention the said Plantations are illegal null and void to all Intents and Purposes whatsoever."—From an Act for preventing Frauds and regulating Abuses in the Plantation Trade, *Statutes of the Realm,* 7:105 (1695-6).

The requirement that colonial acts be referred to the home government for approval or disallowance placed a heavy burden upon English colonial administrators and made it necessary to develop an orderly procedure for reviewing such acts. As the main questions to be determined were frequently of a legal nature, the practice was adopted of referring colonial legislation to the legal advisers of the Crown for an opinion as to its fitness ''in point of law.'' Points of law related to (*a*) whether the colonial legislature exceeded its authority, or (*b*) whether any provisions of the act were unwarranted by the terms of the charter or in conflict with an act of Parliament.[2] The king's counsel were called ''watch-dogs of legality,'' for ''their practiced eyes were quick alike to note undue encroachments upon the domain of individual liberty, and unwarranted violations upon the prerogatives of the Crown.''[3]

The most effective method of controlling colonial laws, however, was by means of instructions to the governors.

---

[2] Elmer Beecher Russell, *The Review of American Colonial Legislation by the King in Council*, Columbia University *Studies in History, Economics and Public Law*, 64 (New York, 1915) 63.

[3] ''In no instance was a recommendation of the attorney or solicitor as to the confirmation or disallowance of an act rejected.''—*Ibid.*, 68. In 1760 the inquiry was submitted to the attorney general and the solicitor general whether or not in certain acts of the Pennsylvania assembly ''there be clauses and provisions . . . . which are not consonant to reason or which are repugnant or contrary to the laws, statutes or rights of England or inconsistent with the King's sovereignty or lawful prerogative or contrary to the allegiance due from the proprietaries or the inhabitants of the said province or not warranted by the power given by the charter to make laws,'' The attorney general and solicitor general advised the Privy Council: ''There may be cases in which particular provisions may be void *ab initio* though other parts of the law may be valid, as in clauses where any act of Parliament may be contraversed or any legal right of a private subject bound without his consent. These are cases the decision of which does not depend on the exercise of a discretionary prerogative, but may arise judicially and must be determined by general rules of law and the constitution of England. And upon this ground it is, that in some instances whole acts of assembly have been declared void in the courts of Westminister Hall, and by His Majesty in council upon appeals from the plantations.''—5 Pennsylvania *Statutes* at Large, 735–737.

Special restrictions were placed around laws emitting bills of credit, or regulating their value in coin, those affecting trade and property rights, and those relating to the prerogative of the king.[4] It is interesting to observe that some of the earliest cases of review of acts by state courts related to paper money legislation[5] and interference with property rights.[6]

Similarities between the expressions used by the law officers of the Crown in making their recommendations to the Board of Trade and the opinions of American state judges when they asserted the right to invalidate legislative acts indicate that the legal doctrines and principles commonly held in England at this time had their counterparts in the legal thought of the colonists. Attempts of the legislatures to pass judgments in individual cases were declared void. Acts were annulled because not properly belonging to the law-making power. Special care was exercised in preventing acts which interfered with property rights.[7] Terms in common use in rendering these opinions were that acts were unjust or unreasonable, or were not in accord with the principles of the English law; retrospective laws were condemned; two or more acts could not be contained under the same title.

It is not surprising that some of the phrases embodying the above principles found their way into the state constitutions and were regarded by the judges as too sacred to be violated. An act of the assembly of Georgia attempting to confer upon certain persons title to lands

---

[4] Russell, *op. cit.*, 89. See reference by the Board of Trade to attorney and solicitor of colonial acts granting decrees of divorce upon "a matter of doubt whether the legislature of the Province of Massachusetts Bay or any other Colony has a power of passing laws of this nature, and consequently whether these acts are not of themselves null and void."

[5] Cf. Trevett v. Weeden, *infra*.

[6] See Frost v. Leighton, Giddings v. Brown, *infra*.

[7] Russell, *op. cit.*, 146.

was disallowed by the English government because a decision,

upon a question of this nature by a partial act of Legislature without any hearing of the parties or any of those Regulations and Exceptions which Justice and Policy have prescribed in all general laws for quieting possessions, is arbitrary, irregular and unjust, and subversive to those principles of the Constitution by which disputes . . . . in all matters of private property . . . . are referred to the decision of the Court of Law.[8]

Colonial acts were reviewed not only from the standpoint of legality but also on grounds of policy and expediency.[9] The Board of Trade in carrying out the provision that colonial laws should conform to the laws of England required that certain formal provisions in the enactment of laws be met, that they conform to the governor's instructions, to the charter as well as to acts of Parliament, and that they embody the standards of justice characteristic of the jurisprudence of England. Though control over colonial acts was often ineffective, "in such policies as the crown chose to maintain consistently and without compromise the colonies learned to acquiesce; for against a disallowance, followed by an instruction to the governor forbidding his assent to any future act of like purpose, the popular party, as a rule, could make little or no headway."[10]

---

[8] *Ibid.*, 155, 156. An act of the assembly of North Carolina, which gave preference to executions upon judgments for local debts was held "contrary to reason, inconsistent with the Laws, greatly prejudicial to the Interests of this Kingdom, and therefore not warranted by the Charter, and consequently void."—*Ibid.*, 148; see also George Adrian Washburne, *Imperial Control of the Administration of Justice in the Thirteen American Colonies, 1684–1776*, Col. Univ. *Studies in History, Economics and Public Law*, 105 (New York, 1923) 49.

[9] The general adoption of the English common law by the colonies was usually disapproved by the home government on the ground that it interfered with the necessary control over colonial laws.—Russell, *op. cit.*, 140 ff.

[10] *Ibid.*, 204; Washburne, *op. cit.*, 50 ff.

Colonial acts when signed by the governor went into effect and were treated as valid until disallowed by the Crown. Disallowance was equivalent to the repeal of the act and hence differed from a veto which prevented a law from going into effect, and from a decision of a court declaring an act invalid, which meant that the act was void at the time of enactment.

The extent to which such an administrative review was exercised is shown by the fact that of 8,563 acts submitted by the colonies 469 or 5.5 per cent were disallowed by orders in council. The weakness of the review lay in the long delays necessary before action could be taken— the average period between the time of an enactment and its disallowance being three years and five months[11]—and the possibilities of evading the orders by the colonial assemblies. ''The power of review exercised by the Privy Council,'' observed Dr. Russell,

was analogous to that assumed by the Supreme Court of the United States after the formation of the new government. The Privy Council, it is true, declared acts void upon grounds other than the contravention of a fundamental law; but it frequently did disallow laws because they conflicted with the colonial charters, or with acts of the British Parliament or the common law of England. Under its tutelage the colonists became accustomed to a limitation upon the power of their legislatures. In this sense the work of the Privy Council constituted at once a precedent and a preparation for the power of judicial annulment upon constitutional grounds now exercised by the state and federal courts in the United States.[12]

---

[11] Russell, *op. cit.*, 221, 222.

[12] *Ibid.*, 227.

2. *Judicial annulment of acts by the Privy Council—*

In addition to the practice of the annulment of colonial acts through review by the Board of Trade and disallowance on his Majesty's order, or as a result of a veto by the governor on advice of the agents of the Crown, there were instances of an indirect annulment when in the settlement of a controversy between individuals as an incident a law was not applied because invalid.[13] It was the latter procedure which formed a direct precedent for the American idea of judicial review of state legislation by the Supreme court.

Acting as a final court of judicature the Privy Council in the case of *Winthrop v. Lechmere,* 1727, held that an act of the colony of Connecticut relating to the division of the property of an intestate among his children was "null and void as being contrary to the law of this realm, unreasonable, and against the tenor of their charter, and consequently the province had no power to make such a law."[14] The Privy Council maintained that in accordance with the common law of England real estate descended to the eldest son, and that it was against reason as well as law[15] that an only daughter should be co-heir with an only son. Thus a colonial act of nearly thirty years' standing was invalidated. Such a procedure had a different effect from disallowance for it rendered void all actions under the law. Since the laws of Connecticut were not laid before the Crown for approbation or dis-

---

13 "Three cases are usually cited as involving the validity of colonial legislative enactments and a diligent search yields no more."—Washburne, *op. cit.,* 184 ff.

14 James B. Thayer, *Cases on Constitutional Law,* 1:136; for an account of this case see Harold D. Hazeltine, "Appeals from Colonial Courts to the King in Council with especial reference to Rhode Island," *Report* to Am. Hist. Assoc. (1894), and Arthur Meier Schlesinger, "Colonial Appeals to the Privy Council," 28 *Pol. Sci. Quart.* (June and Sept. 1912) 440 ff.

15 Hazeltine, *op. cit.,* 319 ff.

allowance, it was contended that there was no other way of enforcing the terms of the charter, which provided that the laws of the colony should not be contrary to the laws of England, than by considering acts beyond the charter as no laws at all.[16] Contrary to the invariable practice the Board of Trade was not consulted in this case. The decision overturned the policy of settling estates which had prevailed in Connecticut since the foundation of the colony, and the colonial government set about vigorously to have the decision of the Privy Council reversed. A case involving a similar issue was appealed from Massachusetts and the statute of that colony relating to intestate estates was upheld.[17] On the strength of this decision the government of Connecticut supported another appeal to the Privy Council and was successful in having the former decree of the Council reversed and the colonial act of 1699 validated.[18] If an appeal on a colonial matter involved the validity of a law or the action of an officer it was regularly referred to the Board of Trade but if a purely judicial question was raised the judicial committee of the Privy Council might settle the question directly.

There seems to be some dispute whether the decisions in such cases as those of *Winthrop v. Lechmere* and *Phillips v. Savage* were in the nature of judicial decrees or whether they were rather legislative or administrative acts similar to the procedure in the disallowance of statutes. As a precedent for authority in courts of justice to declare laws invalid, it appears to make little difference whether these decrees be regarded as legislative or judicial in nature. A cursory examination of English his-

---

[16] *Ibid.*, 36. Cf. also Oliver M. Dickerson, *American Colonial Government 1696–1765* (Cleveland, 1912) 275 ff., on reasons why this law was held void.

[17] Phillips v. Savage, Hazeltine, *op. cit.*, 319–321; Schlesinger, *op. cit.*, 442.

[18] Clark v. Tousey, Hazeltine, *op. cit.*, 321–322; Schlesinger, *op. cit.*, 444.

tory during this period makes it apparent that anything like a well marked separation of powers into legislative, executive, and judicial was lacking. Nevertheless, the fact that a colonial act might be held invalid in the ordinary course of appeal to England, whether considered legislative or judicial or both, was recognized and well understood.

Another objection raised to these cases as precedents for the American doctrine is that the cases were not cited by those who were responsible for the adoption of the American practice of judicial review. The colonists were as a rule not content under the arrangements for appeal of cases to the Privy Council. Frequently they did everything in their power to prevent appeals, refused to carry out the orders of the Council, and criticized the practice of review as one of the chief causes of irritation between the home government and the colonies. It is not suprising then, that colonial and state justices, even if they knew of these decisions did not refer to these precedents when seeking to place limits upon legislative action.

3. *The Privy Council as an appellate court—*

Not only were colonial laws subjected to constant scrutiny to determine whether they conformed to the laws and customs of the common laws and statutes of England, but the Privy Council gradually secured authority and jurisdiction over the colonies as a final court of appeal. By this means the Crown aimed to prevent important changes in colonial administration of the law and to revise the judgments of the local courts when they were detrimental to the interests of the Crown, or were arbitrary. The right of the Crown to hear appeals from colonial courts and to exercise a controlling power over their judicial tribunals was not positively asserted until after 1680. The New York charters of 1664 and 1674 and the New Hampshire commission of 1679 contained provisions with respect to appeals, but it was not until there was an open denial of this right of appeal by certain colonies that the Privy Council decided to permit appeals. The first general regulation of procedure in case of appeal was made by an order in council in 1684. This order provided that sufficient security must be given to prosecute appeals effectually. By orders and commissions the minimum amount involved to warrant an appeal was fixed at £300 and later increased to £500.[19]

On account of difficulties which arose over the attempt of the general assemblies of the colonies to revise the judgments of their supreme courts, the Crown issued an order that in all cases exceeding in value three hundred pounds "no appeal should be heard by the general assembly, as such a practice was inconsistent with the laws and practices of England, but that all appeals from the decisions of the general court should be heard and determined by the King in council."[20] By an order in council of March 9, 1698, the king asserted that it was "the inherent right of his Majesty to receive and determine appeals from all his Majesty's colonies in America; and that they govern themselves accordingly."[21] Further-

---

[19] The practice of appealing colonial cases to the king in Council may be traced to the fifteenth century. The king encouraged the practice and tried to make this method of appeal exclusive. At the same time that the procedure in such appeals was regulated by orders in Council, the courts decided that appeals from the plantations lay only to the king in Council. Jurisdiction of the Council in colonial appeals was not definitely regulated by Parliament until 1833.—Jennett v. Bishop, 1 Vernon 264 (1683) and Fryer v. Bernard, 2 P. Wms. 262 (1724); cf. Norman Bentwich, *The Practice of the Privy Council in Judicial Matters* (ed. 2; London, 1926) 4 ff.

[20] H. D. Hazeltine, "Appeals from Colonial Courts to the King in Council, with especial reference to Rhode Island," *Report* to Am. Hist. Assoc., 1894, 314.

[21] *Ibid.*, 302.

more, the restriction upon appeals in cases not exceeding
three hundred pounds in value was considered not to
preclude his Majesty from hearing appeals when he
should deem it advisable, and this prerogative was frequently exercised by the king.[22] Certain of the colonies
resisted this attempt to establish a court of appeal in
London. The charter colonies in particular refused to
permit appeals claiming that their charters failed to
make provision for such procedure. Finally the contention of the king's counsel was sustained that an English
subject cannot be deprived of his right of appeal by any
specific words or lack of words in the king's grant.

The practice of appeal in judicial matters was regulated by special orders in council and instructions to
colonial governors, and was finally subjected to a requirement of value in excess of five hundred pounds. An appeal had to be taken fourteen days after sentence, with
security to cover costs and damages in case the court's
decree was affirmed. The limitation of five hundred
pounds gave the governors and colonial courts practically
final power in most of the litigation of the day. Governors and assemblies as final courts of appeal[23] took
advantage of this provision and often refused to permit
appeals when the value was practically greater than the
required amount. This reluctance to permit appeals led
to the development of the right to petition the king to

---

[22] Hazeltine, *op. cit.*, 303. For an account of the obstructive methods
of the colonies relating to appeals, consult Schlesinger, *op. cit.*, 292 ff. and
433 ff. The procedure regarding appeals was regulated by provisions in
colonial charters and by colonial legislative acts.

[23] Speaking of Rhode Island, Professor Hazeltine observes ''from the
very first the assembly appears to have regarded itself a judicial tribunal
as well as a legislative body, and during practically all of the colonial
period exercised an appellate jurisdiction over colonial courts, granting or
refusing also appeals to the King in council.''—Am. Hist. Assoc. *Reports*
1894, 326 ff. In the case of Brenton v. Remington the Privy Council in
1710 held a decision of the Rhode Island assembly void for lack of
jurisdiction.

grant permission to appeal, and in 1746 in all the colonies except those in which the courts were established by charters or orders in council the governors were directed to permit appeals to his Majesty in council.[24] Appeals were to be permitted also in certain cases when the amount in controversy was less than five hundred pounds.

The extent of the review of colonial cases by the king in council may be indicated by the experience of Rhode Island. Fifty-nine cases were decided between the years 1735 and 1776.[25] In twenty-four of these cases the decisions of the colonial courts were reversed, modified, or returned with instructions. Since twenty-two cases were dismissed for non-prosecution the reversals or modifications of decisions were approximately seventy-five per cent.[26] The procedure in disposing of cases was as follows:

Every appeal was referred to the privy council's committee on plantation affairs, and before the lords of this committee the case was carefully and fully tried. But the lords of the committee did not always rely on their own judgment alone. They frequently referred cases to the lords commissioners for trade and plantations; and these commissioners, in turn, often sought the advice of the attorney and solicitor general. Reports were then returned from board to board until the committee on plantation affairs made its report to the King and the entire council. The council's advice upon the report was then obtained, and the King, acting upon this advice, issued the final decree in the form of an order in council, either affirming, reversing, or otherwise revising the decision of the colonial court.[27]

---

[24] Hazeltine, *op. cit.*, 309. For provisions in charters and statutes regarding appeals from colonial courts, see *ibid.*, 311 ff.

[25] *Ibid.*, 337. Hazeltine states that he found no record of an appeal case prior to 1706.

[26] For details regarding cases appealed, see *ibid.*, 338 ff.

[27] *Ibid.*, 350. The number of appeals from the colonies varied greatly from 78 from Rhode Island to only a few from North and South Carolina. For the number of appeals from the colonies, see Schlesinger, *op. cit.*, 447.

It was through this practice that the colonists became accustomed to referring their causes to a supreme tribunal for final adjudication.

At times the colonial courts did not hesitate to refuse to give effect to an order of the king or to resist an act of Parliament deemed contrary to their rights as English subjects.

A remarkable decision to this effect was rendered in 1738–1739 by the Superior Court of Judicature of Massachusetts, when the court refused to enforce an order of his Majesty in council, "because the powers of the court derived through the charter and the laws passed to carry the same into effect were in the judgment of the court inadequate for that purpose."[28] The case arose over the cutting of trees for the royal navy under a license granted by the Crown. Though Frost had title to the land his Majesty's agents claimed the right to cut trees of a certain size under a charter granted by the king. Frost brought an action for trespass and though the king's agent was ably represented the court awarded damages for the trees cut. On appeal to the Superior Court of Judicature this decision was affirmed. The representatives of the king then appealed to the Privy Council and secured an order that the judgment be reversed and the money collected by Frost restored. After some delay the Superior Court was of the opinion that considering the royal charter with the laws of the province and the usage and practice of the court, they had no authority to give such an order.[29] A second order from the Privy Council suffered a like fate, despite the fact that the governor,

---

28 Andrew McFarland Davis, "The Case of Frost v. Leighton," *Am. Hist. Rev.*, 2 (January 1897) 229–240.

29 Davis, *op. cit.*, 234.

the council, and the justices were specifically ordered to have the money returned. The attitude of the colonial courts in refusing to give effect to the king's order in council met with approval in the Court of King's Bench, in the case of *Campbell v. Hall,* when an act of the king in council was held to be void as contradictory to and in violation of a previous act.[30]

Another instance in which a colonial court claimed the right to invalidate legislative action, was the case of *Giddings v. Brown.* A Massachusetts town voted its minister a dwelling, and a suit was instituted in 1657 to compel the payment of a tax levied for this purpose. Magistrate Symonds, basing his judgment upon English law and colonial precedents which he regarded as binding, held the vote of the town meeting void. In the course of his judgment he said:

The fundamental law which God and nature has given to the people cannot be infringed. The right of property is such a fundamental right. In this case the goods of one man were given to another without the former's consent. This resolve of the town being against the fundamental law is therefore void, and the taking was not justifiable.[31]

The decision was based upon the ground that fundamental natural law was superior to ordinary legislative enactments, and the court assumed that it was a judicial duty not to give effect to an act contrary to this superior law. The decision of the magistrate was reversed by the General Court and the levy was held valid.[32]

[30] James Bradley Thayer, *Cases on Constitutional Law* (Cambridge, 1895) 1:40–47.

[31] Paul Samuel Reinsch, ''English Common Law in the Early American Colonies,'' *Selected Essays in Anglo-American Legal History* (Boston, 1907) 1:376, 377.

[32] *Hutchinson Papers,* 2:1 ff.

Although there are but few cases recorded in which colonial courts directly and openly refused to enforce the laws of England, the evidence available demonstrates that restraints upon the colonial legislatures were in a few instances enforced by the English courts.[33] It is possible, of course, to exaggerate the influence of these colonial cases, especially since the advocates of the right of the courts to review legislative acts scarcely mentioned them when they searched for precedents to support the idea of judicial guardianship of the fundamental written law. But the practice of having charters and colonial acts interpreted and expounded through judicial decrees of the courts of a superior government, as well as the possibility of such interpretation by the courts as a coordinate branch of the colonial governments, was fairly well known. In fact the colonial authorities, organized originally under charters granted to trading companies, were accustomed to have their charters construed and to have the corporation acts set aside as *ultra vires* through ordinary judicial processes. The acceptance of the next step in the development of the American doctrine of judicial review of legislation was natural and not likely to meet with the serious opposition which attends a significant change in political practice. "This practice taught the colonists," says Professor Hazeltine,

to look more and more to a supreme tribunal for the adjudication of their legal cases, and to accept as law the judicial opinions of that body. It accustomed them to regard the courts of

---

[33] Thayer, *op. cit.*, 131. Chief Justice Whitaker, of South Carolina, in a communication to the Board of Trade made inquiry as follows: "Sometimes acts have been made in Parliament not only contrary to the King's instruction and prerogative, but repugnant to the laws of England. Are these laws void from the beginning or only voidable by his Majesty's disallowance? What are judges to do when they are pleaded in evidence?"— William M. Meigs, *The Relation of the Judiciary to the Constitution* (New York, 1919) 44.

the different colonies as but parts of a judicial system which found a unifying principle in a court of final appeal. In short, with functions similar to those of the council, when the time came to organize a government for themselves.[34]

II. JUDICIAL REVIEW AND AMERICAN DOCTRINES OF NATURAL RIGHTS AND OF FUNDAMENTAL LAWS

It was the resistance to English authority which culminated in the American Revolution, that rendered the conception of a fundamental law and of individual natural rights popular and encouraged judges to regard it as their peculiar duty to guard and defend the superior laws. The doctrine that there were superior laws to which all legislation must conform was eloquently defended by James Otis.

1. *Argument of Otis and appeal to natural rights—*

The occasion for the first notable speech of Otis was a controversy over the right of the Superior Court of Massachusetts to issue general search warrants instead of particular warrants, which had been successfully evaded by those who practiced smuggling goods into the colonies in opposition to the colonial trade acts. When the court was asked to grant general warrants or writs of assistance, Otis, who was the king's advocate in the province, resigned his office and appeared before the court to argue the cause of the Boston merchants.

His attack was begun on the general search warrant by designating this decree of the agents of the Crown as "the worst instrument of arbitrary power, the most destructive of English liberty and the fundamental principles of law, that ever was found in an English law-book." After distinguishing between a special writ

---

[34] Hazeltine, *op. cit.*, 299.

which was legal and a general writ which was opposed
as illegal, Otis concluded:

Thus reason and the constitution are both against this writ.
Let us see what authority there is for it. Not more than one
instance can be found of it in all our law-books; and that was
in the zenith of arbitrary power, namely, in the reign of
Charles II, when star-chamber powers were pushed to an extreme
by some ignorant clerk of the exchequer. But had this writ been
in any book whatever, it would have been illegal. No acts of
Parliament can establish such a writ; though it should be made
in the very words of the petition it would be void. An act
against the constitution is void.[35]

Views expressed in Otis' pamphlet, *The Rights of the
British Colonies Asserted and Proved,* issued in 1764,
were of even greater importance in the growth of precedents favorable to judicial review. The powers of the
legislature, he maintained are limited:

These are their bounds, which by God and nature are fixed,
hitherto have they a right to come, and no further. . . . . These
are the first principles of law and justice, and the great barriers
of a free state, and of the British constitution in particular. To
say the Parliament is absolute and arbitrary is a contradiction.[36]

Otis quoted from Vattel's discourse on constitutions
and aided in popularizing the notion of a fundamental
law in Massachusetts.[37] In fact, it is likely that Otis and
Samuel Adams were responsible for the statement on
fundamental law which by means of the Massachusetts
Circular Letter was sent throughout the colonies. In all
free states, the letter asserted,

the Constitution is fixed; and as the supreme legislative derives
its Power and Authority from the Constitution, it cannot over-

---

35 John Adams, *Works,* 2, Appendix, 525, and Quincy, 521–527, Appendix
by Justice Gray.

36 Otis, *Rights of the British Colonies Asserted and Proved,* 70.

37 Andrew C. McLaughlin, *The Courts, the Constitution and Parties,* 109.

leap the Bounds of it without destroying its own foundation. That it is an essential, unalterable right in nature, ingrafted into the British Constitution, as a fundamental Law . . . . that what a man has honestly acquired is absolutely his own.[38]

The ideas that the written fundamental law must be fixed, that legislative power was limited, and that legislative authority was derived from the constitution, were strongly emphasized.[39] Otis also referred to the opinions of Coke and other English justices for authority that acts of Parliament against natural equity are void, and that acts

against the fundamental principles of the British Constitution are void. . . . . If the reasons that can be given against an act are such as plainly demonstrate that it is against *natural* equity, the executive courts will adjudge such act void. It may be questioned by some, though I make no doubt of it, whether they are not obliged by their oaths to adjudge such acts void.[40]

The prevailing reason offered by those who resisted the enforcement of the Stamp Act, according to the testimony of Governor Hutchinson, was "that the Act of Parliament is against Magna Carta, and the natural rights of Englishmen and therefore, according to Lord Coke, null and void."[41] In February, 1766, the question was raised before a county court in Virginia whether the act of Parliament imposing stamp duties in America was binding on Virginia. The judges are reported to have been unanimously of the opinion that the law did not bind the inhabitants of Virginia, "inasmuch as they conceived said act to be unconstitutional."[42]

---

[38] Otis, *op. cit.*, 70–71; *Writings of Samuel Adams*, 1:185.

[39] *Ibid.*, 1:134, 156, 170.

[40] McLaughlin, *op. cit.*, 79 and Quincy *Reports*, 521 ff.

[41] John Adams, *Works*, 9:390, 391, note, and Appendix. Quincy, 527.

[42] John Bach McMaster, *A History of the People of the United States* (New York, 1900) 5:394.

It was of little moment that the argument of Otis was not in accordance with the law and practice of the English government at that time. The restatement of Coke's theory of judicial supremacy was particularly acceptable to those who were resisting the enforcement of the colonial trade laws enacted by Parliament.[43] An appeal beyond ordinary statutes to a fundamental law held to embody the natural rights of Englishmen furnished a plausible basis for resistance which was rapidly developing into open rebellion. According to Otis and those who shared his views, the courts were to be the guardians of the natural rights of the individual as against the encroachments of the other departments of government. The idea that individual rights should be protected by the courts against arbitrary governmental acts soon met with approval by certain attorneys and judges.

Robin v. Hardaway, 1772.—A case reported by Thomas Jefferson indicated the reliance upon natural law and the theories of Coke during the Revolutionary period. The right of traders to sell the descendants of

---

[43] The reiteration of Coke's theory by text writers helped to support colonial views. See especially the following:

"If a statute be against common right or reason, or repugnant, or impossible to be performed, the common law shall control it, and adjudge it to be void.

"It is to be holden, that a statute contrary to natural equity, as to make a man judge in his own case, is void."—6 *Bacon's Abridgment* Statute (A) 1735.

"So where the words of an act of Parliament are against common right and reason, repugnant, or impossible to be performed, they shall be controlled by the common law."—4 *Comyn's Digest* Parliament (R. 27) 1762-7.

"It appears in our books, that in several cases the common law shall control acts of Parliament, and sometimes adjudge them to be utterly void, for when an act of parliament is against common right and reason, or repugnant, or impossible to be performed, the common law shall control it, and adjudge it to be void."—19 *Viner's Abridgment*, Statutes (E.6) 1741-51.

Indians as slaves, based upon an act of the colony of Virginia of 1692, was involved. In the defense of the Indians their attorney, Mason, maintained that the act of the colony was void because it was contrary to a natural right. He asserted:

All acts of the legislature apparently contrary to natural right and justice, are, in our laws, and must be in the nature of things, considered as void. The laws of nature are the laws of God; whose authority can be superseded by no power on earth. A legislature must not obstruct our obedience to him from whose punishments they cannot protect us. All human constitutions which contradict his laws, we are in conscience bound to disobey. Such have been the adjudications of our courts of justice.[44]

Citing Coke's opinion in *Bonham's Case* and Hobart's opinion in *Calvin's Case*, Mason considered the act of 1682 originally void because contrary to natural right and justice. The appeal to natural right was probably not regarded by the judges as conclusive, since they decided that the act of 1682 was repealed by a subsequent act of 1705. But it was not uncommon for colonial lawyers and colonial courts to regard natural law and the ancient principles of the common law as superior to ordinary legislative acts.[45]

2. *Written constitutions*—

Written constitutions as the foundation of public law in the United States developed from charters granted originally to trading companies. As fundamental acts of political organization the charters were transformed into written constitutions through a group of ideas. Among these were: concepts of a law of nature above all

---

[44] 1 Jeff. (Va.) 109, 114.

[45] Cf. Comment of Paul S. Reinsch in *Select Essays* in *Anglo-American Legal History*, 1:413.

human enactments, a belief in inalienable rights of the individual, a theory of the supremacy of the common law courts, and the English and French ideas of a fundamental written law superior to ordinary statutes, with various theories regarding the separation of powers and the placing of limitations on the powers of government. Though the notion of a written fundamental law may be traced to the Middle Ages, when the people were familiar with charters of liberties granting various rights and privileges, constitutions or written fundamental laws defining the rights of individuals and limiting the governing agents were primarily a development of the seventeenth and eighteenth centuries.[46] It was at this time that the doctrine was introduced into the legal systems of Europe and of America that ''in every government there must be somewhat fundamental, somewhat like a Magna Carta, which should be standing and unalterable.''[47]   In the formation of new governments when a check was sought upon the powers of the executive and of the legislature, and when men were concerned with the necessity of fixing limits to the exercise of public powers, the idea of a fundamental law in the nature of a written document embodying the desired limitations and restrictions was conceived as an effective means for protection against undue governmental interference in private affairs.

Although the ''Agreement of the People,'' prepared and presented to the House of Commons by Cromwell and eventually submitted for popular approval, was an effort to establish a fundamental law in England, the attempt did not meet with success.[48]   It remained for the

---

46 Borgeaud, op. cit., 34.

47 Oliver Cromwell, Letters and Speeches (Carlyle), Part 7, Speech 3 (September 12, 1654).

48 See Borgeaud, op. cit., 6–9.

American colonies to adopt the first written constitutions according to the modern meaning of the term. The colonies were governed under charters which were in the nature of fundamental laws and their governments were in origin merely directorates of corporate trading companies.[49] But a series of local charters and instruments of government gave a new meaning to a written constitution.

The Mayflower Compact, drawn up on the landing of the Pilgrims in Plymouth in 1620, is sometimes styled the first constitution in America, though this is scarcely warranted from the nature of the compact. Recognizing allegiance to the English Crown the signers of this document agreed to maintain order and to submit to all ''Just and equall lawes'' made by their own community.

Drafted in 1639, the Fundamental Orders of Connecticut are frequently called the oldest political constitution in America. By this document a confederation was formed for religious purposes, which provided that in civil affairs the towns were to be governed according to such laws as shall be agreed upon. A scheme of government was drawn up which placed the common affairs of the towns in the hands of a governor and an assembly. The authority of the electors was sanctioned to select their own rulers and to control those elected to office.[50]

The charters granted to the colonies from 1620 to 1700 embodied ideas of later constitutional government such as the representative system with ultimate control by the electors, the separation of the legislative and executive functions, and a beginning was made toward the establishment of an independent judiciary. Various

[49] Herbert L. Osgood, *The American Colonies in the Seventeenth Century* (New York, 1924) 3:509.

[50] Cf. Breckinridge Long, *Genesis of the Constitution of the United States* (New York, 1926).

efforts to bring about a union among the colonies also aided in the formation of concepts relating to a written fundamental law. Beginning with the New England Confederation drafted in 1643, successive charters or plans of union were prepared which emphasized the importance and advantages of a written instrument for organizing and defining intercolonial relations. The framers of the federal and state constitutions found some useful and suggestive ideas in the different plans of union.

A written constitution, however, in the nature of a charter ''guaranteeing the nation against the usurpations of the authorities to whom she necessarily confides the exercise of her sovereign power; guaranteeing also the minority against the omnipotence of the majority,''[51] was essentially a product of the American Revolution. The peculiar significance attached to fundamental laws in the United States took definite and concrete form in the period from 1780 to 1803. It was in this period that the American doctrine of judicial review of legislation was formally announced and accepted as a feature of the public law of the states and of the nation. The gradual emergence of the principles that constitutions are fundamental laws with a peculiar sanctity, that legislatures are limited and receive the commission for their authority from the constitution, and that courts are to be considered the special guardians of the superior written laws may be observed in the evolution of political ideas which accompanied the separation from the British Empire and the establishment of an independent government in America.

---

[51] Borgeaud, *op. cit.*, Introduction.

Chapter IV

COUNCILS OF CENSORS

B EING THUS accustomed to charters or other written instruments of government which organized their political machinery and defined in a general way the powers to be exercised, the colonists, when the occasion came to form their own governments, naturally were inclined to put in written form the fundamentals of their political organizations. Certain political theories accepted and applied by the leaders of the American Revolution gave the peculiar form and content to the first state constitutions.

Among these theories were the doctrine of natural rights, the theory of a social compact, the principle of popular sovereignty, and the right of revolution. The general doctrine of natural rights as formulated in the Declaration of Independence was made more specific by the insertion in some state constitutions of bills of rights containing certain of the individual privileges guaranteed by Magna Carta and the English bills of rights and also privileges regarded essential to the special conditions of the colonies, such as freedom of speech and religious liberty. Embodied in most of the early state constitutions was the idea advanced by Patrick Henry in his argument in the *Parson's Cause,* namely, that government, being formed on a compact or contract to rule for the good of the people, any government which ceases to act for the common good is no longer legitimate and is rightfully overthrown. The compact theory was closely associated with the principle of popular sovereignty, a doctrine expressed in the Massachusetts Constitution of 1780 as follows: "All power residing originally in the people, and being derived from them, the several magistrates and officers of government, vested with authority, whether legislative, executive, or judicial, are their substitutes and agents, and are at all times accountable to them."[1] All the foregoing principles led to the doctrine of resistance against arbitrary power and the justification, if need be, of an appeal to the right of revolution.

It will be seen how the doctrine of the review of legislation by the courts was fostered by the formation and limitation of governments by means of written constitutions, by the doctrines of natural and inalienable rights for the protection of which governments were thought to be primarily formed, and by the necessity of resistance to arbitrary political action in whatever form. Judges were supported in their refusal to enforce acts which they deemed arbitrary by the general belief that it was the duty of every good citizen and all conscientious public officials to resist any encroachments upon the sacred rights of the people. The right of resistance to check the arbitrary exercise of public powers founded on the generally accepted right of revolution was gradually transformed into a normal legal procedure to enforce the limitations on political action defined in the constitution.

I. SUPREMACY OF THE LEGISLATURES IN EARLY STATE GOVERNMENTS

In the early state governments, however, there are many indications that the legislature was regarded as relatively speaking the supreme department, subject to the few limitations inscribed in the constitution. No pro-

---

[1] Art. 5.

vision for the separation of governmental powers was included in some of the first state constitutions and when a clause for this purpose was inserted it had as a rule little practical significance. There was not only, as Madison observed, too great a mixture and consolidation of powers, but also no provision was made for "maintaining in practice the separation delineated on paper."[2]

Whether or not the constitutions contained provisions for the separation of powers, the legislatures frequently revised judicial proceedings, authorized appeals, or interpreted the law for individual cases. Though defective laws often made it incumbent to grant remedies in individual cases the practice was indulged in many times when it was unnecessary.[3] The fact that the legislature controlled the appointment of judges in most of the states and that the terms were short was not conducive to the independence of the judges.

Judge Chipman, of Vermont, speaking of the first state constitutions, observed:

when they constituted the legislature, they considered that its power was necessarily supreme and uncontrollable, and that all constitutional restrictions upon their power were merely directory. No idea was entertained that an act of the legislature, however repugnant to the constitution, could be adjudged void and set aside by the judiciary, which was considered by all a subordinate department of government. And these sentiments generally prevailed until after the Constitution of the United States was promulgated.

---

[2] *The Federalist*, No. XLVII.

[3] Edward S. Corwin, "The Progress of Constitutional Theory Between the Declaration of Independence and the Meeting of the Philadelphia Convention," *Am. Hist. Rev.*, 30 (April 1925) 514. The idea of the supremacy of the legislature is also shown by the provisions in certain states for the amendment of constitutions by the general assemblies. Cf. constitutions of Maryland, 1776, art. 59; of Delaware, 1776, art. 30; and of South Carolina, 1778, art. 44. The procedure for amendment differed somewhat from that employed in passing ordinary acts.

During the first Septenary, the Legislature frequently interfered with the Judiciary department. They passed an act prohibiting the prosecution of any real or possessory action, or any action on contract. They passed acts vacating and annulling judgments. They constituted themselves a Court of Chancery. They appointed a board of Commissioners with full power to decide in a summary manner all disputes relative to the title of lands. They also frequently granted new trials in cases which had been finally decided by the Judiciary. The powers thus exercised by the Legislature with the approbation of a majority of the people, naturally confirmed the idea, that the power of the Legislature was unlimited and supreme. No idea was entertained that the Judiciary had any power to enquire into the constitutionality of acts of the Legislature, or pronounce them void for any cause, or even to question their validity. Indeed, the framers of the Constitution could never have intended to confer on the Courts the power of pronouncing an act of the Legislature void for any cause, when they provided for an annual election of the Judges by the same Legislature who were to pass the laws.[4]

Jefferson commented as follows on the theory of the separation of powers in the Virginia constitution of 1776:

If the legislature assumes executive and judiciary powers, no opposition is likely to be made; nor, if made, can it be effectual; because in that case they may put their proceedings into the form of an act of assembly, which will render them obligatory on the other branches. They have, accordingly, in many instances, decided rights which should have been left to judiciary controversy; and the direction of the executive, during the whole time of their session, is becoming habitual and familiar.[5]

---

[4] D. Chipman (Vt.) *Reports*, preface, 21, 22. Cf. also for observation that in Vermont judicial review was for many years regarded antirepublican.—*Ibid.*, 25, 26. For the practice of legislative supremacy in Rhode Island, see Hazeltine, Am. Hist. Assoc. *Reports*, 1894.

[5] *Writings* (Memorial ed.) 2:163, 164. For criticism of the lack of an adequate theory of separation of powers in Virginia, see Jefferson, *Writings*, 2:160. See also *Proceedings*, relative to the calling of the Con-

The governor was not granted the veto power and could exercise, therefore, no check upon legislative dominance. There was good ground for the observation of Madison that "in republican government the legislative authority necessarily predominates."[6] Even though it was generally agreed that great precautions should be taken against the enterprising ambition of the legislative department, and that constitutions were fundamental enactments and ought not to be violated, it is significant that in the majority of the states no provisions were made for keeping legislative authority within the limits of the fundamental law. The guardianship of written constitutions was left in all but three states to the moral obligation of the members of the assembly and to the protection resulting from the sense of responsibility which the judges, executives, and other officers claimed of right in the course of their regular functions of interpreting and applying the laws.

In tracing the precedents which led in the direction of the American doctrine of judicial review of legislative acts, it is necessary to treat of the peculiar institution known as the council of censors. While there were of course advocates of the doctrine of legislative supremacy, nevertheless the sentiment appeared to be rather general that legislative authority must in certain respects be limited. Though in the first state constitutions the power of suspending the laws or the execution of the laws was not to be exercised except by the legislature, it was also frequently enacted that no part of the constitution should

---

ventions of 1776 and 1790 (Harrisburg, 1825) in the Pennsylvania Council of Censors. In a report issued in 1784, the council charged the legislature with violations of the constitution including numerous instances of interferences with private rights and with the settlement of questions judicial in character.

6 *The Federalist* (Ford ed.) 345.

be altered, changed, or abolished by the legislature.[7] The distinction between fundamental law as embodied in written constitutions and ordinary legislative enactments was only beginning to receive recognition. Constitutions were regarded as binding upon legislatures, yet the obligation to abide by the provisions of a written instrument was conceived to be mainly a moral obligation. The oath prescribed by the New Jersey constitution, which bound the members of the assembly not to assent to any law which appeared to be injurious to the public welfare and not to annul or repeal certain sections thereof, is evidence that members of the assembly were thought to be merely under a moral obligation to preserve the constitution, such as is recognized in European political systems where the courts are in no sense guardians of the fundamental law.

An effort was made in Pennsylvania, New York, and Vermont to protect the fundamental law from encroachments without dependence upon the moral obligation of members of the assembly or the assertion of the right of courts to declare laws invalid. This method of protection was known as the Council of Censors or Council of Revision. A brief survey of the activities of these councils sheds light upon the developing theory of judicial supremacy.[8]

---

[7] Constitution of Maryland; Francis Newton Thorpe, *Constitutions and Charters*, 3 (Washington, 1909) 1690, 1691.

[8] A valuable paper on the subject of the council of censors by Lewis Hamilton Meader was published in the *Pennsylvania Magazine of History and Biography* for October 1898. The author traces the development of the idea of a Council of Censors and gives an account of the history and proceedings of the Councils of Pennsylvania and Vermont.

II. COUNCILS OF CENSORS

1. *Pennsylvania council—*

In the Pennsylvania constitution of 1776, it was provided that the declaration of rights and the constitution ought never to be violated. In order that these provisions might be preserved, every seven years two persons were to be chosen from each city and county of the state who were called a Council of Censors, whose duty it was to inquire whether the constitution has been preserved inviolate in every part; and whether the legislative and executive branches of government have performed their duty as guardians of the people, or assumed to themselves, or exercised other or greater powers than they are entitled to by the constitution.[9]

The council was granted authority to pass public censures, to order impeachments and to recommend to the legislature the repealing of such laws as appeared to them contrary to the principles of the constitution. They also had authority to call a convention if there appeared to them an absolute necessity of amending any article of the constitution which may be defective, explain-

---

[9] Pennsylvania Constitution, 1776, Thorpe, *Charters and Constitutions,* 5:3091, sec. 46: "The declaration is hereby declared to be a part of the constitution of this commonwealth, and ought never to be violated on any pretense whatever." Sec. 47: "In order that the freedom of the commonwealth may be preserved inviolate forever, there shall be chosen by ballot by the freemen of each city and county respectively, on the second Tuesday in October, in the year one thousand, seven hundred and eighty-three, and on the second Tuesday in October, every seventh year thereafter, two persons in each city and county of this state, to be called the Council of Censors; who shall meet together on the second Monday of November next ensuing their election; the majority of whom shall be a quorum in every case, except as to calling a convention, in which two-thirds of the whole number shall agree; and whose duty it shall be to inquire whether the constitution has been preserved inviolate in every part and whether the legislative and executive branches of government have performed their duty as guardians of the people, or assumed to themselves, or exercised other or greater powers than they are entitled to by the constitution; they are also to inquire whether the public taxes have been justly laid and collected in all parts of this commonwealth, in what manner the public monies have been disposed of, and whether the laws have been duly executed.

ing such as may be thought not clearly expressed and adding such as are necessary for the preservation of the right and happiness of the people.

The first council elected under this provision met in November, 1783. A committee of three was designated at once to inquire whether the constitution had been preserved inviolate in every part.[10] The committee noted that the constitution was defective in that it granted an uncontrolled power of legislation which enabled that body "to usurp both the judicial and executive authority, in which case no remedy would remain to the people but by revolution."[11] Numerous amendments to the constitution were proposed, which provided among other things for two houses in the legislature, a single executive, life terms for supreme judges, and no compulsory rotation in office. The vote on these amendments stood yeas 12, nays 9, but the minority claimed that the original vote stood 12 to 10, and that as a consequence the proposals

---

For these purposes they shall have power to send for persons, papers and records; they shall have authority to pass public censures, to order impeachments and to recommend to the legislature the repealing of such laws as appear to them to have been enacted contrary to the principles of the Constitution. These powers they shall continue to have, for and during the space of one year from the day of election and no longer; the said council of censors shall also have power to call a convention, to meet within two years after their sitting, if there appear to them an absolute necessity of amending any article of the constitution which may be defective, explaining such as may be thought not clearly expressed, and of adding such as are necessary for the preservation of the rights and happiness of the people. But the articles to be amended and the amendments proposed and such articles as are proposed to be added or abolished, shall be promulgated at least six months before the day appointed for the previous consideration of the people, that they may have an opportunity of instructing their delegates on the subject.'' For an account of the framing of this constitution, which provided for a unicameral legislature vested with practically supreme power and included other radical features, consult Meader, *op. cit.,* 10–19. The plan for a council of censors is attributed to James Cannon and George Bryan, leaders of the radical element in the convention.— *Ibid.,* 15.

10 *Proceedings relative to the Constitutions of 1776 and 1790 and the Council of Censors,* 68. Also Meader, *op. cit.,* 23–31.

11 *Proceedings,* 70.

were not supported by the necessary two-thirds. Hence they spoke of the subsequent proceedings of the Council as illegal and as establishing an alarming precedent, and they maintained that no appeal could be made to the people to call a constitutional convention.[12]

The session which seemed to have resulted in no action was dominated by the party styling themselves "Republicans" who were opposed to the constitution of 1776. Both the majority and minority prepared reports and appealed to the people in support of their proposals.[13] The majority referred to the people as the sovereigns of Pennsylvania, and advocated a revision of the constitution through other means than the council of censors. A division appeared in the council on the basis of conservatives and radicals. Changes were favored by the conservatives which would have introduced checks and balances and would have more adequately protected property rights. The minority protested that the changes proposed "tend to introduce among the citizens new and aristocratic ranks with a chief magistrate at their head, vested with powers exceeding those which fall to the ordinary lot of kings," and they charged the majority with an attempt to set up class distinctions. Arguments to amend the constitution by the erection of an upper house were answered by many objections and by the advocacy of the existing system of a single legislative assembly. The majority were supported by the eastern counties, composed mainly of the trading and commercial classes, whereas the minority secured its main strength from the western agricultural sections.[14]

---

[12] *Proceedings*, 78.

[13] *Ibid.*, 80–82.

[14] For an account of the party struggles which were waged in Pennsylvania over the early constitutions see "Party Struggles over the Pennsylvania Constitution," by S. B. Harding, Am. Hist. Assoc., *Reports*, 1894, 371.

A second session of the council was held in June, 1784, when a further report was rendered on cases of invasion of the constitution. With regard to the calling of a convention, a committee reported that the constitution of 1776 was "clear in its principles, accurate in its forms, consistent in its several parts and worthy of the veneration of the people of Pennsylvania." Among the laws condemned were the following: (1) acts for seizing goods for the use of the army and settling prices on them, denounced as unconstitutional invasions of the rights of property; (2) acts permitting members of the assembly to hold other offices at the same time; (3) the passing of bills without publication; (4) the assumption of power to appoint to office in cases not granted by the constitution; (5) the withholding of trial by jury; (6) the recognition of the right of Congress to erect corporations.[15] A long list of unconstitutional acts was prepared, with reasons of assent signed by fourteen members and reasons for dissent signed by nine members.[16] The majority again prepared a lengthy report in defense of their proposals, and the minority again dissented, because they said the Council dealt in a great measure with matters "that were never submitted to them, and totally foreign to the nature and design of their appointment."[17]

Because of the fact that eighteen thousand had petitioned against and eight hundred for calling a convention, and because of the fact that this session was dominated by the party known as "Constitutionalists," or those favorable to the constitution of 1776, the committee resolved that there was no necessity to call a convention to alter or amend the constitution.[18] The members lamented the fact that the constitution had intrusted to

---

15 See Harding, *op. cit.*, 387.   17 *Ibid.*, 114.
16 *Proceedings*, 83.   18 *Ibid.*, 124.

them no power of enforcing their decisions. "We can only give our opinion, we can only recommend," they said; "the good sense and virtue of the people are intrusted with the execution."[19] A final appeal was made to the people, in the hope that they would distinguish between the voice of reason and the language of disappointment,[20] and would support the present constitution of the state, which, if properly administered, would give Pennsylvania the best government in the world.

The utter disgust and indignation of the Republicans were voiced by the president of the council, Frederick A. Muhlenberg, when he said: "the rascals know well enough if the intelligent part of the people, and, I assert also, if a majority of the people were properly and equitably represented in the convention, that a change would be the consequence and they would be unhorsed."[21]

The party strife which rent the meetings was largely responsible for the fact that the council speedily declined in public esteem. The general assembly of the state by resolution in March, 1789, voted to call a convention to amend the constitution. Although a minority of seven-

---

[19] *Proceedings,* 124.

[20] *Ibid.,* 126.

[21] Am. Hist. Assoc., *Reports* 1894, 388; President Muhlenberg further expressed his disgust in a letter to his brother on June 28, 1784. After criticizing the Council for not being based upon representation in accordance with the tax burden of the state, he continued: "In brief, the whole thing is a farce, costs the state five thousand or six thousand dollars, keeps the people in a ferment, and is not worth a farthing. I am ashamed to be a member, and if it might not be said 'You forsook the vessel in the storm,' or 'You are afraid to weather it out,' I would have resigned long ere this; perhaps I should do so yet, for I can neither before God nor the world answer for thus wasting my precious time, robbing the State, and doing only mischief. The fellows from the back counties now hope to stay here till next October to draw their 17s. 6d. and to return home with a well filled purse. Some of them will get at the end of the session more money than they ever had in their lives. In short, dear brother, I am losing patience and draw a deep sigh at the corrupt political condition of our State."—Harding, *op. cit.,* 388; also Meader, *op. cit.,* 28–31.

teen members came to the defense of the constitution, the assembly indicated quite emphatically its preference for a convention instead of waiting for the ordinary procedure of a council of censors, which they criticized as a body "not only unequal and unnecessarily expensive but too dilatory to produce the speedy and necessary alterations."[22]   In the constitution which resulted from the deliberations of this convention, the section relative to a council of censors was dropped, and no provision was made either for the guardianship of the fundamental law or its amendment.   Thus came to an end the rather inglorious career of the Pennsylvania council of censors.

2. *Vermont council—*

In the Vermont constitution of 1777 the Pennsylvania provision for a council of censors was incorporated *verbatim,* with the exception that a different method of election was adopted.[23]   The first session of the Vermont council convened in October, 1785. A number of statutes were condemned, among them acts to prevent riots, against counterfeiting, to prevent unseasonable night walking, and to prevent the selling of hides. The council also criticized the assembly for its practice of acting as a court of appeal asserting that, "in all instances where they have vacated judgments, recovered in the due course of law (except where the particular circumstances of the case evidently made it necessary to grant a new trial), [they] have exercised a power not delegated or intended to be delegated to them by the Constitution."[24]   Such proceedings were regarded as contrary to the clause of the Bill of Rights guaranteeing trial by jury and against the interests of the community that "so numerous a body

---

22 *Proceedings,* 133.   24 D. Chipman, *Reports,* preface, 24–26.
23 Thorpe, *op. cit.,* 6:3760.

as the Governor, Council, and General Assembly of the State should be employed in determining causes between party and party."[25] Certain particular acts of this character in which new trials were granted were disapproved. A copy of a revised constitution was prepared with amendments favored by the council. Among the recommendations for amendments it was proposed: first, to have a senate instead of the present executive council; second, to provide a court of chancery distinct from courts of law; third, judges were to hold office during good behavior; fourth, the governor, and the judges of the supreme court were to act as a council of revision to examine all acts before they became law, a provision suggested no doubt by the New York council of revision.[26] The council prepared an address in which the legislature was severely criticized, and in which there was recommended the calling of a convention to amend the constitution. In June, 1786, the convention met and ratified some of the amendments suggested, including provisions that the legislative, executive, and judicial departments be kept distinct and that the governor and the council have a qualified veto power.[27]

At the outset, recognizing that in Vermont the legislature was supreme, the council attempted to do nothing more than to make recommendations to the legislature and to issue an appeal to the people.[28] The enforcement of the constitution was primarily in the hands of the

---

[25] *Journal* of Council of Censors of Vermont, 23.

[26] *Ibid.*, 13–15.

[27] Meader, *Council of Censors*, 43.

[28] The people of Vermont appear to have regarded the constitution as in the nature of an ordinary act of the legislature. It was not until 1796 that the legislature declared the constitution to be the supreme law of the land.—Meader, *Council of Censors*, 42; also Judge Chipman's *Memoirs of Thomas Chittenden*, chap. 5.

legislature, and the practice of revising and annulling judgments of the courts naturally confirmed the notion that the legislature was supreme.[29] This fact, along with the establishment of the council, prevented the judiciary from inquiring into the constitutionality of acts of the legislature.[30] A second session of the council convened in 1792, and proposed some radical changes in the constitution, with a recommendation that a senate replace the executive council so as to provide a bicameral legislative chamber. The council reported that it was happy to find no acts which were unconstitutional or deserving of censure.[31] The convention called to consider the proposed amendments refused to adopt any of them and gave an indication of the lack of popular approval which was soon to bring the council into discredit.

Every seven years a new council was elected, which held up to condemnation acts of the legislature and made

---

[29] 1 D. Chipman, *Vermont Reports*, 13, 22; see also W. F. Dodd, *Revision and Amendment of State Constitutions*, 36, 37. Professor Dodd cites an instance where the legislature clearly violated the constitution without as much as a protest from the Council of Censors. The work of the Council is thus described by Judge Chipman: ''The Council of Censors it appears had learned from experience the necessity of limiting the powers of the Legislature, of prohibiting them from an interference with the Judiciary department, and, for this purpose, inserted the following article in the Constitution which was adopted: 'The Legislative, Executive and Judiciary departments shall be separate and distinct, so that neither exercise the power properly belonging to the other.' Yet as they provided for an annual election of the Judges, it is evident that they considered this article as merely directory. They did not at that time consider such Constitution established by the people, to be in its nature the supreme law of the land, of course paramount to all laws enacted by a Legislature, deriving all their power from the same Constitution. Nor did they conceive that Courts would consider it as such, or, that they would pronounce any act of the legislature void, as being repugnant to the constitution.''—1 D. Chipman, *Reports*, 24, 25; *Vermont State Papers*, 537.

[30] ''Long after the period to which we have alluded [1786],'' says Judge Chipman, ''the doctrine that the Constitution is the supreme law of the land, and that the Judiciary have authority to set aside and pronounce void all acts of the Legislative repugnant thereto was considered anti-republican.''—1 D. Chipman *Reports*, preface, 25, 26.

[31] Meader, *op. cit.*, 44.

recommendations for their repeal and at times offered specific amendments to the constitution. The criticisms of the legislature in granting new trials grew in severity with each succeeding session, and it was noted with much regret that the practice was continued "notwithstanding the repeated animadversions of different councils of censors."[32] The session of 1827, after noting the lack of acceptance of the various recommendations of the council, announced with evidence of much satisfaction "that the highest judicial tribunals have pronounced these acts void, and they have reason to hope this decisive interposition of the courts will hereafter prevent their enactment."[33] In fact after the experience of thirty years men had begun to recognize that the council of censors was a failure.[34]

Amendments to the constitution suggested by the censors in the sessions of 1792, 1814, 1820, and 1827 were promptly defeated by state conventions. And although the council continued to meet to consider the laws in relation to the constitution and to offer amendments, the members appeared unable to account for the failure to adopt any of the many amendments proposed except through the method of electing delegates.[35] The session which convened in 1842 subscribed to the proposition that

it is an attribute of the supreme judicial tribunals to judge of the constitutionality of all laws passed by the legislature, when properly brought before them. They are always to regard the constitution as the fundamental law of the land, and superior

---

[32] *Journal*, session 1827:34–39.

[33] Meader, *op. cit.*, 44.

[34] Williams, *History of Vermont*, 2:400–401, also, 1 Chipman, *Reports*, 20.

[35] *Journal*, 67, session 1834, Mr. Meader thinks "one may reasonably infer that the Councils of Censors were more nearly abreast of the times in governmental affairs while the constitutional conventions represented the conservatism of the state," 53.

to any legislative enactment. Consequently, if the law is not warranted by, or is repugnant to, the provisions of the constitution, as is sometimes the case, the judges are bound to pronounce it inoperative and void.[36]

And it was apparently recognized that in the acceptance of this proposition there was no longer any excuse for a council of censors since its purpose was more effectively fulfilled by a totally different method now firmly intrenched as a part of the judicial system of practically all the states. A proposal to abolish the council, however, was not acted on favorably and perfunctory sessions were held until 1869, when the council was eliminated by a convention, on its own recommendation. The fact that the legislature was recognized as the supreme department of government, and that the function of guarding the constitution was ostensibly intrusted to a council of censors, retarded the acceptance in Vermont of the doctrine that it was the duty of the courts to declare invalid acts contrary to the fundamental law.[37]

3. *New York council of revision—*

New York, in the constitution of 1777, provided for a council of revision with a function similar to that of the councils of censors, but organized the body on a different plan.[38] Assuming that ''laws inconsistent with the spirit of the constitution or with the public good'' might be

---

[36] *Journal*, session 1842, 16.

[37] See *infra*, Dupy v. Wickwire, 168.

[38] New York Constitution, 1777, sec. 3. ''And whereas laws inconsistent with the spirit of this constitution, or with the public good may be hastily and inadvisedly passed: Be it ordained, that the governor for the time being, the chancellor, and the judges of the supreme court, or any two of them, together with the governor, shall be, and hereby are, constituted a council to revise all bills about to be passed into laws by the legislature: and for that purpose shall assemble themselves from time to time when the legislature shall be convened; for which, nevertheless, they shall not receive any salary, or consideration under any pretense whatever. And that all

hastily and inadvisedly passed, the governor, chancellor, and judges of the Supreme Court were constituted a council to review all bills about to become laws. The council was expected to exercise something in the nature of a veto power. Bills which were not approved were to be returned with the objections and might be enacted into law over the veto of the council by a two-thirds vote of each house of the assembly. In case a bill was not returned within ten days it became a law without the approval of the council.

The history of this council is interesting, because it not only exercised a sort of veto power, but was also charged with the special duty of guarding the spirit of the fundamental law. When bills were forwarded to the council and objections were offered, a copy with the signature of the governor was submitted to the house which had last passed the act.[39] During the existence of the council one hundred and sixty-nine bills were returned with objections. Fifty-one of the bills were passed into laws by a two-thirds vote of the legislature; the remain-

---

bills which have passed the senate and assembly shall, before they become laws, be presented to said council for their revisal and consideration; and if, upon such revision and consideration, it shall appear improper to the said council, or a majority of them, that the said bill shall become a law of this state that they return the same, together with their objections thereto in writing, to the senate or house of assembly (in which soever the same shall have originated), who shall enter the objection sent down by the council at large in their minutes and proceed to reconsider the said bill. But if, after such reconsideration, two thirds of the said senate or house of assembly shall, notwithstanding the said objections, agree to pass the same, it shall, together with the objections, be sent to the other branch of the legislature, where it shall also be reconsidered, and if approved by two thirds of the number present, shall be a law.

"And in order to prevent any unnecessary delays, be it further ordained, that if any bill shall not be returned by the council within ten days after it shall have been presented, the same shall be a law, unless the legislature shall, by their adjournment, render a return of the said bill within ten days impracticable; in which case the bill shall be returned on the first day of the meeting of the legislature after the expiration of the said ten days."—Thorpe, *op. cit.*, 5:2628, 2629.

[39] A. B. Street, *Council of Revision of the State of New York*, 7.

ing one hundred and eighteen failed to become laws.[40] Among the vetoes of the council many were based on the ground that the acts were contrary to the constitution. On February 20, 1778, a bill to prevent the exportation of flour, meat, and grain was objected to as "being inconsistent with the spirit of the constitution of this state."[41] Notwithstanding the objections the legislature passed the act. A bill for raising a further sum by tax "from those who, taking advantage of the necessities of their country, have, in prosecuting their private gain, amassed large sums of money to the great prejudice of the public" was objected to as being inconsistent with the spirit of the constitution "because an equal right to life, liberty and property is a fundamental principle in all free societies and states, and is intended to be secured to the people of this state by the constitution thereof."[42] On account of the objections of the council the bill did not become a law.

A series of bills were criticized as being inconsistent with the constitution but were passed by the legislature, notwithstanding the objections of the council. Measures which were thus enacted into law over the council's veto included bills for the sale of forfeited estates; for the organization of the supreme court; for settling estates, which deprived citizens of the right of trial by jury; and for punishing disorderly persons. In the course of objections to a bill for the payment of salaries it was observed that the council found it to be their duty to remind the legislature of the principles of the constitution, and

---

[40] Street, *op. cit.*, 7; a different result is recorded by Thorpe on the authority of Hough. It is stated that the council objected to one hundred and twenty-eight bills, of which seventeen were passed notwithstanding these objections.—5:2629.

[41] For summary of vetoes by the council, see Street, 202 *et seq.*

[42] Street, *op. cit.*, 214–216.

those great maxims relative to the independence of the judiciary department which general experience had proved essential to the public good. But despite the protest this act also was passed.

Measures which failed of enactment because of objections on the ground of unconstitutionality included acts of incorporation, the licensing of coaches, the appropriation of land for highways and streets, restraint in the issuance of lottery tickets, and concerning the judges of the supreme court. In the latter instance a court of five judges was upheld by the council "as a common law principle not subject to change by the legislature." The act was condemned as an effort to place the council in absolute subserviency to the legislature instead of permitting it to act as a check upon their proceedings and to keep them within constitutional bounds.

In 1820 the legislature recommended a convention without submitting the question to the voters. When the bill was referred to the council, the measure was returned with the observation that

the difficulty of acceding to such a measure of reform, without the previous approbation of the constituents of the government, presses with peculiar force and with painful anxiety upon the Council of Revision, which was instituted for the express purpose of guarding the Constitution against the passage of laws inconsistent with its spirit.

The objections were referred to a committee of the House, which reported that it was doubtful "whether the council possessed the constitutional power arbitrarily to object to the passage of bills upon mere opinions, vaguely expressed, respecting their propriety or expediency."[43] The committee believed that it belonged to a convention to

---

[43] Street, *op. cit.*, 391.

determine whether a council independent of the people should be allowed to exercise so dangerous an authority.[44] Although a decided opinion was expressed in favor of curbing the authority of the council of revision, the two-thirds majority necessary for its passage was not secured. By special act the question of a convention was submitted to the people, and as a result New York adopted the constitution of 1821, and the council, which had existed for forty-four years, was abolished.

In New York and Pennsylvania, as in Vermont, the assertion of the right of courts to declare laws invalid was delayed because of the provisions in their constitutions establishing a council of censors or a council of revision. The courts in Pennsylvania on several occasions asserted that they had the power to declare laws invalid, but they did not at any time refuse validity to a legislative act.[45] As late as 1825 this power was denied in the dissenting opinion by Justice Gibson,[46] who afterward became chief justice of Pennsylvania. The first case in which the Supreme Court of New York declared a state law of no effect because in violation of the state constitution is *People v. Foot* in 1821.[47]

The effort to limit legislative power and to maintain the distinction between constitutions as fundamental en-

---

[44] Street, *op. cit.*, 465.

[45] Respublica v. Duquet, 2 Yeats 293 (1799); Emerick v. Harris, 1 Binney 416 (1808); Commonwealth v. Smith, 4 Binney 117 (1811).

[46] Eakin v. Raub, 12 S. & R., 330. See *infra*, 272 *et seq.*

[47] 19 Johns. 58. In Beadleston v. Sprague, 6 Johns. 101 (1810), the supreme court of New York construed a statute so as not to destroy a previously acquired right. Also in Dash v. Van Kleeck, 7 Johns. 477 (1811), an act was construed not to operate retrospectively so as to take away a vested right. And in People v. Platt state acts were held void because in violation of the clause of the federal Constitution relating to the impairment of the obligation of contracts.—17 Johns. 195 (1819). The court of chancery in Gardner v. Newburgh, 2 Johns. Ch. 162 (1816), granted an injunction against the enforcement of a statute relating to eminent domain proceedings until provision was made for awarding just compensation to persons who might be injured thereby.

actments and ordinary statutes, by means of a separately constituted body failed signally in Pennsylvania, accomplished very little in Vermont and, separate from the veto power, was not a successful check on the legislature in New York, since a large percentage of acts, objected to on the ground of unconstitutionality, was enacted into law in that state despite the protests of the council. It is not surprising, then, to find each of the above states abandoning the plan of a council of censors and confiding the guardianship of the fundamental law to the judiciary which in other states had asserted the authority to act as a check upon legislative encroachments. The one device to protect the fundamental law, other than the doctrine of judicial supremacy, to which men turned in the days of the American Revolution,[48] was such a conspicuous failure that it merely tended to strengthen the cause of those who favored judicial guardianship of constitutions. It was the council of revision which was proposed for the federal government in the convention at Philadelphia and which led to most of the discussion in that body relative to the function of the judiciary in relation to the review of legislation.[49]

It was customary to provide in the state constitutions that the fundamental law should never be violated and to prescribe that all powers not delegated by the constitution were "excepted out of the general powers of government and were to remain forever inviolate." The method of preventing violations of constitutions, however, was rarely indicated, but was left to be developed by custom and practical experience.

---

[48] Jefferson embodied the plan of a council of revision in his proposed constitution for the state of Virginia drafted in 1783. See *Writings*, 4:161, 162.

[49] For details of this discussion, see chap. 6.

CHAPTER V

DEVELOPMENT OF THE PRACTICE OF JUDICIAL REVIEW OF LEGISLATIVE ACTS: STATE PRECEDENTS PRIOR TO 1789

THE STATE cases in which the American practice of review of legislative acts was first announced, and which were recognized as precedents in its development and extension, have an important rôle in the legal history of the United States. In order to present the ideas relating to judicial review as conceived by the founders of the American government, it is necessary to give a concise statement of the facts and issues involved in some of the early cases, and to quote from the opinions of the judges justifying their views in passing on the validity of legislative acts. The list as presented is not intended to be exhaustive—for historians are still finding data on new cases—but representative precedents are selected which were known and recognized as instances involving either directly or indirectly the issue of the validity of a legislative act as in conflict with natural law and natural rights or with fundamental written law.[1]

---

[1] The most complete treatment of state cases may be found in James Bradley Thayer, *Cases on Constitutional Law* (Cambridge, 1895) 1:48–80; Brinton Coxe, *Judicial Power and Unconstitutional Legislation* (Philadelphia, 1893) 219–270; Edward S. Corwin, "The Establishment of Judicial Review," 9 *Mich. Law Rev.* (Dec. 1910 and Feb. 1911) 102 and 283, and *The Doctrine of Judicial Review* (Princeton, 1914); and William M. Meigs, *The Relation of the Judiciary to the Constitution* (New York, 1919).

The account of early cases is not confined to definite legal precedents, for a number of cases are included in which no act was held invalid, but in which the judges discussed the issue of judicial review in the form of dicta. Popular impressions and assumptions are likely to form part of the content of legal doctrines and this was particularly true from 1776 to 1820 when the American doctrine of judicial review of legislation was being adopted. There were few volumes of published law reports and the cases relating to judicial review were seldom rendered available for common use and understanding except through reports in the public press. Under such circumstances reports or impressions passed from person to person were frequently the only means by which what now seem like important legal decisions could become known. It is not surprising then to find that the impressions which prevailed regarding cases were often not strictly in accord with the facts. Nevertheless these impressions were in certain instances important factors in determining men's views regarding judicial control over legislation.

1. *Case of Josiah Philips,* Virginia 1778[2]—

In May, 1778, the General Assembly of Virginia, on the recommendation of a committee composed of Jefferson, Smith, and Tyler, passed an act in the form of a bill of attainder against Josiah Philips and a band of outlaws who were accused of instituting a reign of terror among the sparsely settled communities of Virginia. A few weeks after the passage of this act Philips and several of his associates were captured and later executed. In the

---

[2] For an account of the case of Josiah Philips see article by William P. Trent, *Am. Hist. Rev.* (April 1896) 1:444–454; and Jesse Turner, "A Phantom Precedent," 48 *Am. Law Rev.* (March-June 1914) 321.

debates concerning the adoption of the federal Constitution in Virginia the impression prevailed that Philips was condemned and executed under the bill of attainder. It was this alleged procedure which Randolph criticized in the Virginia convention. He maintained that the bill for the attaint of Philips was prepared beforehand and read three times in one day, and that the prisoner was sentenced to death and executed without the privilege of presenting evidence in his behalf.[3] Randolph appears to have misrepresented a number of the facts relating to the case but his inaccurate statements were not controverted by any of those who attempted to defend the action of the assembly, and the impression appeared to prevail that there had been a monstrous violation of the principles of justice.[4]

When Philips was brought to trial according to available evidence the act of assembly was ignored and the outlaws were tried for robbery and condemned in accordance with the regular criminal procedure of the common law.[5] The significance of the case from the standpoint of judicial control over legislation lies in the ground upon which the attorney general ignored the bill of attainder and proceeded to trial. As to the reasons for disregarding the act there seems to be no direct evidence. One explanation is that the attorney general was advised by the judges that the act of attainder was void and that sentence would not be passed under the act. If this explanation be true the case would form an interesting precedent for judicial control over legislative acts. Confirmation for this procedure is found in Judge Tucker's edition of Blackstone published in 1803, in which he commented on the case as follows:

---

[3] 3 Elliot's *Debates*, 66, 67.   [4] Trent, *op. cit.*, 449, 450.   [5] *Ibid.*, 448.

In May, 1778, an act passed in Virginia, to attaint one Josiah Philips unless he should render himself to justice within a limited time; he was taken after the time had expired and was brought before the general court to receive sentence of execution pursuant to the directions of the act. But the court refused to pass the sentence and he was put upon trial according to the ordinary course of law. This is a decisive proof of the importance of the separation of the powers of government, and of the independence of the judiciary; a dependent judiciary might have executed the law, whilst they execrated the principles upon which it was founded.[6]

Another explanation is that Philips was tried and executed according to common law procedure, and not under the bill of attainder, because the time set for the act of attainder to take effect had not expired and that it was necessary to try Philips for an offense under the criminal law. Opinions differ as to which of these explanations of the reasons for the attorney general's action is more nearly correct.[7] Whatever conclusion may be reached regarding the disposition of the case it has a peculiar interest from the standpoint of the developing notion regarding the right of the courts to hold invalid legislative acts considered in conflict with the provisions of written constitutions, though no one regards it as a real precedent.[8] For regardless of the actual facts of the case

[6] 1 *Tucker's Blackstone*, Appendix, 293. Though this work was published fifteen years after the case Judge Tucker as a member of the court and an associate of some of the judges at the time of Philips' trial was familiar with the circumstances of the case.

[7] Professor Corwin rejects this case as having no basis in fact and as a "myth elaborated in an ingenious series of conjectures."—*The Doctrine of Judicial Review*, 71. This judgment fails to give due weight to the influence on legal thinking of incorrect facts and incorrect assumptions when such facts and assumptions are believed to be true. Professor Trent regards the first explanation as on the whole the more reliable and more plausible. Cf. *op. cit.*, 453. Mr. Turner believes that evidence sustains the second explanation. Cf. *op. cit.*, 342.

[8] The Virginia constitution of 1776 had no provision against the passage of acts of attainder.

Judge Tucker's statement made current at the time a view which placed the case among the early precedents favorable to judicial review.[9]

2. *Holmes v. Walton,* New Jersey, 1780—

The courts of New Jersey were pioneers in asserting the principle of judicial control over legislation. *Holmes v. Walton* appears to be the first recorded case where a court definitely invalidated an act because it was deemed to be in conflict with a provision of the written constitution of the state. The case arose over an act of the legislature of 1778 providing for the seizure of goods belonging to the enemy, and granting in such cases a trial by a jury of six men from whose decision no appeal was allowed.[10] In the enforcement of this act an appeal was taken to the supreme court on the ground that a jury consisting of only six men was contrary to law and contrary to the constitution of New Jersey. The case was argued before the supreme court in November, 1779, and judgment was not rendered until September, 1780, ten months after the time of the argument.[11] There is no record of the opinion of the court in the case, but reliable evidence shows that, relying on section xxii of the constitution of 1776, which provided that the inestimable right of trial by jury shall remain confirmed as "a part of the law of this colony without repeal forever," the court held

---

[9] Cf. reference to this case by Justice Yeates, of Pennsylvania, in Emerick v. Harris, 1 Binney's Reports (1808) 415, 420. The reference is based on Tucker's version; also in opinion by Theoderick Bland (*infra,* 269). "It is not at all impossible," says Professor McLaughlin, "that this case may have been later looked upon, despite various distortions of the facts, as a case in which the court asserted its independent right to interpret the constitution."—*The Courts, The Constitution and Parties* (Chicago, 1912) 48.

[10] Wilson's *Laws of New Jersey,* Appendix, v.

[11] Austin Scott, "Holmes v. Walton; The New Jersey Precedent," *Rutgers College Publication,* 5. Published also in 4 *Am. Hist. Rev.* (April 1899) 456.

the statute void.[12] The best direct evidence is in the nature of a petition to the House of Assembly in December, 1780,

complaining that the justices of the Supreme Court have set aside some of the laws as unconstitutional, and made void the proceedings of the magistrates, though strictly agreeable to the said laws, to the encouragement of the disaffected and great loss to the loyal citizens of the state.[13]

Other petitions denouncing the decision were submitted to the assembly and an attempt was made to prevent the removal of such causes to the supreme court.[14] The next session of the legislature, with these protests before it, ratified the action of the court by passing a law requiring justices on the demand of either party to grant a jury of twelve men.[15] From this and other contemporary evidence it is certain that the court refused to give effect to the act, and thus asserted its right as special guardian of the written fundamental law.[16] The decision of the judges was no doubt affected by a section of the constitution which prescribed, in the oath of the members of the legislature, that trial by jury should be held inviolate. But it is significant that a court of justice should assume the rôle of interpreting and enforcing upon members of the legislature the terms prescribed in such oath, and that the judiciary should assert the right to determine the procedure involved in trial by jury according to the meaning of the phrase as used in the constitution.

Professor Scott exaggerates the importance of the case in an attempt to demonstrate its influence on the

---

[12] *Ibid.*, 6, 7.

[13] *Votes and Proceedings of House of Assembly*, 52.

[14] Scott, *op. cit.*, 8, 9; 4 *Am. Hist. Rev.*, 462.

[15] Wilson's *Laws*, Appendix, Act of December 22, 1780.

[16] See reference to the decision in this case by Chief Justice Kirkpatrick in State v. Parkhurst, 4 Halstead (1804) 444. Cf. *supra*, 163.

federal convention in Philadelphia and in the assertion that it takes precedence in point of time of all similar decisions.[17] David Brearly, William Paterson, and William Livingston, members of the federal convention, were prominently connected with the case and were favorable to judicial control over legislation. But of their actual service in the convention in influencing opinion on this matter we have little direct evidence. The resolution, originally drafted by William Paterson, which made the federal laws and treaties the supreme law of the states, binding the judges thereof notwithstanding state laws to the contrary, was incorporated into the final draft of the Constitution from the New Jersey plan,[18] but this resolution did not settle the difficult problem as to the proper guardians of the federal Constitution and laws.

Too much weight can readily be given to the influence of this case in tracing the establishment of the American doctrine. There is danger in according too great emphasis to any one of these early state precedents, particularly because of the fact that most of the decisions were not published until many years later and frequently the opinions which appear so important today were unknown, except to the parties primarily concerned, until an interested court reporter or enthusiastic student brought to light long neglected judicial opinions. It is quite natural that the claims of various states should be urged as taking precedence in the formulation of the American doctrine. But the gradual evolution of ideas relating to judicial review of legislation in Virginia, Rhode Island, South Carolina, and North Carolina before the framing of the

---

17 "The New Jersey Precedent," 17. For comment on the undue importance attributed to this case, see McLaughlin, *The Courts, the Constitution and Political Parties*, 41 n.

18 Elliot's *Debates*, 5:322; "The New Jersey Precedent," 14.

federal Constitution takes away from any one state the particular claim of having introduced the principle in American law. It seems rather that a series of precedents with a cumulative effect, along with a common sentiment in practically all of the states, led men to accept certain ideas which made review of legislative acts by the courts seem necessary.

The New Jersey court must, however, be given credit for definitely supporting a constitutional provision as against a legislative enactment, and for setting, in this respect, a precedent in the development of the American doctrine. That the decision was influential in arousing sentiment in other states is indicated by the comments of Gouverneur Morris. In a reference to this decision in 1785, Morris remarked,

They know that the boasted omnipotence of legislative authority is but a jingle of words. In the literal meaning it is impious. And whatever interpretation lawyers may give, freemen must feel it to be absurd and unconstitutional. Absurd, because laws cannot alter the nature of things; unconstitutional, because the constitution is no more, if it can be changed by the legislature.[19]

In New Jersey, he noted, the judges have pronounced a law unconstitutional and void; but he did not wish to see the courts of Pennsylvania decide upon the constitutionality of acts for fear that such power in the hands of judges would be dangerous.[20]

3. *Commonwealth v. Caton*, Virginia, 1782—

In Virginia, the case of *Commonwealth v. Caton*[21] raised the question whether the courts could declare void

---

[19] Jared Sparks, *Memoirs of Gouverneur Morris* (Boston, 1832) 3:438.

[20] See opinion of Morris favoring judicial review, *Annals* of Congress, 7 Cong., 1 sess., 180, 181.

[21] 4 Call 5.

an act of the assembly. Three men were condemned for treason by the General Court under an act passed in 1776. The house of delegates, by resolution of the 17th of June, 1782, granted them a pardon, and sent it to the senate for concurrence, which was refused. The men continued in jail under the sentence until October, 1782, when the attorney general moved in the General Court that execution of judgment might be entered. The prisoners pleaded the pardon granted by the house of delegates. The attorney general denied the validity of the resolution as the senate had not concurred in it, and the General Court referred the case to the Court of Appeals.

Justice Wythe maintained that, as a member of the court, it was plainly and unmistakably his duty to resist the legislature in an attempted exercise of powers inconsistent with the constitution. In the course of his opinion, he observed:

Although it was said the other day by one of the judges, that, imitating that great and good man Lord Hale, he would sooner quit the bench than determine it, I feel no alarm; but will meet the crisis as I ought; and, in the language of my oath of office, will decide it according to the best of my skill and judgment.

I have heard of an English chancellor who said, and it was nobly said, that it was his duty to protect the rights of the subject against the encroachment of the Crown, and that he would do it at every hazard. But if it was his duty to protect a solitary individual against the rapacity of the sovereign, surely, it is equally mine to protect one branch of legislature, and consequently, the whole community, against the usurpations of the other; and, whenever the proper occasion occurs, I shall feel the duty; and, fearlessly, perform it. Whenever traitors shall be fairly convicted by the verdict of their peers, before the competent tribunal, if one branch of legislature, without the concurrence of the other, shall attempt to rescue the offenders from sentence of the law, I shall not hesitate, sitting in this place to say to the General Court, *Fiat justitia ruat coelum;* and, to the usurping branch of the legislature, you attempt worse than a vain thing; for although you cannot succeed you set an example which may convulse society to its center. Nay more, if the whole legislature, an event to be deprecated, should attempt to over-leap the bounds prescribed to them by the people, I, in adminis-tering the public justice of the country will meet the united powers, at my seat in this tribunal; and, pointing to the consti-tution, will say to them, here is the limit of your authority; and hither shall you go, but no further.[22]

Justice Pendleton was less dogmatic when he said:

How far this court, in whom the judiciary power may in some sort be said to be concentrated, shall have power to declare the nullity of a law passed in its forms by the legislative power, without exercising the power of that branch, contrary to the plain terms of that constitution, is indeed a deep, important and I will add, a tremendous question, the decision of which might involve consequences to which gentlemen may not have extended their ideas. I am happy in being of opinion there is no occasion to consider it upon this occasion; and still more happy in the hope that the wisdom and prudence of the legis-lature will prevent the disagreeable necessity of ever deciding it, by suggesting the propriety of making the principles of the Constitution the great rule to direct the spirit of their laws.[23]

The report states that "Chancellor Blair and the rest of the judges, were of the opinion that the court had power to declare any resolution or act of the legislature or either branch of it, to be unconstitutional and void." But the treason act being regarded as valid, the senate not having concurred in the resolution which was under consideration and as a consequence no statute was before the court, the opinions were in the nature of dicta. As this case involved a defect in the formal requirements as

---

[22] 4 Call 7, 8.   [23] *Ibid.*, 17, 18.

to the passage of a law it comes within a category where review of legislation by courts is generally presumed to exist.

The claim has also been advanced that this was the first case wherein the question relative to the constitutionality of a law was discussed before a judicial tribunal. And the reporter of the volume notes that "the firmness of the judges (particularly of Mr. Wythe) was highly honorable to them: and will always be applauded, as having incidentally fixed a precedent, whereon a general practice, which the people of this country think essential to their rights, and liberty has been established."[24]

4. *Rutgers v. Waddington*, New York, 1784—[25]

Very soon after the judges of Virginia had asserted the right to declare legislative acts invalid, an issue was determined in the mayor's court of New York which involved the judiciary of that state in a memorable controversy. The case arose on an action for trespass brought against Joshua Waddington for the occupancy of a brewery belonging to Elizabeth Rutgers, during part of the period covered by the Revolutionary War, 1778 to 1783. The action was brought under a statute of New York, which provided that any one who left his place of abode, and who had not voluntarily put himself into the power of the enemy, should be entitled to recover in an action of trespass against any person or persons who may have occupied or destroyed his estate.[26] The object of the law was to authorize an action of trespass by owners of property who had vacated the premises during British

---

24 4 Call 20; see Case of Kamper v. Hawkins, 1 Va. Cases 20 (1793) *infra*, 152.

25 J. B. Thayer, *Leading Cases on Constitutional Law*, 1:63; Brinton Coxe, *Judicial Power and Unconstitutional Legislation*, 223.

26 *Sessions Law*, March 17, 1783 (original edition) 283, 284.

possession of the city as against Tory occupants. And no defendant was permitted to plead in justification any military order or command of the enemy. It developed in the trial that from September, 1778, to April, 1780, the premises had been occupied by order of the military commander in charge of the district and that the actual voluntary trespass covered from April, 1780, to March, 1783, the date of the passage of the above act.[27] Hamilton, as attorney for Waddington, argued that the state law was contrary to the Articles of Confederation, to the treaty of peace, and to the law of nations, and therefore null and void.[28]

In the course of their opinion the judges defended the right to interpret statutes reasonably and asserted, that

The supremacy of the legislature need not be called into question; if they think fit positively to enact a law, there is no power which can control them. When the main object of such a law is clearly expressed, and the intention manifest, the judges are not at liberty, although it appears to them to be reasonable, to reject it; for this were to set the judicial above the legislative, which would be subversive of all government.

But when a law is expressed in general words, and some collateral matter, which happens to arise from those general words, is unreasonable, then the judges are in decency to conclude that the consequences were not foreseen by the legislature; and therefore they are at liberty to expound the statute by equity, and only *quod ad hoc* to disregard it.

When the judicial make these distinctions, they do not control the legislature; they endeavor to give their intention its proper effect.

---

[27] For a full history of this case consult "'An account of the Case of Elizabeth Rutgers v. Joshua Waddington," edited with an historical introduction by Henry B. Dawson.

[28] Allan McLane Hamilton, *Intimate Life of Alexander Hamilton* (New York, 1910) 457 ff. and *Works* (Federal ed.) 4:238–240.

This is the substance of the authorities on a comprehensive view of the subject; this is the language of Blackstone in his celebrated *Commentaries,* and this is the practice of the courts of justice, from which we have copied our jurisprudence, as well as the models of our own judicatories.[29]

After having stated the rule of Blackstone regarding legislative omnipotence and having affirmed the doctrine that the supremacy of the legislature need not be called into question, the justices proceeded to disregard that part of the statute which would, as it seemed, operate unreasonably, apparently in an effort to avoid a conflict between the statute and the treaty of peace. A decision was rendered to the effect that although a statute must be regarded as obligatory, collateral matters which arise out of the general words which happen to be unreasonable may be disregarded by the court.[30]

The case involved a recent state statute and the Treaty of Peace of 1783. According to the general impression, one or the other had to give way. And from the fact that the fate of many other suits depended upon the decision, the trial was viewed with grave interest and alarm by the contending parties. It was feared that a conflict between the nation and one of the states concerning the execution of the provisions of the treaty might involve the United States in international difficulties.[31]

---

[29] Pamphlet by Dawson, 40.

[30] Dawson, *op. cit.,* 41.

[31] Coxe, *Judicial Power and Unconstitutional Legislation,* 223. For references to this case, see Hamilton, *Works* (Lodge ed.) 5:227 and 7:198, and Jefferson, *Writings* (Mem. ed.) 16:239–241.

The uncertainty resulting from the decision of Rutgers v. Waddington led Congress to enact resolutions to the effect that the legislatures of the states could not pass any acts limiting or impeding the operation of national treaties which are a "part of the law of the land and are not only independent of the will and power of such legislation but also binding and obligatory on them." The states were urged to repeal all legislation of this character. In a circular of April 13, 1787, to the states it was asserted

The court interpreted the statute so as to avoid a conflict of authorities. Although no act was declared void, and the opinion on the whole was favorable to legislative supremacy, it was commonly thought that the decision resulted in invalidating a portion at least of a state statute, and a determined protest was made at the next session of the House of Assembly and at public mass meetings.

The Whigs, as those were called who belonged to the party in the state under the leadership of Clinton, considered the decision "subversive of good order and the sovereignty of the state"; and on the 13th of September, 1784, a meeting was called to discuss ways and means of bringing the dangers of the decision before the public. As a result of this meeting a committee was appointed of which Melancthon Smith was the leader, to prepare and publish an address to the people of the state.[32] The history and facts of the case were briefly stated and a criticism rendered, which is of no little interest. From the statement of the case as given, it appeared to the committee that the mayor's court had assumed and exercised a power to set aside an act of the state; that it had permitted the vague and doubtful custom of nations to render ineffective a clear and positive statute. "This proceeding," they claimed, "in the opinion of a great part of the citizens of this metropolis, and in our opinion, is an assumption of power in that court, which is inconsistent

---

that "when therefore a treaty is constitutionally made, ratified and published by us, it becomes binding on the whole nation, and superadded to the laws of the land, without the intervention of state legislatures."—*Journals of Congress* (ed. of 1801) 12, March 21 and April 13, 1787.

[32] Matthew L. Davis, *Memoirs of Aaron Burr* (New York, 1837), 2:45. The address was published in the *New York Packet* and the *American Advertiser*, No. 434, Thursday, November 4, 1784. Cf. Dawson's "Account of Rutgers v. Waddington," 25-40.

with the nature and genius of our government, and threatening to the liberties of the people.''[33]

The committee thought that no one could doubt the meaning of the law and denied that a court could give a decision contrary to the plain and obvious meaning of a statute. That there should be a power vested in courts of judicature, whereby they might control the supreme legislative power was thought to be absurd. Such power in courts was held to be destructive of liberty, and to remove all security of property. The design of courts of justice is to declare laws, not to alter them. Whenever they depart from this rule, they confound legislative and judicial powers.[34] In free governments citizens must know the remedies which are imposed by law. But this was regarded as impossible in case courts might set aside statutes. For then no one would know what the law is until he had the opinion of the court.

The reasoning of the court and the reasoning of the legislature, it was observed, might lead to very different conclusions. And as the court reasons last upon the case, it is utterly impossible for any man to know the result, however exactly the law may apply to the case, unless through a tedious and expensive process he obtains the opinion of the court.[35] The arrangements for an independent judiciary were regarded as necessary and essential when judges kept within their proper sphere. For

when they speak the plain and obvious meaning of the law, and do not presume to alter it or to explain it to mean anything or nothing, and while in the duties of their real province, they cannot be too independent; nor ought they to be liable to a remove but for misbehavior. But if they are to be invested with a power

---

[33] Dawson, *op. cit.*, 29, 33.
[34] *Ibid.*, Introduction, xxxiii *passim*.
[35] *Ibid.*, xxxiv.

to overrule a plain law, though expressed in general words, as all general laws are and must be; when they may judge the law unreasonable, because not consonant to the law of nations or to the opinions of ancient or modern civilians and philosophers; for whom they may have a greater veneration than for the solid statutes and supreme legislative power of the state; we say, if they are to assume and exercise such a power, the probable consequences of their independence will be the most deplorable and wretched dependency of the people. That the laws should be no longer absolute, would be in itself a great evil; but a far more dreadful consequence arises, for that power is not lost in the controversy but transferred to judges who are independent of the people.[36]

The principle of the decision was denounced as dangerous to the freedom of government, and the committee believed that a perseverance in that principle would leave legislatures nothing but a name and that the acceptance of such a doctrine would lead to a revolution in government.[37]

October 27, 1784, on motion of Mr. Harper, a resolution was introduced in the state assembly and a vote of censure passed, which recited the decision of the mayor's court and alleged

that the adjudication aforesaid is, in its tendency, subversive of all law and good order, and leads directly to anarchy and confusion, because if a court instituted for the benefit and government of a corporation may take upon them to dispense with, and act in a direct violation of a plain and known law of the state, all other courts either superior or inferior, may do like; and therewith will end all our dear-bought rights, and privileges and legislatures become useless.

Because of the dangers which seemed to inhere in the precedent it was recommended that the council of ap-

---

[36] Dawson, *op. cit.*, Introduction, xxvi *passim*.   [37] *Ibid.*, xxix.

pointment select such persons as mayor of the city of New York as would govern themselves by the known laws of the land.[38] Mr. Waddington, it seems, becoming alarmed at the opposition which developed, accepted an arrangement for compromise, and the case was dropped.[39] The law, however, remained in force until repealed by the legislature.

The rather violent opposition to the judgment of the court, along with the federal issue involved, gave the case a prominence which it scarcely deserves as a precedent in the growth of judicial review of legislation.

5. *Symsbury Case*, Connecticut, 1785—

An action was brought by the proprietors of the town of Symsbury demanding the surrender of a tract of land in the town of New Hartford. The controversy involved a survey which restricted the limits of Symsbury without the consent of the proprietors of the town. Though a survey made with the approval of the general assembly operated to restrict and to limit the extent of the jurisdiction of the town of Symsbury, the court insisted it could not legally operate to curtail the land granted to the proprietors of the town without their consent.[40] Apparently the legislature of the state could have reversed this decision,[41] but it was a significant attempt to check an interference with vested rights by legislative action.

---

38 *Ibid.*, xii.

39 Alexander Hamilton, referring to the decision, remarked: ''Even the suit of Rutgers v. Waddington, after a partial success in the Mayor's Court, was terminated by a compromise, according to the advice of defendant's counsel, owing to the apprehension of an unfavorable issue in the supreme court; and this, notwithstanding the defendant was a British subject.''— *Works* (Lodge ed.), 5:227.

40 Kirby (Conn.) 444–447.

41 See Calder v. Bull, 3 Dall. 386 (1798).

6. *Trevett v. Weeden*, Rhode Island, 1786[42]—

One of the landmarks in the development of judicial control over legislation in the United States is the case of *Trevett v. Weeden*. John Weeden was indicted under a special act of assembly for refusing to receive paper bills of Rhode Island, as an equivalent for silver or gold, in payment for meat sold in his market.[43] The penalty, fixed by the enforcement acts passed by the paper money advocates was one hundred pounds, and the court was to proceed to trial within three days after the complaint was filed, without a jury and without opportunity of appeal from the sentence imposed.[44] James Varnum, who argued the case in behalf of Weeden, prepared a notable brief which indicates perhaps better than any other document prior to the federal Convention, some of the ideas on which reliance was placed in accepting the principle of judicial review of legislative enactments.

Varnum began his argument by asserting that he would attempt to show that the act of assembly was contrary to the fundamental laws of the state, and therefore a mere nullity and void *ab initio*.[45] Trial by jury, he contended "is a fundamental right, a part of our legal constitution" and the legislature cannot deprive the citizens

---

[42] See Charles Warren, ''Earliest Cases of Judicial Review of State Legislation by Federal Courts,'' 32 *Yale Law Jour.* (Nov. 1922) 16 ff.

[43] For an account of the laws which formed the occasion for this case, consult Pelez W. Chandler, *American Criminal Trials* (Boston, 1841) 2:269 ff.

[44] J. B. McMaster, *History of the People of the United States* (New York, 1883) 1:338; McMaster states that ''The framers of this shameful law had hoped by these means to place the goods, the estates, the liberty of every hard money man in the state at the mercy of the courts.'' See also Brinton Coxe, *op. cit.*, 234, and Thayer, *op. cit.*, 73.

[45] ''The case of Trevett against Weeden,'' by James M. Varnum, (Providence, 1787) iv; J. B. Thayer, *Cases on Constitutional Law*, 1:73. See also Frank Greene Bates, *Rhode Island and the Formation of the Union*, Columbia Univ. *Studies in History, Economics and Public Law*, 10 (New York, 1898) 107 ff. Chandler's, *Criminal Trials*, 2:283.

of this right. In arguing for a legislature subject to
limitations, Varnum continued:

> The powers of legislation, in every possible instance, are
> derived from the people at large, are altogether fiduciary and
> subordinate to the association by which they are formed. Were
> there no bounds to limit and circumscribe the legislature; were
> they to be actuated by their own will, independent of the funda-
> mental rules of the community, the government would be a gov-
> ernment of men and not of laws. And whenever the legislators
> depart from their original engagements and attempt to make
> laws derogatory to the general principles they were bound to
> support they become tyrants.[46]

Locke was quoted to the effect that when legislatures act
contrary to the end for which they were constituted, they
are guilty of rebellion. An association of all the people
expressly limited the legislative power which is confined
within the bounds of invariable custom. Using Vattel as
an authority, it was asserted that the legislature cannot
alter the fundamental law for the legislators "derive
their powers from the constitution." How can they
change it, without destroying the foundation of their
authority? "The true distinction lies in this," argued
Varnum,

> that the legislative have the uncontrollable power of making laws
> not repugnant to the constitution; the judiciary have the sole
> power of judging of those laws, and are bound to execute them;
> but cannot admit any act of the legislative as law, which is
> against the constitution.

> The judges are sworn "truly and impartially to execute the
> laws that now are or shall hereafter be made, according to the
> best of their skill and understanding." They are also sworn "to
> bear true allegiance and fidelity to this State of Rhode Island
> and Providence Plantation, as a free, sovereign and independent

---

[46] Varnum, *op. cit.*, xxi. Chandler, *op. cit.*, 306.

State." But this became a State in order to support its funda-mental, constitutional laws, against the encroachments of Great Britain. The trial by jury, as hath been fully shown, is a funda-mental, a constitutional law; and therefore is binding upon the judges by a double tie, the oath of allegiance, and the oath of office. . . . .

Laws are *made* by the General Assembly under the powers they derive from the constitution, but when made they become the laws of the land, as such the Court is sworn to execute them. But if the General Assembly attempt to make laws contrary hereunto, the Court cannot receive them as laws; they cannot submit to them. If they should, let me speak it with reverence, they would incur the guilt of a double perjury.

The life, liberty and property of the citizens are secured by the general law of the State. We will then suppose (as the very nature of the argument allows us to view the subject in every possible light) that the General Assembly should pass an act directing that no citizen should leave his house, nor suffer any of his family to move out of the same, for a space of six months, upon the pain of death. This would be contrary to the laws of nature. Suppose they should enact that every parent should destroy his first-born child. This would be contrary to the laws of God. But upon the common principles, the Court would be as much bound to execute these acts as any others. For if they can determine upon any act that is not law and so reject it, they must necessarily have the power of determining what acts are laws and so on the contrary. There is not a middle line. The legislative hath power to go all lengths, or not to overleap the bounds of its appointment at all. So it is with the judiciary, it must reject all acts of the legislative that are contrary to the trust reposed in them by the people, or it must adopt all.

But the judges, and all others, are bound by the laws of nature in preference to any human laws, because they were ordained by God himself, anterior to any civil or political insti-tutions. They are bound, in like manner, by the principles of the constitution in preference to any acts of the General

Assembly, because they were ordained by the people anterior to and created the powers of the General Assembly.[47]

The gist of Varnum's argument lay in the contention that trial by jury was an ancient right secured to Englishmen through the laws of nature and the laws of God, sanctioned by such enactments as Magna Carta and other great charters. These ancient rights were made a part of the fundamental law of Rhode Island, and the judges were entrusted with the guardianship and preservation of this law. Bacon's abridgment was quoted as supporting the view "that the power of controlling a statute is in the judges; for they have authority over all laws, more especially over statutes, to mold them according to reason and convenience to the best and truest use." Hobart, Plowden, and Lord Coke were cited as authorities for the doctrine advanced, and the argument was concluded with the assertion:

That the trial by jury is a fundamental, and constitutional right ever claimed as such—ever ratified as such—ever held most dear and sacred:—That the legislative derives all its authority from the constitution—hath no power of making laws but in subordination to it—cannot infringe or violate it,—that this act is unconstitutional and void,—that this court hath power to judge and determine what acts of the General Assembly are agreeable to the constitution and, on the contrary, that this Court is under the solemn obligation to execute the laws of the land, and therefore cannot, will not, consider this act as a law of the land.[48]

---

47 Varnum, *op. cit.*, xxv–xxix; Chandler, *op. cit.*, 314–317.

48 Varnum, *op. cit.*, xxxiii *passim.* Chandler, *op. cit.*, 324, 325. The real ground of decision in this case was that the body for the trial of the offense was not the superior court, but one specially constituted. See Judge Thomas Durfee, "Gleanings from the Judicial Supremacy in Rhode Island," contributed to Edward Field's *Rhode Island at the End of the Century*, vol. 3. Frequently the case is considered as having been decided on constitutional grounds and as the first precedent for judicial review. See Cooley, *Constitutional Limitations* ed. 4, 196; James Bryce, *The Ameri-*

The court, Justice Howell rendering the decision, held that the case was not cognizable before them and thus refused to pass on the issue of the conflict between the law and the constitution. But the decision was understood as declaring the enforcement law "repugnant and unconstitutional." No reasons for this opinion were given. Common law precedents that statutes which were contradictory need not be enforced seemed to influence the court in its decision.

Trevett v. Weeden, is an interesting case from the standpoint of objections to judicial review of legislation. The contest between the paper and hard-money advocates was bitterly fought by the leaders of both parties. Excitement ran high, and some of the judges were charged with speaking against the act from the bench.[49] A special session of the legislature summoned by the governor demanded an immediate attendance of the judges to assign their reasons for adjudging an act of the legislature void.[50] The two houses of the assembly joined in this resolution:

Whereas it appears that the honorable, the justices of the Superior Court of Judicature, Court of Assize, etc., at the last September term of said court declared and adjudged an act of the supreme legislature of this state to be unconstitutional, and so absolutely void; and whereas it is suggested that the said judgment is unprecedented in this state and may tend directly to abolish the legislative authority thereof; it is therefore voted and resolved that all the justices of said court be forthwith cited by the sheriffs of the respective counties in which they live or

---

can *Commonwealth,* (earlier editions) 1:244; Arnold, *History of Rhode Island,* 2:525; McMaster, *op. cit.,* 1:337–339; John Fiske, *The Critical Period of American History* (New York, 1895) 175 ff.

[49] McMaster, *op. cit.,* 1:339; Bates, *op. cit.,* chap. 4.

[50] Chandler's *Criminal Trials,* 2:326. The request for the attendance of the judges indicates that in the opinion of the paper money advocates the court had declared the law void.

may be found, to give their immediate attendance on the assembly to assign the reasons and grounds of the aforesaid judgment; and that the clerk of said court be directed to attend this assembly at the same time with the records of the court which relate to the said judgment.[51]

After some delay due to the illness of two justices they finally appeared before the assembly.[52] Judges Howell, Tillinghast, and Hazard defended their judgment. Though willing to render every aid possible to the legislature Judge Howell contended that "for the reasons of their judgment upon any question judicially before them, they were accountable only to God, and their own consciences." Though the defendant had contended that the act was "unconstitutional and void," the judgment of the court merely was that the information was not cognizable before them. The other justices expressed similar views.

After a lively debate the assembly decided that the answers were not satisfactory and a motion was made to dismiss the judges from office. But before a vote was taken three of the judges united in a protest to the governor and the houses of assembly, denying the power of the legislature to call upon them for the reasons of their judgment, maintaining by arguments and authorities of law that they were "accountable to God under the solemnities of their oath of office, and to their own consciences." They answered that while they

disclaim and totally disavow any the least power or authority or the appearance thereof to contravene or control the constitutional laws of the State or acts of the General Assembly . . . . they conceive that the entire power of the construing and judg-

---

51 *Acts and Resolves,* of the General Assembly, 1786–7, 61.

52 According to certain reports only three judges appeared before the legislature. Cf. Charles Warren, "Earliest Cases of Judicial Review of State Legislation by Federal Courts," 32 *Yale Law Jour.* (Nov. 1922) 20. Bates claims all of the judges answered the summons (see 135 ff.).

ing of the same in the last resort is vested solely in the Supreme judiciary of the State,

and as there was reason to apprehend that it was intended by a summary vote of the legislature to dismiss them from office, they asked for and demanded a hearing "as freemen and officers of the State and utterly protested against the exercise of any power in the Legislature to deprive them of their right to exercise the functions of their office."[53]

Varnum then addressed the assembly in defense of the judges. He contended that due process of law required a hearing and a trial before a judge could be deprived of his office and that the assembly being the accuser could not be judge in the case. Following the presentation of the memorial and Varnum's argument, an opinion was requested from the attorney general regarding the right of the assembly to suspend or to remove judges from office. He replied that such removal was not possible except upon a charge of criminality. After further discussion by members of the assembly it was voted, that, though the judges had rendered no satisfactory reasons for their judgment, they were not charged with criminality, and that they be discharged from any further attendance upon the assembly on that account.[54] At the next annual election by the legislature, however, four of the justices who gave the adverse decision, excepting only the chief justice, were dropped, and others favorable to the wishes of the assembly were appointed. Before the new judges took their seats, however, the obnoxious law was repealed and the courts had gained a partial victory.[55]

---

[53] Varnum, "Case of Trevett v. Weeden," xiv; Chandler's *Criminal Trials,* 334 ff.

[54] Chandler's *Criminal Trials,* 2:336 ff.   [55] McMaster, *op. cit.,* 1:339.

As Rhode Island had not adopted a written constitution but was governed under a colonial charter, and as there was no direct provision in the charter with which the legislative act could be held to be in conflict, the opinion and argument of Varnum were based largely upon an overruling law of nature and upon Coke's theory of ancient fundamental enactments which circumscribe the limits of legislative power and which rest for their interpretation with the common law judges. In this respect the case furnishes a less direct precedent than the earlier one in New Jersey. But the decision appears to have been regarded as a genuine instance of judicial review based on the charter as a written constitution and Varnum's pamphlet issued in 1787 gave the case extensive publicity.

7. *Bayard v. Singleton,* North Carolina, 1787[56]—

About the time that the federal Convention began its sessions in Philadelphia a case was decided by the courts of North Carolina, which attracted considerable attention.[57] A confiscation act designed to protect all persons who had purchased lands sold by commissioners of forfeited estates against former Tory owners was contested in an action for the recovery of a house and lot. In all cases of dispute relative to property sold by the commissioner of forfeited estates the court was required to dismiss the suit on motion. Bayard brought suit in May, 1786, to recover a property sold under the terms of the

---

56 Cf. Coxe, *op. cit.,* 249, and Thayer, *op. cit.,* 78; see also Battle's "Address on the History of the Supreme Court," 103 N. C. *Reports,* 445. For reference to an earlier case in North Carolina in which the judges claimed that the legislature did not have authority to remit fines before they were actually paid in the treasury, cf. J. Crawford Biggs, "The power of the Judiciary over Legislation," North Carolina Bar Assoc. *Proceedings,* (1915) 13.

57 1 Martin 42.

confiscation act. The court delayed a decision for about a year[58] and attempted to secure a compromise which would avoid a conflict between the law and the constitution.

Because of the delay in deciding the case of *Bayard v. Singleton* and the contention of the judges in an earlier case that the legislature could not remit fines until they had been actually paid into the treasury, charges were brought against the judges in the legislature in 1786. The judges were asked to appear and be heard in reference to the charges preferred. Judge Ashe declined to attend the assembly stating that the charges were groundless and that in his judicial character he was "righteous and, therefore, bold."[59] Judges Spencer and Williams attended a joint session of the two houses. The charges were considered by two committees and a report that the judges were found not to be guilty of malpractice in office was approved by the assembly. Certain members of the assembly were not satisfied with such a disposition of the charges and they introduced a bill to require that the judges "decide according to the true spirit and meaning of the *Constitution and the general laws of the land.*"[60] The bill was defeated by a decisive vote. That the judges were not influenced by these proceedings is shown by the decision in the Bayard case in the following year.

It was then determined that with much apparent reluctance they were obliged to give their opinion against the dismissal of the suit because of the act of assembly. The court maintained:

---

[58] The delay was due in part to the belief that the next assembly might revise the law.—See 18 *State Records* of N. C., 139.

[59] J. Crawford Biggs, "The Power of the Judiciary over Legislation," North Carolina Bar Assoc., *Proceedings* (1915) 14.

[60] *Ibid.*, 15.

That notwithstanding the great reluctance they might feel against involving themselves in a dispute with the Legislature of the State, yet no object of concern or respect could come in competition or authorize them to dispense with the duty they owed the public, in consequence of the trust they were invested with under the solemnity of their oaths. . . . .

That by the constitution every citizen had undoubtedly a right to a decision of his property by trial by jury. For that if the Legislature could take away this right, and require him to stand condemned in his property without a trial, it might with as much authority require his life to be taken away without a trial by jury, and that he should stand condemned to die without the formality of any trial at all; that if the members of the General Assembly could do this, they might, with equal authority, not only render themselves the Legislators of the State for life, without any further election of the people, from thence transmit the dignity and authority of the legislation down to their heirs male forever.

But that it was clear, that no act they could pass could by any means repeal or alter the constitution, because if they could do this, they would at the same instant of time destroy their own existence as a Legislature, and dissolve the government thereby established. Consequently the constitution (which the judicial power was bound to take notice of as much as of any other law whatever), standing in full force as the fundamental law of the land, notwithstanding the act of which the present motion was grounded, the same act must, of course, in the instance, stand as abrogated and without any effect.[61]

On the dismissal of the motion the case went to trial according to due course of law. One of the counsel for the plaintiff in the case was James Iredell, whose opinions favorable to judicial review were ably presented in his letters.

---

[61] 1 Martin 47.

The notion that legislative power must be curbed is presented with vigor and clearness by James Iredell, as follows:

It was, of course, to be considered how to impose restrictions on the legislature, that might still leave it free to all useful purposes but at the same time guard against the abuse of unlimited power, which was not to be trusted, without the most imminent danger, to any man or body of men on earth. We had not only been sickened and disgusted for years with the high and almost impious language of Great Britain, of the omnipotent power of the British Parliament, but had severely smarted under its effects. We felt in all its rigor the mischiefs of an absolute and unbounded authority, claimed by so weak a creature as man, and should have been guilty of the basest breach of trust, as well as the grossest folly, if in the moment when we spurned at the insolent despotism of Great Britain, we had established a despotic power among ourselves.

I have therefore no doubt, but that the power of the Assembly is limited and defined by the Constitution. It is a creature of the Constitution. (I hope this is an expression not prosecutable.) The people have chosen to be governed under such and such principles. They have not chosen to be governed, nor promised to submit upon any other; and the Assembly have no more right to obedience on other terms than any different power on earth has a right to govern us; for we have as much agreed to be governed by the Turkish Divan as by our own General Assembly, otherwise than on the express terms prescribed.[62]

The constitution appears to me to be a fundamental law, limiting the powers of the Legislature, and with which every exercise of those powers must, necessarily be compared. Without an expressed Constitution the powers of the Legislature would undoubtedly have been absolute (as the Parliament of Great Britain is held to be), and any act passed, not inconsistent with

[62] G. J. McRee, *The Life and Correspondence of James Iredell*, 2:145-146.

natural justice (for that curb is avowed by the judges even in England) would have been binding on the people. The experience of the evils which the American war fully disclosed, attending an absolute power in a legislative body, suggested the propriety of a real, original contract between the people and their future Government, such, perhaps, as there has been no instance of in the world but in America.

Iredell frequently referred to the principle of unbounded legislative power which our constitution condemns. He stated that in England, where the theory of legislative supremacy prevails, ''they are less free than we are.''[63]

In many respects the clearest and frankest statement of the theory of judicial supremacy, as it was developing in American law, is to be found in Iredell's letters. Discussing the nature of a legislature with limited powers, Iredell raised the question as to the remedy in cases of a violation of the constitution and discarded the proposition; first, that the legislature was judge of its own powers, and second, that the whole people could resist in case of oppression on the part of the legislative body. He presented the case of the courts as special guardians of the written fundamental law in the following argument:

These two remedies then being rejected, it remains to be inquired whether the judicial power hath any authority to interfere in such a case. The duty of that power, I conceive, in all cases, is to decide according to the laws of the state. It will not be denied, I suppose, that the Constitution is the law of the State, as well as an act of the Assembly, with this difference only, that it is the fundamental law, and unalterable by the legislature, which derives all its power from it. One act of Assembly cannot repeal the Constitution, or any part of it. For

---

63 McRee, *op. cit.*, 2:148.

that reason, an act of Assembly, inconsistent with the Constitution, is void, and cannot be obeyed, without disobeying the superior law to which we were previously and irrevocably bound. The judges, therefore, must take care at their peril that every act of Assembly they presume to enforce is warranted by the Constitution, since, if it is not, they act without lawful authority. This is not a usurped or a discretionary power, but one inevitably resulting from the constitution of their office, they being judges for the benefit of the whole people, not mere servants of the Assembly. . . . .[64]

The Constitution, therefore, being a fundamental law, and a law in writing of the solemn nature I have mentioned (which is the light in which it strikes me), the judicial power, in the exercise of their authority, must take notice of it as the groundwork of that as well as of all other authority; and as no article of the Constitution can be repealed by a legislature, which derives its whole power from it, it follows either that the fundamental unrepealable law must be obeyed, by the rejection of an act unwarranted by and inconsistent with it, or you must obey an act founded on an authority not given by the people, and to which, therefore, the people owe no obedience. It is not that the judges are appointed arbiters, and to determine as it were upon any application, whether the Assembly have or have not violated the Constitution; but when an act is necessarily brought in judgment before them, they must, unavoidably, determine one way or another.[65]

It really appears to me, the exercise of the power is unavoidable, the Constitution not being a mere imaginary thing, about which ten thousand different opinions may be formed, but a written document to which all may have recourse, and to which, therefore, the judges cannot wilfully blind themselves. This seems also to have been the idea of some of the early Assemblies under the Constitutions, since, in the oath of allegiance are

---

[64] McRee, *op. cit.*, 2:148.
[65] *Ibid.*, 173.

these expressions. "I, A. B., do sincerely promise and swear, that I will be faithful and bear true allegiance to the State of North Carolina, and to the powers and authorities which are or may be established for the government thereof, not inconsistent with the Constitution." (Act of Nov. 1777). In any other light than as I have stated it, the greater part of the provisions of the Constitution would appear to me to be ridiculous, since in my opinion nothing could be more so than for the representatives of a people solemnly assembled to form a Constitution, to set down a number of political dogmas, which might or might not be regarded; whereas it must have been intended, as I conceive, that it should be a system of authority, not depending on the casual whim or accidental ideas of a majority either in or out of doors for the time being; but to remain in force until by a similar appointment of deputies specially appointed for the same important purposes; and alterations should be with equal solemnity and deliberation made.[66]

The effect of Iredell's argument was evident in the court's decision, in the course of which the judges observed "that the obligation of their oaths, and the duty of their office required them in that situation to give their opinion on that important and momentous subject";[67] and concluded that the act in question was invalid because contrary to the constitution which the judicial power was bound to enforce as the fundamental law.[68]

William R. Davie, one of the counsel for the plaintiff, who was threatened by a criminal prosecution for his argument against the law, was in attendance at the convention in Philadelphia when the decision was rendered, and Richard Spaight, also a member of the convention, criticized the action of the court as follows:

---

[66] McRee, *op. cit.*, 2:174.
[67] Bayard v. Singleton, 1 Martin 44.
[68] *Ibid.*, 45.

I do not pretend to vindicate the law which has been the subject of controversy; it is immaterial what law they have declared void; it is their usurpation of the authority to do it, that I complain of, as I do most positively deny that they have any such power; nor can they find anything in the constitution either directly or impliedly, that will support them or give them any color of right to exercise that authority. Besides, it would have been absurd, and contrary to the practice of all the world, had the constitution vested such power in them, as it would have operated as an absolute negative on the proceedings of the legislature, which no judiciary ought ever to possess, and the state, instead of being governed by the representatives in the general assembly, would be subject to the will of three individuals, who united in their own persons the legislative and judiciary powers, which no monarch in Europe enjoys, and which would be more despotic than the Roman decemvirate, and equally insufferable.[69]

Spaight expressed the belief which was generally held at the time that the legislative authority ought to be restricted, but he could see no way to effect this except by the exercise of suffrage at the polls. In this manner, he thought, a legislative act contrary to the constitution and the natural principles of justice could be effectively annulled. According to Iredell the great argument of those in opposition was that

though the assembly have no right to violate the constitution, yet if they do so, the only remedy is either by an humble petition that the law may be repealed, or a universal resistance of the people. In the meantime their act, whatever it is, is to be obeyed, as a law; for the judicial power is not to presume to question the power of any act of assembly.[70]

The discussions aroused and the interest in the case make it one of the most important of the early state prece-

---

[69] McRee, *op. cit.*, 169, 170; see also 103 N. C. *Reports*, 472, 473.

[70] McRee, *op. cit.*, 146.

dents.[71] It is claimed to be the first reported state case in which an act was held void, as contrary to the terms of a written constitution.[72]

8. A Massachusetts precedent—

On July 11, 1788, barely a year after the judgment in the North Carolina case, Cutting wrote to Jefferson commenting upon what he termed "the manly proceeding of a Virginia Court of Appeals." "I may venture to applaud," he continued, "the integrity of the judges who thus fulfill their oaths and their duties. I am proud of such characters."[73] He informed Jefferson that an act of the legislature was declared unconstitutional by the supreme court of Massachusetts, and stated that at the very next session of the legislature the law was formally repealed, although he doubted the necessity of such a procedure.[74] On the basis of a thorough examination of evidence it is claimed that no case can be found at this time in which the legislature on the suggestion of the supreme court repealed a statute because of its unconstitutionality.[75] The absolute supremacy of the legislature

---

[71] *Ibid.*, 2:172 ff., for Iredell's answer to Spaight. This case has also been given high rank among the state precedents. In a history of the courts of the state it is claimed: "These, our earliest judges, are entitled to the eminent distinction of contesting with Rhode Island the claim of being the first in the United States to decide that the courts have the power and duty to declare an act of the legislature, which in their opinion is unconstitutional, to be null and void. The doctrine is so familiar to us, so universally acquiesced in, that it is difficult for us to realize that when it was first mooted, the judges who had the courage to declare it were fiercely denounced as usurpers of power."—103 N. C. *Reports*, 472, 473.

[72] Biggs, *op. cit.*, 18.

[73] This comment probably refers to the Case of the Judges, 4 Call 135.

[74] George Bancroft, *History of the Formation of the Constitution of the United States*, 2 (New York, 1882) 472, 473.

[75] A. C. Goodell, Jr., "An Early Constitutional Case in Massachusetts," 7 *Harv. Law Rev.* (Feb. 1894) 422–424. See also Jesse Turner, "Four Fugitive Cases from the Realm of American Constitutional Law," 49 *Am. Law Rev.* (Nov.-Dec. 1915) 828 ff. Mr. Turner thinks the conclusions of Goodell are scarcely warranted by the available evidence.

after the renunciation of allegiance to the British Crown
makes it unlikely that such a decision could have been
rendered relative to a law contrary to the state constitution.[76] Mr. Goodell comes to the conclusion that the
case to which Cutting referred must have been an action
of debt involving the treaty of peace, and that the act
invalidated was in all probability a state law which was
thought to encroach upon the powers of Congress under
the Confederation.[77] The case has apparently little weight
as a precedent, but the opinion of Cutting shows the
prevalence of the sentiment favorable to the adoption of
Coke's doctrine of common law supremacy, and of judicial review of legislation. The way was being prepared
for the acceptance, as an axiom of public law, of the principle that courts must declare acts invalid, if considered
by them to be contrary to written constitutions. Some
notable state cases aided in crystallizing public opinion
before the federal courts were called upon to meet the
issue.

---

[76] Goodell, *op. cit.*, 424.
[77] *Ibid.*, 424.

CHAPTER VI

THE ISSUE OF JUDICIAL REVIEW OF LEGISLA-
TIVE ACTS IN THE FEDERAL AND STATE
CONVENTIONS, AND IN THE JUDI-
CIARY ACT OF 1789

1. *Federal judicial authority during the revolutionary
period—*

ACCORDING to the opinion generally accepted the case
of *Marbury v. Madison* made the American doctrine of judicial review of legislative acts a feature
of the federal system of constitutional law. A few earlier
precedents served as a background for Marshall's decision,
but the responsibility for introducing the practice as a rule
for the federal courts is placed primarily on the great chief
justice. On account of popular impressions with regard
to the matter, Chief Justice Marshall receives unstinted
praise on the part of those who look upon judicial supremacy as the mainstay of our federal system of government and is subjected to censure by those who think
that judicial supremacy is one of the prime causes of the
unpopularity of American courts. It seems to be the
case in the development of judicial supremacy as in the
origin of other fundamental political and legal institutions, that a few men are able to formulate the notions
which are a part of the common heritage and thereby
receive credit for originality, when in fact they are expressing the generally accepted judgments of their generations. John Marshall's fame as statesman and jurist

will not suffer any real loss when we cease to credit him with more than formulating and announcing well defined and generally accepted notions, in his assertion that the right to declare laws invalid was an indispensable function of the federal judiciary. Marshall's reasoning was put into such an effective form that it has furnished the standard arguments for judicial review despite later demonstrations of his unwarranted assumptions and inaccurate statements of fact.[1]

The gradual acceptance of the doctrine of judicial review in the states had its counterpart in a number of federal precedents before Marshall's accession to the bench of the Supreme Court. The sanction for the right of the federal courts to invalidate acts is regarded as based on Article VI of the Constitution, which declares:

This Constitution, and the laws of the United States which shall be made in pursuance thereof; and all treaties made, or which shall be made under the authority of the United States, shall be the supreme law of the land; and the judges in every state shall be bound thereby, anything in the constitution or laws of any state to the contrary notwithstanding,

and on Section 2 of Article III, which provides that "the judicial power shall extend to all cases, in law and equity, arising under this Constitution; the laws of the United States, and treaties made, or which shall be made, under their authority." But it is necessary to read these sections in their historical development and in the light of some fundamental assumptions and political principles, which Marshall and other men of the time were in the habit of accepting as postulates in order to extract therefrom the meaning which is supposed to give warrant to the judges to consider the validity of acts of Congress.

[1] Cf. opinions of Justices Bland and Gibson, *infra*, 261 *et seq.*

In order to trace these principles and assumptions we shall have to examine the gradual growth of a federal tribunal, the discussion thereon in the convention at Philadelphia, and the chief cases which preceded *Marbury v. Madison,* in the state and federal courts. The first steps toward a federal tribunal were taken when the Continental Congress organized a committee on appeals.

Committee on appeals in Congress.—The idea of a federal judicial tribunal appears to have been first presented by Washington, who recommended to Congress the establishment of a court to take cognizance of prizes captured by Continental vessels. As a result of this recommendation a committee was appointed on January 30, 1777, whose duty it was to determine upon the capture of prizes at sea and other cases arising under international relations.[2] Frequent changes were made in this committee, and because this arrangement proved unsatisfactory, the committee was superseded in January, 1780, by a court of appeals, which continued to hear cases until the final adjournment in 1787.[3] This court considered and determined a few important cases, but its powers were gradually absorbed by the appellate courts of the states.[4] A weakness of the system lay in the fact that the court was obliged to depend upon state officials to enforce its decrees. The decision of the court of appeals in the case of the sloop "Active" was flagrantly disregarded by the authorities of Pennsylvania, with the result that the court lost much of the little power it formerly possessed. It was this tribunal, no doubt, which furnished a model for the Supreme Court of the United States.

---

2 3 *Journals of Congress,* 34.

3 *Ibid.,* 6, 10; see also 131 U. S., Appendix, xiii.

4 131 U. S., Appendix, xix *passim* for an account of the decisions of this court.

In April, 1787, the Congress of the Confederation passed a resolution indicating the trend of affairs relative to the confidence in judicial authority. Because certain laws of the states were complained of by Great Britain, on the ground that they were repugnant to the treaty of peace, the secretary for the Department of Foreign Affairs presented resolutions which were unanimously approved by Congress. It was resolved that the legislatures of the states were not to pass acts interpreting, or construing a national treaty nor in any way to interfere with the operation and execution of the same, because such treaties were held to be part of the law of the land, and as such independent of the power of state legislatures. Furthermore, it was resolved that any acts or parts of acts should be replaced, and

that the courts of law and equity in all causes and questions cognizable by them respectively and arising from or touching said treaty, shall decide and adjudge according to the true intent and meaning of the same, anything in the said acts or parts of acts to the contrary thereof in anywise notwithstanding.[5]

Before the meeting of the federal convention in Philadelphia Congress recommended that the states enact laws in accordance with this plan. A letter from Congress was transmitted to the states urging upon them the passage of an act to enforce the provision. In the course of the letter, it was observed that a general law would be preferable to one that would enumerate all the acts and clauses intended to be repealed:

because omissions might accidentally be made in the enumeration, or questions might arise, and perhaps not be satisfactorily determined, respecting particular acts or clauses about which contrary opinions may be entertained. By repealing in general

---

[5] J. B. Thayer, *Cases on Constitutional Law*, 81; 12 *Journals of Congress* (ed. 1801), 23.

terms all acts and clauses repugnant to the treaty, the business will be turned over to its proper department, viz, the judicial; and the courts of law will find no difficulty in deciding whether any particular act or clause is or is not contrary to the treaty.[6]

Prior to this time judicial authority was exercised almost entirely by state courts. The final tribunals of appeal which were organized by Congress determined a limited number of cases, but gradually deteriorated in public esteem; and the necessity of a court with power to enforce national laws and obligations became increasingly apparent.

Political theories of the time favored judicial restriction of state laws to the point of practical nullification. The same trend of thought regarded the federal courts as the only proper tribunals to determine the validity or invalidity of state laws contrary to the terms of the treaty of peace or the law of nations. In practice a principle was emerging, not sanctioned by any positive enactment, which was destined to place effective limits on the legislative departments. State courts were asserting authority above that of the legislative assemblies. Federal courts were claiming the right to declare void state laws contrary to national laws and treaties, and contrary to the "sovereign rights of peace and war" vested in the Confederate Congress. Before the meeting of the convention in Philadelphia some significant steps had been taken in the direction of the establishment of a review of legislation by American courts.

2. *Judicial authority in relation to legislation in the Philadelphia convention—*

The sentiment of the members of the Constitutional Convention of Philadelphia has become involved in a con-

---

6 12 *Journals of Congress,* 32–36.

troversy which has resulted in an exhaustive examination of the opinions of each member relative to the matter of judicial control over legislation. On the one hand, it is charged that the federal courts usurped the power to declare acts of Congress invalid, on the ground that the sentiment in the federal convention was on the whole unfavorable to the exercise of this right, that a proposition to establish such a right was defeated, and that no express grant of the power was incorporated in the final draft of the Constitution.[7] On the other hand, it is urged that though no express provisions grant explicitly to the federal courts the right to review acts of Congress the authority is clearly implied in certain provisions and the intention of the framers of the Constitution was to have the judiciary exercise such a power. In examining the records of the Convention relative to judicial review, it becomes evident at once that interest centered principally on the question of a council of revision, such as that in operation in New York.[8]

Resolutions submitted on May 29 by Randolph provided that the executive and a convenient number of the national judiciary ought to compose a council of revision with authority to examine every act of the national legislature before it should operate, and every act of a particular legislature before a negative thereon should be final, and that the dissent of the said council should amount to a rejection unless the act of the national legislature were again passed, or that of a particular legisla-

[7] See articles by William Trickett, ''Judicial Dispensation from Congressional Statutes,'' 41 *Am. Law Rev.* (Jan.-Feb. 1907) 65: ''The Great Usurpation,'' 40 *Am. Law Rev.* (May-June 1906) 356. ''Judicial Nullification of Acts of Congress, *North Am. Rev.*, 185 (Aug. 1907) 848; L. B. Boudin, ''Government by Judiciary,'' 26 *Pol. Sci. Quart.* (June 1911) 238; Gilbert E. Roe, *Our Judicial Oligarchy* (New York, 1912) chap. 2; Address by Chief Justice Walter Clark of North Carolina, *Congressional Record*, July 31, 1911.

[8] For an account of the New York council of revision, see *supra*, 82.

ture were again negatived by two-thirds of the members of each branch.[9]

This plan involved some of the ideas of a council of revision such as that of New York and a form of veto of laws. It was defended as a means by which the judiciary might protect itself against the encroachments of the legislature. When this proposal was first brought up for consideration Gerry expressed doubts whether the judiciary ought to form a part of the council, since the courts would have a sufficient check against encroachments by their interpretation of the law, which involved a power of deciding on their constitutionality. In some states, he said, "the judges had [actually] set aside laws as being against the Constitution. This was done with general approbation. It was quite foreign, from the nature of the office, to make them judges of the policy of public measures."[10] Luther Martin also believed the constitutionality of laws would "come before the judges in their proper official character. In this character they have a negative on the laws."[11]

On June 4, by a vote of 8 states to 2, it was decided to drop the plan of a council of revision and to adopt the executive veto instead.[12] Bedford opposed

every check on the legislature, even the council of revision first proposed. He thought it would be sufficient to mark out in the

---

[9] Randolph believed that "our chief danger arises from the democratic parts of our constitution. . . . . None of the constitutions have provided sufficient checks against the democracy." See Max Farrand, *The Records of the Federal Constitution of 1787* (New Haven, 1911) 1:21, 26, 27.

[10] Farrand, *op. cit.*, 97, 98. Rutledge thought the judges ought never to give their opinion on a law until it comes before them.—*Ibid.*, 2:80.

[11] *Ibid.*, 76. This was one of the grounds given by Martin for opposing the Constitution.—Farrand, 3:220.

[12] *Ibid.*, 1:104; 2:76. Rufus King was of opinion that "the judicial ought not to join in the negative of a law because the judges will have the expounding of those laws when they come before them; and they will no doubt stop the operation of such as shall appear repugnant to the constitution."—*Ibid.*, 1:109.

Constitution the boundaries to the Legislative Authority, which would give all the requisite security to the rights of the other departments. The representatives of the people were the best judges of what was for their interest, and ought to be under no external control whatever.[13]

It is not necessary to give in detail the views of the members of the convention on a council of revision.[14] The idea of a council was strongly supported by some and was finally brought up for a second consideration by Wilson and Madison.[15] It was contended that such a council would enable the judiciary better to defend itself against legislative encroachments.

Wilson, on proposing a reconsideration of the council of revision, argued:

The Judiciary ought to have an opportunity of remonstrating against projected encroachments on the people as well as on themselves. It has been said that the Judges, as expositors of the Laws would have an opportunity of defending their constitutional rights. There was weight in this observation; but this power of the judges did not go far enough. Laws may be unjust, may be unwise, may be dangerous, may be destructive; and yet not be so unconstitutional as to justify the judges in refusing to give them effect. Let them have a share in the Revisionary power, and they will have an opportunity of taking notice of these characters of a law, and of counteracting, by the weight of their opinions, the improper views of the legislature.[16]

---

[13] Farrand, *op. cit.*, 1:100, 101.

[14] Those who desire to examine fully the views of individual members may consult Farrand, Charles A. Beard, *The Supreme Court and the Constitution* (New York, 1912), and Horace A. Davis, *The Judicial Veto* (Boston, 1914).

[15] *Ibid.*, 3:73. Madison thought "a law violating a constitution established by the people themselves would be considered by the judges as null and void."—Farrand, *op. cit.*, 2:93. For various opinions expressed by Madison on judicial review, see *infra*, 233 *et seq.*

[16] Farrand, *op. cit.*, 2:73. A year later Wilson suggested that if a law should be made inconsistent with those powers vested by this instrument in Congress, the judges would declare such a law to be null and void.

Mason supported a council for similar reasons.[17]

Ellsworth heartily approved the plan, and it was again strongly supported by Madison because it would be a check on legislative encroachments and it would, moreover, be

useful to the Community at large as an additional check against a pursuit of those unwise and unjust measures which constituted so great a portion of our calamities. . . . . Experience in all the States had evinced a powerful tendency in the legislature to absorb all power into its vortex. This was the real source of danger to the American constitutions; and suggested the necessity of giving every defensive authority to the other departments that was consistent with republican principles.[18]

The notion that definite limits must be fixed for the exercise of legislative powers was frequently expressed by members of the convention. Gerry and others opposed the device of a council of revision because it made the judges, as the expositors of the laws, the legislators, which, in his opinion, ought never to be done.[19] Gouverneur Morris supported the proposal because he concurred in the view that the public liberty was in greater danger from legislative usurpation that from any other source, and that a strong check was necessary to restrain legislative power.[20] Luther Martin believed that the judges would have a negative on the laws in considering their constitutionality, and hence thought the council of revision unnecessary. The motion to establish a council was again defeated.[21]

---

17 Farrand, *op. cit.*, 78.

18 *Ibid.*, 74.

19 See opinion of Gerry, *ibid.*, 75.

20 *Ibid.*, 2:75, 76 *passim*. Morris said, ''he could not agree that the Judiciary, which was a part of the Executive, should be bound to say that a direct violation of the constitution was law.''—*Ibid.*, 299.

21 *Ibid.*, 80.

At a later time the plan for a council was brought up by Madison and was opposed by Pinckney because he regarded the interference of the judges in the legislative business inadvisable. Mercer "disapproved of the doctrine that the judges as expositors of the Constitution should have authority to declare a law void. He thought laws ought to be well and cautiously made, and then be uncontrollable."[22] Dickinson also thought the judges should not have power to set aside a law. The motion of Madison suffered the fate of the earlier efforts, and the idea of a national council of revision was definitely rejected. Among those who opposed judicial review is Benjamin Franklin, who thought it would be improper to put it in the power of any man to negative a law passed by the legislature because it would give him control over the legislature.[23]

From these opinions of members of the convention it appears that the real issue involved and finally determined did not directly settle the matter whether the federal courts were to declare laws of Congress invalid. The arguments favoring this power were presented by a few of the ablest members; on the other hand, there was a well defined opposition to the exercise of such authority by the judiciary.

The control over state laws seems to have received comparatively little consideration by the convention. A proposal that the federal government should have a right of veto on the laws of the states which were deemed in conflict with federal powers was thought to be impracticable.[24] Instead of such a plan Luther Martin presented a resolution which with some minor modifications was

---

[22] Farrand, *op. cit.*, 298 ff.; Elliot's *Debates*, 5:429.
[23] Farrand, *op. cit.*, 1:109.
[24] *Ibid.*, 2:27, 28.

accepted. He moved that the acts of the federal government shall be the supreme law of the respective states and "that the Judiciaries of the several States shall be bound thereby in their decisions, anything in the respective laws of the individual states to the contrary notwithstanding."[25] State courts and state judges were expected to enforce the federal Constitution as a law superior to state enactments, and the language of the Constitution left undetermined whether the fundamental law was to be guarded primarily by the judiciary and to be held in special cases paramount to legislative acts.

But the lack of any express grant to declare laws invalid is not conclusive evidence that this power was to be withheld from the federal judiciary. Without any grant, either express or implied, state courts had exercised the power, and had advanced the view that to declare void a law, considered by the judges as contrary to the constitution, was a duty which judges should not refuse to accept. A similar assumption appears to have been favored by an important group of the federal convention. The views of the members are fully analyzed by various authors from different points of view.[26] Of the fifty-five members of the convention Charles A. Beard estimated that one-third took little or no part in the proceedings. Of the twenty-five men whose character, ability, diligence, and regularity of attendance made them the controlling element in the convention, it is claimed that

---

[25] *Ibid.*, 28, 29.

[26] Charles A. Beard, *The Supreme Court and the Constitution* (New York, 1912); Horace A. Davis, "Annulment of Legislation by the Supreme Court," in *The Judicial Veto* (New York, 1914) chap. 3, and in 7 *Am. Pol. Sci. Rev.* (Nov. 1913) 541; Frank E. Melvin, "The Judicial Bulwark of the Constitution," 8 *Am. Pol. Sci. Rev.* (May 1914) 167; William M. Meigs, *The Relation of the Judiciary to the Constitution* (New York, 1919) chaps. 7, 8; Edward S. Corwin, "The Establishment of Judicial Review," 9 *Mich. Law Rev.* (Dec. 1910 and Feb. 1911) 102, 283.

seventeen out of this selected list declared directly or indirectly for judicial review of legislation.[27] Beard finds only five members who are in any way on record as opposed to judicial nullification of laws, and only one of these appears in the selected list.[28]

Examining the same evidence as Beard, Mr. Davis concludes that the question of judicial review of legislation was intentionally left undetermined by the makers of the Constitution, and that the objections and impressions in the ratifying conventions indicated that there was no intention to give to the Supreme Court the power to annul acts of Congress.[29] In an answer to Davis by Frank E. Melvin, Beard's analysis is not only defended but it is also claimed that other names such as Rutledge and Gorham might be added to the favorable list.[30] There

---

[27] Beard, *op. cit.*, 16 ff. Beard's list of those who indicated directly or indirectly that they were in favor of judicial review are: **Blair*, Franklin, *King, Morris, R.,* Rutledge, Butler, *Gerry, Madison, Paterson,* Sherman, Dayton, Gorham, *Martin, L.,* Pinckney, Chas., *Washington, Dickinson, Hamilton, Morris, G., Randolph, Wilson, Mason,* Pinckney, C. C., *Williamson, Ellsworth, Johnson.*

* Italics indicate those whose views are definitely known.

After presenting the recorded opinions of the individual members, the evidence is thus summarized: ''Of the leading members of the Convention no less than fourteen believed that the judicial power included the right and duty of passing upon the constitutionality of acts of Congress. Satisfactory evidence is afforded by the vote on the judiciary act that three other leading members held to the same belief. Of the less prominent members we find that three expressed themselves in favor of judicial control and three others approved it by their vote on the judiciary act. We are justified in asserting that twenty-five members of the Convention favored or at least accepted some form of judicial control. This number understood that federal judges could refuse to enforce unconstitutional legislation.''—*Ibid.*, 60, 61. As Chief Justice, Brearly, of New Jersey, had declared a law void, see Holmes v. Walton, *supra*, 94; William Paterson, Attorney General, and William Livingston, Governor, apparently concurred in this decision.

[28] Beard, *op. cit.*, 51–55.

[29] A revision of Professor Beard's list is prepared which includes men as either opposed to judicial review or as non-committal, who, it seems to me, on a fair analysis of the evidence, may be considered as favorable to judicial review. See Horace A. Davis, *The Judicial Veto*, 49 ff.

[30] See Farrand, *op. cit.*, 2:79, 80, 298–301.

can be little doubt of the definite acceptance of judicial review by the Convention, thinks Melvin.[31]

Wilson, Ellsworth, Hamilton, Madison,[32] Morris, and King, all of whom are on record at different times as favoring judicial review of legislation, had an important part in giving the Constitution its final form. So far as these men were responsible for the language of the Constitution it is probable that the provisions on judicial powers were so worded as impliedly to sanction the exercise of power by federal courts to declare laws of Congress invalid. It was perhaps deemed advisable to allow the definite assertion of the right to come through judicial interpretation of the language of the Constitution rather than to arouse controversy and suspicion by incorporating a direct grant. Moreover, men who favored the doctrine of judicial review were accustomed to regard it as one of the fundamental principles of republican government and not necessarily based upon an express grant of authority.

It is a mistake, however, to claim that the members of the Philadelphia convention expressed any definite views on the main issue of judicial review of legislative acts.[33]

---

[31] Frank E. Melvin, ''The Judicial Bulwark of the Constitution,'' 8 *Am. Pol. Sci. Rev.* (May 1914) 167–203. The conclusion of Melvin that from thirty-two to forty members of the convention, including nearly every influential member, upheld the right of the courts to declare legislative acts void, places in too favorable a light the evidence supporting judicial control of legislation just as the analysis of Davis gives an interpretation which exaggerates the views unfavorable to the American doctrine.

[32] For a change of opinion by Madison see *infra,* 234 *et seq.*

[33] Professor Corwin reviewing Beard's analysis says, he is ''not convinced by Mr. Beard's data that the Convention of 1787 thought itself to be concluding the constitutional question decided in Marbury v. Madison. On the contrary I believe that the Convention regarded that question as still open when it adjourned.''—7 *Am. Pol. Sci. Rev.* (May 1913) 330. Continuing he says: ''Thus of the twenty-five members set down by Mr. Beard as favoring judicial review of acts of Congress seven are so classified simply on the score of their voting two years after the Convention for the judiciary act of 1789, the terms of which do not necessarily assume any such power, though they do not preclude it. Of another six, only utterances are quoted

Analysis of the opinions pro and con sheds little light on the developing principles and concepts which were rendering judicial control over legislation inevitable in both the federal and state governments. Independent of any expressions of opinion in the federal and state conventions, review of legislation by the courts was likely to be adopted eventually as a feature of the federal government. The contentions for or against usurpation of authority by the courts with respect to control over legislation cannot be settled by an examination of the convention debates.

3. *Issue of judicial review in the debates over the ratification of the federal Constitution.*—Opinions favorable to judicial review of legislative acts as asserted in the federal convention were reiterated in some of the speeches before the state ratifying conventions.[34] Only a few representative opinions can be given.

---

which post-date the Convention, sometimes by several years. Furthermore by far the two most important members of this group are Hamilton and Madison, the former of whom apparently became a convert to the idea under discussion between the time of writing *Federalist* 33 and *Federalist* 78 and the latter of whom is proved by the very language which Mr. Beard quotes to have been unfavorable both in 1788 and 1789. Again, another four are reckoned as favoring the power of judicial review proper on account of judicial utterances antedating the Convention from five to seven years, though these utterances at the time they were made, were in one instance sharply challenged by public opinion and in another by judicial opinion. Only eight of the twenty-five acknowledged the power on the floor of the convention itself, and of these eight, three were pretty clearly recent converts to the idea, while some of them seemed to limit the power to its use as a means of self-defense by the court against legislative encroachment. On the other hand the idea was challenged by four members of the Convention; and although they were outnumbered, so far as the available records show, two to one by the avowed advocates of judicial review, yet popular discussion previous to the Convention had shown their point of view to have too formidable a backing to admit of its being crassly overridden.'' —*Ibid.*, 330, 331.

[34] Beard, *op. cit.*, Chap. III. For a complete list of opinions consult Elliot's *Debates*, Beard's *Supreme Court and the Constitution*, or Davis, *The Judicial Veto*.

John Marshall, in Virginia, inquired whether the legislature can go beyond the delegated powers. "If they were to make a law," he said, "not warranted by any of the powers enumerated, it would be considered by the judges as an infringement of the Constitution which they are to guard. They would not consider such a law as coming under their jurisdiction. They would declare it void."[35] A similar view was expressed by Mr. Grayson,[36] and supported by Mr. Pendleton.[37] In Maryland Luther Martin's letter informed the citizens of that state that "whether, therefore, any laws or *regulations* of the Congress, or any acts of *its President* or *other officers*, are contrary to, or not warranted by, the Constitution, rests only with the judges, who are appointed by Congress, to determine; by whose determinations every state must *be bound*."[38] Wilson, of Pennsylvania, a consistent supporter of judicial review, said:

If a law should be made inconsistent with those powers vested by this instrument in Congress, the judges, as a consequence of their independence, and the particular powers of government being defined, will declare such law to be null and void. For the power of the Constitution predominates. Anything therefore that shall be enacted by Congress contrary thereto will not have the force of law.[39]

In addition to the limitations imposed on the legislatures by natural or revealed law it was maintained by James Wilson that legislative authority must be sub-

---

[35] Elliot's *Debates*, 3:553. Randolph and Henry also approved judicia¹ review.—*Ibid.*, 205, 325, 539–41. "I take it as the highest encomium on this country," Henry exclaimed, "that the acts of the legislature, if unconstitutional are liable to be opposed by the judiciary."

[36] Elliot's *Debates*, 3:567.

[37] *Ibid.*, 548.

[38] Elliot's *Debates*, 1:380.

[39] McMaster and Stone, *Pennsylvania and the Federal Constitution*, 305, 340, 354, 776. McKean is reported to have expressed similar views.

jected to another control—that of an overruling constitution.[40] Wilson thought that in the United States, and in each of the commonwealths of the Union, the legislature by no means possessed supreme power. Instead of being uncontrollable, the legislative authority was placed, he believed, under just and strict control.[41] William R. Davie, of North Carolina, believed that it was the duty of the judges to see that the regulations of the Constitution were obeyed.[42] And Ellsworth, in Connecticut, contended that:

This constitution defines the extent of the powers of the general government. If the general legislature should at any time overleap their limits, the judicial department is a constitutional check. If the United States go beyond their powers, if they make a law which the Constitution does not authorize, it is void; and the judicial power, the national judges, who, to secure their impartiality, are to be independent, will declare it to be void.[43]

The most effective advocate of the developing American ideas on judicial review was Alexander Hamilton. His opinion, formulated in the seventy-eighth number of *The Federalist*, is the clearest presentation of the doctrine of a written constitution as a superior enactment, the preservation of which rests primarily with the judges.

After some observations regarding the judiciary as the weakest of the three departments of government, the

---

[40] Wilson, *Works*, 1:415: "To control the power and conduct of the legislature by an overruling constitution, was an improvement in the science and practice of government reserved to the American states. . . . . The truth is, that in our governments, the supreme, absolute and uncontrollable power remains in the people. As our constitutions are superior to our legislatures; so, the people are superior to our constitutions."—Wilson, Commentaries on the Constitution of the United States of America, 38.

[41] *Ibid.*, 1:189; private citizens were justified, Wilson held, in refusing to obey an unconstitutional act of the legislature although they must abide by the consequences in case of a wrong judgment.

[42] Elliot's *Debates*, 4:155, 156.

[43] Elliot's *Debates*, 2:196.

necessity of the inclusion of the principle of the separation of powers, and the difficulties involved in the maintenance of a coordinate position by the courts, Hamilton maintained that,

The complete independence of the courts of Justice is peculiarly essential in a limited Constitution. By a limited Constitution I understand one which contains certain specified exceptions to the legislative authority; such, for instance, as that it shall pass no bills of attainder, no *ex post facto* laws, and the like. Limitations of this kind can be preserved in practice no other way than through the medium of courts of justice, whose duty it must be to declare all acts contrary to the manifest tenor of the Constitution void. Without this, all the reservations of particular rights or privileges would amount to nothing.

Some perplexity respecting the rights of the courts to pronounce legislative acts void, because contrary to the Constitution, has arisen from an imagination that the doctrine would imply a superiority of the judiciary to the legislative power. It is urged that the authority which can declare the acts of another void must necessarily be superior to the one whose acts may be declared void. As this doctrine is of great importance in all the American constitutions, a brief discussion of the ground on which it rests cannot be unacceptable.

There is no position which depends on clearer principles than that every act of a delegated authority, contrary to the tenor of the commission under which it is exercised, is void. No legislative act, therefore, contrary to the Constitution, can be valid. To deny this would be to affirm that the deputy is greater than his principal; that the servant is above his master; that the representatives of the people are superior to the people themselves; that men acting by virtue of powers may do not only what their powers do not authorize, but what they forbid.

If it be said that the legislative body are themselves the constitutional judges of their own powers, and that the construction they put upon them is conclusive upon the other departments, it may be answered that this cannot be the natural presumption, where it is not to be collected from any particular provision in the Constitution. It is not otherwise to be supposed that the Constitution could intend to enable the representatives of the people to substitute their will for that of their constituents. It is far more rational to suppose that the courts were designed to be an intermediate body between the people and the legislature, in order, among other things, to keep the latter within the limits assigned to their authority. The interpretation of the laws is the proper and peculiar province of the courts.

A constitution is, in fact, and must be regarded by the judges as a fundamental law. It therefore belongs to them to ascertain its meaning, as well as the meaning of any particular act proceeding from the legislative body. If there should happen to be an irreconcilable variance between the two, that which has the superior obligation and validity ought, of course, to be preferred; or, in other words, the Constitution ought to be preferred to the Statute; the intention of the people to the intention of their agents.

Nor does this conclusion by any means suppose a superiority of the judicial to the legislative power. It only supposes that the power of the people is superior to both; and that where the will of the legislature, declared in the statutes, stands in opposition to that of the people, declared in the Constitution, the judges ought to be governed by the latter rather than the former. They ought to regulate their decisions by the fundamental laws, rather than by those which are not fundamental. . . . .

It can be of no weight to say that the courts, on the pretense of a repugnancy, may substitute their own pleasure to the constitutional intentions of the legislature. This might as well happen in the case of two contradictory statutes; or it might as well happen in every adjudication upon any single statute. The courts must declare the sense of the law; and if they should be disposed to exercise *will* instead of *judgment,* the consequence would equally be the substitution of their pleasure to that of the legislative body. The observation, if it prove anything, would prove that there ought to be no judges distinct from that body.

If, then, the courts of justice are to be considered as the bulwarks of a limited Constitution against legislative encroachments, this consideration will afford a strong argument for the permanent tenure of judicial offices, since nothing will contribute so much as this to that independent spirit in the judges which must be essential to the faithful performance of so arduous a duty.

Hamilton thus interpreted the theory of the separation of powers and the placing of limitations on the several departments in the Constitution, and especially on the legislature to involve the independence of the judiciary in respect to the other departments with the privilege and right of declaring void all acts in their judgment contrary to the provisions of the written Constitution.[44] This defense of judicial review of legislation became the standard argument for judges and statesmen. The indebtedness of Chief Justice Marshall to Hamilton is evident in his opinion in the case of *Marbury v. Madison.*[45]

Among others who favored the right of the courts to prevent violations of the provisions of the Constitution, were Samuel Adams, in Massachusetts,[46] Dickinson, in Pennsylvania,[47] Davie and Iredell in North Carolina,[48] and Hansen, in Maryland.[49]

On the other hand, various objections were raised by those who disapproved of the indefinite language in the articles relating to the judiciary. In public addresses and papers of the time the plan of the federal judiciary was

---

44 *The Federalist*, 521–523.
45 1 Cranch 137 (1803).
46 Elliot's *Debates*, 2:131.
47 Paul Leicester Ford, *Pamphlets on the Constitution of the United States* (Brooklyn, 1888) 184.
48 Elliot's *Debates*, 4:156 and Iredell's *Letters of an Elector*, see *supra*, 115.
49 ''They may reflect however, that every judge in the union, whether of federal or state appointment . . . . will have a right to reject any act handed to him as a law, which he may conceive repugnant to the constitution.''—Ford, *op. cit.*, 234.

severely attacked. Elbridge Gerry feared that a Star Chamber was about to be established. He urged:

that there are no well-defined limits of the Judiciary powers, they seem to be left as a boundless ocean, that has broken over the chart of the Supreme Lawgiver. *"Thus far thou shalt go and no further,"* and as they cannot be comprehended by the clearest capacity, or the most sagacious mind, it would be an Herculean labor to attempt to describe the dangers with which they are replete.[50]

Edmund Randolph and George Mason, who with Gerry refused to sign the Constitution, objected seriously to the fact that there were no limitations on the judicial power.[51] Mason was alarmed in that he believed the federal judiciary to be so constructed and extended as to absorb and destroy the judiciaries of the several states.[52] Similar objections were raised by Richard Henry Lee in his letters of a Federal Farmer.[53] There were some who believed that the courts would not be dangerous because they would be obliged to accept and enforce the laws as enacted by Congress.[54] This was not the opinion of Robert Yates, of New York, who opposed the Constitution because of the powers conferred on the judiciary. Among his objections he claimed that

the supreme court then have a right, independent of the legislature, to give a construction to the Constitution and every part of

---

[50] Ford, *op. cit.*, 9.

[51] *Ibid.*, 275. Gerry later expressed an opinion favorable to judicial supremacy. In the debate in Congress regarding the President's power of removal he said: "The judges are expositors of the Constitution and the acts of Congress. Our exposition, therefore, would be subject to their revisal. The judiciary may disagree with us and undo what all our efforts have labored to accomplish. A law is a nullity unless it can be carried into execution: in this case our law will be suspended."—Elliot's *Debates*, 4:393, 403.

[52] *Ibid.*, 329, 330.

[53] *Ibid.*, 398 *et seq.*

[54] C. F. Williams and Melancthon Smith, in New York.—Elliot's *Debates*, 2:330, 334, 338, 378.

it, and there is no power provided in this system to correct their construction or do away with it. If therefore the legislature pass any laws inconsistent with the sense the judges put upon the Constitution, they will declare it void.[55]

Along with the indications of approval of judicial control over legislation in the debates and discussions on the adoption of the Constitution, it is necessary to consider the political opinions and purposes of the men into whose hands the Constitution was placed to carry out its general spirit and meaning. It is well known that the Federalist group which were given charge of the federal government in 1789, and the major portion of those who participated in the Philadelphia convention, intended to establish a system of government that would be stable and would give sufficient protection against the dangers of majority rule.

Washington, Hamilton, Wilson, Ellsworth, and Marshall were among those who were called upon to interpret and apply the provisions of the new Constitution relative to judicial power. They were also leaders among those who believed in safeguarding the rights of property against the leveling tendencies of the radical Democrats. All, with the exception of Washington, are on record as supporters of the view that courts were obliged to declare acts contrary to the fundamental law invalid. It was to be expected that the federal courts as organized by the Federalist party would accept as a principle of their organization that acts contrary to the Constitution must be declared void. Had the government in 1789 been placed in charge of the radicals, such as Patrick Henry, Thomas Jefferson, and Samuel Adams, a different pro-

---

[55] Paul Leicester Ford, *Essays on the Constitution of the United States* (Brooklyn, 1892) 295. Similar views were expressed by an unknown writer in Pennsylvania, see McMaster and Stone, *op. cit.*, 611, 612, 659.

cedure might have been engrafted on our federal law. But some of the radicals and of those of democratic inclinations were at this time advocates of the right of judicial review. Patrick Henry, who feared the centralized power which the new Constitution was about to establish, held that it was "the highest encomium of this country, that the acts of the legislature, if unconstitutional, are liable to be opposed by the judiciary."[56] Even Thomas Jefferson, who later became an outspoken opponent of judicial review, is on record as favoring a council of revision. And in speaking of the executive veto, he said, "I should have liked it better had the judiciary been associated for that purpose, or invested with a similar and separate power."[57] He is also known to have favored a bill of rights because of "the legal checks which it put into the hands of the judiciary."[58] It is, of course, useless to conjecture, but one is inclined to wonder what decision on the matter Jefferson and his party would have favored had the Constitution been placed for its interpretation in the hands of men inclined to his way of thinking. Certain it is that the course of political affairs from 1789 to 1803 resulted in establishing beyond cavil the right of the federal courts to declare acts of Congress invalid, and in developing a spirit of opposition thereto which made Jefferson an inveterate enemy of John Marshall and an uncompromising opponent of judicial supremacy. The judiciary act of 1789 was the first step in the triumph of the Federalist doctrine of judicial authority over acts of Congress.

---

[56] Elliot's *Debates*, 3:324–325.

[57] *Writings* (edited by Ford), 4:475, 476.

[58] *Ibid.*, 5:81.

4. *The Judiciary Act of 1789—*

An act organizing the courts of the United States was passed by both houses of Congress and approved by President Washington on the 24th of September, 1789.[59] Oliver Ellsworth, who was known to favor judicial review of legislation, as chairman of the Senate committee is credited with being largely responsible for the drafting and passage of the act.[60] The Supreme Court was to consist of a Chief Justice and five associate justices, and inferior courts were instituted comprising circuit courts and district courts for the separate states.[61] The jurisdiction of the federal courts and the realm of judicial duties were more definitely outlined than was possible in the draft of the Constitution. In relation to the development of judicial review of legislation in both federal and state governments, the twenty-fifth section of this act is remarkable. It was enacted

that a final judgment or decree in any suit in the highest court of law or equity of a state in which a decision in the suit could be had, where is drawn in question the validity of a treaty or statute of, or an authority exercised under the United States and the decision is against their validity; or where is drawn in question the validity of a statute or an authority exercised under a state, on the ground of their being repugnant to the Constitution, treaties or the laws of the United States and the decision is in favor of their validity, or where is drawn in question the construction of any clause of the Constitution, of a treaty, or a statute of, or commission held under the United States, and the decision is against the title, privilege or exemption specially set up or claimed by either party, under such clause of the said constitution, treaty, statute or commission, may be reexamined and

---

59 *U. S. Statutes* at Large, 1:73–93.

60 *Annals* of Congress, 1:18, 49, 50.

61 *U. S. Statutes* at Large, 1, secs. 1 and 2.

reversed or affirmed in the Supreme Court of the United States upon a writ of error.[62]

The national legislature herein explicitly recognized the right of a state court to declare laws of the United States void, subject to an appeal to the federal Supreme Court, wherein it was intended to vest revisory powers over all decisions affecting the validity of laws or treaties of the federal government. There was an implication in this section that an act of Congress might be held invalid by a state court and rendered effective with the approval of the Supreme Court. The original provision was confined to cases in which a state court decided in favor of the validity of a state law or proceeding. It was necessary to extend the jurisdiction of the federal courts by an amendment to this section to cover decisions by state courts against the validity of state laws on the ground that there was a conflict with federal authority.

Members of the House of Representatives, however, opposed the bill vigorously.[63] The main opposition seemed to center around the sections providing for district courts. The plan establishing separate federal courts to consider cases arising in the various states was attacked as being expensive, cumbersome, and likely to interfere with the normal and regular function of the state judicial systems.[64] It was recognized by the advocates of the bill that the plan proposed would constitute "one of the strongest cements for making this Constitu-

[62] *Ibid.*, 1:85–86.

[63] For the claim that the Judiciary Act was a compromise measure "so framed as to secure the votes of those who, while willing to see the experiment of a Federal Constitution tried, were insistent that the Federal Courts should be given the minimum powers and jurisdiction," see Charles Warren, "New Light on the History of the Federal Judiciary Act of 1789," 37 *Harv. Law Rev.* (Nov. 1923) 53 ff.

[64] *Annals* of Congress, 1:796 ff.

tion firm and compact."[65] The principal ground of opposition was not, however, the right of courts to declare acts invalid, though some objections were raised regarding the extent of the power conferred by the twenty-fifth section of the act.[66] The fear was expressed that there could be no suit or action brought in the state courts that might not "under this clause be reversed or affirmed by being brought within the cognizance of the Supreme Court."[67] The advocates of the section defended the provision and claimed that if a state court should usurp the jurisdiction of federal causes, and by its adjudications attempt to strip the federal government of its constitutional rights, it was necessary that the national tribunal should possess the power of protecting those rights from such invasion.[68]

Whether or not the provision of the Constitution relating to the establishment of inferior federal courts was mandatory upon Congress was also fully discussed. The impression appeared to prevail that Congress had no choice in the matter and that inferior courts must be established. In the course of this debate, Gerry defended the courts as guardians of the fundamental law, when he raised the query whether the judges will not be guided by the Constitution as well as the laws. "The Constitution," he said, "will undoubtedly be their first rule; and so far as your laws conform to that, they will attend to them, but no further."[69]

The fact that statements of this character were not infrequently made, even by the opponents of a strong federal judicial system, seems to indicate that at this day the right of courts of justice to protect judicial powers and to guard the fundamental law from legislative and

---

[65] *Annals*, 1:811.　　[67] *Ibid.*, 815.　　[69] *Annals*, 1:829.
[66] *Ibid.*, 811, 815.　　[68] *Ibid.*, 819.

executive encroachments was part of the legal doctrines of all parties. The opponents of the motion to strike out the section providing for district courts could muster only eleven votes, and recognizing that further opposition was futile, they referred the bill back to the committee and finally passed it without any material amendments.[70] The general agreement that state courts might declare federal laws contrary to the Constitution invalid and the arrangement for appeal of such cases to the Supreme Court, as well as the suggestion that the judiciary was to have an independent constitutional status in order to protect the fundamental law, were evidences of the belief that federal courts, as guardians of the Constitution, might when occasion arose declare both state and federal acts invalid.

---

[70] *Ibid.*, 894.

CHAPTER VII

DEVELOPMENT OF THE PRACTICE OF JUDICIAL REVIEW OF LEGISLATIVE ACTS; STATE PRECEDENTS AFTER 1789

THE ARGUMENTS in the Philadelphia convention over different provisions of the Constitution and the discussions over the ratification of the Constitution frequently referred to the possibility of the review of legislative acts by the courts either with approval or disapproval. Before a case arose in the federal courts involving the validity of an act of Congress a number of state courts decided in favor of judicial review of state enactments.

1. *Ham v. M'Claws*, South Carolina, 1789.—A claim was made that Negro slaves seized by a revenue officer had become forfeited because they were imported contrary to the directions of an act of the legislature. Since settlers who were prevailed upon to enter the state under the sanction of existing law could not possibly know of the terms of a more recent enactment, it was asserted that forfeiture could not be supported in this case even though the act provided for no such exceptions.[1] Citing Coke's *Reports* the attorney for the claimants argued that it was

the duty of the court, in such case, to square its decision with the rules of common right and justice. For there were certain fixed and established rules, founded on the reason and fitness

---

[1] 1 Bay (S. C.) 93, 96.

of things, which were paramount to all statutes; and if laws are made *against* those principles, they are null and void. For instance, statutes made against *common right and reason,* are void. So statutes made against natural equity are void, and so also are statutes made against *Magna Carta.*[2]

The court in its instruction to the jury advised the restriction of the application of the act as follows:

It is clear, that statutes passed against the plain and obvious principles of common right, and common reason, are absolutely null and void, *as far as they are calculated to operate against those principles.* . . . . We are, therefore, bound to give such a construction to this enacting clause of the act of 1788, as will be consistent with justice, and the dictates of natural reason, though contrary to the strict letter of the law; and this construction is, that the legislature never had it in their contemplation to make forfeiture of the negroes in question.[3]

Principles of natural law and reason were used as a guide by the judges rather than any written constitutional provision.

2. *Gilman v. McClary,* New Hampshire, 1791.—There is a reference to a New Hampshire case in 1785 but details regarding it are not available.[4] An interesting decision, however, was rendered by a county court in 1791. In the early state governments trials by the legislature were not uncommon. The general assembly in a few states acted

---

[2] *Ibid.,* 96.

[3] *Ibid.,* 98.

[4] Manuscript record, Superior Court for the County of Rockingham, September, 1791. For data on this case I am indebted to Walter F. Dodd's note in 12 *Am. Hist. Rev.* (Jan. 1907) 348–350. William Plumer, Jr., in his *Life of William Plumer,* 170–172, refers to this case, claiming that his father contended that the law was unconstitutional. This, remarks the biographer, "though not the first, was by far the most important instance in which the court pronounced a law of the state unconstitutional." William Plumer, a member of the New Hampshire legislature in 1785 writes, "I entered my protest singly and alone, against the bill for the recovery of small debts in an expeditious way and manner; principally on

as a final court of appeal. This practice was followed in New Hampshire even after the adoption of the constitution of 1784. It is not surprising then to find that when on a suit for money alleged to be due Nathaniel Gilman from Elizabeth McClary the court decided against Elizabeth McClary, she appealed to the legislature for redress. The petition was considered by a committee in each house and after an opportunity had been accorded to the parties to be heard a bill was passed, in the strange language of the act, "to restore Elizabeth McClary to her law." When the case again came before the Superior Court of the county the following record was made:

It appears to the Court that if the act virtually or really reverses the judgment of this Court it is repugnant to the bill of rights and constitution of this State and if the Act does not reverse the said judgment the Court cannot render another judgment in the same case upon appeal while the first judgment remains in full force. It is therefore considered by the Court that the said act is ineffectual and inadmissible and that the said action be dismissed.

3. *Case of Judges*, Virginia, 1788–1789.—The judges of Virginia aided in popularizing the doctrine of judicial review of legislation. None of the early cases caused more comment or was more widely known than the issue which absorbed the attention of the highest courts of

---

the ground that it was unconstitutional. The courts so pronounced it, and the succeeding legislature repealed the law."—William Plumer, Jr., *The Life of William Plumer*, 59. See also reference to a case in which a special act of the legislature directing a trial of a cause was held void by a justice. —*Memoir, Autobiography and Correspondence of Jeremiah Mason* (reprinted, Kansas City, 1917) 26, and William M. Meigs, "The American Doctrine of Judicial Power and its Early Origin," 47 *Am. Law Rev.* (Sept., Oct. 1913) 684.

In Merrill v. Sherburne (1 N. H. 199, 216) Justice Woodbury also referred to legislative acts granting new trials which were declared void.— Chickering v. Clark, and Butterfield v. Morgan, 1797, and Jenness v. Seavey, 1799.

that state from 1788 to 1793. The case arose over an act of the assembly of 1788[5] establishing district courts and imposing new judicial duties. On the passage of an earlier act of 1784 the question was raised whether it was contrary to the constitution to impose new duties on the judges, provided no additional compensation was granted. The reorganization of the districts under a new act brought the matter before the courts for determination.[6] At the next meeting of the court of appeals, after the passage of the act, a remonstrance was prepared and submitted to the general assembly, in which the justices protested against the statute. Regretting the necessity of rendering an opinion on a conflict between the constitution and an act of assembly they asserted that they found themselves obliged to decide, however their delicacy might be wounded, or whatever temporary inconveniences might ensue, and in that decision to declare *that the constitution and the act are in opposition and cannot exist together; and that the former must control the operation of the latter.*

Special attention was called to the provision for the separation of powers as expressed in the constitution and to the principle that the judges should hold office during good behavior. They insisted that their salaries should remain fixed as long as the duties remain the same, and that their insistence on considering a law void was not an attempt to control the legislature. "They are within the line of their duty," said they, "declaring what the law is, and not making a new law." In case the legislature disapproved of their conduct, the only recourse was an appeal to the people.[7]

Following this remonstrance several new acts of assembly were passed relating to the organization of courts.

---

[5] 12 Hening *Stat.* 535.   [6] 4 Call 135.   [7] *Ibid.,* 141 ff.

But in March, 1789, the judges again protested against an attempt on the part of the legislature to interfere with their independence. In April, 1793, however, the judges elected under the act of December, 1788, decided to proceed to business on the ground that they held their offices under the constitution, and that the new law could not take them away, even were there any intention to do so. Mercer observed that it was not in the power of the legislature to deprive the judges of their offices "except for misbehavior in office, and in the manner prescribed in the constitution."[8] The right of the legislature to reduce the salaries while the duties remained the same, and to require an increase of duty without additional compensation, was denied. The entire issue was reconsidered and exhaustively discussed in *Kamper v. Hawkins*. As the reasons for refusal to enforce the act of the legislature were fully presented by the judges, and as this case was in many respects one of the most important state precedents before the case of *Marbury v. Madison,* the opinions expressed by the judges deserve attention.

4. *Kamper v. Hawkins,* Virginia, 1793.—An injunction to stay the proceedings of a judgment obtained under one of the acts of assembly reorganizing the district courts again brought up the issue whether the acts of assembly regarded as contrary to the written constitution would be accepted and enforced. The judges declaring the act contrary to the letter and spirit of the constitution delivered their opinions separately. Judge Nelson observed:

The difference between a free and an arbitrary government I take to be—that in the former limits are assigned to those to whom the administration is committed; but the latter depends

---

8 *Ibid.,* 150–151.

on the will of the departments or some of them. Hence the utility of a written constitution.

A *Constitution* is that by which the powers of government are limited.

It is to the *governors,* or rather to the departments of *government,* what a *law* is to individuals—nay, it is not only a rule of action to the branches of government, but it is that from which their existence flows, and by which the powers (or portions of the right to govern) which may have been committed to them are prescribed—It is their commission—nay, it is their creator.[9]

He further expressed the conviction that the constitution was comprised of fundamental principles and rules which were of higher authority than legislative acts. Vattel's influence was apparent in the insistence on the fact that the legislature derived its existence from the constitution and that it might not impugn the charter under which it was organized. In case of a presumed conflict between a legislative act and the constitution the query as to whether the court must not give judgment against the claimant was answered that there were three possible lines of conduct.

1st, to refuse to decide the question at all, which would be a dereliction of duty; or

2d, to wait for the legislature to decide whether the act be unconstitutional, which would be contrary to the separation of powers' clause of the constitution.

3d, to decide that the act is void, and therefore that the claimant under it cannot succeed.

The third seemed to him the only reasonable position for judges to take.[10]

To the objection that if the courts declared legislative acts void they thereby assumed legislative powers and

[9] 1 Va. Cases 23, 24.   [10] *Ibid.,* 31.

claimed a superiority over the legislature it was thought that when the cases of individuals were brought before the judges they were bound to decide.[11]

Following a similar line of argument, Judge Roane, who was reputed to be Jefferson's choice for Chief Justice had not Marshall received the appointment from President Adams, asserted that he at first thought that the judges ought to execute the law but that on mature consideration he had changed his opinion. Accepting the proposition that the people are sovereign and that they have fixed limits for the government in a bill of rights and in the body of the Constitution, the difficult question to determine is whose duty it is to decide in case of a conflict between a law and the constitution. Judge Roane believed that:

the judiciary may clearly say, that a subsequent statute has not changed a former for want of sufficient words, though it was perhaps intended it should do so. It may say, too, that an act of assembly has not changed the Constitution, though its words are expressly to that effect; because a legislature must have both the power and will (as evidenced by words) to change the law, and it is conceived, for the reason above mentioned, that the legislature have not power to change the fundamental laws. In expounding laws the judiciary considers *every* law which relates to the subject. Would you have them to shut their eyes against that law which is of the highest authority of any, or against a part of that law, which, either by its words or by its spirit, denies to any but the people the power to change it?[12] . . . .

From the above premises I conclude that the judiciary may and ought to adjudge a law unconstitutional and void, if it be plainly repugnant to the letter of the Constitution, or the fundamental principles thereof. By fundamental principles I understand those great principles growing out of the Constitution, by

---

[11] 1 Va. Cases 30, 32.   [12] *Ibid.*, 38.

the aid of which, in dubious cases, the Constitution may be explained and preserved inviolate; those land-marks, which it may be necessary to resort to, on account of the impossibility to foresee or provide for cases within the spirit but without the letter of the Constitution.[13]

Judge Henry maintained that the doctrine of parliamentary omnipotence could not be held to apply to the state of Virginia, because this doctrine had been repudiated by the convention that framed the state constitution.[14]

The contention that it was an impropriety on the part of the judiciary to decide against a law was disposed of by Judge Tyler, who thought the constitution was a contract between the people and their rulers and by it the latter were to be held to strict account. The enforcement of the contract could not be left with the legislature itself. Judge Henry continued:

I will not in an extra-judicial manner assume the right to negative a law, for this would be as dangerous as the example before us; but if by any legal means I have jurisdiction of a cause, in which it is made a question how far the law be a violation of the constitution, and therefore of no obligation, I shall not shrink from a comparison of the two, and pronounce sentence as my mind may receive conviction . . . .

To conclude, I do declare that I will not hold an office which I believe to be unconstitutional; that I will not be made a fit agent, to assist the legislature in a violation of this sacred letter; that I form this opinion from the conviction I feel that I am free to think, speak and act, as other men do upon so great a question; that as I never did sacrifice my own opinions for the sake of popularity in the various departments I have had the honor to fill, however desirable popular favor may be, when obtained upon honorable principles; so now that I am grown old

---

[13] *Ibid.*, 40.   [14] *Ibid.*, 47, 48.

I cannot depart from these motives which I have both in public and private life made my standard—I concur therefore most heartily with my brothers, who have gone before me, in the last two points, that the law is unconstitutional and ought not to be executed; the injunction therefore must be overruled—and this opinion I form, not from a view of the memorials, nor from the writers who knew not the blessings of free government, but as they were seen and felt throughout the prospect of future times, but from honest reason, common sense and the great letter of a Free Constitution.[15]

In order to substantiate the view that the legislature was subordinate to the constitution, and hence could not change the fundamental laws, Judge Tucker quoted from Paine and Vattel. The objection that the constitution of a state is a rule to the legislature only and not to the judiciary or the executive, was thus refuted:

This sophism could never have obtained a moment's credit with the world, had such a thing as a written constitution existed before the American Revolution. . . . . With us, the constitution is not an "ideal thing, but a real existence: it can be produced in a visible form": its principles can be ascertained from the living letter, not from obscure reasoning or deductions only. The government, therefore, and all its branches, must be governed by the constitution. Hence it becomes the first law of the land, and as such must be resorted to on every occasion where it becomes necessary to expound *what the law is.* This exposition it is the duty and office of the judiciary to make. . . . . It appears to me that this deduction clearly follows, viz. that the *judiciary* are *bound* to take notice of the constitution, *as the first law of the land;* and that whatsoever is contradictory thereto is *not* the law of the land.[16]

Hamilton's defense of the theory of judicial supremacy was quoted as conclusive, and it was assumed as a fact that the judiciary was established "as a barrier against

---

[15] 1 Va. Cases 59, 61, 65–6.   [16] *Ibid.,* 77, 78, 81.

possible usurpation, or abuse of power in the other departments.'"[17] Hence it was taken for granted that the judiciary must be placed in an independent and superior position in order to guard securely the fundamental law.

The judges unanimously agreed that the act reorganizing the district courts could only be executed by those who were judges in accordance with the provisions of the constitution. They presented their remonstrance to the governor with a request that he lay the same before the assembly. Subsequent to the presentation of this remonstrance to the governor all the judges resigned, and afterwards requalified under an act amending the law so as to remove the main grounds for the dispute.

The case attracted wide attention, and the opinions of the judges were presented to the public in book form the following year. The underlying assumptions and principles advocated as a basis for judicial review were clearly formulated. When John Marshall announced the same principles as fundamental doctrines of federal law, it was Virginia statesmen and judges who opposed the principles which her judges had so insistently supported. Judge Roane himself was among those who were persuaded to think that courts were usurping authority when they presumed to declare legislative acts void. It was evidently regarded as a different matter to have state judges declare an act of their own legislature void and to have federal courts declare state acts invalid. The latter involved the bitter antagonisms which were aroused when state powers and privileges were curtailed.

5. *Bowman v. Middleton*, South Carolina, 1792.— Under an act of assembly passed in 1712, a freehold was transferred from one party to another without judicial

---

[17] *Ibid.*, 85–88.

process and without a trial by jury. On the ground that title could not be given under such an act an effort was made to have the act invalidated.[18] The court, refusing to enforce the act,

> were clearly of opinion, that the plaintiffs could claim no title under the act in question, as it was against common right, as well as against *Magna Carta*, to take away the freehold of one man and vest it in another, and that, too, to the prejudice of third persons, without any compensation, or even a trial by the jury of the country, to determine the right in question; that the act was therefore, *ipso-facto*, void; and, that no length of time could give it validity, being originally founded on erroneous principles.[19]

Coke's theory of common law supremacy seemed to influence the judges in their decision.

6. *Austin v. Trustees of the University of Pennsylvania*, Pennsylvania, 1793.—One of the earliest cases in Pennsylvania arose over the attempt of the legislature by a special act to grant title to certain premises. A few months later and before the suit relating to the premises was instituted the legislature repealed the act granting title. For the reasons stated in the preamble of the repealing act, Judge Yeates said he had no difficulty in declaring the former act unconstitutional. The effect of the two acts was held to leave to the judiciary the determination of the rights involved.[20]

7. *State v. ————*, North Carolina, 1794.—A law was enacted that judgments might be obtained by the attorney general by motion against the receivers of public money. When the attorney general moved for judgment under this act against several parties, the judge refused to render judgment because it condemned a man without

---

[18] 1 Bay (S. C.) 252.   [19] *Ibid.*, 254.   [20] 1 Yeates 260, 261.

a hearing. Referring to the fact that the act violated certain sections of the constitution relating to trial by jury, Judge Williams said:

I think the act unconstitutional, and I cannot, as at present advised, give my assent to its being carried into effect—the judges of the land are a branch of government, and are to administer the constitutional laws, not such as are repugnant to the constitution; it is their duty to resist an unconstitutional act. In fact, such an act made by the General Assembly, who are deputed only to make laws in conformity to the constitution, and within the limits it prescribes, is not any law at all.[21]

A few days later the attorney general again moved the court to give judgment and Judges Ashe and McCay, disagreeing with Judge Williams, proceeded on the ground that the act was valid.[22]

8. *Respublica v. Duquet*, Pennsylvania, 1799.—This case raised the question whether the law of 1795, directing the corporation of Philadelphia to pass ordinances to prevent the erection of wooden buildings in certain parts of the city, was constitutional. The chief objection was that the ordinance passed directed a prosecution by

---

[21] 1 Hay (N. C.) 28, 29.

[22] *Ibid.*, 40. Chief Justice Kirkpatrick, of New Jersey, referred in State v. Parkhurst to an earlier case in that state, Taylor v. Reading, in which "a certain act of the legislature, passed March 1795, upon the petition of the defendants, declaring that in certain cases payments made in continental money should be credited as specie, was by this court held to be an *ex post facto* law, and as such unconstitutional, and in that case inoperative."—4 Halstead 427, 444 (1802).

When in 1796 the owners of lots in the city of Charleston attempted to restrain the street commissioners from laying out a new street, an act of the legislature authorizing the proceedings of the commissioners was attacked as taking a freehold for public use without consent, full compensation, or trial by jury. The judges were equally divided in their opinions and the proceedings were allowed to stand. Judge Waties, with whom Judge Burke concurred favored the granting of a writ of prohibition and said: It was painful to him to be obliged to question the exercise of any legislative power, but he was sworn to support the constitution, and this was the most important of all the duties which were incumbent on

indictment and that the legislature could not grant such authority to a corporation. Though the court held the act valid an expression of opinion as a dictum asserted the right to declare acts invalid, as follows: "if a violation of the constitution should in any case be made by an act of the legislature, and that violation should unequivocally appear to us, we shall think it our duty not to shrink from the task of saying such law is void."[23]

9. *Stidger v. Rogers,* Kentucky, 1801.—The constitution of the State of Kentucky provided that trial by jury was to remain inviolate, and that all laws contrary to the constitution were void.[24] An act of assembly of 1799 was held unconstitutional because it empowered a court to ascertain the value of property in a case which, prior to the formation of the constitution, could have been ascertained only by a jury. The court also thought that the act impaired the contract entered into by the parties, and expressed the opinion that an act of the legislature which authorized the court to award damages for the non-

---

the judges. On the faithful performance of this high duty would depend the integrity and duration of our government. If the legislature is permitted to exercise other rules than those ordained by the constitution, and if innovations are suffered to acquire the sanction of time and practice, the rights of the people will soon become dependent on the legislative will, and the constitution have no more obligation than an obsolete law. But if this court does its duty, in giving to the constitution an overruling operation over every act of the legislature which is inconsistent with it, the people will then have an independent security for their rights which may render them perpetual. In exercising this high authority, the judges claim the rights of the people will soon become dependent on the legislative will, If an act of the legislature is held void, it is not because the judges have any control over the legislative power, but because the act is forbidden by the constitution, and because the will of the people, which is therein declared, is paramount to that of their representatives, expressed in any law. As the act under consideration appeared to him to be repugnant to this high will he was bound to say that it ought not to have any operation and that the prohibition should be granted.—Lindsay v. Commissioners, 2 Bay 61–62.

23 12 Yeates 493, 501.
24 2 Kentucky Decisions, 52.

performance of a contract made before the act was passed changed the obligation of the contract and was void.[25] At the same time an act which was regarded as depriving a party of trial by jury in a case in which, before that time, he was entitled to jury trial at law was held contrary to the constitution.[26] And the following year a part of an act relating to penalties and damages for delinquency in the payment of public moneys by clerks of the general court was declared void.[27]

10. *Whittington v. Polk,* Maryland, 1802.—William Whittington claimed that Polk had unjustly deprived him of the office of chief justice of the county courts of eastern Maryland and appealed to the general court to sustain his claim. An act of assembly relating to the administration of justice was involved and counsel contended that such an act repugnant to the constitution is void, and that the court has a right to so declare it. Chief Justice Chase observed that these contentions had not been controverted in any of the cases which had been brought before the courts of Maryland. Though the act was regarded valid, the Chief Justice expressed an opinion on the issue raised by counsel. The government of Maryland he believed, was in the nature of a compact between the people and their agents, the public officers, and

the power of determining finally on the validity of the acts of the legislature cannot reside with the legislature, because such power would defeat and render nugatory all the limitations and restrictions on the authority of the legislature contained in the bill of rights and form of government, and they would become judges of the validity of their own acts, which would establish a despotism, and subvert that great principle of the

---

[25] *Ibid.,* 52.
[26] Enderman v. Ashby, 2 Ky. Decisions (1801) 53.
[27] Caldwell v. The Commonwealth, *ibid.,* 129.

constitution, which declares that the powers of making, judging, and executing the law shall be separate and distinct from each other.

This power cannot be exercised by the people at large, or in their collective capacity, because they cannot interfere according to their own compact, unless by elections, and in such manner as the constitution has prescribed, and because there is no other mode ascertained by which they can express their will. . . .

It is the office and province of the court to decide all questions of law which are judicially brought before them, according to the established mode of proceeding, and to determine whether an act of the legislature, which assumes the appearance of a law, and is clothed with the garb of authority, is made pursuant to the power vested by the constitution in the legislature; for if it is not the result or emanation of authority derived from the constitution, it is not the law, and cannot influence the judgment of the court in the decision of the question before them.

The oath of a judge is "that he will do equal right and justice according *to the law of this state,* in every case in which he shall act as judge."

To do right and justice according to law, the judge must determine what the law is, which necessarily involves in it the right of examining the constitution (which is the supreme or paramount law, and under which the legislature derive the only authority they are invested with, of making laws) and considering whether the act passed is made pursuant to the constitution, and that trust and authority which is delegated thereby to the legislative body.[28]

The assertion of this authority was necessary, it was claimed, to enforce the theory of the separation of powers. These views have a special significance since they were announced only a short time before Marshall's opinion in the *Marbury Case* and Chase was later appointed a justice of the Supreme Court of the United States, where he expressed similar views in a federal case.

---

[28] 1 Harris and Johnson 236, 242, 244.

11. *State v. Parkhurst,* New Jersey, 1802.—Information in the nature of a *quo warranto,* filed by the attorney general against Parkhurst for unlawfully holding the office of clerk of the court of common pleas, involved the construction of various acts of the legislature. Justices Smith and Boudinot of the Supreme Court delivered opinions in favor of the state and rendered judgment against Parkhurst. Chief Justice Kirkpatrick dissented and delivered an opinion which appears to have been sanctioned by the court of appeals, as that court upon a writ of error reversed the decision of the Supreme Court and rendered judgment in favor of Parkhurst. Chief Justice Kirkpatrick thought that the legislature was necessarily bound by the terms of the written constitution. The question whether the judges could declare void a law deemed contrary to the provisions of the written charter, had

been considerably agitated in these United States. It has enlisted many champions on both sides. It is a question equally arising out of every constitution where the legislative power is limited, and where there are certain rights or powers reserved in the hands of the people themselves, over which the legislature has no control.

The oath of the judges required by the legislature enjoining them to decide "agreeably to the *constitution and laws of the state of New Jersey,*" was regarded equivalent to a legislative determination, clearly authorizing the courts to hold void legislative acts deemed by them to be contrary to the constitution.[29]

The opinion of Chief Justice Marshall in the case of *Marbury v. Madison*[30] rendered in 1803 formulated in

---

[29] 4 Halstead 427, 443–445, Appendix. See reference by Chief Justice Kirkpatrick to an earlier case in New Jersey, *supra,* 159; also case of Holmes v. Walton, *supra,* 92.

[30] 1 Cranch 137.

succinct and effective form the main tenets of those who
supported the right of the courts to review legislative
acts. Henceforth the advocates of the American doctrine
in the states had a federal precedent to rely upon and
not infrequently the language of Marshall was used and
his arguments repeated. The steps leading to the *Marbury v. Madison* decision will be sketched in the next
chapter.

12. *White v. Kendrick,* South Carolina, 1805.—An act
of assembly extending the jurisdiction of justices was
adjudged to be unconstitutional,[31] because it violated the
clause of the constitution securing the right of trial by
jury. Referring to Blackstone and the English doctrine
of parliamentary omnipotence, Justice Wilds said that
such political infallibility was not to be attributed to the
legislature except on subjects particularly set apart for
its cognizance. The legislature being a mere creature
with its powers limited we are placed as sentinels to
guard against its encroachments on power not its own.[32]

13. *Trustees of the University of North Carolina v.
Foy,* North Carolina, 1805.—In 1789 the legislature of
North Carolina granted to the trustees of the university
all the property that had theretofore or should thereafter
escheat to the state. In 1800 the legislature repealed the
grant. This repealing act was held void as contrary to
the section of the bill of rights which declared that "no
freeman ought to be deprived of his life, liberty or property, but by the laws of the land."[33] Judge Locke speaking for the court maintained that the university was in a
sense established by the constitution and that it was not
at the mercy of the legislature.[34]

---

[31] 1 Brevard 469. Cf. note, apparently added by the reporter.
[32] *Ibid.,* 471.   [33] 5 N. C. 58.   [34] *Ibid.,* 86.

As this is one of the first cases in which the phrase "law of the land," or "due process of law" was interpreted, the decision has a peculiar interest. The "law of the land" phrase in the bill of rights was held to be a restraint on the legislature and Judge Locke thought that,

members of a corporation as well as individuals shall not be so deprived of their liberties or properties, unless by a trial by jury in a court of justice, according to the known and established rules of decision derived from the common law and such acts of the Legislature as are consistent with the Constitution. Although the trustees are a corporation established for public purposes, yet their property is as completely beyond the control of the Legislature as the property of individuals or that of any other corporation. . . . . The property vested in the trustees must remain for the uses intended for the university, until the judiciary of the country in the usual and common form pronounce them guilty of such acts as will, in law, amount to a forfeiture of their rights or a dissolution of their body.[35]

It is interesting to note how some of the modern ideas involved in due process of law were here suggested.

14. *Decisions in other states.*—The practice of asserting the right of the judiciary to serve as the chief guardians of the fundamental law was recognized and approved in other states. As early as 1805 in Ohio, Judge Pease interpreted an act defining the duties of justices of the peace so that the fifth section, which gave them jurisdiction over sums exceeding twenty dollars, and the twenty-ninth section, which prevented plaintiffs from recovering costs in actions commenced by original writs in the court of common pleas for sums between twenty and fifty dollars, were held void as repugnant to

---

[35] *Ibid.*, 88–89. See dissenting opinion of Judge Hall in which he disapproved of the higher law theories of counsel and the extra-constitutional views of the court.

the Constitution of the United States and of the state.[36]
Similar opinions were rendered by Justices Huntington
and Tod. These decisions became the ground for impeachment proceedings.[37]

In 1807 the supreme court of Tennessee asserted that
the legislature had no right to pass an act perfecting
titles to land, because "it was expressly reserved to
North Carolina, until she had complied with her engagements, after which the power was to reside in the United
States."[38]   Consequently section 7 of the act of 1801
perfecting land titles was held not obligatory.

A somewhat extended approval of the right of review
of legislation was presented in Pennsylvania although
the act of assembly was held valid. Because of a conflict
with the provision of the constitution that "trial by jury
shall be as heretofore and the right remain inviolate,"
a statute extending the jurisdiction of the alderman's
court of Philadelphia was alleged to be void. In rendering judgment favorable to the validity of the act Judge
Yeates again defended the right of the courts to review
legislation. The constitution was considered in the
nature of a compact and

the judiciary power far from being an emanation from the executive, is intended by the American constitutions as a counterpoise
or check to its excesses and those of the legislature. . . . . The
obligation of an oath imposed upon us to support both constitutions would be nugatory if it were dependent upon either of the
other branches of the government, or in any manner subject to
their control; since such control might operate to the destruction
instead of the support of either constitution.[39]

---

36 5 *Western Law Monthly* (June 1863) 3 ff.

37 See William M. Utter, "Judicial Review in Early Ohio," *Miss. Valley
Hist. Rev.* (June 1927) 14:9, and *infra*, 255.

38 Miller's Lessee v. Holt, 1 Overton 243, 244.

39 Emerick v. Harris, 1 Binney 416, 419, 420 (1808).

In 1809 Chief Justice Tilghman remarked that in his judgment the courts could declare acts void provided the conflict between a law and the constitution was plain but he believed there was a grave necessity of exercising the power with great discretion.[40] A few years later Judge Breckenridge also argued in favor of judicial review.[41]

In 1811 the right was again asserted by way of dicta in South Carolina. A case arose over an act of the legislature disqualifying an attorney and preventing him from carrying on his practice because of public employment. It was contended that the act was void because it was an *ex post facto* law; and because it deprived him of a right of freehold "without the judgment of his peers or any law authorized by the constitution." Chancellor Waites in the course of his opinion declared that in a proper case he would not hesitate to declare a legislative act void for,

it is the peculiar and characteristic excellence of the free governments of America, that the legislative power is not supreme; but that it is limited and controlled by written constitutions, to which the Judges, who are sworn to defend them, are authorized to give a transcendent operation over all laws that may be made in derogation of them. This judicial check affords a security here for civil liberty, which belongs to no other government in the world; and if the Judges will everywhere faithfully exercise it, the liberties of the American nation may be rendered perpetual. But while I assert this power in the Court, and insist on the great value of it to the community, I am not insensible of the high deference which is due to the legislative authority. It is supreme in all cases in which it is not restrained by the constitution; and as it is the duty of the legislators as well as of the Judges to

---

[40] Olmsted's Case, 1 Brightly's Report 15.

[41] Case of John Towers, 2 Browne's Reports (Court of Common Pleas, Phila., District, Pa.) 195 (1812).

consult this and conform their acts to it, so it ought to be presumed that all their acts are conformable to it, unless the contrary is manifest. . . . . The validity of a law ought not, then, to be questioned, unless it is so obviously repugnant to the constitution that when pointed out by the judges, all men of sense and reflection in the community may perceive the repugnancy. By such a cautious exercise of this judicial check no jealousy of it will be excited, the public confidence in it may be promoted, and its salutary effects be justly and fully appreciated.[42]

The court refused to declare the act void.

A Vermont court in 1814 refused to read a deposition in a case despite the fact that the legislature had sanctioned the procedure. The act, said the court, is clearly void, because the legislature attempted to render a decision in a particular case—a procedure prohibited by the constitution. The act was also held invalid because it was retrospective in its nature. Even if the legislature should have specially provided that a party should be liable according to the terms of this act such an *"ex post facto* provision would have been void, as being against the constitution of this state, and constitution of the United States and even against the law of nature."[43]

On a similar basis an act of the legislature of New Hampshire, awarding a new trial in an action which had been decided in a court of law, was held to be an exercise of judicial power and also retrospective in its operation, and for these two reasons unconstitutional.[44] Finding the constitutional basis for the court's opinion rather insecure Judge Woodbury noted that the court was induced to rest its opinion "upon general principles."[45]

---

42 Byrne v. Stewart, 3 Des. 466, 476, 477.
43 Dupy v. Wickwire, 1 D. Chipman 237–239.
44 Merrill v. Sherburne, 1 N. H. 199, 204 ff. (1818).
45 *Ibid.*, 211.

The long usage of the legislature in granting new trials was not regarded as a justification for such procedure, when first principles were thought to be violated.

The courts of New York did not come into line until 1819, when it was determined that statutes, so far as they affected the rights of a patent covering both banks of the river Saranac, impaired the obligation of contract and were unconstitutional and void. On the basis of *Fletcher v. Peck*[46] and *New Jersey v. Wilson*[47] the conclusion was held to be irresistible "that the acts in question are unconstitutional and invalid, so far forth as they affect the river Saranac, within the bounds of the patent."[48]

By a gradual development the American doctrine of judicial review of legislation had emerged through colonial and state precedents and dicta of judges into a fairly well understood and accepted principle.[49] Referring on some occasions to an overruling law of nature, on other occasions to the fundamental principles embodied in the great English charters of liberties, and, finally, to formally enacted written instruments, colonial and state courts steadily asserted and maintained the right to invalidate acts, and thus they promulgated for the United States and put into an effective form Coke's theory of the supremacy of the courts. In most of the cases where there was resistance to judicial decrees invalidating legislative acts the court's opinion and judgment were ultimately accepted. Impeachment proceedings and legislative censure only tended to strengthen judicial power. Finally, the fact that the other departments of govern-

---

[46] 6 Cranch 87, 136 (1810).

[47] 7 Cranch 164 (1812).

[48] People v. Platt, 17 Johns. 195, 214, 215.

[49] For critical analyses of the prevailing views, see opinions of Judges Bland and Gibson, *infra*, 261 *et seq*.

ment deferred to the judgment of the courts and accepted their conclusions, although there was no legal requirement that they should do so, tends to show that it was the acceptance of certain fundamental notions of law and government which led men to sanction and support the underlying principles of the American doctrine. The way was prepared for the general adoption of the practice of judicial control of legislative acts before the federal courts were factors to be reckoned with in the law of the United States. It was to be expected that the federal judiciary would follow the plan which had so generally been incorporated into the practice of the states. The adoption of the doctrine by the national judiciary gave added prestige to those who were hastening the day of its general acceptance throughout the states, and made it certain that the principles involved would soon be generally approved as features of the public law of the country.

Chapter VIII

DEVELOPMENT OF THE PRACTICE OF JUDICIAL REVIEW OF LEGISLATIVE ACTS: EARLY FEDERAL PRECEDENTS

THE WAY of the Supreme Court to a position of respect and prominence was rather slow and was marked by reverses which tended to shake the confidence of the people in the highest federal tribunal. Changing personnel, the mingling of the justices in politics, and the long, wearisome, and sometimes dangerous trips on circuits during the first decades had not a little to do with the unpopularity of the court. Chiefly because of the general feeling of uncertainty and distrust Edmund Pendleton, of Virginia, Robert Hanson Harrison, of Maryland, Charles Cotesworth Pinckney, of South Carolina, and Edward Rutledge, of South Carolina, declined to accept commissions to positions on the court. John Rutledge, of South Carolina, Thomas Johnson, of Maryland, John Blair, of Virginia, and Alfred Moore, of North Carolina, resigned their positions and John Jay, of New York, and Oliver Ellsworth, of Connecticut, abandoned the office of Chief Justice. With a reversal of one of the most important decisions by an amendment and with very few controversies of importance to decide, it is not surprising to find that the Supreme Court did not make much of an appeal either to the interest or imagination of the people.[1]

---

[1] Cf. Albert J. Beveridge, *The Life of John Marshall* (Boston, 1919) 3:120, 121. When Chief Justice Jay was tendered a reappointment as Chief Justice by President Adams he wrote: (*Continued on Page 172*)

The reaction which was felt immediately after the adoption of the Constitution resulted in strengthening the powers of the state courts at the expense of federal authority. From 1790 to 1800 only six cases were decided by the court involving questions of constitutional law,[2] and John Marshall, on his appointment in 1801, found only a few cases awaiting adjudication. The Supreme Court had an inauspicious beginning, and there were few indications of those remarkable powers which this tribunal soon began to exercise.

"Such was the temper of the times, that the act to establish the Judicial Courts of the United States was in some respects more accommodated to certain prejudices and sensibilities, than to the great and obvious principles of sound policy. Expectations were nevertheless entertained that it would be amended as the public mind became more composed and better informed; but those expectations have not been realized, nor have we hitherto seen convincing indications of a disposition in Congress to realize them. On the contrary, the efforts repeatedly made to place the judicial department on a proper footing have proved fruitless.

"I left the bench perfectly convinced that under a system so defective it would not obtain the energy, weight and dignity which was essential to its affording due support to the national government; nor acquire the public confidence and respect which, as the last resort of the justice of the nation, it should possess. Hence I am induced to doubt both the propriety and expediency of my returning to the bench under the present system."— George Pellew, *John Jay*, 337, 338.

On August 5, 1792, Edmund Randolph, the Attorney-General, informed Washington that

"it is much to be regretted that the judiciary, in spite of their apparent firmness in annulling the pension law, are not what sometime hence they will be, a resource against the infractions of the Constitution on the one hand, and *a steady asserter of federal rights* on the other. So crude is our judiciary system, so jealous are our state judges of their authority, so ambiguous is the language of the Constitution, that the most probable quarter from which an alarming discontent may proceed is the rivalship of these two orders of judges."—Sparks, *Life and Writings of Washington*, 10:513.

For the contention that the Supreme Court was an important tribunal from the time of the establishment of the Constitution, see Charles Warren, "The Early History of the Supreme Court of the United States, in connection with Modern Attacks on the Judiciary," 8 *Mass. Law Quart.* (1923) 7 ff.

2 See Hayburn's Case, 2 Dallas 409; Chisholm's Executor v. Georgia, 2 Dallas 419; Hylton v. United States, 3 Dallas 171; Hollingsworth v. Virginia, 3 Dallas 378; Calder v. Bull, 3 Dallas 386; Cooper v. Telfair, 4 Dallas 14.

1. *Hayburn's Case,* 1792—

The first case before the federal courts involving the constitutionality of an act of Congress was *Hayburn's Case.*[3] Congress passed an act to regulate the claims to invalid pensions and authorized the judges of the circuit courts to receive and determine upon the applications for pensions, subject to review by the Secretary of War and by Congress.[4] In the New York circuit Justices Jay, Cushing, and Duane were of the opinion "that neither the Legislative nor the *Executive* branches, can constitutionally assign to the Judicial any duties, but such as are properly judicial and to be performed in a judicial manner."[5] Because of the benevolence of the object and in deference to the intention of the legislature, however, the judges agreed to execute the act in the capacity of commissioners. Justices Wilson, Blair, and Peters in the Pennsylvania circuit refused an application for an award and addressed a letter to the President in which they referred to the theory of the separation of powers as implied in the provisions of the Constitution and expressed the opinion that the court could not proceed:

1st. Because the business directed by this act is not of a judicial nature. It forms no part of the power vested by the Constitution in the courts of the United States; the Circuit Court must, consequently have proceeded without constitutional authority.

2nd. Because, if, upon that business, the court had proceeded, *its judgments* (for its *opinions* are its judgment) might, under the same act, have been revised and controlled by the legislature, and by an officer in the executive department. Such revision and control we deem radically inconsistent with the

---

[3] 2 Dallas 409. See Charles Warren, *The Supreme Court in United States History* (Boston, 1922) 1:69 ff.

[4] *U. S. Statutes* at Large, 1:243–245.

[5] 2 Dallas 410; and *American State Papers,* Misc., 1:51.

independence of that judicial power which is vested in the courts; and, consequently, with that important principle which is so strictly observed by the Constitution of the United States.

These, Sir, are the reasons for our conduct. Be assured that, though it became necessary, it was far from being pleasant. To be obliged to act contrary, either to the obvious directions of Congress, or to a constitutional principle, in our judgment equally obvious, excited feelings in us, which we hope never to experience again.[6]

In the North Carolina circuit, Justices Iredell and Sitgreaves sent a similar communication to the President in which it was contended that the revision provided for in the act by the Secretary of War "subjects the decision of the court to a mode of revision which we consider to be unwarranted by the Constitution," and with regard to the provision permitting an ultimate appeal to Congress, the Justices said "we beg leave to add, with all due reference, that no decision of any court of the United States can under any circumstances, in our opinion, agreeable to the Constitution, be liable to a revision or even suspension by the Legislature itself."[7] The justices suggested that it might be possible to administer the act as commissioners but on this point they had grave doubts. As no application was made to the justices in this circuit, there was no occasion for a decision on the direct issue.

---

[6] 2 Dallas 411. This decision of the justices in the Pennsylvania circuit has been styled the "First Hayburn Case" to distinguish it from a later case before the federal Supreme Court, when the attorney general presented a motion for a mandamus to compel the circuit court of Pennsylvania to hear the petition of Hayburn. The motion was held under advisement until Congress had removed the objectionable features of the act. For full discussion of these cases see Max Farrand, "The First Hayburn Case," *Am. Hist. Rev.*, 13 (Jan. 1908), 281–285. Professor Farrand concludes that there "would seem to be no reasonable doubt that on April 11, James Wilson, John Blair, and Richard Peters declared the Invalid Pension Act of 1792 unconstitutional" and that the case of Vanhorne's Lessee (*infra*, 179) was thus anticipated by three years.

[7] 2 Dallas 412.

The decision of the judges in the Pennsylvania circuit led the Attorney General to appeal to the Supreme Court for a mandamus to compel the judges to act on a petition by William Hayburn. The justices refused to act on the motion of the Attorney General but on a motion presented on behalf of Hayburn, they observed that they would hold the motion under advisement until the next term. No decision was pronounced, however, as the legislature at an intermediate session, provided in another way for the relief of the pensioners.[8] It is therefore apparent that the Supreme Court did not render a judgment on the validity of the pension act. The significance of the case arises from the decision of the circuit judges for the Pennsylvania district and the opinions expressed by individual justices. Similar issues were raised in other cases.

Chandler v. the Secretary of War.—The claim of John Chandler for a pension under the act of Congress being approved by Justices Iredell and Law acting as commissioners, was refused by Henry Knox, Secretary of the Treasury. In the meantime Congress passed another act changing the procedure in presenting the evidence on claims and authorized the Secretary of War and the Attorney General "to take such measures as may be necessary to obtain an adjudication of the Supreme Court of the United States on the validity of any such rights claimed under the act aforesaid by the determination of certain persons styling themselves commissioners."[9] Following this instruction the Attorney General applied for a mandamus to compel the secretary to place on the pension list all the names approved by the justices on the circuits. The Supreme Court refused to act on this motion and then an application was made to compel the

[8] *Ibid.*, 409, 410; Farrand, *op. cit.*, 281; and Warren, *op. cit.*, 78 ff.
[9] 1 *U. S. Statutes* at Large, 324.

secretary to place the name of John Chandler on the list. On February 14, 1794, the court decided that a mandamus could not be issued to the Secretary of War for the purpose desired.[10] Chief Justice Marshall apparently had this case in mind in his comments on the Invalid Pension Act in the case of *Marbury v. Madison.*[11]

United States v. Yale Todd.—Under the terms of the same act involved in the *Chandler Case* the case of the *United States* versus *Yale Todd* was docketed by consent in the Supreme Court. Yale Todd had previously appeared before Chief Justice Jay and Justices Cushing and Law, who acting as commissioners had ordered payment of a pension. In the presentation of the case before the Supreme Court it was agreed that if the justices had no authority to act as commissioners the judgment should be awarded for the United States. Without stating the grounds for the decision judgment was rendered in favor of the United States. Little attention was paid to the record in this case until 1851 when a similar case arose

---

[10] *Annals* of Congress, 7 Cong. 1 sess. 904 and argument of Charles Lee in Marbury v. Madison, 1 Cranch 137, 149. For an account of this case see Gordon E. Sherman, "The Case of John Chandler v. The Secretary of War," 14 *Yale Law Jour.* (June 1905) 431.

[11] This opinion seems now, for the first time, to be taken up in this country.

It must be well recollected that in 1792 (1 *Stats.* at Large, 243), an act passed, directing the secretary of war to place on the pension list such disabled officers and soldiers as should be reported to him, by the circuit courts, which act, so far as the duty was imposed on the courts, was deemed unconstitutional; but some of the judges thinking that the law might be executed by them in the character of commissioners, proceeded to act, and to report in that character.

This law being deemed unconstitutional at the circuits, was repealed, and a different system was established; but the question whether those persons who had been reported by the judges as commissioners, were entitled, in consequence of that report, to be placed on the pension list, was a legal question, properly determinable in the courts, although the act of placing such persons on the list was to be performed by the head of a department.

That this question might be properly settled, Congress passed an act in February 1793 (1 *Stats.* at Large, 324), making it the duty of the secretary

over an act granting the District Judge of Florida authority to settle Spanish claims arising under the provisions of a treaty.[12]

Chief Justice Taney who delivered the opinion in the *Case of Ferreira*, dismissing the appeal for want of jurisdiction, added a note to the case referring to the judgment on the application of Todd. The Chief Justice summarized the judgments in the Hayburn and Todd cases as follows: "That the power proposed to be conferred on the Circuit Courts of the United States by the act of 1792 was not judicial power within the meaning of the Constitution, and was, therefore unconstitutional, and could not be lawfully exercised by the courts.'"[13]

---

of war, in conjunction with the attorney general, to take such measures as might be necessary to obtain an adjudication of the supreme court of the United States on the validity of any such rights, claimed under the act aforesaid.

After the passage of this act, a mandamus was moved for, to be directed to the secretary of war, commanding him to place on the pension list, a person stating himself to be on the report of the judges.

There is, therefore, much reason to believe, that this mode of trying the legal right of the complainant was deemed by the head of a department, and by the highest law officer of the United States, the most proper which could be selected for the purpose.

When the subject was brought before the court, the decision was, not that a mandamus would not lie to the head of a department directing him to perform an act, enjoined by law, in the performance of which an individual had a vested interest; but that a mandamus ought not to issue in that case; the decision necessarily to be made if the report of the commissioners did not confer on the applicant a legal right.

The judgment, in that case, is understood to have decided the merits of all claims of that description; and the persons, on the report of the commissioners, found it necessary to pursue the mode prescribed by the law subsequent to that which had been deemed unconstitutional, in order to place themselves on the pension list.

The doctrine therefore, now advanced, is by no means a novel one.— Marbury v. Madison, 1 Cranch 171, 172.

[12] United States v. Ferreira, 13 Howard 40 (1851).

[13] 13 Howard 52, 53. On the basis of this note the Todd case is included in the list of cases in which statutes and ordinances were held void, inserted as an appendix to 131 U. S. Reports. See also reference to this case by Justice Shiras claiming that an act of Congress was held unconstitutional in *in re* Sanborn, 148 U. S. 222, 224 (1893). For the claim that Chief Justice Taney's statement is misinterpreted in so far as it is contended that

Both the *Chandler Case* and the *Todd Case* were test cases under the act of 1793; in the first case the name had not been placed on the roll by the Secretary of War and in the second case the court held against the rights of those whose names had been placed on the list.[14] Though the Invalid Pension Act was not directly held void the refusal to enforce the act by certain justices was equivalent to an invalidation of the statute.

As this was the first instance in which a federal court refused to enforce a law of Congress, "the novelty of the case produced a variety of opinions with respect to the measures to be taken on the occasion." A committee of five was appointed by Congress to enquire into the facts and to report. No further action seems to have been taken except to repeal the original act. Many favorable opinions were expressed; others regretted that "the humanity of Congress had been thwarted by the action of the judges."[15] James Wilson was thought to be largely responsible for the refusal of the justices to carry out the provisions of the act of Congress.

---

he asserted the act of 1792 had been declared unconstitutional in the *Todd* case, see Jesse Turner, "Four Fugitive Cases from the Realm of American Constitutional Law," 49 *Am. Law Rev.* (Nov.-Dec. 1915) 830 ff. The main issue in the Todd application seems to have been whether the acts of the justices as commissioners under the act of 1792 which had now been repealed, were valid.

Professor Thayer in discussing this note observed that the decision in this case was rather that the theory adopted by some of the judges which gave them authority to act as commissioners was untenable; and that the act of 1792 was not directly held to be unconstitutional. See Thayer, 1 *Cases on Constitutional Law* 105, note; also Farrand, "The First Hayburn Case," 13 *Am. Hist. Rev.* 282, 283; and David Hunter Miller, "Some Early Cases in the Supreme Court of the United States," 8 *Va. Law Rev.* (Dec. 1921) 108 ff.

14 Cf. David Hunter Miller, *op. cit.*, 108, 119.

15 For threats of impeachment of the justices, see Bache's *General Advertiser* for April 20, 1792, and Frenau's *National Gazette* for April 16, 1792. For opinions in the anti-Federalist papers favorable to the opinions of the judges, see Warren, *op. cit.*, 73 ff.

Under the English practice at this time it would have been proper to call on the judges for a service of this kind, and under the colonial and state practice it was not uncommon for the legislature to place non-judicial duties upon the judges. But a new theory of the separation of powers was emerging and with this came a different view of the relation of the judges to the other departments of the government.[16]

2. *Vanhorne's Lessee v. Dorrance,* 1795—

Justice Paterson, in the circuit court of the United States for the Pennsylvania district, delivered a charge to a jury in which he discussed the relative position of the legislature, the courts, and the constitution.[17] Coke and Blackstone were cited as authorities that in England the power of Parliament is unlimited. Though some of the judges have had the boldness to assert that an act of Parliament made against natural equity was void, the general opinion is that the validity of an act of Parliament cannot be disputed, and must be obeyed. In England, observed Justice Paterson, there is no written constitution by which a statute can be tested,

But in *America* the case is widely different: Every state in the union has its constitution reduced to written exactitude and precision.

What is a constitution? It is the form of government, delineated by the mighty hand of the people, in which certain first principles of fundamental laws are established. The Constitution is certain and fixed; it contains the permanent will of the people, and is the supreme law of the land; it is paramount to the power of the Legislature, and can be revoked or altered only

---

[16] See especially, Cases of Judges, 2 Call. 139 (1789) and Kamper v. Hawkins, 1 Va. Cases 23 ff.

[17] Vanhorne's Lessee v. Dorrance, 2 Dallas 304.

by the authority that made it. The life-giving principle and the death-doing stroke must proceed from the same hand. What are legislatures? Creatures of the Constitution; they owe their existence to the Constitution; they derive their powers from the Constitution; it is their commission; and, therefore, all their acts must be conformable to it, or else they will be void. The Constitution is the work, or will of the people themselves, in their original, sovereign, and unlimited capacity. Law is the work or will of the legislature in their derivative subordinate capacity. The one is the work of the Creator, and the other of the Creature. The Constitution fixes limits to the exercise of legislative authority, and prescribes the orbit within which it must move. In short, gentlemen, the Constitution is the sun of the political system, around which all legislative, executive, and judicial bodies must revolve. Whatever may be the case in other countries, yet in this there can be no doubt, that every Act of the Legislature, repugnant to the Constitution, is absolutely void. . . . .

I take it to be a clear position; that if a legislative Act oppugns a constitutional principle, the former must give way, and be rejected on the score of repugnance. I hold it to be a position equally clear and sound, that, in such case, it will be the duty of the Court to adhere to the Constitution, and to declare the act null and void. The Constitution is the basis of legislative authority; it lies at the foundation of all law, and is a rule and commission by which both legislator and judges are to proceed. It is an important principle, which, in the discussion of questions of the present kind, ought never to be lost sight of, that the judiciary in this country is not a subordinate but a coordinate branch of the government.[18]

An act of assembly of Pennsylvania known as the quieting and confirming act was denounced as interfering with the natural, inherent, and inalienable right of private property, and was therefore regarded inconsistent

---

[18] 2 Dallas 308–310.

with the constitution of the state and the Constitution of the United States. The importance of property rights, whose security and safety led men of the time to welcome with enthusiasm the check upon popular assemblies which judicial supremacy promised, was thus supported by Justice Paterson.[19]

Because the state law was regarded as a manifest outrage upon the inviolability of property rights, the jury was instructed to consider the confirming act as unconstitutional and void. This case is usually considered the first instance in which the federal courts held a state act void.[20]

3. *Ware v. Hylton*, 1796—

One of the important controversies in which the Supreme Court was called upon to render a decision during Washington's administration was that raised by *Ware v. Hylton*.[21] The treaty of peace was held superior in effect

---

[19] *Ibid.*, 310.

[20] Mr. Warren claims to have found two decisions in the circuits which precede the case of Vanhorne's Lessee. They are: Barnes v. William West (U. S. C. C., 1791 and 1792)—an ejectment proceeding arising out of an attempt to satisfy a mortgage by tender of paper money. Chief Justice Jay, and Justices Wm. Cushing and D. J. Henry Marchant decided that the plea claiming that the mortgage had been satisfied was bad. The decision resulted in the non-enforcement of the state legal tender law. Champion and others v. Silas Casey and others involved a special state law giving an extension of time in which to settle accounts with creditors and an exemption from arrest and attachments. In a suit by British merchants the federal Circuit Court held insufficient a plea based on this law. Though no opinion was rendered by the court, contemporary accounts claimed that the state law was held void so far as these proceedings were concerned because the law impaired the obligation of contracts. The Lower House of the state legislature acquiesced in this decision by voting that no more exemptions would be granted from arrests and attachments for private debts. It is claimed that this is the first instance in which the federal courts held a state statute void as in conflict with the federal Constitution. See Charles Warren, "Earliest Cases of Judicial Review of State Legislation by Federal Courts," 32 *Yale Law Jour.* (Nov. 1922) 23 ff.

[21] 3 Dallas 198 (1796): "The splendid eloquence of Patrick Henry, the great reasoning faculties of John Marshall at the bar and the powerful dissenting opinion of Iredell were employed in vain to convince the court that

to all state enactments in conflict therewith when it was decided that British creditors could recover debts previously owing to them by American citizens, notwithstanding a payment into a state treasury. The justices differed as to whether Virginia had the sovereign power during the Revolution to confiscate British property within its territory but Justices Chase, Paterson, Wilson, and Cushing agreed that whatever power Virginia possessed, the acts of the state became subject to the treaty when it was ratified and its provisions must be enforced as the supreme law notwithstanding any state laws in conflict therewith. In fact, it was the judgment of the court that all state acts in conflict with the treaty were null and void.

Iredell dissented holding that "the acts of the legislature of the state, in regard to the subject in question, so far as they were conformable to the constitution of the state, and not in violation of any article of the confederation (where that was concerned) were absolutely binding *de facto*" and the subsequent adoption of the treaty of peace did not affect the rights involved."[22] Though the court adopted the nationalist view in this judgment, the language of the Constitution and the express authority of the federal courts gave reasonable support for the conclusion reached.

Chase took occasion to reiterate the doctrine that when the Declaration of Independence was announced the separate sovereignty of each state was reduced only so far as specific powers were granted to the federal government in the Constitution. In answer to the contention

Congress had no power to make a treaty that could operate to annul a legislative act of any of the states, and thus destroy rights acquired under such act."—Hampton L. Carson, *The History of the Supreme Court of the United States with Biographies of All the Chief and Associate Justices* (ed. 2; Philadelphia, 1902), 1:169–170.

[22] 3 Dallas 256 ff.

of counsel, chiefly Marshall and Campbell, that a legislature could not destroy rights acquired by or vested in individuals, Chase replied "the legislatures of the states have often exercised the power of divesting rights vested, and in some instances of almost annihilating the obligation of contracts, as by tender laws." Although it was not necessary to render a judgment on this point, there was here forecasted the great issue as to the protection of vested rights which came before the court when Marshall was Chief Justice.

In two other cases, *Hylton v. the United States*,[23] 1796, and *Hollingsworth v. Virginia*,[24] 1798, acts of Congress were attacked as being unconstitutional, and it was assumed in the argument that the court had the power to declare the acts invalid. The statutes were upheld as constitutional. But the opinion that courts could invalidate legislative acts was gaining such popularity that it was to be expected that the national judiciary under Federalist control would, at the earliest favorable opportunity, assume the special guardianship of the fundamental law.

4. *Calder v. Bull*, 1798—

In 1798 a case was appealed to the Supreme Court to test the validity of a state law having a retroactive effect. The legislature of Connecticut had passed a law setting aside a decree of a court of justice which had refused

---

[23] 3 Dallas 171. Justice Chase remarked that "only one question is submitted to the opinion of this court: whether the law of Congress, of the 5th of June, 1794, entitled, 'an act to lay duties upon carriages, for the conveyance of persons' is unconstitutional and void?" and that "it is unnecessary at this time, for me to determine, whether this court, constitutionally possesses the power to declare an Act of Congress void, on the ground of its being made contrary to, and in violation of the Constitution," but if the court have such a power, I will never exercise it, but in a clear case."— *Ibid.*, 172, 175.

[24] *Ibid.*, 387.

validity to a will. As a result of the law a new trial was held by the same court and the will approved. In appeals to the superior and supreme courts of the state this decree was affirmed. In the meantime more than eighteen months had elapsed and by the state law of limitations the right of appeal had lapsed. On appeal to the Supreme Court of the United States it was contended that the Connecticut law granting a new hearing in this case was an *ex post facto* law and was prohibited by the federal Constitution.

Justice Chase was satisfied that the Supreme Court had no jurisdiction to determine whether any law of the state legislature contrary to the state constitution was void, but declined to express an opinion whether they could declare void an act of Congress contrary to the federal Constitution.[25] "If I ever exercise the jurisdiction," he remarked, "I will not decide any law to be void, but in a very clear case."

He reiterated the view expressed in earlier cases that as a self-evident proposition the several state legislatures retained all the powers delegated to them by the state constitutions, which were not expressly taken away by the Constitution of the United States, all the powers delegated by the people of the United States to the federal government were defined, and no constructive powers could be exercised by it. After asserting that all non-delegated powers remained with the states, Chase then turned to the realm of political philosophy and defended the proposition that there were implied limitations upon the legislative power as a general principle of the social compact, as follows:

---

[25] 3 Dallas 386, 388. Cf. also opinion of Justice Iredell that if an act of Congress or of the legislature of a state violates constitutional provisions it is unquestionably void.

I cannot subscribe to the omnipotence of a state legislature, or that it is absolute and without control; although its authority should not be expressly restrained by the constitution, or fundamental law, of the State. The people of the United States erected their Constitutions, or forms of government, to establish justice, to promote the general welfare, to secure the blessings of liberty; and to protect their persons and property from violence. The purpose for which men enter into society will determine the nature and terms of the social compact; and as they are the foundation of the legislative power, they will decide what are the proper objects of it: the nature and ends of legislative power will limit the exercise of it. This fundamental principle flows from the very nature of our free Republican governments, that no man should be compelled to do what the laws do not require, nor to refrain from acts which the laws permit. There are acts which the Federal, or State, legislature cannot do, without exceeding their authority. There are certain vital principles in our free Republican governments, which will determine and overrule an apparent and flagrant abuse of legislative powers; as to authorize manifest injustice by positive law; or to take away that security for personal liberty, or private property, for the protection whereof the government was established. An act of the Legislature (for I cannot call it a law) contrary to the great first principles of the social compact, cannot be considered a rightful exercise of legislative authority. The obligation of a law in governments established on express compact, and on republican principles, must be determined by the nature of the power, on which it is founded. A few instances will suffice to explain what I mean. A law that punishes a citizen for an innocent action, or, in other words, for an act, which, when done, was in violation of no existing law; a law that destroys, or impairs, the lawful private contracts of citizens; a law that makes a man a judge in his own cause; or a law that takes property from A and gives it to B. It is against all reason and justice for a people to intrust a legislature with such powers; and, therefore, it cannot be presumed that they have done it. The genius, the nature, and the spirit, of our state governments, amount to a prohibition of such acts of legislation; and the general principles of law and reason forbid them. The legislature may enjoin, permit, forbid, and punish; they may declare new crimes; and establish rules of conduct for all its citizens in future cases; they may command what is right, and prohibit what is wrong; but they cannot change innocence into guilt; or punish innocence as a crime; or violate the right of an antecedent lawful private contract; or the right of private property. To maintain that our Federal or State legislatures possess such powers, if they had not been expressly restrained, would, in my opinion, be a political heresy altogether inadmissible in our free republican governments.[26]

This was good Federalist doctrine especially in the minds of those who thought it necessary to limit legislative power with respect to contracts and property interests. It was essential to dull the teeth of democracy to preserve personal and property interests. And when constitutional provisions were not definite or specific enough to protect these interests from popular control the theory of implied limitations was called into play, thus placing additional limits on legislative powers to those prescribed in the written fundamental law.

But Justice Chase did not believe that the *ex post facto* clause of the federal Constitution was inserted to secure the citizen in these rights and interests. In his judgment the term *ex post facto* was intended to be limited to acts regulating crimes and criminal procedure. And although Chase thought the federal and state legislatures did not have the power to deprive citizens of rights vested in them by existing laws "unless for the benefit of the whole community; and not making satis-

---

[26] 3 Dallas 386–9 (1798). See opinion of Chase in the general court of Maryland that a state act was void as in conflict with the bill of rights of the state constitution, Egan v. Charles Co. Ct., 3 H. and McH. 169, 170 (1793).

faction" he believed that no vested right had been disturbed.

Justice Paterson agreed with the theories of Chase and remarked at the conclusion of his opinion,

I had an ardent desire to have extended the provision in the Constitution to retrospective laws in general. There is neither policy nor safety in such laws; and, therefore, I have always had a strong aversion against them. It may in general be truly observed of retrospective laws of every description, that they neither accord with sound legislation, nor the fundamental principles of the social compact. But on full consideration, I am convinced, that *ex post facto* laws must be limited in the manner already expressed; they must be taken in their technical, which is also their common and general acceptation, and are not to be understood in their literal sense.[27]

Justice Iredell concurred in the result but not in the reasoning of these justices. He expressed an opinion favorable to the review of legislative acts and against the theory of interpreting implied limitations on legislative powers. Referring to the limits which the written constitutions of the United States have marked for legislatures he said:

If any act of Congress, or of the Legislature of a state, violates those constitutional provisions, it is unquestionably void; though, I admit, that as the authority to declare it void is of a delicate and awful nature, the Court will never resort to that authority, but in a clear and urgent case.

But he thought that a court could not declare a law void, merely because it was in their judgment, contrary to the principles of natural justice. There are then but two lights in which the subject can be viewed:

1st. If the legislature pursue the authority, their acts are valid. 2d. If they transgress the boundaries of that authority,

---

[27] 3 Dallas 397.

their acts are invalid. In the former case, they exercise the discretion vested in them by the people, to whom alone they are responsible for the faithful discharge of their trust; but in the latter case, they violate a fundamental law, which must be our guide, whenever we are called upon as judges to determine the validity of a legislative act.[28]

The judgment of the court was against bringing the protection of vested interests under the *ex post facto* provision of the federal Constitution. It remained for future justices to find a method of protecting property and contracts and to develop as an effective restraint on legislative powers the theory of implied limitations which Chase defended and Iredell opposed.

5. *Cooper v. Telfair,* 1800—

The constitutionality of a state statute was again raised on an appeal from the circuit court of the United States for the district of Georgia.[29] Under acts of the Georgia legislature several men had been expelled from the state, and their property had been confiscated. It was argued on trial that the acts of the state were repugnant to the constitution of Georgia and therefore void. The circuit court refused to set aside the laws, and the Supreme Court affirmed this decision. In case of a conflict between the Constitution and a law Justice Washington thought "the presumption, indeed, must always be in favor of the validity of laws, if the contrary is not clearly demonstrated." Along the same line Justice Paterson said: "To authorize this court to pronounce any law void it must be a clear and unequivocal breach of the Constitution, not a doubtful and argumentative application." Justice Cushing was of the opinion that the Supreme Court had the same power to declare the law void as the

---

[28] 3 Dallas 399.   [29] 4 Dallas 14 (1800).

courts of Georgia possessed, but did not think that the case warranted the exercise of such power. Justice Chase observed:

> Although it is alleged that all acts of the legislature, in direct opposition to the prohibitions of the Constitution, would be void; yet, it still remains a question, where the power resides to declare it void? It is, indeed, a general opinion, it is expressly admitted by all this bar, and some of the Judges have individually in the Circuits decided that the Supreme Court can declare an act of Congress to be unconstitutional and therefore invalid; but there is no adjudication of the Supreme Court itself upon the point. I concur, however, in the general sentiment with reference to the period, when the existing constitution came into operation.[30]

The members of the Supreme Court were finally led to favor a power of review of all federal and state laws, and to insist upon declaring the same void when deemed to be contrary to the provisions of the federal Constitution. It was left for Chief Justice Marshall, whose judicial opinions were always expressed in an assertive and lucid style, to summarize the arguments in favor of this feature of the American system of government. But before the Supreme Court was called upon to deal directly with the issue, an important controversy arose which gave expression to the prevailing sentiment of the time regarding judicial authority.

6. *Kentucky and Virginia resolutions*—

In the discussions which arose over the Alien and Sedition laws, passed by a Federalist administration and bitterly opposed by the Anti-Federalists, the resolutions drawn up by Thomas Jefferson, adopted by the Kentucky legislature, and submitted to the other states, contained a doctrine distinctly opposed to the idea of a national

---

[30] 4 Dallas 19.

sovereignty with a final interpreting organ in the central government. It was declared that the states had been united under a compact in which the states became members of the Union formed by the compact. The resolution went on to declare

that the government created by this compact was not made the exclusive or final judge of the extent of the powers delegated to itself. Since that would have made its discretion, and not the Constitution, the measure of its powers; but that, as in all other cases of compact among parties having no common judge, each party has an equal right to judge for itself, as well as of infractions as of the mode and measure of redress. . . . And that in cases of a deliberate, palpable, and dangerous exercise of other powers, not granted by the said compact, the states, who are parties thereto, have the right and are in duty bound, to interpose, for arresting the progress of the evil, and for maintaining within their respective limits, the authorities, rights and liberties appertaining to them.[31]

A similar series of resolutions, somewhat less radical in spirit, was prepared by Madison and adopted by the Virginia Assembly.[32]

Replies from the states.—These resolutions were submitted to the other state assemblies, and in a number of instances were branded as an unjustifiable interference with the general government, and as a dangerous tendency which was to be spurned by all loyal citizens.[33] Rhode Island replied that the Constitution of the United States "vests in the federal courts, exclusively, and in the Supreme Court of the United States, ultimately, the authority of deciding on the constitutionality of any act or law of the Congress of the United States."[34] Massachusetts

---

31 Thomas Jefferson, *Works*, 8:459.
32 Madison, *Works*, 4:507.
33 "Reply of Delaware to Virginia," Elliot's *Debates*, 4:532.
34 "Reply of Rhode Island to Virginia," *ibid.*, 533.

resolved: ''That this legislature are persuaded that the decision of all cases in law and equity arising under the Constitution of the United States, and the construction of all laws made in pursuance thereof, are exclusively vested by the people in judicial courts of the United States.''[35] The house of representatives of Pennsylvania was of the opinion that the people of the United States ''have committed to the supreme judiciary of the nation the high authority, of ultimately and exclusively deciding upon the constitutionality of all legislative acts.''[36] All the replies prepared by Federalists in the states north of the Potomac not only condemned the resolutions but also in nearly every instance referred more or less directly to the federal judiciary as the proper authority to decide on the validity of acts of Congress. South of the Potomac the Republicans failed to secure expressions of approval of the resolutions but prevented any formal disapproval of them.[37]

7. *Cases in inferior federal courts*—

When in the trial of Callender under the Alien and Sedition Act, Attorney General Wirt argued before the jury that the act of Congress on the basis of which the indictment was brought, was unconstitutional, Justice

---

[35] ''Reply of Massachusetts to Virginia,'' Elliot's *Debates*, 4:534.

[36] *Journal* of House of Representatives of Pennsylvania, 9:198. In the states whose legislative bodies voted to condemn the Virginia and Kentucky resolutions many refused to join in the vote of censure. A number of Republicans in all the states apparently approved the principles of the resolutions, in so far as they denied to the federal judiciary the authority to decide on the validity of acts of Congress.

[37] For opinions favorable to the Virginia and Kentucky Resolutions, consult account of F. M. Anderson, ''Contemporary Opinion of the Virginia and Kentucky Resolutions,'' *Am. Hist. Rev.*, 5 (Oct. 1899 and Jan. 1900) 46, 235. See Madison's *Report* before the Virginia legislature on the replies of the other states in which he claimed that the people of each state instead of the people of the United States were parties to the compact and hence might decide on violations of the terms of the compact.—*Ibid.*, 242.

Chase refused further argument on this point and read
a memorandum in defense of the view that the judges
alone might decide on the constitutionality of an act of
Congress. He concluded that

the judicial power of the United States is the only proper and
competent authority to decide whether any statute made by congress (or any of the state legislatures) is contrary to, or in
violation of, the federal Constitution. . . . . I believe that it
has been the general and prevailing opinion in all the Union
that the power now wished to be exercised by a jury, properly
belonged to the federal courts.[38]

An act of North Carolina of 1715, which required
claims against the estates of deceased persons to be filed
within seven years, was held to be repealed by implication
in 1789 when a shorter period of limitation was fixed. In
1799 the legislature by another act declared the law of
1715 had not been repealed and was still in force. This
latter act was held void in the North Carolina Circuit by
Chief Justice Marshall and Justice Potter. Citing the
provisions of the bill of rights relating to the separation
of powers, Marshall asked,

Does it belong to the judiciary to decide upon laws when
made, and the extent and operation of them; or the legislature?
If it belongs to the judiciary, then the matter decided by this
act, namely, whether the act of 1789 be a repeal of the 9th section of 1715, is a judicial matter, and not a legislative one. The
determination is made by a branch of government, not authorized by the constitution to make it, and is therefore, in my
judgment, void.

The act of 1799 was also held void as in violation of the
contract clause of the federal Constitution.[39]

---

[38] United States v. Callender, 25 Fed. Cases 239, 256–257 (1800) and
Wharton, *State Trials*, 688.

[39] Ogden v. Witherspoon, 18 Fed. Cases 618, 619 (1802) and 2 Hayw.
(N. C.) 227.

Judge Iredell, upholding a state act relative to land titles, remarked,

I admit, as strongly as any man can assert, that if this act of assembly is plainly unwarranted by the constitution, it is totally void as being passed without authority, the authority of the legislature being, in certain cases, restricted by a superior power which must of course be obeyed . . . . when the constitution says one thing and an act of assembly another, the judges must say the former law is in force and not the latter, because the former is a supreme law unrepealable and uncontrollable by the authority which enacted the latter.

The term *ex post facto,* Justice Iredell claimed, did not apply to retrospective acts of a civil nature and the courts could not hold a statute void merely because contrary to the principles of natural justice.[40]

8. *Marshall's opinion in the case of Marbury v. Madison, 1803—*

The position of the court and the relation between the three departments of our government were argued by Chief Justice Marshall in the case of *Marbury v. Madison.*[41] William Marbury, who had been appointed by President Adams to the office of justice of peace in the District of Columbia, asked the Supreme Court to issue a mandamus to Secretary of State Madison, who, according to the instructions of President Jefferson, refused to turn over the commission. The appointment was confirmed and the commission was signed and sealed, but through an oversight had not been delivered.

The Judiciary Act of 1789 authorized the Supreme Court to issue writs of mandamus to persons holding

---

[40] Minge v. Gilmour, Federal Cases, No. 9631. North Carolina Circuit, 1798. 17 Fed. Cases 440, 442.

[41] 1 Cranch 137.

office under the authority of the United States. Marbury's application for the writ of mandamus raised three questions, namely, was he entitled to his commission, was mandamus a proper remedy, and could the Supreme Court grant a writ of mandamus in an original proceeding? By a curious method of approach Chief Justice Marshall answered the first two questions in the affirmative and then denied that the court had jurisdiction of the issue by holding the above section of the Judiciary Act invalid.

Marshall was personally interested in the cause and on this ground should have declined to pass upon the issue. The commission in controversy was made out during the time when Marshall was holding two offices, Secretary of State and Chief Justice. Marshall himself was responsible for the failure to deliver the commission. Regarding the matter he wrote: "I should, however, have sent out the commissions which had been signed and sealed but for the extreme hurry of the time and absence of Mr. Wagner who had been called on by the President to act as his private secretary."[42] Under these circumstances it was rather inappropriate for the Chief Justice to participate in the decision of the case and especially to render the opinion of the court.[43] Moreover, the act of Congress in controversy could have been so interpreted as to sustain its validity. But in the opinion of Marshall the time seemed appropriate to announce certain principles of constitutional interpretation.

The question was presented, claimed the Chief Justice, whether the authority given to the Supreme Court by the Judiciary Act of 1789, authorizing the courts of

---

[42] Beveridge, *The Life of John Marshall*, 3:124.

[43] See J. A. C. Grant, "Marbury v. Madison Today," 23 *Am. Pol. Sci. Rev.* (Aug. 1929) 673 ff.

the United States to issue writs of mandamus to public officers,[44] was warranted by the Constitution in its application to the original jurisdiction of the Supreme Court; or, in other words, whether an act which, according to the judgment of the members of the court, was repugnant to the Constitution, could become a law of the land. The court, in an opinion delivered by the Chief Justice, thought that

The question whether an Act repugnant to the Constitution can become the law of the land, is a question deeply interesting to the United States; but, happily, not of an intricacy proportioned to its interest. It seems only necessary to recognize certain principles, supposed to have been long and well established, to decide it.

That the people have an original right to establish, for their future government, such principles as, in their opinion, shall most conduce to their own happiness, is the base on which the whole American fabric has been erected. The exercise of this original right is a very great exertion; nor can it nor ought it to be frequently repeated. The principles, therefore, so established, are deemed fundamental. And as the authority from which they proceed is supreme, and can seldom act, they are designed to be permanent.

This original and supreme will organizes the government, and assigns to different departments their respective powers. It may either stop here, or establish certain limits not to be transcended by those departments.

The government of the United States is of the latter description. The powers of the legislature are defined and limited; and that those limits may not be mistaken, or forgotten, the Constitution is written. To what purpose are powers limited, and to what purpose is that limitation committed to writing, if these limits may at any time, be passed by those intended to be restrained? The distinction between a government with limited

---

[44] *U. S. Statutes* at Large, 1:73, sec. 13. See U. S. v. Lawrence, 3 Dallas 42, recognizing the validity of this section.

and unlimited powers is abolished, if those limits do not confine the persons on whom they are imposed, and if acts prohibited and acts allowed are of equal obligation. It is a proposition too plain to be contested, that the Constitution controls any legislative Act repugnant to it; or, that the legislature may alter the Constitution by an ordinary Act.

Between these alternatives there is no middle ground. The Constitution is either a superior paramount law, unchangeable by ordinary means, or it is on a level with ordinary legislative Acts, and, like other Acts, is alterable when the legislature shall please to alter it.

If the former part of the alternative be true, then a legislative Act contrary to the Constitution is not law; if the latter part be true, then written constitutions are absurd attempts, on the part of the people, to limit a power in its own nature illimitable.

Certainly all those who have framed written constitutions contemplate them as forming the fundamental and paramount law of the nation, and, consequently, the theory of every such government must be, that an Act of the Legislature, repugnant to the Constitution, is void.

This theory is essentially attached to a written constitution, and is consequently to be considered, by this court, as one of the fundamental principles of our society. It is not, therefore, to be lost sight of in the future consideration of this subject.

If an Act of the Legislature, repugnant to the Constitution, is void, does it, nothwithstanding its validity, bind the courts, and oblige them to give it effect? Or, in other words, though it be not law, does it constitute a rule as operative as if it was a law? This would be to overthrow in fact what was established in theory; and would seem at first view, an absurdity too gross to be insisted on. It shall, however, receive a more attentive consideration.

It is emphatically the province and duty of the judicial department to say what the law is. Those who apply the rule to particular cases, must of necessity expound and interpret that rule. If two laws conflict with each other, the courts must decide on the operation of each.

So, if a law be in opposition to the Constitution; if both the law and the Constitution apply to a particular case, so that the court must either decide that case conformably to the law, disregarding the Constitution, or conformably to the Constitution, disregarding the law, the court must determine which of these conflicting rules governs the case. This is of the very essence of judicial duty.

If, then, the courts are to regard the Constitution and the Constitution is superior to any ordinary Act of the Legislature, the Constitution, and not such ordinary Act, must govern the case to which they both apply.

Those, then, who controvert the principle that the Constitution is to be considered, in court, as a paramount law, are reduced to the necessity of maintaining that courts must close their eyes on the Constitution, and see only the law.

This doctrine would subvert the very foundation of all written constitutions. It would declare that an Act which, according to the principles and theory of our government, is entirely void, is yet, in practice, completely obligatory. It would declare that if the legislature shall do what is expressly forbidden, such Act, notwithstanding the express prohibition, is in reality effectual. It would be giving to the legislature a practical and real omnipotence, with the same breath which professes to restrict their powers within narrow limits. It is prescribing limits, and declaring those limits may be passed at pleasure.

That it thus reduces to nothing what we have deemed the greatest improvement on political institutions, a written constitution, would of itself be sufficient, in America, where written constitutions have been viewed with so much reverence, for rejecting the construction. But the peculiar expressions, of the Constitution of the United States furnish additional arguments in favor of its rejection.

The judicial power of the United States is extended to all cases arising under the Constitution.

Could it be the intention of those who gave this power, to say that in using it the Constitution should not be looked into? That a case arising under the Constitution should be decided without examining the instrument under which it arises?

This is too extravagant to be maintained.

In some cases, then, the Constitution must be looked into by the judges. And if they can open it at all, what part of it are they forbidden to read and to obey?

There are many other parts of the Constitution which serve to illustrate this subject.

It is declared that "no tax or duty shall be laid on articles exported from any state." Suppose a duty on the export of cotton, of tobacco, or of flour; and a suit instituted to recover. Ought judgment to be rendered in such a case? Ought the judges to close their eyes on the Constitution, and see only the law?

The Constitution declares "that no bill of attainder or *ex post facto* law shall be passed."

If, however, such a bill should be passed, and a person should be prosecuted under it, must the court condemn to death those victims whom the Constitution endeavors to preserve?

"No person" says the Constitution, "shall be convicted of treason unless on the testimony of two witnesses to the same overt act, or on confession in open court."

Here the language of the Constitution is addressed especially to the courts. It prescribes, directly for them, a rule of evidence not to be departed from. If the legislature should change that rule, and declare one witness, or a confession out of court, sufficient for conviction, must the constitutional principle yield to the legislative Act?

From these, and many other selections which might be made, it is apparent that the framers of the Constitution contemplated that instrument as a rule for the government of courts, as well as of the legislature.

Why otherwise does it direct the judges to take an oath to support it? This oath certainly applies in an especial manner to their conduct in their official character. How immoral to impose it on them, if they were to be used as the instruments, and the knowing instruments, for violating what they swear to support!

The oath of office, too, imposed by the legislature is completely demonstrative of the legislative opinion on this subject. It is in these words: "I do solemnly swear that I will administer justice without respect to person, and do equal right to the poor and to the rich; and that I will faithfully and impartially discharge all the duties incumbent on me as according to the best of my abilities and understanding, agreeably to the Constitution and laws of the United States."

Why does a judge swear to discharge his duties agreeably to the Constitution of the United States, if that Constitution forms no rule for his government—if it is closed upon him, and cannot be inspected by him?

If such be the real state of things, this is worse than solemn mockery. To prescribe, or to take this oath, becomes equally a crime.

It is also not entirely unworthy of observation, that in declaring what shall be the supreme law of the land, the Constitution itself is first mentioned; and not the laws of the United States generally, but those only which shall be made in pursuance of the Constitution, have that rank.

Thus, the particular phraseology of the Constitution of the United States confirms and strengthens the principle supposed to be essential to all written constitutions, that a law repugnant to the constitution is void; and that courts, as well as other departments, are bound by that instrument.

The political aspects of this decision are obvious on any careful examination of the reasoning. Propositions and postulates involved in the judgment are:

1. A written constitution is a law of superior obligation and consequently any acts contrary thereto must be invalid.

There was almost universal agreement to this proposition, but it left the main issue undetermined.

2. A written constitution with limitations on the powers of government necessitates the exercise of judicial review.

This is a postulate based on certain political theories which the adoption of many written constitutions has demonstrated may as well be determined otherwise.

3. The oath of the judges to support the Constitution requires that the justices follow the Constitution and disregard any conflicting statute.

This proposition fails to take into account that the officers of all three departments take the same oath and that by similar reasoning the members of Congress and the Executive could refuse to accept a decision of the Supreme Court with which they disagreed.

It assumes that the determination of the validity of a law is a mechanical and necessitous matter in which personal or individual judgments do not enter instead of a delicate and difficult question frequently with serious political implications on which lawyers and statesmen may well disagree.

4. Legislative acts contrary to the Constitution are *ipso facto* void, consequently the courts are obliged to disregard such statutes.

This proposition assumes that, constitutional provisions being laws of a superior order and statutes being laws of an inferior order, when a conflict arises the court whose duty it is to apply all laws and resolve conflicts of laws must enforce the superior law.

Again there is failure to take into account the borderline case where judgments differ as to whether there is a real conflict.

Moreover, this proposition fails to distinguish between the categories of *political laws* unenforceable by courts and *ordinary laws* which it is the duty of judges to interpret and apply. This well-known distinction has resulted in placing all constitutional provisions outside of the pale of judicial authority in many European countries and John Marshall himself was quick to recognize that certain parts of the federal Constitution were political in character and hence unenforceable by the judiciary. The real issue here is whether a conflict between a constitution and a statute can be regarded as a case within judicial cognizance. Prevailing theories and practice in foreign countries have ruled that such a conflict is not a case for judicial action.

If certain provisions of the Constitution are political in nature and unenforceable, why are not all provisions in this category and by what authority do courts accept cases under some provisions and refuse them under other provisions?

Why should a legislative act passed in due form, following all of the designated rules of procedure be considered as never having been passed or *ipso facto* void? Is it not an unusual presumption for the officers of one department to consider the acts of the officers of another department of no avail? In fact, as indicated by Justices Bland and Gibson and other opponents of judicial review, every argument in favor of judicial review was based on assumptions or postulates which assumed the whole ground of the dispute.[45] The arguments in opposition and the underlying theories and assumptions relative to judicial review will be considered later.

---

[45] "This decision," says Professor Corwin, "bears many of the earmarks of a deliberate partisan coup."—*The Doctrine of Judicial Review*, 10.
"No words in the Constitution gave the Judiciary the power to annul legislation," Beveridge, *op. cit.*, 3:114.

Many commentators think that the issue of the constitutionality of the act of Congress might have been entirely avoided by the court had the judges desired to do so.[46] It is generally understood that the section of the judiciary act of 1789 authorizing the Supreme Court to issue writs of mandamus was not intended to apply to the original jurisdiction of the Court.[47] The authority condemned in this case has since been upheld by Congress and the federal courts. But Marshall, who was an ardent Federalist, was aware of a rising opposition to the theory of judicial control over legislation, and he no doubt concluded that the wavering opinions on federal judicial supremacy needed to be replaced by a positive and unmistakable assertion of authority.

The opinion of Marshall settled the doubt regarding the attitude of the federal courts on the right of judicial nullification of congressional acts in a manner that was clear and decisive. In it the Chief Justice asserted Coke's theory of judicial supremacy and declared that the Supreme Court was the final interpreter and guardian of the federal Constitution. The decision became authority

---

[46] "Marshall's opinion in the case of Marbury v. Madison was a shrewd political manifesto, rather than a logical foundation for the decision of that highly technical case." Horace A. Davis, "Annulment of Legislation by the Supreme Court," 7 *Am. Pol. Sci. Rev.* (Nov. 1913) 543.

"The learned Chief Justice did pass upon a constitutional question involving the authority of a coordinate branch of the government, the executive, in a case he had no right so much as to entertain if his own decision was correct. . . . The learned Justice really manufactured an opportunity to declare an act void." Andrew C. McLaughlin, "Marbury v. Madison Again," 13 Am. Bar Assoc. *Jour.* (March 1928) 156, 157.

"So far, then, as practical results were concerned, the case of Marbury v. Madison had now come to the point where it was of no consequence whatever to anyone. It presented only theoretical questions, and, on the face of the record, even these were as simple as they were unimportant. This controversy, in fact, had degenerated into little more than "a moot case" as Jefferson termed it twenty years later."—Beveridge, *Life of John Marshall*, 3:124–125; see also Warren, *op. cit.*, 1:240.

[47] For recognition of the right of the court to issue a mandamus in an appellate proceeding, see United States v. Peters, 5 Cranch 135.

in the federal government for the proposition—which had already been adopted in a majority of the states and which was destined to form a distinct feature of the whole political system of the United States—that a constitution is a fundamental law, that legislative and executive powers are limited by the terms of this fundamental law, and that the courts as interpreters of the law are expected to preserve and defend constitutions as inviolable acts, to be changed only by the people through the amending process.

Although President Jefferson did not accept as final the opinion of the Chief Justice, and although the power to invalidate an act of Congress was not again exercised for more than fifty years, nevertheless the statement of the doctrine of judicial review of legislative acts served as a forceful precedent for the judges who hesitated to assert such authority in dealing with state enactments. Soon after 1803 it was taken for granted that the right to declare invalid statutes which were regarded as contrary to the written fundamental law was the special privilege and duty of every court, state and federal. There was opposition, to be sure, to the acceptance of this authority, but the opponents were eventually obliged to submit to the assertions of those who unwaveringly supported judicial control over legislation.

Chapter IX

LEGAL THEORIES AND PRINCIPLES INVOLVED IN THE ESTABLISHMENT OF THE AMERICAN DOCTRINE OF JUDICIAL REVIEW OF LEGISLATIVE ACTS

I T IS DIFFICULT to find an adequate explanation of the reasons for the adoption of the peculiar practice which has come to be known as the American doctrine of judicial review of legislation. Justice Gibson, of Pennsylvania, claimed that John Marshall, in defending the principle of judicial review of acts of Congress, assumed the whole ground in dispute, namely, that the opinions of judges on constitutional questions were necessarily superior to the opinions of legislators, and then gave spurious reasons for his conclusions. Those who favored judicial review of legislation frequently arrived at their judgments because of inarticulate assumptions or partisan political views as to government and law and seldom analyzed clearly the grounds for their judgments. Most of the reasons customarily advanced for the assertion of such authority by judges ignored the main issue, as Justices Bland and Gibson contended.[1] It was generally conceded at this time that constitutions were made up of superior principles or laws and that all public authorities were to be guided by their provisions. There was general agreement that constitutional provisions were laws and were to be interpreted and applied as such. But not all

---

[1] Cf. *infra*, 261 *et seq.*

laws are alike in significance and application. The courts have found provisions in constitutions that have only political significance and are not susceptible of strict legal applications.[2] Why were not all provisions of constitutions *political laws* as they are generally considered to be in Europe, and hence primarily to be interpreted and applied by legislatures as the dominant European practice requires? If the constitution was the voice of the people—a political theory, as we are aware, without much practical basis—why were not the representatives of the people the natural expositors of these laws.[3] The fact of the matter is that judicial review of legislation was adopted as a practical device to meet a particular situation by shrewd men of affairs who knew what they wanted and who seldom expressed clearly the reasons which prompted their conclusions. Furthermore, the arguments for judicial review were based upon principles of political faith and inner motives of conduct which were seldom made articulate when American political and legal institutions were in the process of formation.

The attempt to account for judicial review of legislation as a result of the abuse of powers by early state legislatures[4] fails to give due weight to other factors operating independent of legislative mistakes or indiscretions which undoubtedly aided in strengthening the position of the courts. Judicial review was supposed to

---

[2] Cf. *infra*, 476.

[3] How has it come about, argued John Breckinridge, of Kentucky, in defending the Kentucky Resolutions of 1798, that the judges, the servants of the people and delegated specific powers by the constitution are considered to have rights above the people and their representatives?—E. D. Warfield, *The Kentucky Resolutions of 1798* (New York, 1887) 94, 95.

[4] See Edward S. Corwin, *The Doctrine of Judicial Review* (Princeton, 1914) preface. ''The judges were, it seems, not acting strictly on precedent. Indeed, the striking fact is that they commonly did not refer to precedents; but they thought alike and along similar lines.''—Andrew C. McLaughlin, *The Courts, the Constitution, and Parties* (Chicago, 1912) 29.

result primarily from certain common assumptions or from general principles. Among these principles were the assurance that rights belonged to the individual which no government dared violate with impunity—a form of the ancient natural rights' philosophy; that consequently there were limits to all governmental powers and these were especially applicable to legislatures; that it was the duty of all persons and especially the judges to resist any interference with such rights,[5] a form of the revolutionary doctrine of resistance to arbitrary governmental acts; and, that a constitution was a type of higher law emanating more directly from the people and was to be enforced by the courts as law.

1. *Doctrines of natural law and natural rights*—

The American idea of a written constitution as well as its counterpart the American doctrine of judicial review of legislation are in a certain measure developments from the medieval and modern notions of natural law and natural rights. The will of the people as well as that of all of their agents must be exercised subordinate to fundamental ideas and principles of right. Ancient ideas of natural law and their applications in the eighteenth century in England, France, and America have been traced elsewhere and need be referred to only incidentally.[6] It suffices to say that among the prevailing ideas at the time when the American doctrine of judicial review originated was the rather general acceptance of the notion that there were natural and inalienable rights which could not justly be interfered with by govern-

---

5 ''When the government violates the rights of the people, insurrection is for the people and for each portion of the people the most sacred of rights and the most indispensable of duties.''—Declaration of Rights in French constitution of 1793, art. 35.

6 Cf. *supra*, 29 *et seq.*

ments.[7] To resist such interferences was the duty of every citizen and especially every public officer.[8]

The term constitution was employed during colonial times not only to refer to charters or written instruments but also to the permanent principles upon which governments were then conceived to be founded.[9] There was a common political conviction of the time that these permanent principles on which governments were based could be changed only by the people.[10] With the emphasis on written charters came also a revival of the medieval notion of the supremacy of law.[11] Coke's version of the supremacy of the common law as the embodiment of reason, which it was the duty of courts to apply regardless of acts of the king or Parliament to the contrary was readily espoused in America. Judicial review was originally thought to result from the revolutionary right of

---

[7] Professor McLaughlin writes "of the prevalence of the Revolutionary opinion that natural law was real *law*, that natural justice was a real constitutional limitation, and that the legislative body in every free state is limited by fundamental principles of individual right and liberty."— *Op. cit.*, 78.

[8] James Wilson thought the right of resistance and revolution should be "taught as a principle of the Constitution of the United States and of every state in the Union."—*Works* (Andrew's ed.) 1:18.

[9] "No free government or the blessing of liberty can be preserved to any people but by . . . . frequent recurrence to fundamental principles."— Virginia Constitution, 1776.

"A frequent recurrence to fundamental principles . . . . is absolutely necessary to preserve the blessings of liberty and keep a government free."—Pennsylvania Constitution, 1776.

[10] The prevalence of this conviction is shown by the fact that nine out of twelve of the constitutions adopted from 1776 to 1778 were drafted by legislative bodies specially authorized to act by the voters. See Walter Farleigh Dodd, *The Revision and Amendment of State Constitutions* (Baltimore, 1910) 234.

[11] Thomas Paine, in defending his suggestion for the framing of a Continental Charter, offered the following plan for proclaiming the charter: "Let a day be solemnly set apart for proclaiming the Charter; let it be brought forth placed on the divine law, the word of God; let a crown be placed thereon, by which the world may know that so far we approve monarchy that in America law is King."—*Political Writings of Thomas Paine* (1835) 1:45, 46.

anyone to refuse obedience to acts contrary to common right and reason. It was in Coke's opinions and writings that legal sanction might be found for the assertion of a sort of political authority by judges. Thus judges were given a primary place in the political order. A premise on which certain arguments for judicial review of legislation were predicated was an inclination to confide in judges and to distrust legislators.

2. *Distrust of legislative power*—

At the time of the formulation of the American doctrine of judicial review and its general adoption as a feature of state and federal public law, certain ideas were prevalent which aided greatly in making the exercise of this power by the courts acceptable to government officials and to a majority of the electors, who were then chiefly the property holders of their communities. Foremost among these ideas was a distrust or a fear of legislative power. In the first state constitutions there were many indications that the legislative power was the object of popular confidence. But by 1787 it seemed to be commonly believed that "the greatest danger to liberty arises from the expanding power of the legislative body."[12] In the Philadelphia convention Madison expressed fears regarding the development toward legislative supremacy in the states. "The Legislative department," he remarked, "is everywhere extending the sphere of its activity, and drawing all power into its impetuous vortex." The founders of our republics "seem never to have recollected the dangers of legislative usurpations, which, by assembling all power in the same hands, must lead to the same tyranny as is threatened by executive

---

[12] Charles E. Merriam, *American Political Theories* (New York, 1906) 109, 110.

usurpations.'"[13] It was the opinion of Madison that any project of usurpation by either the executive or the judiciary would be immediately defeated, since the legislative department would necessarily hold the controlling power. There was no doubt in his mind that legislative authority ought to be restricted, and that the means of security against this authority was the great problem to be solved. The people, in his judgment, ought to indulge all their jealousy and exhaust all their precautions against the enterprising ambition of the legislative department.

Certain colonial charters and the early state constitutions aimed to restrict the executive power and to make the judiciary subordinate, but this tendency gave way to a desire to strengthen the executive and to increase the importance of the judiciary in order to offset the actual and supposed dangers and excesses of legislatures. The evils which were experienced from what was termed an excess of democracy or the dangers of the leveling spirit, and the turmoil held to be due to the turbulence and follies of popular rule,[14] inclined the conservative leaders of political thought to favor carefully defined limitations on the legislative power. There were wide differences of opinion as to the proper corrective, but as to the necessity of restrictions there was general agreement among prominent statesmen of the time.

Moreover, there was more concern as to the restrictions under which governments should operate than as to the functions to be performed. Governments were to be prohibited from interfering with freedom of person, security of property, freedom of speech and of religion. The guaranty of liberty was, therefore, to give the rulers as little power as possible and then to surround them

---

[13] *The Federalist* (Ford's ed.), 328.

[14] Cf. opinions of Gerry and Randolph, *Madison Papers* 2:753–758.

with numerous restrictions—to balance power against power. Though the original assertion of the authority to declare legislative acts void was fostered by ideas of the supremacy of the judges in the application of a superior law of reason, the theory of the separation of powers with a consequent feeling of independent authority on the part of the judges was of considerable influence in the assertion of the right of courts to hold legislative acts void.

3. *Theory of the separation of powers—*

In the declaration of rights formulated for the state of Massachusetts in 1780 is to be found this significant section:

In the government of this commonwealth, the legislative department shall never exercise the executive and judicial powers, or either of them; the executive shall never exercise the legislative and judicial powers, or either of them; the judicial shall never exercise the legislative and executive powers, or either of them; to the end it may be a government of laws and not of men.[15]

The concluding phrase was probably suggested by an ancient idea reiterated by Harrington when he maintained that in a monarchy man is not governed by the law, but law by the man, whereas in a republic man is governed by another man but all in common are governed by the laws.[16]

Though the state constitutions of 1776 concentrated authority to a considerable extent in the legislatures, a number of devices were inserted to prevent the influence of the personal element in government—to repress the inevitable tendency, as it was then thought, for govern-

---

15 Thorpe, *Federal and State Constitutions*, 3, Pt. 1, art. 30.
16 James Harrington, *Oceana and Other Works* (ed. 3) 396.

ment to become arbitrary and oppressive. Not only did these constitutions provide that the "legislative, executive and judiciary ought to be forever separate and distinct,"[17] but they also placed certain prohibitions and restrictions upon the exercise of governmental powers. Such restrictions in the form of declarations of rights were to be jealously guarded and strictly preserved. Although in the majority of cases no provision was made for the enforcement of these restrictions, various safeguards were proposed.[18] Officers in the executive and legislative departments were to have short terms and were usually not to have the privilege of reelection. The people were to have the right to petition the legislature and if the privilege to secure redress failed, there remained, so they held, the right "to reform the old or establish a new government." In the language of the Maryland constitution "the doctrine of non-resistance against arbitrary power and oppression, is absurd, slavish, and destructive of the good and happiness of mankind."[19]

It remained for the judges to give effect to these provisions by asserting their own independence and insisting upon their interpretation of constitutions as superior to that of the other departments. A number of state courts had already taken steps in this direction. The rather extraordinary theory of judicial independence and semi-superiority which was emerging was generally supported by the Federalist political leaders, and was eventually announced as a federal constitutional doctrine. The theory of the separation of powers was accorded

---

[17] Constitution of Maryland, sec. 6; Thorpe, 3:1687. Constitution of Georgia, art. 1; *Ibid.*, 2:778. Constitution of Virginia, sec. 5; *Ibid.*, 7:3813
[18] See Councils of Censors, chap. 4, *supra.*
[19] Thorpe, 3:1677.

greater significance because of the correlative idea of the necessity of checks and balances in adjusting the relations of departments.

The introduction into American constitutions of the idea of checks and balances proved an aid to the courts in establishing their supremacy as final interpreters of the fundamental laws, written and unwritten.

4. *Theory of checks and balances—*

While the general rule in other countries has been to centralize authority and to place supreme power in one department, usually in the legislature, it was the deliberate purpose of the founders of the American system to separate the powers of government and, so far as possible, to divide authority. The view of dividing and limiting public power was clearly stated by Jefferson in the following dictum:

All the powers of government—legislative, executive, and judiciary—result in the legislative body. The concentrating these in the same hands is precisely the definition of despotic government. It will be no alleviation that these powers will be exercised by a plurality of hands, and not by a single one. One hundred and seventy-three despots would surely be as oppressive as one. Let those who doubt it turn their eyes on the republic of Venice. As little will it avail us that they are chosen by ourselves. An elective despotism was not the government we fought for, but one which should not only be founded on free principles, but in which the powers of government be so divided and balanced among several bodies of magistracy, as that no one could transcend their legal limits, without being effectually checked and restrained by the others.[20]

In a summary of all of the various checks devised in the federal system, John Adams was constrained to speak of them as a ''complication and refinement of

---

20 *Works*, 3:223.

balances, which for anything I recollect is an invention of our own.''[21] The ends arrived at in framing the governments of 1776–1800 were, truly, ''to divide and restrict power; to secure property; to check the appetite for organic change, and to guard individual liberty against the tyranny of the multitude.''[22] To secure these ends by devising an effective check upon legislative usurpations was one of the founders' chief purposes. As protection to person and property was the great end of government,[23] the prime consideration was to limit governmental action so far as private rights are concerned. It was commonly held that the individual had much more to fear from possible usurpations by the executive and legislative departments than by the judiciary. The colonists, in order to accomplish the end of protecting individual rights, accepted the seventeenth-century opinions that courts had the power to declare void an act of Parliament contrary to the common law or the principles of natural justice; and they used this idea for political purposes after it had ceased to have any real weight as a legal principle in England or on the continent of Europe. The acceptance of the idea of the review of legislative acts by the courts was thought necessary also in order to protect the rights of minorities.

5. *Necessity to afford protection to minorities*—

To protect minorities against the dangers of oppression by majority rule was another purpose which the founders of the American government set about to accomplish. The necessity of a check upon majorities was expressed cogently by James Iredell:

---

[21] John Adams, *Works*, 6:467.

[22] Lecky, *Democracy and Liberty* (London, 1899) 1:9.

[23] Samuel Adams, *Works*, 1:69.

The pleasure of a majority of the Assembly! God forbid! How many things have been done by majorities of a large body in heat and passion that they themselves afterwards repented of? Besides, would the minority choose to put themselves in the power of a majority. None, therefore, could have even a chance of being secured, but sycophants that will forever sacrifice reason, conscience and duty to the preservation of a temporary popular favor. Will this not put an end to all freedom of deliberation, to all manly spirit, and prove the utter extinction of all real liberty. . . . . In a republican government (as I conceive) individual liberty is a matter of the utmost moment, as, if there be no check upon the public passions, it is in the greatest danger. The majority, having the rule in their own hands, may take care of themselves, but in what condition are the minority, if the power of the other is without limit? These considerations, I suppose, or similar ones, occasioned such express provisions for the personal liberty of each citizen, which the citizens, when they formed the Constitution, chose to reserve as an unalienated right, and not to leave at the mercy of any assembly whatever. The restriction might be attended with inconvenience; but they chose to risk the inconvenience, for the sake of the advantage.[24]

Iredell no doubt expressed the view of conservative leaders generally when he insisted that every citizen should have a ''surer pledge for his constitutional rights than the wisdom and activity of any occasional majority of his fellow citizens, who, if their own rights are in fact unmolested, may care very little for his.''[25]

The danger of oppression by majority rule was much to be feared, according to Madison. In the tenth number of *The Federalist* Madison presented as the chief characteristic of the federal system a device by which the spectacles of turbulence and contention and the distrust of public engagements and alarm for private rights, felt

---

[24] McRee, *Letters of Iredell*, 147, 173.
[25] *Ibid.*, 175.

throughout the states, would be obviated because of checks upon the rules of the majority. He contended that the political system to be established must take into account the conditions of natural inequality which prevail among men. These conditions of inequality were evidenced primarily by the differences in the facility of acquiring property. The unequal distribution of wealth which necessarily results, Madison believed, would lead to parties and cliques; and since the great mass of people would be without property, they would combine in support of their common interests, in which case the rights of property and the public liberty would not be secure.[26] The chief danger, Madison thought, was not to be apprehended "from the acts of government contrary to the sense of its constitutents, but from the acts in which the government is the mere instrument of the major number of the constituents." Hence, he concluded that the majority "must be rendered, by their number and local situation, unable to concert and carry into effect schemes of oppression," and the new Constitution was defended because among its many merits it secured the rights of the minority against the "superior force of an interested and overbearing majority."[27]

Madison was for a long while skeptical as to the advisability of constituting the judiciary as a check upon the legislature and as the prime defender of the minority, although he held the opinion, so generally supported at the time, that the protection of individual rights from all undue interference was the prime purpose of government. The conviction of leaders among both conservatives and radicals that the judiciary would become the greatest bulwark for the protection of individual interests because

---

[26] Elliot's *Debates*, 5:387.
[27] *The Federalist* (Ford's ed.), 55.

it secured the rights of the minority, was undoubtedly
one of the chief reasons for the adoption by the courts
of the right to declare laws invalid. It was commonly
believed that "not until the adoption of the federal
Constitution, with its restraints on state powers and a
supreme court to enforce them, was there any true check
given to the state legislatures or true protection given
to minorities." Back of these political doctrines was a
pervading belief, made more assertive by the tendency
of state legislatures to interfere rather indiscriminately
with the rights of property and contract, that property
rights were not secure with unlimited power in legislative
bodies.

6. *Protection to be accorded to property rights*—

Men were inclined to look favorably upon the courts
as censors of legislative powers because they were convinced that property was a sacred right, which it was
the supreme function of the government to preserve and
protect. Some of the earliest and most emphatic statements favorable to the American doctrine of judicial
review were called forth by an attempt on the part of legislatures to interfere with property rights. Acts were
regularly held void which ran counter to the political
axiom of the day, that property should not be interfered
with except where public necessity clearly demanded, and
then only on condition that the owner should have been
previously and equitably indemnified. Among the early
cases relating primarily to property rights are *Giddings
v. Brown; Bayard v. Singleton; Vanhorne's Lessee v.
Dorrance.*[28]

Political leaders of the eighteenth century were
primarily concerned with the safeguarding of the rights

---

[28] Cf. *supra*, 57, 112, 179.

of private property. According to Gouverneur Morris, "life and liberty were generally said to be of more value than property. An accurate view of the matter would, nevertheless, prove that property was the main object of society."[29] It was a prime consideration, as Madison noted, to provide against the dangers of the time when a great majority of the people would be without property of any sort. Hamilton thought that the Senate would preserve the rights of property and the interests of the minority against the demands of the majority.[30] But Hamilton, like many others of a conservative and aristocratic cast, placed his faith for the protection of property and the rights of minorities in the judiciary, the department which was revered above all others as a defense against popular rule. The right of the judiciary to declare laws invalid, and thus to check the rapacity of legislative assemblies, was in the opinion of many to be the chief cornerstone of a governmental structure planned with particular reference to preserving property rights inviolate and to assuring a special sanction for individual liberties.

That it was the intention of the framers of the American system of government to limit legislative powers, to protect minorities, and to preserve property rights there can be no doubt.[31] But these political notions would not have resulted in the adoption of the practice of the review of legislative acts by the courts except for the prevalence of certain other ideas and assumptions relating to written constitutions and to fundamental laws.

---

[29] Elliot's *Debates*, 5:278; see also 243 and 280 for similar opinions by Madison and King.

[30] *Ibid.*, 203.

[31] See Charles A. Beard, *The Supreme Court and the Constitution* (New York, 1912), especially, chap. 4, and J. Allen Smith, *The Spirit of the American Government* (New York, 1907) chaps. 1–3.

7. *Written constitutions as fundamental laws—*

It was customary to claim that the provisions of the written constitution were equivalent to laws in the ordinary acceptation and meaning of the term. Since under English common law usage it was the duty of the courts to interpret and apply laws, so they must interpret and apply the fundamental laws. Hence legislatures, not being courts, could not interpret written constitutions. Moreover, the belief was prevalent that the written constitution was *law* of a superior and more fundamental character than legislative acts and that the courts as the authorized interpreters of the law must define and apply the fundamental law. This theory made the judge a mechanical agent for comparing two grades of enactments.

What was termed "a new epoch in the history of civil institutions" had resulted in the formulation of the principle that a constitution is a written compact in which

the sovereignty of the people and the responsibility of their servants are principles fundamentally and unequivocally established; in which the powers of the several branches of government are defined and the excess of them, as well in the legislature as in other branches, finds limits, which cannot be transgressed without offending against the greater power from whom all authority, among us, is derived; to-wit, the people.[32]

A constitution "unalterable but by the same high power which established it"[33] was beginning to be distinguished from all other law, and the first principle which was to give constitutional law in the United States a peculiar sanctity was recognized as a distinct feature of American

---

[32] Tucker's *Blackstone*, 1:88, note (ed. 1803).
[33] James Iredell, "Letters to an Elector," McRee, 2:145.

jurisprudence, namely, the distinction between fundamental laws and ordinary acts passed by the legislature.

Written constitutions were soon to be adopted as
fundamental laws in many countries, and it was necessary that other principles be developed in connection with
the idea of a written document as comprising superior
and paramount laws in order to give the doctrine of judicial review its unique importance in the United States.

The notion of limited legislative powers soon took
concrete form in the opinions rendered in American state
courts. The justices of North Carolina, quoting Vattel
with approval, held that the legislature could not "repeal
or alter the Constitution, because if they could do this,
they would at the same instant of time destroy their own
existence as a Legislature, and dissolve the government
thereby established."[34]

The justices of Virginia were even more determined
in their insistence that the legislature is "not sovereign
but subordinate," that the people have established a
fundamental law in the constitution which gives the legislature its authority and existence, and that the legislature
may not infringe this constitution without endangering
the liberties of the people.[35]

That written constitutions set certain limits to the
power of the legislature and that acts beyond those limits

---

[34] Bayard v. Singleton, 1 Martin 42, 45 (1787).

[35] "I consider the people of this country as the only sovereign power.—
I consider the legislature as not sovereign but subordinate; they are subordinate to the great constitutional charter which the people have established as a fundamental law, and which alone has given existence and
authority to the legislature. . . . . But if the legislature may infringe this
Constitution, it is no longer fixed; it is not this year what it was the last;
and the liberties of the people are wholly at the mercy of the legislature.
. . . . The supposed '*omnipotence of parliament*,' which is an abominable
insult upon the honor and good sense of our country, as nothing is omnipotent as it relates to us, either religious or political, but the *God of Heaven*
and our Constitution." Opinions of Judges Roane, Henry, and Tyler,
Kamper v. Hawkins, 1 Va. Cases 20, 36, 38, 60.

were nullities was repeated and approved frequently before it was definitely accepted and announced as a principle to be followed by the federal judiciary. The principle which had slowly been taking form in American law was summarized by Judge Tucker as follows:

Should Congress attempt to pass a law contrary to the Constitution of the United States, or should the state legislature make a similar attempt against it, or against the state constitution; such acts, though clothed with all the forms of laws, would not be law, nor repeal in any measure what was established by a higher authority, to-wit that of the people.[36]

Referring to the rule of Blackstone relative to the absolute and uncontrollable power of Parliament, Tucker observed that in America, constitutions being the act of the people and not of the government, the legislature can possess no power over the other branches of government where the principles of the constitution are concerned. Judge Tucker maintained that this was a distinction which had been introduced into the governments of the western hemisphere and which placed them in a class superior to that of the other governments of the world. Tucker's *Blackstone* was published in 1803, and this statement of the American doctrine had evidently been prepared before Marshall delivered his opinion in the case of *Marbury v. Madison*.

But the principles that constitutions are fundamental or paramount laws, superior to any ordinary legislative acts, and that the legislative power is defined and limited, would not have been sufficient to lead to the establishment of the American doctrine of judicial review of legislation. Both of these principles have been accepted in other nations without the development of the type of judicial

---

[36] Tucker's *Blackstone*, 1:88.

supremacy which is peculiar to the United States. It was the formulation and the adoption of a third principle to complement and support these two ideas which brought into operation the noteworthy characteristic of American constitutional law.

8. *Judges as guardians of written constitutions*—

In a majority of governments it is a settled principle that the judges may not question the authority of a coordinate legislative body. It is the duty of courts to accept as final every legislative act passed in due form and submitted to them for interpretation. This principle that legislation is superior to adjudication, which is the basic idea of the practice of legislative supremacy, was firmly established in England prior to the American Revolution, and has since been accepted by most countries which have adopted written constitutions. Switzerland adopted a written constitution as the basis of a federal system of government and refused to accept the idea that the judges may scan the authority of the legislative department and refuse to enforce acts which in their judgment are not within constitutional limits. As a general rule the judgment of the legislative branch of government as to the meaning of the constitution appears to take precedence over the judgments of the courts. The legislature is the chief guardian of the terms of the constitution as well as of the scope of its own powers.

How, then, did the people of the United States come to adopt a principle that had been only tentatively approved in a few European nations and in no instance had been put into successful operation? The opinions of the judges themselves indicate the gradual evolution of the idea that courts were to become the special guardians of written constitutions. This feature of the American doctrine developed slowly and in its development molded the character of our political institutions more than any other principle adopted by the founders of government in state and nation.

The origin of a superior and paramount law which rests for its final interpretation with the conscience of the judges, though it is the result of the interaction of a variety of opinions and theories, was a direct product of the doctrines resulting from the conflict between the King of England and Sir Edward Coke. The extravagant claims of Coke favoring the supremacy of common law courts have never been sanctioned in England, either by the courts of justice or by the other departments of government. But despite the fact that the dicta of the courts favoring a common law supremacy were deliberately discarded when the English nation settled its long quarrel over the royal prerogative, Coke persisted in placing his extreme views in his works. And on account of his prestige and learning his *Institutes* were widely used by lawyers and judges, and especially in America, where the doctrine of common law supremacy appeared to give encouragement and the weight of authority to those who were imbued with the conviction that both the legislative and executive branches must be held in check.

The doctrine of Coke, formulated chiefly as dicta in cases brought before his court and read into earlier cases reported by him, became the prime authority for the guiding principle of the American doctrine of judicial supremacy. Some of the "exorbitant and extravagant opinions" which the king had advised Coke to remove from his *Reports* after his deposition from the bench[37] were passed on to the American colonists for a different

---

[37] Gardiner, *History of England from the Accession of James I to the Outbreak of the Civil War 1603 1642* (New York, 1899–1901).

reception than they were accorded in the country of their origin.

9. *Coke's doctrine of the supremacy of the common law as interpreted by the courts—*

The gradual and effective crystallization of opinion favoring Coke's doctrine of judicial supremacy is seen in some state decisions in which was raised the question of the power of the judiciary over that of the legislature. In 1789 the supreme court of South Carolina felt that it was the duty of the court to square its decision with justice and the dictates of natural reason. Coke was quoted to the effect that statutes against common right and reason and statutes against natural equity or against Magna Carta were void.[38] Similarly a judge of the same state noted that while it was painful to him to be obliged to question the exercise of any legislative power, he was sworn to support the constitution, and this was the most important of all duties that were incumbent upon him. When an act, in his judgment, was repugnant to the fundamental law, "he was bound to say, that it ought not to have any operation."[39]

The influence of Coke's theory was apparent before 1688. In Massachusetts there was a steady and persistent opposition to the exercise of the royal prerogative over colonial affairs. A definite and formal approval of his doctrine of judicial supremacy was recorded in an early case before a Massachusetts court where the resolution of a town meeting was held void and not enforced by the magistrate.[40] In the period preceding the American Rev-

---

[38] Ham v. McClaws, 1 Bay 93, 98 (1789).

[39] Lindsay v. Charleston Commissioners, 2 Bay 61–62 (1796).

[40] Giddings v. Brown, 1 *Selected Essays in Anglo-American Legal History*, 376. Cf. *supra*, 57.

olution, Jefferson noted that ''Coke's Lyttleton was then the universal law book for students and a sounder Whig never wrote nor one of profounder learning in the ortho-dox doctrines of the British Constitution.''[41] The doctrine of Coke was applied by James Otis in his well-known argument on Writs of Assistance. In opposing general search warrants, sanctioned by an act of Parliament, Otis maintained that reason and the Constitution were both against this kind of writ.[42] The theory of the su-premacy of law as interpreted by lawyers and judges was thereby made an issue of significance to all the colonies in their resistance to the home government, and the theory was advanced at a moment when it was sure to draw to itself widespread popular attention.

The popularity of the doctrine of review of legisla-tion in 1776 is evidenced in the charge of Justice Cushing to a Massachusetts jury to ignore certain acts of Parlia-ment as void and inoperative. He was supported in his view by John Adams.[43] So in 1772 Mason, citing opinions of Coke and Hobart, argued that judges are ''in con-science bound to disobey'' all enactments which con-tradict the laws of nature and the laws of God.[44] The principle that courts must interpret statutes so as to give them a reasonable interpretation was accepted and fol-lowed as the ruling principle in some important colonial cases.[45]

That Coke's theory had crystallized into a well defined doctrine prior to the meeting of the federal convention in Philadelphia is apparent in the argument of Varnum

41 Corwin, *op. cit.*, 105.

42 John Adams, *Works*, 9:525.

43 Corwin, *op. cit.*, 106.

44 Robin v. Hardaway, Jefferson (Va.) Reports, 109, 114.

45 Cf. Rutgers v. Waddington, *supra*, 98.

in the Rhode Island case of *Trevett v. Weeden,* 1786. Varnum began with the proposition that the legislature derived all its authority from the constitution, that any laws which were in violation of the fundamental law were unconstitutional and void, and then followed Coke's idea to its logical result by affirming that it was the business of the court "to judge and determine what acts of the general assembly were agreeable to the constitution."[46]

Varnum insisted that the legislature could pass only laws that were not repugnant to the written instrument and that the courts could not accept as law any unconstitutional act. If the judges should attempt to enforce a law which seemed to them repugnant to the constitution, he declared that they would violate their oaths.[47]

Three guiding principles of the American doctrine of judicial review, namely, that written constitutions are fundamental and superior laws, that legislative powers must necessarily be defined and limited, and that judges are the special guardians of the fundamental law, were so well formulated that their acceptance as tenets of state and federal law was assured. Although the opinion of Chief Justice Marshall, announcing the doctrine of judicial review as a principle of federal law, was for some time referred to by his political opponents as "obiter dicta," it was definitely accepted as a principle of the national government, and forcefully asserted as an indispensable feature of every effective written constitution. All the state courts could thereafter rely upon it in placing an interpretation upon state statutes in conflict with constitutions.

---

[46] Brinton Coxe, *Judicial Power and Unconstitutional Legislation* (Philadelphia, 1893) 241.

[47] *Ibid.,* 242.

By 1803 it was asserted in the federal courts and in a majority of the supreme courts of the states that a written constitution was a mandatory direction to the judges, who in taking an oath to support the fundamental law obligated themselves to refuse to enforce a legislative act which they regarded as contrary to any of the provisions of the written paramount law. The principles were put into the form of a seemingly unanswerable argument: the people, as the ultimate sovereign, have established written limitations upon the legislature in the nature of fundamental laws; all acts contrary to these limitations are not law; it is for the judiciary to say what the law is, and if two rules conflict, to decide which governs; the judiciary are to declare a legislative act void which conflicts with the constitution. The judiciary must in the nature of the case declare laws repugnant to the constitution invalid or a written constitution becomes a "solemn mockery." The theory of judicial review was held to be essentially attached to a written constitution, and any other interpretation was considered not only likely to lead to ruin, but also impossible to contemplate as a reasonable proposition. The legal duty of every judge was regarded as clear and unmistakable, that whether acting as judge of a state or of a federal court he was bound to treat as void every unconstitutional act when the issue was fairly presented in a case before him. Emerging from a notion of an overruling law of nature or law of God, through a concept of a law fundamental and unalterable, which was vitalized by Coke's theory of the supremacy of common law courts, a doctrine of judicial review of legislation was incorporated in state and federal systems in order to place effective limitations and restrictions upon the legislative and executive departments of government.

The idea for which Coke had struggled so persistently in England, which had proved impossible to attain in his own country—that the common law as interpreted by the courts shall be superior to the king and Parliament—was accepted and put into operation about two centuries later with modifications necessitated by the enactment of written constitutions, in the development and adoption of the American doctrine of judicial supremacy.[48]

---

[48] Professor McLaughlin presents the following summary of principles which characterized the thinking of those who aided in the establishment of judicial review of legislation:

In seeking for the historical background of judicial authority in America I have found it necessary to emphasize a series of fundamental principles which entered into the warp and woof of Revolutionary thinking. As I have said more than once, I am not attempting to make out that each one of these principles, or all of them, demand, by absolute logical necessity, the exercise of the power of the courts to refuse to be bound by legislative enactment. My contention only is that such were the antecedents and that some of these notions or principles were of surpassing influence in the minds of the men of Revolutionary days. The chiefest among the principles I have given are these: first and foremost, the separation of powers of government and the independence of the judiciary, which led courts to believe that they were not bound in their interpretation of the constitution by the decisions of a collateral branch of the government; second, the prevalent and deeply cherished conviction that governments must be checked and limited in order that individual liberty might be protected and property preserved; third, that there was fundamental law in all free states and that freedom and God-given right depended on the maintenance and preservation of that law, an idea of the supremest significance to the men of those days; fourth, the firm belief in the existence of natural rights superior to all governmental authority, and in the principles of natural justice constituting legal limitations upon governmental activity, a notion that was widely spread and devoutly believed in by the young lawyers and statesmen of the Revolutionary days who were to become the judges of the courts and the lawyers that made the arguments; fifth, the belief that, as a principle of English law, the courts would consider that an act of Parliament contrary to natural justice or reason was void and pass it into disuse, a belief which was especially confirmed by the reference to Coke. Back of all of these ideas was a long course of English constitutional development in which judges had played a significant part in constitutional controversy; in English history courts had held an influential if not an absolutely independent position; Parliament itself had long played the rôle of a tribunal declaring existing law rather than that of a legislative body making new law. The principle of legislative sovereignty as a possession of Parliament was, on the other hand, a comparatively modern thing.—*The Courts, The Constitution and Parties* (Chicago, 1912) 105, 106.

10. *Suggested limitations on judicial review*—

To render the exercise of judicial review more accept-able to the public the judges announced certain restric-tions or self-imposed limitations which were supposed to qualify the assertion of this power by the courts. Though these limitations were not seriously observed, since their strict application would have rendered the invalidation of acts practically impossible, they did serve to allay some of the fears regarding the dangers inherent in according such transcendent authority to judges who were usually not directly responsible to public sentiment.

First, it was asserted that the violation of the consti-tution must be plain and clear. This view at various times was stated in the form that every presumption is in favor of the validity of an act and that the discrepancy between the law and the constitution must be clear beyond a reasonable doubt.[49]

Chief Justice Marshall, in holding a state act invalid, referred to this attitude on the part of judges (an atti-tude, indeed, which his associates on the bench and others thought he failed to act upon in his own opinions):

The question, whether a law be void for its repugnancy to the constitution, is, at all times, a question of much delicacy, which ought seldom, if ever, to be decided in the affirmative, in a doubtful case. The court, when impelled by duty to render such a judgment, would be unworthy of its station, could it be unmindful of the solemn obligations which that station imposes. But it is not to be on slight implication and vague conjecture that the legislature is to be pronounced to have transcended its powers, and its acts to be considered as void. The opposition between the constitution and the law should be such that the

---

[49] See Judge Chase in Hylton v. United States, 3 Dall. 171 (1796); Cooper v. Telfair, 4 Dall. 14, 18 (1800); Byrne v. Stewart, 3 Des. 466, 477 (1812).

judge feels a clear and strong conviction of their incompatibility with each other.[50]

Second, it was asserted that the power of review of legislation in courts of justice did not mean a supremacy of the judiciary over the legislature. Hamilton found that some objections to the exercise of power to declare laws invalid, were due to a fear that the doctrine would imply a superiority of the judiciary to the legislative power. It was urged that an authority which can declare the acts of another void must necessarily be superior to the one whose acts may be declared invalid. In reply to this objection he asserted that this power by no means supposes a superiority of the judicial to the legislative power, "it only supposes that the power of the people is superior to both; and that where the will of the legislature declared in its statutes, stands in opposition to that of the people, declared in the Constitution, the judges ought to be governed by the latter rather than the former."[51] James Wilson, an ardent champion of judicial control, also claimed that no superiority of courts was involved in declaring statutes void. The court does not, he affirmed, decide directly upon the doings of the legislature. It simply decides whether there are conflicting laws, and if so merely announces that the higher law demands obedience.[52] The justices, too, disavowed any intention to assert the superiority of the judiciary over the legislature, maintaining that the judges claimed no judicial supremacy and that they were only the administrators of the public will. If an act of the legislature is held void, they said, it is not because the judges have any control over the legislature, but because the act is forbidden by

[50] Fletcher v. Peck, 6 Cranch 87, 128 (1810).

[51] *The Federalist*, 522.

[52] *Works* (Federal ed.) 1:415.

the constitution, and because the will of the people is paramount to that of their representatives.[53] Not only was the superiority of the judiciary denied, but also, it was asserted that each department is the constitutional judge of its own powers.[54] The view which Hamilton so ably presented in his defense of judicial authority soon received the affirmation of the courts. And it came to be the accepted view that courts, when they refuse to enforce legislative acts, do not assume a superior authority.

Third, it was recognized that to give the courts the right to refuse to enforce a legislative act was placing an important prerogative in the hands of the judiciary; hence it was necessary to give assurance that the exercise of this power was not likely to lead to abuses which in the nature of things would be irremediable. Hamilton tried to allay the fear regarding the abuse of power on the part of the judiciary by insisting that the judiciary would necessarily be the weakest of the three departments and that the people would have nothing to fear from the judges who would protect rather than interfere with individual liberties.[55] Judges also refused to give advisory opinions on constitutional questions and insisted that a decision would be given only in an actual case when the rights of private persons or corporations were involved.

The American doctrine of judicial review of legislation, as it came to be applied by state and federal courts, was sanctioned because it was contended by proponents of the doctrine that judges would refuse to exercise the power to declare laws void except in cases where a mani-

---

[53] Lindsay v. Commissioners, 2 Bay 61 (1796).

[54] White v. Kendrick, 1 Brevard 370 (1805).

[55] *The Federalist*, 518–520, and *supra*, 138 *et seq.* See on this point Whittington v. Polk, 1 Harris and Johnson 236 (1802).

fest duty required judicial interference. It was maintained, by those supporting judicial review, that the legislature and judiciary are coordinate departments, that each department in the exercise of its proper functions is supreme, and that one department could not be subjected to the control of another. The courts, it was asserted, were obliged to declare legislative acts contrary to the constitution void, but this did not mean that judicial power was superior to that of the legislature.

By limiting the exercise of the power to cases regularly brought before the courts for deliberation; by recognizing that certain political acts of the executive and legislature were beyond judicial control; in the main, by confiding the basis for invalidating acts to the express provisions of written constitutions, and by avoiding a controversy in doubtful cases and hence invalidating very few laws in the early history of judicial supremacy, it was not difficult to convince the people of the necessity and efficacy of the power and to allay fears regarding the dangers of its abuse. The majority of the people were persuaded that judicial supremacy was an indispensable feature of republican government, because there was an ingrained fear of executive power, and the legislative department was losing in public esteem, and because men seemed primarily concerned with limitations and restrictions on the functions of government. Although the foregoing canons were not strictly observed and might, at the discretion of the judges, be entirely disregarded, nevertheless the impression prevailed that judicial review of legislation was confined within narrow limits and restricted to but few subjects.

CHAPTER X

OPPOSITION TO THE THEORIES AND THE PRACTICE OF JUDICIAL REVIEW OF LEGISLATION IN THE STATE AND FEDERAL GOVERNMENTS

I. OPPOSITION TO THE REVIEW OF ACTS OF CONGRESS AND OF ACTS OF STATE LEGISLATURES BY THE FEDERAL COURTS

THOUGH the prevailing sentiment of the leaders of all parties was favorable to the authoritative exercise of review of legislative acts by the courts, there was no time when there was not a determined opposition by an insistent minority. It was frequently insisted that the assertion of such authority by the judges was a usurpation of power, since no express grant of review was given in written constitutions, and since it was too vital a matter to be determined from mere interpretations and implications.

Opposition to the review of legislative acts by the judiciary was expressed along various lines. First, it was claimed, that, in accordance with the English practice and the prevailing custom in the states during the Revolutionary period, the legislature was supreme so far as final powers were regarded as belonging to the government. Second, the authority to pass judgment on the validity of legislative acts was considered as outside of the jurisdiction of the courts of justice because of the political character of the controversies, and as not within the duties and functions of courts viewed either historically or practically. Third, constitutions were regarded as emanating from the people and whether they provided for a framework of government with a distribution of powers or for a guaranty of individual rights, the people and their representatives were thought to be the best interpreters of the provisions of the fundamental law. These and other arguments were urged with vigor by those who saw grave dangers in the adoption of the principle of judicial supremacy.

In order to make the case for judicial review of legislation seem more plausible certain authorities on judicial history have asserted that opposition to the doctrine did not arise until partisan lines were clearly drawn as between the Federalists and Anti-Federalists and that this opposition is to be attributed to partisan and personal motives.[1] A cursory survey of the legal literature of the period refutes this contention.

1. *Opinions of James Madison—*

James Madison was one of those who strove earnestly in the federal convention to have the executive and the judges act as an advisory council on legislative matters. He was disappointed by the refusal of the convention to adopt a provision for such a council, and regretted this action because he thought the establishment of such a body "would have precluded the question of a judiciary annulment of legislative acts."[2] He seems to have accepted judicial control only with limitations. When the jurisdiction of the Supreme Court was under discussion,

---

[1] Charles Warren, *The Supreme Court in United States History*, 1:256.
[2] *Writings*, 8:406.

he doubted ''whether it was not going too far to extend the jurisdiction of the Court generally to cases arising under the Constitution and whether it ought not to be limited to cases of a judicial nature.'' The right of expounding the Constitution in cases not of this nature ought not, he thought, to be given to that department.[3]

The refusal of the convention to establish a council of revision left the judiciary paramount, and he thought this result certainly undesirable, as is evidenced by his comment on the proposed Virginia constitution of 1788. ''In the state constitutions and indeed in the federal one also,'' he said,

no provision is made for the case of a disagreement in expounding them [the laws] ; and as the courts are generally the last in making the decision, it results to them, by refusing or not refusing to execute a law, to stamp it with its final character. This makes the Judiciary Department paramount in fact to the legislature, which was never intended and can never be proper.[4]

He fully approved the right of the courts to pass upon constitutional questions in cases of a judicial nature, but believed that this did not preclude the other departments from declaring their sentiments on matters of constitutionality.

His views were more fully expressed in the House of Representatives on the question of granting to the President the power of removal. He thought that a decision with regard to a doubtful part of the Constitution might come with as much propriety from the legislature as from any other department of government.[5] It was his belief

---

[3] Max Farrand, *The Records of the Federal Convention,* 2:430.

[4] *Writings* (Hunt ed.) 5:293, 294.

[5] Elliot's *Debates,* 4:354, House of Representatives, June 16, 1789. For confirmation of this view see Myers v. United States, 272 U. S. 52 (1926) and especially comments of Chief Justice Taft 136 ff.

that such a decision would become the permanent exposition of the Constitution.[6] When the objection was raised that the legislature had no right to expound the Constitution, but must defer all doubtful questions of constitutional interpretation to the judiciary, Madison replied, "I beg to know upon what principle it can be contended that any one department draws from the Constitution greater powers than another, in marking out the limits of the powers of the several departments."[7] In reply to the contention that an act of Congress might be ignored by the courts, Madison declared that "nothing has yet been offered to invalidate the doctrine, that the meaning of the Constitution may as well be ascertained by the legislative as by the judicial authority."[8] It is, therefore, a fair question," he said,

whether this great point may not as well be decided, at least by the whole legislature, as by part—by us, as well as by the executive or the judicial. As I think it will be equally constitutional, I cannot imagine it will be less safe that the exposition should issue from the legislative authority than any other; and the more so, because it involves in the decision the opinions of both of those departments whose powers are supposed to be affected by it. Besides, I do not see in what way this question could come before the judges to obtain a fair and solemn decision; but even if it were the case that it could, I should suppose, at least while the government is not led by passion, disturbed by faction, or deceived by any discolored medium of sight, but while there is a desire in all to see and be guided by the benignant ray of truth, that the decision may be made with the most advantage by the legislature itself.[9]

According to this view Congress was to have the right to interpret the Constitution and to give it a construction

---

[6] Elliot's *Debates*, 4:378. [8] *Ibid.*, 399.
[7] *Ibid.*, 382. [9] *Ibid.*, 383.

of its own which the judiciary would be bound to respect. The opinion of Madison, though apparently acquiesced in by other members of Congress, was answered with assertions supporting the theory that the courts were to be the final interpreters of the fundamental law.[10]

That Madison was somewhat uncertain as to his opinions on judicial review is shown by his views on the controversy over the Alien and Sedition laws and later observations on the authority of the judiciary. If the distinction is kept in mind between review by a coordinate department, such as by the Supreme Court over acts of Congress or by a state supreme court over an act of a state legislature, and review by a superior court in a federal system over an inferior court, some seeming inconsistencies disappear. Madison doubted whether the final decisions on constitutional questions with respect to the delimitation of powers between the nation and the states could be left to the states. On the other hand, he disapproved the policy of giving the courts too extensive powers in the interpretation of the federal Constitution, particularly with respect to the powers of Congress.[11]

The federal judiciary was rebuked, for holding that a state could be brought before a federal court on a suit by a citizen of another state,[12] by the adoption of the Eleventh Amendment to the Constitution. But a conflict which arose in New Hampshire[13] and the controversy over the Alien and Sedition laws led to the assertion by certain state assemblies that the people of the United States "have committed to the supreme judiciary of the nation the high authority of ultimately and conclusively

---

10 For representative opinions, see Warren, *op. cit.*, 1:83, 84.
11 Cf. *supra*, 190.
12 Chisholm's Executor v. State of Georgia, 2 Dallas 419 (1793).
13 Penhallow v. Doane's Administrators, 3 Dallas 54 (1793).

deciding upon the constitutionality of all legislative acts.''[14]

It was in the discussions which arose over the Kentucky and Virginia resolutions in the various state legislatures that the rising Republican or Democratic party took a firm stand against the Federalist doctrine that the Supreme Court was the final arbiter on matters involving the interpretation of the Constitution. In the northern states the Federalists were in a majority, and they adopted in each state a strong expression of disapproval of the resolutions submitted from the states south of the Potomac. None of the southern commonwealths sent replies, and the Republicans of New Jersey, New York, and Massachusetts disapproved the Federalist doctrine that the Supreme Court was the final arbiter on matters of constitutionality.[15] Contemporary accounts show that the Republicans fully indorsed the protesting features of the Virginia and Kentucky resolutions and accepted in part the reasoning upon which the remedy was grounded, though many did not go to the full extent of supporting the extreme measures proposed by these resolutions.[16]

Madison espoused the Republican doctrines with certain qualifications. To the claim that the judicial

---

[14] *Journal* of House of Representatives of Pennsylvania, 9:198.

[15] Cf. F. M. Anderson, ''Contemporary Opinions of the Virginia and Kentucky Resolutions,'' *Am. Hist. Rev.* (Oct. 1899) 5:46 ff. See especially resolution offered by Pennington in the New Jersey House and amendments presented in New York Assembly,—*ibid.*, 54–56.

[16] *Ibid.*, 237. ''But when they pass laws beyond the limits of the Constitution . . . . we do not ask a repeal, but ought to make a legislative declaration that, being unconstitutional, they are void and of no effect. Let it be granted that honest judges may refuse to act upon them; but Congress itself, if it be possessed of virtue and wisdom, will on the representations of the state legislatures expunge their unconstitutional proceedings from the annals of the United States.''—John Breckinridge in defense of the Kentucky Resolutions, Ethelbert D. Warfield, *The Kentucky Resolutions of 1798* (New York, 1887) 94.

authority is to be regarded as the sole expositor of the Constitution, Madison replied:

First, that there may be instances of usurped power, which the forms of the Constitution would never draw within the control of the judicial department; secondly, that if the decision of the judiciary be raised above the authority of the sovereign parties to the Constitution, the decisions of the other department, not carried by the forms of the Constitution before the judiciary, must be equally authoritative and final with the decisions of that department.

Though admitting a superiority of the decisions of the judicial department over the other departments in relation to questions of a judicial nature under the Constitution, Madison insisted that such judicial decisions cannot bind the parties to the constitutional compact "from which the judicial as well as the other departments hold their delegated trusts."[17] He insisted that the state legislatures had the right to declare the meaning of the federal Constitution, though to carry such declarations into effect might require an amendment to the Constitution,[18] and argued:

On the subject of an Arbiter or Umpire, ... there can be none, external to the U. S. more than the individual States; nor within either, for those extreme cases, or questions of passive obedience and non-resistance, which justify and require a resort to the original rights of the parties to the compact. But that in all cases, not of that extreme character, there is an Arbiter or Umpire, as within the Government of the States, so within that of the U. S. in the authority constitutionally provided for deciding controversies concerning boundaries of right and power.[19]

---

17 James Madison, "Report of the Committee to whom were referred the replies of the states to the Virginia Resolution concerning the Alien and Sedition Laws."—*Writings*, 6:351, 352.

18 *Writings*, 6:402, 403.

19 *Writings*, 9:342, 343. Letter to Joseph C. Cabell, Aug. 16, 1829.

At another time Madison asserted that conflicts of power between the federal and state governments must be decided by the federal judiciary, subject in cases of extreme usurpations to "an appeal from the cancelled obligations of the constitutional compact, to the original rights and the law of self-preservation."[20] He thought that the final decisions as to constitutional controversies could not be left to the individual states without imperiling the Union itself.[21]

Charles Pinckney expressed the extreme Republican doctrine:

On no subject am I more convinced, than that it is an unsafe and dangerous doctrine in a republic, ever to suppose that a judge ought to possess the right of questioning or deciding upon the constitutionality of treaties, laws, or any act of legislature. It is placing the opinion of an individual, or of two or three, above that of both branches of congress, a doctrine which is not

---

[20] *Ibid.*, 398. "With respect to the supremacy of the Judicial power on questions occurring in the course of its functions, concerning the boundary of Jurisdiction between the U. S. and individual States, my opinion in favor of it was as the 41 No. of the Federalist shows, of the earliest date; and I have never ceased to think that this supremacy was a vital principle of the Constitution as it is a prominent feature in its text."—*Writings*, 9 :476.

[21] An opinion favorable to judicial supremacy was expressed by Madison in 1834 as follows:

"As the Legislative, Executive, and Judicial departments of the United States are co-ordinate, and each equally bound to support the Constitution, it follows that each must, in the exercise of its functions, be guided by the text of the Constitution according to its own interpretation of it; and, consequently, that in the event of irreconcilable interpretations, the prevalence of the one or the other department must depend on the nature of the case, as receiving its final decision from the one or the other, and passing from that decision into effect, without involving the functions of any other.

It is certainly due from the functionaries of the several departments to pay much respect to the opinions of each other; and, as far as official independence and obligation will permit, to consult the means of adjusting differences and avoiding practical embarrassments growing out of them, as must be done in like cases between the different co-ordinate branches of the legislative department.

But notwithstanding this abstract view of the co-ordinate and independent right of the three departments to expound the Constitution, the Judicial

warranted by the constitution; and will not, I hope, long have any advocates in this country.[22]

The Federalists looked upon such expressions of opinion as detrimental to the existence of the Union, and in Massachusetts an editor who published the Republican doctrines was arrested, tried, and imprisoned.[23] It was in this discussion that the argument was resorted to that the American doctrine of judicial review was a necessity because any other conclusion would result disastrously, and it was made to appear that the very basis of the Union hinged on the acceptance of the doctrine. The Republicans were charged with seeking a dissolution of the Union and were shown scant courtesy wherever the Federalist party was in power. With the advent into power of the Democratic party and of their leader Jefferson, who formerly seemed to favor judicial review,[24] the attack upon the American doctrine was made one of the major political issues of the day.

---

department most familiarize itself to the public attention as the expositor, by the order of its functions in relation to the other departments; and attracts most the public confidence by the composition of the tribunal.

It is the Judicial department in which questions of constitutionality, as well as of legality, generally find their ultimate discussion and operative decision: and the public deference to and confidence in the judgment of the body are peculiarly inspired by the qualities implied in its members; by the gravity and deliberation of their proceedings; and by the advantage their plurality gives them over the unity of the Executive department, and their fewness over the multitudinous composition of the Legislative department.

Without losing sight, therefore, of the co-ordinate relations of the three departments to each other, it may always be expected that the judicial bench, when happily filled, will, for the reasons suggested, most engage the respect and reliance of the public as the surest expositor of the Constitution, as well in questions within its cognizance concerning the boundaries between the several departments of the Government as in those between the Union and its members.''—*Writings*, 6:349.

[22] Wharton's *State Trials*, 412 (1799).

[23] Cf. Anderson, *op. cit., Am. Hist. Rev.*, 5:61–63.

[24] ''The laws of the land,'' Jefferson wrote, ''administered by upright Judges, would protect you from any exercise of power unauthorized by the Constitution of the United States.''—*Writings* (Ford ed.), 7:281.

2. The views of Thomas Jefferson and of leading Democrat-Republicans—

The history of the progress of the Supreme Court in power and authority began with the advent of John Marshall to the Supreme Bench in 1801. This period also marked the beginning of a determined opposition to the court by the executive department. It is well known that Marshall and the majority of his associates were ardent Federalists, and wrought a manifest revolution in developing the authority and defining the duties of the central government. The reorganization of the judicial system with the opportunity of appointing to the new places justices in sympathy with Federalist principles, and the evident intention to foster the development of national power through the courts were particularly odious to Jefferson. It was expected that the office of Chief Justice would be filled by Jefferson, and Judge Spencer Roane, a loyal Republican, appears to have been slated for the position.[25] The resignation of Ellsworth gave John Adams the opportunity, after John Jay had declined a reappointment,[26] to call to this high office the ablest of southern Federalists; and from the day of Marshall's appointment Jefferson planned for his removal and aimed to curb the powers of his court. Two bitterer political enemies "never lived within the bounds of the Old Dominion than Jefferson and Marshall."[27]

Judge Roane, Thomas Ritchie, and John Taylor, of Caroline, along with Jefferson, waged the battle against federal judicial power in Virginia and made the opposition to the American doctrine of judicial review of legis-

[25] Wm. E. Dodd, "Chief Justice Marshall and Virginia," *Am. Hist. Rev.* (July, 1907) 12:776, 777.

[26] Warren, *op. cit.*, 1:172 ff.

[27] Dodd, *op. cit.*, 776.

lation a national issue. In a letter to Mrs. John Adams, Jefferson said:

I did consider his [Mr. Adams'] last appointments to office as personally unkind. They were from among my most ardent political enemies, from whom no faithful cooperation could ever be expected; and laid me under the embarrassment of acting through men whose views were to defeat mine, or to encounter the odium of putting others in their places. It seemed but common justice to leave a successor free to act by instruments of his own choice.[28]

At another time Jefferson lamented the fact that his enemies had retired into the judiciary and that there the remains of Federalism were to be preserved and from that battery all the works of Republicanism were to be beaten down and destroyed. In his first annual message the President brought to the particular attention of the members of Congress the judiciary system of the United States, and especially that portion of it recently erected.[29] On the advice of the President and under the leadership of his party, the law under which the federal judicial system was remodeled was repealed,[30] but the Supreme Court, in charge of the newly appointed Chief Justice, was thought to be protected by the Constitution and hence was excepted from the attack which was directed at the state and minor federal courts.

The power of impeachment had been held out in the debates prior to the adoption of the Constitution, as the natural and effective method of keeping the judicial power under control. That power was now to be exercised by the majority party to prevent the interference of the courts with the undoubted will of the people. It was generally believed that "if the judges of the Supreme

---

28 *Works*, 10:85.   29 *Ibid.*, 9:340.   30 U. S. *Stat.*, 2:132.

Court should dare, as they had done, to declare an act of Congress unconstitutional, or to send a mandamus to the Secretary of State as they had done,''[31] it would be the duty of the House of Representatives and the Senate to remove them for exceeding their constitutional limits. In 1804 several Pennsylvania justices were brought to trial. The administration regarded these cases of such importance that several influential Republicans took up the case against the judges. After a long struggle, the state senate refused to declare the judges guilty, three less than the required two-thirds voting in favor of impeachment.[32] The issue was finally put to the test in the trial of Justice Chase, who had been indiscreet and was certainly guilty of conduct unbecoming to a judicial officer. In a charge to a grand jury he had used this language:

You know, gentlemen, that our state and national institutions were framed to secure to every member of the society, equal liberty and equal rights; but the late alterations of the federal judiciary by the abolition of the office of the sixteen circuit judges, and the recent change in our State constitution, by the establishment of universal suffrage, and the further alteration that is contemplated in our State judiciary (if adopted) will, in my judgment, take away all security for property and personal liberty. The independence of the national judiciary is already shaken to its foundation, and the virtue of the people alone can restore it. The independence of the judges of this state will be entirely destroyed if the bill for the abolition of the two supreme courts should be ratified by the next general assembly. The change of the State Constitution, by allowing universal suffrage, will, in my opinion, certainly and rapidly destroy all protection to property, and all security to personal liberty; and our repub-

---

[31] John Quincy Adams, *Memoirs*, 1:322.

[32] Henry Adams, *History of the United States* (New York, 1921), 2: 219–220.

lican constitution will sink into a mobocracy, the worst of all possible governments.[33]

Jefferson soon wrote to Nicholson, suggesting that "this seditious official attack upon the principles of our Constitution" ought not to pass unpunished. The House of Representatives immediately voted that Justice Chase be impeached. Party feelings were at a high pitch throughout the trial and the case seemed to center not so much on the removal of Chase as on the possibility of the Democrats placing a curb upon Chief Justice Marshall and the federal courts.[34] The trial was conducted unwisely, and as no criminal actions were shown in the conduct of the judge, the whole proceeding failed of its object.[35] Justice Chase was acquitted, impeachment was proved impractical for partisan purposes, and the result was that Congress was not inclined to interfere in future controversies between the executive and the courts. Resolutions to make all judges removable by the President on the joint vote of both houses were frequently presented by the Republicans, but sufficient support could not be mustered to secure favorable action.[36]

With Jefferson's antagonism to Marshall and to the federal judiciary well known, it was to be expected that the Republicans would make an effort to curb the growing powers of the courts. The attack of the Republicans was outlined first in the debate over the repeal of the act of the previous administration reorganizing the judiciary,[37] and took more definite form in the impeachment proceedings. Republicans charged the Federalists with

---

[33] *Annals* of Congress, 1804–1805, 673–676; Henry Adams, *op. cit.*, 2:148.

[34] *Ibid.*, 2:226.

[35] *Ibid.*, chap. 10, "Trial of Chase."

[36] H. V. Ames, *Amendments to the Constitution*, 149–151.

[37] The main object of the act of 1801 was the reorganization of the circuits with the purpose of relieving the Supreme Court Justices of circuit

an attempt to establish a department of the government in which they could intrench themselves and could continue to support the principles of irresponsibility which they cherished.[38] It was thought to be the aim of the Federalists to set up "a permanent corporation of individuals invested with ultimate censorial and controlling power over all the departments of the government, over legislation, execution, and decision, and irresponsible to the people."[39] Through Chief Justice Marshall and the Supreme Court this censorial and controlling power was to be exercised.

Republicans opposed this design of the Federalists, maintaining that it was directly contrary to the principles of representative government. According to one of the Republican leaders they believed that each department ought to be independent, but that no department ought to be independent of the nation itself. It was emphatically denied that the Constitution authorized courts of justice to control the other departments of the government.[40]

---

duties. Cf. Max Farrand, "The Judiciary Act of 1801," 5 *Am. Hist. Rev.* (July 1900) 682 ff.

Prior to 1801 there were seventeen districts with a district judge in each. Fourteen of these districts were grouped into three circuits—Eastern, Middle, and Southern.

The act of 1801 added five new districts; four resulted from the division of former districts in New York, Pennsylvania, Virginia, and Tennessee. The fifth district was made out of the territories of Ohio and Indiana. The twenty-two districts were divided into six circuits and to relieve the Supreme Court Justices of circuit duties, circuit judges were to be appointed for this purpose. There were to be three judges for each of five circuits and one for the Western thereby creating sixteen circuit judgeships to be appointed by President Adams. To fill the positions in the circuits six of the district judges were promoted. The other positions were filled by personal friends or political adherents of the President. To the vacant district judgeships three senators and one representative were selected.

Though reorganization of the judiciary was necessary in certain respects this act was then and has since been regarded as a party measure enacted for the primary purpose of securing Federalist judges in the new circuit courts.

[38] Adams, *op. cit.*, 1:287. [40] *Annals* of Congress, 7 Cong., 1 Sess., 59.
[39] *Ibid.*, 289, 290.

The long debate on this repealing act brought forth some notable defenses of an independent judiciary whose duty it was to check the legislature in case it should pass laws in violation of the constitution. The powers of government were limited, and if those limits were exceeded, it was contended that there was the utmost necessity that timely checks should be interposed. And for this special purpose, it was thought, an independent judiciary was established "to save the people from their most dangerous enemy, to save them from themselves." The proposition that judges may not declare laws invalid was denounced as merely a step toward making the legislature supreme and thus letting loose the tyranny of the mob.

Gouverneur Morris who formerly opposed judicial review insisted that "the decision of the Supreme Court *is*, and of necessity *must* be, final. . . . . If the legislature may decide conclusively on the constitution, the sovereignty of America will no longer reside in the people but in Congress, and the Constitution is whatever they choose to make it."[41]

On the other hand, Republicans argued that all departments of government must ultimately depend on public opinion and that no branch should be made independent of the popular will. They wished to know whether the judiciary was intended to be a coordinate or a paramount body. The object of courts of law, it was held, was to settle rights between suitors, not to protect people against the abuses of legislative and executive

---

[41] *Annals* of Congress, 7 Cong., 1 Sess., 180, 181.

Morris raised and answered the query: "Did the people of America vest all power in the Legislature? No; they had vested in the judges a check intended to be efficient—a check of the first necessity, to prevent an invasion of the Constitution by unconstitutional laws—a check which might prevent any faction from intimidating or annihilating the tribunals themselves."— Cf. Benton, *Abridgment of Debates in Congress*, 2:550.

powers.[42] The Federalist view of judicial supremacy, they contended, would submit the entire sovereignty of the nation to the control of the judiciary, and whatever the other departments might do, they thought, the courts might undo. This theory of judicial control which was intended to place all governmental functions dependent upon the will of judges who were independent of the law and of the nation and uncontrollable except through an amendment to the Constitution or a revolution, was held as justly reprehensible. Apprehensions of the exercise of arbitrary power were put in a strong light. "I have no fear of usurpation of power by the legislature," said one representative, "for this branch is biennially responsible to the people; nor have I any fear of usurpation of power by the executive, for his term is limited to four years; but I fear this check-department of the government will grasp at all power." And the probable usurpations of power by courts with the authority to declare laws invalid were vividly depicted.[43]

To counteract the argument that the repeal of the judiciary act of 1802 would be unconstitutional Senator Breckinridge of Kentucky insisted that "this pretended power of the courts to annul the laws of Congress cannot possibly exist . . . . the legislature have the exclusive right to interpret the Constitution in what regards the law-making power, and the judges are bound to execute the laws they make.[44]

Senator Breckenridge was one of those who were willing to stand out against the prevailing opinion of the time. In fact he introduced a bill to reorganize the whole judicial system of the country.[45] He opposed the doctrine that courts of justice might refuse to enforce acts of

[42] *Annals* of Congress, 7 Cong., 1 Sess., 25–186, 510–985.
[43] *Ibid.*, 552.   [44] *Ibid.*, 179.   [45] Elliot's *Debates*, 4:440.

Congress and in defense of his measure he formulated a series of propositions denying the right which courts were regularly inclined to assert. He argued,

> To make the Constitution a practical system, the power of the court to annul the laws of Congress cannot possibly exist. My idea of the subject in a few words, is . . . . that the Constitution intended a separation only of the powers vested in the three great departments, giving to each the exclusive authority of acting on the subject committed to each; that each is intended to revolve within the sphere of its own orbit, is responsible for its own motion only and is not to direct or control the course of others; that those for example, who make the laws, are presumed to have an equal attachment to and interest in the Constitution, are equally bound by oath to support it, and have an equal right to give a construction of it; that the construction of one department, of the powers particularly vested in that department, is of as high authority, at least, as the construction given it by any other department; that it is in fact more competent to that department to which such powers are exclusively confided, to decide upon the proper exercise of those powers, than any other department to which such powers are not entrusted and who are not consequently under such high and responsible obligation for their exercise; and that therefore, the legislature would have an equal right to annul the decisions of the court founded upon their construction of the Constitution.[46]

Although he found that the courts were inclined to give decisions which obstructed the operation of a law, he contended that such a law is not the less obligatory because the organ through which it was to be executed had

---

[46] Elliot's *Debates*, 4:444. Senator Breckenridge contended that "the legislature have the exclusive right to interpret the Constitution in what regards the law-making power, and the judges are bound to execute the laws they make. For the Legislature would have at least an equal right to annul the decisions of the courts, founded on their construction of the Constitution as the courts would have to annul the act of the Legislature, founded on their construction."—*Annals* of Congress, 179 (Feb. 3, 1802).

refused its aid. On the basis of these propositions he reached the conclusion that a prolonged conflict between two departments of government would result in a determination of the question as to where the sovereign power of legislation resided.

Republicans seemed aware of the danger to their cause in leaving the Supreme Court in the hands of Marshall and men of the Federalist party.[47] The sessions of the Supreme Court were virtually suspended for fourteen months, but after the unsuccessful issue of the impeachment cases the Republicans appeared to recognize their inability to cope with the great stronghold of Federalism, the national judiciary.[48] Chief Justice Marshall announced one of the primary Federalist principles, that of judicial review of acts of Congress, in the Marbury opinion, and seemingly took some satisfaction in recognizing officially the failure of the Republican efforts to curtail judicial powers.

President Jefferson did not submit so readily as Congress. In referring to the *Marbury Case,* he said: "The federal judges declared that commissions signed and sealed by the President were valid although not delivered. I deemed delivery essential to complete a deed—and withheld delivery of the commissions. They cannot issue a mandamus to the President or legislature, or to any other officers."[49] Ignoring entirely the decision of the court, Jefferson referred to it later as an "obiter dissertation" of the Chief Justice.[50] As President, he continued to follow his own interpretation of the Constitution, or that interpretation with which he thought the people were most in sympathy. He realized, as probably few men of the time did, that the Supreme Court

---

[47] Adams, *op. cit.,* 2:152.   [49] *Works,* 10:396; 11:141; 12:256.
[48] *Ibid.,* 143.   [50] *Ibid.,* 12:257.

would become, as a result of such decisions, the final judge of its own authority.

The personal antagonism between Jefferson and Marshall did not result in an open breach until Burr's trial. When Marshall sent a subpoena to the President to produce certain papers in court, Jefferson refused on the ground that the executive would not be independent of the judiciary, "if he were subject to the commands of the latter and to imprisonment for disobedience; if the several courts could bandy him from pillar to post, and withdraw him entirely from his constitutional duties."[51] Marshall's reproof of the executive was thought to be "not altogether respectful to the coordinate branch of government."[52] Jefferson insisted that if Marshall should suffer Burr to escape, he should be removed from office. When Burr was finally acquitted, Jefferson was determined that Marshall must be punished. With the President's approval an amendment was prepared that all judges of the United States should hold office for a term of years, and should be removed by the President on address by two-thirds of both houses. Jefferson maintained that this amendment would bring under control the court which "proclaims impunity to that class of offenders which endeavor to overturn the Constitution and are themselves protected in it by the Constitution itself."[53] His refusal to accept as final the opinion in the *Marbury Case* and his declination to appear before the court in the Burr conspiracy trial have since been recognized as valuable precedents necessary for the independence of the executive in the American constitutional system.

On his return to private life Jefferson became an uncompromising foe of Marshall and an outspoken opponent of the practice of judicial nullification. On May 25,

---

51 *Works*, 10:404.   52 Adams, *op. cit.*, 3:446.   53 *Works*, 10:387.

1810, writing to Madison relative to an appointment to the Supreme Court, he warned the new President against "the cunning and sophistry" of the Chief Justice, and intimated that it would be difficult to find a man with enough firmness of character to maintain his independence by the side of Marshall. In a letter to Judge Tyler, whose cause he was urging at this time, he wrote:

We have long enough suffered under the base prostitution of law by party passions in one judge and the imbecility of another. In the hands of one the law is nothing more than an ambiguous text, to be explained by his sophistry into any meaning which may subserve his personal malice. Nor can any milk-and-water associate maintain his own dependence, and by a firm pursuance of what the law really is, extend its protection to the citizens or the public.[54]

Not a word in the Constitution, he insisted, had given the power of final interpretation to the judges rather than to the executive or legislative branches.

His feelings grew in intensity with every decision from the court which affected the fundamental rights claimed by the states. When the opinions favoring national authority, such as *McCulloch v. Maryland, Dartmouth College v. Woodward,* and *Cohens v. Virgina,* followed in close succession, his letters, contained frequent references to the courts. To Judge Spencer Roane, who granted a modified form of the federal judicial veto, Jefferson wrote, September 6, 1819, that

In denying the right they usurp of exclusively explaining the Constitution, I go further than you do. . . . . If this opinion be sound, then indeed is our Constitution a complete *felo-de-se.* For intending to establish three departments, coordinate and independent, that they might check and balance one another, it has given, according to this opinion, to one of them alone, the

---

[54] *Ibid.,* 11:142.

right to prescribe rules for the government of the others, and to that one, too, which is unelected by, and independent of, the nation. For experience has already shown that the impeachment it has provided is not even a scarecrow.[55]

The Constitution on this hypothesis is a mere thing of wax in the hands of the judiciary, which the judges may twist and shape into any form they please.[56] According to Jefferson's construction of the Constitution, each department was meant to be truly independent and to have an equal right to decide for itself what was the meaning of the Constitution in the cases submitted to its action.

In 1820 a work was presented to Jefferson in which the judges were considered as the ultimate arbiters of all constitutional questions. This, Jefferson held, was a "very dangerous doctrine indeed, and one which would place us under the despotism of an oligarchy. Our judges are as honest as other men and not more so. They have with others the same passions for party, for power, and the privilege of their corps."[57] Their power, he thought, is the more dangerous because they are in office for life, and are not responsible, as are the legislative and executive departments, to the people through the elective control. It is contended that the Constitution restrains the authority of the judges to judicial duties as it restrains the executive and legislative to their respective duties. But regardless of this principle, the judges, he thought, undertook to dictate to the executive in the discharge of his duties.

Jefferson regularly expressed the fear that the courts of the United States were attempting to break down the constitutional barriers between the coordinate powers of the state and the Union. In his autobiography, prepared

---

[55] *Works*, 12:136, 137.   [56] *Ibid.*, 137–138.   [57] *Ibid.*, 162.

in 1821, he discussed the draft of the Constitution submitted to the Philadelphia convention and certain amendments thereto. He then referred to an amendment which was overlooked at the time, and in the omission of which lurked the danger that was leading to the destruction of the combination of national powers in a general government and independent powers in the states.[58] This amendment, which was intended to submit the federal judiciary to a practical and impartial control, Jefferson regarded as indispensable to the continuance of federal government in the United States. He wrote:

> It is not enough that honest men are appointed judges. All know the influence of interest on the mind of man, and how unconsciously his judgment is warped by influence. To this bias add that of the *esprit de corps*, of their peculiar maxim and creed that "it is the office of a good judge to enlarge his jurisdiction," and the absence of responsibility, and how can we expect impartial decisions between the general government, of which they are themselves so eminent a part, and an individual state from which they have nothing to hope or fear? We have seen, too, that, contrary to all correct example, they are in the habit of going out of the question before them, to throw an anchor ahead and grapple further hold for future advances of power. They are then, in fact, the corps of sappers and miners, steadily working to undermine the independent rights of the states, and to consolidate all power in the hands of that government in which they have so important a freehold estate.[59]

Becoming greatly aroused as decision after decision was announced, approving the extension of the powers of the various departments of the federal government, he was convinced that the judges would soon be in a position "to lay all things at their feet."

---

[58] *Works*, 12:121, 122.

[59] *Ibid.*, 122.

II. OPPOSITION TO THE REVIEW OF STATE LAWS BY STATE
    COURTS

No less significant were the arguments in opposition
and the resistance to judicial authority over legislation
aroused by the opinions of state justices and the decisions
of state courts. The criticisms of the assertion of this
extraordinary authority by judges and the methods of
resistance adopted in some of the early precedents have
been dealt with in preceding chapters. Other representative objections and critical appraisals of the developing
doctrine of judicial supremacy deserve to be considered.

Opposition to judicial review was rather pronounced
in Connecticut. After stating that the judges are as likely
to declare laws void which are clearly constitutional as
the legislature to pass unconstitutional laws, Mr. Swift
maintained that,

The legislature must be considered as the supreme branch of
the government. Previously to their passing any act, they must
consider and determine whether it will be compatible with the
constitution. Being the supreme power, and bound to judge
with respect to the question, in the first instance their decision
must be final and conclusive. It involves the most manifest
absurdity, and is degrading to the legislature, to admit the idea,
that the judiciary may rejudge the same question which they
have decided, and if they are of a different opinion, reverse the
law, and pronounce it to be a nullity. It is an elevation of the
judiciary over the heads of the legislature; it vests them with
supreme power, and enables them to repeal all the laws, and
defeat all the measures of government. Whenever a law is
passed by the legislature, the first business of the courts will be
to decide whether it be constitutional and valid. The lowest
courts must permit the question to be seriously and deliberately
agitated before them, respecting the validity of the law, and
then they must solemnly decide whether an act passed by the

legislature, can be deemed binding, till it has received the sanction of the supreme judiciary, and has been declared to be constitutional . . . . where the judiciary are independent of the people and the legislature, and hold their offices by an appointment of the supreme executive, it is a total prostration of the government, to vest them with a power of deciding that legislative acts are null. The legislature will lose all regard and veneration in the eyes of the people, when the lowest tribunals of judicature are permitted to exercise the power of questioning the validity, and deciding on the constitutionality of its acts. . . . . A principle so dangerous to the rights of the people, and so derogatory to the dignity of the legislature, cannot be founded in truth and reason.[60]

Judge Chipman, of Vermont, expressed similar views,[61] and Chief Justice Kirkpatrick, of New Jersey, spoke of the issue of judicial review as enlisting "many champions on both sides."[63] But more serious objections to the practice of judicial review were raised in other states.

1. *Conflicts in Ohio and Kentucky—*

The opposition to judicial authority which involved an attack upon the doctrine that it was the function of the judiciary to guard constitutions, was supported by the democratic sentiment in the frontier states of Ohio and Kentucky. As early as 1808 in Ohio a strong sentiment was aroused against a few judges who ventured to declare a state law unconstitutional. A part of an act of the legislature, extending the jurisdiction of justices of the peace to cases involving less than fifty dollars, was held to be repugnant to the Constitution of the United

---

[60] Zephaniah Swift, *A System of the Laws of the State of Connecticut* (Windham, 1795), 1:52–53.

[61] Cf. *supra*, chap. 4.

[62] 4 Halstead 444, 5.

States and the constitution of the state of Ohio, and therefore null and void.[63]

Judge Pease and his associates declared this act void. A committee of the legislature was appointed to investigate this decision. The committee reported that the law was constitutional and the decision of the court erroneous, but it was their opinion that the courts had the right to judge of the constitutionality of statutes.[64] On the part of the report regarding a recognition of the right to hold statutes void, the legislature could not agree and the charges against the judges were dropped.

A case involving the interpretation of the same act came before the State Supreme Court and this court declared the law void as in violation of the provisions of the federal and state constitutions guaranteeing trial by jury. At the next meeting of the assembly a committee appointed in the house to investigate the decision reported a resolution "that the judges of this state are not authorized by the constitution to set aside any act of the legislature by declaring the law unconstitutional and void."[65] The resolution was approved in the house by a vote of eighteen to twelve but was defeated in the senate. At the next election Huntington, who had rendered an opinion against the constitutionality of the justice of peace act, was elected governor and the issue of judicial supremacy was extensively discussed in the campaign.[66] Though Huntington secured a majority of the votes the

---

[63] Chase's *Statutes of Ohio*, 1:39, act of Feb. 12, 1805. Sketch of Hon. Calvin Pease, 5 *Western Law Monthly*, 3 (June 1863), and Joseph H. Hixson, "The Judicial Veto in Ohio," Thesis (MS), Ohio State University, 1922.

[64] *House Journal* of the Fifth General Assembly, 78. For an account of this controversy I am indebted to William T. Utter, "Judicial Review in Early Ohio," *Miss. Valley Hist. Rev.*, 14:8 ff.

[65] *House Journal* of the Sixth General Assembly, 43 ff.

[66] Utter, *op. cit.*, 12 ff.

legislature elected at the same time was unfriendly to the courts. Another house committee was appointed to inquire into the official conduct of Huntington, Tod, and Pease. The committee reported articles of impeachment against both Tod and Pease mainly on the ground that they had asserted the right to declare void acts of the legislature. During the trial of the judges in the senate the arguments for and against judicial review were fully presented.[67] The friends of the judges followed the standard arguments, such as formulated by Hamilton and Marshall. On the other hand the opponents denied that judicial review resulted by necessary implication from the nature of written constitutions. They called attention to the difficulties of knowing what the laws are until the courts have declared their validity and deplored the danger of making the courts virtually omnipotent. It was admitted that the legislature was bound by the constitution but it was denied that that body was required to accept the courts' interpretation of the meaning of that instrument. The vote of the senate on both cases was fifteen to nine in favor of conviction—one vote less than the required two-thirds majority. Only a temporary victory had been gained, for the legislature passed a resolution indicating its intention to replace the judges at the expiration of their terms and in 1810 three new judges were elected to the Supreme Court who were reputed to be supporters of the authority of the legislature rather than the courts.[68] The legislative victory was made more complete by passing an even more drastic act than the one which had been declared unconstitutional.

The resistance to the doctrine of judicial veto of laws was maintained with even greater ardor in Kentucky.

---

[67] Utter, *op. cit.*, 15 ff. [68] *Ibid.*, 22.

Although the right had been asserted by a Kentucky court in 1801,[69] the opposition to the practice did not result in any positive action until the decision was rendered by Judge Clark, in 1822, on the validity of the relief laws. The session of the Kentucky legislature which met in 1820 passed a series of laws providing an easy method for the release of obligations which were burdening the debtor class of the state. One of these laws was contested before Judge Clark on the ground that it was in violation of the Constitution of the United States and the constitution of the state. Judge Clark granted an order which was interpreted as a refusal to enforce the law and stated the reasons for his decision.[70]

When this decision became known, the Kentucky house of representatives which was then in session protested that,

Whereas this house is informed that Judge James Clark has given a decision in contravention of the laws of this commonwealth, called the indorsement and replevin laws, and therein grossly transcended his judicial authority and disregarded the constitutional powers of the legislature of this commonwealth: Therefore, Resolved that a committee be appointed to inquire into the decision of the said Judge, and report thereon to this house.[71]

In a few days the chairman, Mr. Slaughter, reported for the committee. The principles and doctrines of Judge Clark's opinion were denounced as

incompatible with the constitutional powers of the legislative department of this government, subversive of the best interests of the people, and calculated in their consequences to disturb the tranquillity of the country, and to shake the public confidence

---

[69] Stidger v. Rogers, Kentucky Decisions, 52 ff. Cf. *supra*, 160.

[70] Williams v. Blair, Niles *Register*, 23, Supplement, 153.

[71] *Ibid.*, 155.

in the institutions and measures of the government, called for by the condition and the necessities of the people. That the judicial department has a power, beyond control, to defeat the general policy of the state, deliberately adopted by the representatives of the people within the pale of their authority, is a position which your committee are not prepared to admit.[72]

The committee recommended the removal of Judge Clark from office and proceedings toward impeachment were immediately instituted. Several days were granted to the Judge to file an answer and a vote was then taken, which resulted in an acquittal: 59, less than the necessary two-thirds, voting in favor of and 35 against the motion. The governor in his message of the following year approved the laws and also denounced the courts for refusing to enforce the legislative acts.[73] In the same year, the court of appeals upheld the decision of the lower court,[74] with the result that the contest was continued in a political fight at the polls. The people of the state were separated into two distinct organizations, the "old court party" and the "new court party." The elections resulted in a complete victory for the "new court party" and the issue gradually passed out of Kentucky politics.[75]

When the judges of the highest court of Georgia undertook to invalidate an act, the legislature passed a resolution as follows, which expressed the resentment felt at the assumption of such powers by judges:

Whereas, John McPherson Berrien, Robert Walker, Young Gresham and Stephen W. Harris, judges of the Superior Court, did, on the 13th day of January, 1815, assemble themselves together in the city of Augusta, pretending to be in legal con-

---

[72] *Ibid.,* 155.
[73] *Ibid.,* 156.
[74] Lapsley v. Brashear, 4 Litt. (Ky. Repts.) 47.
[75] Collins, *History of Kentucky,* 1:218 *et seq.*

vention, and assuming to themselves . . . . the power to determine on the constitutionality of laws passed by the general
assembly, and did declare certain acts of the legislature to be
unconstitutional and void; and . . . . the extraordinary power
of determining upon the constitutionality of acts of the state
legislature, if yielded by the general assembly whilst it is not
given by the constitution or laws of the state, would be an
abandonment of the dearest rights and liberties of the people,
which we, their representatives, are bound to guard and protect
inviolate;

Be it therefore resolved, That the members of this general
assembly view, with deep concern and regret, the aforesaid conduct of the said judges . . . . and they can not refrain from an
expression of their entire disapprobation of the power assumed
by them of determining upon the constitutionality of laws regularly passed by the general assembly, as prescribed by the constitution of this state; we do, therefore, solemnly declare and
protest against the aforesaid assumption of powers, as exercised
by the said judges, and we do, with heartfelt sensibility, deprecate the serious and distressing consequences which followed such
decision; yet we forbear to look with severity on the past, in
consequence of judicial precedents, calculated in some measure
to extenuate the conduct of the judges, and hope that for the
future this explicit expression of public opinion will be obeyed.[76]

Though there was widespread opposition to the doctrine of review of legislative acts by the courts the underlying principles advanced in support of the doctrine were
seldom critically examined. There were many indications
that opinions were rather evenly divided as to the acceptance of judicial review but owing to its unusual and
novel features most of the discussion centered around its
defense. Among the men who systematically examined
the arguments or principles in favor of the American

---

[76] Simeon E. Baldwin, *The American Judiciary* (New York, 1905),
112, 113.

doctrine of judicial review and pointed out the weaknesses and fallacies of the reasoning involved are Judge Theodorick Bland, of Baltimore, Maryland, and Justice Gibson of Pennsylvania. A résumé of these opinions places in clearer light the postulates and assumptions on which the arguments for judicial review were based.

2. *Opinion of Judge Bland*—

Judge Bland's opinion was rendered in 1816 and although reprinted in pamphlet form because of the interest it aroused seems to have been given little consideration by writers on the American practice of declaring laws invalid.

"The right of courts to declare laws invalid," observed Judge Bland, "is one that has been much talked of among the people, and frequently mentioned in the courts of justice, but I have rarely seen it treated with that care and close attention, which its nature and dignity seemed to demand."[77] Despite the belief that the matter had been determined by the courts of the state and of the United States, Judge Bland did not regard the matter as settled. Though yielding obedience to superior and overruling authority he doubted the constitutional correctness of these judgments, and believed that a statement of his convictions might cause judges to enter with great caution upon the exercise of the right, if not to a reconsideration of the reasoning on which the earlier favorable opinions were founded.

An act of the legislature of Maryland which invested county courts with original equity jurisdiction in all cases in which the courts of chancery had power to act gave

---

[77] Theodorick Bland, *The Opinion of Judge Bland on the Right of the Judiciary to declare an act of Assembly Unconstitutional and also, on the Constitutionality of the Act investing the County Courts with Equity Jurisdiction* (Baltimore, 1916), preface.

262 AMERICAN DOCTRINE OF JUDICIAL SUPREMACY

the occasion for the presentation of Judge Bland's views.[78] The act proposed such radical changes in the organization and powers of the judiciary, that it was thought necessary to examine whether the act was in accordance with the constitution. To Judge Bland the act of the legislature was clearly an interference with the method of trial by jury as protected by the declaration of rights of the state constitution. Considering the law in violation of the constitution the query was first raised, Have the judges a right to pronounce an act of assembly unconstitutional and void? Being aware that the question had been settled in favor of the courts Judge Bland claimed that "the public mind does not repose in quiet under the determination that has been given,"[79] and that the grounds of such extraordinary authority in courts should be reexamined again and again.

Turning to the arguments in defense of judicial review of legislation Judge Bland noted that the opinion of Hamilton in the seventy-eighth number of *The Federalist* seemed to regard the right as flowing from the tenure of the judicial office and a constitution with limits on the governmental powers. In the Invalid Pension case the judges who refused to execute the law, instead of advancing any reason or authority to prove that the judiciary had a right to annul a law, seemed rather to take the right for granted, and adduced reasons to show that such a right ought to be exercised in that case.[80] Justice Paterson's opinion in *Vanhorne's Lessee v. Dorrance* was characterized as eloquence rather than logical argument. Though John Marshall was credited with advancing all

---

[78] Evans and Dwinn v. Randall and Payson, Baltimore County Court, March 1816.

[79] *Opinion*, 11.

[80] *Opinion*, 12.

the possible arguments in favor of judicial review in *Marbury v. Madison,* no precedents were cited and the issue was dealt with in a general way "with consequences asserted and positions assumed."[81]

Judge Bland distinguished between two types of judicial review, one legal in character, involving refusal to execute a law as a matter of right and duty; the other revolutionary in character, when officers resist the enforcement of the law because they deem the laws inimical to the public welfare, and make an appeal to the people to sustain their action. The latter method was regarded as a policy upheld by the doctrine favoring resistance against arbitrary power sanctioned as a rule by the bills of rights. This distinction, though frequently underlying the arguments in favor of review of legislation by the courts, was seldom clearly recognized. Judicial review

presumes a right in one department to construe, control, or vacate the acts of another department, which is itself invested with discretionary power to determine on the limitations and circumstances under which it may or may not act; it presumes specific limitations to be imposed on one set of agents, which such agents may interpret and are enjoined strictly to observe; and yet supposes a power in another set of organs, also to expound such limitations, and to annul any acts that may run counter to them.[82]

Judge Bland here referred to the fallacy of the assumption that judges as agents of the people may pass on the acts of legislatures as agents of the people, the powers and limitations of each being defined in the written constitution.

The issue was then confined to the right of the courts of justice of Maryland to declare acts of the assembly

---

[81] Cf. opinion of Judge Gibson, *infra,* 272.   [82] *Opinion,* 14.

void.[83] Certain principles or axioms were recognized in the constitution of Maryland, namely, that sovereignty resides in the people; that the written constitution expressing the will of the people must be considered as a rule of government for all; and that the provision for the separation of powers imposes the duty on each department not to encroach on the rights and powers of the other departments. The propriety of accepting the doctrine of judicial review was then examined, first, as to the theory of the separation of powers; second, as to the principle of checks and balances; third, as to the limitations on public officers.

There were, Judge Bland found, two prevailing views concerning the separation of powers. One group of political writers contended that there were only two departments of power, that which makes, and that which executes the laws, the judiciary being considered as only a part of the executive.[84] Other writers maintained that there could be no liberty where the legislative and executive powers were united in the same authorities or if the power of judging was not separated from the legislative and executive powers. It was the former theory which was applied in England. And as the state constitutions were adopted in the light of the English practice it was very likely intended to follow the English custom which did not permit the courts to declare an act of Parliament void. Montesquieu's interpretation of the English system so far as it was accepted in America was intended merely to keep the departments distinct, with each under the injunction to respect the ambit of authority of the others.

---

[83] *Ibid.,* 16 ff.

[84] For a modern interpretation of the separation of powers along similar lines, see Frank J. Goodnow, *Politics and Administration* (New York, 1900).

As evidence of the common opinion it was noted that the papers of *The Federalist* dealing with the theory of the separation of powers do not refer in any way to the right of the judiciary to survey the acts of the other departments, and that—

The supremacy of the legislative power within its sphere, was admitted to be an obvious and necessary consequence of its very organization, and the only legitimate check upon its abuse of power, was, its being divided into several branches, and made immediately responsible to the people for the public agents of one department were not, at that time, deemed more virtuous or trustworthy, than those of another. The security chiefly relied on, was the nature and manner of the grant of power, and the responsibility to the people for its misuse.[85]

Though the state constitution specifically provided for various checks upon the several departments there was no basis for an implied or presumed right of one department to determine whether the other departments have exceeded their limits.[86] According to Judge Bland,

instead of a reasonable check, this claim of the judiciary introduces a fundamental discordancy of principle; for even those who advocate this doctrine must admit, that the judiciary may, by means of such a check, at any time, arrest the further progress of the government, by declaring its revenue laws, or any other of equal importance, which can be drawn within its control, to be wholly unconstitutional.[87]

This prophecy came nearer to a forecast of future developments than the claim that the power would seldom be exercised.

The next argument that was refuted was the contention of Hamilton and Marshall that courts must exercise such authority to enforce the limits on departments as

---

[85] *Opinion*, 19, 20.   [86] *Ibid.*, 20 ff.   [87] *Ibid.*, 23.

defined in the written constitution.[88] In taking issue with this dictum Judge Bland stated in an effective form the Democratic-Republican doctrine. "The right to enforce the observance of limitations," he maintained,

> rests with, and belongs exclusively to the people, and cannot, in any manner, be enforced by the judiciary. A constitutional limitation is then, the voice of the people addressed to the public agents respectively, in relation to their separate and distinct duties. . . . . It is the business and duty, of each department to attend to the constitution, only so far as regards its own proper checks and limitations, and not as relates to those of others.[89]

Since the constitution in no respect makes the legislature accountable to the judiciary for the execution of its duties "it follows, therefore, that the judicial department can have no right to re-establish any prostrated legislative boundary, or to confine that department within the limits assigned to it."[90] Referring to the doctrine announced by Marshall, that "the President is invested with certain important political powers, in the exercise of which he is to use his own discretion, and is accountable only to his country in his political character, and to his own conscience,"[91] Judge Bland could see no distinction between the legislature and the executive in this respect and doubted whether any clear dividing line could be drawn between discretionary and non-discretionary duties, hence he concluded that "the general assembly are invested with discretion to judge of the true extent of the limitations to their legislative power, for the exercise of which they are accountable only to the people; their deci-

---

88 Cf. Marbury v. Madison, 1 Cranch 137, 176 (1803).

89 *Opinion*, 24, 25.

90 *Ibid.*, 26.

91 Marbury v. Madison, 1 Cranch 137, 165 (1803).

sions, therefore, as to the constitutionality of a law must be conclusive."[92] "Suppose," he continued, "the judicial department should declare a law to be invalid, and the people, to whom the legislators are expressly and specifically made *accountable* for their conduct, should approve of it as being valid, beneficial and expedient— such a case would not be unlike that of having a man first accused and punished, and then tried and acquitted."[93]

Instead of judicial review resulting from the circumstances and nature of things and arising from the "very essence of judicial duty,"[94] Judge Bland observed that

to lay down a rule applicable to a case, or to all cases, is a legislative act; to prescribe rules of conduct, either by enacting new laws, or by altering or abolishing the old, are legislative acts; the legislature may apply the constitution to a proposed law, but it should in no instance apply the rule to the case. "It is emphatically the province and duty of the judicial department, to say what the law is," not what it shall be; it introduces, alters, or abolishes no rule; its functions are passive; it has none of the attributes of the legislative department. In a case where the will of the legislature declared in its statutes, stands in opposition to that of the people declared in the constitution, the judicial department is invested with no new or extraordinary powers; it stands in no new point of relationship to the other departments, nor can it, by such a state of things, acquire any legislative or other power which it had not before; its character is, according to the constitution, immutable. To ascertain how far any bill, which the general assembly may propose to pass into a law, may be constitutional or otherwise, is exclusively the duty of the legislators; who, alone, are accountable for any error or misconduct in so doing. The right and duty of comparing the constitution with the proposed law, of interpreting both, and deciding how far they accord, is directly and necessarily involved

---

[92] *Opinion*, 26.
[93] *Ibid.*, 26, 27.
[94] Marbury v. Madison, 1 Cranch 137, 178.

in the power to legislate, and is a part of it. The chief object
of legislative construction, is to ascertain the limits within which
rules may be laid down; the principal object of judicial interpretation, is to find the proper rule for the case. The right and
duty in the one instance, is necessary and direct; in the other,
it is incidental only. But they are incompatible, they cannot
exist together; for, if they did, exposition might be retorted
upon exposition, without end. The direct legislative right of
interpretation, must then, be final and conclusive. To say, therefore, that the court must decide the case according to the constitution or the law, is taking for granted what is not conceded.
The previous conclusive and binding decision of the legislature,
has left the court no such alternative; it can have no right to
re-examine and adjudicate upon that which has already been
determined by the proper and only authority accountable for
such an act.[95]

The power to determine what laws may be constitutionally passed is essentially a legislative power and if
the courts review the laws they necessarily assume legislative authority. In this line of reasoning Judge Bland
adopted the logic which is now generally accepted in all
countries which have rejected judicial review of legislation and have adopted legislative supremacy. The legislative right of interpretation on constitutional questions
must be final and conclusive. The degrading and humili-
ating position in which the legislature was placed by
accepting the Federalist theory of judicial review was
foreshadowed in the prediction that every court, every
justice of the peace, and every officer acting judicially
may determine upon the constitutionality of a law and
may thereby check legislative authority.

The oath of the judges to support the constitution was
considered by exponents of judicial review as additional

---

[95] *Opinion*, 27, 28.

evidence that the judges were to disregard an act which they deemed invalid.[96] But Judge Bland replied, "oaths of office, from their very nature, cannot either increase or diminish the powers or duties of the officer by whom they are taken. They are only solemn promises to perform duties which exist independently of such oaths."[97] And since all officers take the same oath the above argument is "stript even of the semblance of plausibility."

The claim that the theory was essentially attached to a written constitution was considered as without any foundation and from the very object of a written constitution "a directly contrary inference seems to be fairly deducible." The sole object of a written constitution is to make the principles and primary rules of government so plain and explicit that they may not readily be ignored or mistaken. If certain principles are put into writing why would not so fundamental and vital a matter as judicial review of legislation be made definite and specific by being put into writing.

Because the judicial check on the other departments of government must necessarily be ineffective in restraining them with respect to political issues and because certain violations of the constitution could rarely, if ever, be made a ground for a case before the court, judicial review could not operate evenly and fairly in the protection of the rights of citizens.[98] Instances were cited in which laws seriously interfered with individual rights and no protection was accorded by the judiciary. The mischievous results which might ensue from the practice of courts in declaring legislative acts void was, Judge Bland thought, well illustrated in the decisions of the

[96] Marbury v. Madison, 1 Cranch 137, 180.

[97] *Opinion*, 30.

[98] Judge Bland refers to the case of Josiah Philips (*supra*, 89) and comments on Tucker's version of the case.

Supreme Court of the United States invalidating state
laws because they were in conflict with the contract clause.
Grave consequences would result if legislative acts granting charters to corporations were held to be contracts
under this provision. A distinction was made as to the
charters of quasi-public corporations, such as turnpike
companies, which should be regarded as political contracts, subject to be canceled or repealed whenever the
public good might require. The opinion of Chief Justice
Marshall in the case of *Fletcher v. Peck*[99] was criticized
and especially because it ignored the well settled rulings
of English law, which were founded on justice and reason
and permitted a consideration of a mistake or fraud in
any legislative grant or transfer of property. And Judge
Bland concluded:

From which it does appear to me, that it is, in general, by
no means so estimable and efficacious as is commonly believed;
that it may be productive of great mischief; that there are cases
in which, if it were enforced in the manner some have contended,
it would become a cloak for fraud and iniquity; and that, in
all cases, its operation, in its present form, is too tardy and too
much obstructed by technical difficulties.

It lies not within the limits prescribed to the opinions I may
deliver here, to enter upon a discussion, whether this judicial
check ought, or ought not, to exist. But this much I may be
allowed to say, with deference to the opinions of others, that it
would be much better for the people that it did not exist at all,
than, that it should be allowed in its present form. A judicial
check upon the abuse of legislative power, such as this; which
can only be exercised under the encumbrance of technical forms;
which, after laying dormant for half a century, or more, may
be called up to invalidate a law which has been deemed perfectly constitutional by the community during all that time;
which is not coextensive with the power it assumes the right to

---

[99] 6 Cranch 87 (1810).

curb, not having the means and capacity to draw within its
control some legislative acts which strike directly at the very
heart of the Republic, while it stretches itself about others, so
as to prevent the general assembly from doing justice to the
pecuniary interests of the state, is not that kind of safeguard
to the rights and liberties of the people, on which they should be
induced to rely with implicit confidence. Yet, I have no doubt,
that there are cases, and a mode, in which the information and
experience of the judicial department might be brought to act
as a useful check and auxiliary to the legislative power. But it
is admitted on all hands, that no such judicial right *is specifically
and expressly given,* and it does appear to me, *that it cannot be
derived either from the genius or any of the provisions of the
constitution of Maryland.*[100]

Following a brief summary of the decisions of the courts
of Maryland and of the United States Judge Bland said
"to this weight of authority, I feel myself therefore compelled to submit."[101]

He then turned to the question of the validity of the
state act under consideration. Taking into account the
practice of chancery jurisdiction in England and in Maryland prior to the Revolution, it was asserted that the
intention of the constitution was to establish one chancery
court, from which there was to be no appeal. In so far
as the new act gave original equity jurisdiction to the
county courts and permitted equity cases to be taken to
the court of appeals it violated express provisions of the
constitution which clearly distinguished between a chancellor and common law judges. The act was also regarded
as a violation of the provision of the bill of rights which
guaranteed a jury trial to all citizens in trials at common
law, because the act destroyed the distinction between
common law and equity procedure, and because it placed

---

[100] *Opinion,* 62.   [101] *Ibid.,* 65.

new and unwarranted duties on common law judges. Consequently Judge Bland declined to accept the equity jurisdiction imposed upon him by the state law and suggested that his opinion on the constitutionality of the law might be either reversed or affirmed by the court of appeals. In either case, he observed, he would abide by the wisdom and superior judgment of the appellate court.

Less than ten years later similar arguments were cogently expressed in a dissenting opinion by Justice Gibson. These opinions in opposition to judicial review of legislation are in many respects more logical and accurate types of legal argument than Hamilton's reasoning in *The Federalist* or John Marshall's opinion in *Marbury v. Madison*. They demonstrate most of the defects in the arguments favoring the review of legislative acts by the courts, but the dominant trend of political thinking was directed into other channels and the able opinions of Judges Bland and Gibson received comparatively little support.

3. *The dissenting opinion of Justice Gibson*—

One of the most effective attacks upon the doctrine of judicial review of legislative acts as expounded by its supporters was embodied in the dissenting opinion of Justice Gibson in the case of *Eakin v. Raub* in the Supreme Court of Pennsylvania,[102] wherein he joined Judge Bland in condemning all the reasons which were usually presented as rendering review of legislation advisable and necessary. According to the judgment rendered by the court, no constitutional question was involved, but since some doubts, relative to the judicial right to set aside legislative acts, were raised in the argument, Chief

---

[102] Eakin v. Raub, 12 Sergeant and Rawle (Penn. Repts.) 330.

Justice Tilghman in his opinion observed that he adhered to the opinion

that when a judge is convinced, beyond doubt, that an act has been passed in violation of the constitution, he is bound to declare it void, by his oath, by his duty to the party who has brought the cause before him, and to the people, the only source of legitimate power, who, when they formed the constitution of the state, expressly declared that certain things *were excepted out of the general powers of government and should forever remain inviolate.*[103]

Justice Gibson was impelled by the remarks of the Chief Justice to express in a dissenting opinion his views on the right of the judiciary to declare legislative acts void. After making a distinction between acts which were regarded as being repugnant to the constitution of a particular state and acts repugnant to the Constitution of the United Sates, Justice Gibson remarked that he was aware that a right to declare all unconstitutional acts void was generally held as a professional dogma, but, he thought rather as a matter of faith than of reason. Having once embraced the same doctrine, he wished to state the arguments that impelled him to abandon it.[104] No judge, he said, except Chief Justice Marshall in *Marbury v. Madison* had ventured to discuss the right in question, although the judiciary had all along claimed the privilege of exercising the right. The opinion of Judge Paterson, in *Vanhorne's Lessee v. Dorrance,*[105] was characterized as abounding in beautiful figures and metaphorical illustrations without any real basis in argument. It was claimed that in the determination of this question precedents ought to count for absolutely nothing. The constitution being a collection of fundamental laws, not to be departed from in practice nor altered by judicial

---

[103] 12 S. and R. 339.   [104] *Ibid.*, 345, 346.   [105] 2 Dallas 307 (1795).

decision, instead of assuming the right in question the judge who asserted it ought to be prepared to maintain it on the principle of the constitution.[106]

Justice Gibson claimed that where a government exists by virtue of a written constitution the judiciary does not necessarily derive any other than its ordinary and appropriate powers.[107] Our judiciary is constructed on the principles of the common law, and in adopting any organ or instrument of common law, we take it with just such powers as were incident to it at common law, except where they are expressly or by necessary implication abridged or enlarged in the act of adoption. On this principle the powers of the judiciary have to do with the judicial execution of the municipal law, or the administration of distributive justice, without extending to anything of a political cast whatever. "I take it, therefore," said Justice Gibson,

that the power in question does not necessarily arise from the judiciary being established by a written constitution, but that this organ can claim, on account of that circumstance, no powers that do not belong to it at the common law; and that, whatever may have been the cause of the limitation of its jurisdiction originally, it can exercise no power of supervision over the legislature, without producing a direct authority for it in the constitution, either in terms or by irresistible implication from the nature of the government; without which the power must be considered as reserved, along with the other ungranted portions of the sovereignty, for the immediate use of the people.[108]

A different rule holds with regard to state laws contrary to the Constitution of the United States. The authority of the judiciary over an act of an assembly or

---

[106] 12 S. and R. 356.
[107] *Ibid.*, 346.
[108] *Ibid.*, 347.

a state constitution which is in conflict with the Constitution laws or treaties of the United States is recognized by implication at least, in the Constitution itself. The states agreed to certain limitations of their own sovereignty in the adoption of the federal Constitution. These limitations were to be made effective against the states through the instrumentality of their judges. The federal Constitution declares that the Constitution and the laws of the United States shall be the supreme law of the land and that the judges in every state shall be bound thereby.[109] This, Justice Gibson thought, was a grant of a political power, and was evidence that no state law should be executed contrary to the Constitution, laws, or treaties of the United States. He then analyzed in order the standard reasons advanced favorable to the review of legislative acts by the courts.

(*a*) *The constitution is a law of superior obligation.*[110]— As the constitution of the state contains no express grant of the power to nullify state laws, it must therefore be established by implication from the fact that the state constitution is a law of superior obligation; and in case of a conflict an act of the legislature would have to give way to the constitution. This Justice Gibson conceded, but it is a fallacy, he claimed, to suppose that a conflict can arise before the judiciary. He defined a constitution as an act of extraordinary legislation, by which the people established the structure of their government; and a statute as an act of ordinary legislation, the provisions of which were to be executed by the executive or the judiciary. The constitution, he found, contained no practical rules for the administration of justice, with which alone the judiciary had to do. It is generally true that

---

[109] Art. 6, sec. 2.   [110] 12 S. and R. 347.

the provisions of a constitution are to be carried into effect immediately by the legislature, and only mediately if at all, by the judiciary. In certain specific cases where the provisions of the constitution deal with judicial processes or procedure, the language is directed to the courts and they may well resist any change to the contrary by the legislature. In all other cases, there is no other rule to guide the courts in the interpretation of the law beyond the act of assembly under consideration. The constitution and the act of assembly do not furnish conflicting rules applicable to the point before the court; nor is it at all necessary that one or the other should give way.[111]

(b) *The power is necessary in order to uphold a written constitution.*[112]—The argument that such a power in the judiciary is necessary to secure the principles of a written constitution was readily refuted. The fear that the legislature would become arbitrary and that constitutions would be thereby rendered useless, called for a determination of the purpose of a written constitution. Such documents could have no other purpose than to outline certain principles and to affirm definite rights, which were thus brought to the particular attention of the people. Principles of government no longer need depend wholly upon tradition and the vague notions of those in authority. But Justice Gibson believed there was no magic or inherent power in parchment and ink to protect principles from violation. In the business of government, he thought a recurrence to first principles was necessary, and for this purpose he regarded a written constitution as an instrument of inestimable value. It served the purpose, also, of rendering these principles

---

[111] 12 S. and R. 348.
[112] *Ibid.*, 354, 355.

familiar to the mass of the people, and tended to arouse public opinion, which was considered as the only effectual safeguard against legislative usurpation. The constitution of Pennsylvania, he noted, had withstood the shocks of strong party excitement for thirty years, without a single case of the exercise of this right by the judiciary.[113]

(c) *Legislative acts are ipso facto void.*—The theory which was frequently accepted during the first period of the American government, that legislatures possessed no inherent right of legislation but derived all authority from the people in the form of grants in written constitutions, was met by Justice Gibson with equal vigor. On this theory the constitution fixed the sphere of action of the legislature, and no law could be valid for which power was not granted. The conclusion then followed that acts not warranted by the constitution were not acts of the people and were therefore *ipso facto* void. A law that is *ipso facto* void is regarded as if it never had been, and must be entirely ignored. But Justice Gibson regarded it as an audacious claim to assert that the deliberate and well matured judgment of one of the regularly constituted departments of government, expressed in the form of acts passed under a strict observance of the principles of the constitution, should be rejected as *ipso facto* void.[114] All respect was demanded for the acts of the judiciary when a law was declared unconstitutional. The legislature must acquiesce even though it may think the construction of the judiciary wrong. This claim rested solely on the ground that the legislature ought to respect the judgment of a coordinate department of the government. Why should not the same respect be rendered to the judgment of the legislature? It will not be pretended

---

[113] 12 S. and R. 354, 355.   [114] *Ibid.*, 349.

"that the legislature has not at least an equal right with the judiciary to put a construction on the constitution, nor that either of them is infallible; nor that either ought to be required to surrender its judgment to the other.''[115]

(*d*) *The refusal to execute an unconstitutional law.*— But the advocates of judicial nullification ask: "Do not the judges do a positive act in violation of the constitution, when they give effect to an unconstitutional law?" The fallacy of this question lay, said Justice Gibson, in supposing that the judiciary adopts the acts of legislature; whereas the enactment of law and the interpretation of it are two separate acts, and as the judiciary is not required to concur in the enactment, neither is it responsible for the breach of the constitution which may be the consequence of the enactment. The fault is imputable to the legislature and on it the responsibility rests.[116] This argument, he regarded, as nothing more than a repetition of the claim that an "unconstitutional law is *ipso facto* void,'' since a refusal to enforce a law can be based only on the right of one department to assert authority over the other departments. No such right is recognized in the branches of the national government, except in the judiciary.[117]

(*e*) *The oath of judges to support the constitution.*— That the judges are sworn to support the constitution, and are bound by it as the law of the land, was another argument in favor of this particular type of judicial review. In reply Justice Gibson observed that if the official duty of a judge does not comprehend an inquiry into the authority of the legislature, the oath in support of the constitution gives him no such special prerogative. The basis of every argument in favor of the right of the

---

[115] *Ibid.*, 349.   [116] *Ibid.*, 354.   [117] *Ibid.*, 351.

judiciary was found, in last analysis, to be an assumption of the whole ground in dispute. Even if the oath of a judge is to secure support of the constitution in the discharge of his official duty, it can apply only to the exercise of ordinary judicial powers. The constitution was intended to furnish a rule of construction where a particular interpretation of a law would conflict with some constitutional provision, and wherever possible such interpretation was to be avoided. The oath was more probably designed to secure the powers of each of the different branches from being usurped by any of the others, such as to prevent the House of Representatives from erecting itself into a court of justice, or the Supreme Court from attempting to control the legislature. In this view, the oath of the judges may be used with equal force against the right of the judiciary. ''The official oath, then, relates only to the official conduct of the officer, and does not prove that he ought to stray from the path of his ordinary business to search for violations of duty in the business of others; nor does it, as supposed, define the powers of the officer.''[118]

(*f*) *Cases must be free from doubt.*—The power of judicial veto was said to be restricted to cases that were free from doubt or difficulty. But Justice Gibson maintained that the abstract existence of a power cannot depend on the clearness or obscurity of the case in which it is to be exercised; for this question cannot present itself before the existence of the power shall have been determined. No considerations of policy ought to influence the exercise of this right.[119]

The notion of a complication of counterchecks had been carried to an extent, in theory, of which the framers

---

[118] 12 S. and R. 353.
[119] *Ibid.*, 352, 353.

of the Constitution never dreamt. When governmental powers were distributed to the appropriate branches, all things incident to the exercise of these powers were committed to each branch exclusively. The checks upon each department were definitely provided for so as to maintain the essential features of the principle of the separation of powers. Had it been intended to have the judiciary serve as an additional check, the matter would surely not have been left in doubt. The judges would not have been left to stand on the insecure ground of public opinion as to constructive powers. They would have been placed on the impregnable ground of an express grant, and as a consequence would not have been compelled to resort to the debates in the convention, or to the opinion that was generally entertained at the time, in order to uphold the assertion of such remarkable powers.[120] Justice Gibson claimed that what he wished to impress upon the attention particularly was,

the necessity of yielding to the acts of the legislature the same respect that is claimed for the acts of the judiciary. Repugnance to the constitution is not always self-evident; for questions involving the consideration of its existence require for their solution the most vigorous exertion of the higher faculties of the mind, and conflicts will be inevitable if any branch is to apply the constitution after its own fashion to the acts of all others. I take it, then, the legislature is entitled to all the deference that is due to the judiciary; that its acts are in no case to be treated as *ipso facto* void, except where they would produce a revolution in the government; and that, to void them, requires the act of some tribunal competent under the constitution (if any such there be) to pass on their validity. All that remains, therefore, is to inquire whether the judiciary or the people are that tribunal.[121]

---

[120] *Ibid.*, 351, 352.
[121] *Ibid.*, 350.

Since the judiciary was not expressly constituted as the judge of constitutionality, it must derive such authority from the reasonableness or fitness of the thing. But as legislation peculiarly involves the consideration of the limitations placed upon the law-making power, and the interpretation of the laws involves only the construction of the laws as enacted, it would seem to follow that the construction of the constitution belongs primarily to the legislature, which ought to have the authority to judge the constitutionality of is own acts.[122]

(*g*) *Power rests with the people to keep legislation within constitutional limits.*—Though it was claimed that the judiciary was a coordinate department and was in no sense superior to the other departments, it was difficult to see how such a contention could be true if the judges were to define the limits of the other departments.[123] And then one of the chief weaknesses in the arguments supporting judicial review was pointed out:

The constitution and the *right* of the legislature to pass the act, may be in collision. But is that a legitimate subject for judicial determination? If it be, the judiciary must be a peculiar organ to revise the proceedings of the legislature, and to correct its mistakes; and in what part of the constitution are we to look for this proud preeminence? Viewing the matter in the opposite direction, what would be thought of an act of assembly in which it should be declared that the Supreme Court had, in a particular case, put a wrong construction on the Constitution of the United States, and that the judgment should therefore be reversed? It would doubtless be thought a usurpation of judicial power. But it is by no means clear that to declare a law void which has been enacted according to the forms prescribed in the constitution is not a usurpation of legislative power. It is an act of sovereignty;

---

[122] *Ibid.,* 350.
[123] *Ibid.,* 350, 351.

and sovereignty and legislative power are said by Sir William Blackstone to be convertible terms. It is the business of the judiciary to interpret the laws, not scan the authority of the lawgiver; and without the latter it cannot take cognizance of a collision between a law and the constitution. So that to affirm that the judiciary has a right to judge of the existence of such collisions, is to take for granted the very thing to be proved.[124]

To assume that the validity of a legislative act can be made an issue before the court with the possibility of rendering a judgment in the ordinary course of the trial of a case, regardless of the inevitable political implications, thereby placed the judges in a position of superiority and rendered other arguments or defenses of judicial review largely superfluous.

Judge Gibson concluded:

For these reasons, I am of the opinion that it rests with the people, in whom full and absolute sovereign power resides, to correct abuses in legislation, by instructing their representatives to repeal the obnoxious act. What is wanting to plenary power in the government, is reserved by the people for their own immediate use; and to redress an infringement of their rights in this respect would seem to be an accessory of the power thus reserved. It might, perhaps, have been better to vest the power in the judiciary; as it might be expected that its habits of deliberation, and the aid derived from the arguments of counsel, would more frequently lead to accurate conclusions. On the other hand, the judiciary is not infallible; and an error by it would admit of no remedy but a more distinct expression of the public will, through the extraordinary exercise of the right of suffrage—a mode better calculated to attain the end, without popular excitement. It may be said, the people would not notice an error of their representatives. But they would as probably do so as notice an error of the judiciary; and, besides, it is a *postulate* in the theory of our government, and the very basis

---

[124] 12 S. and R. 348.

of the superstructure, that the people are wise, virtuous and competent to manage their own affairs; and if they are not so, in fact, still every question of this sort must be determined according to the principles of the constitution, as it came from the hands of its framers, and the existence of a defect which was not foreseen, would not justify those who administer the government in applying a corrective in practice which can be provided only by a convention.[125]

In this opinion one argument in favor of the principle of judicial review of legislative acts was frankly admitted, namely, that the laws of the nation were to be supreme and that the laws of the states repugnant to any national law should give way; and that the judiciary was an appropriate body to determine when there was a conflict between the two grades of law. So much was at least implied in the words of the Constitution. Every other feature of judicial review, especially that practice by which the Supreme Court established the right to set aside laws of Congress, as well as the practice by which the state courts asserted a revisory authority over the general assemblies of the states, had been, according to the opinion of Chief Justice Gibson, developed out of the theories, assumptions, and constructive interpretations of the judges. In many respects Justice Gibson dealt with the arguments and assumptions favoring judicial review along lines similar to those of Judge Bland.

Few men of the time realized that the acceptance of one feature of the practice of nullifying legislative acts—the fact that the courts of both state and nation were probably expected to deal with a conflict between a state law and a national law—did not necessarily involve the acceptance of the other feature of the practice, that a judicial decision must be regarded as final and authorita-

---

[125] 12 S. and R. 355, 356.

tive even above the legislatures of state and nation. The latter, however, was generally considered as a necessary result of the former, and the difference in importance between the two propositions was seldom noted. The opinions of Judges Bland and Gibson appear to be the most thorough critical examinations of the theories and principles of judicial review of legislation by men who opposed judicial supremacy on the grounds of principle and policy. There were many who disapproved of the principle of judicial review but seldom were their reasons put into clear and articulate form and the alternative methods of preserving the fundamental law were often ill defined.

In 1845 this opinion was quoted in an argument of counsel before the supreme court of the state. Gibson, who had been advanced to the position of chief justice, remarked: "I have changed that opinion for two reasons. The late convention, by their silence, sanctioned the pretensions of the court to deal freely with the acts of the legislature; and from experience of the necessity of the case."[126] Another of those who opposed the American practice of judicial nullification, and one who cogently expressed the reasons for his opposition, was impelled to fall in line with the trend of public opinion, in spite of misgivings that the nation on this issue was heading in the wrong direction. Any one who carefully considers the opinions of Judges Bland and Gibson can readily perceive that reason and logic had comparatively little weight with those who resolutely set about to make judicial review of legislation a part of the American political system.

---

[126] Norris v. Clymer, 2 Penna. St. 277, 281.

CHAPTER XI

OPPOSITION TO THE THEORIES AND THE PRACTICE OF JUDICIAL REVIEW OF LEGISLATION IN STATE AND FEDERAL GOVERNMENTS

(*Continued*)

III. RESISTANCE TO THE REVIEW OF STATE ACTS BY THE FEDERAL COURTS

SINCE the decision in the case of *Marbury v. Madison* had little effect on legal developments at the time and no other act of Congress was held void until 1856, the serious controversies over the review of legislation by the federal courts arose over the nullification of acts of the states by the national judiciary. A brief review of a few of the conflicts between state and federal authorities will indicate another phase of the opposition to judicial review.

The act organizing the courts of the United States that was passed in 1789,[1] defined the jurisdiction of the federal courts more definitely than was possible in the draft of the Constitution. The twenty-fifth section of this act explicitly recognized the right of a state court to declare laws of the United States void, subject to an appeal to the Supreme Court of the United States, wherein it was intended to vest revisory power over de-

---

[1] U. S. *Stats.* 1:73–93. On the changes made in the draft bill in the course of the passage through Congress consult, Charles Warren, ''New Light on the History of the Federal Judiciary Act of 1789,'' 37 *Harv. Law Rev.* (Nov. 1923) 49.

cisions affecting the validity of the laws or treaties of the federal government.[2] This section has been called "a logical preparation for the independent right of the federal court to deny the validity of congressional enactments,"[3] but it is apparent that the federal courts were not expressly granted such authority.

At the time of the establishment of the federal government in 1789 there was a lively sense of jealousy among the people of the states regarding the authority of national officers. Few cases were brought to the federal courts for adjudication and most of these related to admiralty and maritime matters, concerning which there was rather general agreement that the state courts could not settle matters effectively and finally. It was not long, however, before the states began to assert themselves against what they deemed to be the dangers lurking in encroachment on their rights by the federal courts. In 1802 Nathaniel Macon, speaking in the House of Representatives, referred to the issuance of a writ to the supreme court of North Carolina, directing a case then pending in the state court to be brought to the federal court. The state judges, he claimed, "refused to obey the summons and laid the whole proceeding before the legislature, who approved their conduct." Whether or not Macon referred to an authentic case, he expressed a sentiment which was to become popular in other states.

---

2 Cf. *supra*, 144–145.

3 Andrew C. McLaughlin, *The Courts, the Constitution and Parties*, 18. "It may reasonably be thought that the Constitution has not *expressly* given the judiciary the power to disregard unconstitutional Acts of Congress, and it may be surmised that this express giving of the power was purposely avoided, as in some other cases, where Madison intimates, and even says in terms, that the Constitution was silent from motives of expediency, of set purpose leaving a given result to be reached by inference and construction."—James Bradley Thayer, in review of Brinton Coxe, *Judicial Power and Unconstitutional Legislation*, 7 *Harv. Law Rev.* (Jan. 1894) 380.

1. *Conflict with Georgia—*

In 1793, the Supreme Court became involved in a controversy with the state of Georgia, with the result that the main contention of one of its decisions was directly overruled by an amendment to the Constitution. Hamilton, Marshall, and Madison had expressed the opinion that the highest authority of a state could not be called before the bar of a federal court.[4] Nevertheless, following a practice adopted in earlier controversies, Georgia was sued and on appeal to the Supreme Court, Edmund Randolph, the Attorney General, argued that, unless the state of Georgia caused an appearance to be entered, in behalf of the state, judgment should be directed against the state and damages awarded.[5] Although the Attorney General was an advocate of the doctrine of state sovereignty, he did not regard submission to the authority of the Supreme Court as a limitation of sovereignty. On the refusal of the state to accept service, judgment was entered against the state in a decision which vigorously maintained the principle of national sovereignty. Justice Blair claimed in his opinion that "when a State, by adopting the Constitution, has agreed to be amenable to the judicial power of the *United States,* she has, in that respect, given up her right of sovereignty."[6] Justice Wilson thought the question might be resolved to the maxim "Do the people of the *United States* form a Nation?" and asserted that in the adoption of the Constitution the individual states had renounced any claim that they might have had on the possession of sovereign pow-

---

[4]For the opinion of Hamilton, see *The Federalist* (Ford ed.) 81:545, 546; opinion of Marshall, 3 Elliot's *Debates* 555, "I hope that no gentleman will think that a state will be called at the bar of a federal court"; opinion of Madison, *ibid.*, 522.

[5] Chisholm v. Georgia, 2 Dallas 419 (1793).

[6] 2 Dallas 452.

ers. He maintained that sovereignty in a strict sense belonged to the people of the United States, and that neither the states nor the federal authorities could lawfully claim this high prerogative. It was his opinion that Georgia was not a sovereign state, and since she had granted a full measure of general powers to the central government, she therefore made herself amenable to the judicial authority under the Constitution.[7] In a dissenting opinion, Justice Iredell denied the soundness of the arguments of the majority of the court and held that no such action against a state could be legally maintained.[8]

The attitude of the court in assuming jurisdiction in the case was regarded as unconstitutional and extrajudicial. It was feared that a precedent might be set, which "would effectually destroy the retained sovereignty of the states, and would actually tend in its operation to annihilate the very shadow of state government and to render them but tributary corporations to the government of the United States."[9] The court rendered its opinion on February 18, 1793. The whole country was aroused; the worst fears of those who had opposed the adoption of the Constitution, it was asserted, were being realized. The Eleventh Amendment was immediately proposed and hurriedly carried through Congress. The decision of the court was generally regarded as "dangerous to the peace, safety and independence of the states."[10] A bill which passed the Georgia house of assembly, but apparently was not favorably acted on by the senate, declared that federal marshals attempting to execute the writ of the Supreme Court against the state of Georgia

---

[7] *Ibid.*, 453 ff.

[8] *Ibid.*, 429 ff.

[9] Herman v. Ames, *State Documents on Federal Relations* (Philadelphia, 1906) 7.

[10] Resolves of Massachusetts, *Massachusetts Archives*, 9:108.

"are hereby declared to be guilty of felony, and shall suffer death without the benefit of clergy by being hanged."[11] A prolonged controversy was avoided by the proposal and adoption of the Eleventh Amendment.[12]

2. *Conflict with New Hampshire*—

Again, as early as 1793, the federal judiciary came into conflict with one of the New England states. The case grew out of the capture of a vessel, the "Susanna," by the brigantine "McClary." The admiralty court of New Hampshire condemned the cargo of the vessel and ordered it to be sold.[13] In a trial before the federal Court of Appeals in cases of capture, a decision was rendered October 1777, adverse to the contention of the state. The case was dropped until 1793, when an issue was brought before the Circuit Court of the United States for the district of New Hampshire, and the decision of the Court of Appeals was upheld. On appeal to the Supreme Court of the United States the decision of the inferior court was affirmed. The legislature of the state, immediately after the decision of the Circuit Court, issued a remonstrance practically asserting the sovereignty of the state and denying the jurisdiction of the federal courts.[14] Following the decision of the Supreme Court, the legislature sent another communication to Congress objecting seriously to "a violation of state independence and an unwarrantable encroachment by the courts of the United States." The remonstrance contained a complete denial

---

[11] Ames, *op. cit.*, 10.

[12] "The judicial power of the United States shall not be construed to extend to any suit in law or equity, commenced or prosecuted against one of the United States by citizens of another state, or by citizens or subjects of any foreign state."

[13] For history of this case see Penhallow v. Doane's Administrators, 3 Dallas 54–69 (1793).

[14] *American State Papers*, Misc. 1:79.

of a federal judicial authority superior to that of the
state, prior to 1788. The legislature regarded Congress
as merely an advisory body, and it resolved ''not to submit the laws made before the existence of the present
government by this (then independent state) to the adjudication of any power on earth.'' The legislature also
threatened to resist an attempt to execute an ''unconstitutional decree of a court instituted by a former Congress, and which, in its effects, would unsettle property
and tear up the laws of the several states.''[15]

3. *Contest with Pennsylvania*[16]—

The case of the sloop ''Active'' in which Gideon Olmsted tried to secure an award of the value of a vessel and
cargo taken from the British by him and his companions
during the Revolutionary War brought about a determined conflict with the state of Pennsylvania. When the
federal district court for Pennsylvania ordered the payment to Olmsted of the money due on the sale of the ship
and cargo, the state passed a law requiring that the
money be paid into the state treasury and authorizing
the governor to resist any process which might issue from
any federal court. For five years Judge Peters refused
to issue a mandate to carry out the court's order. Olmsted then appealed to the Supreme Court for a mandamus, which was granted by Chief Justice Marshall.[17]

The Chief Justice found that an act of the state required the governor to use any means which he might
think necessary to protect the rights of the state and to

---

[15] *American State Papers*, Misc., 1:124.

[16] For the history of this case from standpoint of the United States,
see United States v. Peters, 5 Cranch 115. For the state, see *American
State Papers*, Misc., 2:2–7; *Annals*, 11 Cong., 2 sess., Appendix, 2253–2269;
Ames, *op. cit.*, 45 ff.—Hampton L. Carson, ''The Case of the Sloop Active,''
17 *Green Bag* (Jan. 1895) 17.

[17] McMaster, *A History of the People of the United States*, 5:403–6.

insure the person and property of the litigants against any process whatever, issued from a federal court.[18] After stating the facts, he declared:

> If the legislatures of the several states may, at will, annul the judgments of the courts of the United States, and destroy the rights acquired under those judgments, the constitution itself becomes a solemn mockery; and the nation is deprived of the means of enforcing its laws by the instrumentality of its own tribunals. So fatal a result must be deprecated by all; and the people of Pennsylvania, not less than the citizens of every other state, must feel a deep interest in resisting principles so destructive of the Union and in averting consequences so fatal to themselves.[19]

The ultimate right to determine the jurisdiction of the courts of the Union was not, he said, placed by the Constitution in the several state legislatures but in the Supreme Court of the United States. Consequently, it was asserted, that the state of Pennsylvania could claim no constitutional right to resist the legal process which might be directed from the Supreme Court.

President Madison was asked to intervene on behalf of the state. His reply that "the executive of the United States is not only unauthorized to prevent the execution of a decree sanctioned by the Supreme Court of the United States, but is especially enjoined by statute to carry into effect any such decree where opposition may be made to it,"[20] served as a warning to the state authorities. They realized that the state must either submit to

---

[18] United States v. Peters, 5 Cranch 115, 135, 136. Cf. Ross v. Rittenhouse, 2 Dallas 160 (1792) in which Chief Justice McKean of the Supreme Court of Pennsylvania denied the authority of the Committee on Appeals of the Continental Congress to reverse the decision of the trial court in the state; also refusal of McKean to allow the case to be removed to a federal district or circuit court, Respublica v. Cobbett, 3 Dallas 467 (1798).—See 5 *Journals* of Congress 64 ff.

[19] 5 Cranch 136. [20] *Works*, 2:438, 439.

the judicial decree or resist the federal government by force of arms. The state legislature then made a conciliatory move which resulted in an amicable settlement of the case. Submission was turned to humiliation, however, when the decree was not only executed but the state officers were also tried for forcibly obstructing the execution of the laws of the nation and were sentenced to fine and imprisonment.[21] The fact that the sentence was remitted by the President, because of his belief that the men had acted under a mistaken sense of duty, did not serve to allay the sense of humiliation which the state suffered. The resolutions adopted during the time that the marshal delayed in serving his writ show that the absence of a clear statement in the Constitution as to where lay the authority to give a final interpretation of the Constitution and laws when federal relations were involved, was regarded as a serious defect in the federal system as devised by the Philadelphia Convention.

In a report submitted to the Senate, June 11, 1809, the legislature of the state claimed that "in resisting encroachments on their rights they are not acting in the spirit of hostility to the legitimate powers of the United States Court, but are actuated by a disposition to compromise, and to guard against future collisions by an amendment to the Constitution."[22] After reviewing the history of the *Olmsted Case* and attempting to vindicate the policy pursued, they submitted a series of resolutions. "It is to be lamented," one resolution read, "that no provision is made in the Constitution for determining disputes between the general and state governments by an impartial tribunal." It was further resolved,

---

[21] See pamphlet, *Trial of General Bright in the Circuit Court of the United States* (Philadelphia, 1809).

[22] *American State Papers*, Misc., 2:2.

that from the construction which the United States' Courts give to their powers, the harmony of the states, if they resist encroachments on their rights, will frequently be interrupted; and if to prevent this evil, they should, on all occasions yield to stretches of power, the reserved rights of the states will depend on the arbitrary power of the courts.[23]

The authorities of the state feared that the acceptance of the principle announced by the court would mean the ultimate destruction of the federal nature of our government. They could not accept the idea that the federal government was to be the sole judge of the extent of its own powers, particularly if the courts were to set aside state laws as freely as the laws of the national congress. At the same time the legislature of the state suggested an amendment to be submitted to the states, favoring the establishment of an impartial tribunal to arbitrate difficulties between the state and federal governments.

The recommendation of Pennsylvania was rejected in notices of disapproval from a majority of the states.[24] Virginia adopted a reply in which it was claimed that the suggestion of Pennsylvania for the establishment of an impartial tribunal to arbitrate between state and nation was uncalled for, because "a tribunal is already provided by the Constitution of the United States, to wit; the Supreme Court, more eminently qualified from their habits and duties, from the mode of their selection and from the tenor of their offices, than any other tribunal which could be erected."[25] In the face of this reply Virginia could not

---

23 *Ibid.,* 6.

24 See *Journal of Senate of Pennsylvania,* 1809–10 for typical replies from the states; Ames, *op. cit.,* 5 ff.; Charles Warren, "Legislative and Judicial Attacks on the Supreme Court of the United States—A History of the Twenty-Fifth Section of the Judiciary Act," 47 *Am. Law Rev.* (Jan-Feb. 1913) 5.

25 Act of General Assembly of Virginia, 1809–10, 102.

hope for much assurance of support when in the next few years she found herself in a similar contest over the appellate jurisdiction of the court whose ability and impartiality had been so highly praised.

4. *Contest with Virginia*—

(a) *Martin v. Hunter's Lessee.*

A controversy involving timber and tobacco lands formerly owned by Lord Fairfax extended over nineteen years and finally the Virginia court of appeals decided against the Fairfax claimants.[26] On the basis of interference with rights violated under federal treaties a writ of error was sought from the Supreme Court. Chief Justice Marshall, because of personal interest, refused to take any part in the trial of the case. Justice Story, rendering the opinion for the majority of the court, Justice Johnson dissenting, held that the state had not acquired title to the land and hence could give no title to Hunter.[27] Accordingly a mandate was directed to the judges of the Virginia court of appeals to enter judgment for Martin.

The Virginia court under the leadership of Judge Roane and backed by a strong public sentiment refused to obey the order of the Supreme Court and replied that

the court is unanimously of opinion, that the appellate power of the Supreme Court of the United States does not extend to this court, under a sound construction of the constitution of the United States;—that so much of the 25th Section of the act of Congress to establish the judicial courts of the United States, as extends the appellate jurisdiction of the Supreme Court to this

---

[26] See Hite v. Fairfax, 4 Call 42 (1786) in which John Marshall argued that Fairfax had been illegally deprived of his property. Marshall acquired a personal interest in the Fairfax estate.—Beveridge, *The Life of John Marshall*, 4:145 ff.

[27] Fairfax's Devisee v. Hunter's Lessee, 7 Cranch 603 (1813).

court, is not in pursuance of the constitution of the United States.[28]

When the Virginia court of appeals, following this declaration, resisted the exercise of authority over the state by a federal tribunal, the Supreme Court, in the opinion rendered by Justice Story, upheld the jurisdiction of the courts of the Union by reasoning which was thoroughly national in tenor.[29] After paying a tribute of respect to the authority of the state court which was under review, Justice Story proceeded with federal doctrines as follows: "the Constitution of the United States was ordained and established, not by the states in their sovereign capacities, but emphatically, as the preamble of the Constitution declares, by 'the people of the United States'."[30] The people had a right to make the power of the state governments subordinate to those of the nation and this right they have exercised in numerous instances as may be seen by reference to the provisions of the Constitution. Part of the authority surrendered by becoming members of the federal compact was the privilege of determining the final validity of laws which were in conflict with the federal Constitution.[31] Story found that the argument was advanced that

an appellate jurisdiction over state courts is inconsistent with the genius of our governments, and the spirit of the Constitution. That the latter was never designed to act upon state sovereignties, but only upon the people, and that if the power exists, it will materially impair the sovereignty of the states, and the independence of their courts.[32]

---

[28] Hunter v. Martin, 4 Munf. 3, 58 (1813).

[29] Martin v. Hunter's Lessee, 1 Wheaton 304 (1816).

[30] *Ibid.*, 324.

[31] *Ibid.*, 325–7.

[32] *Ibid.*, 342, 343.

In reply he asserted:

It is a mistake that the Constitution was not designed to operate upon states, in their corporate capacity. It is crowded with provisions which restrain or annul the sovereignty of the states in some of the highest branches of their prerogatives. . . . . When, therefore, the states are stripped of some of the highest attributes of sovereignty, and the same are given to the United States; when the legislatures of the states are, in some respects, under the control of congress, and in every case are, under the Constitution, bound by the paramount authority of the United States; it is certainly difficult to support the argument that the appellate power over the decisions of state courts is contrary to the genius of our institutions. The courts of the United States can, without question, review the executive and legislative authorities of the states, and if they are found to be contrary to the Constitution may declare them to be of no legal validity. Surely the exercise of the same right over judicial tribunals is not a higher or more dangerous act of sovereign power.[33]

One fact alone, Justice Story thought, ought to settle the issue regardless of any grant to the federal government, namely, the necessity of uniformity in decisions relative to the Constitution of the United States. Because, on an examination of the Constitution, no clause could be found which limited the courts in the exercise of such power, Justice Story observed, "we dare not interpose a limitation where the people have not been disposed to create one."[34] In the judgment of the court, therefore, the appellate power of the United States extended to cases pending in state courts.

The Supreme Court had now asserted its authority as a board of arbitration between the federal and state authorities. Following the opinion in the case of *Marbury v. Madison,* any encroachment on the part of Con-

[33] 1 Wheaton 343, 344.   [34] *Ibid.,* 346, 348, 350.

gress or the President could be prevented by the court; while the opinion of Justice Story was authority for the doctrine that any act of a state—legislative, executive, or judicial, even the final voice of the people in the state constitutional convention—could be set aside if considered by the Supreme Court to be in conflict with the provisions of the federal Constitution. The state authorities did not finally submit until the case was re-argued and the decision re-affirmed in the case of *Cohens v. Virginia*,[35] in 1821, when Chief Justice Marshall affirmed Justice Story's opinion.

(b) Cohens v. Virginia.

Congress authorized the corporation of the city of Washington to establish a lottery the proceeds from which were to be used for municipal purposes. Under the city ordinance lottery tickets were sold in Virginia contrary to a state law. An indictment under the state law from the quarter sessions court of the borough of Norfolk was appealed to the Supreme Court of the United States on the ground that the borough court was the highest court of the state having jurisdiction of the case.

Counsel for the state argued that a law for the District of Columbia was not a law of the United States in the sense used in the Constitution, that the lottery law was merely a municipal ordinance and the proceeds were to be used for municipal purposes, that the state of Virginia was necessarily a party in the case and that the Supreme Court was prevented from taking appellate jurisdiction by the Eleventh Amendment. It was also contended in the argument that the appellate jurisdiction of the Supreme Court applied only to cases brought from the inferior federal courts and that there was concurrent

---

[35] 6 Wheaton 264.

jurisdiction in state and federal courts to determine questions relating to the validity of the laws of Congress. Marshall, delivering the opinion, determined the question in favor of national supremacy.

They maintain [he asserted] that the nation does not possess a department capable of restraining peaceably, and by authority of law, any attempts which may be made, by a part, against the legitimate powers of the whole; and that the government is reduced to the alternative of submitting to such attempts, or of resisting them by force. They maintain that the constitution of the United States has provided no tribunal for the final construction of itself, or of the laws or treaties of the nation; but that this power may be exercised in the last resort by the courts of every state in the Union.

The Chief Justice noted that the Constitution declares the laws, treaties, and public acts of the United States to be the supreme law of the land and that the judges in every state shall be bound thereby, anything in the Constitution or laws of any state to the contrary notwithstanding, and

this is the authoritative language of the American people; and, if gentlemen please, of the American States. . . . . The general government, though limited in its objects, is supreme with respect to these objects. This principle is a part of the constitution and if there is anyone who denies its necessity, no one can deny its authority.[36]

Though a sovereign and independent state may not be sued without its consent, such liability to suit is a portion of sovereignty that may be surrendered. The judicial department is authorized to decide all cases of every description, arising under the Constitution or laws of the United States. From this general grant of jurisdiction, no exception is made of those cases in which a state may

---

[36] 6 Wheaton 381.

be a party. "We think," Marshall affirmed, "that a case arising under the Constitution or laws of the United States is cognizable in the courts of the Union whoever may be the parties to the case."[37]

In the judgment of Marshall, the necessity or reasonableness of the power to be exercised by the federal courts was not to be regarded as conclusive, though this consideration should not be overlooked when the principles of the constitution were to be restricted for the purpose of destroying the instrument itself. The mischievous consequences of the construction claimed on the part of Virginia must, he thought, be given great consideration. In many states the judges were dependent for office and salary on the will of the legislature and could not therefore maintain that independence necessary for the determination of constitutional questions.[38] The Constitution was framed for ages to come and was designed to approach immortality as nearly as human institutions could approach it, hence the necessity for fixed, uniform principles of interpretation.[39] On the dangers of dissolution, which were graphically depicted by the counsel for the state, Marshall observed that

whenever hostility to the existing system shall become universal, it will be also irresistible. The people made the Constitution, and the people can unmake it. It is the creature of their will. But this supreme and irresistible power to make and unmake resides in the whole body of the people . . . . the attempt of any of the parts to exercise it is usurpation, and ought to be repelled by those to whom the people have delegated the power of repelling it.[40]

Taking into account the number of state governments, the conclusion was reached that twenty independent courts of final jurisdiction over the same causes arising

---

[37] *Ibid.*, 383. [38] *Ibid.*, 385–387. [39] *Ibid.*, 387. [40] *Ibid.*, 389.

under the same laws was a hydra in government, from which nothing but contradictions and confusion could proceed. Such a construction would reduce to a nullity almost the entire Constitution and must in the consideration of that instrument be held untenable. The jurisdictional question having been determined the case was argued on its merits. Marshall then upheld the fine of the local court because he claimed that the intent of Congress was to confine the lottery law to the District of Columbia; it therefore could not be enforced in Virginia.

This opinion bears the earmarks of a political manifesto designed to humiliate the states and to strengthen the forces of nationalism. A relatively insignificant cause was made the occasion for one of Marshall's strongest Federalist pronouncements.[41] However much these may have helped to weld the states into an enduring Union they served to arouse a bitter antagonism that needed only an appropriate incentive to foster the spirit of civil strife. Virginia had lost her case and the national government had gained a decisive victory, for the Eleventh Amendment, adopted to protect state authority, was reduced by interpretation to a very insecure basis for the maintenance of state independence.

The conflicts which involved Marshall and the federal courts in a controversy with the state of Virginia resulted in a series of attacks against the national judiciary and the American doctrine of judicial review of legislation. The decision in the case of *Martin v. Hunter's Lessee* has been styled the first "pass at arms between the Virginia school of states rights' advocates and the great chief justice."[42] The federal court attempted to demonstrate

---

[41] Cf. Beveridge, *op. cit.*, 4:342 ff.

[42] Wm. E. Dodd, "Chief Justice Marshall and Virginia," *Am. Hist. Rev.* (July 1907) 12:779.

that a state was subordinate to the Union; the state judges refused to obey the national authority.

Denials that the federal courts had the right to declare acts of Congress invalid seem to have appeared frequently in the South.[43] Three years after the *Martin Case,* opposition to this principle of federal law was again strongly aroused over the decision in the case of *McCulloch v. Maryland.* Judge Roane, who was among the Virginia judges that helped to establish the American doctrine of judicial review in that state,[44] had since come to the conclusion that such power was not an inherent function of the judiciary and that courts in exercising such authority were usurping power. In the *Richmond Enquirer* he took up the cause of the state, supported the position of the Virginia and Kentucky resolutions, and insisted that the federal courts were not the ultimate arbiters on matters of constitutionality. Roane lamented that the Supreme Court, which was supposed to be Republican in sentiment, was becoming the champion of a new Federalism.[45] Copies of his articles were sent to Jefferson and Madison with a request for an expression of their opinions. Madison declined to answer, and Jefferson heartily indorsed Roane's opinions, but begged to be excused from participating in contests of opinion.[46] Monroe was also approached, but as President he could take no direct part in the controversy.[47]

Aroused by these attacks, Chief Justice Marshall wrote to Story, "our opinion in the Bank case has aroused the sleeping spirit of Virginia, if indeed it ever sleeps."

---

[43] Dodd, *op. cit.,* 780.

[44] Case of Judges, 4 Call 139; and Hamper v. Hawkins, 1 Va. Cases 38–40.

[45] Dodd, *op. cit.,* 780–781.

[46] *Works,* 12:135–137.

[47] Dodd, *op. cit.,* 781.

He deplored the fact that the legislature was about to take up the matter with a view to action similar to that of the Virginia and Kentucky resolutions. In order to counteract these attacks of the Republicans he urged his friends to indorse the position and doctrines of the Supreme Court, maintaining that if Republicanism triumphed, "the Constitution would be converted into the old confederation."[48]

When Marshall in the case of *Cohens v. Virginia* in 1821 required the state of Virginia through its highest court to submit to the jurisdiction of the federal court despite the Eleventh Amendment, Judge Roane's attacks were renewed. In other countries, he said,

the judiciary is the weakest of the several departments of government, and has been limited to the mere causes brought before it: ours aspires to a more elevated function. It claims the right not only to control the operations of the coordinate departments of the government, but also to settle exclusively the chartered rights of the states.[49]

In a series of papers he tried to show the necessity of maintaining the sovereignty of the state and warned his fellow-citizens that the nation was in danger if Marshall's decision stood. John Taylor supported the opinion of Roane in works[50] which were warmly commended by Jefferson, who took occasion several times to express his hearty approval of Roane's attack on Marshall and on the federal courts.

Jefferson, the most formidable opponent of Marshall and the Federalist principles of interpretation adopted by the Supreme Court, expressed his opinion on the case

---

[48] *Ibid.*, 781.

[49] *Ibid.*, 783.

[50] Cf. *New View of the Constitution of the United States* (Washington, 1823) and *Constructions Construed and Constitutions Vindicated* (Richmond, 1820).

which Virginia had lost. In a letter to William Johnson in June, 1823, he reviewed the history of the contest between the Federalists and the Anti-Federalists. With regard to the query whether the Supreme Court had advanced beyond its constitutional limits, he replied that age disqualified him from replying fully and that the examination had already been very well done. He then referred to certain papers prepared by Judge Roane, which had appeared in the *Enquirer* under the name of Algernon Sydney:[51]

I considered these papers maturely as they came out, and confess that they appeared to me to pulverize every word which has been delivered by Judge Marshall, of the extra-judicial part of his opinion; and all was extra-judicial, except the decision that the act of Congress had not purported to give to the corporation of Washington the authority claimed by their lottery law, of controlling the laws of the states within the states themselves. But unable to claim that case he could not let it go entirely, but went on gratuitously to prove that notwithstanding the eleventh amendment, a state could be brought as a defendant to the bar of his court; and again, that Congress might authorize a corporation of its territory to exercise legislation within a state and paramount to the laws of that state.[52]

This doctrine of Marshall, Jefferson thought, "was so completely refuted by Roane, that if he can be answered, I surrender human reason as a vain and useless faculty given to bewilder and not to guide us."[53] The practice of Chief Justice Marshall, "of traveling out of his case to prescribe what the law would be in a moot case not before the court," was regarded as very irregular and censurable.[54] To bear out these criticisms *Marbury v. Madison* was cited. In this case the court determined at once that, being an original process, they did not have cognizance

---

[51] *Works*, 12:252–259.   [52] *Ibid.*, 255.   [53] *Ibid.*, 255.   [54] *Ibid.*, 256.

of it, and therefore the question before them was ended. But the Chief Justice went on to lay down what the law would be, if they had jurisdiction over the case. "The object was clearly to instruct any other court having the jurisdiction what they should do if Marbury should apply to them."[55] Although the court could not issue a mandamus to the President or legislature, said Jefferson, "this case of *Marbury v. Madison* is continually cited by bench and bar as if it were settled law." As a partial remedy for the dangers with which Jefferson thought this practice was replete, he advocated as an amendment, that each judge should give his individual opinion on all issues concerning the constitutionality of laws.

Roane led the people of Virginia to think that Marshall was the arch enemy of his native state, and that under his direction the national government was adopting a policy decidedly detrimental to the state. Marshall evidenced his alarm at the situation.

The opinion of the Supreme Court in the Lottery case [he wrote] has been assaulted with a degree of virulence transcending what has appeared on any former occasion. . . . . There is on the subect no such thing as a free press in Virginia and of consequence the calumnies and misrepresentations of this gentleman (Roane) will remain uncontradicted and will by many be believed to be true. He will be supposed to be the champion of state rights, instead of being what he really is, the champion of dismemberment.

Referring to Jefferson's criticisms, he said:

I cannot describe the surprise and mortification I have felt at hearing that Mr. Madison has embraced them (these Virginia views) with respect to the judicial department. . . . In support of the sound principles of the Constitution and of the Union of

---

[55] *Ibid.*, 256, 257.

the States not a pen is drawn. In Virginia the tendency of things verges rapidly to the destruction of the government and the reestablishment of a league of sovereign states. I look elsewhere for safety.[56]

Marshall felt that there was a concerted effort to convert the government into a league similar to the Confederation and he attributed the whole attack to Jefferson. In his message of December, 1821, Governor Randolph condemned the Supreme Court for arrogating to itself ''the high authority to judge exclusively in the last resort how far the federal compact is violated, and to arraign before it, not only the decisions of the state courts, but the states themselves.''[57] The controversy was made an issue in other states and conditions appeared so alarming that Marshall warned the friends of the Union to be more on the alert.

A plan of cooperation to resist the encroachments of the federal judiciary seems to have been considered by Virginia, Kentucky, and Ohio, and steps were taken to bring the whole matter to the attention of the states and of Congress. Roane drafted an amendment to the national Constitution, which was to be proposed to the Virginia assembly and then to be sent to the other states for their indorsement. The amendment proposed and indorsed by the state was as follows:

That the judicial power of the United States shall not be construed to extend to any case in which a state shall be a party, except in controversies involving the rights of a state and to which such state shall claim to be a party. That no appeal shall be construed to lie to any court of the United States from any decision rendered in the courts of a state.[58]

This amendment seems to have received no support outside of Virginia, and the plan to remove Marshall and

---

[56] Dodd, *op. cit.*, 784.   [57] *Ibid.*, 785.   [58] *Ibid.*, 786.

curb the powers of the federal courts was doomed to failure. Roane died six months afterward, thinking that his work had been in vain. But South Carolina soon took up the cause where Roane left off, and ''continued an agitation which forced Calhoun to recant his ardent nationalism in 1828, and which swept the South two decades later into Texas annexation, ceasing not until the Roane-Marshall debate was settled in the awful tribunal of civil war.''[59]

5. *Protest of Ohio*—

Resistance to the act establishing a national bank continued in Ohio even after the settlement of the controversy in Maryland and the complete victory there of the national authorities. The general assembly of Ohio had passed a law levying a tax of $50,000 on each branch of the bank of the United States established in the state. The tax was meant to be prohibitive and the amounts were to be speedily collected. Two branches refused to pay the tax and the state authorities forcibly seized the sum of $100,000 from one of the banks. Suits were begun and criminal prosecutions instituted against the officers of the state, and while the suits were under consideration the general assembly met. Reports and resolutions were drawn up and sent to the Senate and House of Representatives. At the same time an act was passed to withdraw from the bank of the United States the protection of the laws of the state.[60] On an appeal to the Supreme Court of the United States the former decision was reaffirmed and the state laws declared null and void.[61]

In a report submitted to Congress from the state, the objection was raised that the state was reduced to the

---

[59] Dodd, *op. cit.*, 787.
[60] Ames, *op. cit.*, 93, 94.
[61] Osborn v. Bank of the United States, 9 Wheaton 738 (1824).

level of an ordinary citizen and made answerable in inferior tribunals. As the auditor of the state was sued, it was contended that, in everything but name, the state was the actual defendant.[62] It was asserted that the principle of the proceedings secured to the federal tribunals every power supposed to be taken from them by the Eleventh Amendment.[63] The committee reported that they were "aware of the doctrine that the federal courts are exclusively vested with jurisdiction to declare, in the last resort, the true interpretation of the Constitution of the United States." But to this doctrine in the latitude contended for, they never could give their consent.[64]

The report further stated that after the adoption of the Eleventh Amendment the courts of the United States ceased to be the proper constitutional tribunals to investigate and determine the power and authority of the states under the Constitution of the United States. *Marbury v. Madison* and *Fletcher v. Peck* were cited as cases wherein a decision of the Supreme Court of the United States was not conclusive on great questions of political rights and political powers.[65] The propositions of Chief Justice Marshall in the decision of *McCulloch v. Maryland* were then summarized and respectively denied. As a result of this decision the committee thought that "the government of the Union may, and undoubtedly will, progressively draw all the powers of the government into the vortex of its authority."[66] The report continued:

It is important to glance at the train of implications with which this doctrine is connected. The power to create the bank implies the power to preserve it. This power to create is, itself, derived by implication . . . . and the power to preserve implies

---

[62] Senate *Documents*, 16 Cong., 2 sess., 12, Nos. 72, 6, 7, 8.
[63] *Ibid.*, 10.   [65] *Ibid.*, 17, 18.
[64] *Ibid.*, 11.   [66] *Ibid.*, 22.

a choice in selecting the means of preservation, and upon the doctrine of the court, all these powers are supreme, to the operation of which, the constitutions and laws of the states can oppose no obstacle. It is certainly difficult to see the point where these implications terminate or to name the power which they leave to the states unimpaired.[67]

The report closed with a series of resolutions denying federal jurisdiction over the state in the case under consideration and protesting against the doctrine "that the political rights of the separate states that compose the American Union and their powers as sovereign states, may be settled and determined in the Supreme Court of the United States."[68]

6. *Kentucky and Green v. Biddle—*

In Kentucky a decision of the federal Supreme Court thoroughly aroused opposition to that judiciary. An act of the state of Kentucky concerning the title to certain land grants which involved an agreement with the state of Virginia was held to be repugnant to the Constitution of the United States as in violation of a contract between the two states.[69] The legislature of Kentucky adopted a long report with a separate series of resolutions relative to the above decision and submitted a remonstrance to Congress. A protest was entered against what was termed "the erroneous, injurious and degrading doctrines of the opinion of the Supreme Court of the United States."[70]

Three justices were absent, however, at the time the opinion was rendered in the Supreme Court, and only

---

67 *Ibid.*, 25.

68 *Ibid.*, 34.

69 Green v. Biddle, 8 Wheaton 1 (1823).

70 For history of this conflict, see Ames, *op. cit.*, 17–23.

three out of the four present concurred in the decision. A recommendation was therefore made that no constitutional question relating to the validity of laws of Congress or of the laws of the states should be determined unless two-thirds of the members of the court concurred in the decision. In the report to Congress the state maintained that:

It is the principle which that decision established at which they shudder, and with which they can never be reconciled. The people of Kentucky can bear anything but degradation and disfranchisement. They cannot bear to be construed out of their right of self-government; they value their freedom above everything else and are as little inclined to be reasoned out of it, as they would be to surrender it to foreign force.[71]

On the failure of Congress to grant the relief desired by the state authorities, the issue was again brought before the legislature in 1825 by a message from the governor. The house of representatives sent an inquiry to the governor, asking information regarding the proper procedure to follow in order

to refuse obedience to the decisions and mandates of the Supreme Court of the United States, considered erroneous and unconstitutional, and whether, in the opinion of the executive, it may be advisable to call forth the physical power of the state to resist the execution of the decisions of the court, or in what manner the mandate of said court should be met by disobedience.[72]

As the governor was not inclined to assume the responsibility for the use of force, a feeble resistance was continued until 1831, when a second decision of the Supreme Court was accepted as final by the state authorities.[73]

---

[71] Senate *Documents*, 18 Cong., 1 sess., 4, no. 69, 8.

[72] *Niles Register*, 19:228, 229.

[73] Hawkins v. Barney's Lessee, 5 Peters 457.

The seriousness of the contest between the states and the federal government over the jurisdiction of the federal courts was indicated by the tendency of counsel for the states to threaten the dissolution of the Union if the federal courts continued to coerce the states.[74]

7. *Judicially construed limitations on the powers of the states—*

The Supreme Court of the United States not only asserted the right to determine the validity of the laws of Congress and to set aside state laws in conflict with express provisions of the federal Constitution, treaties, or laws, but under the direction of Chief Justice Marshall this tribunal was also inclined to place other unexpressed limitations upon the realm of state authority.

The legislature of Georgia, influenced by notoriously corrupt methods, granted to certain companies large tracts of land for a nominal return. When the fraudulent practices of the land speculators were exposed, a newly elected legislature passed a repealing act in which the former law was declared null and void and all claims arising thereunder were annulled. In addition to the original companies, which included investors from many states, new companies were formed to defend the investors' interests. One of the companies secured the advice of Hamilton who claimed that the repealing act violated the contract clause of the Constitution and he predicted that "the courts of the United States . . . . will be likely to pronounce it so."[75] Following this suggestion there was a persistent program to bring a case

---

[74] See Elkison v. DeLiesseline, Fed. Cas. No. 4366 (1823) in which Justice Johnson held void a state law authorizing the seizure and imprisonment of free negroes brought into the state on board a foreign vessel.

[75] Beveridge, *op. cit.*, 3:584.

before the Supreme Court presided over by Chief Justice Marshall who was known to be in sympathy with the views of Hamilton. The case which was finally brought to the federal courts was considered by many to be a feigned case.[76] On the second hearing of the case Chief Justice Marshall held, on the basis of the provision, that no state shall impair the obligation of contracts, that when a law is in its nature a contract, a repeal of the law cannot divest rights acquired under the law. It was the opinion of the court that "the state of Georgia was restrained either by general principles which are common to our free institutions, or by the particular provisions of the Constitution of the United States, from passing a law whereby" an estate could be constitutionally and legally impaired.[77] The fact that the Supreme Court failed to consider the fraudulent methods used in securing the original grant and that a legislative act transferring title to property was held to be an irrepealable grant, contrary to the prevailing rules of English law, brought the charge that the decision of the Supreme Court was inspired by partisan motives.

The case of *Dartmouth College v. Woodward*[78] extended the limitation already imposed. It was therein held that a charter granted to a private institution or corporation was a contract, and that such conract could not be impaired by future legislation unless the right had been reserved in the original grant. By a series of acts the legislature of New Hampshire had reorganized the form of control and management of Dartmouth College, which had been conducted thus far under the provisions

---

[76] See comment of Justice Johnson, 6 Cranch 147 (1810).

[77] 6 Cranch 87, 139. By a vote of 46 to 54 an attempt to censure the Supreme Court for this action was defeated in the House of Representatives.

[78] 4 Wheaton 518 (1819).

of a charter granted by the King of England. The state
claimed that there was no limitation in the constitution
of the state or the fundamental law of the United States
which interfered with the control of such corporations,
and the state supreme court held the state laws valid.[79]
On the basis of that clause in the Constitution which
denied the right of states to impair the obligation of
contracts, the case was appealed to the Supreme Court
of the United States.[80] The attorney-general on behalf of
the state claimed that this provision was intended to
affect private contracts only, and the rights acquired
under them. He regarded the appeal as an attempt to
extend the obvious meaning of the Constitution and to
apply it by a species of legal fiction to a class of cases
which had always been under government control.[81] After
the argument and first consideration of the case Chief
Justice Marshall announced that the court could not
agree and that the case would be continued until the next
term, which meant the following year. Though no definite
information is available it is generally believed that the
vote of the judges was five to two against the old college.
The friends of the college set to work to convert the opponents and conducted what Senator Lodge has called a

---

[79] In supporting the state law Chief Justice Richardson held that the
charter of the college was in the nature of a public corporation and that
the clause of the federal Constitution relating to the impairment of contracts was not intended to limit the power of the states over their officers
or their own civil institutions.—65 New Hampshire 473–624.

[80] On the efforts of Webster to get a case before the Supreme Court,
see John M. Shirley, *The Dartmouth College Causes and the Supreme Court
of the United States* (St. Louis, 1879). ''I saw Judge Story as I came
along. He is evidently expecting a case which shall present all the questions. . . . . The question we must raise in one of these actions, is whether
by the general principles of our governments the state legislatures be not
restrained from divesting vested rights. This, of course, independent of
constitutional provision respecting contracts . . . . on general principles, I
am very confident the court at Washington would be with us.''—Daniel
Webster, 1 Webster's *Private Correspondence*, 282–3.

[81] 4 Wheaton 609.

"decorous political campaign."[82] Webster's argument before the Supreme Court was printed and distributed freely among those who might influence the opinions of the judges. Justice Story was readily won over to the side of the college and seems to have aided Webster.[83] Through Chancellor Kent of New York, an ardent Federalist, influence was brought to bear on Justice Johnson. So effective was the effort to change the views of the Justices that when the court convened about eleven months later all the justices had been won over to the side of the college except Duvall and Todd. When Chief Justice Marshall rendered his opinion, after refusing to hear William Pinkney plead for a reargument, Todd was absent on account of illness and Duvall dissented without filing an opinion. Chief Justice Marshall, following the reasoning of Webster, the counsel for the old corporation, gave it as his opinion that the state had attempted to divest the property of a private corporation, and that this particular type of legislation was meant to be prohibited by the federal Constitution.

The case for the trustees and the state was poorly argued and some of the essential facts were not clearly presented on the record: had the Chief Justice and the majority of the justices followed the record and the facts, which were then well known, the charter to Dartmouth College would not have been declared a contract under the protection of the federal Constitution.[84]

The cases of *Fletcher v. Peck* and *Dartmouth College v. Woodward,* formed the beginning of an extensive series of restrictions upon state legislation, made possible

[82] *Life of Webster* (American Statesmen Series, 1883) 91.

[83] Shirley, *Dartmouth College Causes* (St. Louis, 1879) 201.

[84] Jesse F. Orton, "Confusion of Property with Privilege, Dartmouth College Case," *The Independent* (August 19 and 26, 1909).

through the fact that many laws may be attacked on the
ground of infringement of property rights—a good part
of which was now placed entirely beyond the control
of the state legislature. The decision aligned on the
side of nationalism the economic interests of corporate
organizations.[85]

The clause in the Constitution which authorizes Congress to regulate commerce was likewise so interpreted
as to take a large part of commercial relations out of the
jurisdiction of the state. The court defined commerce to
include traffic and general commercial intercourse, and
held that the primary regulation of such intercourse belongs to Congress and not to the states. As a result of
the decision in *Gibbons v. Ogden*,[86] the acts of the legislature of the state of New York, granting to Livingston
and Fulton the exclusive navigation of all waters by fire
or steam within the jurisdiction of the state, were held to
be repugnant to the Constitution, and the control of all
such navigable waters was placed within the jurisdiction
of the federal government. In the case of *Brown v. Maryland*,[87] the court maintained that a tax on the original
importer of an article before it had become a part of
the general property of the state was a tax on commerce
and therefore prohibited by the Constitution. The states
had already been prohibited from taxing the bank of

---

85 ''The sacredness of contract, the stability of institutions, and above
all, Nationalism in government, were to John Marshall, articles of creed as
holy as any that ever inspired a religious enthusiast.''—Beveridge, *op. cit.*,
4:221.

These decisions of the Supreme Court were characterized as ''the bulwark of American individualism against democratic impatience and Socialistic fantasy.''—Sir Henry Maine, *Popular Government*, 248. See similar
prediction by Justice Story in letter to Chancellor Kent, Aug. 21, 1819,
Life and Letters (ed. by W. W. Story), 1:331, and opinion of John Fiske
in *Essays, Historical and Literary*, 1:379.

86 9 Wheaton 1 (1824).

87 12 Wheaton 419 (1827).

the United States,[88] on the ground that the power to tax involved the power to destroy; that the power to destroy might defeat and render useless the power to create, and that there was a plain repugnance in conferring on one government a power to control the constitutional measures of the other. "Whenever the terms in which a power is granted to Congress, or the nature of the power, require that it should be exercised exclusively by Congress," claimed Chief Justice Marshall, "the subject is as completely taken from the state legislatures as if they had been expressly forbidden to act on it."[89] On the great subject of contracts, commerce, and taxation, the state governments were forced to submit to important restrictions imposed by the Constitution as interpreted by the federal Supreme Court.

8. *The Supreme Court in defense of nationalism*—

At the same time the Supreme Court was establishing its position as the final court of appeal in cases of conflict of authorities between state and national officers, and construing implied restrictions on the states, it was also strengthening the position of the national government by the development of the Federalist doctrine of implied powers. The American political system was inaugurated under a written constitution which stated in general terms the powers which were to be exercised by the federal government. Along with the specific grants of power to the national Congress it was further provided that Congress shall make all laws which shall be necessary and proper for carrying into execution the foregoing powers.[90] On the interpretation of this clause the Fed-

---

[88] McCulloch v. Maryland, 4 Wheaton 316 (1819).

[89] Sturges v. Crowninshield, 4 Wheaton 193 (1819).

[90] Art. 1, sec. 8.

eralists and the Anti-Federalists differed greatly. The latter favored a strict construction of the Constitution, holding that only those powers were granted by the Constitution which were absolutely necessary and indispensable to the conduct of the government. The former upheld every means necessary and desirable to carry into effect the powers of the central government, and favored a broad interpretation of the general grants of power given by the Constitution. The issue took a definite form in the policy of Hamilton favoring the establishment of a national banking system. The greatest objection raised against the bill presented on the recommendation of Hamilton was on the ground of unconstitutionality. In order to determine the course of the executive, President Washington had asked for a written opinion from his cabinet officers on the constitutionality of the measure.[91] Jefferson denied the right of the general government to pass such a law because no express grant warranted it. The measure was not indispensable to the execution of the powers allotted to the nation and, in his judgment, the right to enact such legislation remained by the Constitution exclusively with the states.[92]

Hamilton argued for the constitutionality of the proposed law and formulated in his opinion the doctrine of implied powers which Marshall later developed in actual cases. He regarded the powers granted to the central government as expressed and implied, the latter being as effectually delegated as the former. The implied powers were defined as the instrument or means of carrying into effect the specified powers. These implied powers included those means which were *needful, requisite, incidental,* or *conducive* to the exercise of any express power.

---

[91] *Works* (Federal ed.), 2:443, 444.
[92] *Ibid.*, 197.

The criterion of constitutionality was then given as the end to which the measure related as a means. If the end be clearly comprehended within any of the specified powers, and if the measure has an *obvious relation* to that end, if it is *not forbidden by any particular provision of the Constitution,* it may safely be deemed to come within the compass of the national authority.[93] This method of reasoning apparently reversed the principle of delimitation of powers as defined in the Tenth Amendment. When the doctrine of implied powers was adopted it was relatively easy to find among the express powers granted to Congress a power to which a particular measure might be related as a means, and then the measure was constitutional unless there was an express prohibition in the Constitution. The revolutionary character of this proposition was not fully recognized, at the time it was first adopted by the Supreme Court.

McCulloch v. Maryland.

Hamilton's plan for a national bank was adopted in spite of constitutional objections. Not until 1819, however, under a second national bank act, was the issue presented to the Supreme Court for consideration, in the case of *McCulloch v. Maryland.*[94] The general assembly of Maryland had passed an act to impose a tax on all banks or branches thereof in the state of Maryland not chartered by the state legislature. As a result of the attempt to execute this law against a branch of the national bank in Baltimore a case was brought on appeal to the federal Supreme Court. The counsel for the state argued that the bank of the United States was not necessary or indispensable to the carrying on of the operations

[93] *Works, op. cit.,* 444–493.
[94] 4 Wheaton 316 (1819).

of the federal government; that the Constitution did not emanate from the people, but as the act of sovereign and independent states; that the acts of Congress chartering and protecting the bank of the United States were not warranted by the Constitution. The states of the Union, it was claimed, had not surrendered themselves, in this manner, by implication, to the Congress of the United States and to such corporations as Congress might create. Corporations not chartered by the state, wholly exempt from taxation, are utterly at variance with every principle of government of the United States. The national act was characterized as an overwhelming invasion of state sovereignty not warranted by any express grant from the Constitution,[95] and the federal government is thereby ''to hold a power by implication and ingenious inference from general words in the Constitution, which it can hardly be believed would have been suffered in an express grant.''[96] In answer to the argument that the state would be likely to abuse the power if the right to tax were granted, were placed the propositions, first, that if the states have the power this court cannot take it from them through the fear that they may abuse it; secondly, that the fear of abuse applies just as effectually against permitting and absolute authority in the general government as in permitting a certain degree of control in the states.[97]

Chief Justice Marshall regarded the issue raised as a most vital one to the constitutional system of the country, and assumed that

it must be decided peacefully, or remain the source of hostile legislation, perhaps hostility of a still more serious nature; and if it is to be so decided, by this tribunal alone can the decision

---

[95] 4 Wheaton 337.   [96] *Ibid.*, 345.   [97] *Ibid.*, 348.

be made. On the Supreme Court of the United States has the Constitution of our country devolved this important duty.[98]

Because of the long acceptance of the national bank acts, both by the legislative and by the judicial departments, he thought the acts ought not to be lightly set aside. He reasoned that

if any one proposition could command the universal assent of mankind, we might expect it would be this—that the government of the Union, though limited in its powers, is supreme within its sphere of action. This would seem to result, necessarily, from its nature. It is the government of all; its powers are delegated by all; it represents all; and acts for all. Though any one state may be willing to control its operations, no state is willing to allow others to control them. The nation, on those subjects on which it can act, must necessarily bind its component parts.[99]

The government is acknowledged by all to be one of enumerated powers. But questions respecting the extent of the powers actually granted are perpetually arising and will probably continue to arise as long as our system shall exist. Hence,

we think the sound construction of the constitution must allow to the national legislature that discretion, with respect to the means by which the powers it confers are to be carried into execution, which will enable that body to perform the high duties assigned to it, in the manner most beneficial to the people. Let the end be legitimate, let it be within the scope of the constitution, and all means which are appropriate, which are plainly adapted to that end, which are not prohibited, but which consist with the letter and spirit of the constitution, are constitutional.[100]

Although the Chief Justice regularly insisted that the government of the United States was one of enumerated

---

[98] 4 Wheaton 400, 401.
[99] *Ibid.*, 405.
[100] *Ibid.*, 421.

powers and that those powers not granted were denied, he used language which indicated that he was willing to allow a very wide latitude in the choice of means by the legislative authority. Following the reasoning of Hamilton, he claimed, that

where the law is not prohibited, and is really calculated to effect any of the objects entrusted to the government, to undertake here to enquire into the degree of its necessity, would be to pass the line which circumscribes the judicial department, and to tread on legislative ground. This court disclaims any pretension to such a power.[101]

That such a construction of the Constitution should be preferred as would render its operations extremely difficult, hazardous and expensive, seemed to him incredible. He deplored the baneful influence of the narrow construction of the Constitution supported by the state and exposed, as he thought, the absolute impracticability of maintaining the central government on such a restricted basis.[102]

The national banking system was upheld, the state was prohibited from taxing this corporation of the United States, and it was declared that the national government should be not confined to the execution of the powers strictly enumerated in the Constitution. Marshall pleaded for a "natural" interpretation of the words of the Constitution. In *Gibbons v. Ogden* he again asserted:

If they contend for that narrow construction which, in support of some theory not to be found in the constitution, would deny to the government those powers which the words of the grant as usually understood, import, and which are consistent with the general views and objects of the instrument; for that narrow construction which would cripple the government, and render it

---

[101] 4 Wheaton 423.   [102] *Ibid.*, 417, 418.

unequal to the objects for which it is declared to be instituted, and to which the powers given, as fairly understood, render it competent; then we cannot perceive the propriety of this construction, nor adopt it as the rule by which the Constitution is to be expounded.[103]

On account of the conflicts with the states from 1809 to 1830, numerous measures were introduced in the Senate and House of Representatives with the intent to restrict the powers and jurisdiction of the federal courts. The failure of the impeachment of Chase prompted John Randolph to propose an amendment in March, 1805, to have the judges removed by the President on the joint address of both houses of Congress. Similar amendments were presented in the years 1806, 1811, and 1816, but failed to receive sufficient consideration at any time to be brought to a final vote. The great controversy with Virginia brought forth a proposal to have the Senate act as an appellate court in cases involving the states as parties, and the attempts to curb federal judicial power, all of which were unsuccessful, ended in a futile effort to amend the Constitution by limiting the term of office of federal judges.[104] A series of amendments suggested by the states had met a similar fate. The authority of the court, however, was soon to be curtailed somewhat by the leaders of the Democratic party.

---

[103] 9 Wheaton 1, 188 (1824).

[104] Herman v. Ames, ''Amendments to the Constitution,'' Am. Hist. Assoc. *Reports*, 1896, 144 ff.

Chapter XII

JUDICIAL REVIEW OF LEGISLATION AND JACKSONIAN DEMOCRACY

Opposition to the Federalist Principles of Constitutional Interpretation

Prior to 1825 the friends of the doctrine of judicial review of legislation were seldom seriously alarmed over the protests of those who denounced the control of courts over legislation. The resistance of the Democratic party and the confirmed opposition of Jefferson did not hinder the federal courts from interfering freely with the legislative enactments of the states; and later when the policies of the time were tending in the direction of a stronger national government, this same party found the Supreme Court an effective ally in the development of some of its leading projects. Judicial review had been accepted as a feature of the political system of the states. The rise of a new democracy revived the attacks on the Federalist principles of judicial review of legislation.

1. *Views of Martin Van Buren*—

When the wave of enthusiasm which carried Jackson into the office of President began to assert itself in the government, it was to be expected that the Supreme Court would come in for its share of censure. Everything of an aristocratic or conservative nature was subject to condemnation by the Democrats. The life tenure of the Supreme Court justices and the extraordinary powers claimed for the judiciary were two features of the old order which the Jacksonian type of Democrat heartily disapproved. The rise of a regular party organization with radical views led to a renewal of the attacks upon the doctrine of judicial veto of laws. Martin Van Buren, one of the leaders of the new democracy, objected vigorously to the way in which the old Federalist party had secured the control of the judiciary and had held to this department as an ark of future safety which the Constitution placed beyond the reach of public opinion. He was "exasperated at the guarded and sly manner in which they [the courts] put forth the doctrines of the old Federal party without assuming the responsibility of affirming them."[1] Deploring the prevailing attitude of the time, he said:

A sentiment I had almost said of idolatry for the Supreme Court has grown up, which claims for its members an almost entire exemption from the fallibilities of our nature, and arraigns with unsparing bitterness the motives of all who have the temerity to look with inquisitive eyes into this consecrated sanctuary of the law. . . . . I have been brought up in an opposite faith, and all my experience has confirmed me in its correctness. . . . . I believe the judges of the Supreme Court (great and good men as I cheerfully concede them to be) are subject to the same infirmities, influenced by the same passions, and operated on by the same causes, that good and great men are in other situations. I believe they have as much of the *esprit de corps* as other men. Those who think otherwise form an erroneous estimate of human nature; and if they act upon that estimate, will soon or late, become sensible of their delusion.[2]

On April 7, 1826, Van Buren expressed an opinion in the Senate which was intended to call attention to the

---

[1] Van Buren, *Inquiry into the Origin and Cause of Political Parties in the United States* (New York, 1867) 362.

[2] Edward M. Shepard, *Martin Van Buren*, "American Statesmen Series" (New York, 1916) 136, 137.

dangers inherent in the American doctrine of judicial review. His remarks were prefaced by the admission that "there exists not upon this earth, and there never did exist, a judicial tribunal clothed with powers so various and so important as the Supreme Court."[3] Since the acts of Congress depended upon the court for their execution, and since the court could determine whether an act is in accord with the Constitution or not, the veto of the Court, it was claimed, might absolutely suspend nine-tenths of the acts of the national legislature. Although the power had been rarely exercised, its existence and an occasional interference were enough to serve as such a positive barrier as to be greatly deplored. Van Buren protested:

Not only are the acts of the national legislature subject to its review, but it stands as the umpire between the conflicting powers of the general and state governments. That wide field of debatable ground between those rival powers is claimed to be subject to the exclusive and absolute dominion of the Supreme Court. The discharge of the solemn duty has not been infrequent, and certainly not uninteresting. In virtue of this power, we have seen it holding for naught the statutes of powerful states, which had received the deliberate sanction, not only of their legislatures, but of their judicatories. . . . . You have seen such statutes abrogated by the decisions of this court, and those confident in the wisdom and power of the state authorities plunged in irremediable ruin . . . . decisions final in their effect and ruinous in their consequences. I speak of the power of the court, not of the correctness or incorrectness of its decisions. With that we have nothing to do.[4]

---

3 Elliot's *Debates,* 4:485.

4 *Ibid.,* 485. Van Buren claimed that, "It has from the beginning been the constant aim of the leading Federalists to select some department in our political system, and to make it the depository of power which public sentiment could not reach nor the people control." Relative to Hamilton's lack of respect for the people he said: "This distrust of the capacity and disposition of the masses . . . . retained its hold upon his strong mind and ardent

After dealing with the fact that the highest authorities of almost every state in turn had been rebuked by the court in the exercise of this prerogative, Van Buren indicated the weakness of his objections by the admission that "the authority has been given to them, and this is not the place to mention its exercise."[5] Regarding the independence of the judges, Van Buren maintained, "the only effectual and safe remedy will be to amend the Constitution so as to make the office elective, and thus compel the judges, like the incumbents of the Executive and Legislative departments, to come before the people at stated and reasonable periods for a renewal of their commissions."[6] It remained for President Jackson and Chief Justice Taney to indicate the method by which the principles announced by Chief Justice Marshall might be modified and the Federalist doctrine of judicial review restricted.

2. *Second Conflict with Georgia—*

The last great controversy with which the Supreme Court had to deal while under the direction of Chief Justice Marshall was a conflict with the state of Georgia over the Indian question. The issue arose through an attempt of the state authorities to secure control over the

---

feelings when he bequeathed it to his political disciples, and it has been the shibboleth of their tribe ever since. In a large degree wealthy and proud of their social position, their fear of the popular will and desire to escape from popular control, instead of being lessened, is increased by the advance of the people in education and knowledge. Under no authority do they feel their interests to be safer than under that which is subject to the judicial power, and in no way could their policy be more effectually promoted than by taking power from those departments of the government over which the people have full control and accumulating it in that over which they may fairly be said to have none." Van Buren, *Inquiry into the Origin and Cause of Political Parties in the United States,* 275, 329–330.

5 Elliot's *Debates,* 487.

6 *The Autobiography of Martin Van Buren* (ed. by Fitzpatrick), *Report,* Am. Hist. Assoc. (Washington, 1920) 2:184, 5.

land of the Creek Indians. The governor and legislature of Georgia openly defied the President of the United States and resisted the assertion of his authority under treaties with the Indians. Congress was not inclined to stand by President Adams, and Georgia proceeded against the Indians according to her own discretion.[7] After the contest had continued for more than two years, during which time a voluminous correspondence had merely tended to reveal the weakness of federal power and to arouse the wrath of the state authorities, the suggestion was made that the whole case be turned over to the Supreme Court of the United States.

The governor advised the state representatives in Congress that he could not acknowledge a power in the federal government to bring before its judicial tribunals for trial and judgment the governor, judges, or representatives of the state. He was not wanting, the governor claimed, in confidence in the Supreme Court of the United States, in all cases falling within its acknowledged jurisdiction. But according to his conception the Supreme Court was not made the arbiter in controversies involving rights of sovereignty between the states and the United States. The states could not therefore consent

to refer to the Supreme Court, as of right and obligation, questions of sovereignty between them and the United States, because that court, being of exclusive appointment by the government of the United States, will make the United States the judge of their own cause; this reason is equally applicable to a state tribunal.[8]

The failure of Congress to support the President in his attempt to enforce the treaties and uphold national

---

[7] House *Executive Documents*, 19 Cong., 2 sess., 4, no. 59; *Reports* of House Committees, 3, no. 98.

[8] *Niles Register*, 32:20.

authority finally led to the acknowledgment of the contention of the state and brought an end to the Creek controversy.

The success in the case of the Creeks led the authorities of Georgia to attempt to secure the lands of the Cherokee Indians. With the tacit support of the United States government, the Indian tribe drew up a constitution and took steps in the direction of setting up an independent government. This was directly in line with the past policy of the national government toward the Indians, to treat them as independent communities within the states to be dealt with by the national government and then only by treaty. Georgia retaliated by an act of assembly incorporating the land of the Cherokee nation into the territory of the state, and annulling all laws as well as the constitution of the newly formed nation.[9]

The opportunity to bring the question at issue before the Supreme Court was soon presented when, in the execution of the statutes over the Cherokee territory, an Indian by the name of Corn Tassel was tried, convicted, and sentenced to death. On an appeal to the Supreme Court a writ of error was granted with the purpose of bringing the case before the federal courts for reconsideration.

The governor, having received the order from the court, submitted a message in which he referred to a communication,

purporting to be signed by the Chief Justice of the United States, and to be a citation of the state of Georgia to appear before the Supreme Court, ... to answer to that tribunal for having caused a person who had committed murder within the limits of the state, to be tried and convicted therefor, and he

---

[9] *Ibid.*, 38:328, 329.

declared it to be his intention to resist the execution of the writ with whatever force the laws have placed at my command.[10]

The legislature immediately resolved, "that they view with feelings of deepest regret, the interference by the Chief Justice of the Supreme Court of the United States, in the administration of the criminal laws of the state, and that such an interference is a flagrant violation of her rights," and further that the governor and every other officer of the state are hereby requested to disregard any mandate that may be served upon them, proceeding from the Supreme Court of the United States, for the purpose of arresting the execution of any criminal laws of the state.[11] The order of the Supreme Court was ignored and Tassel was executed according to the verdict of the state tribunal.[12]

A later case was dismissed by the Supreme Court for want of jurisdiction but with some caustic remarks to the effect that if courts were permitted to indulge their sympathies, a case better calculated to excite them could scarcely be imagined.[13] The request of the Indians was denied, however, because the court believed that

the bill requires us to control the legislature of Georgia, and to restrain the exertion of its physical course. The propriety of such an interposition by the court may well be questioned. It savors too much of the exercise of political power to be within the province of the judicial department. . . . . If it be true that wrongs have been inflicted and that still greater ones are to be apprehended, this is not the tribunal which can redress the past or prevent the future.[14]

---

10 *Niles Register*, 38:338.

11 *Ibid.*, 338.

12 *Ibid.*, 353.

13 Cherokee v. The State of Georgia, 5 Peters 1, 15 (1831).

14 *Ibid.*, 15. In this case Martin Van Buren observed that Marshall after having decided that the Supreme Court did not have jurisdiction "went on

A new law of the state making more stringent regulations for the Cherokee territory was defied by several missionaries who were working among the Indians, with the result that they were tried, convicted, and sentenced to imprisonment.[15] On an application to the Supreme Court another writ was issued demanding that the authorities of the state appear before the court. Governor Lumpkin, instead of obeying the writ, referred the whole matter to the legislature in a message which is typical of the attitude assumed when the courts of the nation asserted jurisdiction over matters with which the state governments were inclined to deal and to admit of no interference.

My respect for the Supreme Court of the United States [said the governor] as a fundamental department of the federal government, induces me to indulge the earnest hope, that no mandate will ever proceed from that court, attempting or intending to control one of the sovereign states of this union, in the free exercise of its constitutional, criminal or civil jurisdiction.[16]

The object of the proceeding was considered to be nothing less than an attempt to call into question and to overthrow the essential jurisdiction of the state.

---

notwithstanding, as he did in the famous case of Marbury v. Madison, to deliver an extra-judicial opinion upon one of the material points of the case, and declared that so much of the argument [of counsel] as was intended to prove the character of the Cherokees as a state, as a distinct political society, separated from others, capable of managing its own affairs, and governing itself has, in the opinion of a majority of the Judges, been completely successful.'' The question of the right of the Indians to their lands, he intimated ''might, perhaps be decided by the Court in a proper case with proper parties.'' The political implications of the case were indicated by the fact that Mr. Peters, the Supreme Court reporter, decided to publish the case immediately, separately from the regular Supreme Court reports and to give what he termed Mr. ''Wirt's great argument in behalf of the Cherokees,'' which had been taken down by stenographers employed for the purpose.— *Autobiography,* 2:291, 292.

[15] *Niles Register,* 38:244–248.

[16] *Niles Register,* 40:313.

The Supreme Court not only assumed jurisdiction but decided the case against the state.[17] In the opinion submitted by Chief Justice Marshall, the court declared that the treaties and laws of the United States contemplated the Indian territory as completely separated from that of the state and provided that all intercourse with the Indians should be carried on exclusively by the government of the Union. The Cherokee nation, then, is a distinct community, occupying its own territory with boundaries accurately described, in which the laws of Georgia have no right to enter save with the assent of the Cherokees themselves, or in conformity with treaties and with the acts of Congress. The whole intercourse between the United States and this nation is, by our Constitution and laws, vested in the government of the United States. The act of the state of Georgia under which the plaintiff was prosecuted is consequently void and the judgment a nullity.[18]

The mandate which was issued in accordance with this decision was totally disregarded by the state authorities. Opinions were quoted in the press of the state strongly favoring the use of force, and frequent references were made to the dangers of judicial despotism.[19] The case was supposed to demonstrate the absurdity of the doctrine that the federal courts were granted a supreme control over the states.

In the controversy with the Creeks the state authorities succeeded in gaining control of the lands because Congress failed to uphold President Adams in his attempt to enforce the treaties with the Indians. In the Cherokee difficulty the Supreme Court was humiliated

---

17 Worcester v. The State of Georgia, 6 Peters 515 (1832).

18 6 Peters 560, 561.

19 *Niles Register*, 42:78.

because President Jackson supported the policy of the state government. In his first annual message, on December 8, 1829, the President informed the country that

if the general government is not permitted to tolerate the erection of a confederate state within the territory of one of the members of this Union against her consent, much less could it allow a foreign and independent government to establish itself there. . . . . Actuated by this view of the subject, I informed the Indians inhabiting parts of Georgia and Alabama that their attempt to establish an independent government would not be countenanced by the Executive of the United States, and advised them to emigrate beyond the Mississippi or submit to the laws of those states.[20]

As a result of the lack of unity of action among the departments of the federal government, Georgia felt at liberty to resist judicial mandates and enforce her own laws regardless of orders from the federal courts. The missionaries were finally pardoned by the governor, and the great question at issue was settled by an act of Congress providing for the removal of the Indian tribes to the territory beyond the Mississippi River.[21] A few references to the controversy are to be found in the campaign literature of the time, the failure of the President to secure the enforcement of federal judicial decrees being used as the basis of a political attack on Jackson and his party.[22]

---

[20] James D. Richardson, *Messages and Papers of the Presidents* (New York, 1911) 2:457, 458.

[21] *U. S. Statutes* at Large, 4:411, 412 (1830).

[22] *Works* of Daniel Webster, 1:269; Niles, *op. cit.*, 43:140. It was in connection with the Worcester case that Jackson is reported to have declared that he would not enforce the decree of the court. There is doubt whether Jackson made such an assertion. Henry Clay and others, perhaps, for political purposes gave publicity to the report that the President had indicated his disapproval of the attitude of the Supreme Court.—Horace Greeley, *The American Conflict* (Chicago, 1864) 1:106; Charles Warren, *The Supreme Court in United States History* (Boston, 1922) 2:219.

Georgia's successful resistance in this dispute was a victory for the Democrats, and, together with the bank controversy where the authority of the Supreme Court was successfully challenged from another quarter, may be looked upon as the beginning of a new era in the history of the court: an era when questions heretofore determined by the court were voluntarily turned over to the political departments of the government; when the doctrine of implied powers, under which the authority of the federal government had been enlarged, received a more restricted application; when the states were given greater freedom from interference by the federal judiciary. There was also a reversal of some of the nationalistic policies of Hamilton and Marshall and a return to the principles of Jefferson and Jackson. The Federalist party lost control of its only stronghold—the Supreme Court; the Democratic party, for the first time, held full sway in all departments of the government. Four of the fundamental policies of the party pointed toward a strict construction of the Constitution: the treatment of the Indians, the refusal of the United States government to take part in internal improvements, the reduction of the tariff, and the attack upon the national bank.

3. *The attitude of President Jackson—*

The issue on the continuance of the national bank raised a constitutional question of prime importance. The Supreme Court, in the cases of *McCulloch v. Maryland*[23] and of *Osborn v. United States' Bank*,[24] had upheld the United States government in the establishment of a national bank and had checked the authority of the states to interfere with the institution. The great argument against the bank on the ground of its unconstitutionality

---

[23] 4 Wheaton 316 (1819).   [24] 9 Wheaton 738 (1824).

had been brushed aside by the court in the formulation of the famous implied power doctrine. The bank continued to do business under a charter granted by Congress.

Jackson and his party associates detested the bank. Its power, prestige and, it was charged, some of its money had been used to support the administration of President Adams. The corporation was attacked on all sides, but in no way so emphatically as on the issue of its unconstitutionality. In spite of a special message from the President against the bank, both houses of Congress voted to recharter the corporation.[25] In the forceful veto with which Jackson returned the bill to Congress we have the President's opinion on judicial powers:[26]

It is maintained by the advocates of the bank that its constitutionality in all its features ought to be considered as settled by precedent and by the decision of the Supreme Court. To this conclusion I cannot assent. . . . . If the opinion of the Supreme Court covered the whole ground of this act, it ought not to control the coordinate authorities of this government. The Congress, the Executive and the Court must each for itself be guided by its own opinion of the Constitution. Each public officer who takes an oath to support the Constitution swears that he will support it as he understands it, and not as it is understood by others. It is as much the duty of the House of Representatives, or the Senate, and of the President, to decide upon the constitutionality of any bill or resolution which may be presented to them for passage or approval, as it is of the Supreme Court, when it may be brought before them for judicial decision. The opinion of the judges has no more authority over Congress than the opinion of Congress has over the judges; and, on that point, the President is independent of both. The authority of the Supreme Court must not, therefore, be permitted to control the Congress or the executive when acting in their legislative

---

[25] Senate *Journal*, 22 Cong., 1 sess., 451–453.

[26] Richardson, *Messages and Papers of the Presidents*, 2:581, 582.

capacities, but to have only such influence as the force of their reasoning may deserve.

The President continued to the effect that the question of the kind or necessity of a banking institution was a subject exclusively for legislative consideration. It was the province of the President and the legislature to determine whether a banking institution was necessary and to fix the powers and duties of such an institution, and from their decision there was no appeal to the courts.[27] In short, the President insisted that the legislative and executive departments as well as the courts had the authority to determine the constitutionality as well as the expediency of a national bank.

4. *Change in the personnel of the Supreme Court—*

Chief Justice Marshall lived to see the reversal of certain principles upon which he had been building a unique constitutional structure. He had seen his efforts toward the enlargement of the field of authority of the central government and the restriction of the scope of action of the states of the Union, sanctioned by the nation. He had taken advantage of the opportunity to lay the foundation for a strong central government, construing powers from the vague and indefinite provisions of a written instrument which left many questions unde-

---

[27] Senate *Journal*, 22 Cong., 1 sess., 439. Certain writers attempt to limit the scope of Jackson's reference to constitutional questions as applying only to his authority to veto laws. They cite an opinion of Chief Justice Taney (*Maryland Hist. Mag.*, March 1915, 10:23) to sustain this view. That this was not the current impression regarding the message may be seen from the comment of Daniel Webster, who criticised this message as follows: ''The President, if the principle and reasoning of the message be sound, may either execute or not execute the laws of the land, according to his sovereign pleasure. He may refuse to put into execution one law, pronounced valid by all branches of government, and yet execute another which may have been by constitutional authority pronounced void.''— *Works* (National ed.) 2:122.

termined because of its brevity and also through fear lest its adoption might be jeopardized. His appeal for broad and liberal principles of interpretation rested on the grounds of expediency and necessity, and under the peculiar conditions of the time his arguments were used with remarkable effect.

But the closing years in the career of the Chief Justice were embittered by persistent opposition to his policies. Georgia had successfully defied the authority of the court with the sympathetic support of the President and both houses of Congress. The President, moreover, had turned the force of his logic against the doctrine that the Supreme Court was the final interpreter of the Constitution. A still greater disappointment arose when, after careful consideration of two cases—one relative to a bank controversy[28] and the other concerning the regulation of commerce[29]—the Chief Justice was obliged to announce that

the practice of this court is not (except in cases of absolute necessity) to deliver any judgment in cases where constitutional questions are involved, unless four judges concur in opinion,

---

[28] Briscoe v. Bank of Kentucky, 8 Peters 118 (1834) and 11 Peters 257 (1837).

On the final disposition of this case Justice Story dissenting said: "When this cause was formerly argued before this court, a majority of the judges, who then heard it, were decidedly of the opinion that the act of Kentucky establishing this bank, was unconstitutional and void, as amounting to an authority to emit bills of credit for and on behalf of the state, within the prohibition of the constitution of the United States. In principle it was thought to be decided by the case of Craig v. the State of Missouri, 4 Peters 410. Among that majority was the late Chief Justice Marshall; a name never to be pronounced without reverence. The cause has been again argued, and precisely upon the same ground as the former argument. A majority of my brethren have now pronounced the act of Kentucky to be constitutional. I dissent from that opinion; and retaining the same opinion which I held at the first argument in common with the Chief Justice, I shall now proceed to state the reasons on which it is founded."—11 Peters 257, 328 (1837).

[29] City of New York v. Miln, 11 Peters 102 (1837).

thus making the decision a majority of the whole court. In the present cases four judges do not concur in opinion as to the constitutional question which has been argued. The court, therefore, directs these cases to be reargued at the next term under the expectation that a larger number of the judges may then be present.[30]

This was a confession on the part of Chief Justice Marshall that the Federalist control of the judicial branch of the national government was losing ground. A change in the political tenor of the government was affecting the trend of constitutional interpretation. The advocates of the extreme form of the American practice of judicial veto of state laws, which tended toward the enlargement of national control through the doctrine of implied powers and placed limitations on the realm of state action through an extensive application of a few general principles of the Constitution, became alarmed. Reviewing the progress of the federal judiciary in 1838, the *Democratic Review* asserted that nearly every state had been brought up for sentence and had been forced to pass through "the Caudine forks of a subjugation which has more than revived the suability of states." Forty cases were styled "political fulminations" upon which the great fabric of judicial architecture was built.[31] Federal judicial authority was checked in the contest with Georgia and was arrested through the political revolution which gave Jackson and Van Buren an opportunity to change the personnel of the Supreme Court. The wave of democracy which swept over the country had a similar result upon the attitude of the state courts toward the developing practice of judicial supremacy.

---

[30] 8 Peters 121 (1834). Justices Johnson and Duvall were absent when these cases were argued.

[31] Lalor, *Cyclopaedia of Political Science*, 2:649, 650.

With the appointment of Roger B. Taney to the Supreme Court, the dominant influence of Marshall and his oldtime associates ceased. Justice Taney had served in the cabinet under President Jackson at the time of the controversy over the national bank, and was known to be in sympathy with the main policies of the Democratic party. His appointment was purposely planned to place at the head of the court a justice who stood for a strict construction of the Constitution, a greater respect for the rights of the states, and a lessening of judicial interference in the public affairs of the nation. Although Chief Justice Taney did not control the policy of the court as completely as Marshall had directed its course in the previous period of American constitutional history, nevertheless his opinions indicate clearly the tendencies of the time.

5. *Maintenance of the rights of the state—*

The earlier opinions of Chief Justice Taney were characterized by a strict adherence to the language of the Constitution, the doctrine of implied powers was narrowly interpreted, and the principles of convenience and expediency were used to restrict the rapidly developing powers of the central government rather than to enlarge them. He was especially anxious to allow the freest exercise of authority by the states which a strict interpretation of the Constitution would permit. The result of such a policy was not likely to involve the federal courts in contests over assertion of authority either with the states or with other departments of the federal government. For a period of twenty years the main point to be considered in constitutional interpretation was the method by which conflicts might be avoided and judicial powers restricted in the opinions of a court controlled by men under the influence of Democratic doctrines.[32]

A significant feature of the opinions handed down by Chief Justice Taney was his insistence upon the maintenance of the reserved rights of the states. His main contention was that the states could not be restrained within narrower limits than those fixed by the Constitution of the United States, and that within these limits they were the sole judges of what was best for their own interest.

When the majority opinion of the court, delivered by Justice Story a few years before his resignation, maintained that the power of legislation on the subject of fugitives from labor was exclusively in Congress, Chief Justice Taney agreed in the judgment, but denounced a part of the opinion of Story as an unjustifiable interference with state legislation.[33] In the absence of any express prohibition, he could perceive no reason for establishing one by implication. Later the Chief Justice took a firmer stand in preserving the integrity of state authority.[34] The states had attempted to regulate the liquor traffic and had come into conflict with the principles laid down by the Supreme Court in the case of *Brown v. Maryland*.[35] Some of the principles upheld in earlier cases were discarded by the Chief Justice in the words:

It is equally clear that the power of Congress over this subject does not extend further than the regulation of commerce

---

[32] Referring to the change in the personnel and decisions of the Supreme Court after Jackson's inauguration as President, Professor and Mrs. Beard remark: "Thus, in solemn decisions, Jacksonian judges from agrarian states broke down the historic safeguards thrown around property rights by the letter of the Constitution and the Jurisprudence of John Marshall."—*The Rise of American Civilization* (New York, 1927) 1:689.

[33] Prigg v. Commonwealth of Pennsylvania, 16 Peters 539, 626-633 (1842).

[34] License Cases, 5 Howard 504 (1847).

[35] 12 Wheaton 419 (1827).

with foreign nations and among the several states; and that beyond these limits the states never have surrendered their power over trade and commerce, and may still exercise it free from any controlling power on the part of the central government. Every state, therefore, may regulate its own internal traffic according to its own judgment and upon its own views of the interest and well-being of its citizens.[36]

Men of the time agreed that the regulation of commerce was given exclusively to the general government, and that even if Congress did not regulate, the states could not; if Congress enacted legislation, all state laws to the contrary had to give way; but the real issue was whether the states could regulate at all. The Supreme Court had been inclined toward the view of an exclusive grant to Congress. The Chief Justice answered this contention by stating that

the controlling and supreme power over commerce with foreign nations and the several states is undoubtedly conferred upon Congress. Yet, in my judgment, the states may nevertheless, for the safety or convenience of trade, or for the protection of the health of its citizens, make regulations of commerce for its own ports and harbors, for its own territory; and such regulations are valid unless they come into conflict with the laws of congress.[37]

This judgment of Chief Justice Taney was upheld by later decisions on commercial questions.[38]

The doctrine of implied powers belonging to the federal government and the correlative doctrine of implied prohibitions on the states, as defined by Chief Justice Marshall, were repudiated or restricted in their implications by the Supreme Court.

---

[36] License Cases, 5 Howard 579.

[37] *Ibid.*, 579.

[38] See Leisy v. Hardin, 135 U. S. 100 (1890) and in re Rahrer, 140 U. S. 545 (1891).

6. Change in the attitude of state courts—

Restrictions upon the supervisory power of the federal courts over state statutes were not the only check which the Jacksonian democracy aimed to place upon the developing practice of the supremacy of the courts. As a result of the victory of the Democrats in a majority of the commonwealths a corresponding change in attitude is to be noted in the state courts. Judges were inclined to recognize the principle of legislative supremacy, and the sparing use of the authority to nullify acts from 1830 to 1860 proves that the new type of democracy was not disposed to tolerate any serious barriers to the enforcement of the rule of the people. The right of courts to invalidate legislative enactments, after the first wave of enthusiasm which brought its adoption, was indeed scarcely used before the Civil War in any but a few states as an effective check upon legislative power. The practice of judicial review was confined during this period mainly to four states, North Carolina, Massachusetts, New York, and New Hampshire.[39] In New York from 1830 to 1845 only five decisions were rendered invalidating acts or portions thereof, and in Massachusetts, for the same period, only one important statute was held void.

Great care was taken to preserve the authority of the judiciary to limit legislative power, but neither state nor federal courts were inclined so to exercise authority as to interpose a serious barrier to the activity of legislatures. Some far-reaching claims had been made by the courts of New York in asserting the authority to defend vested rights and to interpose limitations on the basis of

---

[39] Cf. Edward S. Corwin, "The Establishment of Judicial Review," 9 *Mich. Law Rev.* (Feb. 1911) 315, and "The Doctrine of Due Process of Law before the Civil War," 24 *Harv. Law Rev.* (March 1911) 366.

natural law theories.[40] And in North Carolina the phrase "the law of the land," was construed as a restriction upon legislative action.[41] But in these states the period of democratic ascendancy tended to restrict the barriers which the courts had set up. The development and extension of judicial control over legislation into an effective check upon many fields of legislative activity was deferred until the period subsequent to the Civil War.

A departure from the rule of deferring to the popular judgments, which prevailed for almost three decades, was the effort of the Supreme Court under Chief Justice Taney to settle the slavery issue regardless of the fact that the court's decision required an overturning of a statute of many years' standing. This decision involved the federal judiciary in the first of a series of controversies which ceased only with the complete restoration of peace in all parts of the United States.

Before the outbreak of the Civil War other states at various times resisted the decisions and decrees of the Supreme Court. The Supreme Court of California went on record as refusing to obey a writ of error of the Court,[42] but its action was later condemned by the state legislature. South Carolina inserted a section in its Nullification Ordinance designed to prevent any appeals to the Supreme Court on legal questions arising out of the interpretation of the ordinance.[43] In 1859 Wisconsin refused to enforce the Fugitive Slave Law and resisted the efforts of the federal courts to compel its enforcement. Booth, who was held for trial before a United States

---

[40] Dash v. Van Kleeck, 7 Johns. 477, 499 (1811).

[41] Hoke v. Henderson, 2 Dev. 1 (1833).

[42] Johnson v. Gordon, 4 Cal. 368 (1854).

[43] This provision was held void by the state supreme court in State v. McCready, 2 Hill 1 (1834).

district court, was released on a writ of habeas corpus on the ground that the Fugitive Slave Law was void, and the state supreme court affirmed this decision. A writ of error issued by Chief Justice Taney ordering the state court to forward its proceedings for review was ignored. The Supreme Court of the United States assumed jurisdiction notwithstanding this refusal and reversed the decision of the lower court.[44] The state courts refused to recognize or enforce this judgment and the legislature approved their action by passing a resolution denying that the Supreme Court was granted authority to assume jurisdiction over the state courts. Accepting the compact theory of government the legislature insisted that the states must be ultimate judges of the infractions of the Constitution.[45]

From 1789 to 1860 the jurisdiction of the federal courts under the 25th section of the Judiciary Act resulted in vigorous protests from two-thirds of the states and in several instances almost led to armed resistance. Vigorous efforts in Congress to repeal this section of the Judiciary Act failed to secure any change in the law. There was a determined attempt to repeal the 25th section of the Judiciary Act in 1831, after the Supreme Court had held void the Missouri law authorizing the issue of loan certificates[46] and had attempted to interfere with Georgia's jurisdiction over the Cherokee Indians. The justices feared at times that the jurisdiction of the court over the states was in serious danger.[47] But in most of the controversies with the states the federal judiciary came out victorious and with the Democratic control of

---

[44] Ableman v. Booth, 21 Howard 506 (1858).

[45] Laws of Wis., 1858, 247, 248 and Ames, *op. cit.*, 303.

[46] Craig v. Missouri, 4 Peters 410 (1830).

[47] Warren, *op. cit.*, 163.

the Supreme Court resistance from the states was reduced to a minimum until the slavery controversy involved the court once more in the turmoil of politics and let loose the spirit of defiance which had been suppressed for several decades.

Evidence of the impending crisis which a long line of conflicts with the states over the extensive powers exercised by the federal courts particularly in the way of limiting state authority and extending national powers had aroused to a pitch little short of war, is shown in a type of judicial opinion rendered by a Georgia justice in 1854.

Justice Banning, who held valid a state tax on gross sales so far as it applied to imports, despite the decision of the Supreme Court in *Brown v. Maryland*,[48] prepared a lengthy opinion which he said represented his own views.[49] He argued against the Hamilton-Marshall doctrine of implied powers and reviewed the cases in which the states had resisted the decrees of the Supreme Court. The power to annul state laws, he claimed, was not expressly given to the federal government. Consequently, "The Supreme Court of the United States has no jurisdiction over this court or over any department of the government of Georgia. This Court is not a United States Court; and therefore, neither the government of the United States, nor any department of it, can give this Court an order."[50] The Supreme Court of Georgia is therefore, co-equal and coordinate with the Supreme Court of the United States. Reference was made to the fact that the courts of Georgia treated with contempt the claim of jurisdiction over them by the Supreme Court of

[48] 12 Wheaton 419 (1827).
[49] Padelford v. Savannah, 14 Ga. 438 (1854).
[50] 14 Ga. 499.

the United States. And Judge Banning added, "in this course, on the part of the Judiciary, the Legislature and the Executive concurred—indeed cooperated. And the people approved the conduct of the whole."[51] The decisions rendered by John Marshall and other justices of Federalist inclinations were styled "political decisions made by partisan judges," which will be overruled as the present majority of justices belong to a different school of politics. Since all constitutional decisions are more or less political and partisan in character, it was thought that the ultimate tribunal on such questions should be the people.

When, a few years later, the Supreme Court of the United States decided a slavery controversy favorably to the South, Southern statesmen came to the defense of the federal judiciary while the way was being prepared in the Northern states for defiance of and resistance to national judicial authority.

---

[51] *Ibid.*, 506.

CHAPTER XIII

POLITICS AND FEDERAL CONSTITUTIONAL LAW

1. *The personnel of the court and dissenting opinions*—

AMERICAN constitutional law, a great teacher of property law once observed, is more politics than law.[1] Certainly the political character of federal constitutional law is evidenced by the differences of opinion on many of the issues decided by the courts and particularly in those cases in which federal or state laws were declared unconstitutional. The close relations of the Supreme Court of the United States to politics may be discerned from the influence and control over the court exercised by the President and Congress and by the persistent divisions within the membership of the court as indicated by dissents. Since a written constitution deals primarily with matters of special political import, it is to be expected that its interpretation will be directed in a large measure by political influences. The doctrine of judicial supremacy has greatly increased the political significance of the Supreme Court in American governmental affairs.

President Washington, who was careful in making his selections for public office, exercised peculiar care in his nominations for the members of the Supreme Court. All the first five appointees to the Supreme Bench were supporters of the Constitution either in the federal con-

---

[1] See Felix Frankfurter, "The Constitutional Opinions of Justice Holmes," 29 *Harv. Law Rev.* (April 1916) 683.

vention or in the state conventions, and were known to be actively in sympathy with the Federalist principles of politics to which Washington adhered. Jay's Federalist inclinations were evidenced in numerous public statements and records. Cushing was a pronounced Federalist. Wilson, although somewhat democratic in certain opinions, was classed as a Federalist on the big issues which divided the parties. Blair was a friend of Washington and a Federalist in his political thinking. The remaining appointees of President Washington—Iredell, Johnson, Paterson, Ellsworth, and Chase—are all characterized by their biographers as ardent Federalists. Thus Washington himself "initiated the system of appointing political adherents, and political adherents only to places on the Supreme bench. That system has seldom been departed from."[2]

It was a bench of judges whose opinions in politics conformed to those of the Federalist party that rendered the decision in *Chisholm v. Georgia*,[3] affirming the doctrine of national as against state sovereignty and the right of maintaining a suit against a state. Iredell alone supported the view which had been announced while the Constitution was being adopted and in which the popular uprising which soon wrote into fundamental law the Eleventh Amendment, was anticipated.

John Adams, too, appointed to the court men whose Federalist inclinations were previously well established. The Federalists were evidently bent on securing federal supremacy by means of the judiciary and it was generally conceded that when defeated in the elections, they hoped, through the judiciary, to exercise a check on the other

---

[2] W. D. Coles, "Politics and the Supreme Court of the United States," 27 *Am. Law Rev.* (March-April, 1893) 183.

[3] 2 Dall. 419 (1793).

branches of the government. As Federalists the justices supported so far as their judicial offices would permit the main principles of that party. Nationalism was upheld as against local interests and state rights, and federal authority was to be expanded by application of the principles of the common law and of international law. The Federalist theories of the separation of powers and the independence of the courts were enunciated as legal principles with the design chiefly to serve as a check upon the growing powers of the legislature. As a culmination of these principles the doctrine was announced that courts could declare legislative acts void, if regarded by the judges as in conflict with the provisions of the Constitution, and that they should protect vested rights from legislative attacks even though no provisions of the Constitution prevented such legislation.[4] The courts thus were regarded as the champions of one national consolidated government and of the conservative groups which demanded a check on the other departments of government particularly to protect property and contracts.[5]

But the enunciation of good Federalist doctrines as principles of constitutional law was not the only evidence of partisanship on the part of the judges. Wharton gives an account of the political trials which followed soon after the adoption of the Constitution, in which it was held that by the common law the federal courts had the power to punish offenses against the laws of the United States or the law of nations.[6] Justice Chase was such an

---

[4] For thirty-four years it is claimed, John Marshall labored unceasingly to counteract the political principles of Thomas Jefferson. See W. D. Lewis, *Great American Lawyers* (Philadelphia, 1907) 2:337, and Martin Van Buren, *Inquiry into the Origin and Cause of Political Parties in the United States*, 282.

[5] See Beveridge, *Life of John Marshall*, 3:11.

[6] *State Trials* 1 ff., also Henfield's case.

extreme partisan and so overbearing in his conduct of trials that vigorous protests were made. In one of the trials under the Alien and Sedition Law the attorneys for the defense withdrew from the case, and the Philadelphia bar after inquiring into Chase's behavior at this trial resolved not to appear before him while on circuit. In other cases every point presented by the defense the Justice swept aside in a contemptuous manner.[7] And it was the practice of the judges to dilate on the duty of loyalty to the federal government and to laud the virtues and beneficence of the Constitution. The charges to grand juries were often political harangues designed to uphold the Federalist ideals of government and to set opposition to these ideals in the light of traitorous and rebellious conduct.

The close of President Adams' administration was marked by a series of events destined to completely enmesh the federal courts in the whirlpool of partisan politics. First of these events was the resignation of Ellsworth in time to permit Adams to appoint a Federalist as his successor and thus thwart Jefferson's design to nominate Spencer Roane for this post.[8] The fact that it was necessary for Marshall to hold two offices for one month contrary to a prohibition in the Constitution did not disturb Federalist leaders in carrying out their political program. A second event of greater political significance was the enactment of a law reorganizing the judiciary and the filling of many positions created by the act with Federalist friends and sympathizers. With the rush of the concluding days of the administration taken up in confirming nominations to these positions and the

---

[7] See Ensminger Mowry, ''Political and Party Aspects of the National Judiciary, 1789–1801,'' *Am. Hist. Mag.*, 3:83, 331, 471, at 95, and Coles, *op. cit.*, 191 ff.

[8] Beveridge, *op. cit.*, 3:114.

signing and delivering of commissions, the stage was set for a political conflict involving the entire federal judicial establishment, which engrossed much of the time and attention of the new administration for a number of years. The story of the repealing act with the consequent political alignments has been treated elsewhere.[9]

Senator Beveridge observed that Marshall had gradually become the leader and spokesman for the Federalist party and that, while serving at the same time as Secretary of State and Chief Justice, he was using all his energy and ability to save the defeated remnants of his party from utter rout.[10] According to Justice Story, Marshall was

in the original, genuine sense of the word a Federalist—a Federalist in the good old school in which Washington was the acknowledged head and in which he lived and died. In the maintenance of the principles of that school, he was ready at all times to stand forth the determined advocate and supporter. On this subject he scorned all disguise; he affected no change of opinion; he sought no shelter from reproach.[11]

It was not expected that Marshall would leave his stern and persistent principles of Federalism behind when he went on the bench. By his decision in the *Marbury Case,* by his conduct of the Burr trial, and by a series of constitutional decisions, Marshall "labored ceaselessly to counteract Jefferson's constitutional principles," clothing in constitutional law and making a part of our federal system of government some of the waning and popularly discarded doctrines of Federalism.[12] When Chief Justice

---

[9] Cf. *supra,* 244 *et seq.*

[10] See especially, *The Life of John Marshall,* 2:558–564; also, Mowry, "Political and Party Aspects of the National Judiciary, 1789–1801," *Am. Hist. Mag.,* 3:83, 331, 471.

[11] Joseph Story, *Miscellaneous Writings,* 649 ff.

[12] Mowry, *op. cit.,* 3:83, 331 and 471.

Marshall is credited with putting life into the Constitution or with being the creator of the Constitution, little else is meant than that the familiar tenets of Hamiltonian Federalism were incorporated into our constitutional structure while full sanction for the process was given by the Supreme Court.[13] In view of the supposed detachment and impartiality of judges it is rather strange to have biographers refer to Marshall's constitutional opinions as "state papers of the first rank," as embodying "constructive judicial statesmanship," and to describe him as devoting his energies as a judge "to strengthen and enlarge the powers of the national government," and as the "constructing architect of American nationalism."[14]

Jefferson, Madison, and Monroe appointed only Democrats or, as they were then called, Democratic-Republicans, to the vacancies on the court. By 1815, in accordance with the wishes of Jefferson, the court had become Democratic in political affiliations, that is, a majority of its members were supporters of Jefferson at the time of their appointment.[15] But, owing to the fact that Justice Johnson changed in his political thought to a mild form of Federalism and that Justice Story was won over from his earlier political views to become a defender of Federalism and the advocate of Marshall's policies and,

---

[13] Much of the prestige of Marshall rests upon the success with which he injected "emotional drive" into the doctrine that "the constitution deals with great governmental powers to be exercised to great public ends" and thereby gave the weight of judicial sanction to one of the primary tenets of Federalism.—Cf. Frankfurter, "The Constitutional Opinions of Justice Holmes," 29 *Harv. Law Rev.* (April 1916) 683, 685.

[14] See Beveridge, *Life of John Marshall*, 3, preface, 15, 75, 109, 132, 178; 4:117, 169; and Edward S. Corwin, *John Marshall and the Constitution* (New Haven, 1921) 122. Marshall expressed his prejudice and opposition to Jefferson when he wrote, "the Democrats are divided into speculative theorists and absolute terrorists, with the latter I am disposed to class Mr. Jefferson."—Beveridge, *op. cit.*, 3:11.

[15] Cf. William E. Dodd, "Chief Justice Marshall and Virginia," *Am. Hist. Rev.* (July 1907) 12:776 ff.

also, that the other Democratic appointees were unequal to the task of placing a check on the strong position and determination of the Chief Justice, the complaint was frequently raised that the Supreme Court, which was supposed to be Democratic in sentiment, had become the bulwark of a new Federalism.[16] The first real change in the political affiliations of the members of the court came with the appointments of President Jackson. Five vacancies were filled with Democrats—McLean 1828, Baldwin 1830, Wayne 1835, Taney and Barbour 1836— and in order to make Democratic control secure, Congress, on March 3, 1837, passed an act increasing the number of justices from seven to nine. The Democrats were thus doing what the Federalists had done a generation before.[17]

For twenty-eight years the appointments continued to be adherents of the Democratic party with one exception, that of Justice Curtis, a Whig who was appointed by President Fillmore. The Chief Justice and his associates ceased to support the extreme measures of protection to be accorded to vested rights in accordance with the Dartmouth College decision,[18] began to interpret more narrowly the Federalist doctrine of implied powers, and to use the principles of convenience and expediency to restrict the rapidly developing powers of the central government, rather than to enlarge them. For a period of more than twenty years the court was influenced in its opinions by men who held Democratic views just as it was influenced in the earlier period by the dominance of the Federalists. The court continued under Democratic

---

[16] Cf. Dodd, *op. cit.*, 776 ff.

[17] Sutherland, "Politics and the Supreme Court," 48 *Am. Law Rev.* (May-June 1914) 390, 396.

[18] See Charles River Bridge Case, 11 Peters 420 (1837).

control until the great upheaval of the Civil War brought about a change both in personnel and in point of view.

Because it was called upon to deal with fiercely contested political issues, the Supreme Court was regarded as a stronghold that it was necessary to control in order to assure political success. The Federalists saw to it that no "Jacobin" contaminated the high judicial chamber. To the Democratic-Republicans only faithful party members were considered for vacancies on the bench, and when a reformed Democratic party came into power, the court was soon reconstituted with Democrats of the new school. It has come to pass then that "Congresses and Senates, and Presidents have used the Supreme Bench as constituting a part of the political machinery of the great parties of the country"[19] and, while it may be too much to say that on the bench the justices continue to be politicians and to stand by their party in questions that would materially affect its success, there is enough evidence to demonstrate that partisan influences have been at work in the Supreme Court chamber. Moreover, evidences of these partisan influences which are apparent in certain opinions and judgments of the court are no less in evidence in the differences of opinion manifested by the members of the Supreme Court in their dissenting opinions.

During the first decade after 1789 it was the custom in the majority of cases for the justices to render opinions seriatim, each justice stating the reasons which impelled him to render judgment. The prevalence of this custom may be indicated by the following table of important cases prior to the August term, 1800:

[19] Morgan, "Partisanship in the Supreme Court," *North Am. Rev.*, 132:181.

<table>
<tr><td>SERIATIM</td><td>UNANIMOUS</td></tr>
</table>

SERIATIM	UNANIMOUS
State of Georgia v. Brailsford, 1st	State of Georgia v. Brailsford, 3d
State of Georgia v. Brailsford, 2d	Glass v. Sloop Betsey
Chisholm, Exr. v. Georgia	United States v. Lawrence
Bingham v. Cabot, evenly divided on two points	Hills v. Ross
	McDonough v. Dannery
Penhallow v. Doane's Administrator	Beyer v. Michel
	Brown v. Van Braam
Talbot v. Janson	Hollingsworth v. Virginia
Hylton v. United States	
Ware v. Hylton	
Fenemore v. United States	
Calder v. Bull	
Cooper v. Telfair	
Priestman v. United States	

Such important issues as were raised in *Chisholm v. Georgia, Hylton v. United States,* and *Ware v. Hylton* were determined by a common judgment arrived at through different methods of reasoning. No justice succeeded in becoming the oracle for the judgments and opinions of the courts.

The first dissenting opinion was delivered by Justice Thomas Johnson.[20] It was soon followed by the only great dissent in the first ten years of the court's work—that of Justice Iredell in the *Chisholm Case*.[21] "I am now decidedly of opinion," asserted Iredell, "that no such action as this before the court can legally be maintained."

With the accession to the bench of John Marshall as Chief Justice in 1801 the practice of delivering opinions *seriatim* was abandoned.[22] The striking change in atti-

---

[20] State of Georgia v. Brailsford, 2 Dallas 402 (1792). Cf. also for differences in reasoning of justices.

[21] 2 Dallas 419.

[22] "I rejoice in the example you set of *seriatim* opinions," wrote Jefferson to Justice William Johnson, "and I have heard it often noticed and always with high approbation. Some of your brethren will be encouraged to follow it occasionally, and in time it may be felt as a duty, and the sound practice of the primitive court be again restored."—*Works* (Fed. ed.) 12:259.

tude and opinions of the court, which resulted from Marshall's appointment can be appreciated only by a comparison with preceding years.[23] Twenty-four cases are reported in volume 1 of the Reports by Cranch. The opinions rendered by the court in these cases are distributed as follows:

Chief Justice	13
Chase	1
Paterson	1
(Chief Justice refrained from taking part because he had tried the case in lower court.)	
Judgments by the court without opinions	9

The opinions by Chief Justice Marshall were as a rule brief, dealing concisely with the specific issue before the court. If there were divergent views on the questions litigated the members of the court refrained from making their views public. In the case of *Abercrombie v. Dupuis* the court voted that the issue involved had been decided in an earlier case and "they did not think proper to overrule that case."[24] The Chief Justice accepted this judgment with the comment that "he did not know how his opinion might be if the question were a new one." Individual opinions were subordinated to the necessity of upholding a judicial decision previously announced. The reporter spoke of this significant change in terms of the highest praise.[25]

In a government which is emphatically styled a government of laws [he noted] the least possible range ought to be left for the discretion of the judge. Whatever tends to render laws certain, equally tends to limit that discretion. . . . . Every case

---

[23] In Talbot v. Seeman, 1 Cranch 1, Beveridge observes that Marshall disregarded the custom of the delivery of opinions by the justices *seriatim* and assumed the function of presenting the views of the court.—*Life of John Marshall*, 3:16.

[24] 1 Cranch 342 (1803).

[25] 1 Cranch, Preface.

decided is a check upon the judge. He cannot decide a similar case differently without strong reasons, which, for his own justification, he will wish to make public.

The same preponderance of opinions by Marshall appears in the second volume of Cranch's Reports. Twenty-one causes were considered and adjudged by the court. The decisions were distributed as follows:

Chief Justice	14
Cushing	1
(Minor opinion of a few lines.)	
Judgments by the Court without opinion	5

The Chief Justice declined to take part in the hearing of the case *McIlvaine v. Coxe's Lessee*[26] because of the fact that he was previously interested in the case and had formed an opinion on the issue. The case was argued February 1804; no opinion was rendered until February 1808. In the *United States v. Fisher*,[27] Justice Washington was unable to concur in the opinion and judgment rendered by the court. An opinion in the form of a dissent was filed with a frank confession of high respect for the court's judgment:

In any instance where I am so unfortunate as to differ with this court, I cannot fail to doubt the correctness of my own opinion. But if I cannot feel convinced of the error I owe it in some measure to myself, and to those who may be injured by the expense and delay to which they have been exposed, to show at least that the opinion was not hastily or inconsiderately given

In 3 Cranch, opinions were delivered as follows:

Marshall	26
(One dissent from result.)	
Judgments without opinion	6
Seriatim opinions	5
(In all of which Marshall did not participate.)	

---

[26] 2 Cranch 280 (1805).   [27] 2 Cranch 358, 397 ff.

And in 4 Cranch:

Marshall	32
Judgments without opinion	6
Johnson	2
(Marshall did not participate.)	
Chase	1
(Marshall did not participate.)	

On one occasion Cushing, Chase, Livingston, and Johnson disagreed with some of the conclusions of the Chief Justice,[28] and in one case Chase and Livingston dissented.[29] When Marshall held that the stipulation in a treaty "that free ships shall make free goods" does not imply the converse that "enemy ships shall make enemy goods," Justices Story and Johnson dissented.[30] Justice Story expressed regret that he was unable to agree with the majority of the court but held it an indispensable duty not to surrender his own judgment because the weight of opinion was against him.[31] From 1816 there was a striking unanimity in the decisions of the court. Marshall, Story, and Washington were the leaders in supporting the Federalist leanings of the court on constitutional issues. But the other justices usually agreed with the exception of a dissent by Duvall without opinion in the *Dartmouth College Case*.[32] Occasionally Justice Johnson assumed a critical attitude toward the conclusions of the Federalist Justices. Concurring in the decision but not in the reasoning in *Martin v. Hunter's Lessee* he said:

I flatter myself that the full extent of the constitutional revisory power may be secured to the United States, and the benefits of it to the individual, without ever resorting to compulsory or

---

28 Rose v. Himely, 4 Cranch 241 (1808).
29 Hudson v. Guestier, 4 Cranch 293 (1808).
30 The Nereide, 9 Cranch 389 (1815).
31 *Ibid.*, 455.
32 4 Wheaton 518, 713 (1819).

restrictive process upon the state tribunals; a right which, I repeat again, Congress has not asserted; nor has this court asserted, nor does there appear any necessity for asserting.[33]

Marshall's only dissent from the majority was rendered in the case of *Ogden v. Saunders*.[34] In an important case involving state insolvent laws it was impossible to render a judgment in which all the members of the court agreed. Justices Washington, Thompson, Johnson, and Trimble rendered opinions and Marshall, Duvall, and Story dissented. On the first disposition of the case Johnson, Marshall, Duvall, and Story united in a judgment whereas Washington, Thompson, and Trimble dissented. When in a later case this difference of opinion was referred to as leaving the main issue unsettled, Marshall took occasion to state that the opinion rendered by Johnson in giving judgment established principles which were no longer open to controversy but were the settled law of the court and Justice Story also announced that this opinion must be deemed final and conclusive.[35]

The dominance of Chief Justice Marshall over the views of the court from 1801 to 1835 is shown by a summary of the opinions on constitutional questions. Thirty-six opinions were rendered by Marshall in twenty-three of which there were no dissents. During this period dissenting opinions were rendered as follows: Johnson, 8; Washington, 2; Thompson, 5; Story, 1; Duvall, 2; Marshall, 1; Baldwin, 2; McLean, 1.[36] Only a few of these dissenting opinions are significant in the development of constitutional law.

---

[33] 1 Wheaton 304, 381 (1816).

[34] 12 Wheaton 213 (1827).

[35] See Justice Story's comment in Boyle v. Zacharie and Turner, 6 Peters 635, 643 (1832).

[36] Hampton L. Carson, ''Great Dissenting Opinions,'' Am. Bar Assoc. *Reports* (1894) 273.

When President Jackson changed the personnel and political affiliations of the justices by the appointment of McLean, Baldwin, Wayne, and Taney and there was a reversal of opinion in the cases of *New York v. Miln*,[37] *Briscoe v. Bank of Kentucky*,[38] and the *Charles River Bridge Case*,[39] Justice Story attempted to uphold the Federalist point of view. In his dissent in the latter case, he observed, "I have the consolation to know that I had the entire concurrence upon the same grounds of that great constitutional jurist, the late Mr. Chief Justice Marshall." Chief Justice Taney did not attempt to rule the court and to deliver the sole opinion for the court on constitutional issues. The early practice of delivering seriatim opinions was resumed and dissents became more frequent. Justices Thompson and Story disagreed with the majority of the court that no injunction should be issued to restrain Georgia from enforcing its laws with respect to the Cherokee Indians.[40] Chief Justice Taney seldom dissented.[41] In *Prigg v. Pennsylvania*,[42] regarding the control over fugitive slaves, he concurred in rendering the judgment but vigorously disagreed with the reasoning of Justice Story.

The divergences of opinion on constitutional questions as well as on other issues which frequently involved significant political controversies from 1841 to 1860 are discovered in the opinions of Justice Daniel, who was a representative of the Virginia states-rights' school. Justice Daniel delivered the opinion of the court in eighty-

---

37 11 Peters 102 (1837).

38 Ibid., 257.

39 *Ibid.*, 420.

40 Cherokee Nation v. State of Georgia, 5 Peters 1 (1831).

41 See opinions in Wheeling Bridge Case, 9 Howard 647 (1850), and Rhode Island v. Massachusetts, 12 Peters 657 (1838).

42 16 Peters 539 (1842).

four cases and dissented in one hundred and eleven. These dissents dealt chiefly with questions of slavery,[43] of internal improvements,[44] of relations of the national government to the states,[45] of the jurisdiction of circuit courts,[46] and of the admiralty jurisdiction of the district courts.[47] The expanding admiralty jurisdiction of the district courts called for Justice Daniel's severest criticisms. He lost no opportunity to put himself on record as opposed to the extension of admiralty jurisdiction and its encroachments upon the common law and the right of trial by jury.[48]

Referring to the majority opinion in the *Passenger Cases* Justice Daniels said:

Impressed as I am with the mischiefs with which that decision is believed to be fraught, trampling down as it seems to me to do some of the strongest defenses of the safety and independence of the States of this confederacy, it would be worse than a fault in me could I contemplate the invasion in silence.[49]

Similar views were expressed by Justice Campbell who insisted that the powers of Congress were limited to the express grants in the Constitution, and that, there-

---

[43] Prigg v. Commonwealth, 16 Peters 539 (1842), and Scott v. Sandford, 19 Howard 393 (1856).

[44] Searight v. Stokes, 3 Howard 151, 180 (1845), and Neil, Moore & Co. v. State of Ohio, 3 Howard 720 (1845).

[45] License Cases, 5 Howard 504 (1846); Passenger Cases, 7 Howard 283; Cooley v. Board of Wardens, 12 Howard 299 (1851); and Wheeling Bridge Case, 13 Howard 518 (1851).

[46] McNutt v. Bland, 2 Howard 9 (1844), and Rundle v. Delaware & Raritan Canal Co., 14 Howard 80 (1852).

[47] Waring v. Clarke, 5 Howard 441 (1846).

[48] For the data regarding the dissents of Justice Daniel I am indebted to H. B. Brown, "The Dissenting Opinions of Mr. Justice Daniel," 21 *Am. Law Rev.* (Nov.-Dec. 1887) 888, 889. Though differing from the views of Justice Daniel, Mr. Brown concludes, "As an example of moral courage the career of Mr. Justice Daniel has few if any parallels in the judicial history of the country."—*Ibid.*, 900.

[49] 7 Howard 283, 494 (1849).

fore, there were no implied powers and he claimed that
the federal government was the mere "agent" of the
States.[50]

2. *Federalist principles of politics made a part of federal constitutional law*[51]—

By the time of the election of Andrew Jackson to the
Presidency the main principles of Hamiltonian Federalism had become a part of American constitutional law.
Among the features of the Federalist program especially
relating to the judiciary were: (1) a strong federal government whose powers were to be expanded by an "implied power" doctrine permitting those things to be
assumed by the federal government which might be
deemed of national importance;[52] (2) a judiciary independent of the other departments and in many respects
independent of the nation itself; (3) a doctrine of judicial
review of legislation whereby the judicial department,
independent of any effective popular control, through its
function as guardian and protector of the fundamental
law, could hold in check all departments of the government including the representatives of the people;[53] (4) a
theory of the preservation of vested rights whereby acquired rights might be protected by these independent
courts regardless of whether or not constitutions ex-

---

[50] Brown, *op. cit.*, 869.

[51] Portions of the following pages have been taken from my article,
"Histories of the Supreme Court of the United States written from the
Federalist Point of View," 4 *Southwestern Pol. and Soc. Sci. Quart.* (June
1923) with the permission of the editors.

[52] Cf. Hamilton's "Opinion on the Constitutionality of a National
Bank," *Works* (ed. 1851), 4:104 ff. See opinion of Marshall in McCulloch
v. Maryland, 4 Wheaton 516 (1819), in which this doctrine was adopted as
a principle of construction.

[53] See Hamilton's argument in No. 78 of *The Federalist*, which was
adopted by Chief Justice Marshall in Marbury v. Madison, 1 Cranch 137
(1803).

pressly provided for such protection.[54] The doctrine of judicial supremacy became the main feature of this program.

The basic ideas of the program were formulated by such men as James Wilson[55] and Alexander Hamilton, were adopted as principles of constitutional interpretation when John Marshall served as Chief Justice of the Supreme Court, and were espoused by Joseph Story[56] and James Kent with a determination to see that they were safely incorporated as fundamental principles of public law throughout the United States. Kent[57] and Story helped to give currency to these ideas and to put them under a common law cloak. Webster in his arguments before the Supreme Court and in his orations helped to impress them upon the people.[58]

---

[54] See Opinion of James Wilson on the protection of vested rights, 7 *Jour. Am. Bar Assoc.* (March 1921) 125 ff. and opinion of Alexander Hamilton, Beveridge, *The Life of John Marshall*, 3:568 ff. Cf. adoption of these views by Chief Justice Marshall in Fletcher v. Peck, 6 Cranch 87 (1810); also Edward S. Corwin, "The Basic Doctrine of American Constitutional Law," 12 *Mich. Law Rev.* (Feb. 1914) 247.

[55] Cf. L. H. Alexander, "James Wilson," 183 *North Am. Rev.* (1906) 971.

[56] It is to be noted that Story was appointed by Jefferson and was thought to be a Democratic-Republican. There were indications that he was turning Federalist before his appointment to the Supreme Court and he soon became stronger in the advocacy of Federalist principles than Marshall himself. See, for example, his opinions in Martin v. Hunter's Lessee, 1 Wheaton 304 (1816); Dartmouth College v. Woodward, 4 Wheaton 518 (1819); and Charles River Bridge v. Warren Bridge, 11 Peters 420 (1887). Writing to Kent relative to the *Dartmouth College Case*, Story urged him "to lay before the public in a popular shape, the vital importance to the well-being of society, and the security of private rights of the principles on which that decision rested. Unless I am very much mistaken these principles will be found to apply with an extensive reach to all the great concerns of the people, and will check any undue encroachments upon civil rights, which the passions or the popular doctrines of the day may stimulate our state legislatures to adopt."—*Life and Letters*, 1:331.

[57] 1 *Commentaries* 456 (ed. 12); Dash v. Van Kleeck, 7 Johns. 477, 498 (1911); and Gardner v. Newburgh, 2 Johns. 162, 167 (1816). See also, Corwin, 12 *Mich. Law Rev.* 261 ff.

[58] *Works*, 3:29–32.

Beginning with the defeat of John Adams by Thomas Jefferson for the Presidency the advocates of Federalism began propaganda to the effect that the fate of the Union depended upon a complete acceptance of the principles of this party: the defeat of Federalism would ultimately mean the downfall of the Union: the espousal of Federalism was the sole method of saving the Union and of preventing the "ruin of the wise, rich and good."[59] Opponents were not only condemned but were to be despised as enemies of the Union itself. The Federalist cult which has had a profound effect on American life[60] is seen in its most extreme form in the development of the authority and prestige of the Supreme Court.

It is, of course, difficult to refute the contention that Federalism with its dogma of judicial supremacy saved the Union and that the views in opposition, had they been adopted, would have destroyed the Union. Jefferson and many of his followers, after believing in a somewhat mild form of judicial review of legislation and in certain other checks on popular rule, came to the conclusion, as a result of political experience, that on vital issues it was better that the will of the people, or more literally that the will of the electorate, ought to prevail rather than to set up an oligarchy of judges or other officials who

---

59 Fisher Ames, *Works* (ed. by Seth Ames; Boston, 1854) 316.

60 "Political intolerance" became "a leading characteristic of the entire Federal party."—S. E. Morison, *Harrison Gray Otis*, (New York, 1913) 1:155. The leading Federalists had one idea, namely, to suppress democracy, Jeffersonian democracy was, they thought, "a prelude to universal chaos." —*Ibid.*, 265. See also prophecy of Robert Goodloe Harper, "the principles on which the Federalists have acted must be adopted, their plans must be substantially pursued or the government must fall to pieces."—*Ibid.*, 211; and comment of Fisher Ames as to "Federalists, who alone will or can preserve liberty, property or Constitution."—*Works*, 298, 316. The Federalist party ceased to exist from 1820 to 1828 when the more liberal members of the party joined the Democrats and the conservatives entered the newly formed Whig party. Federalism as a social cult survived for many years the downfall of the party.—Morison, *op. cit.*, 2:248 ff.

were presumed to know what the people wanted. Just as Hamilton, Marshall, and Webster thought it better from the standpoint of political expediency to keep certain matters, especially those relating to property and contracts out of the hands of the electorate, so the Democrats on the same grounds tended to favor ultimate popular control even over private rights. Despite the reversal of opinions under the leadership of Democratic justices, in most respects the Hamilton-Marshall theories were adopted in American constitutional law and the Jeffersonian popular control theory was discarded, at least, so far as fundamental personal and private rights are concerned.[61] But it is significant that a modified form of the Democratic theory has been in operation in England since the adoption of the cabinet or parliamentary system of government. Property, contracts, and vested rights in England are protected so far as the people through their representatives in Parliament choose to protect them and the voters through the ballot may when they see fit over-

---

[61] Jeffersonian Democrats, though led by political experience to oppose judicial review of legislation in the nation and in the states and to deny the validity of the doctrine of implied limitations on legislatures to protect property and vested rights, did not feel sure of their ground and developed rather slowly concrete proposals to take the place of judicial supremacy. The cabinet system of England had not been effectively developed and Jefferson was not likely to turn to this nation for guidance. But during the debate over the Judiciary Act in 1802 something approaching the cabinet form of government was suggested as the proper alternative to the judicial check. This idea was later advocated by Jefferson and put in more concrete form in the controversy between the executive and the courts over the bank issue in Jackson's administration. Senator White expressed Jackson's view as to the main issue: "The honorable Senator argues that the Constitution has constituted the Supreme Court a tribunal to decide great constitutional questions such as this; and that when they have done so the question is put to rest, and every other department of the government must acquiesce. This doctrine I deny. The Constitution vests 'the judicial power in a Supreme Court, and in such inferior courts as Congress may from time to time ordain and establish.' Whenever a suit is commenced and prosecuted in the courts of the United States, of which they have jurisdiction, and such suit is decided by the Supreme Court—as that is the court of last resort, its decision is final and conclusive between the parties. But as an authority it does not bind either the Congress or the President of the

turn or recall judicial decisions.[62] With some slight exceptions the Democratic or popular control theory has 'been adopted in other English-speaking countries like Canada, Australia, and South Africa where there are no bills of rights and few special or implied limitations on legislatures.[63] The same theory forms a constituent part of the government of France and of many constitutions based upon the French system.[64] In fact the majority of the countries of the world with the growth of democratic government have accepted the doctrine of fairly complete popular control over public affairs similar to that ad-

---

United States. If either of these coordinate departments is afterwards called upon to perform an official act, and consciously believes that performance of that act will be a violation of the Constitution they are not bound to perform it, but, on the contrary, are as much at liberty to decline acting as if no such decision had been made. . . . . If different interpretations are put upon the Constitution by the different departments, the people is the tribunal to settle the dispute. Each of the departments is the agent of the people, doing their business according to the powers conferred; and where there is disagreement as to the extent of these powers, the people themselves, through the ballot boxes, must settle it.''—See Van Buren, *''Inquiry into the Origin and Causes of Political Parties in the United States,''* (New York, 1867) 329, 330.

62 Cf. Taff Vale Ry. v. Amalgamated Society of Railway Servants, (1901) A. C. 426 and Trades Disputes Act of 1906 which nullified that decision; also re Grand Trunk Arbitration, 57 D. L. R. 8 (1921) involving the question of the valuation of the plant in an agreement by which the Canadian government took over the Grand Trunk Railway system.

The opinions of the arbitrators, Sir Walter Cassels and Sir Thomas White, give the English-Canadian point of view favoring public interests. Justice Taft in his dissent states a representative American point of view as to the necessity of protecting vested rights. ''The only adjudicated cases,'' says Justice Taft, ''on the subject of fixing railway rates are in the United States. There are no English cases. There are no Canadian cases.'' Such questions are not settled by the courts in England and Canada.

63 It is a significant fact that the doctrine of affording special protection to vested rights through judicial control was deliberately rejected by Canada and Australia.

64 There seems to be a movement in France to adopt certain features of the American doctrine of judicial review of legislation but most Frenchmen are opposed to combining with this principle the special protection of property and contracts which makes the American doctrine unique among governmental systems of the world. See Lambert, ''Le government des juges et la lutte contre la législation sociale aux États-Unis'' (Paris, 1921). Also, Larnaude in *Bulletin* de la Société de Législation Comparée, 31 (1901–1902), 175–229, 240–257.

vocated by the Jeffersonian Democrats. Outside of the United States it is rarely conceived as possible that courts will interpose their judgment to check the matured policies of the legislative and executive departments. A recent movement to extend the authority of courts and to accept the primary principles of the American doctrine of judicial review seems to have affected but little the prevailing system of legislative supremacy.[65]

Would the democratic theory of popular control, which has been so long practiced in the British Empire and has been so generally adopted elsewhere, have proved destructive if adopted in the United States? No one can say. But some conjectures may be in order.

If more complete ideas of popular control had prevailed the process of centralization would no doubt have moved more slowly with perhaps some temporary setbacks. It is doubtful whether a broad construction of the Constitution so as to extend the powers of the federal government would have become such a grave political issue from 1815 to 1835 when the court was to a large extent the center of attack.[66] It was in this period when the court in its political inclinations had marked Federalist tendencies while the other departments of government were under Democratic control, that resistance to federal encroachments developed a spirit of bitterness which often brought threats of rebellion.[67] The states feared federal encroachments on commerce and transportation, on slavery, and on internal improvements, and the senti-

---

[65] See "Some Phases of the Theory and Practice of Judicial Review of Legislation in Foreign Countries," 24 *Am. Pol. Sci. Rev.* (Aug. 1930) 583 ff.

[66] See letters of Jefferson relating to the judiciary and publications of John Taylor of Virginia "Construction Construed and Constitution Vindicated"; "New Views of the Constitution," and "Tyranny Unmasked."

[67] Cf. contest over Cohens v. Virginia, Beveridge, *The Life of John Marshall*, 2:7 ff. and 2:83-84 regarding resistance of South Carolina in 1823.

ment was frequently expressed that it was better to endure rebellion than to become "slaves of a great consolidated government." Marshall and other Federalist leaders tried to make it appear that an attack on the centralizing tendencies of Congress and of the Supreme Court was an attack upon the Union. The Federalists under the leadership of Marshall and Webster wished to convert, by means of interpretation, what was thought by the majority of the people to be a confederate form of government with the center of gravity in the states, to a federal government with undoubted national supremacy and an unlimited opportunity for development of federal powers.[68] When a court participated in the settlement of such a grave political issue it necessarily became subject to acrimonious public attacks. And the fact that this department was beyond the ordinary reach of popular control made the resentment of opponents of its decisions having political implications all the greater. It was quite generally believed that the court was "silently absorbing rights of the states, and destroying those of the people, without attracting that attention which the magnitude of the interests required."

If Democratic policies had prevailed, the spirit of bitterness which developed from the covert undermining of state powers would have had a more natural outlet and the determination to protect the states' powers and rights at any cost would have had less to feed upon. With a more natural and easy outlet for political feelings and prejudices and greater free play for particularist tendencies may it not have been that the issues of expansion and of slavery could have been dealt with and settled without such long, severe, and bitter controversies?

---

[68] See W. W. Willoughby, *The American Constitutional System* (New York, 1904) chaps. 2, 3.

Again, if the Federalist doctrines of protection to vested rights and of implied limitations on legislatures in favor of private rights of person and of property had been rejected, the economic and industrial development of the country through private capital, would, of course, have been less rapid. Public interests would have prevailed where private interests gained ascendancy under the Federalist régime. Private property and corporate interests would not have become so impregnably intrenched as to be in many respects quite beyond public control. The political situation as to labor and capital and the protection of private rights would probably be somewhat as it has been in England for several centuries and as it has been in Canada since 1867, and similar to what it is in many other countries which have never adopted the doctrine of vested rights superior to and beyond governmental authority.

Constitutional lawyers, freed from the traditionalist policy of sustaining nationalism regardless of all facts and theories to the contrary, are beginning to recognize more frankly the methods by which Congress and the Supreme Court transformed a government basically confederate in character with supreme authority in the states to a federation with supreme powers in the national government.[69] And some of the blame which has

---

[69] Recognizing that the Constitution did not expressly provide for a change from the old Confederation to a new Federation by leaving certain questions of supremacy of authority undetermined, Professor Willoughby has pointed out that ''the circumstance that the Constitution was so indefinitely worded that it could be interpreted as creating a National State, without doing too much violence to the meaning of terms, enabled the people, through Congress and the Supreme Court, to satisfy their desire for political unity without a resort to open revolutionary means. Still it must be conceded by those who take this view, that however peaceably and gradually the transformation to a Federal State was effected, the change was necessarily revolutionary in character. It does not help them to point to the manner in which its steps were clothed in apparent legal form.''—

been attributed to the Democratic party for preparing the way for Civil War, will have to be borne by the Federalists and Nationalists who as the Kentucky legislature charged "reasoned" the people of the states out of their powers. Distinct advantages were gained by the adoption of judicial supremacy and by the giving of such large responsibilities to the courts in the development of the American political system. The bitter contests which arose over the establishment of federal supremacy over the state authorities and the confusion of issues which resulted from the Civil War, have tended, however, to discredit and to condemn unduly the doctrines espoused by the democratic or liberal parties. Each of the great conflicting groups in American life has left a marked impression on our legal doctrines and political practices. A fair appraisal of legal history will accord a due measure of credit to those who opposed as well as to those who favored the doctrine of judicial supremacy.

W. W. Willoughby, *The American Constitutional System* (New York, 1904) 32, 33.

"If a State should differ with the United States about the construction of them (provisions of the Constitution relating to the distribution of powers) there is no common umpire but the people, who adjust the affair by making amendments in the constitutional way, or suffer from the defect. In such a case the constitution of the United States is federal; it is a league or treaty made by the individual States, as one party, and all the States as another party. When two nations differ about the meaning of any clause, sentence, or word in a treaty, neither has an exclusive right to decide it; they endeavor to adjust the matter by negotiation, but if it cannot be thus accomplished, until a reference be had to the mediation of other nations, and arbitration or a state of war. There is no provision in the constitution, that in such a case the Judges of the Supreme Court of the United States shall control and be conclusive: neither can the Congress by a law confer that power. There appears to be a defect in this matter, it is a *casus omissus*, which ought in some way to be remedied. Perhaps the Vice-President and the Senate of the United States; or commissioners appointed, say one by each State, would be a more proper tribunal than the Supreme Court. Be that as it may, I rather think the remedy must be found in an amendment of the constitution."—Chief Justice McKean of Pennsylvania in Respublica v. Cobbett, 3 Dallas 467, 473, 474 (1798).

Chapter XIV

JUDICIAL REVIEW OF LEGISLATION IN THE CIVIL WAR PERIOD

I. Lincoln and Judicial Supremacy

1. *Dred Scott decision—*

As early as 1848 it was suggested in Congress that the issues involved in the slavery controversy should be turned over to the Supreme Court for final determination. It was generally believed, however, that the court, in accordance with its policy of avoiding political issues, would not render a judgment even if it were possible to present the questions in the form of a case. A decision of the Supreme Court would not satisfy both parties and would be disregarded, as had been the case in the bank controversy. Certain members of Congress intimated that, although the people had respect for the Supreme Court, they were not willing to leave the decision on so vital an issue to a court so large a proportion of which was opposed to slavery.[1] Nevertheless from 1848 to 1856 the idea of settling the slavery issue by judicial determination was evident in several cases which were brought before the state courts.[2] And the Chief Justice of the United States, with a majority of his associates, was finally prevailed upon to announce the decree that the power of Congress over the territories acquired since the adoption of the Constitution was limited by all its provi-

---

[1] *Debates of Congress* (abridgment), 16:225–229.
[2] *Ibid.*, 226.

sions in favor of private rights, that the Missouri Compromise Act of 1820 was necessarily unconstitutional, and that Congress could not prohibit slavery within the territories.[3]

Two members of the court rendered dissenting opinions in which they denounced the decision as an attempt to foist the individual opinions of the members of the Supreme Court upon the country under the cloak of constitutional interpretation. As soon as the decision was announced, it was seized upon by both of the leading parties to be used for political purposes. The opinion of the Chief Justice was circulated by the Democrats, the dissenting opinion of Justice Curtis by the Republicans.[4] On the one side, it was maintained that, "whoever resists the final decisions of the highest judicial tribunal aims a deadly blow to our whole republican system of government."[5] On the other hand, the opinion of Chief Justice Taney was denounced as deserving of no more respect than a pro-slavery stump speech delivered during the recent presidential campaign. The contest was soon thrust into the political arena by the series of debates between Stephen A. Douglas and Abraham Lincoln, in which the Dred Scott decision was one of the most important matters discussed.

Lincoln, in a speech at Springfield, Illinois, as the Republican candidate for United States Senator made his first public attack upon the Supreme Court's decision. He gave a history of what he regarded as the "complete legal machinery," that is, the combination between Senator Douglas, the President of the United States, and

---

3 Dred Scott v. Sandford, 19 Howard 393 (1856).

4 James Ford Rhodes, *History of the United States* (New York, 1902–20) 2:264.

5 Douglas to the grand jury at Springfield, Illinois, published in the New York *Times*, June 23, 1857.

the members of the Supreme Court, by which slavery was to be forever fastened upon the country. He impressed the idea upon the assembly by an illustration of framed timbers, the parts of which are made at different times and placed by different workmen, but which when brought together fit exactly and form so complete a structure in every part as to indicate that there must have been a common plan.[6] Only one more decision, Lincoln said, was necessary to force slavery upon the states. That decision was sure to come unless the people met and overthrew the power of the dynasty which had perpetrated upon the country the first infamous decision.[7]

When taken to task by Judge Douglas for his resistance to a decision of the Supreme Court, Lincoln replied that he was not resisting the decision, or attempting to interfere with property by taking Dred Scott from his master.

All that I am doing [Lincoln said] is refusing to obey it as a political rule. If I were in Congress and a vote should come up on a question whether slavery should be prohibited in a new territory, in spite of the Dred Scott decision, I would vote that it should. . . . . Somebody has to reverse that decision, since it is made, and we mean to reverse it, and we mean to do it peaceably.[8]

Lincoln condemned Judge Douglas because he insisted that this extraordinary decision was to be accepted by Congress and obeyed by everybody. The instance of the national bank was cited wherein a decision of the Supreme Court was overruled by the other departments of the government.[9]

---

[6] *Lincoln and Douglas Debates* (ed. by Sparks) 1–5.

[7] *Ibid.*, 6.

[8] *Ibid.*, 29, 30.

[9] *Ibid.*, 30, 31.

As the debate continued, Lincoln found it necessary to take even stronger ground. He read from the letter of Jefferson in which the idea was denounced that the judges must be regarded as the final arbiters on all constitutional questions, and were to be held in higher esteem than other men; and in which the assertion was made that "the Constitution has erected no such single tribunal, knowing that, to whatever hands confided, with the corruptions of time and party, its members would become despots."[10] Lincoln then remarked: "Thus we see the power claimed for the Supreme Court by Judge Douglas, Mr. Jefferson holds, would reduce us to the despotism of an oligarchy. Now, I said no more than this; in fact, never quite so much as this; at least I am sustained by Mr. Jefferson."[11] The instances wherein Supreme Court decisions had been disregarded and overturned were frequently cited with approval.

When attacked as to the way he proposed to resist the court's decision, Lincoln replied:

We oppose the Dred Scott decision in a certain way, upon which I ought perhaps to address you a few words. We do not propose that when Dred Scott has been decided to be a slave by the court, we, as a mob, will decide him to be free, ... but we nevertheless do oppose that decision as a political rule which shall be binding on the voter to vote for nobody who thinks it wrong, which shall be binding on the members of Congress or the President to favor no measure that does not actually concur with the principles of that decision. . . . . We propose so resisting it as to have it reversed if we can, and a new judicial rule established upon this subject.[12]

Lincoln charged Douglas with favoring Supreme Court decisions when he liked them and opposing them when

---

10 *Works*, 12:163.   11 *Debates*, 92, 93.   12 *Ibid.*, 299.

he did not like them,[13] and called his attention to the fact that the Cincinnati platform, which the Judge was advocating unqualifiedly, disregarded a "time-honored decision of the Supreme Court, in denying the power of Congress to establish a national bank."[14] In the opinion of Lincoln, the Dred Scott decision would never have been made had not the party that was responsible for it been previously sustained at the polls.[15]

The most direct attack upon the decision by Lincoln was embodied in a speech in which he referred to it as follows:

My friends, I have endeavored to show you the logical consequences of the Dred Scott decision, which holds that the people of a territory cannot prevent the establishment of slavery in their midst. I have stated, which cannot be gainsaid, that the grounds upon which this decision is made are equally applicable to the free states as to the free territories, and that the peculiar reason put forth by Judge Douglas for indorsing this decision, commit him in advance, to the next decision and to all other decisions coming from the same source. . . . . What constitutes the bulwark of our own liberty and independence? . . . . Our reliance is in the love of liberty which God has implanted in us. Our defense is in the spirit which prized liberty as the heritage of all men, in all lands everywhere. Destroy this spirit and you have planted the seeds of despotism at your own doors. Familiarize yourselves with the chains of bondage, and you prepare your own limbs to wear them. Accustomed to trample on the rights of others, you have lost the genius of your own independence and become the fit subjects of the first cunning tyrant who rises among you. And let me tell you, that all these things are prepared for you by the teachings of history, if the elections shall promise that the next Dred Scott decision and all future decisions will be quietly acquiesced in by the people.[16]

---

13 *Ibid.*, 94.   15 *Ibid.*, 279.
14 *Ibid.*, 280.   16 *Works* (ed. by Nicolay and Hay) 11:109–111.

In a few of his later addresses Lincoln referred with ridicule to the "Dred Scott Supreme Court."[17] The following year the Republican party resolved in its platform

that the new dogma that the Constitution of its own force carries slavery into any or all territories of the United States is a dangerous political heresy, at variance with the explicit provisions of that instrument itself, with contemporaneous exposition, and with legislative and judicial precedent; is revolutionary in its tendency, and subversive of the peace and harmony of the country,[18]

and rewarded one of the ablest opponents of that dogma with the nomination to the Presidency.

In his first inaugural address President Lincoln indicated the attitude which the government under his administration would assume toward the Dred Scott decision as well as toward other instances of judicial interference in political affairs. The President announced a modified form of the Jacksonian doctrine:

I do not forget the position, assumed by some, that constitutional questions are to be decided by the Supreme Court; nor do I deny that such decisions must be binding in any case, upon the parties to a suit, as to the object of that suit, while they are also entitled to very high respect and consideration in all parallel cases by all other departments of the government. And while it is obviously possible that such decision may be erroneous in any given case, still the evil effect following it, being limited to that particular case, with the chance that it may be overruled and never become a precedent for other cases, can better be borne than could the evils of a different practice. At the same time, the candid citizen must confess that if the policy of the government, upon vital questions affecting the whole people, is to be irrevocable fixed by decisions of the Supreme Court, the instant

---

[17] *Debates*, 380.
[18] Edward Stanwood, *History of the Presidency* (Boston, 1898) 293.

they are made, in ordinary litigation between parties in personal actions, the people will have ceased to be their own rulers, having to that extent practically resigned their government into the hands of that eminent tribunal. Nor is there in this view any assault upon the court or the judges. It is a duty from which they may not shrink to decide cases properly before them and it is no fault of theirs if others seek to turn their decisions to political purposes.[19]

2. *Judicial interference with the President's military administration*—

An occasion soon arose in which the President was obliged to put into practice his theory regarding judicial authority. In order to make it possible to bring federal troops through the hostile state of Maryland the President by an executive order suspended the writ of habeas corpus. John Merryman, of Baltimore, was arrested on the charge of acting in hostility to the government of the United States. He was lodged in Fort McHenry under the direction of General Cadwalader. On a petition to Chief Justice Taney for a writ of habeas corpus an order was granted to which General Cadwalader failed to respond, claiming that he was "duly authorized by the President of the United States to suspend the writ of habeas corpus for the public safety."[20] The Chief Justice then issued a writ of attachment with the purpose of bringing the general before the court to answer for contempt in refusing to produce the body of Merryman. The federal marshal, however, informed the Chief Justice that he was not permitted to enter the fort and received no answer to the writ.[21]

---

[19] *Works,* 6:179–180.

[20] Edward McPherson, *The Political History of the United States of America, during the Great Rebellion* (Washington, 1876) 154.

[21] McPherson, *op. cit.,* 154.

The whole proceeding appeared to take the Chief Justice by surprise, with the result that he issued a hasty order and indicated that he would prepare an opinion to sustain his action. In the oral statement justifying the order of the court Taney remarked that the President of the United States could not suspend the privilege of the writ of habeas corpus nor authorize a military officer to do so; and that a military officer had no right to arrest and detain a person not subject to the rules of war for an offense against the laws of the United States, except by judicial authority and subject to its control.[22] Taney maintained that the marshal had the power to summon the *posse comitatus* to seize and bring into court the party named in the attachment; but as it was apparent that he would be resisted by a force notoriously superior to the *posse comitatus,* the court had no power under the law to order the necessary force to compel the appearance of the party.[23]

The Chief Justice later submitted a written opinion in which he charged that the President not only claimed the right to suspend the writ of habeas corpus himself, at his discretion, but to delegate that authority to a military officer and leave it to him to determine whether he would obey judicial process. No official notice, Taney declared, had been given that the President claimed this power or that he had exercised it in the manner indicated. He thought that it was admitted on all hands that the privilege of the writ of habeas corpus could not be suspended except by act of Congress.[24]   After offering a carefully prepared argument in favor of the position assumed by the court, the Chief Justice concluded with the opinion that if such a state of affairs was permitted

---

22 *Ibid.,* 155.   23 *Ibid.,* 155.   24 *Ibid.,* 155.

to exist, "the people of the United States are no longer living under a government of laws, but every citizen holds life, liberty, and property at the will and pleasure of the army officers in whose military district he may happen to be found."[25]

In such a case, Taney said, "my duty was too plain to be mistaken. I have exercised all the power which the Constitution and laws confer on me, but that power has been resisted by a force too strong for me to overcome." With the possibility that the instructions might have been misunderstood, Taney ventured to turn the record of the whole proceeding over to the President with the reflection that it would then remain for him, in the fulfillment of his constitutional obligation, to determine what measures he would take to uphold the judicial department of the government.[26]

In the meantime the President had submitted the question to his attorney-general, from whom he received the opinion that when a dangerous insurrection threatens the very existence of the nation, the President has the discretionary power to arrest and hold in custody "persons known to have criminal intercourse with the insurgents, or persons against whom there is probable cause for suspicion of such criminal complicity,"[27] and that the President has power to suspend the privilege of the writ of habeas corpus as to persons arrested under such circumstances, since he is especially charged by the Constitution with the preservation of the public safety and is the sole judge of the emergency which requires prompt action; and for any breach of trust he is responsible to the high court of impeachment, but to no other tribunal.[28] Acting on this view, the order of General Cad-

---

[25] *Ibid.*, 158.   [27] *Ibid.*, 159.

[26] *Ibid.*, 158.   [28] *Ibid.*, 161.

walader was upheld and the right of judicial interference denied. In a proclamation issued in February 1862, President Lincoln referred to this incident when he said that "the judicial machinery seemed as if it had been designed not to sustain the government, but to embarrass and betray it."[29]

At the opening of the December term of court in 1861, the attorney-general informed the justices that their lawful jurisdiction was practically restrained, their just power diminished, and their beneficent authority to administer justice according to law was successfully denied and resisted in a large portion of the country.[30] It remained to be seen whether the judicial department would quietly acquiesce while the political departments of the government were waging the contest for the preservation of the Union. Several of the justices were known to be opposed to the methods of the President in the conduct of the war. When the *Prize Cases* came before the Supreme Court in 1862, wherein the question was raised whether the President had a right to institute a blockade of ports in possession of persons in armed rebellion against the government,[31] there were apprehensions lest the judiciary might interfere with the course which the executive was pursuing. The court, however, by a majority of one, in an opinion based upon the principles of international law relating to belligerents, affirmed the policy of President Lincoln. Three of Lincoln's appointees, Justices Swayne, Miller, and Davis gave a majority for the government. Four Democratic members of the court, Chief Justice Taney, Justices Nelson, Catron, and Clifford dissented.

---

[29] *Works*, 7:101.   [31] 2 Black 635 (1862).
[30] 1 Black 9.

Justice Grier, in delivering the opinion of the court, declared that it was not the less a civil war because it was called an insurrection by the one side and the insurgents were considered as rebels or traitors.[32] According to his opinion, the character and nature of the resistance to be used against the insurrection had to be determined by the President, and the courts were of necessity obliged to recognize as final the decisions and acts of the political departments of the government.[33]

The court regarded the contest as in the realm of war between nations, with all its attending consequences, and thus placed the national authorities in a much stronger position than would otherwise have been possible. The judicial department realized the necessity of upholding the military authorities and appreciated the fact that most of the questions arising out of the state of warfare did not belong to the realm of duties allotted to courts of justice. A dissenting opinion was prepared by Justice Nelson. After a graphic description of the nature of the state of war, Justice Nelson declared that by our Constitution the power to bring about such a condition is lodged in Congress.[34] In order that a war may legally exist, it must be recognized or declared by the war-making power of the government. No power short of this could change the legal status of the government or the relations of its citizens from that of peace to a state of war.[35] Accordingly, the conduct of affairs during the first period of the rebellion was designated as a personal war, and it was claimed that the actual state of war did not come into existence until after the act of Congress, on the 13th of July, 1861, went into effect.[36] In short,

---

[32] *Ibid.*, 669.   [35] *Ibid.*, 689.

[33] *Ibid.*, 669, 670.   [36] *Ibid.*, 694, 695.

[34] *Ibid.*, 688.

said the dissenting justices, the President had no right to declare war nor did he possess the constitutional power to institute a blockade.

For some radical remarks at a Democratic mass meeting, Vallandigham, a Democratic leader of Ohio, who criticized the conduct of the war, was arrested under a military order and thrown into prison.[37] After a mere form of a trial which resulted in a sentence for detention until the end of the war, an attempt was made to bring the matter to a close by sending the prisoner over to the Confederacy. The whole proceeding was an extreme assertion of military authority and caused considerable difficulty for the administration.[38]

The Supreme Court, in an appeal which was brought to free Vallandigham, with the Republican majority supporting the President, did not feel inclined to interfere, although the arrest was made under circumstances similar to those which led the court later to deny this authority to the executive. Regardless of the fact that the military order was issued with full knowledge that there was an act of Congress covering the case, three members of the court concurred in the result of this opinion that the court had no power to review the proceedings of a military commission ordered by a general of the United States.[39]

The greatest difficulty, however, arose through criticisms of the party press. Resolutions of condemnation were frequently forwarded to President Lincoln. The tenor of these criticisms is shown in a summary of one series of resolutions when a political gathering in Ohio

---

[37] For history of this case see Rhodes, *op. cit.*, 4:246–255.

[38] *Ibid.*, 248.

[39] *Ex parte* Vallandigham, 1 Wallace 243 (1863). Justice Miller took no part in the argument or decision.

inquired whether he really claimed that he might override all the guaranteed rights of individuals, on the plea of conserving the public safety, whenever he chose to say the public safety required it.[40] Although Lincoln confessed that he regretted the necessity of arresting Vallandigham, and doubted whether he would have ordered his arrest, nevertheless he decided to assume the responsibility for the whole proceeding.

When the war was brought to a successful conclusion, the Supreme Court felt at liberty to deliver an opinion more nearly corresponding to the sentiments of its members.[41] It was then announced by Justice Davis, one of Lincoln's appointees, that the federal authority, having been unopposed in the state of Indiana, and the federal courts being open for the trial of offenses and redress of grievances, the usages of war could not under the Constitution afford any sanction for the trial by a military tribunal of a citizen in civil life no matter what the offense.[42] Although the proceedings were known to have the fullest sanction of the executive department of the government, the judgment was rendered without a dissenting voice. Several members of the court, however, took exception to the extreme position of Justice Davis, when he insisted that neither Congress nor the President had the power to authorize a military commission to proceed to trial and judgment under the conditions which existed in Indiana.

---

[40] *Works*, 9:3, 4.
[41] *Ex parte* Milligan, 4 Wallace 2 (1866).
[42] *Ibid.*, 126, 127.

II. FEDERAL COURTS AND THE POLICY OF CONGRESS TOWARD RECONSTRUCTION

Immediately after the close of the Civil War stringent laws were passed against those who had taken part in the rebellion. A provision of the constitution of Missouri, adopted in 1865, prescribed an oath to be taken by officers, teachers, preachers, and all those serving in any public capacity, or by any one desiring to participate in the election of such officers.[43] The oath was directed against all those who had assisted in the rebellion, and practically disqualified any person who had manifested in the least his adherence to the cause of the enemies of the United States. There was a severe penalty for continuing in public service without taking the oath. Under the authority of this provision, Cummings, a Catholic priest, was sentenced to pay a fine of five hundred dollars and to be committed to jail until the costs were paid. The supreme court of Missouri affirmed the judgment and the case was brought into the courts of the United States on a writ of error.[44]

About the same time Congress prescribed a similar oath for all attorneys and counselors desiring to appear before the courts of the United States. Garland had been admitted to practice before the Supreme Court previous to the war. He participated in the rebellion and after his return demanded admission without the formality of taking the oath prescribed by Congress.[45] Counsel contended that the provisions of the constitution of Missouri

---

[43] Cummings v. Missouri, 4 Wallace 279 (1866).

[44] *Ibid.*, 281, 282.

[45] *Ibid.*, 335–337.

and of the law of Congress were contrary to the Constitution of the United States both as bills of attainder and as *ex post facto* laws. The court held that the states could not, under the form of creating a qualification or attaching a condition, in effect inflict a punishment for a past act which was not punishable at the time it was committed.[46] The provision of the constitution of Missouri and of the law of Congress instead of requiring a qualification relative to the duties of the office imposed a punishment for past conduct. Although the prohibition of *ex post facto* laws was aimed at criminal cases, it could not be evaded by giving a civil form to that which was in substance criminal. As a result of the principles thus announced, the court held that the provisions of the Constitution and the law of Congress were both bills of attainder and *ex post facto* laws, and as such null and void.

A dissenting opinion by Justice Miller concurred in by the Chief Justice and two associate justices applied to both cases. Referring to the English bills of attainder, it was claimed that "a statute, then, which designates no criminal, either by name or description—which declares no guilt, pronounces no sentence, and inflicts no punishment—can in no sense be called a bill of attainder."[47] As to *ex post facto* laws, "all the cases agree that the term is to be applied to criminal cases alone, and not to civil proceedings."[48] The dissenting justices could see nothing in the nature of a punishment in the oaths required. They held that Congress had the right to prescribe the oath as a qualification for all those who wished to take part in the administration of the government, and that the state, in the exercise of its exclusive power over the

[46] 4 Wallace 319 (1866).   [48] *Ibid.*, 390.
[47] *Ibid.*, 390.

subject of religion, could so control public morals and public order as to exclude from preaching or teaching all those who had shown any disposition to oppose the government of the United States.[49]

Up to the time of the test oath cases, the Supreme Court was not inclined to apply the clause in the Constitution prohibiting bills of attainder and *ex post facto* laws to the protection of the individual in the realm of civil rights.[50]   Justice Miller in his dissent, which applied to both cases, commented as follows: ''The act which has just been declared to be unconstitutional is nothing more than a statute which requires of all lawyers who propose to practice in national courts, that they shall take the same oath which it exacted of every officer of the government civil or military.''[51]   The opinion of the majority was condemned inferentially by Justice Miller in the remark that ''I have endeavored to bring to the examination of the great questions of constitutional law involved in this inquiry those principles alone which are calculated to assist in determining what the law is, rather than what, in my judgment, it ought to be.''[52]

When Congress indicated its intention to pursue extreme measures toward the reconstruction of the governments of the southern states, regardless of the objections of President Johnson, several states attempted to prevent the execution of these acts by appealing to the Supreme Court. Mississippi filed a bill in equity asking the Supreme Court to enjoin Andrew Johnson perpetually from

---

[49] 4 Wallace 396–399.

[50] See Watson v. Mercer, wherein it was held that ''*ex post facto* laws relate to penal and criminal proceedings which impose punishments or forfeitures, and not to civil proceedings which affect private rights retrospectively.''—8 Peters 110 (1834).

[51] 4 Wallace 385.

[52] *Ibid.*, 399.

executing certain reconstruction acts.[53] Georgia also filed a bill to enjoin the enforcement of these laws.[54] Both appeals were denied on the ground that the bills required the interference of the court in a political issue, which was plainly contrary to previous practice. Though the acts of the President and Congress were admitted to be subject to the cognizance of the Supreme Court in proper cases, these were not regarded as cases for judicial interference. The situation appeared to be fraught with too serious political consequences for the court to interfere, lest the excitement over reconstruction should be increased by meddling on the part of the Supreme Court. Five of the nine justices were known to be opposed to the congressional policy of reconstruction. The arrest of McCardle by a military commission in Mississippi under the provisions of one of these acts led to an appeal to the Supreme Court. The first question raised was with regard to jurisdiction, which was decided in favor of the Supreme Court in an opinion by Chief Justice Chase. The Chief Justice claimed that prior to the passage of the act of 1867 appellate jurisdiction was exercised over the action of inferior courts by habeas corpus. As this authority had not been removed, no doubt was entertained that an appeal might be taken from the judgment of the circuit court to the Supreme Court.[55]

Alarmed at the dangers of an adverse decision and determined to admit of no interference, Congress passed an act which practically took away jurisdiction over the McCardle case.[56] It was then argued that the act of Congress was a manifest assault upon the judicial

---

[53] State of Mississippi v. Johnson, 4 Wallace 475 (1866).

[54] State of Georgia v. Stanton, 6 Wallace 50 (1867).

[55] 6 Wallace 324 (1867).

[56] United States *Statutes* at Large, 15:44, March 27, 1868.

department of the government and therefore unconstitutional. The act was thought to be equivalent to the doctrine that the Supreme Court should never give judgment in any case contrary to the views of the majority in Congress.[57] When the case was again presented, Chief Justice Chase held that the court was not at liberty to inquire into the motives of the legislature. The court originally had been granted jurisdiction, and now that, by an act of Congress this jurisdiction had been taken away, it was quite clear that the court could not proceed to pronounce judgment in this case.[58] The sentiment in Congress relative to the exercise of the right of declaring legislative acts void was aroused to such an extent that this decision was the only one which could have averted a serious contest between the two departments. The opinions of a few members of Congress indicated the tendency of the time to disregard judicial decisions. The McCardle case is frequently cited as a precedent to sustain the authority of Congress to prevent the validity of its acts from being considered by the Supreme Court under its appellate jurisdiction.

In the session of Congress after the decision had been rendered in the *Milligan Case,* in the consideration of a reconstruction bill, Thaddeus Stevens severely criticized the attitude of the Supreme Court. The late decision of the Supreme Court of the United States, he maintained, had rendered absolutely indispensable immediate action by Congress upon the question of the establishment of governments in the rebel states,—"that decision, although in terms not as infamous as the Dred Scott decision, is yet far more dangerous in its operations upon the lives and liberties of the loyal men of this country.''[59]

---

[57] 7 Wallace 510 (1868).   [58] *Ibid.,* 515.

[59] *Congressional Globe,* 39 Cong., 2 Sess.,351, January 3, 1867.

One member reminded the house that those desiring clemency might appeal to the Supreme Court for such protection as a majority of that body were inclined to grant to rebels, and begged the House to commit itself to no such folly.[60] But in discussing the possibility of interference from the Supreme Court, he remarked, "that court should recollect that it has had bad luck with its political decisions. The people of this country thus far have preferred to govern the country themselves and let the court attend to its law business. Both of its great political opinions have been overruled by an appeal to the ballot box."[61]

In the discussion of a proposed amendment to the Constitution another member took occasion to deliver an harangue against the court and the executive when told that the Supreme Court of the United States would strike down the amendment. That supreme tribunal of justice, he thought, had no power to give a decision, for it was a political question in which a court might in no way interfere. The decision of Congress, he declared, was final and conclusive over every judicial tribunal in the land. Neither the executive nor the judicial departments had any voice in the matter: any right to challenge the authority of the people.[62]

On January 21, 1867, a bill was introduced requiring a unanimous decision by the court on questions involving the constitutionality of laws.[63] Later a similar bill came up for consideration. Williams of Pennsylvania noted that there was a case now pending in the Supreme Court of the United States which demanded immediate action

---

[60] *Congressional Globe*, 255.

[61] *Ibid.*, 255.

[62] *Ibid.*, 501, 502, January 16, 1867.

[63] *Ibid.*, 616.

by the House. Such a decision, he thought, would simply awaken both houses to the necessity of defending the legislative power which is the true sovereign of the nation.[64] On the issue whether decisions on questions of constitutionality ought to be given by a unanimous opinion or by a two-thirds majority, Mr. Williams argued that a dissent implies doubt and most lawyers would agree that in cases where there is a dissent among the members of the court, the opinion of the dissenting judges would almost invariably be found to be the better one.[65]

Some time earlier a bill had been offered for the purpose of providing that certain persons should not hold the office of attorney or counselor in any court of the United States. This bill was presented in direct opposition to the decision of the Supreme Court. It was believed that, if the judges of the highest tribunal would not by proper regulations protect themselves from the contamination of conspirators and traitors against the government, the legislative department should exercise its power to declare who should be admitted to practice in the courts of the Union.[66] In reply it was argued that such a law would be a palpable and manifest usurpation of the powers delegated to the great conservative department of the government.[67]

On the consideration of a supplementary reconstruction bill, on January 28, 1868, it was claimed that the idea which had gone forth (that the judiciary could render a decision on the subject of reconstruction) was a strange one. The members of Congress did not suppose that it was intended for one or five members of the Supreme Court to regulate the political interests and relations of the country. If the Supreme Court should decide the

---

[64] *Congressional Globe, op. cit.*, 478.   [66] *Ibid.*, 646, 647.
[65] *Ibid.*, 479.   [67] *Ibid.*, 488.

reconstruction acts unconstitutional, the moral effect would be injurious; and if the Supreme Court should deliberately usurp the authority of the legislature, Congress had the right to withdraw from it all supervisory power over the reconstruction acts.[68]

The expression of such opinions in Congress, together with the act passed over the President's veto removing the *McCardle Case* from the jurisdiction of the court, was sufficient warning that Congress would allow no interference in the program which had been planned. The legislature hereafter dealt with a free hand in the districts where the reconstruction acts applied. Congress had, it was claimed, "subdued the Supreme Court" and brought it to a realization of the fact that the state of war had not fully passed away, and that the independence of departments with the Supreme Court as final interpreter of the Constitution and laws could not be tolerated in dealing with the states of the confederacy. With this issue the series of conflicts begun in 1850 came to a close and affairs began to approach more nearly the pre-war condition. The principles affirmed by the Democrats from 1830 to 1850 and the loss of prestige due to the Dred Scott decision, as well as the complete subordination of judicial authority during the war period, seemed to indicate that judicial supremacy was losing ground. But the ascendancy of the executive department during the war and the supremacy of the legislative department in the period of reconstruction were soon to be superseded by an era in which the courts gradually assumed a stronger position than had been possible at any previous time.

---

[68] *Congressional Globe, op. cit.,* 791.

III. Results of Changes in the Personnel of the Court

The result of a policy of caution in exercising judicial authority over legislative acts was that, up to 1830, as against more than a score of the acts of state legislatures, only one act of Congress had been declared unconstitutional, though some justices also refused to enforce the Invalid Pension Act. In the period from 1830 to 1860, one act of Congress was declared unconstitutional, and only a few acts of state legislatures. The Civil War policies increased the total by eleven cases in which Congressional acts were denied validity. The caution in refusing enforcement of legislative acts had been so strictly observed, and with so few exceptions, that Chief Justice Waite could claim that

every possible presumption is in the favor of the validity of a statute, and this continues until the contrary is shown beyond a rational doubt. One branch of the government cannot encroach on the domain of another without danger. The safety of our institutions depends in no small degree on a strict observance of this salutary rule.[69]

With the passing of war problems and reconstruction policies the judicial department was soon restored to its former prestige and gradually resumed its oldtime functions. The issue of federal versus state sovereignty, which had given the court in the first few decades such a commanding position in our government, was solved for the time being. The process of nationalization begun by the Federalist party and continued by Congress

---

[69] Sinking-Fund Cases, 99 U. S. 700, 718 (1878).

and the Supreme Court was now completed by force of arms. New problems awaited the court. The construction of the three amendments recently made a part of the Constitution was awaited with much interest. A reviving industrial life called for the settlement of a group of problems for which precedents were lacking. The court slowly became involved in the determination of business and economic policies. As a result, since 1870 our national judiciary has entered a comparatively new and untried field for courts of justice. Not only has it been obliged to act as arbiter between the state and federal authorities but it has also been called upon to assume the immensely more difficult function of guiding the public regulation and control of the organized activities of economic and social life. An increasing number of decisions by a divided court, long and elaborate opinions with equally long dissenting opinions, a tendency to reverse former decisions, and often an uncertainty as to the exact nature of decisions, all are evidences of an attempt to apply old constitutional principles to relatively new conditions and to develop new canons of interpretation.

Beginning with the *Legal Tender Cases*[70] there was a tendency to divide on the determination of great constitutional controversies. The matter of taxation of corporations engaged in inter-state traffic, the determination and application of the new amendments to the Constitution, whether applicable particularly to the African race or to every person and corporation in the United States, the right of state legislatures to regulate rates of compensation for the services of corporations doing business which affects the public, the right of Congress to enact

---

[70] 12 Wallace 457 (1870).

an income tax law, the regulation of the liquor traffic
by the states, the enforcement of the anti-trust laws, the
treatment of colonial possessions, the right of the states
to regulate hours of labor, the determination of what
is contempt of court, are a few of the more important
issues on which the Supreme Court has not been able to
speak with the definiteness and assurance that characterized federal judicial decisions in the time of Chief Justice
Marshall.

President Lincoln appointed five members of the
Supreme Court, Noah H. Swayne, 1861, Samuel F. Miller,
1862, David Davis, 1862, Stephen J. Field, 1863, and
Salmon P. Chase, 1864. For the third time, Lincoln, like
Washington and Jackson, had the opportunity, through
the appointment of new members, to change the general
point of view and attitude of the Court. Justice Swayne
was a Democrat in politics, who became a nationalist and
joined the Republican party. Samuel F. Miller was an
ardent Republican and a firm supporter of the doctrines
of the new Federalism. Though a Republican at the time
of his appointment David Davis was inclined to be an
independent in politics and later joined the Democratic
party. A close friend of Lincoln, Davis, it is claimed,
was largely responsible for Lincoln's nomination as
the Republican candidate for the Presidency. After
Lincoln's election Judge Davis accompanied him to
Washington and was the President's adviser until he
was appointed to the Supreme Court. When Congress
created a new circuit comprising the Pacific Coast states,
on the recommendation of the Senators and Congressmen
of all of the states in the district, Lincoln appointed
Stephen J. Field, a Democrat—one of the few instances
in which a President has appointed to the Supreme
Bench, one who belonged to a different political party.

The last of Lincoln's appointments, Salmon P. Chase, was a Whig with democratic leanings. He joined the Republican party because of his views on the slavery issue. It was charged that Lincoln appointed Chase to the office of Chief Justice in order to remove a rival from the political field and to counteract the opinions of Taney.

An increase in dissents may be noted with the term of court held in 1861. With the deaths of Justices Daniel and McLean and the resignation of Justice Campbell there were three vacancies. Only one position was filled —by the appointment of Swayne. Most of the opinions were rendered during this term by Nelson and Grier and dissents were rather frequent. Before the next term the two vacancies were filled by the appointments of Miller and Davis. With the addition of a tenth member of the court, Field of California was appointed, who did not take his seat until the following year. During this term the trial of cases involving matters relating to war and other political issues resulted in twenty dissents rather evenly distributed among seven of the justices. As the majority of the court was still of the democratic faith most of the seventeen dissents during the 1863 term were made by the new justices, Miller, Swayne, and Davis. Dissents at this time were recorded as a rule without opinions.

At the beginning of the 1864 term Chief Justice Taney died and was succeeded by Chase. With the resulting change in the political affiliations of the members of the court, Justices Clifford and Nelson became the chief dissenters. Different from the Marshall period the delivery of opinions was usually evenly distributed among the justices who actively participated in the term's work. During the 1865 term the opinions of the court were distributed as follows:

Chief Justice Chase	12	Justice Grier	6
Justice Clifford	9	Justice Miller	10
Justice Davis	8	Justice Nelson	11
Justice Field	7	Justice Swayne	10

Justices Grier and Field disagreed more frequently than the other justices with the majority opinion. From this time Miller becomes one of the leading dissenters, though the Democratic members, Clifford and Nelson, indicate rather frequent disagreement with the opinions and judgments of the court.[71] The total number of dissents for a term was increasing.

One of the direct results of the appointments by President Lincoln was the reversal of the policy and decisions of the Supreme Court at the outbreak of the war and the consequent support of the war policies of the President. In the Dred Scott decision the Supreme Court had undertaken to limit and restrict the powers of Congress and the President in dealing with the great slavery controversy. When both Congress and the President ignored the court's decision, there was no attempt by the reconstituted court to offer resistance. Furthermore, the futile attempt of Chief Justice Taney to deny to the President the authority to suspend the writ of habeas corpus was soon to be followed by an approval of the exercise of extraordinary executive power and authority in the *Prize Cases*,[72] when the appointees of President Lincoln, Justices Swayne, Miller, and Davis, turned the balance in favor of the government as against the Democratic members of the court, Justices Taney, Nelson, Catron, and Clifford. In the *Vallandigham Case*,[73] the court again supported the administration by denying that it had power to review by certiorari the proceedings

---

[71] See Philip Greely Clifford, *Nathan Clifford: Democrat* (New York, 1922) chap. 10.
[72] 2 Black 635 (1862).   [73] 1 Wallace 243 (1863).

of a military commission ordered by an officer of the United States army.

It was a court composed of a Republican majority that gave its support and sanction to the extraordinary military powers assumed by President Lincoln and supported Congress in the radical measures of Reconstruction which the party leaders in Congress had determined upon. It is true that the court swerved from the path of unquestioned support of the other departments in placing a stamp of disapproval upon a military court in Indiana long after the circumstances had passed which rendered extreme measures by the executive necessary,[74] and interfered somewhat with several measures of Reconstruction in declaring invalid the test oaths prescribed by the state of Missouri and by an act of Congress.[75] It is noteworthy that President Lincoln's appointees, Justices Swayne, Davis, and Miller, dissented in both of these decisions. Justice Field's opinion in these cases ''was assailed by the Republican press, and by an overwhelming majority of the House of Representatives, with a bitterness which at the present day seems incredible.'' And when the Supreme Court was warned as to the probable result of an interference with Congressional Reconstruction, the Republican appointee to the office of Chief Justice joined with the other members of the court in accepting the result and inferentially in submitting to the general policy of Reconstruction as enacted into law by Congress.[76]

A notorious instance of the influence of partisan appointments to the Supreme Court is involved in the

---

[74] *Ex parte* Milligan, 4 Wallace 2 (1866).

[75] Cummings v. the State of Missouri, 4 Wallace 277; *ex parte* Garland, 4 Wallace 333.

[76] *Ex parte* McCardle, 7 Wallace 510 (1868).

method by which the Legal Tender acts were ultimately declared constitutional and a strongly supported policy of the Republican party upheld. It is impossible to give here the full details of the passage of the Legal Tender acts under the direction and with the reluctant assent of the then Secretary of the Treasury, Mr. Chase; of the first condemnation of the acts by a court, with Chase and the former Democratic members lined up against the three Republican members, Miller, Swayne, and Davis; and the ultimate reversal of this decision after President Grant had appointed two more Republican members to the court.

Legal Tender Cases—

In order to meet the exigencies of the war, the national government had enacted two laws which made United States notes legal tender in the payment of all debts, public and private. These statutes had been the law of the land for a period of almost seven years when they were assailed before the Supreme Court on the charge of unconstitutionality. The majority of the court were of the opinion that there was in the Constitution no express grant of legislative authority to make any sort of credit currency a legal tender in payment of debts contracted before the passage of the acts of 1862 and 1863, and that these acts were so far inconsistent with the spirit of the Constitution and therefore prohibited by it. Chief Justice Chase, who rendered the decision, then took occasion to state the reasons for his change of attitude since the time when, as Secretary of the Treasury, he had favored this form of legislation.

The decision indicated that the court was inclined to insist that its interpretation of the Constitution on the financial policy of the government was superior to that of Congress and the President.[77] Three justices dissented, with the remark that such an opinion of the court, annulling the law after years of general acceptance, substituted the court's ideas of policy for judicial construction and presented an indefinite code of ethics for the national legislature.[78]

A reconstituted court held the laws valid on the theory that, since there were no prohibitions against such enactments by Congress, the matter should be left to the discretion of the legislative department.[79] Laws, the court maintained, were not to be annulled unless there was no room for reasonable doubt regarding invalidity. In the affirmation of the *Legal Tender Cases* a few years later, the Supreme Court not only upheld the previous decision,[80] but stated so forcefully the argument for an almost unrestricted power of Congress that, had the principle of this particular case prevailed, there would have been little chance for judicial control of the acts of the legislative department of the federal government.

The first Legal Tender decision was regarded as an attack on sound Republican doctrine made by five judges with Democratic affiliations while the Republican justices had strongly defended the faith. "Senators and Representatives," says Mr. Rhodes, "denounced it as being as infamous as the Dred Scott decision. The influence of the Pennsylvania Railroad and other large corporations which had outstanding bonds of issue prior to 1861 was used against it."[81] The opinion for reversal was

---

[77] Hepburn v. Griswold, 8 Wallace 603 (1869).

[78] *Ibid.*, 623, 624, 638.

[79] Legal Tender Cases, 12 Wall. 457 (1870); Justice Field in his dissent defended the doctrine that in matters relating to private rights the courts were intended to revise the determinations of the other departments of government.—See p. 648.

[80] Juilliard v. Greenman, 110 U. S. 421 (1883).

[81] Rhodes, 6:265.

written by Justice Strong and concurred in by Justice Bradley and the three dissenters in the first case. When the proposal to reopen the case came before the court, Chief Justice Chase and Justice Miller came near to an open wrangle while sitting on the bench.[82]

Although the charge of Chase that the court was reorganized with the purpose of securing a reversal of the first *Legal Tender Case* has been denied, the conservative view on partisanship is discriminatingly presented by Professor Hart in his life of Chase.

If by packing [says Professor Hart] is to be understood the appointment of men whose views on political questions were likely to be those of the administration, the charge is true, and is equally true of President Lincoln and all of his successors down to 1886; for during that whole period no Supreme Court judge was designated who was not of the same political party as the President for the time being.[83]

Then after giving the circumstances leading to the appointment of Justices Strong and Bradley,[84] two judges known to favor the legal tender acts, Professor Hart concludes:

Though the President and the Attorney General stand absolved from a deliberate purpose of changing a majority of four to three into a minority of four to five, there can be no reasonable doubt, that the President and his advisers intended, as vacancies occurred in the court, to fill them with men who would reflect the opinions of the Republican party, and that party had declined to commit itself even to a speedy restoration of the notes to a gold basis. It was true that Strong, as state judge in Pennsylvania, had rendered a decision in favor of the constitutionality

---

[82] *Ibid.*, 269.

[83] Albert Bushnell Hart, *Salmon Portland Chase* (New York, 1899) 399, 400.

[84] To fill these vacancies Attorney General E. R. Hoar and E. M. Stanton were first nominated, but Stanton died within a few days and the Senate rejected Hoar.

of the legal tenders, and so had most of the judges in the sixteen other states before whom the question had come. Yet there was no lack of good lawyers in the Republican party who had not committed themselves upon the question. Had it been the purpose of the President to choose two judges who would balance each other, he could have found two such men; he and his advisers, with few exceptions, desired the legal tender act to stand, and the appointments were taken to mean that it would be reaffirmed.

The Republican party, supported by the business interests of the country, had determined to have the legal tender acts stand and they were resolved to have no interference, not even from the Supreme Court itself.[85] The reversal was no doubt regarded as justified, partly because Justice Grier, who first joined the Republicans in pronouncing in favor of the acts, changed to the side of the Chief Justice—an act which led all the judges to suggest that he ought to resign. Nevertheless, with Justice Grier out, the first decision was rendered by a vote of 4 to 3 with a majority of one—a number which has turned the scale in more than one important constitutional controversy. With the change in political attitude by the members of the court and the antagonisms aroused thereby, with President Grant's appointments causing a reversal of the court's position in the *Legal Tender Cases,* and with the participation along partisan lines of certain of the justices in the Electoral Commission established to settle the Hayes-Tilden controversy, the Supreme Court came to be looked upon as an organ for carrying out the dominant will of the majority party.

---

[85] Cf. Rhodes, *op. cit.,* 6:266. For refutation of charge of packing the court, see *ibid.,* 270 ff.

Chapter XV

CHANGE IN SCOPE AND SIGNIFICANCE OF JUDICIAL REVIEW OF LEGISLATION

1. Restricted use of authority to review acts prior to 1860—

FOR NEARLY a century after the establishment of the federal government in 1789 the review of legislation by the federal and state courts had resulted in the failure to uphold relatively few statutes. The exceptional instances in which acts were declared void related chiefly to the invasion of property rights, to the denial of trial by jury, to the exercise of what was regarded as judicial powers by the legislature, and to interference with the inviolability of contracts—all matters in which the eighteenth-century patriots were greatly interested and concerning which they were particularly sensitive. The courts in a narrow field stepped in to protect the individual from encroachment in matters where interference was seriously resented.[1]

---

[1] *Summary of Laws invalidated by state courts from 1776 to 1819*

1.	Organization of courts and judicial procedure	6
2.	Denial of trial by jury	4
3.	Taking of private property	3
4.	Contrary to constitution as fundamental law	2
5.	Obligation of contract	1
6.	Bill of attainder	1
7.	Lack of proper procedure in passage of act	1
		18

This table does not include a complete list of acts held void by state courts in this period, but the cases are sufficiently representative to indicate the character of the laws which were then rendered null and void by the refusal of courts to enforce them.

In the few states for which a record has been made of the laws declared void the authority to nullify acts was used very sparingly. Justice Woodward noted that for nearly fifty years under the Pennsylvania constitution of 1790 no act of the legislature was held void. Though judges claimed the power, and said they would exercise it in clear cases, no case arose which in their judgment

---

Acts of Congress invalidated by federal courts from 1789 to 1888
(Based on table in U. S. Reports, 131, Appendix)

Relating to organization and procedure of courts	7
Effort to exercise powers not granted in Constitution	6
Interference with state powers	2
Ex post facto law	1
Interfering with rights of citizen	1
Unjust penalties	1
Denial of trial by jury	1
	19

With the exception of the extraordinary decree issued in the Dred Scott case, which is not included in the above table, all the acts or portions of the acts of Congress invalidated by the courts before 1868 related to the organization and jurisdiction of courts. Denying the power of Congress to make notes legal tender was the first departure from this rule.

Acts of State Legislatures invalidated by Federal Courts prior to 1888
(Based on list furnished in U. S. Reports, 131, Appendix)

Impairing obligation of contract	50
Interference with interstate commerce	50
State interference with federal powers by means of taxation	16
Interference with powers of courts and judicial procedure	3
Act in conflict with treaty	3
Ex post facto law	3
Denial of right of suffrage	1
Taking property without due process	1
Denial of trial by jury	1
	128

Laws of territorial legislatures in excess of powers granted and acts of confederate states which were held void are not included.

A summary of this character gives no indication as to the weight or importance of judicial decisions invalidating acts, but it is especially noteworthy that the total of state enactments invalidated to 1888 should be so largely based on two provisions of the Constitution—the clause relating to the regulation of commerce and the one prohibiting the states from impairing the obligation of contracts.

was clear enough to justify the exercise of the power.[2]
For forty-five years under the New York constitution of
1777 only one act was held void and for the next twenty-
five years under the constitution of 1821 six acts were
refused application. Beginning with the constitution of
1846 an average of two statutes a year was denied
validity.[3]

The hesitancy to assert such an extraordinary prerogative was apparent also in other states. In Connecticut there was only one case[4] prior to the constitution of
1818 and in Massachusetts after the decision invalidating
an act in 1813[5] no law was declared void for thirty-four
years.[6] But the change which was coming both in the
attitude of the judges and in the sentiment regarding
legislatures was shown by the fact that ten laws were set
aside in Massachusetts from 1850 to 1860.

Following the impeachment proceedings against
Judges Tod and Pease[7] no law was declared void in Ohio,
so far as the official records show, until 1835.[8] In this
case the Supreme Court held void as contrary to the state
and federal constitutions a section of a tax law in so far
as it attempted to levy a higher tax rate on dividends

---

[2] Sharpless v. Mayor of Philadelphia, 21 Penna. St. 147, 183 (1853).

[3] Edward S. Corwin, ''The Extension of Judicial Review in New York,''
15 *Mich. Law Rev.* (Feb. 1917). 285. ''From 1840 on, judicial review
became a considerable factor of constitutional government in New York.
From that date till the Civil War there were probably more statutes invalidated in New York on constitutional grounds than in all the other states
of the Union combined. But the great extension of judicial review in New
York, as in other states, has taken place since 1870.''—Corwin, *op. cit.*, 303.

[4] Symsbury Case, Kirby (Conn.) 1785.

[5] Holden v. James, 11 Mass. 396.

[6] Sohier v. Mass. General Hospital, 3 Cush. 483 (1849).

[7] Cf. *supra*, 255 et seq.

[8] Joseph H. Hixson, *The Judicial Veto in Ohio*, Thesis (MS), Ohio State
University, 1922. See State of Ohio v. Commercial Bank of Cincinnati,
7 Ohio Rep. 125 (1835).

than was provided in a law incorporating a bank. During the same year the court denied authority to the legislature to interfere with property rights so as to change the character of a tract devoted to the public use.[9]

From 1802 to 1851, when a new constitution was adopted in Ohio there are only seven reported cases in which acts of the legislature were held void and one city ordinance was invalidated:

1 held void for impairing the obligation of contracts.

4 held void for invading the rights of private property.

3 held void for infringing on the jurisdiction of the courts.[10]

A change in the attitude of the judges in the consideration of legislative measures, the beginning of a restrictive policy toward legislative enactments through numerous express constitutional restrictions, and the construction of implied limitations become apparent in the states at about the Civil War period. A similar change in attitude began about the same time in the federal courts and became more marked two decades later.

2. *Opinions favoring an extensive judicial review*—

Indications of the new point of view may be discovered in occasional dicta of justices prior to 1860 and in the nullification of a few state acts without express constitutional warrant for such action. Doctrines of superior natural laws or of fundamental laws which aided in the

---

[9] Town of Gallipolis v. Trustees of Town of Gallipolis, 7 Ohio Rep. 217 (1835).

[10] Hixson, *op. cit.*, 23, 24. The new constitution dealt more specifically with the protection of private property, prohibited the assembly from granting divorces, from exercising any judicial powers not expressly conferred, and from authorizing a city, county, or town to become a stockholder in a corporation, or to raise money or to loan its credit to a corporation.

evolution of the American concepts of written constitutions also gave sanction for the construction of implied limitations to restrict legislative activities. Such implied limitations were conceived as resulting from the nature of the social compact,[11] from the fundamental principles of free republican governments, or from the spirit of a written constitution. The development of these implied limitations and some of the consequences which followed in the evolution of the American doctrine of judicial review of legislation have been considered elsewhere.[12]

These limitations were applied by the judges to protect vested rights of property.[13] And by the opinions of Chief Justice Marshall definite restrictions were placed upon the authority of the state to change the terms of contracts either of individuals or of corporations.[14] Chancellor Kent and Justice Story developed these ideas into a policy of placing general restrictions on legislative authority favorable to the protection of vested civil rights.[15]

In 1811 Justice Kent maintained that such rules of construction must be followed:

---

[11] Justice Chase in Calder v. Bull, 3 Dallas 386 (1798).

[12] "The Law of Nature in State and Federal Judicial Decisions," 25 *Yale Law Jour.* (June 1916) 617; and in "Judicial Review of Legislation in the United States and the Doctrines of Vested Rights and Implied Limitations on Legislatures," 2 *Texas Law Rev.* (April and June 1924) 257, 387 and 3 *ibid.* (Dec. 1924) 1; see also my monograph on *The Revival of Natural Law Concepts* (Cambridge, 1930); Parts II and III.

[13] Symsbury Case, Kirby (Conn.) 444, 447 (1785); Ham v. McClaws, 1 Bay (S. C.), 93, 98 (1789); Vanhorne's Lessee v. Dorrance, 2 Dallas 304, 310 (1795); Trustees of University of North Carolina v. Foy, 2 Hay. (N. C.) 310, 312 (1804).

[14] Fletcher v. Peck, 6 Cranch 87 (1810); Dartmouth College v. Woodward, 4 Wheaton 518, 628 (1819).

[15] Dash v. Van Kleeck, 7 Johns. (N. Y.) 477, 505 (1811); Gardner v. Newburgh, 2 Johns. Ch. 162, 166 (1816); Terrett v. Taylor, 9 Cranch 43, 52 (1815); Wilkinson v. Leland, 2 Peters 627, 658 (1829).

as are agreeable to those settled rules which the wisdom of the
common law has established for the interpretation of statutes,
as is not inconvenient, nor against reason, and injures no person.
A statute is never to be construed against the plain and obvious
dictates of reason. The common law, says Lord Coke, adjudgeth
a statute so far void; and upon this principle the Supreme
Court of South Carolina proceeded, when it held that the courts
were bound to give such a construction to a statute as was consistent with justice, though contrary to the letter of it. . . . . It
is not intended that we have any express constitutional provision
on the subject; nor have we any for numerous other rights dear
alike to freedom and to justice. An *ex post facto* law, in the
strict technical sense of the term is usually understood to apply
to criminal cases, and this is its meaning when used in the Constitution of the United States; yet laws impairing previously
acquired civil rights are equally within the reason of that prohibition, and equally to be condemned. We have seen that the
cases in the English and in the civil law apply to such rights;
and we shall find upon further examination, that there is no
distinction in principle, nor any recognized in practice, between
a law punishing a person criminally for a past innocent act or
punishing him civilly by divesting him of a lawfully acquired
right. The distinction consists only in the degree of the oppression, and history teaches us that the government which can deliberately violate the one right soon ceases to regard the other.[16]

The authority of common sense and the reason of civilized
states was regarded as sufficient to cause "not only the
judicial, but even the legislative, authority to bow with
reverence to such a sanction."[17] In the opinion of Judge
Kent the act of the legislature was to be considered as
not having been passed. This case became a ruling precedent for the principle that legislatures irrespective of

---

16 Dash v. Van Kleeck, 7 Johns. 502, 505.
17 *Ibid.*, 508.

constitutions could not divest individuals of lawfully acquired civil rights.[18]

In a subsequent case Chancellor Kent decided that upon the authority of Grotius and Pufendorf and other continental writers ''compensation was due the owner of property taken by the state even in the absence of any constitutional provision to that effect; that compensation was due one whose property was not taken, but damaged, by the state; and that the power of eminent domain could be exercised for public purposes only.''[19] According to Kent's notion, the police power was surrounded by the same limitations.[20] These views developed into the doctrine which Kent so forcefully expounded that statutes must be construed in accordance with the principles of the common law because it is not to be presumed ''that the legislature intended to make any innovation upon the common law further than the case absolutely required.''[21] And this doctrine found its way eventually into the case law of the United States in the form that ''statutes in derogation of the common law are to be strictly construed.''[22]

In addition to the theory developing in the state courts that certain classes of statutes were to be deemed void as in derogation of the common law, the federal courts were gradually evolving other effective checks on state legislation. The first of these was discovered in the

---

[18] For a discussion of the doctrine of vested rights as ''the foundational doctrine of constitutional limitations in this country,'' see Edward S. Corwin, ''Due Process of Law before the Civil War,'' 24 *Harv. Law Rev.* (March and April 1911) 366, 460.

[19] Corwin, *op. cit.*, 378.

[20] 2 *Comm.* 328–330.

[21] 1 *Comm.* 564; also Pound, ''Common Law and Legislation,'' 21 *Harv. Law Rev.* (April 1908) 383, 401.

[22] 1 *Bouvier Inst.*, sec. 88.

relatively minor provision in the federal Constitution that no state should pass a law impairing the obligation of contracts. This brief restriction, intended primarily to prevent sectional strife and to make impossible the confiscation of private property and the repudiation of debts, was used, by Chief Justice Marshall's interpretation in the well-known cases of *Fletcher v. Peck*[23] and *Dartmouth College v. Woodward*,[24] as a means of strengthening vested rights against legislative and executive interference. Under this limitation corporate charters and franchises were held to be contracts and hence beyond repeal unless made so by express reservation of such power in charters. Since many charters were granted for an indefinite period, the theory that these instruments were in the nature of contracts which could not be revoked placed the effective regulation of corporations beyond the power of legislatures. It was this restriction and the wide scope given to the clause granting Congress the control of interstate commerce under what was known as the implied power doctrine,[25] that made state regulation of corporations extremely difficult, and placed some far-reaching limitations on the legislative activity of the states. It was under the authority of these decisions, according to Justice Cole of the Iowa Supreme Court, that "more monopolies have been created and perpetuated, and more wrongs and outrages upon the people effected, than by any other single instrumentality of the government."[26]

On the whole the practice of holding legislatures in check on the theory that vested rights of property should

---

[23] 6 Cranch 87.
[24] 4 Wheaton 519.
[25] See *supra*, 315–317.
[26] Dubuque v. Railroad Co., 39 Ia. 95, 96 (1874).

be protected whether constitutional provisions so required or not made little headway either in the state or federal courts until the decade prior to the Civil War.[27] Before 1860 state justices, however, concluded that the spirit of free government and the principles of written constitutions prohibited legislatures from depriving citizens of their property or seriously interfering with their contract rights.[28] The supreme court of New York gave its approval to the doctrine of implied limitations when a prohibition law was declared void. "When the rights have been acquired by the citizen under existing laws," it was asserted, "there is no power in any branch of the government to take them away."[29] The doctrine of affording judicial protection to vested rights was soon brought under a constitutional cloak by construing it as a requirement of due process of law.

The period from 1860 to 1890 was characterized by a return to a condition somewhat similar to that from 1789 to 1825 when devices to limit legislative power were popular with the leaders of the Federalist party. Unlimited faith in legislatures did not produce the results anticipated, and the indiscriminate manner in which valuable rights and privileges were often corruptly bartered away by legislators, led the states, in the adoption of new constitutions, to set up a strict control of legislative action. Each constitution contained a long list of matters on which legislatures were definitely forbidden to act and special limits were placed on the public borrowing power. Constant interference with the local affairs of cities

---

27 For some unusual cases see Goshen v. Stonington, 4 Conn. 209 (1822); Regents v. Williams, 9 G & J (Md.) 365, 403 ff. (1838).

28 Sohier v. Massachusetts General Hospital, 3 Cush. 483 (1849); White v. White, 5 Barb. 474 (1849).

29 Wynehamer v. New York, 13 N. Y. 378 (1856).

was to be prevented by many restrictions designed to safeguard municipal home rule.[30]

The popular distrust of legislative power which began during the second quarter of the nineteenth century tended to increase after 1870 and encouraged every effort to curb legislative activity. Courts found ready approval for the limitations which they were disposed to enforce against legislative interference in private affairs. The doctrine that legislatures could not pass laws which impaired vested rights was applied with new vigor in Massachusetts after 1860,[31] and was readily accepted and extended during the next decade in order to restrict legislative control over property rights. Restrictions imposed by the law of nature were revived by state and federal courts[32] so as to place additional limits to the range of legislative interposition in private affairs. And in the effort to prohibit special and class legislation primary reliance was placed upon the judiciary to hold in check inconsiderate and reckless legislatures.

As the champions of vested rights and the defenders of individual privilege from the legislative tinkering so commonly despised, the courts were not only restored to a place of high public esteem, but they soon became largely immune from criticism, while the American doctrine of judicial supremacy, regaining all its former popularity, was lauded as the protecting arm of the government and the highest product of the Anglo-Saxon

---

[30] Theories of *laissez faire* in economics and politics became prevalent again. For restrictions in a typical constitution cf. Pennsylvania, 1873, Thorpe, 3126; and New York, 1894, Thorpe, 2707.

[31] Cf. Wildes v. Vanvoorhis, 81 Mass. 139 (1860); Denny v. Matoon, 84 Mass. 361 (1861).

[32] For the introduction in the states of the rule that statutes in derogation of the common law are void, cf. Pound, ''Common Law and Legislation,'' 21 *Harv. Law Rev.* 400. Cf. also opinion of Justice Miller, Loan Association v. Topeka, 20 Wallace 655 (1874).

mind in the realm of law. The way was thus prepared for the development, from the general phrases of fundamental laws, of implied limitations on legislative and executive officers.

3. *Due process of law and the extension of judicial review*—

The phrases "due process of law" and "the equal protection of the laws" are the most significant expressions in American constitutional law. Due process of law, which formerly referred in England to a method of procedure in criminal trials, was eventually considered as procedure according to ancient customary law, and after 1689 might be changed by parliamentary enactment as well as by judicial decisions. When the term "due process of law" or the "law of the land" was inserted in the American state constitutions it was accepted with the usual English significance. Both in England and in the American states there were occasional broad claims for due process as a guaranty of good government and of principles of justice and reasonableness. But in practice these words were chiefly used as a protection to individuals against summary and arbitrary executive action. With the exception of Coke's extravagant claims they were not regarded as a check on legislative authority.

It was not long before state judges began to apply the law of the land provision of their constitutions in a few cases in accordance with the broad interpretation, as a guaranty against arbitrary political action,[33] requiring equality in the operation of the laws,[34] condemning

---

[33] North Carolina v. Foy, 2 Hay 310 (1804); Rodney L. Mott, *Due Process of Law* (Indianapolis, 1926) 192 ff.

[34] Bank of State v. Cooper, 2 Yerg. 599 (Tenn.) 605, 606 (1831).

retrospective legislation,[35] and protecting the natural rights of the individual.[36] The comparatively few precedents of this type made little impression on the developing principles and concepts of American law during the first half-century. It was not until due process of law was interpreted as sanctifying the ancient common law and its procedure,[37] and as requiring judicial action to take away property rights, that the term acquired anything more than a nominal significance in American constitutional law.[38] Changes in economic and political conditions accompanying the Civil War and the constructive interpretations of judges and of text writers such as Cooley in his *Constitutional Limitations* aided in transforming due process of law so as to accord protection to private rights against either executive or legislative action considered arbitrary or unreasonable.[39] The revolutionary character of the change did not become apparent until the state courts had applied this limitation to the varied forms of political action affecting economic and social life and the Supreme Court of the United States had reversed itself in the application of the "due process" clause of the Fourteenth Amendment.

Though the phrase "due process of law" was inserted in the Fifth Amendment as a limitation on the federal government no act of either the executive or the legislature was condemned prior to 1860. Only one case involved any serious consideration of the meaning of the term and

---

[35] Hoke v. Henderson, 15 N. C. 1, 15 (1833).

[36] In re Dorsey, 7 Porter (Ala.) 293, 377, 378 (1838).

[37] State v. Simons, 2 Spears 761, 767 (1844) and Taylor v. Porter, 4 Hill 140, 146 (1843).

[38] Wynehamer v. New York, 13 N. Y. 378 (1856).

[39] In Illinois from 1870 to 1915 there were 789 cases involving constitutional questions; 115 of these arose under the due process clause; and, in 257 cases acts or parts of acts were held void.

in this case the administrative procedure in question was held proper.[40] Due process of law was held, however, to be a restraint on the legislature as well as the executive and to require a procedure which had the sanction of settled usage both in England and in this country.

At the time of the adoption of the Fourteenth Amendment to the federal Constitution there were two interpretations to the proviso that no state shall "deprive any person of life, liberty or property, without due process of law, nor deny to any person within its jurisdiction the equal protection of the laws." A group of Radical Republicans wished to place supervisory authority in the national government over all state powers. On the other hand, a majority of the Republican party and practically all Democrats regarded the amendments as a means of securing civil rights and equal protection of the laws to Negroes. The discussions in Congress and in the states shed little light as to the meaning intended to be conveyed by these terms, though a preponderant majority of the people belonged to the latter group. When Congress attempted to nationalize the protection of civil rights the Supreme Court rejected the Radical Republican interpretation and adopted the conservative opinion of both Democrats and Republicans—that the amendment was designed primarily to protect the Negro race in their newly acquired rights.[41]

According to this interpretation "due process of law" would have had little effect in limiting the functions of the states. Four justices dissented, however, and speaking through Justice Field they thought that it was the intention of the Fourteenth Amendment to "protect the

---

[40] Murray's Lessee v. Hoboken Land and Improvement Co., 18 Howard 272 (1855).

[41] The Slaughter-House Cases, 16 Wall. 36 (1872).

citizens of the United States against the deprivation of their common rights by state legislation.''[42] Though the amendment received a restricted application it will be seen that the dissenting opinion by a gradual process of interpretation became the prevailing view of the court. But for the time being the majority of the Supreme Court justices discouraged litigation under the amendment. Only thirty-five cases were considered in sixteen years and most of these were either unimportant or trivial.[43]

When the claim was made that the owner of property affected with a public interest is entitled to a reasonable compensation for its use and that what is reasonable compensation is a judicial and not a legislative question, the answer was given that the practice has been otherwise, that ''in countries where the common law prevails it has been customary from time immemorial for the legislature to declare what shall be reasonable compensation under such circumstances, or, perhaps more properly speaking, to fix a maximum beyond which any charge made would be unreasonable.''[44] Though this power may be abused, for the protection against abuses by legislatures the court replied, ''the people must resort to the polls, not the courts.''[45] In short, the issue was regarded as a political question, and was to be determined finally by the political departments of the government. Justices Field and Strong dissenting favored the judicial determination of such questions.

The attitude of the majority of the Supreme Court seemed to be in favor of allowing a rather free hand in

---

[42] *Ibid.*, 89.

[43] Charles M. Hough, ''Due Process of Law—Today,'' 32 *Harv. Law Rev.* (Jan. 1919) 218.

[44] Munn v. Illinois, 94 U. S. 113, 133 (1876) and the Granger Cases, 94 U. S. 155, 164, 179 (1876).

[45] *Ibid.*, 134. See also *The Revival of Natural Law Concepts*, 148 ff.

matters of legislative discretion.[46] One decision had affirmed the doctrine that in most matters of policy and expediency, when there was no direct prohibition in the Constitution, Congress had final authority. Another had denied that the new amendments to the Constitution were intended to shield property owners or individuals from that government control which had existed before the Civil War. And the Supreme Court had finally refused to restrict the attempts of the states to regulate monopolies and deal with exclusive corporations even when such legislation had fixed a maximum charge which was believed to be unreasonable. The legislatures of the states and of the nation were thus to be free to deal with the important issues of policy which an era of peace, prosperity, and expansion had brought up for solution.[47]

Some years earlier there were indications of a change in the judicial attitude of liberality toward state enactments. In a contest over state aid to railroads by taxation Justice Miller held that when a tax can no longer be justly claimed to have a public character, the law authorizing it is beyond the legislative power. In support of the natural law theory as a basis for invalidating statutes, Justice Miller said:

It must be conceded that there are rights in every free government beyond the control of the state. A government which recog-

---

[46] Munn v. Illinois, 94 U. S. 136. In Stone v. Wisconsin, 94 U. S. 181, 186 (1876), it was again maintained by the minority that the Court's decision was wrong and that "it will justify the legislature in fixing the price of all articles and the compensation for all services. It sanctions intermeddling with all business and pursuits and property in the community, leaving the use and enjoyment of property to be regulated according to the discretion of the legislature."

[47] Before a rather distinct change of attitude is noticeable in the decisions of the federal courts an important case was determined in favor of a high degree of discretionary power to be exercised by the national legislature in the unanimous approval of an income tax. Springer v. United States, 102 U. S. 586 (1880).

nized no such rights, but held the lives, the liberty, and the property of its citizens subject at all times to the absolute disposition and unlimited control of even the most democratic depository of power, is, after all, but a despotism of the many— of the majority, but none the less a despotism. The theory of our governments, state and national, is opposed to the deposit of unlimited power anywhere.[48]

There can be no lawful tax, he maintained, which is not laid for a public purpose, and the determination of what is a public purpose was asserted to be a judicial and not a legislative question. Justice Clifford took occasion to criticize the majority opinion on the ground that

courts cannot nullify an act of the state legislature on the vague ground that they think it opposed to a general latent spirit supposed to pervade or underlie the Constitution, where neither the terms nor the implications of the instrument disclose any such restrictions. Such a power is denied to the courts, because to concede it would be to make the courts sovereign over both the Constitution and the people, and convert the government into a judicial despotism. . . . . Unwise laws and such as are highly inexpedient and unjust are frequently passed by legislative bodies, but there is no power vested in a circuit court, nor in this court, to determine that any law passed by a state legislature is void if it is not repugnant to their own constitution or the Constitution of the United States.[49]

Indications that the justices were being prevailed upon to change their views in relation to the authority of the states in the regulation of public utilities were apparent in dicta.[50] But the reversal of the former opinions of the court did not take place until 1889.

---

[48] Loan Association v. Topeka, 20 Wall. 655, 663 (1875).

[49] *Ibid.*, 669, 670. See *The Revival of Natural Law Concepts*, 155, 156.

[50] See comment of Chief Justice Waite in Stone v. Farmers' Loan and Trust Co., 116 U. S. 307 (1886); Spring Valley Waterworks v. Schottler, 110 U. S. 347 (1886); Justice Gray in Dow v. Beidelman, 125 U. S. 680 (1888).

The state of Minnesota had placed in the hands of a commission the power to determine the reasonableness of railroad rates, and from the decision of the commission there was no appeal. The opinion of the commission was final and conclusive as to what were to be lawful, equal, or reasonable charges. In accordance with the language of the Supreme Court in earlier cases this was regarded by the state as a legislative question, left solely to the discretion of the state and therefore not subject to judicial review. The corporation, however, resisted the action of the commission and claimed that under the provisions of the Fourteenth Amendment the statute of the state was in conflict with the federal Constitution.

The contention of the corporation was upheld by the majority of the court in an opinion of Justice Blatchford, because in his judgment the state law deprived the company of its rights to a judicial investigation by due process of law, and substituted therefor, as an absolute finality, the action of a railroad commission, which, in view of the powers conceded to it by the state court, could not be regarded as clothed with judicial functions or as possessing the machinery of a court of justice.[51] The question of the reasonableness of a rate of charge for transportation by a railroad company, involving the element of reasonableness both as regards the company and as regards the public, the court held was eminently a question for judicial investigation. If the company was deprived of its power of charging reasonable rates for the use of its property, and such deprivation took place in the absence of an investigation by judicial machinery, the whole procedure was a deprivation of property without due process of law and a denial of equal protection of the

---

[51] Chicago, Milwaukee & St. Paul Railway Co. v. Minnesota, 134 U. S. 418 (1890).

laws.[52] Justices Bradley, Gray, and Lamar joined in a dissenting opinion. It was asserted that the majority view of the court practically overruled *Munn v. Illinois* and other railroad cases; that the governing principle of those cases was that the regulation of railroad rates is a legislative and not a judicial question. The argument of Justice Bradley was summed up as follows:

But it is said that all charges should be reasonable, and that none but reasonable charges should be exacted; and it is urged that what is a reasonable charge is a judicial question. On the contrary, it is preeminently a legislative one, involving considerations of policy as well as of remuneration, and is usually determined by the legislature fixing a maximum of charges. . . . . If this maximum is not exceeded, the courts cannot interfere. Thus the legislature either fixes the charges at rates which it deems reasonable, or merely declares that they shall be reasonable; and it is only in the latter case, where reasonableness is left open, that the courts have jurisdiction of the subject. I repeat: when the legislature declares that the charges shall be reasonable, or, which is the same thing, allows the common-law rule to that effect to prevail, and leaves the matter there, resort may be had to the court, to inquire judicially whether the charges are reasonable. Then, and not till then, is it a judicial question. But the legislature has the right, and it is its prerogative, if it chooses to exercise it, to declare what is reasonable. This is just where I differ from the majority of the court. They say in effect, if not in terms, that the final tribunal of arbitrament is the judiciary, I say it is the legislature. I hold that it is a legislative question, not a judicial one, unless the legislature or the law (which is the same thing) has made it judicial. . . . . It is

---

[52] *Ibid.*, 458. Justice Miller concurred in the judgment, expressing his own views, which differed from the majority opinion, but not sufficiently, he thought, to call for a dissenting opinion; by this time he had become sufficiently imbued with the necessity of favoring the exercise of an extensive judicial review to aid in a reversal of the doctrines formerly announced by the court.

always a delicate thing for the courts to make an issue with the legislative department of the government, and they should never do so if it is possible to avoid it. By the decision now made we declare, in effect, that the judiciary, and not the legislature, is the final arbiter in the regulations of fares and freights of railroads and the charges of other public accommodations. It is an assumption of authority on the part of the judiciary which, it seems to me, with all due deference to the judgment of my brethren, it has no right to make. . . . . It is complained that the decisions of the board are final and without appeal. So are the decisions of the courts in matters within their jurisdiction. There must be a final tribunal somewhere for deciding every question in the world. Injustice may take place in all tribunals. All human institutions are imperfect—courts as well as commissions and legislatures. Whatever tribunal has jurisdiction, its decisions are final and conclusive unless an appeal is given therefrom. The important question always is, what is the lawful tribunal for the particular case? In my judgment, in the present case, the proper tribunal was the legislature, or[53] the board of commissioners which it created for the purpose. . . . .

It may be that our legislatures are invested with too much power, open, as they are, to influences so dangerous to the interests of individuals, corporations and society, but such is the constitution of our republican form of government; and we are bound to abide by it until it can be corrected in a legitimate way. If our legislatures become too arbitrary in the exercise of their powers, the people always have a remedy in their hands, they may at any time restrain them by constitutional limitations. But so long as they remain invested with the powers that ordinarily belong to the legislative branch of government, they are entitled to exercise those powers, amongst which, in my judgment, is that of the regulation of railroads and other public means of

---

[53] Justice Bradley noted that an invasion of property rights involving fraudulent behavior or a direct confiscation of property would undoubtedly call for interference by the courts because the Constitution clearly provided for protection against such invasions.

intercommunication, and the burdens and charges which those who own them are authorized to impose upon the public.[54]

The decisions in the *Loan Association* and the *Minnesota Railroad Cases* indicated that it was the intention of the federal courts to review and control the legislative enactments of the states, especially so far as they related to the ownership, control, and disposition of private property. Precedents were established which gave encouragement to individuals and corporations to appeal beyond legislatures to the citadel of judicial protection. Courts were henceforth to accept the responsibility of approving or disapproving enactments which resulted from the attempt of the states to bring under subjection the harmful tendencies which inevitably follow in the wake of a rapid social and industrial development.

The issue thus raised as to the powers which belong to the legislative department of government and those which rightfully belong to the judicial department was determined in favor of the judiciary by the deciding vote of one or two members of the Supreme Court. Unquestionably each party in the controversy could turn to the past and cite precedents to bear out the interpretation which seemed from its point of view to be the only correct conclusion. In the interpretation of the contract clause of the Constitution and the due process of law provision the courts suggested the possibility of a censorship over a wide field of state legislation. The general terms of the Fourteenth Amendment relative to the deprivation of life, liberty, or property without due process of law and the denial of equal protection of the laws gave in the opinion of certain justices the desired sanction to encourage the courts to participate in the determination of

---

[54] 341 U. S. 462–463, 465, 466.

governmental policies. On the other hand, able jurists and statesmen could find sufficient precedents in the past and strong arguments from the standpoint of reason to maintain that courts were exceeding their rightful function when they assumed to determine questions of policy by declaring void, as unwise or unjust, acts of legislatures because the acts were held to be contrary to rather vague and indefinite constitutional provisions. It was the firm belief of these justices that the time-honored function of courts and the special powers allotted to our own judiciary did not require the determining of the justice or injustice, the expediency or the inexpediency, of legislation. Courts might find it necessary to consider extreme cases involving a direct confiscation of property or fraudulent methods resulting in an injury to private rights, but the mere question of the difference of opinion regarding compensation for services which the state ought lawfully to regulate was held to be wholly beyond the realm of judicial inquiry. Warning was given regarding the dangers and difficulties which a wide judicial review would create.

The phrases "due process of law" and "the equal protection of the laws" were not only given a new meaning by applying them to legislative acts and administrative procedure but the substantive content of the words was enlarged. First, the eighteenth-century notion of fundamental rights excepted from the powers of government[55] was revived. "The limit of the full control which the state has in the proceedings of its courts both in civil and criminal cases," said Justice Peckham, "is subject only to the qualification that such procedure must not work a denial of fundamental rights or conflict with spe-

---

[55] See Corfield v. Coryell, Fed. Cas. No. 3, 230 (1823) and Terrett v. Taylor, 9 Cranch 43, 52 (1815).

cific and applicable provisions of the federal Constitution.''[56] Second, action which the justices regarded as arbitrary was held to violate the due process and equal protection requirements of the Fourteenth Amendment. Chief Justice Fuller described this requirement when he maintained that the action of the states must be exerted "within the limits of those fundamental principles of liberty and justice which lie at the base of all our civil and political institutions. Undoubtedly the amendment forbids any arbitrary deprivation of life, liberty, or property, and secures equal protection to all under like circumstances in the enjoyment of their rights."[57] Third, the principle of reasonableness was applied to many types of legislative and administrative action. Primarily the requirement of reasonableness was held applicable to the powers of the state for the protection of the public health, order, morals, and welfare, or what is generally regarded as comprised within the police power.[58]

4. *Results of the extension of the meaning of due process of law—*

With judicial review of legislative enactments applied via due process of law to the main lines of public regulation of business and economic conditions, it was not long before the Fourteenth Amendment took its place as the foremost feature of the federal Constitution, so far as limitations on the powers of the states are concerned.

---

[56] West v. Louisiana, 194 U. S. 258, 263 (1904). Cf. Robert P. Reeder, "Constitutional and Extra-Constitutional Restraints," 61 *Univ. of Pa. Law Rev.* (May 1913) 441.

[57] In re Kemmler, 136 U. S. 436, 448 (1889); see also Justice Moody in Twining v. New Jersey, 211 U. S. 78, 100 (1908).

[58] See Justice Peckham in Lochner v. New York, 198 U. S. 45, 56 (1898); Justice Hughes in Chicago, Burlington & Quincy R. R. Co. v. McGuire, 219 U. S. 549, 56 (1910); and Ray A. Brown, "Due Process of Law, Police Power and the Supreme Court," 40 *Harv. Law Rev.* (May 1927) 943, 966.

Whereas for the first twenty years after the adoption of the amendment about one case a year on the average arose under its provisions, it was not long before thirty or more cases were adjudicated in the same period. In such important fields of state power as eminent domain, taxation, public utility regulation, and the police power, state and local acts were attacked before the Supreme Court in more than six hundred cases to the year 1910.[59]

Most of the cases coming under this amendment have arisen since 1896. From 1900 to 1913 there were four hundred and nine opinions or about thirty-one a year. Out of a total of more than six hundred cases only twenty-eight dealt with the rights of the Negro race for whose protection the amendment was primarily enacted. More than half the cases have come to the court on appeals of public utility interests and other corporate organizations asking protection from the acts of the legislatures and administrative agencies of the states.[60]

Gradually the prohibitions involved in due process of law were held applicable to substantive law as well as to legal procedure, to executive, administrative, and judicial acts as well as to legislation, and to corporations as well as to natural persons.[61] Writing in 1919, Judge Hough

---

[59] Charles Wallace Collins, *The Fourteenth Amendment and the States*, (Boston, 1912) 183. See also summary of Judge Hough in 32 *Harv. Law Rev.* (Jan. 1919) 229, and my article on ''Judicial Review of Legislation in the United States and the Doctrines of Vested Rights and of Implied Limitations on Legislatures,'' 3 *Texas Law Rev.* (Dec. 1924) 1.

[60] Collins, *op. cit.*, 183 and *The Revival of Natural Law Concepts*, 183, from which an extract is used with the permission of the Harvard University Press.

[61] Willis, ''Due Process of Law under the United States Constitution,'' 74 *Univ. of Pa. Law Rev.* (Feb. 1926) 337, 338. Mr. Willis claims that by attacking all forms of state legislation before the Supreme Court corporations are attempting to undermine our dual form of government.—*Ibid.*, 342. The Fourteenth Amendment, in the judgment of Mr. Collins was to be a charter of liberty for human rights, but it operates today to protect primarily the rights of property. It has become the Magna Carta of organized capital. It ''gives to the federal government undefined and illimitable control over

believed, that "the direct appeal of property to due process of law had for the most part failed. . . . . The indirect appeal through liberty is still going on. . . . . But it is dying, and the courts, when invoked today under the due-process clause, are doing little more than easing the patient's later days.''[62] That this prediction is not being fulfilled is shown by the fact that since 1920 more acts in the field of social and economic legislation have been invalidated under the due-process clauses than were set aside from 1868 to 1920.[63]

Phrased in percentages this means [says Mr. Brown] that from 1868 to 1912 the Court has held against the legislature in a very little more than six per cent of the cases; from 1913 to 1920 in a little more than seven per cent of the cases; while since 1920 the Court has held against the legislature in twenty-eight per cent of the cases.

And if we go behind the decisions and look at the votes of the individual judges in each case, we will find the same startling increase in the number of opinions adverse to the validity of legislation under the due process clauses. In the period up to 1921 the judicial vote was cast approximately ninety per cent in favor of the various statutes considered, and only ten per cent against. Since then, however, the favorable vote has shrunk to about sixty-nine per cent and the adverse vote grown to thirty-one per cent.[64]

---

every phase of state activity. It throws into the hands of the Supreme Court of the United States more power over the states than does all the rest of the Constitution combined.'' Collins, *op. cit.*, 146 ff.

[62] ''Due Process of Law—Today,'' 32 *Harv. Law Rev.* 218, 233. For similar judgments regarding the decline of significance of this phrase, consult Charles Warren, ''The Progressiveness of the United States Supreme Court,'' 13 *Col. Law Rev.* (April 1913) 294 and Robert E. Cushman, ''The Social and Economic Interpretation of the Fourteenth Amendment,'' 20 *Mich. Law Rev.* (May 1922) 737, 757 ff.

[63] Ray A. Brown, ''Due Process of Law, Police Power, and the Supreme Court,'' 40 *Harv. Law Rev.* (May 1927) 943 ff.

[64] *Ibid.*, 944, 945.

Due process of law also became the medium for the incorporation of the natural rights' philosophy of the Declaration of Independence into the federal Constitution.[65] Through the dicta of Justices Field and Brewer a basis was predicated for the acceptance of the natural rights' doctrine and the development of the concepts of liberty of contract or of the right to pursue a calling, which was appropriated and applied by the state courts[66] before it received the approval of a majority of the justices of the Supreme Court.[67] The extremes to which the doctrine of liberty of contract may be carried are illustrated in the cases of *Lochner v. New York*[68] in which a New York law fixing a ten-hour day in bakeshops was held void, and *Adkins v. Children's Hospital*[69] in which an act of Congress providing for the fixing of a minimum wage for women in certain employments was nullified.

Building on the foundations of early years when the statutes invalidated related to a very restricted group of subjects, widening the terms of the Fourteenth Amendment, and developing common and natural law limitations, the courts, federal and state, have exercised a decided check on legislative power in refusing sanction to bills not properly passed, to statutes which deny the equal protection of the laws and which deprive owners of property without due process of law, to class and special legislation, and to other types of enactments which would have been well within legislative competence in the early

---

[65] See Justice Field's dissent in Butchers' Union Co. v. Crescent City Co., 111 U. S. 746, 756 (1883) and dicta in Barbier v. Connolly, 113 U. S. 27, 31 (1885).

[66] Cf. Roscoe Pound, ''Liberty of Contract,'' 18 *Yale Law Jour.* (May 1909) 454.

[67] Allgeyer v. Louisiana, 165 U. S. 578, 591 (1897); Coppage v. Kansas, 236 U. S. 1 (1915).

[68] 198 U. S. 45 (1904).

[69] 261 U. S. 525 (1923).

days of judicial review. The character of these decisions and the numerous restrictions thereby placed on legislative assemblies have made it possible for the courts to invade the field of public policy and to act as super-legislatures.[70]

Through the broad guaranties of the federal and state constitutions the courts have to a large degree acquired the right of final determination as to the laws which shall or shall not be enforced. "It is not what the legislature desires, but what the courts regard as juridically permissible," claims Dean Pound, "that in the end becomes law. Statutes give way before the settled habits of legal thinking which we call the common law. Judges and jurists do not hesitate to assert that there are extra-constitutional limits to legislative power which put fundamental common law dogmas beyond the reach of statutes."[71]

The legislative activity of American courts which has resulted from this extension of the right of review has now become a commonplace fact of our political thought. The significance of the fact was forcefully stated by President Roosevelt in one of his messages to Congress in which he declared: "The chief lawmakers in our country may be, and often are, the judges, because they are the final seat of authority."[72] The extent to which the restrictive power of courts over law-making has influenced the trend of governmental activity in the United States has only begun to receive consideration. The acts of Congress which have been invalidated by the federal courts and the acts of state legislatures which have been

---

[70] Justice Brandeis dissenting in Burns Baking Co. v. Bryan, 264 U. S. 504, 533 (1923).

[71] "Law in Books and Law in Action," 44 *Am. Law Rev.* 27.

[72] December 8, 1908.

rendered null and void and the restrictions which have been placed on legislative and executive activity by the knowledge that the courts would in all probability not approve a particular line of governmental action, form the limitations which make unique the constitutional system of the United States.

The list below of cases declared invalid by federal and state courts[73] indicates the character of enactments which have been nullified by judicial judgment, but these cases by no means exhaust the limitations placed upon the realm of political activity by the adoption of the American doctrine. On account of the fact that courts might

---

[73] Summary of Laws held void by State and Federal Courts according to the list prepared by the New York Library, 1903–1908:

	1903	1904	1905	1906	1907	1908	Total
Lack of clear title	10	8	7	13	7	10	55
Denial of equal protection of laws	9	4	1	6	10	6	36
Class and special legislation	4	7	8	19	7	8	53
Lack of power and refusal to follow constitution	5	5	8	18	11	1	48
Deprival of property without due process of law	5	15	4	9	11	5	49
Interference with judicial powers	4	2	8	5	12	1	32
Lack of uniformity in taxation	0	5	2	7	7	2	23
Impairing obligation of contract	2	1	2	5	8	3	21
Interference with interstate commerce	1	5	3	2	5	3	19
Not valid exercise of police power	1	0	2	7	2	1	13
Relating to elections	0	0	0	2	5	2	9
Denial of freedom of contract	3	2	3	0	0	0	8
Attempt to confer legislative powers	0	1	3	2	0	2	8
Taking property for private purposes	0	0	2	1	4	1	8
Exemption from taxation	2	1	0	0	1	1	5
Taxation for private purposes	1	0	0	1	2	0	4
Interference with federal power	1	0	0	1	2	0	4
Interference with personal liberty	2	0	0	0	0	1	3
Ex post facto laws	1	1	0	0	0	0	2
Total	51	57	53	98	94	47	400

Subjects on which there were only a few decisions are omitted. Where a number of reasons were given for invalidating an act, the one first mentioned was used in making the classification. The above table gives no indication of the nature of the acts held void. For example, some extraordinary decisions have been based upon the first topic, lack of a clear title; in fact, the famous New York decision in the case of *in re* Jacobs, which is held responsible for placing an effective barrier in the way of tenement legislation, was held void largely on the ground that the title did not properly describe it. Nevertheless it is possible by such a summary as given above to readily perceive that new grounds have been discovered on which legislative acts may be invalidated.

hold acts invalid, the debates in legislative halls have more frequently centered on the subject of constitutionality than on the issue of policy or expediency. Such vital matters as a national monetary system, a protective tariff, internal improvements, slavery, and a host of minor national issues were discussed primarily with relation to constitutionality and only secondarily with relation to public policy. In the state legislatures the judiciary committees which were expected to divine the opinions of the judges as to the validity of proposed laws set the stamp of disapproval and ultimate defeat upon hosts of legislative projects. Single judicial decisions may have closed for years entire fields of political action. The laws which were declared invalid form an interesting phase of American judicial history. But the exact limits which have been imposed on the other branches of government by judicial supremacy are extremely difficult to estimate. Suffice it to say that the chief interest of lawyers and statesmen in America has frequently been in the direction of seeking the limits and bounds of legislative power rather than in the issues of policy and expediency which result in giving untrammeled consideration to the public good.

The popular impressions that the judiciary through the power of invalidating legislative acts has become a great barrier in the way of industrial and social reform has led to criticisms of the court and renewed objections to the American doctrine of judicial supremacy.

CHAPTER XVI

RECENT CRITICISMS OF THE PRACTICE OF JUDICIAL REVIEW OF LEGISLATIVE ACTS

THE EXTENSION of the practice of declaring laws invalid by means of implied limitations discovered by state and federal judges, the widening of the scope of the Fourteenth Amendment, with the consequent restrictions on the legislative powers of the states, and a series of reactionary decisions by state justices—these brought forth finally a renewal of the criticisms of the American doctrine of judicial review of legislation in the United States.

After the attacks by Jefferson and the Democrats of the early nineteenth century, the federal courts with but few exceptions were immune from destructive criticisms. Among the manifold proposals for amendment to the federal Constitution there are few that relate to judicial powers and organization. The series of attacks on the federal judiciary by the Democrats from 1800 to 1830 led to the introduction of amendments to limit the jurisdiction of the federal courts, to provide a more expeditious mode of removal of judges, and to secure shorter terms of office. None of these received serious consideration in Congress. During the first ninety years of the history of the United States only four amendments were proposed to change the manner of the selection of the judges.[1] With the exception of a change in the method of the selection of the judges, the state judicial departments were equally immune from the movements of reconstruction which seriously affected the operation of other branches of the government.

The opposition of Jackson and of Lincoln was directed more at particular decisions of which they disapproved than at the general powers and jurisdiction of the courts. Neither of these attacks had any serious influence upon the doctrine of judicial review as a feature of the American political system. Under Chief Justice Taney and the Democratic ascendancy the powers of the judiciary were restricted, and during the Civil War period civil processes had to give way when necessity seemed to require the dominance of the military power; but by 1870 normal conditions began to prevail and the courts set out anew to limit legislative powers and to restrict governmental activity. This period of expansion of judicial power culminated in the last decades of the nineteenth century and brought about renewed attacks upon the American doctrine of judicial review of legislation. Protests have come from many sources: from the justices themselves, from labor leaders, from liberals and radicals, and from various political parties.

1. *Criticisms by dissenting justices—*

In the application of the doctrine of judicial review of legislative and administrative acts, the federal courts of the United States have not infrequently been criticized for usurping part of the functions of the legislature. A survey of the decisions of the Supreme Court of the United States on constitutional issues since 1870 reveals

---

[1] Herman v. Ames, "The Proposed Amendments to the Constitution of the United States during the First Century of its History." Am. Hist. Assoc. *Reports*, 1896, 144, 146.

a well considered and deep-seated conviction in the minds of a number of justices that the federal courts were interfering with matters not properly within the judicial realm.

Objections on the part of the justices to the extensive judicial censorship which was proposed by extending the application of the Fourteenth Amendment to the protection of corporations and to the preservation of property rights so as to make private rights largely immune from governmental regulation have been noted. Dissenting opinions of federal justices have frankly condemned the policy of decisions which, it is alleged, have practically resulted in legislation by judicial judgments and have tended to weaken that respect for the federal judiciary, which was so marked a characteristic of preceding years.

Justice Harlan in the *Income Tax Cases* raised the inquiry, "Is the judiciary to supervise the action of the legislative branch of the government upon questions of public policy?"[2]

In my judgment [he said] to say nothing of the disregard of the former adjudications of this court, and of the settled practice of the government—this decision may well excite the gravest apprehensions. It strikes at the very foundation of national authority, in that it denies to the general government a power which is, or may become, vital to the very existence and preservation of the Union in an emergency.[3]

Other dissenting justices characterized the majority opinion and judgment as fraught with immeasurable danger and as approaching a national calamity.[4]

---

[2] Pollock v. Farmers Loan and Trust Co., 158 U. S. 601, 679 (1895). In the following pages I have used, with the permission of the editors, some portions of my article "Judicial Criticism of Legislation by Courts," 11 *Mich. Law Rev.* (Nov. 1912) 26 ff.

[3] Pollock v. Farmers Loan and Trust Co., 158 U. S. 671.

[4] *Ibid.*, 695.

Speaking for the minority in the *Insular Cases* Chief Justice Fuller noted that

briefs have been presented at this bar, purporting to be on behalf of certain industries, and eloquently setting forth the desirability that our government should possess the power to impose a tariff on the products of newly acquired territories so as to diminish or remove competition. That, however, furnishes no basis for judicial judgment. . . . . After all, these arguments are merely political, and political reasons have not the requisite certainty to afford rules of judicial interpretation.[5]

And Justice Harlan thought ''the People of the United States who ordained the Constitution never supposed that a change could be made in our system of government by mere judicial interpretation.''[6] When the constitutional requirement of jury trial was held not to be applicable to Hawaii the minority believed that the Constitution

without any declaration to that effect by Congress became the supreme law for that country, and, therefore, it forbade the trial and conviction of the accused for murder otherwise than upon a presentment or indictment by a grand jury and the unanimous verdict of a petit jury and by a unanimous verdict of a petit jury . . . . and that any other construction of the Resolution is forbidden by its clear, unambiguous words and is to make, not to interpret the law.[7]

In the much discussed case wherein the Supreme Court by a five to four vote gave its sanction to an act of Congress prohibiting traffic in lottery tickets in interstate commerce Chief Justice Fuller observed:

I regard this decision as inconsistent with the views of the framers of the Constitution, and of Marshall, its great expounder. Our form of government may remain notwithstanding legisla-

---

[5] Downes v. Bidwell, 182 U. S. 244, 374, 375 (1901).

[6] *Ibid.*, 386, 387.

[7] Hawaii v. Mankichi, 190 U. S. 197, 248, 249 (1903).

tion or decision, but, as long ago observed, it is with governments as with religions, the form may survive the substance of faith.[8]

In a case relative to state taxation of national bank stock, Justices Fuller, Brewer, Brown, and Peckham, dissenting from a majority opinion rendered by Justice White, maintained that "in the face of the plain words of the Constitution and statutes, the clear language of the Supreme Court of California, and the absence of allegation or proof of actual discrimination, this court, by its opinion, strikes down the whole system of California for the taxation of shares of national banks."[9] It was a matter to be deplored, thought the minority, that, to all intents and purposes, the Supreme Court by its decision was granting a favor to national bank property denied to all other property in the country. A similar criticism was made by Justice Harlan with the concurrence of Chief Justice Fuller and Justices White and McKenna, when a decision was rendered on the issue whether a state can impose a tax upon railway companies whose lines lie wholly within the state, where a part of the gross receipts is derived from passengers and freight coming from or destined to points without the state. The minority maintained that the Supreme Court of the United States should have accepted the interpretation which the Supreme Court of Texas placed upon the statutes in question.[10]

When it was maintained that due process of law was denied a Kentucky corporation by a tax upon its rolling stock permanently located in other states and employed in the prosecution of its business, Justice Holmes re-

---

[8] Lottery Case, 188 U. S. 321, 375 (1903).

[9] Justice Brewer in San Francisco National Bank v. Dodge, 197 U. S. 70, 108 (1905).

[10] Galveston Harrisburg, etc., Ry. Company v. Texas, 210 U. S. 217, 228 (1908).

marked: "It seems to me that the result reached by the court probably is a desirable one, but I hardly understand how it can be deduced from the Fourteenth Amendment.'"[11] The state of Kansas decided to levy a charter fee upon all foreign corporations doing business within the state, but on appeal to the Supreme Court by the Western Union Telegraph Company and the Pullman Company, it was decided that such a fee was a tax and as such an interference with interstate commerce. Justices Holmes, Fuller, and McKenna dissented. Justice Holmes' criticism was extremely frank:

I think that the tax in question, for I am perfectly willing to call it a tax, was lawful under all the decisions of this court until last week. From other points of view, if I were at liberty to take them, I should agree that it deserved the reprobation it received from the majority. But I have not heard and have not been able to frame any reason that I honestly can say seems to me to justify the judgment of the court in point of law. In the opinion of certain justices the state's power to tax has been curtailed by judge-made restrictions.[12]

The federal courts have been inclined to extend their jurisdiction into what was formerly regarded as the exclusive field for the state governments. A Chicago corporation appealed from an action of the board of equalization to prevent the assessment and collection of a tax, on the ground that the procedure was in violation of the Fourteenth Amendment. The case was brought before the circuit court without any effort being made to take advantage of the right of appeal provided in the

---

[11] Union Refrigerator Transit Co. v. Kentucky, 199 U. S. 194, 211 (1905). "It is difficult to prove," says Professor Beale, "that a practice which has prevailed in half the states of the Union for a century was contrary to due process of law."—"Jurisdiction to tax," 32 *Harv. Law Rev.* (April 1919) 587, 592.

[12] Pullman Co. v. Kansas, 216 U. S. 56, 77 (1910). See also Western Union Telegraph Company v. Kansas, 216 U. S. 1 (1910).

state courts. Justices Holmes and Moody felt constrained to dissent from the sanction which the Supreme Court accorded to the action of the lower court. "I should have thought," Justice Holmes suggested, "that the action of the state was to be found in its constitution, and that no fault could be found with that until the authorized interpreter of the constitution, the supreme court, had said that it sanctioned the alleged wrong."[13]

When the Supreme Court was asked to grant a writ of *habeas corpus* to secure the release of the attorney-general of Minnesota from commitment by the circuit court of the United States for disobeying an order to cease criminal proceedings under a state statute, Justice Harlan signified in a lengthy opinion his objections to the majority decision upholding the action of the lower court. The principle of the majority, according to Justice Harlan,

would inaugurate a new era in the American judicial system and in the relations of the national and state governments. It would enable the subordinate federal courts to supervise and control the official action of the states as if they were "dependencies" or provinces. . . . . I am justified, by what this court has heretofore declared, in now saying that the men who framed the Constitution, and who caused the adoption of the Eleventh Amendment, would have been amazed by the suggestion that a state of the Union can be prevented, by an order of a subordinate federal court, from being represented by its attorney-general in a suit brought by it in one of its own courts.[14]

The readiness with which the federal courts have taken jurisdiction of rate cases involving the extent of state powers was also condemned by Chief Justice Fuller and Justice Harlan. In their opinion cases of this char-

---

[13] Raymond v. Chicago Traction Co., 207 U. S. 20, 41 (1907).
[14] *Ex parte* Young, 209 U. S. 123, 175, 204 (1908).

acter are precipitated into a Circuit Court of the United States without even an honest effort to abide by the state procedure for the judicial determination of such cases. The opportunity for railroad companies to invoke the power of the federal courts in order to put a stop to proceedings in a state tribunal before the matter had been brought to the highest court of the state was thought to be without warrant in federal law.[15]

At another time the decision of the highest court of a state relative to a deed conveying the coal under a tract of land was held not to be binding upon federal courts in a similar action based on almost identical facts and circumstances. Justices Holmes, White, and McKenna felt called upon to criticize the wide latitude accorded to Circuit Courts in dealing with state matters. Justice Holmes said:

I think it a thing to be regretted if, while in the great mass of cases the state courts finally determine who is the owner of land, how much he owns and what he conveys by his deed, the courts of the United States, when by accident and exception the same question comes before them, do not follow what for all ordinary purposes is the law. . . . . But I suppose it will be admitted on the other side that even the independent jurisdiction of the Circuit Courts of the United States is a jurisdiction only to declare the law, at least in a case like the present, and only to declare the law of the State. It is not an authority to make it.[16]

---

[15] Prentis v. Atlantic Coast Line Co., 211 U. S. 210, 237 (1908). The Virginia State Corporation Commission, acting in the capacity of a court, had determined railway passenger rates, and an injunction had been granted by a circuit court. The Supreme Court in an opinion by Justice Holmes reversed the decree of the lower court on the ground that the case should have been presented first to the state courts. The minority concurred in reversing the judgment, but dissented from the opinion.

[16] Kuhn v. Fairmont Coal Co., 215 U. S. 349, 370 (1910). See also Tullock v. Mulvane, 184 U. S. 497, 523, 572 ff. (1902) in which three justices claimed that no one has such a vested interest in the views of this court upon a question of general law that he may complain of the refusal of a state court to accept those views.

In a case where an owner of real property abutting
on a street in New York City sued to enjoin the use of
an elevated railway unless the fee value of certain ease-
ments of light, air, and access were paid, the Supreme
Court was about evenly divided on the issue. Justices
McKenna, Harlan, Brewer, and Day agreed on an opinion. Justice Brown concurred in the result, but not in
the opinion. Chief Justice Fuller and Justices White,
Peckham, and Holmes dissenting, asserted in an opinion
by Justice Holmes that the rights sustained by the majority were wholly a construction of the courts.[17] Continuing, he stated that the plaintiff, in order to maintain
his contention, must claim that

he has a constitutional right, not only that the state courts shall
not reverse their earlier decisions upon a matter of property
rights, but that they shall not distinguish them unless the distinction is so fortunate as to strike a majority of this court as
sound. . . . . The legislature and the court of appeals of New
York said that the statute assailed was passed for the benefit of
the public using the street, and I accept their view.[18]

It was asserted that a right set up by implication through
a decision of a court of justice of a state should not be
held as final and superior to the legislative power of the
state so as to render invalid a law passed in the interest
of public policy.

When a decision of the Circuit Court relative to the
validity of an Illinois anti-trust act, because it granted
an exception to agricultural products or live stock in the
hands of the producer or raiser, was reviewed, the act
was held to be in violation of the clause of the Fourteenth
Amendment requiring equal protection of the laws. Jus-

---

17 Muhlker v. Harlem R. R. Co., 197 U. S. 544 (1905).

18 197 U. S. 574. See also dissent by Justice Harlan in Vicksburg v.
Waterworks, 202 U. S. 453, 472–473 (1906).

tice McKenna dissented from the opinion of the court, declaring that classifications of this character are entirely proper and that a wide latitude must be left to the discretion of the legislature in dealing with such matters. Courts are not to determine, he thought, whether laws are arbitrary, oppressive, or capricious,

indeed, whether such combinations are evils or blessings, or to what extent either, is not a judicial inquiry. . . . . To consider their effect would take us from legal problems to economic ones, and this demonstrates to my mind how essentially any judgment or action based upon these differences is legislative and cannot be reviewed by the judiciary.[19]

The control over acts of Congress through the exercise of judicial review of legislation has also aroused judicial criticism. In the review of the conviction of Senator Burton for a violation of the federal law against bribery, Justices Brewer, White, and Peckham dissented from the opinion sustaining the conviction with the observation that it seems clear "that the construction now given writes into the statute an offense which Congress never placed there. It is a criminal case, and, in such a case above all, judicial legislation is to be deprecated."[20]

A Philippine act made criminal the entry of a false statement by a public official. On a review of the Supreme Court of the Philippines affirming a conviction for falsification in accordance with this act, the Supreme Court held the act void as in violation of the clause of the Philippine bill of rights prohibiting cruel and unusual punishments. Justice White, with the concurrence of Justice Holmes, recorded a vigorous dissent. He thought that if legislation defining and punishing crime is held repugnant to constitutional limitations because it "seems

---

[19] Connolly v. Union Sewer Pipe Co., 184 U. S. 540, 571 (1902).
[20] Burton v. United States, 202 U. S. 344, 400 (1906).

to the judicial mind not to have been sufficiently impelled by motives of reformation of the criminal," the legislative power is impotent to control crime. Since the decision subjected to judicial control the degree of severity with which authorized modes of punishment might be inflicted, it seemed to the minority, "that the demonstration is conclusive that nothing will be left of the independent legislative power to punish and define crime."[21] The direct result of the decision, it was maintained, was to expand the judicial power by endowing it with a vast authority to control the legislative department in the exercise of its rightful discretion. The doctrine that, "by judicial construction constitutional limitations may be made to progress" so as ultimately to include that which was not intended, was condemned.

In defining the authority of the Interstate Commerce Commission, the majority opinion of the court in a series of cases was held so to restrict the powers of the commission as to make it, in the opinion of Justice Harlan

a useless body for all practical purposes, and to defeat many of the important objects designed to be accomplished by the various enactments of Congress relating to interstate commerce. . . . . It has been left, it is true, with power to make reports, and to issue protests. But it has been shorn, by judicial interpretation, of authority to do anything of an effective character.[22]

Justice Day, with the concurrence of Justices Harlan and McKenna, dissented from a judgment against the right of the Interstate Commerce Commission to require testimony from a railway manager, contending that too narrow a construction was given to the act of Congress

---

[21] Weems v. United States, 217 U. S. 349, 388, 411 (1910). See Keller v. United States, 213 U. S. 138, 149 (1909) and opinions of dissenting Justices in Kepner v. United States, 195 U. S. 100, 134 (1904).

[22] Interstate Commerce Commission v. Alabama Midland Railway Company, 168 U. S. 144, 176 (1897).

conferring power upon the Interstate Commerce Commission to conduct investigations of the affairs of corporations. It was the opinion of the minority that Congress had conferred a power on the commission, which was withheld by a judicial decision.[23]

No cases have aroused more criticism or presented more difficult issues than those having to do with the relations between labor and capital. Here, too, the charge of judicial legislation is brought against the final interpreters of American public law. In *Lochner v. New York,* where the majority in an opinion by Justice Peckham maintained that there was no reasonable ground for interfering with the liberty of person or the right of free contract by determining the hours of labor in the occupation of a baker,[24] Justices Harlan, White, Day, and Holmes dissented. "Whether or not this be wise legislation," Justice Harlan maintained, "it is not the province of the court to inquire. Under our system of government, the courts are not concerned with the wisdom or policy of legislation." They did not regard it as within the function of the court to determine what was sound economic theory in the realm of labor legislation, hence it was claimed that the court had transcended its function when it assumed to annul the statute of the state of New York.[25] Justice Holmes, who joined in the dissent, prepared a separate opinion which presented the principle upon which cases of this character were thought to belong to the legislative branch of the government:

This case is decided upon an economic theory which a large part of the country does not entertain. If it were a question whether I agreed with that theory, I should desire to study it

---

[23] Harriman v. Interstate Commerce Commission, 211 U. S. 407, 423 (1908).

[24] 198 U. S. 45 (1905).   [25] *Ibid.,* 69.

further and long before making up my mind. But I do not conceive that to be my duty, because I strongly believe that my
agreement or disagreement has nothing to do with the right of
a majority to embody their opinions in law. It is settled by
various decisions of this court that state constitutions and state
laws may regulate life in many ways which we as legislators
might think as injudicious, or, if you like as tyrannical as this,
and which equally with this interfere with the liberty to contract. . . . . The Fourteenth Amendment does not enact Mr.
Herbert Spencer's Social Statics. . . . . But a constitution is
not intended to embody a particular economic theory, whether
of paternalism and the organic relation of the citizen to the state
or of *laissez faire.* It is made for people of fundamentally differing views, and the accident of our finding certain opinions
natural and familiar or novel and even shocking ought not to
conclude our judgment upon the question whether statutes embodying them conflict with the Constitution of the United
States.[26]

In *Adair v. United States* the majority held that personal liberty as well as the right of property was invaded
without due process of law by the act making it a criminal
offense against the United States for an interstate carrier to discharge an employee because of his membership
in a labor organization. Justice McKenna dissented in
an opinion which included the remark that Congress could
not restrain the discharge of an employee and yet could,
to enforce a policy of unrestrained competition between
railroads, prohibit reasonable agreements between them
as to the rates at which merchandise should be carried.
The query was then raised whether rates and agreements
might be restricted for the public welfare to the end that
business might prosper while much needed relief to labor-

---

[26] 198 U. S. 75, 76. ''Courts and legislation sometimes have recognized
that the so-called freedom to contract or not may be made illusory by the
economic situation of one of the parties.''—See opinion of Justice Holmes,
Continental Wall Paper Co. v. Voight & Sons Co., 212 U. S. 227, 271 (1909).

ing men was prevented by prejudice and antagonism "intrenched impregnably in the Fifth Amendment of the Constitution against regulation in the public interest."[27] Justice Holmes also said that the statute was constitutional. "I could not pronounce it unwarranted," he said, "if Congress should decide that to foster a strong union was for the best interest not only of the men, but of the railroads and the country at large."[28]

Similarly the act of Congress designed to make the carrier liable for the injury or death of an employee which resulted from the negligence of a fellow-servant was declared unconstitutional. Justices Moody, Harlan, McKenna, and Holmes dissented from the judgment of the court as announced in the opinion of Justice White. Justice Moody in the course of his opinion said:

The Court has never exercised the mighty power of declaring the acts of a coordinate branch of the government void except where there is no possible and sensible construction of the act which is consistent with the fundamental organic law. The presumption that other branches of the Government will restrain themselves within the scope of their authority, and the respect which is due to them and their acts admit of no other attitude from this court. . . . . But the economic opinions of the judges and their views of the requirements of justice and public policy, even when crystallized into well-settled doctrines of law, have no constitutional sanctity. They are binding upon succeeding judges, but while they may influence, they cannot control legislators. Legislators have their own economic theories, their views of justice and public policy, and their views when embodied in written law must prevail.[29]

Justice Holmes signified his dissent likewise on the ground that, as it was possible to read the words in such

---

[27] Adair v. United States, 208 U. S. 161, 189, 190 (1908).
[28] *Ibid.*, 192.
[29] Employers' Liability Cases, 207 U. S. 463, 509, 537, 541 (1908).

a way as to save the constitutionality of the act, they should have been taken in that narrower sense.[30]

A series of cases resulting from the enforcement and interpretation of the *Sherman Anti-Trust Law* for the regulation of trusts and monopolies brought forth an almost continuous line of dissents from the Supreme Court justices. The Sherman law was enacted in 1890, but the prosecution of the Sugar Trust by the government was not upheld by the Supreme Court.[31] The enforcement of the law was not undertaken in a serious way until the Trans-Missouri Freight Association was declared illegal.[32] The court held that an agreement among railways doing interstate business for the purpose of fixing rates and fares was illegal as coming within the prohibitions of the Sherman Act. Justice Peckham, delivering the majority opinion, held that the act of 1890 was intended to include every contract or combination in restraint of trade. With respect to the argument that only contracts restraining trade unreasonably were intended to be comprehended within the terms of the act, Justice Peckham observed:

We are asked to read into the act by way of judicial legislation an exception that is not placed there by the law-making branch of the government, and this is to be done upon the theory that the impolicy of such legislation is so clear that it cannot be supposed Congress intended the natural import of the language it used. This we cannot and ought not to do.[33]

---

[30] For a favorable view on the constitutionality of a similar law after Congress had changed the phraseology to meet the court's objections, see Second Employers' Liability Cases, 223 U. S. 1 (1912).

[31] United States v. E. C. Knight Company, 156 U. S. 1 (1895).

[32] United States v. Trans-Missouri Freight Association, 166 U. S. 290 (1897).

[33] *Ibid.*, 166 U. S. 340 (1897).

The position of the majority was claimed by Justice White to be equivalent to an assertion that the act of Congress itself was unreasonable and that an effort to include all contracts would result in prohibiting all trade. The construction now given the act, Justice White maintained, "disregards the whole current of judicial authority and tests the right of contract by the conceptions of that right entertained at the time of the year-books, instead of by the light of reason and the necessity of modern society."[34] Regardless of this protest against the majority, the Missouri case was upheld two years later with four justices again dissenting,[35] and also five years later in the Northern Securities case.[36] Speaking for four members of the majority in the latter case, Justice Harlan said that the court could not limit the law to unreasonable restraints without invading the field of the legislative department of the government. He maintained that if the law as enacted was detrimental to business and the country, Congress ought to remedy the defect and not the Court. Justice Brewer, though joining with the majority in giving judgment, took issue with the opinion of Justice Harlan, contending that instead of including all contracts, reasonable or unreasonable, in restraint of trade, the ruling should have been that the contracts presented were unreasonable restraints, and as such within the scope of the law. Justice White dissented from the majority view and with him were Chief Justice Fuller, Justices Peckham and Holmes. The conclusions of the majority were held to be "utterly inconsistent with earlier decisions and practices of the government."

[34] 166 U. S. 343, 355.

[35] United States v. Joint Traffic Association, 171 U. S. 505, (1898).

[36] Northern Securities Co. v. the United States, 193 U. S. 197 (1904).

It was the adoption of the minority view as expressed in the *Trans-Missouri,* the *Joint Traffic Association,* and the *Northern Securities Cases,* as the judgment and opinion of the Court in the *Standard Oil* and *Tobacco Trust Cases* that led to the conclusion of Justice Harlan that the federal courts were usurping the legislative functions of the government.

Dissenting in part from the reasoning of the majority of the court in the *Standard Oil Case,*[37] Justice Harlan claimed that

the court, by its decision, when interpreted by the language of its opinion, has not only upset the long settled interpretation of the Sherman Anti-trust Act, but has usurped the constitutional functions of the legislative branch of the government. . . . . After many years of public service at the National Capitol, and after a somewhat close observation of the conduct of public affairs, I am impelled to say that there is abroad, in our land, a most harmful tendency to bring about the amending of constitutions and legislative enactments by means alone of judicial construction.[38]

He rendered a similar opinion in the case of *United States v. American Tobacco Company.*[39]

According to the first line of decisions, the act of Congress was interpreted literally as prohibiting every contract or combination in restraint of trade, and the policy or impolicy and wisdom or unwisdom of such a law were thrown back on Congress. The more recent cases have confined the law to unreasonable restraints only, and have confided to the judicial branch of the government the prerogative of determining what are unreasonable restraints. The legality or illegality of business

---

[37] Standard Oil Company v. United States, 221 U. S. 1 (1911).
[38] *Ibid.,* 106.
[39] *Ibid.,* 189.

combinations rests on the discretion of the judicial conscience. It is this conclusion that Justice Harlan so emphatically opposed as inconsistent and impossible for the judicial branch of the government.[40]

Decisions of a character that have called forth evidences of judicial censure have been also severely condemned by the press and from the public platform. Mr. Bryan, in his speech which won for him the nomination for the Presidency in 1896, exclaimed:

They criticize us for our criticism of the Supreme Court of the United States. My friends, we have not criticized, we have simply called attention to what you already know. If you want criticisms, read the dissenting opinions of the court. There you will find the criticisms. They say that we passed an unconstitutional law, we deny it. The income tax law was not unconstitutional when it was passed; it was not unconstitutional when it went before the Supreme Court for the first time; it did not become unconstitutional until one of the judges changed his mind, and we cannot be expected to know when a judge will change his mind.

When the bakers resisted the enforcement of a Nebraska statute providing for standard sizes for loaves of bread with an allowance for an excess over the specified standards, the Supreme Court condemned the act as an unreasonable and unnecessary restriction upon the use of private property.[41]

After an extensive summary of evidence showing the practical necessity of the prohibition of excess weights as a means of preventing short weights, Justice Brandeis, dissenting, concluded:

[40] The extent of recent objections and criticisms is shown by the fact that from 1901 to 1907, when 77 cases were decided, 29 decisions were rendered by a vote of 5 to 4; 45 by a vote of 6 to 3; and 3 by a vote of 5 to 3. Cf. John R. DosPassos, ''The United States Supreme Court and the Commercial Era,'' 17 *Yale Law Jour.* (June 1908) 573, 577.

[41] Burns Baking Company v. Bryan, 264 U. S. 504, 533 (1923).

The evidence contained in the record in this case is, however, ample to sustain the validity of the statute. There is in
the record some evidence in conflict with it. The legislature and
the lower courts have, doubtless, considered that. But with this
conflicting evidence we have no concern. It is not our province
to weigh evidence. Put at its highest, our function is to determine, in the light of all facts which may enrich our knowledge
and enlarge our understanding, whether the measure enacted in
the exercise of an unquestioned police power and of a character
inherently unobjectionable, transcends the bounds of reason.
That is, whether the provision as applied is so clearly arbitrary
or capricious that legislators acting reasonably could not have
believed it to be necessary or appropriate for the public welfare.

To decide, as a fact, that the prohibition of excess weights
"is not necessary for the protection of the purchasers against
imposition and fraud by short weights"; that is "is not calculated to effectuate that purpose"; and that it "subjects bakers
and sellers of bread" to heavy burdens, is in my opinion, an
exercise of the powers of a super-legislature—not the performance
of the constitutional function of judicial review.[42]

The New York legislature having passed a law to
remedy notorious abuses in the resale of theater tickets,
because in its judgment the matter was of sufficient public interest to warrant public regulation, the Supreme
Court declared the law void on the ground that the
act was an unwarranted interference with a private
business.[43]

Justice Holmes said in a dissenting opinion,

I think the proper course is to recognize that a state legislature
can do whatever it sees fit to do unless it is restrained by some
express prohibition in the Constitution of the United States or
of the State, and that courts should be careful not to extend such

---

[42] 264 U. S. 533, 534.

[43] Tyson and Brother v. Banton, 273 U. S. 418 (1927). As authority for
this view Wolff Co. v. Industrial Court, 262 U. S. 522, 536 (1922) was cited.

prohibitions beyond their obvious meaning by reading into them conceptions of public policy that the particular court may happen to entertain—I am far from saying that I think this particular law a wise and rational provision. That is not my affair. But if the people of the State of New York speaking their authorized voice say they want it, I see nothing in the Constitution of the United States to prevent their having their will.[44]

When the majority of the court held that Minnesota could not assess an inheritance tax on the transfer of bonds and certificates of indebtedness issued by the state and cities of Minnesota and kept in that state, when the decedent was domiciled and resided in New York, where the will was probated, Justice Holmes observed: "A good deal has to be read into the Fourteenth Amendment to

---

[44] Tyson and Brother v. Banton, 273 U. S. 446. Some characteristic protests in recent cases are as follows: "I cannot agree that constitutional rights may be sacrificed because of public necessity, nor taken away because of emergencies which might result in disaster or inconvenience to public or private interests."—Justice Day, dissenting in Wilson v. New, 243 U. S. 332, 372 (1917).

"To read into it [The Constitution] a requirement of uniformity more mechanical than is educed from the expressed requirement of equality in the Fourteenth Amendment seems to me extravagant."—Justice Holmes, dissenting in Knickerbocker Ice Co. v. Stewart, 253 U. S. 149, 166 (1919).

"To strike down this inspection law, instead of limiting the sphere of its operation, seems to me a serious curtailment of the functions of the state, and leaves the farmers of North Dakota defenseless against what are asserted to be persistent, palpable frauds."—Justice Brandeis, dissenting in Lemke v. Farmers' Grain Co., 258 U. S. 50 (1922).

"I had thought that the propriety of the exercise of a power admitted to exist in some cases was for the consideration of Congress alone and that this Court always disavowed the right to intrude its judgment upon questions of policy or morals."—Justice Holmes, dissenting in Hammer v. Dagenhart, 247 U. S. 251, 280 (1918).

"The known purpose of this Amendment was to get rid of nice questions as to what might be direct taxes, and I cannot doubt that most people not lawyers would suppose when they voted for it that they put a question like this to rest. I am of opinion that the Amendment justifies the tax."—Justice Holmes, dissenting in Eisner v. Macomber, 252 U. S. 189, 220 (1920).

"It is surely not clear that the enactment exceeds the power granted by the Sixteenth Amendment. And, as this court has so often said, the high prerogative of declaring an act of Congress invalid, should never be exercised except in a clear case."—Justice Brandeis, dissenting in Eisner v. Macomber, 252 U. S. 189, 238 (1920).

give it any bearing upon this case. The Amendment does not condemn everything that we may think undesirable on economic or social grounds.''[45] And when a similar decision was rendered during the same term, he again expressed his disapproval as follows:

I have not yet adequately expressed the more than anxiety that I feel at the ever increasing scope given to the Fourteenth Amendment in cutting down what I believe to be the constitutional rights of the states. As the decisions now stand I see hardly any limit but the sky to the invalidating of those rights if they happen to strike a majority of this Court as for any reason undesirable. I cannot believe that the Amendment was intended to give us *carte blanche* to embody our economic or moral beliefs in its prohibitions. Yet I can think of no narrower reason that seems to me to justify the present and the earlier decisions to which I have referred. Of course the words ''due process of law'' if taken in their literal meaning have no application to this case; and while it is too late to deny that they have been given a much more extended and artificial signification, still we ought to remember the great caution shown by the Constitution in limiting the power of the states, and should be slow to construe the clause in the Fourteenth Amendment as committing to the Court, with no guide but the court's own discretion, the validity of whatever laws the states may pass.[46]

Though it is not unusual for judges to differ in the interpretation and application of legal terms and principles the persistence of dissents in the cases arising under the ''due process'' and ''equal protection'' phrases of the Fourteenth Amendment and under the commerce clause indicates that, as President Roosevelt insisted, the judges are acting in a quasi-legislative capacity. The determination of economic and social policies whether

---

[45] Farmers Loan and Trust Co. v. Minnesota, 280 U. S. 204 (1929).
[46] Baldwin v. Missouri, 281 U. S. 586, 595 (1930).

by judges or legislators is certain to bring differences of opinion and to result in frequent reversals or modifications of former judgments. Persistent dissents during the past few decades bear witness to the fact that judges in the exercise of their broad powers through the application of the doctrine of judicial supremacy are acting to a limited extent, as Justice Brandeis suggests, in the rôle of super-legislators. If the doctrine that legislation should be held valid unless the invalidity appears evident beyond a rational doubt has any significance, then the insistence on the part of three or four members of the court that a statute is valid ought to cause the majority to hesitate to declare the statute void. It is the failure to understand how five judges can agree that an act of Congress is unconstitutional "beyond rational doubt," when four of their associates who have heard the same arguments declare that the validity seems "absolutely free from doubt" that has tended to weaken the respect for the decisions of the Supreme Court on constitutional issues.[47]

2. *Criticisms of Labor Leaders*—

The most persistent criticisms of the attitude of American courts in limiting and restricting legislative powers have come from labor leaders and from various groups of Liberals and Radicals. "The one symptom among workingmen which most definitely indicates a class feeling," it was observed some years ago, "is a growing distrust of the integrity of the courts."[48] This discontent has been fostered in a large measure by the fact that statutes for the social and industrial betterment of labor-

---

[47] Cf. comments of Justice Clarke in 9 Am. Bar Assoc. *Jour.* (Oct. 1923) 691.

[48] Jane Addams, 13 *Am. Jour. of Sociology* (May 1908) 772.

ers have often met with disapproval and ultimate defeat at the hands of the courts. Labor unions have not infrequently gone on record as condemning particular decisions and as in favor of abrogating the power of the courts to nullify laws on the ground of unconstitutionality.

A special committee report of the American Federation of Labor on the decisions of the courts claimed that "a judicial oligarchy is threatening to set itself above the elected Legislatures, above the people themselves." "What confronts the workers of America," the committee reported,

is not one or several casual court decisions favoring the interests of property as against human rights of labor, but a series of adjudications of the highest tribunal of the land, successively destroying a basic right or cherished acquisition of organized labor, each forming a link in a fateful chain consciously designed to enslave the workers of America.

Among the cases considered were: *Hitchman Coal and Coke Co. v. Mitchell,*[49] *Duplex Printing Press Co. v. Deering,*[50] *Truax v. Corrigan,*[51] *American Steel Foundries v. Tri-City Central Trades Council,*[52] *Hammer v. Dagenhart,*[53] *United Mine Workers of America v. Coronado Coal Co.*[54] Thus it is claimed, "by six decisions the United States Supreme Court, composed of nine men without direct mandate from the people and without responsibility to the people, has set aside a congressional enactment which clearly expressed the will of a vast majority of the people, and all but outlawed the activities of organized labor."[55]

---

[49] 245 U. S. 229 (1917).
[50] 254 U. S. 443 (1921).
[51] 257 U. S. 312 (1921).
[52] 257 U. S. 184 (1921).

[53] 247 U. S. 251 (1918).
[54] 259 U. S. 344 (1922).
[55] Am. Fed. of Labor, *Proceedings* (1922) 371, 372.

The committee recommended among other things, an amendment providing that if the United States Supreme Court decides that an act of Congress is unconstitutional, or by interpretation asserts a public policy at variance with the statutory declaration of Congress, then if Congress by a two-thirds majority repasses the law, it shall become the law of the land. An easier method of amending the Constitution of the United States was also proposed.

At the Thirty-Eighth Annual Convention of the American Federation of Labor, the following resolution was passed:

WHEREAS, The sole right to make or unmake laws is vested in legislative bodies or the direct vote of the people by the Constitution of the United States; and

WHEREAS, The preservation of this right is essential if we are to remain a self-governing people; and

WHEREAS, Courts of the United States without constitutional authority or legislative sanction have assumed the power to invade the prerogatives of the legislative branch of the government by unmaking and rendering invalid laws enacted by the people or their legislative representatives, the exercise of this power setting aside on many occasions the desires and aspirations of the people as expressed through legislation, even when such measures had the approval of the majority of the people, their legislative representatives, and the President of the United States; an action which would be impossible in any other democratically governed nation; therefore, be it

RESOLVED, That the Executive Council be and is hereby instructed to have a study made of the successive steps which have been taken by our Federal and Supreme Courts, through which, without constitutional authority, and in opposition to the action of the Constitutional Convention, they laid hold on power which they now exercise; that the results of such study be prepared in pamphlet form and distributed to the affiliated organizations and given such other form of publicity as may be deemed advisable; and that legal counsel be consulted with so that an adequate measure may be prepared and introduced to Congress, which will prevent any invasion of the rights and prerogatives of the legislative branch of our government, by the judiciary.

As a result of this resolution a thorough study was made of judicial review of legislation and particularly of its effects in relation to social and industrial legislation.[56]

A few instances may be cited to indicate the basis for the antagonism of labor leaders to the courts and to so-called judicial legislation. In 1884 the New York courts by refusing validity to a sweatshop law set a barrier in the way of effective tenement legislation.[57] The decision became a precedent in other states and was bitterly assailed as a "bulwark of protection of private property rights against public interests."[58] In 1895 the court of Illinois refused to allow an act to stand which restricted the hours of labor for women to eight hours a day[59] and thus set an effective obstacle in the way of this type of industrial legislation. A reversal of this decision only partly restored the respect for the courts which the earlier judgment had fostered among labor leaders. Obstructions which resulted from the invalidating of stat-

---

[56] Jackson H. Ralston, *Study and Report for American Federation of Labor upon Judicial Control over Legislatures as to Constitutional Questions* (ed. 2; Washington, 1923).

[57] *In re* Jacobs, 98 N. Y. 98 (1885).

[58] Kelley, *Ethical Gains through Legislation*, 231.

[59] Ritchie v. People, 155 Ill. 98 (1895); for a reversal of this decision see Ritchie & Co. v. Wayman, 244 Ill. 509 (1910). "It remained," says Florence Kelley, "for the Supreme Court of Illinois to discover that the amendment to the Constitution of the United States passed for the purpose of guaranteeing the negro from oppression has become an insuperable obstacle to the protection of women and children." Kelley, *op. cit.*, 141. For a similar change favorable to labor legislation see People v. Williams, 189 N. Y. 131 (1907) holding void a law prohibiting night work for women and People v. Charles Schweinler Press, 214 N. Y. 395 (1915).

utes passed to regulate hours and conditions of labor on public works[60] by the New York courts were finally removed by a constitutional amendment adopted in 1905. An eight-hour law applicable to mines and smelters was held unconstitutional by the Colorado Supreme Court,[61] under conditions that were criticized as not likely to inspire confidence in judicial tribunals.[62] A notorious case of this character was the New York bakeshop law which was finally invalidated by the federal Supreme Court.[63] Although based upon the findings of a commission of the legislature and sustained by a majority of the state supreme court, the law was held to interfere with private rights and was nullified by the federal Supreme Court. The vigorous protests of the dissenting justices and subsequent decisions favorable to labor tended to allay in part the resentment of labor leaders toward the national judiciary.[64]

The phrase "liberty of contract" has furnished the basis for setting aside numerous important legislative acts relative to labor. American judges imbued with an inherent distrust of social legislation whose creed was that of the eighteenth-century individualists, and who desired to minimize the function of the state, disapproved: (1) legislation forbidding employers from interfering with

---

[60] People v. Coler, 166 N. Y. 1 (1901); People v. Orange County Road Construction Co., 175 N. Y. 84 (1903); People v. Grout, 179 N. Y. 417 (1904).

[61] *In re* Morgan, 26 Col. 415 (1899).

[62] Cf. Groat, "Attitude of the Courts toward Industrial Problems," 44 *Annals* of the Am. Acad. of Pol. and Soc. Sci., 105.

[63] *Ibid.*, p. 106; Lochner v. New York, 198 U. S. 45 (1905).

[64] "A survey of the decisions by the Supreme Court of the United States, in which questions affecting labor were involved, discloses the fact that in the last 40 years there have been 21 cases decided by a vote of four to five or four to four, 13 of these, or nearly two-thirds of the total, falling within the last 10 years." Lindley D. Clark, "Labor laws that have been declared Unconstitutional," *Bulletin* of Bureau of Labor Statistics, No. 321 (1922) 7.

the membership of their employees in labor unions; (2) legislation prohibiting the imposition of fines upon employees; (3) legislation providing for the mode of weighing coal in order to fix the compensation of miners; (4) legislation against company stores, requiring employers to pay wages in money; (5) legislation as to the hours of labor.[65] There were, no doubt, good grounds for invalidating some of the acts in question, but, says Dean Pound, "one cannot read the cases in detail without feeling that the great majority of the decisions are simply wrong, not only in constitutional law, but from the standpoint of the common law, and even from that of a sane individualism."[66]

Writing of the decision of the Supreme Court of the United States in the *Minimum Wage Case,* one of the latest unfavorable judgments of the court on labor legislation, Samuel Gompers, President of the American Federation of Labor, advised the people of the United States to take away the usurped power of the court.[67]

Summaries have been prepared of the statutes and ordinances relating to labor which have been held unconstitutional either entirely or in part.[68] The list includes a long line of enactments affecting the contract of employment, the examination and registration of workmen, the employment of women and children, rates and payments of wages, hours of labor, liability acts, protection to employees and to labor organizations.[69] From a careful

---

[65] Roscoe Pound, "Liberty of Contract," 18 *Yale Law Jour.* (May 1909) 481, 482.

[66] Pound, *op. cit.,* 482.

[67] *Am. Federationist* (1923), 399.

[68] *Bureau of Labor Bulletin,* 21:916. Lindley D. Clark, *Labor Laws Declared Unconstitutional.* For summary of the nature of these acts, see 924 ff. To 1922 about 300 separate laws or ordinances affecting labor had been declared void by state and federal courts.

[69] Clark, *op. cit,* 922–924.

estimate of the effect of these decisions it is a common observation that labor has borne the brunt of the restrictive attitude of the courts toward legislative activity, and that there is warrant for the persistent hostility of labor organizations to the American doctrine of judicial supremacy.

The attitudes of American courts in the consideration of labor cases is affected by the theory that law is based on certain principles of justice that are eternal and immutable. While judges, lawyers, and textbook writers have been wont to hold that law and right are unchanging concepts, an industrial upheaval has taken place which is nothing short of a complete revolution.[70]

Written constitutions were framed at a time when the philosophy of individualism was dominant. The terms liberty, equality, justice, natural and inalienable rights, as embodied therein, were the result of a period when competition was regarded as the prime law and practice of industry.[71] With these written constitutions remaining in much the same form as first adopted and with terms that acquired their meaning in concepts of eighteenth-century individualism, courts have been called upon to meet conditions in which the entire organization of industry and the general point of view on social questions have completely changed. Today we find courts and jurists in America applying rules of common law individualism and insisting upon views of liberty and equality with scant consideration of their relation to actual life. Judges imbued with eighteenth-century natural law notions, who insist upon a theory of equality of rights and liberty of contract in the face of notorious economic facts to the

---

[70] Groat, *Attitude of American Courts in Labor Cases*, 360. For the conclusions of the author of this valuable study, see chap. 22.

[71] Groat, *op. cit.*, 361.

contrary, are frequently held up to ridicule and condemnation.[72] The mass of workers have come to feel that it is not constitutions which stand in their way but the opinions of reactionary judges who seek to hold legislatures within the bounds of their own economic and political predilections.

The contrast between the social viewpoint evident in modern progressive legislation and the restrictive attitude of the judiciary in the protection of private rights was clearly manifested in the decision of the New York court on the Workmen's Compensation Act. "If such economic and sociologic arguments as are advanced here in support of this statute can be allowed to subvert the fundamental idea of property," a New York justice exclaimed, "then there is no private right entirely safe, because there is no limitation upon the absolute discretion of legislatures, and the guaranties of the Constitution are a mere waste of words."[73]

A significant type of criticism was the signed protest of fourteen instructors in public law in American universities against the decision in the *Ives Case*. It was their judgment, "that a compensation plan as moderate and carefully guarded as that embodied in the law of New York is entirely constitutional, and they regard it as their duty to inform the public that there is a professional opinion entitled to consideration which differs from that expressed by the Court of Appeals of New York, and

---

[72] Cf. Pound, ''The Scope and Purpose of Sociological Jurisprudence,'' 24 *Harv. Law Rev.* (June 1911) 591, 611; also 25 *Harv. Law Rev.* (Dec. 1911) 140, 146. See also Groat, *op. cit.*, chaps. 21, 22. Florence Kelley in *Ethical Gains through Legislation*, condemned ''the belated and anti-social decisions'' which result from the fact that the judicial mind has not kept pace with the strides of industrial development.—142 ff.

[73] Justice Werner in Ives v. South Buffalo Ry. Co., 201 N. Y. 271, 295 (1911).

which may and should be urged upon the courts of other jurisdictions.''[74]

The burning question which confronts wage earners and social reformers,[75] according to Mrs. Kelley, is the necessity of acquainting the judges of the courts of last resort with the changes which affect the life, health, and happiness of the working people, and of checking the tendency of judges to ''set themselves against the manifest and enlightened will of the community in matters of social, economic or commercial progress.''[76]

In recent years the objections and resentment of labor leaders toward the courts has centered around the use and abuse of the injunction in labor controversies. And efforts of organized labor have been directed toward legislation to limit the use of the injunction in such cases.[77]

However, certain courts have been inclined to uphold industrial regulations and the Supreme Court of the United States has with few exceptions sustained labor legislation. But unfortunately many decisions which have been artificial and reactionary in tendency have aided in engendering a disrespect for courts and law which is one of the marked characteristics of American community life.[78]

---

[74] *The Outlook*, 98:710.

[75] Kelley, *op. cit.*, 255.

[76] Mayor Gaynor, quoted in *The Outlook*, October 5, 1912, 102:250.

[77] See Felix Frankfurter and Nathan Greene, *The Labor Injunction* (New York, 1930).

[78] Summarizing the review of acts of Congress by the Supreme Court, Mr. Ralston concludes that ''as a protection to the individual the jurisdiction has been almost a failure. As a political institution it has been frightfully dangerous. As a method of social review it has been destructive of human life. We may thus conclude that no adequate reason exists for its continuance.''—''Judicial Control over Legislatures as to Constitutional Questions'' (ed. 2) 40.

3. *Usurpation Theory and the Opposition of Liberals and Radicals—*

One of the chief lines of attack upon the American practice of judicial supremacy lies in the contention that the power to declare laws invalid was established in the United States through a usurpation of authority by the federal and state judiciaries. This claim has been supported by judges, jurists, and many members of liberal political parties. Dean Trickett of the Dickinson Law School called the assertion of this authority the "Great Usurpation."[79] That such a power is the very essence of judicial duty, Dean Trickett thought, was to assume the whole ground of dispute at the outset. He denied that courts ought to have the power to sit in judgment on the conformity of acts of Congress. "Judicial duty has plenty of scope, without invading the province of Congress, and without arrogating the authority to brand it either with ignorance, or with disregard of the sense of the constitution."[80] Chief Justice Marshall thought it apparent that "the framers of the Constitution contemplated that instrument as a rule for the government of the courts, as well as of the legislature." Surely such was the intention. "But it by no means follows," says Dean Trickett,

that they intended that all the other branches of the government should sacrifice their own understanding of the Constitution for that of the court, or that the court should, so far as it could, nullify executive and legislative acts which, though expressing

---

[79] 40 *Am. Law Rev.* (May-June 1906) 356. "By usurping the power to declare laws unconstitutional and by presuming to read their own views into statutes without regard to the plain intention of the legislature, they have become in reality the supreme law-making and law-giving institution in our government."—Senator Robert M. LaFollette in Introduction to Gilbert E. Roe, *Our Judicial Oligarchy* (New York, 1912).

[80] Trickett, *op. cit.*, 373.

the honest, intelligent and patriotic judgment of those who enacted them, should clash with its conception of the Constitution.[81]

The judges, no less than Congressmen or the President, may be mistaken concerning the Constitution; and the plan of promulgating laws whose validity the officers and people cannot know until, at some indefinitely remote time, a case is made for the court, is intolerably inconvenient, and productive of enormous injustice, especially since one decision of the court is no guarantee that it may not be repudiated later.[82]

The power authoritatively to interpret the Constitution is held to be virtually the power to make it. Practically, asserted Dean Trickett, "the Constitution is made for us, from time to time, by the nine lawyers who are judges of the Supreme Court. They make it, while, like the Roman haruspices, they think, as do others, that they are only divining the intention of the Numen, the dead men of 1787."[83] There is no trace to be found, he believed, in the work of the constitution-makers of an intention to constitute courts as censors of the work of Congress, and to furnish no censor for the acts of the courts.[84]

---

[81] Trickett, *op. cit.*, 376.

[82] *Ibid.*, 377.

[83] "Judicial Nullification of Acts of Congress," *North Am. Rev.*, 185 (Aug. 1907) 85.

[84] "The fathers never intended to confer such an extraordinary jurisdiction, then unknown, else they would have provided for it in the constitution. It is an usurpation of judicial power. The exercise of this unwarranted and usurped governmental power against the public interest, against the public health, safety and life, has done more than any other single thing to arouse the present popular hostile feeling toward our courts of last resort. . . . .

"From 1902 until 1908 the respective supreme courts of the different states of this Union declared not less than 468 different statutes unconstitutional, and these are mainly statutes in the interest of social and industrial justice, public health, safety and life . . . . the judiciary has become in fact and in law the supreme power over and above the legislature, over and above the executives, and even over and above the people."—Judge R. M. Wanamaker, "The Recall of Judges," Illinois State Bar Assoc. *Proceedings* 1912, 174, 181 ff.

Chief Justice Clark, of North Carolina, also claimed that, "the subsequent action of the Supreme Court in assuming the power to declare acts of Congress unconstitutional was without a line in the Constitution to authorize it, either expressly or by implication." Had the Convention given such power to the courts, Justice Clark believed, it would certainly not have left its exercise final and unreviewable. The judges, he declared, not only have never exercised such power in England, but they do not exercise it in most other countries which, like the United States, have written constitutions. The placing of unreviewable power in the hands of men not elected by the people and holding office for life, is characterized as the most complete denial of popular control of government. Such vast political power, he contended

cannot safely be left in the hands of any body of men, without supervision or control by any other authority whatever. If the President errs, his mandate expires in four years, and his party as well as himself is accountable to the people at the ballot box for his stewardship. If members of Congress err, they, too, must account to their constituents. But the federal judiciary hold for life, and though popular sentiment should change the entire personnel of the other two great departments of government, a whole generation must pass away before the people could get control of the judiciary, which possesses an irresponsible and unrestricted veto upon the action of the other departments.[85]

---

[85] *Congressional Record*, July 31, 1911. Justice Clark several years earlier had presented an arraignment of judicial supremacy.—See 39 *Arena* 148. "The power, thus construed to be in a court, or indeed in the hands of one man, to accomplish such an act as this without any review or possibility of review and without any words in the Constitution conferring it, is so exorbitant and unprecedented that it needs no argument to demonstrate that it ought not to be tolerated, and cannot safely be permitted to continue."—Walter Clark, "Government by Judges," Senate *Doc.* 610, 63 Cong., 2 sess., 1914. For a presentation of the usurpation theory consult J. Allen Smith, *The Spirit of American Government*, chaps. 1–5.

A Justice of the Supreme Court of New York joined those who contend that the framers of the Constitution never intended that the Supreme Court should have power to declare a law of Congress unconstitutional.[86] The claim that courts usurped the power to declare laws invalid has been taken up by different groups of Liberals and Radicals and has been developed into a portion of their political creed. Advocates of the Socialist party maintained that the provisions of the Constitution contain no reference whatever to any such powers either expressly or by obvious implication, and that the great majority of the framers never suspected that a general power of the judiciary to control legislation could be interpreted into the Constitution.[87] Arguing for the cause of the Progressive party, another writer contended that the framers of the Constitution could not have assumed that the courts would exercise such supervisory power over legislation as they exercise. "The debates in the Convention," he stated, "negative any such idea as does the fact that the attempt to exercise such power by the State Courts over State Statutes had been sharply rebuked by the people."[88] "The American people fancy," says another disputant, "that they are a free and independent democracy, when, in fact, they are living under a usurping judicial autocracy. . . . . The system has grown so gradually and so insidiously and has been so taken for granted as correct that the people have failed to take alarm. It is strange, but the judiciary have in

---

[86] John Ford "Judicial Usurpation" 30 *Am. Federationist* (April 1923) 306, 307.

[87] L. B. Boudin, "Government by Judiciary," 26 *Pol. Sci. Quart.* 248. Cf. also Allan L. Benson, "The Usurped Power of the Courts" and *Our Dishonest Constitution.*

[88] Roe, *op. cit.*, 27.

fact usurped the power to repeal any law, under the plea that it is unconstitutional.''[89]

The most persistent criticisms of the American doctrine of judicial supremacy were made in the campaign for the Presidency by Robert M. LaFollette. Reference will be made later to these criticisms and to suggestions for reform, with a consideration of proposals to change the system of judicial review as it operates in the United States.

Not only is there a widespread belief that the courts originally usurped the authority to declare legislative acts void but there are also frequent claims that the justices are invalidating acts because they disapprove of the wisdom or expediency of the acts and that the provisions of statutes are not enforced by the courts because the judges disagree with legislative policies.[90] In effect, the justices are exercising legislative functions.[91]

---

[89] Henry N. Starr, quoted in *The Outlook,* October 5, 1912, 102:250. ''We condemn all unjust assumption of authority by inferior Federal Courts in annulling by injunction the laws of the States, and demand legislative acts by Congress which will prohibit such usurpation and will restrict to the Supreme Court of the United States the exercise of power in cases involving State legislation.''—Platform of the People's Party, St. Louis, 1908. Among the political demands in the Socialist National Platform of 1912 was the following:

''The abolition of the power usurped by the Supreme Court of the United States to pass upon the constitutionality of the legislation enacted by Congress.''

For the presentation of evidence favorable to the ''usurpation theory'' as applied to the federal courts, cf. ''Annulment of Legislation by the Supreme Court,'' by Horace A. Davis, 7 *Am. Pol. Sci. Rev.* (Nov. 1913) 541.

[90] Cf. Roe, *op. cit.,* 123 ff.

[91] ''Judicial decisions are often founded upon the peculiar personal views on economics and social problems of individual judges which, when expressed in a prevailing opinion become precedents for future decisions and are taken as the declared public policy of the American people.''— John Ford, ''Judicial Usurpation,'' 30 *Am. Federationist* (April 1923) 308. ''Backed by and charged with the enforcement of the due-process clause of the Fifth and Fourteenth Amendments, the Supreme Court of the United States is the American substitute for the British House of Lords. It con-

Judge Bruce stated the main contention of the liberal and progressive parties when he asserted that:

though we have advocated a court control and have expressed the belief that the American courts have not been guilty of a usurpation of power in passing upon the validity of statutes and in applying the test of the constitutions, we still believe that there is much foundation for the claim that at times they have imagined constitutional limitations where none have existed, and that to this extent they have been usurpers. Often in the past, though not so often today, they have failed to realize that they are servants of specific, definite and written constitutions and not the servants of any abstract theories of governmental and individual rights; they have failed to realize the fact that, since in America we have enumerated and formulated our basic rights and have definitely prescribed the powers and the limitations of government, we have left no room for the assumption that the courts are the guardians of any supposed natural rights or of any supposed super-constitution. We may make the general statement that in a legal sense in America men and women have no natural and inalienable rights except insofar as our written constitutions have guaranteed them; that the Federal Congress has no powers except those which have been expressly delegated to it, or which are reasonably necessary to the carrying out of those which have been so delegated; and that the power of the legislatures of the several states is supreme except where that power has been limited by their own constitutions or by that of the central government.[92]

---

stitutes the real and only conservative second chamber for each of the state governments.''

It is a second chamber organized ''to defeat the popular will as expressed in legislation when that will appears to endanger what the court may regard as a fundamental requirement of the social structure itself.''

''The attempted legalistic formulae which the court itself uses are the most obvious frauds.'' In the exercise of judicial review of legislation rigid formulae of law are abandoned and judges act as juries and legislatures.— Albert M. Kales, ''New Methods in Due Process Cases,'' 12 *Am. Pol. Sci. Rev.* (May 1918) 241, 243.

[92] Andrew A. Bruce, *The American Judge* (New York, 1924) 54, 55.

Recognizing that most of the errors of the courts have arisen from their application of the due process and equal protection clauses Judge Bruce thinks that

it was never intended, nor is it ever necessary, that on questions of fact and of necessity and where the legislatures, acting within their special domain, have fairly and clearly spoken, the courts should oppose their ideas and their judgments to those of the popular assemblies. The members of the legislatures come fresh from the people. They can appoint committees and they can investigate. Usually they are practical men of affairs. It would seem that their opinions and judgments upon a question of fact and of expediency are as reliable as those of the more or less cloistered judges. They, at any rate, are acting within the scope of their general jurisdiction.[93]

Opponents of judicial review have gained little headway in convincing the American people that judicial supremacy is based upon a usurpation of authority. But whether a usurpation or not, the Liberal and Radical parties have been opposing in every conceivable way what is termed the veto power of American courts over legislation as "one of the most cruel and ruthless checks upon democracy permitted by any civilized people."[94]

Finally the most serious charge brought against the courts in the exercise of judicial supremacy is the criticism that by this means property is impregnably intrenched through legally construed barriers which render democratic government impossible. "The fact is," asserted President Hadley, of Yale University, "that private property in the United States, in spite of the dangers of unintelligent legislation, is constitutionally in a stronger position as against the government and the government authority, than is the case in any country of

---

[93] *Ibid.*, 57, 59.
[94] William Allen White, 67 *Am. Mag.*, 412.

Europe.''[95] Rights and immunities of property holders were protected, he asserts, against legislative interference by two events in our constitutional history, the *Dartmouth College Case* in 1819 and the passage of the Fourteenth Amendment to the Constitution in 1868. The development of this feature of the American constitutional system is called ''fortuitous'' because neither the judges who decided the *Dartmouth College Case* nor the legislators who passed the Fourteenth Amendment had any idea how these things would affect modern industrial situations. But the *Dartmouth College Case,* which rendered contracts inviolable, as beyond legislative control and direction, and the Fourteenth Amendment, which was enacted to secure equal rights to the Negroes, together have placed property beyond government control and have given corporations an almost untrammeled field in which to conduct their operations and to perpetrate wrongs with apparent impunity. ''Under these circumstances,'' President Hadley continues,

it is evident that large powers and privileges have been constitutionally delegated to private property in general and to corporate property in particular. . . . . The general status of the property owner under the law cannot be changed by the action of the legislature or the executive, or the people of a state voting at the polls, or all three put together. It cannot be changed without either a consensus of opinion among the judges, which should lead them to retrace their old views, or an amendment of the Constitution of the United States by the slow and cumbersome machinery provided for that purpose, or, last—and I hope most improbably—a revolution. . . . .

When it is said, as it commonly is, that the fundamental division of powers in the modern state is into legislative, execu-

---

[95] ''The Constitutional Position of Property in America,'' 64 *Independent* (April 16, 1908) 834.

tive and judicial, the student of American institutions may fairly note an exception. The fundamental division of powers in the Constitution of the United States is between voters on the one hand and property owners on the other. The forces of democracy on one side, divided between the executive and legislature are set over against the forces of property on the other side, with the judiciary as arbiter between them; the Constitution itself not only forbidding the legislature and executive to trench upon the rights of property, but compelling the judiciary to define and uphold these rights in a manner provided by the Constitution itself.[96]

The practical check upon legislation set up by the courts in defense of property rights has, it is believed, served a valuable purpose in the experiment of universal suffrage under essentially new conditions. The voter was omnipotent as long as he did not interfere with property rights. Officers might be elected and the policies of government freely changed as long as the rights of property were not invaded.[97]

A conviction that courts have been the custodians of privilege and property, many times to the detriment of the life, health, and the common rights of mankind, and that the judiciary has become a powerful barrier in the path of social and industrial reform has led to persistent attacks upon the American practice of judicial control over legislation.

---

[96] *The Independent, op. cit.,* 836. "The whole American political and social system is based on industrial property right, far more completely than has ever been the case in any European country."—See Arthur T. Hadley, *Undercurrents in American Politics* (New Haven, 1915) 33 ff.

[97] Hadley, *op. cit.,* 837, 838.

CHAPTER XVII

PROPOSALS TO REMEDY THE DEFECTS IN THE AMERICAN PRACTICE OF JUDICIAL VETO OF LEGISLATION

IN VIEW OF the almost continuous criticisms which have been made of the authority which the courts have asserted since the eighteenth century to declare legislative acts void it is difficult to explain why so little consideration has been given to methods to restrict the exercise of such powers and to formulate ways of depriving the judges of this prerogative. The practices and procedure of foreign countries which shed light on the weaknesses of the American system of judicial review and the critical analyses by foreign commentators have received scant attention. Though a number of proposals to remedy some of the defects in the American practice of vetoing legislation have been made few of them have received serious public consideration. Among the proposals for reform which have been advocated at various times the following deserve brief attention:

1. The changing of unpopular court decisions by constitutional amendments.

2. The requirement of an extraordinary majority to nullify legislative acts.

3. The principle of self-limitation or the adoption of a self-denying ordinance by the judges themselves.

4. The education of judges along the lines of economics, sociology, and political science for the development of a social point of view.

5. The recall of judges or of judicial decisions.

6. Abolition of judicial review of legislative acts.

Though each of these proposals has been advocated by different groups that have been criticizing the authority exercised by judges in the United States, none of them has appeared as a satisfactory solution and none so far has commended itself so as to be generally accepted or seriously to affect the practice of nullifying legislative acts by judicial decisions.

1. *Changing judicial decisions by constitutional amendments—*

Though the theory is prevalent that the voters can change by means of a constitutional amendment any unpopular or unsatisfactory decision of the highest courts, this remedy is so difficult of application that it has not commended itself to those who feel that too great limitations are placed on popular control of public affairs through the judicial review of legislative enactments. Most of the state constitutions are difficult to amend. Moreover, it is unlikely that there is sufficient general discontent over an unpopular decision to secure disapprobation by more than half of the electors who participate in elections. Furthermore, many constitutional questions involve technical matters on which voters find it impossible to form a judgment. As the disposition of the voter is to vote "no" on any proposition which is doubtful and on which his opinions are vague, few decisions of the highest courts have been reversed by constitutional amendments.[1] The process of adopting constitutional amendments has shown as a rule a marked conservative attitude on the part of the voters. This attitude is likely

---

[1] Cf. Walter Farleigh Dodd, *Revision and Amendment of State Constitutions* (Baltimore, 1910).

to be exaggerated on questions involving legislative and administrative policies. It took twenty years to reverse a decision of the Supreme Court of the United States denying the power of Congress to levy an income tax and, though certain state decisions have been reversed in a shorter time, this remedy appears so cumbersome and difficult of application that it does not commend itself as a feasible remedy to meet situations which require effective and direct action.

Nevertheless there has been a tendency not only to secure reversals of decisions of the Supreme Court of the United States but also of state courts by constitutional amendments. The attempt to reverse the Child Labor decision of the federal Supreme Court was such a failure, however, that friends of progressive labor legislation have little prospect of securing their aims through constitutional amendments.

2. *The requirement of an extraordinary majority to invalidate acts—*

In practice the judges have seldom declared a statute void unless at least a majority of the full bench joined in the judgment, but this self-imposed limitation has not satisfied some of the opponents of judicial review. Several resolutions were introduced in Congress in 1823 and 1824 proposing to require the concurrence of at least seven judges in any opinion that concerned the validity of state or federal legislation.[2] Martin Van Buren proposed a bill to require the concurrence of seven judges

---

[2] See Resolution by Senator Johnson of Kentucky, *Annals*, 18 Cong., 1 sess., 28; also Petition of Kentucky legislature to 'Congress "to organize the Supreme Court of the United States that no constitutional question . . . . involving the validity of State laws, shall be decided by said court unless two-thirds of all the members belonging to said court shall concur in such decision." Acts of Kentucky (Dec. 29, 1823); Herman V. Ames, *State Documents on Federal Relations*, 107.

out of ten and to have each judge prepare a separate opinion. The proposal was later changed to require a decision by five out of seven judges to invalidate a state statute.[3] The question of the constitutional authority of Congress to enact such a measure seems to have received little consideration in the debates on these proposals. Growing out of the fear that the Supreme Court would declare the Reconstruction Acts void, a bill requiring a unanimous decision of the judges on the validity of a law was presented to Congress in 1867,[4] and a year later the House of Representatives passed a bill requiring a two-thirds vote of the members of the Supreme Court to declare a law void. Following the *Income Tax Case* another bill was presented to require the concurrence of all the justices to declare an act of Congress invalid.[5]

Proposals to place limitations on the authority of the federal courts to invalidate acts were again renewed about 1910. In 1911 Senator Bourne offered a resolution to require a unanimous decision to declare an act of Congress void,[6] and in 1921 a constitutional amendment was proposed to require the concurrence of all but two justices in cases reviewing legislative acts.[7] A series of resolutions were presented in 1923 to restrict the court in passing on the validity of legislative acts and to provide for legislative recall of judges.[8]

---

[3] 18 Cong., 1 sess., 336, 2513, 2635; 19 Cong., 1 sess., 423 and 445. For reference to similar proposals in Congress, see Charles Warren, *Congress, the Constitution and the Supreme Court* (Boston, 1925) 218 ff.

[4] 40 Cong., 2 sess., 478 and 616.

[5] 54 Cong., 1 sess., 5441.

[6] Charles Wallace Collins, *Fourteenth Amendment and the States* (Boston, 1912) 184.

[7] Congressional Digest, 271; Mannie S. Culp, "A Survey of the Proposals to Limit or Deny the Power of Judicial Review by the Supreme Court of the United States," 4 *Indiana Law Jour.* (March and April 1929) 386, 474.

[8] 67 Cong., 4 sess., H. J. Res. 436.

Senator Borah proposed and advocated a similar resolution in 1923 as follows:

That in all suits now pending, or which may hereafter be pending, in the Supreme Court of the United States, except cases affecting ambassadors, other public ministers, and consuls and those in which a State shall be a party, where is drawn in question an Act of Congress on the ground of repugnancy to the Constitution of the United States, at least seven members of the court shall concur before pronouncing said law unconstitutional.[9]

A bill similar in purport introduced by Representative McSwain aimed not only to restrict the court in passing on acts of Congress but also on state acts.

Objections to five to four decisions of the Supreme Court are not confined to labor leaders, liberals, and social reformers.[10] Former Justice John H. Clarke expressed the view of many judges and lawyers, when he asserted that

these five to four decisions have been a focus for criticism of the Court for now half a century, beginning promptly upon the rendering of the second legal tender decision in 1871 over-ruling the first one in the year before. The income tax decision reversal in 1895 by the change of the vote of a single Justice arrested the

---

[9] 68 Cong., 1 sess., S. B. 1197.

[10] "It seems to me wise that a law should not be declared unconstitutional except by a court of last resort and there only if all, or at least three-fourths of the court concur in so holding. It must be admitted that judges (unconsciously perhaps) often seem to decide laws unconstitutional because they deem such laws unwise."—Chief Justice Orrin H. Carter, "The Courts and Unconstitutional Law," Illinois Bar Assoc., *Proceedings* (1912) 409.

"To the lay mind it would seem that when from one to four members of the court were clearly of the opinion that an act of Congress was constitutional a reasonable doubt of the soundness of their conclusions should have been raised in the minds of the majority, particularly as in questions of fact such reasonable doubt is presumed to exist in the jury box until unanimity of opinion has been obtained."—Jackson H. Ralston, "Study and Report for the American Federation of Labor upon Judicial Control over Legislatures as to Constitutional Questions," *Report* to Am. Fed. of Labor (ed. 2; Washington, 1923) 65.

attention of the country as never before to this infirmity in our highest court and the several recent decisions of cases involving economic and social problems have given emphasis to the contention that in the interpretation of the Constitution an unparalleled and fateful power often becomes centered in a single man.

It should be recognized that this is a criticism that is gaining head throughout the country and that it has in it elements of popular appeal which others have not had which render it formidable. It can be expressed in a single crisp sentence, which the man in the street can instantly understand, and which carries an implication of one man power which he is likely instinctively to resent. One man power in soldiers, kings and even in judges has so often proved an agency of injustice and oppression that fear of it is universal. And it should not be forgotten that many a good cause, many a good political institution, even, has been wrecked by a deceitful but taking slogan.

There are many men who think that this new assault upon the Court constitutes a very real danger that this power which they believe most essential to the welfare of our country may be taken away from it or be so modified as to greatly impair our entire system of government, and who also believe that this danger may be avoided in a manner consonant with the best traditions of the Court, by a slight extension in practice of the often repeated self-denying limitation, that Acts of Congress shall not be held invalid save when their conflict with the Constitution is "entirely clear."

The Supreme Court has many times declared itself bound by this rule but never more strongly than in the recent Minimum Wage decision in which it was said "that every possible presumption is in favor of the validity of an act of Congress until overcome beyond rational doubt," and that "only clear and indubitable demonstration" that a statute is in conflict with the Constitution will justify its being declared invalid.

But after making this statement, the opinion proceeds to the conclusion that the Act of Congress involved in the case (an exercise of police power applicable to the District of Columbia) was unconstitutional and void although the Chief Justice and Mr. Justice Sanford declared in a carefully reasoned dissenting opinion that in their judgment "on the basis of reason, experience and authority," the act was valid, and although Mr. Justice Holmes declared that in his judgment the power of Congress to enact the law "seems absolutely free from doubt." Mr. Justice Brandeis did not sit in the case but his judicial history renders it clearly a five to four decision.

Treating this much emphasized rule as a reality and not a mere form of words, it is difficult for men not steeped in legalistic thinking and forms of expression to understand how five judges can agree that an Act of Congress is unconstitutional "beyond rational doubt" and that by "clear and indubitable demonstration" they have shown it to be so, when four of their associates, equally able and experienced judges, who have heard the same arguments on the same record declare that to them "upon the basis of reason, experience and authority" the validity of the Act "seems absolutely free from doubt."

This rule is of the utmost importance to our country. It has been, in terms, an essential limitation upon the power to declare Acts of Congress or of state legislatures invalid for more than a century and almost fifty years ago Chief Justice Waite said: "The safety of our institutions depends in no small degree upon a strict observance of it."

It is no new suggestion that if the Court would give real and sympathetic effect to this rule by declining to hold a statute unconstitutional whenever several of the Justices conclude that it is valid—by conceding that two or more being of such opinion in any case must necessarily raise a "rational doubt"—an end would be made of five to four constitutional decisions and great benefit would result to our country and to the Court.

To voluntarily impose upon itself such a restraint as this would add greatly to the confidence of the people in the Court and would very certainly increase its power for high service to the country. Anyone at all acquainted with the temper of the people in this grave matter must fear if the rule is not observed in some such manner, a greater restraint may be imposed upon the Court by Congress or by the people, probably to the serious detriment of the nation.[11]

The Constitution of Ohio contains the provision that, "no law shall be held unconstitutional and void by the supreme court without the concurrence of at least all but one of the judges, except in the affirmance of a judgment of the court of appeals declaring a law unconstitutional and void."[12] By an amendment to the constitution of North Dakota, adopted in 1918, it is provided "that in no case shall any legislative enactment or law of the State of North Dakota be declared unconstitutional unless at least four [out of five] of the judges shall so decide,"[13] And in 1920 a proviso was approved in Nebraska requiring the assent of five out of seven judges.[14] Similar amendments were considered in other states.[15]

The requirement of an extraordinary majority of the justices to nullify legislative acts, though frequently advocated as a proposal, is designed to meet only those exceptional cases where legislative acts have been declared invalid by a closely divided court such as the five to four decisions common in the determination of labor cases. It is singular that the objection to this proposal is often made to the effect that it would interfere with the principle of majority rule, regardless of the obvious fact that the judgment of a court of seven or nine members

11 "Judicial Power to Declare Legislation Unconstitutional," 9 Am. Bar Assoc. *Jour.* (Oct. 1923) 691, 692.

12 Art. 4, sec. 2. For a review of some of the cases affected by this provision see note on "Minority Control of Court Decisions in Ohio," by W. Rolland Maddox, 24 *Am. Pol. Sci. Rev.* (Aug. 1930) 638. Apparently the writer of the note is not in sympathy with the proposals to limit the right of the courts to review legislation.

13 *Laws*, 1919, 503.

14 Art. 5, sec. 2.

15 Cf. Laws of Minnesota (1913) 893; Massachusetts Constitutional Convention *Debates*, (1917–18) 1:453; and Illinois Constitutional Convention, *Bulletins*, No. 10, 857 ff.

on the validity of a law enacted by the representatives of all of the people is scarcely in line with the principle of majority rule in governmental matters. If the principle of majority rule is so sacred and should be preserved it would seem that the judgment of Congress both as to the policy and validity of legislative enactments should be given greater weight. This proposal, however, to limit the number of dissenting justices, would meet such a small part of the cases which are regarded as vital in the practice of nullifying legislative acts that the device is not regarded as a satisfactory solution for the main defects of judicial control over legislation.

3. *The principle of self-limitation*—

The principle of self-limitation has been advocated on the ground that it would be better for the judges themselves to refuse to accept jurisdiction or to decline the rendering of judgments on matters affecting in an intricate way political and economic policies. Some suggest that the term ''political'' questions might be employed and that the courts under this phrase might defer to the judgment of legislatures where doubtful matters of public policy are involved.

The general adoption of the practice of the review of legislative acts by the judges in the United States was accomplished by men who had definite political convictions and who lost no opportunity to impress those convictions upon constitutions, statutes, and judicial decisions. Shrewd leaders among the statesmen and judges who favored judicial review realized that such unusual authority in courts of justice must not only be clothed in the garb of a popular mandate but also that every effort must be made to show how exceptional and limited the exercise of this authority would necessarily be. Hence certain self-imposed limitations were announced as conditioning judicial review of legislative acts.

Despite the obvious political implications of the assertion of such powers by judges it was customary to insist from the time of Hamilton's classic defense of the American doctrine, that such authority was purely judicial. To bear out this dictum Chief Justice Marshall contended that the courts will not interfere with the necessary range of discretion of another department. Consequently, political acts and certain discretionary powers of executive officers were not to be within the range of judicial review.[16] At various times the Supreme Court has placed in the realm of political questions and hence not subject to judicial review, the negotiations in relation to treaties, issues arising out of the status and conditions of war, matters connected with the admission and deportation of aliens, jurisdiction over territory, recognition of states and governments, and the assurance of peace and order in a state when threatened by an insurrection.[17]

Since the courts of most European countries have regarded any issue on the constitutionality of a law, when it was a question of the competence of a coordinate governmental department, as a political question outside of the jurisdiction of a court of justice, this exception might have been extended to all major constitutional issues by the judges of American courts.

---

[16] Oliver P. Field, ''The Doctrine of Political Questions in the Federal Courts,'' 8 *Minn. Law Rev.* (May 1924) 485; Maurice Finkelstein, ''Judicial Self-Limitation,'' 37 *Harv. Law Rev.* (Jan. 1924) 338 and 339; 138 *Harv. Law Rev.* (Dec. 1925) 221; Melville F. Weston, ''Political Questions,'' 38 *Harv. Law Rev.* (Jan. 1925) 296.

[17] See Marbury v. Madison, 1 Cranch 137, 165, 166 (1803); Foster v. Neilson, 2 Peters 253 (1829); Luther v. Borden, 7 Howard 1 (1849); Mississippi v. Johnson, 4 Wall 475 (1866); Pacific States Telephone Co. v. Oregon, 223 U. S. 118 (1912).

What is regarded as a "wholesome instinct among judges" not to interfere with so-called political questions might readily be extended so as to leave to other departments of government the final word on the policy or wisdom of legislation.[18] This has been demonstrated to be a precarious device. When both the federal and state courts had been nullifying many labor laws and laws regulating social affairs, it was proposed by President Roosevelt and others that, through the pressure of public opinion, it should be impressed upon the judges that in the long run the public will must prevail in the fundamental regulations of social and economic affairs, and that judges should not restrict legislative activities by implied limitations but should rather give a free hand to legislative bodies to pass such laws as seem desirable to regulate public and private conduct.[19] But after national

---

[18] No matter in what terms the opinion of jurists have been couched says Mr. Finkelstein, it is apparent that it is the fear of consequences or the lack of adequate data that has impelled the courts to refrain from entering upon the discussion of the merits of prickly issues. It seems to us that these very considerations should have compelled the refusal by the courts to take jurisdiction of cases raising the question of the constitutionality of social and industrial legislation. It is difficult for the courts, dependent as they are upon counsel for their facts, to have before them the material considerations that have caused state legislatures to pass a limited-hour day for laborers, or a minimum wage law for women and children. The legislative industrial policy of a state or nation can hardly even be stated in classical legal terminology. It would therefore seem the better statesmanship to have included all of these questions in the general category of "political questions."—37 *Harv. Law Rev.* 363. In answer to Mr. Finkelstein, Mr. Weston believes that the constitution defines the dividing line between political and justiciable questions and that the court has no choice to either take or refuse jurisdiction. Mr. Weston gives about as good a defense as is possible for the mechanical approach to the interpretation of constitutional provisions. It is apparent, however, that he does not give due weight to the wide ranges of choice possible in applying the indefinite phrases of written constitutions.—38 *Harv. Law Rev.*, 1296.

[19] "The people themselves must be the ultimate makers of their own Constitution, and when the agents differ in their interpretations of the Constitution, the people themselves should be given a chance after full and deliberate judgment, authoritatively to settle what interpretation it is that their representatives shall thereafter adopt as binding."—Theodore Roosevelt, *Sen. Doc.* No. 904, 62 Cong., 2 sess.

and state campaigns had been conducted on this issue and a seeming reaction had taken place against the wide and varied use of the right of courts to nullify legislative acts, and after it seemed that the principle of self-limitation was to serve as an effective and practical device by which the judges would themselves limit their powers, a reversal of attitude has taken place. The courts are again construing new limitations on legislative, executive, and administrative authorities and are interpolating more extensive restrictions on governmental powers. The suggestion then that the judges can be depended upon in the long run to limit their powers seems rather illusory.

4. *Education of lawyers and judges—*

There are many who believe that the only feasible remedy to meet the present evils of judicial supremacy is to bring about a better system of education of lawyers and judges, to develop a scientific attitude in the study of law, and to broaden the basis of legal education so as to include training on social and economic issues. If, as Mark Twain suggested, "Solomon's justice depends upon how Solomon is raised," it is regarded as necessary to begin early the proper training of those who are in preparation for judicial positions. But, though much may be gained through a better system of legal education, and though a more varied training, especially along social and economic lines, would help to correct some of the narrow legalistic and individualistic thinking of American judges, this device also is likely to fail to meet adequately some of the difficulties in the situation. One of the problems involved in the attempt to find a remedy was stated suggestively by Thomas Jefferson when he wrote,

It is not enough that honest men are appointed judges. All know the influence of interest on the mind of man, and how unconsciously his judgment is warped by influence. To this bias add that of the *esprit de corps* of their peculiar maxim and creed that "it is the office of a good judge to enlarge his jurisdiction," and the absence of responsibility, and how can we expect any impartial decisions between the general government of which they themselves are so eminent a part and the individual state from which they have nothing to hope or fear?

Jefferson was dealing with the well-known tendency of the federal courts to approve the extension of the powers of the federal government under the implied-power doctrine. The process of "undermining" the rights of states, as he called it, was carried on with the approval and assistance not only of the federal courts but of Congress and of the Executive until, by the arbitrament of war, nationalism won over the rights of the states to exercise their independent judgment in governmental matters regarded as federal or national in character. As the occasions have become less frequent for judges to enlarge their jurisdiction in dealing with the extension of federal powers, a new principle is being applied, that of developing implied limitations on legislative powers. And the judges are again engaged in the enlargement of their jurisdiction through restriction of the avenues of popular control and through further limitations, by interpretations, on the direction of public affairs by legislative, executive, or administrative officers. These restrictions are applied today chiefly in the extension of the meaning of the terms "due process of law" and "equal protection of the laws," together with certain broad implications of the doctrine of the separation of powers, as well as new and varied applications of the doctrine of according protection to vested rights. Constitutions have been termed "contracts" between the people and their government, and judicial interpretation is being utilized to change the terms of the contract to the detriment at times of the rights of the people. Along with the admonition to the people to respect constitutions and laws there should go a similar admonition to judges to confine themselves to the clear and direct duty of the interpretation of the laws and to restrict their jurisdiction so as not to expand the vague terms of written constitutions, thereby placing unexpressed limitations on popular sovereignty.

If the fundamental object of government is the preservation of the rights of private property,[20] judicial review of legislative acts should have a prime place in a governmental system. From long practice and from their peculiar capabilities courts are better adapted to protect rights of property than to give protection and security to the individual and to those social values which come in the wake of a highly developed industrial civilization. Judicial review of legislation as practiced in America exaggerates the undue emphasis which the common law system already places on the protection of property and prepares the way for those whose property rights are in the least disturbed to bring pressure on the courts as their citadel of protection.

Judicial review in a certain sense encourages a disrespect for law. A citizen who feels aggrieved by the enforcement of a law is warranted in resisting its enforcement in the hope that the law may eventually be declared void. Those who can afford to take chances in contesting a law can hold up its effective enforcement for many

---

[20] See Blackstone's *Comm.*, 2:139; Justice Harlan in Chicago, Burlington and Quincy Ry. Co. v. Chicago, 166 U. S. 239 (1897); and the argument of Rufus Choate in Pollock v. Farmers Loan and Trust Co., 157 U. S. 534 (1894).

years until the final court of appeal puts its stamp of approval or disapproval on the law. Obedient citizens who invest money or enter into contracts on the strength of an act that is later declared unconstitutional, may suffer serious losses and inconveniences. To permit the determination of the validity or invalidity of a law by a procedure which may require from five to twenty years and may entail a great expense to be borne often by private individuals, some of whom may profit thereby, is to cast a shadow of doubt and uncertainty on the whole process of the administration and enforcement of law.

Americans are imbued with the habit of submission to law and of respect for the courts. This is a commendable habit and one which should receive encouragement and sanction. But submission to law as law whether reasonable or unreasonable, without a critical analysis of the grounds on which the legal precepts and decisions are based, is deplorable. James Madison supporting the adoption of the federal Constitution raised the query:

Is it not the glory of the people of America, that whilst they have paid a decent respect to the opinions of former times and other nations, they have not suffered a blind veneration for antiquity, for custom, or for names, to over-rule the suggestions of their own good sense, the knowledge of their own situation, and the lessons of their own experience?[21]

The creative spirit which inspired the philosophy and principles of the Revolution, formulated the features of the federal Constitution, formed the background for the nationalist opinions of John Marshall, and made institutions to fit the conditions then existing and changed them freely both by amendment and interpretation, is now frowned upon when modern nation builders seek to adjust

---

[21] *The Federalist*, No. 4.

these laws to the radical changes of more than a century. The ideas of the Fathers which in their own time were characterized by the marked fluidity of their content and subjected to constant scrutiny and revision, are today put forth as doctrines of eternal validity which the body politic of today must be made to fit regardless of the inapplicability of the patterns and formulas to present conditions.

5. *Recall of judges and of judicial decisions—*

Chief among the proposals to bring the courts under control is the movement for the recall of judges. California, Oregon, Colorado, Nevada, and Kansas, have adopted amendments to their constitutions providing for the recall of all officers, including the judges. The state of Arizona was permitted to come into the Union only after removing a similar section from its constitution, but soon thereafter adopted a provision for recall of all elective officers, including judges. A proposal has been presented to amend the national Constitution so as to make possible the recall of all federal justices. But many who believe in the recall of other state officers feel that this device will result disastrously when applied to the judiciary. Hence states such as Idaho, Louisiana, Michigan, and Washington adopted amendments for the recall of state officers and excepted the judges. Nevertheless the belief that the judiciary must be subjected to effective popular control, although recall of judges may not be practicable, has led to the advocacy of the recall of judicial decisions.[22]

---

[22] In the excitement over the trial of Justice Chase, Chief Justice Marshall suggested the advisability of having Congress pass upon unsatisfactory judicial decisions rather than to impeach judges.—Beveridge, *Life of John Marshall,* 3:177.

In speaking before the constitutional convention at Columbus, Ohio, President Roosevelt said:

There is one kind of recall in which I earnestly believe, and the immediate adoption of which I urge. . . . . When a judge decides a constitutional question, when he decides what the people as a whole can or cannot do, the people should have the right to recall that decision if they think it is wrong.

His plan was further elaborated in a speech at Carnegie Hall, New York, when he said:

I am proposing merely that, in a certain class of cases, involving the police power, when a State court has set aside as unconstitutional a law passed by the Legislature for the general welfare, the question of the validity of the law—which would depend, as Justice Holmes so well phrases it, upon the prevailing morality or preponderant opinion—be submitted for final determination to a vote of the people, taken after due time for consideration. And I contend that the people, in the nature of things, must be better judges of what is the preponderant opinion than the courts, and that the courts should not be allowed to reverse the political philosophy of the people.

The proposal was defended as a simple device to use in the event of a clash between the state legislature and the court as to the constitutionality of an act for the general welfare, when the people themselves shall be permitted "to decide what the true interpretation of the constitution is." If the state decision is not sustained, the popular verdict shall be final, subject only to action by the Supreme Court of the United States.[23]

---

[23] *The Outlook*, March 23, 1912. "We hold that the people themselves should be given the right to say finally and conclusively whether they do or do not agree with these decisions, and whether these decisions are or are not to stand as the law of the land. . . . . If the legislature takes one view of the powers defined by the Constitution and the court takes another view, then it should be the right of the people to decide between their two sets of servants and say which is correct."—Theodore Roosevelt, "The Right of the People to Review Judge-Made Law," *The Outlook*, 107 (Aug. 1911) 855, 856.

In accordance with the recommendation of Mr. Roosevelt, the Progressive platform included the following section relative to the courts:

The Progressive party demands such restriction of the power of the courts as provides: 1. That when an act passed under the police power of the state is held unconstitutional under the state constitution by the courts, the people, after an ample interval for deliberation, shall have an opportunity to vote on the question whether they desire the act to become law, notwithstanding such decision; 2. That every decision of the highest appellate court of a state declaring an act of the legislature unconstitutional shall be subject to the same review by the supreme court of the United States as is now accorded to decisions sustaining such legislation.[24]

The state of Colorado was the first commonwealth to enact this ingenious proposition into law. By an amendment adopted in 1912, the Supreme Court was to continue to exercise the power to declare any law of the state as in violation of the constitution of the state or the Constitution of the United States; but before such decision became binding, it was made subject to approval or disapproval by the people. The method of securing a referendum on the decision was that within sixty days a petition signed by not less than 5 per cent of the qualified electors might request that the decision be submitted to the people for adoption or rejection—the procedure in such election to be the same as in case of constitutional amendments. In case any such laws are approved by a

---

[24] For a discussion of this proposal from the point of view of its advocates, consult W. L. Ransom, *Majority Rule and the Judiciary* (New York, 1912). ''The demand is not that the Court be deprived of all power to pass on the constitutionality of legislation, but that it be deprived solely of its power of final veto. What is demanded is that the people finally may be able to outvoice the Supreme Court and write their will into law in spite of the Supreme Court.''—Samuel Gompers in Washington *Times,* Sept. 29, 1924.

majority of the electors, they shall become a part of the law of the state, notwithstanding the decision of the Supreme Court. This provision was held void by the state supreme court on the ground that it violated the federal Constitution and that it did not accord with privileges of a law higher than the constitution.[25]

In addition to possible modifications of judicial supremacy through the recall of judges and a proposed recall of a limited class of judicial decisions, the Progressive and Liberal parties uniformly favor an easier method for the amendment of constitutions. Mr. Roosevelt in his speech before the Progressive convention at Chicago said:

Whenever in our constitutional system of government there exist general prohibitions that, as interpreted by the courts, nullify, or may be used to nullify, specific laws passed, and admittedly passed, in the interest of social justice, we are for such immediate law, or amendment to the constitution, if that be necessary, as will thereafter permit a reference to the people of the public effect of such decision under forms securing full deliberation, to the end that the specific act of the legislative branch of the government thus judicially nullified, and such amendments thereof as come within its scope and purpose, may constitutionally be excepted by vote of the people from the general prohibitions, the same as if that particular act has been expressly excepted when the prohibition was adopted. This will necessitate the establishment of machinery for making much easier of amendment both the national and the several state constitutions, especially with the view of prompt action on certain judicial decisions—action as specific and limited as that taken by the passage of the eleventh amendment to the national constitution.

The Progressive platform pledged the party "to provide a more easy and expeditious method of amending the

---

[25] People v. Western Union Co., 70 Col. 90 (1921), and People v. Max, 70 Col. 100 (1921).

federal constitution.'' During the campaign of Robert M. LaFollette for the presidency the issue of subjecting court decisions that nullified legislative acts to a revision either by Congress or by the people was extensively discussed.[26] Senator LaFollette declared it to be his purpose to abolish the ''tyranny and usurpation of the courts including the practice of nullifying legislation in conflict with the political, social, or economic theories of the judges.'' To carry out this purpose he proposed an amendment to the federal Constitution with the following provisions:

No inferior federal judge shall have authority to hold void a law of Congress on the ground that it is unconstitutional. If the Supreme Court assumes to decide any law of Congress unconstitutional, or by interpretation undertakes to assert a public policy at variance with the statutory declaration of Congress, which alone under our system is authorized to determine the public policies of government, the Congress may, by reenacting the law, nullify the action of the Court.

Thereafter the law would remain in full force and effect precisely the same as though the Court had never held it to be unconstitutional.

LaFollette did not win the presidency but many of the voters who cast their ballots for him no doubt were influenced by his stand in opposition to judicial supremacy. And those who had been accustomed to think of the doctrine of judicial review of legislation as the cornerstone

---

[26] The LaFollette platform contained the following provision: So long as judges are the final makers of statute and constitutional law, government by the people becomes government by a judicial oligarchy. The people are the source of all power, and we favor the extension of the recall to the judiciary, with safeguards as to lapse of time between the petition and the vote. . . . . We favor such amendment to the Constitution as will permit a change to be made therein by a majority of the states, provided a majority of all the votes cast in the country shall be in favor of its adoption. An amendment may be initiated by a majority in Congress, or by ten states acting either through the legislators thereof or through a majority of the electors voting thereon in each state.

of the American system of government regarded the campaign as a warning to renew their efforts to convince the people of the necessity and efficacy of a judicial check on governmental powers.

Formerly when laws were enacted by legislatures and amendments were adopted by the people discriminations between constitutional and statutory laws were readily made. But such a condition no longer exists. Important provisions of state constitutions are now made subject to change by legislative act. But of more significance is the fact that the difference between constitutions and statutes is less marked, especially on account of the use of the referendum on ordinary statutes. In states such as Oregon and Oklahoma the initiative and referendum are applied alike to ordinary statutes and constitutional amendments, and the distinction in procedure is not such as to attach unusual sanctity to changes in the fundamental law. In fact, the great expansion of state constitutions and the inclusion therein of minute details of legislative procedure have long since brought about a departure from the former intrinsic differences between constitutions and statutes.

What will be the attitude of the courts toward such legislation as has received the sanction of the people at the polls has not as yet been definitely determined. Although the courts have indicated that they will exercise control over the referendum, it is not likely that judicial review will be a serious check upon such law-making. Courts will, no doubt, be more likely to give their sanction to laws which have received popular approval, and especially so since their power of control may be largely dispensed with by a simple change in title and procedure which will make the measure a constitutional amendment.

There are indications, however, which would lead to the belief that the courts will exercise rather strict control over measures adopted directly by the people.[27]

The agitation to render the amending process more easy, the overturning of judicial decisions of state courts by means of amendments, the placing of statute law-making on practically the same basis as constitution making, and, finally, the adoption of the recall of judges and judicial decisions indicate a feeling in which many concur that judicial control over legislation should be confined to narrower limits.

6. *Proposals to abolish judicial review of legislation*—

The possibility of Congressional action to deprive the Supreme Court of jurisdiction of all questions relating to the constitutionality of acts of Congress has been considered on only a few occasions. Congress asserted its control over the Supreme Court when it removed from the jurisdiction of the court the validity of certain acts.[28] In 1868 a law was passed over the President's veto prohibiting the Supreme Court from passing on the constitutionality of reconstruction laws. The prohibition, which was inserted as a rider to a revenue measure, read:

That so much of the act approved February 5, 1858, as authorizes an appeal from the judgment of the Circuit Court to the Supreme Court of the United States, or the exercise of any such jurisdiction by said Supreme Court on appeals which have been, or may be hereafter taken, be, and the same is hereby repealed.

---

[27] For reference to decisions, see Dodd, *The Revision and Amendment of State Constitutions*, 255, 258.

[28] *Ex parte* McCardle, 7 Wall 506 (1868). Horace A. Davis, *The Judicial Veto*, 115 ff. A. W. Richter, ''A Legislative Curb on the Judiciary,'' 21 *Jour. of Pol. Econ.* (April 1913) 281.

The attorney general had expressed an opinion that the reconstruction laws were unconstitutional. He also refused to prosecute individuals under these laws.

McCardle, who was arrested by the military authorities for criticizing their conduct in a Mississippi paper, claimed protection under the Constitution, and appealed to the Supreme Court. When the *McCardle Case* came before the Supreme Court, Chief Justice Chase, rendering the opinion of the court, said:

It is quite true, as was argued by the counsel for the petitioner, that the appellate jurisdiction of this court is not derived from the acts of Congress. It is, strictly speaking, conferred by the Constitution. But it is conferred ''with such exceptions and under such regulations as Congress shall make. . . . .''

We are not at liberty to inquire into the motives of the legislature. We can only examine into its power under the constitution, but the power to make exceptions to the appellate jurisdiction of this court is given by express words.

What, then, is the effect of the repealing act upon the case before us? We cannot doubt as to this: Without jurisdiction the court cannot proceed at all in any cause. Jurisdiction is power to declare the law, and when it ceases to exist, the only function remaining to the court is that of announcing the fact and dismissing the cause. And this is not less clear upon authority than upon principle.

It is quite clear, therefore, that this court cannot proceed to pronounce judgment in this case, for it has no longer jurisdiction of the appeal; and judicial duty is not less fitly performed by declining ungranted jurisdiction than in exercising firmly that which the constitution and the laws confer.

In a subsequent case restricting the application of this act, Justice Chase observed:[29]

The effect of this act was to oust the court of its jurisdiction of the particular case then before it on appeal and it is not to be

---

[29] *Ex parte* Yerger, 8 Wall 85 (1868).

doubted that such was the effect intended. Nor will it be questioned that legislation of this character is unusual and hardly to be justified except upon some imperious public exigency.

A similar measure was proposed when Senator Owen presented a bill to reenact the Child Labor Law with a clause prohibiting the Supreme Court from invalidating it.[30] It would be an interesting question for the Supreme Court to decide if Congress were to pass a law depriving the court of jurisdiction in all cases involving the validity of acts of Congress, in so far as such questions arise under the appellate jurisdiction of the court.

Few constitutional questions arise under the original jurisdiction of the court. Congress is granted by the Constitution control over the appellate jurisdiction of the federal courts, and Congress has not undertaken to limit the court's review of its acts under appellate jurisdiction except in one instance. So far as this case may be regarded as a precedent Congress may seriously restrict the court's power to declare its acts void. The justices are now more assertive and more disposed to defend their privileges and prerogatives, hence an act to limit their right to declare acts void might be refused application, and then only a constitutional amendment could take away this authority.

---

[30] 65 Cong., 2 sess., 7433. At another time Senator Owen proposed to prohibit judicial review of acts of Congress by the following provision:

That from and after the passage of this act federal judges are forbidden to declare any act of Congress unconstitutional. Any judge who declares any act passed by the Congress of the United States to be unconstitutional is hereby declared to be guilty of judicial usurpation and guilty of violating the constitutional requirement of good behavior upon which his tenure of office rests, and shall be held by such decision to have vacated his office.— 64 Cong., 2 sess., 1068. See Maurice S. Culp, "A Survey of the Proposals to Limit or Deny the Power of Judicial Review by the Supreme Court of the United States," 4 *Indiana Law Jour.* (April 1929) 386, 487; also Walter Clark, "Judicial Supremacy Unwarranted by the Constitution," *The Public* (June 29, 1918) 21:821–822.

No state has undertaken to deny the power of judicial review to its courts, though such action has been sponsored by various groups during the last few decades.[31] Mr. Ralston, in the report prepared for the American Federation of Labor, offered the following proposals relating to judicial review of legislation:

1. The Supreme Court of the United States and State and National Courts generally shall have no power to pass upon the constitutionality of congressional enactments. The courts of the respective states shall have no power to pass upon the constitutionality of the enactments of their respective legislatures, except so far as such enactments are contrary to the National Constitution or to National Laws or treaties, which are given constitutional recognition.

2. The Supreme Court shall retain its jurisdiction to declare unconstitutional any acts of executive and inferior judicial powers in excess of legislative authority, and a like jurisdiction over acts of state legislatures, including acts of commissions, and the state courts shall possess and retain power to pass upon the constitutionality of the acts of counties, cities, towns, and administrators of whatever nature.

3. The Supreme Court of the United States, in the exercise of its jurisdiction to declare an act of the state legislature or of any state or federal agency including the judiciary, to be unconstitutional, shall only do so by the acquiescence of considerably more than a bare majority of its members. Three-fourths of the entire membership of the court should concur to such end, and the like requirement shall hold as to the highest courts of the states.[32]

Speaking of these and other proposals to limit the authority of the Supreme Court to review and declare

---

[31] Among the planks of the Socialist party at the beginning of the twentieth century was a clause favoring ''the abolition of the power usurped by the Supreme Court of the United States to pass upon the constitutionality of legislation enacted by Congress.''

[32] Jackson H. Ralston, ''Judicial Control over Legislatures as to Constitutional Questions,'' 54 *Am. Law Rev.* (March-April 1920) 225.

void acts of Congress with no recourse except amendment to the Constitution, President Coolidge expressed the view which accords with the prevailing sentiment of the people of the United States as follows:

Such a proposal would make the Congress finally supreme. In the last resort its powers practically would be unlimited. This would be to do away with the great main principle of our written constitution, which regards the people as sovereign and the government as their agent, and would tend to make the legislative body sovereign and the people its subjects. It would to an extent substitute for the will of the people, definitely and permanently expressed in their written constitution, the changing and uncertain will of Congress. That would radically alter our form of government and take from it its guarantee of freedom.

7. *Defense of judicial supremacy—*

Since its adoption more than a century ago, the doctrine of judicial supremacy has been ably defended as an indispensable feature of the American system of government. In tracing the development of the practice of judicial review, the arguments in its favor have been analyzed, and certain phases of the defense have been elaborated on in order to meet the attacks of the critics.

The theories of limited government and of the consequent separation of governmental powers, along with the American doctrine of judicial supremacy, furnished the incipient legal basis for the protection of civil liberties and individual rights which has come to be regarded as the feature *par excellence* of the government of the United States. The importance of this feature of the American system was suggested in the assertion that this judicial check affords a security for civil liberty; ''which belongs to no other governments in the world; and if the judges will everywhere faithfully exercise it, the liberties of the American nation may be rendered perpetual."[33]

The right of courts to declare laws invalid was one of the chief reasons which inspired certain men to express reverence for the federal Constitution. In the words of James Wilson, the control of the legislature by an over-ruling constitution, adopted by the people and interpreted by judges, "was an improvement in the science and practice of governments reserved to the American states."[34] The authors of *The Federalist* believed that a new era in government would be inaugurated with the adoption of the federal Constitution. Tucker, in his edition of Blackstone, likewise claimed that a new epoch in the history of civil institutions was introduced by the Revolution, and for the first time reduced to practice in the American constitutions.

In order to impress upon the people the efficacy of the American doctrine of judicial review judges announced that "the integrity and duration of the government depended upon the faithful performance of this high duty."[35] This opinion, which was frequently advanced in the beginning of judicial review, was put into eloquent language by Daniel Webster, when he said:

No conviction is deeper in my mind than that the maintenance of the judicial power is essential and indispensable to the very being of this government. The Constitution without it would be no constitution; the government, no government. I am deeply sensible, too, and, as I think, every man must be whose eyes have been open to what has passed around him for the last twenty years, that the judicial power is the protecting power of the whole government.[36]

---

[33] Byrne v. Stewart, 3 Des. 466, 476 (1812).
[34] Elliot's *Debates*, 2:432.
[35] Lindsay v. Charleston Commissioners, 2 Bay 38, 61 (1796).
[36] *Works*, 3:176.

The superior qualities of the doctrine of limited government based on a written constitution, in which individual rights were regarded of supreme importance and protected by the judicial department against encroachments from the executive or the legislature, have frequently been commended by both American and European publicists. The usual American view was expressed by Francis Lieber who defined liberty as "protection or checks against undue interference, whether this be from individuals, from masses or from government."[37] And he put into concise form the controlling doctrine of the legal system of the United States during the nineteenth century. Everything in favor of the authority of government was to be closely construed, while everything that pertained to the security of the citizen and the protection of the individual was to be interpreted broadly, for it is the very nature of public power to increase, while the citizen needs protection. When civil liberty is protected by restrictions upon legislative and executive power which are upheld by the courts of justice, Lieber thought that all

constitutional questions are decided in a natural, easy, legitimate and safe manner, according to the principle of the supremacy of the law and the independence of justice. It is one of the most interesting and important evolutions of the government of law, and one of the greatest protections of the citizen. It may well be called a very jewel of Anglican liberty, one of the best fruits of our political civilization.[38]

That the individual has a realm of activity within which government shall neither encroach nor permit encroachments,[39] is considered the crowning feature of the

---

[37] Lieber, *Civil Liberty and Self-government* (Phila., 1859), 37–40.
[39] Lieber, *op. cit.*, p. 164.
[39] Burgess, *Political Science and Constitutional Law* (New York, 1913) 1, chap. 4.

United States system of government. The constitutional, independent, non-political judiciary, and the supremacy of the judiciary over the other departments in all cases where private rights are concerned, make our judicial system "the most momentous product of modern political science."[40] In the judgment of Professor Burgess,

it is difficult to see how the guaranty of individual liberty against the government itself could be made more complete. Its fundamental principles are written by the state in the constitution; the power to put the final and authoritative interpretation upon them is vested by the state in a body of jurists, holding their offices independently of the political departments of the government and during their own good behavior; while finally, recourse to the sovereign itself is open if all other defenses fail. This is the special point in which the constitutional law of the United States is far in advance of that of the European states. . . . . And while it must be confessed that we can learn much from the European constitutions in the organization of government and in the details of administration, yet for a clearly defined and well secured civil liberty, ... one which can defy government, and still be subject to the state, one which can do more for civilization upon many sides, and upon many of its finer sides than the best ordered government which the world has ever produced,—Europe must come to us, and take lessons in the school of our experience.[41]

The one distinguishing mark of American common law jurisprudence has been characterized as that of an "unlimited valuation of individual liberty and respect for individual property."[42] It is apparent that this mark of distinction was made the cornerstone of the jurisprudence of the United States.

---

[40] Burgess, "The Ideal of American Commonwealth," 10 *Pol. Sci. Quart.*, 422.

[41] Burgess, *Political Science and Constitutional Law.* 1:179, 264.

[42] Berolzheimer, *System der Rechts und Wirtschafts-philosophie*, 2:160.

The opinion which Americans have so generally held until recent years has been confirmed by the observations of European writers. De Tocqueville observed that the power of American courts to declare laws invalid constituted one of the most powerful barriers against the tyranny of political assemblies, and he lauded this practice as the "most favorable to liberty and to public order."[43]

To this favorable opinion of a continental writer at an early period of American history was added the testimony of two of the greatest English authorities who made a special study of the institutions of the United States. James Bryce in his great work *The American Commonwealth,* commented favorably on the supremacy of the judiciary: "It is nevertheless true that there is no part of the American system which reflects more credit on its authors or has worked better in practice. It has had the advantage of relegating questions not only intricate and delicate, but peculiarly liable to excite political passions to the cool, dry atmosphere of judicial determination."[44] Professor Dicey, who was an advocate of the system of legislative supremacy for the British Empire, believed that a federal system demanded some such power as that exercised by the federal supreme court, and that "the glory of the founders of the United States is to have devised or adopted arrangements under which the Constitution became in reality as well as in name the supreme law of the land."[45]

The recent criticisms of the practice of judicial supremacy and the arguments against the American doctrine have called forth numerous opinions and declara-

---

[43] *Democracy in America,* 1:129–130.

[44] *The American Commonwealth* (New York, 1912) 1:256, 257.

[45] Dicey, *Law of the Constitution,* 154.

tions of approval of this feature of our government. When the Democratic party made the attack on the judiciary one of the planks of its platform in 1896, a national committee was formed and a campaign inaugurated to affirm confidence in the integrity and justice of the courts and to insist that the preservation of the independence and full constitutional prerogatives of the judiciary is essential to the maintenance of the American system of government.

The American practice of judicial supremacy was defended as the sole guaranty of national permanence and was lauded as "the last and crowning political growth of our Anglo-Saxon civilization."[46] It is claimed "that every constitutional convention in every state in this country has not only confirmed the power of the judicial department, but has vindicated the courts by adding limitation after limitation to the legislature." Although only one state has a constitutional provision giving the courts specific power to declare laws void,[47] all officers have uniformly accepted the exercise of this authority as necessary and indispensable. Bar associations, lawyers, and public men, generally have come to the defense of the courts, maintaining that the power to declare laws invalid was not a usurpation and that its continuance is essential to the safety and endurance of the American Republic.[48]

The proposal to recall judges brought a renewal of the expressions of confidence in courts and judges. The arguments in opposition to the recall and in defense of

---

[46] John Woodward, ''The Courts and the People,'' 7 *Col. Law Rev.* (Dec. 1907) 559.

[47] Georgia, Constitution, sec. iv, par. 2.

[48] Cf. Blackburn Esterline, ''The Supreme Law of the Land,'' 40 *Am. Law Rev.* (July-Aug. 1906) 566, in answer to Dean Trickett's article ''The Great Usurpation''; and James B. McDonough, ''The Alleged Usurpation of Power by the Federal Courts,'' 46 *Am. Law Rev.* (Jan.-Feb. 1912) 45.

the American doctrine were formulated by President Taft in his veto of the recall section of the Arizona constitution.[49] This provision of the Arizona constitution was denounced as so "pernicious in its effect, so destructive of independence in the judiciary, so likely to subject the rights of the individual to the possible tyranny of a popular majority," and therefore so injurious to the cause of free government, that the President felt obliged to give his disapproval to the act granting statehood. The President defended the necessity for placing the will of the majority under controlling checks in order to secure the rights of the minority. "No honest, clear-headed man, however great a lover of popular government," he observed,

can deny that the unbridled opinion of the majority of a community converted hastily into law or action would sometimes make a government tyrannical and cruel. Constitutions are checks upon the hasty action of the majority. They are the self-imposed restraints of a whole people upon a majority of them to secure sober action and a respect for the rights of the minority. . . . . In order to maintain the rights of the minority and the individual and to preserve our constitutional balance, we must have judges with courage to decide against the majority when justice and law require.

The proposal to recall judicial decisions led to some of the most emphatic encomiums on the judiciary and in support of the prerogative of the courts to annul legislative acts.[50]

---

[49] Special Message, August 15, 1911.

[50] See, Resolution adopted unanimously by the American Bar Association: "This Association records its opposition to any proposal to limit the power of the Supreme Court of the United States to sustain and enforce the Constitution as the supreme law of the land, as against any act of congress in conflict therewith."—10 Am. Bar Assoc. *Jour.* (Jan. 1924) 29.

Justice Cardozo, who supports the American practice of judicial review, places his defense on the following basis :[51]

the utility of an external power restraining the legislative judgment is not to be measured by counting the occasions of its exercise. The great ideals of liberty and equality are preserved against the assaults of opportunism, the expediency of the passing hour, the erosion of small encroachments, the scorn and derision of those who have no patience with general principles, by enshrining them in constitutions, and consecrating to the task of their protection a body of defenders. By conscious or subconscious influence, the presence of this restraining power, aloof in the background, but none the less always in reserve, tends to stabilize and rationalize the legislative judgment, to infuse it with the glow of principle, to hold the standard aloft and visible for those who must run the race and keep the faith.

Great maxims, if they may be violated with impunity, are honored often with lip-service, which passes easily into irreverence. The restraining power of the judiciary does not manifest its chief worth in the few cases in which the legislature has gone beyond the lines that mark the limits of discretion. Rather shall we find its chief worth in making vocal and audible the ideals that might otherwise be silenced, in giving them continuity of life and of expression, in guiding and directing choice within the limits where choice ranges. This function should preserve to the courts the power that now belongs to them, if only the power is exercised with insight into social values, and with suppleness of adaptation to changing social needs.

---

[51] Benjamin N. Cardozo, *The Nature of the Judicial Process* (New Haven 1921), 92-94.

CHAPTER XVIII

SOME THEORIES AND FICTIONS INVOLVED IN THE APPLICATION OF JUDICIAL REVIEW OF LEGISLATION

1. *Mechanical application of law versus the theory of free legal decision—*

THE CENTRAL problem in American constitutional interpretation is the continued and perennial controversy in the administration of justice over the place and function of the judge. Two theories as to the place and function of the judge have been prevalent in the growth of legal organization and practice. According to one theory, the judge as a seeker of the truth, from divine and other sources, discovers the principles on which his conclusions bearing on a case may be based and from which a judgment follows, subject to no variance or turning. From another viewpoint, the judge gathers his conclusions from his own concepts and conscience influenced largely as these are by his training and experience, and by the social and economic conditions surrounding him and the litigants whose controversies are to be settled. The former of these theories, when carried to an extreme, is known as the "mechanical theory"; the latter, as the theory of "free legal decision." The former has prevailed, particularly in Anglo-American legal systems; the latter is more common in continental European countries where the civil law prevails.[1]

---

[1] In the following pages a few extracts from my article on "General Observations on the Effects of Personal, Political, and Economic Influences in the Decisions of Judges," 17 *Ill. Law Rev.* (June 1922) 96 ff., are used with the permission of the editors of that journal.

In Anglo-American jurisdictions the conflict between the mechanical theory and the theory of free legal decision has been waged over the nature and scope of judicial legislation and the relation of judges to public policy in declaring legislative acts void. Those who support the mechanical theory hold that it is not the function of the judge to make or to change the law. This theory refuses to recognize anything but formulated legal rules and the facts and circumstances of a specific case. The advocates of mechanistic ideas in the United States have become the exponents of the idea of "a government of laws and not of men" and they deprecate the tendency to depart from definite legal rules in the administration of justice. They see grave dangers in the theory of free legal decision and oppose such devices because they believe that the human element is undependable and that in administering justice little discretion should be accorded to the judge.[2]

These two main theories have been customarily accepted with respect to the growth of American constitutional law. According to the mechanical theory, American public law is the result of the development of established principles through rigid deduction. In this development, the rules of construction are plain and easy of application. It is the function of the courts to determine by logical processes the decisions predetermined by the law-giver. Thus, Justice Charlton claimed that a violation of a constitutional right ought to be as obvious to the comprehension of everyone "as an axiomatic truth; as that the parts are equal to the whole."[3] Justice Story became a proponent of the same view:

---

[2] Justice Cardozo believes that in the field of American constitutional law the method of free legal decision is dominant. *The Nature of the Judicial Process* (New Haven, 1921), 17.

[3] Grimball v. Ross (Ga.), T. U. P. Charlton 175, 178 (1808). See also Byrne v. Stewart (S. C.), 3 Des. 466, 477 (1812).

What is to become of constitutions of government if they are to rest, not upon the plain import of their words, but upon conjectural enlargements and restrictions to suit the temporary passions and interests of the day. . . . They are not to be frittered away to please the demagogues of the day. They are not to be violated to gratify the ambition of political leaders; they are to speak the same voice now and forever.[4]

Imbued with this philosophy Justice Brewer thought "the Constitution is a written instrument. As such its meaning does not alter. That which it meant when adopted it means now," and Chief Justice Taney believed that in its present form it speaks not only in the same words but with the same meaning and intent as when it came from the hands of its framers.[5]

With the advocates of this view, the personality of the judge disappears in the mechanical process of deduction involved and there results the phenomenon of a "government of laws and not of men." The mechanical theory of constitutional law has had many advocates and not a few lawyers today are its devoted followers.[6] Devotees of such a mechanical, necessitous construction of constitutional law continue to render lip service to the old adage that the wisdom and justice of legislative acts are entirely outside of the province of courts and judges.

---

[4] Story, *"Commentaries on the Constitution,"* 2:653. "The rules of construction are plain and simple of application. They are in substance identical, whether the instrument for interpretation be a statute or a contract."—Justice Lurton, "A Government of Law or a Government of Men?" *North Am. Rev.* 193 (Jan. 1911) 24.

[5] South Carolina v. United States, 199 U. S. 437, 448 (1905) and Scott v. Sandford, 16 Howard 393, 426 (1856).

[6] See comment of Elihu Root in *The Independent*, 72:704; also Justice Lurton, *op. cit.*, 20. "The power of the Supreme Court," says Mr. Carson, "is never exercised for the purpose of giving effect to the will of the legislature, or in other words, to the will of the law": Hampton L. Carson, "The Supreme Court of the United States," 1:8. Chief Justice Taft, in the opinion of the majority of the Supreme Court in Truax v. Corrigan, 257 U. S. 312 (1921) presents the mechanical theory in its familiar terminology.

They affect to believe with Chief Justice White

that no instance is afforded from the foundation of the government where an act which was within a power conferred was declared to be repugnant to the constitution because it appeared to the judicial mind that a particular exertion of constitutional power was either unwise or unjust.[7]

There are those, however, to whom the mechanical theory has appeared manifestly inadequate and untrue to life, employed, it is thought, rather as a "childish fiction" by the judges and their followers. That no political prejudices have swayed the judges is, they think, to maintain that they are exempt from the customary weaknesses of human nature and above the influences which operate most powerfully in determining the opinions of other men. To the opponents of the mechanical theory, the notion that the courts are automatons or judicial slot machines, registering verdicts in purely mechanical fashion, has seemed impossible and quite contrary to the facts. As advocates of the theory of free legal decision, they take it for granted that the application of the law by judges with human outlook, interests, and passions involves of necessity a freedom of choice and that in this choice all the complex elements that determine human conduct hold sway. The point of view of those who accept the theory of free legal decision is well expressed in President Roosevelt's message to Congress in December, 1908:

The chief law-makers in our country may be, and often are, the judges, because they are the final seat of authority. Every time they interpret contract, property, vested rights, due process of law, liberty, they necessarily enact into law parts of a system of social philosophy; and since such interpretation is fundamental, they give direction to all law-making. The decisions of

---

[7] McCray v. United States, 195 U. S. 27, 54 (1904).

the courts on economic and social questions depend upon their
economic and social philosophy.[8]

In the terms of the theory of free legal decision, the
law is, as a justice of the Supreme Court aptly called it,
"a progressive science" in which it is the duty of judges
to foster and direct the process. And it is the business of
judges by so-called constructive decisions to see that the
law is made to accord with that somewhat uncertain and
elusive thing known as "preponderant public opinion."
In this view it becomes the function of the judges to
legislate and to guide by public policies,—in fact, to
see that the law accords with the dominant social and
political doctrines.

The result in a large number of cases cannot be
reached, it is contended, by a strict and logical application of a constitutional text, but instead the courts must
decide upon the basis of external facts of which judicial
notice is taken. Much depends on the extent to which
such facts are recognized and considered. Moreover,
where the words of the Constitution such as *due process
of law* have no technical significance and the judges must
seek a conclusion without definite guidance, the interpretation which is adopted is necessarily influenced by the
lives, thoughts, and inherited traditions of those who are
to find the meaning.[9]

---

[8] Emphasizing the same thought at a dinner to Justice Harlan after
twenty-five years' service on the Supreme Bench, President Roosevelt said:
"For the judges of the Supreme Court of the land must be not only great
jurists, but they must be great constructive statesmen, and the truth of
what I say is illustrated by every study of American statesmanship, for
in not one serious study of American political life will it be possible to
omit the immense part played by the Supreme Court in the creation, not
merely the modification, of the great policies through and by means of
which the country has moved on to her present position."—37 *Am. Law
Rev.* (Jan.-Feb. 1903) 93.

[9] Dodd, W. F., "The Problem of State Constitutional Construction,"
20 *Col. Law Rev.* (June 1920) 636. Speaking of the judges, Justice Cardozo observes, "all their lives, forces which they do not recognize and

Judicial legislation, whether it operates in public or in private law, is imbued with certain characteristics which have been suggestively analyzed by Professor Dicey:

The courts or the judges, when acting as legislators, are, of course, influenced by the beliefs and feelings of their time, and are guided to a considerable extent by the dominant current of public opinion; Eldon and Kenyon belonged to the era of old Toryism as distinctly as Denman, Campbell, Erle and Bramwell belonged to the age of Benthamite liberalism. But whilst our tribunals, or the judges of whom they are composed, are swayed by the prevailing beliefs of a particular time, they are also guided by professional opinions and ways of thinking which are to a certain extent independent of and possibly opposed to the general tone of public opinion. The judges are the heads of the legal profession. They are advanced in life. They are for the most part persons of a conservative disposition. They are in no way dependent for their emoluments, dignity, or reputation upon the favor of the electors, or even of ministers who represent in the long run the wishes of the electorate. They are most likely to be biased by professional habits and feeling than by the popular sentiment of the hour. Hence, judicial legislation will often be marked by certain characteristics rarely found in acts of Parliament.[10]

Judicial legislation thus aims at the maintenance of the logic or the symmetry of the law and great care is exercised in order to secure consistency. It aims also at securing certainty rather than the development of law and tends toward the maintenance of a fixed legal system.

---

cannot name, have been tugging at them—inherited instincts, traditional beliefs, acquired convictions; and the resultant is an outlook on life, a conception of social needs, a sense in James's phrase of the 'total push and pressure of the cosmos', which, when reasons are nicely balanced, must determine where choice shall fall.''—Cardozo, *The Nature of the Judicial Process*, 12, 13.

[10] A. V. Dicey, *Lectures on the Relation between Law and Public Opinion in England during the Nineteenth Century* (London, 1914) 361, 362.

It frequently results also that ideas of expediency or policy accepted by the courts may differ considerably from the ideas which at a given time have acquired predominant influence among the general public.[11] The morality of courts may be higher than the morality of traders or of politicians, but it has, of course, often happened that the ideas entertained by the judges have fallen below the highest and most enlightened public opinion of a particular time.[12] As a general rule, judge-made law represents the conviction of an earlier age and is characterized by conservatism.[13]

That American law exhibits these characteristics is the opinion of authorities here and abroad.[14] Professor Lambert, of the University of Lyons, in a recent monograph expresses the opinion that the natural conservatism of lawyers and judges is peculiarly exemplified in the law of the United States where, under the prevailing doctrines of the construction of statutes and of judicial review of legislative acts, the courts have attempted to uphold the traditional doctrines of the common law and to support the individualistic conceptions of the eighteenth century.[15] Under the guise of the touchstones of reasonableness and expediency, American judges have defended the principles and standards of the past against the permeation of social and economic reforms.[16] "The

---

11 Dicey, *op. cit.*, 365.

12 *Ibid.*, 365.

13 *Ibid.*, 367.

14 See Roscoe Pound "Common Law Legislation," 21 *Harv. Law Rev.* (April 1908) 383; "Puritanism and the Common Law," 45 *Am. Law Rev.* (Nov.-Dec. 1911) 811; and "The Need of a Sociological Jurisprudence," 19 *Greenbag* (1907) 607.

15 "Le gouvernement des juges et la lutte contre la législation sociale aux États-Unis" (Paris, 1921) 53 ff.

16 *Ibid.*, 222 ff.

judicial control of the constitutionality of laws,'' he observes,

with its two complements, the construction of laws in the American manner and government by injunctions, is without doubt the most perfect instrument of social statics to which one could actually have recourse to curb the agitation of labor leaders and to hold the legislature in check from going too rapidly in the direction of economic radicalism.[17]

One need refer only to some typical labor cases to note the effect of personal opinions and ''the potency of mental prepossessions.''[18] When a majority of five judges held that the common law rules governing the assumption, respectively, by employer and employee, of the risk of employment and the consequences to flow therefrom were not by the Fourteenth Amendment placed beyond the reach of the state's power to alter them as rules of future conduct through legislation designed to promote the general welfare, four justices imbued with nineteenth-century concepts of legal and moral philosophy expressed the opinion that the judgment of the court is a menace to all rights and subjects them unreservedly to personal conceptions of public policy.[19] Likewise, when a majority of the court thought undisputed facts and indubitable inferences from them required the issuance of an injunction to prevent members of a labor union from attempting by peaceable means to gain a foothold in a mine run on a non-union basis, three members of the court thought the union members were acting clearly within their legal rights.[20] Again, when the Arizona civil code took away

[17] *Ibid.*, 224.

[18] Cf. Louis D. Brandeis ''The Living Law,'' 10 *Ill. Law Rev.* (Feb. 1916) 461.

[19] Cf. note on Arizona Copper Co. v. Hammer, 33 *Harv. Law Rev.* (1919–1920) 87.

[20] Hitchman Coal & Coke Co. v. Mitchell, 245 U. S. 229 (1917).

the remedy of injunction in certain controversies between employer and employees, Chief Justice Taft, speaking for the majority, contended that the Arizona law deprived an owner of a business of his property without due process of law. The Chief Justice fell back on such general phrases as "this is a government of laws and not of men" and "no man is above the law," to support the conclusion which, he thought, followed inevitably therefrom. But four justices believed that no person had a vested right in any rule of law, let alone such an exceptional and extreme remedy as the injunction. Justice Brandeis showed by a formidable array of citations that the injunction as a remedy was a recent development in its application to labor cases, that it was rarely used in other English-speaking countries, and that its use had been restricted in a number of states.[21] As these cases are read with all of their implications, one need not be reminded that the judges are primarily expressing their personal opinions upon contested issues of public policy. That the court had passed beyond the line where the measuring stick of the law normally applied, impressed Justice Holmes in his dissent when he remarked,

There is nothing that I more deprecate than the use of the Fourteenth Amendment beyond the absolute compulsion of its words to prevent the making of social experiments that an important part of the community desires, in the insulated chambers afforded by the several states, even though the experiments may seem futile or even noxious to me and to those whose judgment I most respect.[22]

It is customary, in such opinions, for the justices to insist that they have arrived at their conclusions by a process of deductive reasoning from apparently fixed

---

21 Truax v. Corrigan, 257 U. S. 312 (1921).
22 *Ibid.*, 312.

premises supposed to be established by prior cases. "The fact that on the last analysis the decision really turns upon notions of policy entertained more or less consciously or unconsciously by the members of the court is thus thrown into the background."[23] The extreme to which courts and judges will go in their effort to place checks in the path of labor legislation is indicated in the development of the judge-made concept "liberty of contract," which was conceived as a judicial device to protect the laborers from legislative onslaughts upon their natural and inalienable rights.[24]

An intense personal hostility against the policy of such legislation often leads the judges to seek in vague constitutional phrases some catchwords which would warrant the declaration of the lack of power for legislative regulation.[25] Thus due process of law, equal protection of the laws, obligation of contracts with the consequent protection to vested rights are phrases vague enough to permit the justices to bring under the cloak of law or perhaps more accurately of legal phraseology their well settled opinions of social and economic policy and thereby to create a test by which to destroy or uphold legislation according to the special standards of judicial wisdom and fairness.

---

[23] Walter W. Cook "Privileges of Labor Unions in the Struggle for Life," 17 *Yale Law Jour.* (April 1918) 779, 783; see *ibid.*, 800. "No man has seen more plainly that the Court was measuring the legislature's reasons by its own intellectual yardstick than has Justice Holmes; none more keenly perceived that the notations thereon marked those results of environment and education which many men seem to regard as the will of God or the decrees of fate."—Charles M. Hough, "Due Process of Law—Today," 32 *Harv. Law Rev.* (Jan. 1919) 232.

[24] Cf. Roscoe Pound "Liberty of Contract," 18 *Yale Law Jour.* (May 1909) 454.

[25] Adkins v. Children's Hospital, 261 U. S. 525 (1923), and especially dissenting opinions of Chief Justice Taft and Justice Holmes. Cf. Felix Frankfurter "Hours of Labor and Realism in Constitutional Law," 29 *Harv. Law Rev.* (Feb. 1916) 353.

If the judges in the interpretation and application of constitutional law are to act in an increasing degree in a semi-legislative capacity it becomes of paramount importance that some of the criteria of those holding political offices must to a greater degree than in the past be applied to them. More attention should be given to the personal, political, and economic affiliations of those selected for the federal judiciary, the constant scrutiny of public opinion should be directed upon such decisions as are of political or economic significance, and the manifold social and political ramifications of constitutional issues should be minutely and critically analyzed. Such an analysis involves the development of a new constitutional interpretation in which many factors now either neglected or scantily considered by constitutional commentators will receive more adequate consideration.

While in theory, then, we have often been led to believe that constitutional law has been developed solely through the application of the rules of formal logic in accordance with well established principles, in reality it has been to a considerable extent the result of human forces in which the personality of the judges, their education, associations, and individual views were of prime importance. The former of these two elements, legal logic, tradition and precedent, has received extended and adequate treatment at the hands of lawyers and political scientists; the latter, the element of free conception, in which individual views and personal notions have influenced and have frequently predetermined judicial decisions, has received scant attention.[26]

---

[26] In a discussion of "The Spirit of Our Judges," E. V. Abbott claims "we are overawed by the authority of their position; we let them do many things which they have no business to do; we do not sufficiently examine their decisions to note what they are doing; we are too lenient when we do criticise and we are content to leave them at all times in a

2. *Traditional statements in defense of judicial review of legislation—*

The traditional statements in support of the theory and practice of judicial review of legislative acts are either unsound in theory or they do not fit the facts when the modern practice of judicial review is carefully examined.

First, written constitutions of the American type require that the courts invalidate acts deemed contrary to the provisions of the fundamental law. That written constitutions with defined limitations on governmental powers do not inevitably require judicial review of legislative acts, is apparent since a majority of the countries of the world which have written constitutions do not allow their courts to exercise this extraordinary power.

Second, judicial review of legislative acts is an essential requirement in order to preserve the federal features of the American government. It is difficult to defend the claim that the federal courts have been the chief defenders of the federal features of the American system of government. Though the federal courts have in many instances upheld the powers of the states as against the authority of the federal government, it is a well-known fact that there has taken place an almost continuous encroachment on the powers of the states in behalf of the national government—a process of absorption of powers which in the main has received the approval of the federal Supreme Court. In short, as pointed out years ago by John Sharp Williams, the process of federal usurpation has

position of practically irresponsible power'':54 *Am. Law Rev.* (March-April 1920) 231, 240. ''If the judges continue,'' says Dean Lewis, ''to act as elder statesmen and to veto acts which shock their sense of justice and fairness, it becomes imperative that public criticism and control be more actively exercised.''—See *Proc.* of Acad. of Pol. Sci. (Jan. 1913) 3:45.

been about equally sanctioned by presidents, by congresses, and by the federal courts. At the same time that state powers have thus been limited and restricted along many lines the Supreme Court has by a process of judicial legislation construed a group of implied limitations restricting the powers of the states. The federal censorship over state legislation which Justice Miller feared might result from the Fourteenth Amendment is now an established feature of public law.

Third, judicial review of legislative acts is a necessary requirement in order to preserve individual liberties against the rule of the majority and to protect individuals and groups against invidious attacks by public officers or departments of the government. The courts have thus been conceived as a check designed to protect the people against themselves; to prevent hasty and ill-considered action; and to preserve a field of individual liberty beyond the pale of governmental interference. This feature of judicial review is most frequently emphasized as the one which more than any other justifies a judicial surveillance of legislative and executive acts. It is difficult here also to make out a good case favorable to the courts as the special protectors of the inalienable rights and liberties of individuals.

The illegal practices of government departments in the United States or what has been called "the lawless enforcement of the law" by courts, individual justices, and prosecutors during and since the recent war are a discouraging commentary on modern methods for the protection of individual rights. In the midst of great stress and excitement individual rights may receive scant protection regardless of written constitutions, courts with judicial review of legislative acts, and other protective agencies of government. The time has not come to evaluate the extent to which all of the departments of the government of the United States violated the rule of law during and since the war. Judging by the encroachments upon individual rights and privileges made indiscriminately there are times when there are few things the government may not do if public exigencies are regarded as requiring extreme action.[27] It is easier to show that the courts through the doctrine of judicial review of legislation have protected property and contract rights with greater persistence and regularity than they have preserved individual rights.

Fourth, judicial review of legislative acts results in the settlement of matters of constitutional interpretation in the dry, mechanical, and impartial atmosphere of a court instead of under the partisan turmoil of the political forum. Constitutional questions are thus conceived to be primarily legal and thus become subject especially to the quiet and orderly process of the judicial forum.

The contention that judicial review of legislative acts defers matters of constitutional interpretation to the impartial atmosphere of a court fails to take into account the fact that the settlement of many great constitutional issues which are political in character have involved the courts in political controversies. European countries usually have refused to adopt judicial review of legislative enactments because it is thought that courts are thereby necessarily involved in political conflicts and the evil effects of partisanship.

---

[27] ''Whenever pressure has reached a given intensity, on one pretext or another, courts have enforced or dispensed with constitutional limitations with quite as much facility as have legislatures, and for the same reasons. The only difference has been that the pressure which has operated most directly upon courts has not always been the pressure which has swayed legislatures, though sometimes both influences have combined.''—See, Brooks Adams, *Theory of Social Revolutions* (New York, 1914) Chap. II.

It is significant that the grounds which are most frequently advanced for the adoption and continuance of this practice as a feature of the American government are the main reasons given in other countries for rejecting the American plan. Moreover, the arguments favorable to the practice of review of legislation in the United States are usually stated in such form as to defend the authority wielded in the exercise of these powers a generation or more ago, whereas judicial review today is comparable in only a few minor respects with the practice before the Civil War.

The warnings of the great constitutional lawyer, James Bradley Thayer, however, may well cause us to ponder on the tendency to lean too heavily on the courts.

Great and, indeed, inestimable, as are the advantages in a popular government of this conservative influence,—the power of the judiciary to disregard unconstitutional legislation [he claimed], it should be remembered that the exercise of it, even when unavoidable, is always attended with a serious evil, namely the correction of legislative mistakes comes from the outside, and the people lose the political experience, and the moral education and stimulus that come from fighting the question out in an ordinary way, and correcting their own errors. If the decision in Munn v. Illinois, and in the "Granger Cases," twenty-five years ago, and in the "Legal Tender Cases," nearly thirty years ago, had been different; and the legislation there in question, thought by many to be unconstitutional and by many more to be ill advised, had been set aside, we should have been saved some trouble and some harm. But I venture to think that the good which came to the country and its people from the vigorous thinking that had to be done in the political debates that followed, from the infiltration through every part of the population of sound ideas and sentiments, from the rousing into activity of opposing elements, the enlargement of ideas, the strengthening of moral fibre, and the growth of political experience which came out of it all,—that all this far more than outweighed any evil which ever flowed from the refusal of the court to interfere with the work of the legislature.

The tendency of a common and easy resort to this great function, now lamentably too uncommon, is to dwarf the political capacity of the people, and to deaden its sense of moral responsibility. It is no light thing to do that.

What can be done? It is the courts that can do most to cure the evil; and the opportunity is a very great one. Let them resolutely adhere to first principles. Let them consider how narrow is the function which the constitutions have conferred on them,—the office merely of deciding litigated cases; how large, therefore, is the duty entrusted to others, and above all to the legislature. It is that body which is charged, primarily, with the duty of judging of the constitutionality of its work. The constitutions generally give them no authority to call upon a court for advice; they must decide for themselves, and the courts may never be able to say a word. Such a body, charged, in every State, with almost all the legislative power of the people, is entitled to the most entire and real respect; is entitled, as among all rationally permissible opinions as to what the Constitution allows, to its own choice. Courts, as has often been said, are not to think of the legislators, but of the legislature,—the great, continuous body itself, abstracted from all the transitory individuals who may happen to hold its power. It is this majestic representative of the people whose action is in question, a coordinate department of the government, charged with the greatest functions, and invested, in contemplation of law, with whatsoever wisdom, virtue, and knowledge the exercise of such functions requires.

To set aside the acts of such a body, representing in its own field, which is the highest of all, the ultimate sovereign, should be a solemn, unusual, and painful act. Something is wrong when it can be other than that. And if it be true that the holders of legislative power are careless or evil, yet the constitutional duty of the court remains wholly untouched; it cannot rightly undertake to protect the people, by attempting a function not its own. On the other hand, by adhering to its own place a court will help, as nothing else can, to fix the spot where responsibility rests, viz., on the careless and reckless legislators, and to bring down on that precise locality the thunderbolt of popular condemnation. The judiciary, today, in dealing with the acts of coordinate legislatures, owes to the country no greater or clearer duty than that of keeping its hands off these acts whenever it is possible to do it. That will powerfully help to bring the people and their representatives to a sense of their own responsibility.[28]

Under no system, he thinks, can the courts go far to save the people from ruin. We are much too apt to think of the judicial power of disregarding acts of the other departments as our only protection against oppression and ruin. But it is remarkable how small a part this played in any of the debates on the federal Constitution. The chief protections were a wide suffrage, short terms of office, a double legislative chamber, and the so-called executive veto.[29]

3. *Legal fictions in the application of judicial review of legislation—*

Sir Henry Maine in his well-known work on *Ancient Law* devoted a chapter to certain legal fictions which were characteristic of the early stages in the development of the common law. Legal fictions are defined as assumptions or postulates[30] which conceal or attempt to conceal

---

[28] *Thayer's Marshall*, 103, 110 and *Legal Essays* (Boston, 1908) 39–41.

[29] *Thayer's Marshall*, 64; *Legal Essays*, 11–12. For the weaknesses of Marshall's reasoning in the *Marbury Case*, see Thayer, *Essays*, 15.

[30] A postulate differs from a *law* and a *canon* as follows:

"(a) It requires the intervention of *a will*. There is no compulsion about adopting it; if it is not willed, it is no necessity of thought. If it is willed on the other hand, it can not only appear to be universal, but can maintain itself against an indefinite amount of hostile experience.

"(b) It thus seems to be in a way 'independent' of experience. Experience is allowed to confirm it but not to invalidate it, and it is none the worse, if events do not wholly conform to it, so long as they conform suffi-

the fact that a rule of law has undergone change. The fact is that, although the letter of the law remains the same, the law in its operation has been radically changed. The fiction is that the law remains as before, fixed and unchangeable. These fictions, it is claimed, perform the twofold office of transforming a system of law and at the same time concealing the transformation.

A notable instance of such a fiction was thus described: With respect to that portion of our legal system which is embodied in our law reports, we habitually employ a double language and entertain dual and inconsistent ideas. When a group of facts comes before an English court for adjudication the whole course of the discussion between the judge and the advocates assumes that no question can be raised which will call for the application of any principles but old ones, or of any distinctions but such as have long since been allowed. It is taken for granted that there is somewhere a rule of law which will cover the facts of the dispute before the court and that if such a rule has not been discovered, it is only because the necessary patience, knowledge, or acumen have not been applied to its detection. Yet the moment the judgment has been rendered and reported, unconsciously or unavowedly a new train of thought has resulted. It is at once admitted that the new decision has modified the law. The rules applicable have, it is assumed, become more elastic. In fact they have changed.

Such fictions, it is noted, are particularly congenial to the infancy of society, since they satisfy the desire for improvement and at the same time do not offend the superstitious aversion to change which is always present.

---

ciently not to impair its usefulness. Thus the mere discrepancy of experience does not refute a postulate. Hence it is often supposed to be 'self evident'."—F. C. S. Schiller, *Formal Logic; A Scientific and Social Problem* (London, 1912) 126.

To revile them as merely fraudulent, Sir Henry Maine thinks, is to betray ignorance of their peculiar office in the historical development of law, but on the other hand, he observes, there can be no doubt of the general truth that it is far from satisfactory to try to effect an "admittedly beneficial object by so rude a device as a legal fiction."

Just as the common law in theory was held to provide in its ancient and sometimes archaic principles, without change or modification, for every controversy arising out of the relations of men in society, so one may find in the practice of our federal and state courts in the interpretation of constitutions, the prevalence of fictions similar in nature to the legal fictions as defined by Sir Henry Maine.

The practice by which courts of justice have regularly exercised the high function of declaring legislative acts void in the United States is based on the theory that the courts interpret and uphold constitutions in which the will of the people was originally formulated. The power thus asserted by courts of justice was considered a prime necessity in order to enact the popular will into law. The literature of the formative period of the American government is pervaded with the idea that the rule of the people was established by virtue of written constitutions. Regardless of the fact that the judiciary, an appointive body, and one quite remotely responsible to the people, was charged with the special function of declaring the meaning of the written instrument, it was frequently asserted that by this special means the rule of the people was effectively established.[31] According to this fiction,

---

[31] A common type of misrepresentation is indicated by the claim that the issue relating to judicial review of legislation is not an issue as between legislatures and courts but between legislatures and the people. See Frederick Green, "The Judicial Censorship of Legislation," 47 *Am. Law Rev.* (Jan.-Feb. 1913) 90, 91.

even when federal and state constitutions were adopted with little or no popular sanction and when they could be amended with the greatest difficulty, the courts rendered decisions binding all departments and assured the public that it was the rule and sovereignty of the people that prevailed.[32]

The claim is that the people have determined by constitutional enactment the powers, privileges, and limits of the government under which they desire to live. The constitution is then to be regarded as a written document whose terms and principles have a meaning which is fixed and immutable save as modified or revised through the process of amendment prescribed in the instrument itself.

It was to be one of the prime functions of the judicial department to preserve the mandate of the people, unaltered and inviolate. In the exercise of the function of guardianship for the people the courts regarded it as their duty to refuse to give effect to laws which in their judgment contravened the fundamental laws. Thus legislatures and executive officers occasionally had to submit to the declaration of justices that certain acts of theirs were void and could not be upheld in the determination of a suit between private parties. In the seventy-eighth number of *The Federalist,* Hamilton maintained that, "where the will of the legislature declared in its statutes, stands in opposition to that of the people, declared in the Constitution, the judges ought to be governed by the latter rather than by the former. They ought to regulate their decisions by the fundamental laws, rather than by those which are not fundamental."

---

[32] "Our people have never parted with their sovereignty, and our courts are here to guard it."—Frederick J. Stimson, *The American Constitution as it Protects Private Rights* (Scribner's, 1923) 26.

This doctrine was reaffirmed by Chief Justice Marshall in the *Marbury Case* when it was held that the will of the people in the Constitution must be regarded as superior to the acts of the legislature by courts of justice whose business it is to determine what the law is. It was announced as a principle, ''supposed to be essential to all written constitutions,'' that a law repugnant to the Constitution is void, and that it is the duty of justices to so declare it. Since the logic and directive influence of Alexander Hamilton, John Marshall, and their associates accorded so well with the opinion of an influential class of political leaders who were zealously upholding the rights of property and the privileges of private individuals, it was established as a settled practice in the United States that courts of justice were intended to be the final interpreters of the will of the people as expressed in written constitutions.[33] Consequently legislative acts held by judges to be contrary to these constitutions were to be rendered null and void in the process of judicial decisions. By this device, it was constantly claimed, written constitutions might be preserved unaltered and the sovereignty of the people might be maintained. One of the chief theories in the establishment of the supremacy of the judiciary in the United States was formulated into a constitutional dogma.

During the years when this doctrine was first announced there were many prominent citizens who regarded such an assumption of power by the courts of justice as ''inconsistent with the nature and genius of

---

[33] ''The courts place the act by the side of the Constitution with the purpose and the desire to uphold it if it can be reasonably done, but, under the obligation, if there is an irreconcilable conflict, to sustain the will of the people expressed in the Constitution, and not the will of the legislators who are but the agents of the people.''—Justice Allen in State v. Knight, 169 N. C. 333, 352 (1915).

our government and threatening to the liberties of the people.'' The theory was denounced as an adroit scheme to place our government in the hands of a minority, to give property holders undue advantages, and to take the final voice on governmental affairs out of the hands of the people. Where such power had been exercised by courts it was frequently criticized as a usurpation of authority. In 1815 the legislature of Georgia filed a protest against a decision of the court of appeals of the state as follows: ''the extraordinary power of determining upon the constitutionality of acts of the state legislature, if yielded by the general assembly whilst it is not given by the constitution or the law of the state, would be an abandonment of the dearest rights and liberties of the people, which we, their representatives, are bound to guard and protect inviolate.'' There were many at the time who preferred to reserve unto themselves the right to determine what they wanted in government rather than to dispose of this authority to a select body of judges over whose decisions it was very difficult to exercise any control.

Jefferson who became an uncompromising opponent of the theory which accorded to the judiciary the right to refuse to enforce legislative acts, thought the justices were inclined to interpret the provisions of constitutions to suit their own individual opinions on governmental policy and expediency. He believed the federal Constitution was becoming a thing of wax in the hands of the judiciary, which the justices were shaping according to their own peculiar notions. It appeared inevitable to him that the judiciary would express opinions on matters of government under the cloak of interpreting the voice of the people as enacted in constitutions. Then too he recognized that if Hamilton's doctrine of implied powers as belonging to the federal government was adopted by the judiciary and sanctioned by the nation there would result a wide latitude for interpretation in the courts. Jefferson and his associates, who were not inclined to distrust popular government and who thought that on all important issues the popular will ought as a rule to prevail, saw in this assumption of the courts what they regarded as a serious danger. They insisted that this rule gave to one department, the judiciary, the right to prescribe rules for the government of the other departments. Moreover it gave to an appointive body, over which the people had little or no control, the right to place a relatively final interpretation on the Constitution. It seemed that here was a chance for the courts under the guise of interpreting the will of the people to thwart and interfere effectively with the real popular will. Jefferson maintained that conflicts between the departments involving the ultimate interpretation of the Constitution ought to be settled by an appeal to the people. The theory that the courts were merely giving effect to the will of the people as enacted in constitutions in refusing to enforce legislative acts was in the judgment of many Democrats a mere subterfuge to enforce federal and aristocratic doctrines in order to perpetuate the wishes of the property-holding and commercial classes.

Justice Gibson of Pennsylvania thought it an audacious claim to assert that the deliberate and well-matured judgment of one of the regularly constituted departments of government, expressed in the form of acts passed under a strict observance of the principles of the Constitution, should be rejected as *ipso facto* void. He regarded the basis of every argument in favor of the right of the judiciary as an assumption of the whole ground in dispute. In his judgment the interpretation of constitutions belonged primarily to the law-making departments with the reserve power in the people to correct any abuses which were not in accord with the popular will. The judges, it was held, were far from infallible and on account of the fact that judicial errors could be corrected only by constitutional amendments the prevailing practice was regarded as too cumbrous to be feasible. There were frequent protests against individual decisions and occasional criticisms of the general doctrine of judicial resistance to legislative acts largely because it was believed that the courts were assuming authority not granted, that they were enforcing interpretations not warranted by the language of the fundamental laws, and that they were actually exercising supreme or sovereign powers.

It was suggested from the beginning of the exercise of judicial review that the practice of final interpretation of constitutions by courts of justice was an assumption not definitely sanctioned in either constitution or statute and that the guardians of fundamental laws supposed to be immutable were in a position to exercise a remarkable influence in discovering what the fundamental law had to say regarding specific problems and important political controversies. Recently charges have been accumulating that the guardians of the Constitution are inclined to find new and heretofore unknown meanings in the terms of the fundamental law. The claim is made that justices attempt to impress upon the laws of the country their own views of social and industrial policies. Even the judges themselves in numerous dissenting opinions claim that there are not infrequent evidences of an intention to legislate by means of judicial decisions in order to change the meaning of the law so as to accord with

individual opinions regarding social policy. While interpreting constitutions intended, at least in theory, to
speak with the same voice, the justices of our courts have,
it appears, like the priests of the Delphic oracle in Greece,
impressed upon the laws their own personal and political
views. The result is that certainty has sometimes given
way to hesitation and definiteness of law to vague and
ill-defined opinions which require the frequent assistance
of the interpreters.

Yet justices are wont to assert that the federal Constitution is a written instrument, and as such its meaning
does not alter. They say: that which it meant when
adopted it means now; as long as it continues to exist
in its present form, it speaks not only in the same words,
but with the same meaning and intent with which it spoke
when it came from the hands of its framers.

The theory is that constitutions mean the same yes-
terday, today, and forever and that the courts of justice
have the plain and humble duty of declaring the one and
original meaning to be found therein. The fact is that
the fundamental laws have been modified in meaning and
application to accord with the marvelous changes in the
developments of more than a century. The courts have
regularly performed this function, all the while disclaim-
ing any right or authority to make changes. The fact is
that constitutions change in meaning from time to time.
The fiction is that they are unchangeable, except by the
process of amendment. Under the guise of this fiction the
courts have progressively modified our fundamental law
and have attempted to bring it into harmony with the
conditions of modern society.

Another doctrine of American constitutional law has
been scarcely less significant than the theory that the
courts declare the voice of the people as enacted in consti-

tutions. This doctrine is: that although courts constantly declare laws void and thereby refuse to give them effect in suits between private parties they exercise no control over the legislature. In the first argument favoring judicial supremacy Hamilton insisted that the right to declare acts void as in conflict with the Constitution did not mean a superiority of the judicial over the legislative authority. There was, Hamilton claimed, in an issue before the judiciary involving the validity of legislation, merely a conflict between two laws—the one fundamental, the other derivative. The courts only decided which law applied and if it was the Constitution, the statute had to give way. When attention was called to the fact that the authority of the Supreme Court with such a prerogative would be superior to that of the legislature and that "the errors and usurpations of the Supreme Court of the United States will be uncontrollable and remediless," Hamilton replied that such an opinion was made up altogether of false reasoning upon misconceived facts. Chief Justice Marshall in the *Marbury Case* reiterated the doctrine of Hamilton and argued, first, that constitutions were intended to be superior to ordinary legislative acts, and, second, that courts of justice in private controversies between individuals were obliged to determine which law applied, the Constitution or the statute. No intimation was given that this was the exercise of a superior authority determining the competence of an inferior. Marshall seemed to suggest that the court in a kind of automatic manner without taking any real part in the contest determined which should prevail, a legislative act or the Constitution. Much emphasis was placed upon the opinion that the judiciary was a coordinate branch of the government and as such must be permitted to exercise this peculiar authority. The doctrine of Hamilton and

Marshall accorded with the views of a majority of the bench and bar of their time and was duly incorporated in the system of public law in the United States.[34]

Not only was it asserted that the courts exercise no control over legislatures in declaring their acts void but also that they were merely performing a judicial function. Lord Bryce expressed the prevailing opinion of more than a century, when he wrote: "It is therefore no mere technicality to point out, that the American judges do not, as Europeans are apt to say, control the legislature, but simply interpret the law. . . . . The will that prevails is the will of the people expressed in the Constitution which they had enacted."[35] This doctrine has been so thoroughly impressed upon our political thought that a noted foreign writer on law found that "although it is natural to say the Supreme Court pronounces acts of Congress invalid, but in fact this is not so. The court never pronounces any opinion whatever upon an act of Congress." The authority of the court, it is held, can be exercised only in the discharge of the judicial function of hearing and deciding causes in controversies between private parties.[36] The courts of the United States, it was continuously asserted, do not enter into a conflict with the legislature, they merely secure to each kind of law its due authority. The courts do not even preside over a conflict, "for the relative strength of each kind of law has been settled already. All the court does is to

---

[34] The following statement by Lord Bryce is typical of those commonly made by bench and bar in America: "It is therefore obvious that the question, whether a congressional statute offends against the Constitution, must be determined by the courts, not merely because it is a question of legal construction, but because there is nobody else to determine it. Congress cannot do so, because Congress is a party interested. . . . . The President cannot, because he is not a lawyer and he also may be personally interested."—*The American Commonwealth*, 1:247.

[35] *Ibid.*, 1:253.

[36] A. V. Dicey, *The Law of the Constitution*, 159, 160.

declare that a conflict exists between two laws of different degrees of authority. Then the question is at an end, for the weaker law is extinct.''[37] Courts do not invalidate statutes, they merely pronounce them void because contrary to over-ruling law.[38] Consequently it is urged that the courts exercise no control over legislation; they merely interpret constitutions.[39]

It is astonishing how long this fiction continues as a dogma of lawyers, even after its errors and misrepresentations have been repeatedly exposed.[40] Foreign as well as American commentators, although recognizing that the rule is neither desirable nor possible in the governments of other countries, whether federal or centralized, nevertheless pay deference to the traditional view that in the nature of the case the courts of the United States cannot do otherwise than declare acts of the legislature invalid.

In most countries the power wielded by the American courts is regarded as a political power and, as a consequence, is denied to their judiciaries.[41] Bench and bar, as well as the American public generally, have stoutly maintained that the courts were simply and solely exercising judicial power despite the fact that political and

---

[37] Bryce, *op. cit.*, 249.

[38] Francis Lieber, *Civil Liberty and Self-Government* (New York, 1859) 164.

[39] ''August as are the functions of the Court, surely they do not go one step beyond the administration of justice to individual litigants.''— John W. Davis, ''Present Day Problems,'' Am. Bar Assoc. *Jour.* (Sept. 1923).

[40] Cf. James B. Thayer, ''The Origin and Scope of the American Doctrine of Constitutional Law,'' 7 *Harv. Law Rev.* (Oct. 1893) 130, where it is noted that ''so far as the grounds for this remarkable power are found in the mere fact of a constitution being in writing or in judges being sworn to support it, they are quite inadequate.''

[41] At an early day De Tocqueville noted that ''the political powers which the Americans have intrusted to their courts of justice are immense.''— *Democracy in America*, 1:128.

social policies of great import were determined by the judiciary. Calling a power judicial does not change its nature, and the fiction that the courts exercise only judicial power in the United States no longer passes unchallenged as it did for scores of years.

That the exercise of this authority by the courts virtually placed them in a position superior to the legislature was recognized at an early day. A committee in New York in 1784 condemned a decree of the Mayor's court by which a state statute had been partly annulled, as an absurd attempt to control the supreme legislative power of the state. The design of the courts of justice, the committee thought, was to declare laws not to alter them, "whenever they depart from this design of their institution, they confound legislative and judicial powers." When a similar decision was given by the court in North Carolina, Richard Spaight, a prominent member of the bar, thought that "the state instead of being governed by the representatives in the general assembly was subject to the will of three individuals who united in their own persons the legislative and judiciary powers, which no monarch in Europe enjoys."

On this issue Jefferson expressed alarm. He thought that according to this theory the Constitution had not established three departments, coordinate and independent, but that it had given to one department the right to prescribe rules for the government of the others. This power in the hands of judges he regarded the more dangerous because judges were as a rule in office for life and were not responsible to the people through the elective control. Jefferson believed that such a doctrine would place our government "under the despotism of an oligarchy." He could conceive of no other reliable rule than to have the judges confine themselves strictly to judicial duties, leaving an issue between departments to be determined by a popular mandate. No one claimed, Chief Justice Gibson remarked, that the judiciary is of superior rank to the other departments. He could not see, however, how the power which gave law to the others could be of no higher rank than the one which was obliged to submit. The business of the judiciary, he thought, was to interpret and administer the laws, not to scan the authority of the lawgiver.

As it now appears the warnings of the opponents of judicial review have been more than realized in the powers exercised by the judiciary. Today the courts are commonly recognized as superior to the other departments of government and they take a decisive part in the legislative progress. They openly direct governmental activity by determining the trend of legislation affecting many phases of modern society. They have in fact come to treat as unconstitutional practically all legislation which they deem unwise. It has also long since been discovered by the advocates for social and political reforms along many lines, strongly supported by an active public sentiment voicing the wishes of a majority of the electorate, that the greatest barrier in the way of improvement of social and economic conditions is met with in the judiciary where lawyers and justices conservatively inclined insist on upholding the existing order and thereby defeating the popular will. It is openly announced that it is part of the judicial duty to check measures socialistic in intent or otherwise not in accord with progress as judicially understood.

The theory, however, remains the same. In the language repeated only a little less freqently than formerly, the courts merely interpret constitutions which embody the will of the people. The facts are that they mold constitutions, through judicial decisions, so as to enact into law their own views of political policy and expediency; that the other departments are constantly bound by constitutions and laws as defined and modified by the courts; and that no legislative act can be effectively enforced when not in accord with judicial opinions. The fiction is that the judiciary is one of the three departments of government, each exercising independent authority under constitutional limits and that no control is exercised over the authority of the legislature. The theory is that the courts exercise only judicial power. The fact is that they exercise in the course of their manifold functions every form of governmental power, legislative, executive, administrative, and judicial. The theory is that "every possible presumption is in favor of a statute, and this continues until the contrary is shown beyond a rational doubt." In practice statutes have merely the form of law until judicial approval is given.

The theory of the separation of powers which, it is claimed, predicates a basis for judicial review of legislation, if practically applied would make such review impossible. Friends of judicial review interpret the separation of power principle as placing limits on the legislative and executive departments but practically none on the courts.[42] To accept the doctrine of judicial review of legislation is tantamount to a recognition that the departments are no longer coordinate.[43] In France and

---

[42] See Jackson H. Ralston, "Judicial Control over Legislatures as to Constitutional Questions," 54 *Am. Law Rev.* (Jan.-Feb. 1920) 12 ff.

[43] "To allow judges, among other powers, to determine the constitutionality of laws and the legality of administrative acts would destroy the equilibrium of the three departments of the government and would place the other departments under the tutelage of the justices. Not only does

other European countries where Montesquieu's theory of the separation of powers was also applied it was taken for granted that this theory prevented the courts from reviewing legislation, for such authority necessarily involved legislative powers and placed political functions on the judges.

It is usually taken for granted that in a controversy between two private parties the validity of an act of the legislature may be made an issue and a judgment on this issue rendered by the court. But the real question whether in an ordinary suit the acts of two of the main departments of the government, the legislature and the executive, may be drawn into the controversy and questioned by a coordinate branch of the same government seldom received any consideration. In many countries it is insistently asserted that no such issue as the validity of a legislative act can be raised before the ordinary courts in the course of the usual controversies that arise for determination. To take for granted such a matter of grave controversy is simply an example of the type of reasoning to which Justice Gibson referred when he claimed the friends of judicial review assumed the whole ground under dispute at the beginning of their arguments.

Another assumption that has constantly been accepted in the reasoning on judicial review of legislation is that that only is law in the real sense which the courts accept and apply as such. Hence a written constitution could only be law if its provisions were ultimately interpreted and applied by the courts.[44] Such an assumption has

such a plan make the judges masters of the other departments but it also encourages encroachments on the legislative and executive functions by the courts.''—Jean Cruet, *Étude juridique de l'arbitraire gouvernmental et administratif* (Paris, 1906) 452 ff.

[44] Herbert Pope, ''The Fundamental Law and the Power of the Courts,'' 27 *Harv. Law Rev.* (Nov. 1913) 45.

some warrant in the claim that in common law jurisdictions what the courts interpret and apply as such is law. On the other hand it fails to take into account the political character of much of public law and the inherent difficulty of treating political matters in the same category as ordinary private civil affairs.

It is singular how the assumption has been acquiesced in that, when certain judges consider a law is void, it must necessarily be regarded as void by everybody concerned. There are often great differences of opinion among legislators, executives, and judges as to what constitutional provisions mean. Frequent dissenting opinions by justices in the courts declaring acts void, a contrary judgment by justices in other courts, and a change in viewpoint by subsequent judges examining the same law, might, one would think, cast a good deal of doubt upon judicial judgments on the validity of legislation. The treatment of compulsory minimum wage legislation illustrates how a few justices may place an almost insuperable barrier in the way of carrying out a program for which there is a very decided favorable public sentiment.[45]

---

[45] Prior to the unfavorable decision of the Supreme Court (by a 5 to 3 vote, Justice Brandeis not participating) in the *Adkins Case* twenty-nine state judges supporting the judgments of state legislatures thought a compulsory minimum wage act was not a violation of due process of law and only four judges held a contrary opinion. Analyzing the personal attitude and opinions of the justices of the Supreme Court, Professor Powell claims that had the minimum wage law come before the Court a few years earlier it would have been declared valid. ''Suffice it to say that minimum-wage legislation is now unconstitutional,'' he observes, ''not because the Constitution makes it so, not because its economic results or its economic propensities would move a majority of judges to think it so, but because it chanced not to come before a particular Supreme Court bench which could not muster a majority against it and chanced to be presented at the succeeding term when the requisite, but no more than requisite, majority was sitting. In the words of the poet, it was not the Constitution but a measureless malfeasance which obscurely willed it thus—the malfeasance of chance and of the calendar.''—''The Judiciality of Minimum Wage Legislation,'' 37 *Harv. Law Rev.* (March 1924) 545.

Aristotle called a judge "living justice," a phrase which has been translated by an Italian jurist into *"l'aequitas cerebrina,"* with respect to the process of judicial law-making. A well-known legal authority finds at work in American constitutional law the process *"l'aequitas cerebrina."* Due process of law, he concludes:

is what the Supreme Court says it is. Most of the rest of the Constitution is not far different. What Marshall said of its minor ingredients applies in many instances to major ingredients as well. The decisions and opinions here reviewed show that in deducing these ingredients the Supreme Court seldom finds its judgment greatly restricted by the language of the instrument which is our formal fundamental law."[46]

These fictions or assumptions have been recognized and accepted so long that bench and bar have come to regard them as indispensable to a written constitution.[47] Chief Justice Marshall insisted that they must be considered as necessary to a fundamental law which is written and this opinion has regularly been quoted with approval even after scores of written constitutions have been adopted in nations which have refused to accept the doctrine of judicial supremacy. Yet defenders of the American doctrine of judicial supremacy continue to repeat the opinion of Marshall in the face of apparent facts to the contrary. When an opinion suits the occasion and answers a useful purpose it seems to make little difference whether

---

[46] Thomas Reed Powell, ''The Supreme Court and the Constitution,'' 35 *Pol. Sci. Quart.* (Sept. 1920) 439.

[47] ''Spurious interpretation'' as Dean Pound calls the procedure—a process of putting something into a legal text and later drawing it out with a seeming air of discovery. It is essentially a legislative process made necessary in formative periods by the paucity of principles, feebleness of legislation, and rigidity of rules characteristic of archaic law. It is a form of fiction or ''juristic chemistry'' which has prospered in American constitutional interpretation.—''Spurious Interpretation,'' 7 *Col. Law Rev.* (June 1907) 379, 382.

facts controvert it. The opinion because it is acceptable continues to sway the minds of men regardless of the potency and significance of contrary evidence.[48]

It rarely happened that the apparent fact of government by the judiciary in the United States was openly and avowedly expressed. To Professor Burgess we are indebted for a forceful statement of the philosophy underlying the American doctrine and of the postulates which have prevailed in American political thought. Professor Burgess says:

It is then the consciousness of the American people that law must rest upon justice and reason, that the constitution is a more ultimate formulation of the fundamental principles of justice and reason than mere legislative acts, and that the judiciary is a better interpreter of those fundamental principles than the legislature, it is this consciousness which has given such authority to the interpretation of the Constitution by the Supreme Court. . . . . I do not hesitate to call the governmental system of the United States the aristocracy of the robe; and I do not hesitate to pronounce this the truest aristocracy for the purposes of government which the world has yet produced.[49]

What may be termed government by the judiciary, the aristocracy of the robe, or the supremacy of the judiciary, is unquestionably the most significant principle of the politics and public law of the United States.

---

[48] "Underlying all variant systems of thought in a given epoch are always certain fundamental assumptions which are unconsciously presupposed."—W. W. Cook, "Scientific Method and the Law," 13 Am. Bar Assoc. *Jour.* (June 1927) 303. "It may seem incredible," says Professor Cook, "but it is still possible for eminent members of the bar to assert that all a court does in deciding doubtful cases is to deduce conclusions from fixed premises, the law; or what comes to the same thing to assert that all the Supreme Court of the United States does in holding a statute of Congress unconstitutional is to apply by logic a preexisting rule found in the Constitution."—*Ibid.*, 307.

[49] Burgess, *op. cit.*, 365.

Thus our constitutional history furnishes instances of the same kind of fictions which Sir Henry Maine found in the development of the common law. A well matured scheme of government has continued to meet every emergency and solve every difficulty with few substantial changes. In theory we are living under the federal Constitution as it came from the hands of its framers in 1787. All our problems have been solved by the simple application of principles long since settled. The Constitution means the same that it meant when it was adopted in 1787. The Supreme Court sits as the interpreter of the Constitution, as an augur of the voice of the people who instituted our governmental system more than one hundred years ago.[50]

In practice the Constitution has been profoundly changed with only occasional recourse to the difficult process of amendment. Some provisions have become obsolete. Others have been admittedly so changed by interpretation that the obvious meaning has been practically lost in a complex system of decisions each in turn modifying the original rule. A remarkably complete and well developed system of law has been built upon a few general phrases in the Constitution. Our constitutional law has been progressively developed while the process has been concealed beneath language that gave little indication of the actual changes which were being made.

Generations of American statesmen, publicists, and lawyers have accepted these doctrines that the courts in interpreting and defending constitutions as against legislative acts were upholding the will of the people, and

---

[50] ''The Court does not claim nor does it possess a substantive power of holding acts of Congress unconstitutional. The exercise of such power is simply incidental to exercise of general judicial power conferred upon it by the Constitution.''—Charles Warren, *Congress, the Constitution and the Courts* (Boston, 1925) 62, 63. Mr. Warren repeats the fictions involved in this reasoning seemingly unaware that they are fictions.

that, in the exercise of such power the judiciary was merely an independent, coordinate department of the government, which exercised no control over legislation. The assertion is continuously repeated that these doctrines are ''a necessary and inevitable incident of our form of government, and of our written constitutions, limiting and controlling the exercise of the powers of government by public officials.'' How these opinions secured such a firm hold upon the American mind and remained almost undisputed for so long a time is one of the problems of legal history. The development of these fictions as primary principles of constitutional interpretation in America is new proof of the fact that ideas which in the beginning have a very slight basis in reality may continue to exercise a profound influence long after the conditions which produced the ideas have disappeared.

It is necessary to consider today the features of the American constitution and of its growth which, as Lord Birkenhead suggests, were the result of the ''contemporary political atmosphere'' and which if the Fathers had had greater vision would probably have been changed.[51] To him it is a question for the future to determine whether the barriers which the framers of American constitutions placed upon the complete freedom of legislative assemblies will prove equal to the emergencies as they arise and will be as adaptable to the stress and strain of political exigencies as the more flexible and more democratic arrangements of the British Constitution. ''Your constitution,'' he remarked,

is expressed and defined in documents which can be pronounced upon by the Supreme Court. In this sense your judges are the masters of your executive. Your constitution is a cast iron docu-

---

[51] Earl of Birkenhead, ''Development of the British Constitution in the last fifty years,'' 9 Am. Bar Assoc. *Jour.* (Sept. 1923) 578.

ment. It falls to be construed by the Supreme Court with the same sense of easy and admitted mastery as any ordinary contract. This circumstance provides a breakwater of enormous value against ill-considered and revolutionary change.

On the other hand so far as England is concerned, thinks Lord Birkenhead,

the genius of the Anglo-Saxon people has again, rightly or wrongly, refused to shackle in the slightest degree the constitutional competence of later generations . . . . any law of Great Britain can be altered by any Parliament and no court may challenge the constitutional force of an act of Parliament. It is on the whole premature to decide whether you or we have been right.[52]

In the eighteenth century and early nineteenth century the right to invalidate acts was regarded as an indispensable axiom of public law. With the great political controversies engendered by the antagonism between Hamilton and Jefferson, two views of government were succinctly outlined which made this doctrine one of the grounds of difference. According to one view, which Hamilton, Marshall, and Webster championed, and which for the time being prevailed in the development of state and national governments, democratic government required specific checks and balances to protect property rights and to guard the interests of minorities. The champions of this view, who regarded popular government with considerable alarm, uniformly sustained the courts in the exercise of power to declare laws invalid.

According to the other view, advanced by a few of the patriots of 1776, championed particularly by Jefferson after the federal courts were safely launched in the hands of his bitter opponents—the Federalists—and sanctioned on several occasions by Jackson and Lincoln,

---

[52] *Ibid.*, 579.

ultimate popular rule must prevail on all great matters of government, and judicial decisions cannot irrevocably bind the people. Recent advocates of this view regard the check of a fundamental law guarded and protected by the judicial department as a barrier in the path of popular rule. When constitutions are so difficult of amendment that this barrier prevents important measures of legislation desired by a great portion of the people, it is claimed that this power of the courts is essentially out of harmony with modern democratic notions and that unless constitutions can be changed more readily so as to permit desired legislation the doctrine of judicial supremacy must be abandoned.

The philosophy of those who favor the present system of reviewing legislation in the United States along with its assumptions and postulates and with its obvious inconsistencies, embodies a marked phase of fear psychology. Ruin, chaos, and destruction, they think, would inevitably result from any attempts to place the courts of the United States in their normal position of deciding controversies in accordance with predetermined rules, principles and precedents. Legislatures and executives would at once set about to take away the liberties of the people and an uncontrolled despotism would result. This form of argument has an ancient heritage and is as inconclusive as it is unfounded. Of course legislatures and executives have at times abused their powers but so have courts. Where individual rights are most seriously infringed the courts usually join with the other departments in enforcing these infringements. What is needed as an offset to this fear psychology is a generous spirit of trust in the people. Not that the voice of the people is the voice of God or that it is always reliable and invariably inures to the public welfare, but that in the long run the voice of the people is more to be relied upon than that of some self-appointed guardians whose chief claim to eminence is an arrogant confidence that they are endowed with a political acumen not vouchsafed to ordinary human beings.

Despite a tendency to discredit legislative chambers, in most countries there is a rather implicit confidence in legislative bodies as representing the opinions and ideas of the people. Hence when legislative acts come before the courts every presumption is in favor of the policy and validity of the enactment. Courts will not presume to question the force of such acts unless an express authority to do so is conferred upon them and then only when the clear language of the fundamental law leaves no other alternative. In the United States the founders of governments distrusted the people and their representative bodies, the legislatures. They thought liberty and property would be safer in the hands of appointed judges. Despite progressive steps in the direction of popular government and democracy, this distrust of American legislatures has become more marked and the determination of political matters has been to an even greater degree, entrusted to judges. Today, at a time when most governments are based on a belief in and a trust of representative bodies, American governments are essentially characterized by a distrust of legislative chambers and a confidence in judges as ultimate political arbiters.[53]

---

[53] "I know of no safe depository of the ultimate powers of the society but the people themselves; and if we think them not enlightened enough to exercise control with a wholesome discretion, the remedy is not to take it from them, but to inform their discretion by education. This is the true corrective of abuses of constitutional power."—Thomas Jefferson to William Charles Jarvis, September 28, 1820. "The people are the rightful masters of both Congress and the courts—not to overthrow the Constitution, but to overthrow the men who pervert it."—Abraham Lincoln in Debate with Douglas, 1854.

There was nothing inexorable about many of the limitations which the courts, and through their decisions the public, have come to regard as the very essence of written constitutions. By their own decisions and opinions the justices indicated in many cases that their conclusions might as well have been against the establishment of such limitations and favorable to legislative powers by giving to the language of constitutions their plain and obvious construction instead of reading into them a considerable portion of the philosophy and principles of limited government. As the justices have in large measure taken upon themselves the function of judicial censorship of legislative acts, they also hold in their hands the most effective and satisfactory remedy. Following the time-honored traditions as to the functions of judges and the practice of courts generally throughout the world, judicial review of legislative acts might be confined to the normal function of defining and applying the express requirements of written constitutions, concerning which few serious controversies arise, without any necessity for radical changes in existing laws or drastic curtailment of judicial authority relative to the review of legislative enactments.

APPENDIX I

Acts of Congress Invalidated by the Supreme Court of the United States

Congress has passed only a small number of statutes which the Supreme Court has seen fit to declare void. Few of these were on matters which were controversial and in less than a dozen cases was the issue of such importance as to arouse serious public discussion. The instances in which acts were held void were as a rule moot cases, as *Marbury v. Madison,* or on trivial matters which if necessary could easily be obviated by Congress, or on matters on which a sober second thought of Congress would have brought a repeal, as has happened in many instances not dealt with by the judiciary. By the most favorable interpretation about ten cases are usually listed in which individual rights were protected by checking Congressional powers. But on close analysis several of these border on the kind of interpretation which Justice Holmes once remarked is designed to help criminals to escape just punishment; or, by a meticulous or broad interpretation of certain provisions of the bill of rights, these cases have made it extremely difficult to secure the information necessary to prevent fraud and to enforce criminal penalties under federal laws. Other cases included in this list can scarcely be regarded as rendering protection to individual rights without a rather strained interpretation.

On the other hand, the exercise of this authority has in several instances involved the courts in the politics and partisanship of the time and has occasioned severe criticisms or condemnations of the judiciary.

The list that follows is confined to cases in which the validity of an act of Congress was directly in issue and not merely incidentally considered. Cases are not included in which the act was upheld but its application restricted by the Court. No effort has been made to include the decisions of lower federal courts holding acts of Congress invalid, though in some instances such decisions have in effect invalidated congressional enactments.[1]

1. *Hayburn's Case*, 1792,[2] *Chandler v. The Secretary of War*, 1794,[3] and *United States v. Todd*, 1794.[4]

Congress provided that the federal justices of the circuit courts should pass upon applications for pensions by disabled soldiers and should submit their opinions on the applications in writing to the Secretary of War. By section 4 of this act the Secretary of War was authorized, if he suspected imposition or mistake, to withhold the name of the applicant from the pension list, and to report his decision to Congress. 1 *Stat.* 243, 1792.[5]

The justices refused to carry out the provisions of this act as justices, but all except Justice Wilson agreed to act as commissioners outside of court. The justices of the Pennsylvania circuit declined to act on a petition for a pension because in their judgment the act of Congress was invalid. Though applications for relief were presented to the Supreme Court by Hayburn, Chandler and Todd the court did not pass on the issue of the constitutionality of the act, since Congress in the meantime repealed sections 2 to 4 of the previous law and authorized the district judges to pass on the applications and transmit them to the Secretary of War by whom they were to be referred to Congress. 1 *Stat.* 324, 1793.

Though the case of *United States v. Todd* is frequently listed as the first case in which an act of Congress was held void, it is evident that the issue was never clearly presented or passed upon by the Supreme Court.[6]

2. *Marbury v. Madison*, 1 *Cranch* 137 (1803)—

Section 13 of the Judiciary Act of 1789 provided that the Supreme Court shall have the power to issue writs of mandamus in cases warranted by the principles and usages of law, to any courts appointed, or persons holding office, under the authority of the United States. 1 *Stat.* 81, sec. 14, 1789.

---

[1] See in re Atchison, 284 Fed. 604 (1922) holding secs. 21 and 22 of the Clayton act unconstitutional.

[2] 2 Dallas, 409.

[3] See comments of Chief Justice Marshall in Marbury v Madison; 1 Cranch 137, 171, 172 (1803).

[4] 13 Howard, 52 ff.

[5] The references to acts of Congress are to *United States Statutes* at Large.

[6] See *supra*, 173 *et seq.*

On an original motion for a writ of mandamus to the Secretary of State to direct the delivery of a commission as justice of peace in the District of Columbia, this provision was held void as an illegal attempt to extend the original jurisdiction of the Supreme Court beyond the grant of authority in the Constitution, Art. III, Sec. 2, clause 2. An application for a mandamus to compel the Secretary of State to deliver a commission for an office was dismissed for want of jurisdiction.[7]

Opinion rendered by Chief Justice Marshall.[8]

3. *Scott v. Sandford*, 19 *How.* 393 (1857)—

Section 8 of the act of March 6, 1820, providing for the admission of Missouri into the Union, prescribed that in all territory of the Louisiana Purchase north of 36° 30' north latitude, not included within the limits of Missouri, "slavery and involuntary servitude, otherwise than in the punishment of crimes, whereof the parties shall have been duly convicted, shall be, and is hereby, forever prohibited." 3 *Stat.*, 548.

In a case involving the effect of this proviso on a slave who had been taken into a free state and territory and had been returned to the slave state of Missouri, this section was held void in so far as it attempted to prevent a citizen from owning slaves in this territory since Congress does not have the authority to control ownership of other property.

The proviso, which had been in force for thirty-four years, was declared "inoperative and void" by an act of Congress passed in 1854 (10 *Stat.* 289), a short time after the suit had been instituted in the United States' Circuit Court.

Chief Justice Taney rendered the opinion of the court. Concurring opinions were presented by Justices Wayne, Nelson, Grier, Daniel, and Catron. Justices Curtis and McLean dissented and in lengthy opinions held the proviso valid.

4. *Gordon v. United States*, 2 *Wall.* 561; 117 *U. S.* 697, *appendix* (1865)—

By an act of February 24, 1855 (10 *Stat.* 612), Congress provided for the establishment of a Court of Claims. On March 3, 1863, this act was amended so as to provide for an appeal to the Supreme Court in cases wherein the amount in controversy exceeded three thousand dollars, and no amount was to be paid on a claim until an appropriation therefor shall be estimated by the Secretary of the Treasury, and Congress shall make an appropriation for its payment. 12 *Stat.* 766, 768, secs. 5 and 14.

---

[7] The court had previously taken jurisdiction under this provision, see 1 Cranch 148 ff.

[8] The opinion of the court was rendered by a unanimous vote of the judges unless notation of concurring and dissenting opinions is made.

In 1865 the Supreme Court dismissed a case for want of jurisdiction with the observation that a majority of the court (Justices Miller and Field dissenting) thought that under the Constitution no appellate jurisdiction over the Court of Claims could be exercised by this court. No opinion was rendered at the time but a copy of a paper supposed to represent the reasoning on which the opinion was based was found among the papers of Chief Justice Taney and was printed as an appendix to 117 *U. S. Reports.*

The following year Congress repealed section 14 of the act of 1863 (14 *Stat.* 9) and the Supreme Court has since accepted jurisdiction on cases appealed from the Court of Claims on the ground that it now exercises the functions of a court. See *United States v. Klein* 13 Wall. 128 144 (1872).

5. *Ex parte Garland,* 4 *Wall.* 333 (1867)—

By an act passed July 2, 1862, Congress prescribed a test oath for all persons seeking employment in the civil, military, or naval departments of the public service. 12 *Stat.* 502, 503. In January 1865 the act was amended to apply to all attorneys and counsellors practicing in the courts of the United States. 13 *Stat.* 424, C. 20.

In so far as this act was designed to apply to those who had been admitted to practice in the federal courts before its passage it was held void as a bill of attainder and an *ex post facto* law. It was held also that the act could not apply to the petitioner since he had received a full pardon from the President for his participation in the Rebellion.

Justice Field delivered the opinion of the court.

Chief Justice Chase and Justices Miller, Swayne, and Davis dissented on the ground that Congress and the state legislatures possess authority to exclude from the practice of law those who are regarded as disloyal to the government and that the requirement of an oath of loyalty from those admitted to practice did not amount to a violation of the bill of attainder or *ex post facto* clauses of the Constitution.

6. *Reichart v. Felps,* 6 *Wall.* 160, (1868)—

Under authority of an act of the Continental Congress certain grants of land in the Northwest territory were confirmed. Congress in 1812 enacted a law (2 *Stat.* 677, 678, chap. 22) authorizing commissioners to revise and reexamine certain of these confirmations. By this board the claim of title of Felps was rejected. Held that the act of Congress interfered with titles previously granted and confirmed by the authorized agents of the government. An act which had been on the statute book for fifty-five years was rendered of no effect. Justice Grier delivered the opinion of the court.

7. *The Alicia,* 7 *Wall.* 571 (1869)—

An act of Congress of June 30, 1864, provided for appeals in prize cases to be taken directly from the district courts to the Supreme Court and that causes pending in the circuit courts might be transferred to the Supreme Court. 13 *Stat.* 311, sec. 13.

Held on a proceeding to transfer such a case that ''an attempt was inadvertently made to give to this court a jurisdiction withheld by the Constitution'' and hence that the order for transfer was without effect. The Supreme Court could take cognizance of prize cases only under its appellate jurisdiction. Constitution, Art. II, sec. 2.

Chief Justice Chase delivered the opinion of the Court.

8. *Hepburn v. Griswold,* 8 *Wall.* 603 (1870)—

Two acts of Congress (12 *Stat.* 345, sec. 1 and 12 *Stat.* 710, sec. 3) provided that United States notes should be ''legal tender in payment of all debts, public and private within the United States.'' In a case involving the validity of this provision the court held that in so far as Congress attempted to make such notes legal tender for the payment of pre-existing debts the acts were unconstitutional, the power to make a credit currency legal tender not being expressly granted by the Constitution and not being a legitimate implied power under Art. I, sec. 8 of the Constitution.

Chief Justice Chase delivered the opinion of the court.

The members of the court divided 5 to 3, three of the justices, Miller, Swayne, and Davis, joining in a dissent. After the appointment by President Grant of two justices known to be favorable to the issuance of legal tender notes, a rehearing of the case was ordered (Knox v. Lee, 12 Wall. 457) and by a vote of 5 to 4 the above provision was held valid. Justice Strong delivered the opinion of the court, Justice Bradley concurring and Chief Justice Chase and Justices Field, Clifford, and Nelson dissented.

9. *United States v. DeWitt,* 9 *Wall.* 41 (1870)—

A section of the Internal Revenue Act of 1867 (14 *Stat.* 471, 484, sec. 29) made it a misdemeanor punishable by fine and imprisonment for any person to sell oil made from petroleum, for illuminating purposes inflammable at less temperature or fire test than one hundred and ten degrees Fahrenheit. In testing the validity of an indictment under this act the circuit court certified to the Supreme Court the question as to the validity of the act of Congress. The court held that the act could not apply within the states as it was an interference with internal trade and could not be considered as coming within the scope of the power to tax or to regulate commerce.

Chief Justice Chase delivered the opinion of the court.

10. *The Justices v. Murray,* 9 *Wall.* 274 (1870)—

An act of Congress relating to *habeas corpus* and regulating proceedings in certain cases provided for the removal of a cause, after judgment by a state court, to the circuit court of the United States for a retrial on the facts and the law (12 *Stat.* 756, 757, sec. 5). This portion of the act was held void on the ground that under the Seventh Amendment "no fact tried by a jury shall be otherwise reexamined in any court of the United States than according to the common law." A judgment by a circuit court awarding a mandamus for a removal of a case under the act was reversed.

Justice Nelson delivered the opinion of the court.

11. *Collector v. Day,* 11 *Wall.* 113 (1871)—

Under federal income tax acts (13 *Stat.* 223, 281, 282, 479 ff.; 13 *Stat.* 479 ff; 14 *Stat.* 137 and 477) levies were made on the salaries of state judges. In a suit to recover an amount of a tax on salary paid under protest it was held that the levy of the tax was invalid as a tax on a necessary instrumentality of a state government (applying the principle announced in McCulloch v. Maryland, 4 Wheaton, 316, 427 and Weston v. Charleston, 2 Peters 449, 466) and as an interference with the reserved rights of the states.

Justice Nelson delivered the opinion of the court.

Justice Bradley dissenting, thought that the federal government should be permitted to tax all officers, federal and state, and that it would be practically impossible to determine what are necessary instrumentalities of the state government.

12. *United States v. Klein,* 13 *Wall.* 128 (1872)—

A proviso was inserted in the appropriation act of July 12, 1870 (16 *Stat.* 230, 235), that no pardon or amnesty granted by the President shall be admissible in evidence by any claimant in the court of claims, that proof of loyalty shall be made according to the terms prescribed in the proviso irrespective of any executive proclamation, and that where judgments have been rendered on any other proof of loyalty than that prescribed, the Supreme Court shall dismiss the case on appeal for want of jurisdiction.

It was provided in an earlier act that, in proceedings before the Court of Claims under the Abandoned and Captured Property Act (12 *Stat.* 820), any one who had accepted a pardon from the President shall be deemed guilty of participation in rebellion against the government and the court shall dismiss the suit.

In a contest before the Court of Claims relating to abandoned or captured property involving the validity of the proviso of the act of July

12, 1870, it was held void because it attempted to restrict the effect of the pardoning power of the President in a way the Constitution does not warrant, and because it prescribed rules of decision for the judicial department in pending cases.

Chief Justice Chase delivered the opinion of the court.

Justices Miller and Bradley, dissenting, agreed with the majority opinion that the proviso was void in so far as it attempted to prescribe for the judiciary the effect of an act of pardon or amnesty by the President, but refused to accede to a part of the opinion and judgment that under the Abandoned and Captured Property Act, a former owner who had participated in the rebellion had an interest in property or its proceeds when it had been sold and paid into the treasury. The title to such property they believed had completely passed from its original owner.

13. *United States v. Railroad Co.*, 17 *Wall.* 322 (1873)—

Section 122 of the Internal Revenue Act of June 30, 1864, as amended (13 *Stat.* 233, 284; 14 *Stat.* 98, 138) provided that railroads and certain other companies indebted for money for which bonds shall have been issued upon which interest is stipulated to be paid shall be subject to pay a tax of 5 per cent on the amount of all such interest. This tax was held to be levied on the creditors or stockholders of corporations and not upon the corporations. The city of Baltimore having loaned money to the Baltimore and Ohio Railway Company, the tax to be paid would have to be levied on the revenues of the city. Held that a city exercises part of the sovereign or governmental powers of the state and as such is exempt from federal taxes.

Justice Hunt delivered the opinion of the court.

Justice Bradley concurred in the judgment on the ground that Congress did not intend to tax property belonging to states or municipalities and approved the reasoning so far as it held the tax a levy on stock and bond holders.

Justices Clifford and Miller dissented from the opinion and judgment for the reason that they regarded the property involved as used by the city in its private proprietary capacity and as such subject to be taxed like other private property.

14. *United States v. Reese*, 92 *U. S.* 214 (1876)—

An act of Congress (16 *Stat.* 140) provided a penalty for election officers in state and local elections who obstructed any citizen from qualifying as a voter or refused to receive the vote of any citizen who had duly qualified as a voter. Two election inspectors were indicted under this act. On appeal to the Supreme Court it was held that the terms of the act, not being confined to punishment for unlawful discrimination on account of race, color, or previous condition of servitude, are beyond the authority granted by the Fifteenth Amendment, and hence are void. The act was also held to be too indefinite and vague to be enforced as a penal statute.

Chief Justice Waite delivered the opinion of the court.

Justices Clifford and Hunt dissented. Justice Clifford believed that the indictment was illegal because the evidence was not clear that the necessary requirements for voting had been fulfilled, the Enforcement Act being in his judgment a valid exercise of Congressional power. Justice Hunt upheld the act and sustained the validity of the indictment.

For repeal of the above provisions, see 28 *Stat.* 36 (1894).

15. *United States v. Fox*, 95 *U. S.* 670 (1878)—

A federal bankruptcy law had a proviso that any person respecting whom bankruptcy proceedings are commenced, who within three months before their commencement under the false pretense of dealing in the ordinary course of trade obtained on credit from any person goods or chattels with intent to defraud was subject to a penalty of imprisonment (14 *Stat.* 517, 539; *R. S.* 5132 subsec. 9). The question of constitutionality being raised on an indictment under this proviso, the court held sec. 9 invalid because the provision did not relate to a matter of federal concern, not being limited to acts committed in contemplation of bankruptcy. The proviso had no relation to the execution of a power granted to Congress and hence was not within the jurisdiction of the United States. If the statute was intended to apply to acts committed in contemplation of bankruptcy no such limitation was expressly provided.

Justice Field rendered the opinion of the court.

16. *Trade Mark Cases*, 100 *U. S.* 82 (1879)—

An act of Congress passed in 1870 aimed to protect those who had trademarks fulfilling the requirements of federal law (16 *Stat.* 198, 210; *R. S.* secs. 4937–4947). A subsequent act made fraudulent use of a trademark a crime and subject to punishment (19 *Stat.* 141). On several indictments the circuit courts certified to the Supreme Court the question of the validity of these provisions. The provisions relating to trademark legislation were held void because not comprehended within any of the express powers granted to Congress. The chief contention was that the acts did not come within the power to regulate commerce since they were not confined to the use of trademarks in foreign or interstate commerce.

Justice Miller delivered the opinion of the court.

A new act (21 *Stat.* 502, 1881) confined to foreign commerce was held valid. See Leschen Rope Co. v. Broderick, 201 *U. S.* 166 (1906).

17. *United States v. Harris,* 106 *U. S.* 629 (1883)—

Congress provided a punishment in cases where two or more persons conspired to deny to any person the equal protection of the laws (17 *Stat.* 13, 14; *R. S.* 5519). The Supreme Court held this provision void because its terms related exclusively to the action of private persons without reference to the laws of the state or their administration by state officers. The Civil War amendments to the Constitution were considered applicable primarily to rights interfered with by state action.

Justice Woods rendered the opinion of the court.

Justice Harlan regarded the case as not properly before the court on jurisdictional grounds.

18. *Civil Rights Cases,* 109 *U. S.* 3 (1883)—

Congress attempted to secure the full and equal enjoyment of the accommodations and facilities of inns, public conveyances, theaters, and other public amusements to citizens of every race and color (18 *Stat.* 335, 336). In passing on a series of indictments under this act the Supreme Court held the act void because it was not warranted by the Fourteenth Amendment—this amendment being a prohibition on state action or acts done under state authority and not intended to prevent the illegal acts of individuals. The denial of rights involved were also held not to be within the prohibitions of the Thirteenth Amendment as they had nothing to do with slavery or involuntary servitude.

Justice Bradley delivered the opinion of the court.

Justice Harlan dissenting charged the majority of the court with sacrificing the substance and spirit of the recent amendments to the Constitution ''by a subtle and ingenious verbal criticism.'' Justice Harlan believed that Congress was authorized to enact laws to protect people against the deprivation of any of their civil rights because of their race. Cf. Butts v. Merchants and Miners' Transportation Co. 230 *U. S.* 126 (1913) in which the entire act was declared unconstitutional. The act could be applied neither in the territories nor in the states.

19. *Boyd v. United States,* 116 *U. S.* 616 (1886)—

An amendment to the customs revenue laws authorized a court of the United States on motion of the government attorney to require the defendant to produce in court his private papers or else the allegations of the attorney might be taken as confessed (18 *Stat.* 187, sec. 5). In an action for forfeiture of certain goods for fraud in connection with customs invoices the defendant was required to produce an invoice in court. On appeal it was held that an action for forfeiture of goods being essentially a criminal proceeding this section of the revenue laws was invalid as being a violation of the Fourth Amendment, prohibiting unreasonable searches and seizures, and the Fifth Amendment, preventing a person from being a witness against himself in a criminal case.

Justice Bradley delivered the opinion of the court.

Justice Miller and Chief Justice Waite sustained the judgment of the court but held the section in violation of the Fifth Amendment only. It was thought no search and seizure were involved in the proceedings under the act.

20. *Baldwin v. Franks,* 120, *U. S.* 678 (1887)—

Sec. 5519 of the *Revised Statutes* (17 *Stat.* 13, 14) which was held void in United States v. Harris 106 U. S. 629 (see also United States v. Reese 92 U. S. 214) was held invalid for the punishment of those who conspire to deprive aliens of the rights guaranteed to them in a state by the treaties of the United States. Justices Harlan and Field dissented and took exception in particular to the reasoning which applied certain valid provisions of the federal statutes to citizens and not to aliens. Justice Harlan did not accept the reasoning of the majority as to the invalidity of sec. 5519.

Chief Justice Waite delivered the opinion of the court.

21. *Callan v. Wilson,* 127 *U. S.* 540 (1888)—

Congress in its capacity as a legislature for the District of Columbia attempted to dispense with a petit jury in prosecutions by information in the police court (*Rev. Stat.* Dist. of Col., sec. 1064). Callan was tried, without a jury, on a charge of conspiracy to prevent a person from pursuing his calling, and sentenced to pay a fine. On appeal to the Supreme Court it was held that jury trial as used in the Constitution meant jury trial in the common law sense and the term must be construed as relating not only to felonies but also to certain classes of misdemeanors. The possibility of a jury trial by the Supreme Court of the District was held not sufficient to meet the constitutional requirement and the crime of conspiracy was considered not a petty or trivial offense in the trial of which jury trial might be dispensed with.

Justice Harlan delivered the opinion of the court.

22. *Counselman v. Hitchcock,* 142 *U. S.* 547 (1892)—

Sec. 860 of the *Revised Statutes* (15 *Stat.* 37) provided that any evidence obtained from a person by means of a judicial proceeding shall not be used in any court of the United States or in any proceedings before other federal officers in respect to any criminal action. In an investigation concerning certain alleged violations of the Interstate Commerce Act, Counselman, who refused to answer questions which he claimed might incriminate him, was declared in contempt of court.

The Supreme Court reviewed the proceedings and held that the self-incrimination clause of the Fifth Amendment was not limited to protection to the individual in a prosecution against himself but applied to any investigation which might tend to show that he himself had committed a crime. Sec. 860 was held not to supply complete protection from all the perils against which the constitutional prohibition was designed to guard and was not a full substitute for that prohibition.

Justice Blatchford delivered the opinion of the court.

For the repeal of this section, see 36 *Stat.* 352 (1910).

23. *Monongahela Navigation Co. v. United States,* 148 *U. S.* 312 (1893)—

Congress provided for the condemnation of a lock and dam on a navigable stream (25 *Stat.* 400, 411) and stipulated that in the proceedings the value of the franchise accruing from the collection of tolls should not be considered.

When the Navigation Company contested these proceedings the Supreme Court held that the just compensation requirement of the Fifth Amendment in eminent domain cases requires that the full and exact equivalent of present value must be returned to the owner. The determination of what is just compensation is not for Congress but is left to the court. A franchise was held to be a vested right and was to be accorded protection just as other kinds of property.

Justice Brewer delivered the opinion of the court.

Two justices, Shiras and Jackson, did not participate in the decision.

24. *Pollock v. Farmers' Loan and Trust Co.,* 157 *U. S.* 429 and 158 *U. S.* 601 (1895)—

The section of the revenue act of 1894 (28 *Stat.* 509, C. 349) which provided for levying taxes upon rents or income derived from real estate was held a direct tax within the meaning of Art. I, sec. 2, of the Constitution and hence invalid because the act did not meet the requirement of apportionment among the states in accordance with population, and the levy of a similar tax upon income derived from the interest on bonds issued by a municipal corporation was declared void as a tax upon the power of the state and its instrumentalities to borrow money.

Chief Justice Fuller delivered the opinion of the court. Justice Field in a separate opinion maintained that he regarded the law as also a violation of the due process clause of the Fifth Amendment and as contrary to other implied limitations on the authority of Congress to levy taxes.

Dissenting opinions were rendered by Justices White and Harlan who believed that the term ''direct taxes'' as used in the Constitution was intended to apply only to capitation taxes and taxes on land. See Hylton v. United States 3 Dall. 171.

The members of the court being equally divided as to whether the entire Income Tax Act was void and as to other questions raised in the argument no opinions were expressed on these issues.

On a rehearing the entire Income Tax Act, secs. 27–37 of C. 349 of the revenue law of 1894, was held void, on the ground that an income tax regardless of the sources upon which it was levied was a direct tax under the language of the Constitution.

Chief Justice Fuller delivered the opinion of the court.

Dissenting opinions were rendered by Justices Harlan, Brown, Jackson, and White. Justice Harlan claimed that by reversing the earlier law and practice of the government the majority of the court rendered it necessary to amend the Constitution to secure principles of right, justice, and equality in federal taxation, and he insisted that policy and economic considerations rather than law actuated the majority in their conclusions.

The Sixteenth Amendment to the Constitution promulgated in 1913 reversed in part the effect of this decision.

25. *Wong Wing v. United States*, 163 *U. S.* 228 (1896)—

In 1888 Congress provided (25 *Stat.* 476, 479) for a summary hearing before any judge or commissioner, of Chinese persons regarded unlawfully within the United States and for their deportation, if found guilty. An act of 1892 (27 *Stat.* 25) authorized a penalty, for Chinese persons who were convicted of being unlawfully within the United States, of imprisonment at hard labor for a period of not exceeding one year and deportation thereafter. A Chinaman claiming unlawful detention under this act applied to the Supreme Court for release. The acts were held void as in conflict with the Fifth and Sixth amendments to the Constitution because an infamous punishment was inflicted without presentment or indictment by grand jury and without a public trial by a petit jury and the party was not granted a judicial hearing according to the requirements of due process of law.

Justice Shiras delivered the opinion of the court. A concurring opinion was given by Justice Field.

Justice Brewer took no part in the decision.

26. *Kirby v. United States*, 174 *U. S.* 47 (1899)—

An act passed by Congress in 1875 (18 *Stat.* 479) made embezzlement from the United States or the receipt of stolen property with knowledge a felony with appropriate penalties. Section 2 of the act provided that in a prosecution for the receipt of stolen goods a judgment of conviction against the embezzler shall be conclusive evidence that the property was stolen from the United States. This section was held void in so far as a party was not duly confronted with witnesses against him as required by the Sixth Amendment of the Constitution.

Justice Harlan delivered the opinion of the court. Justices Brown and McKenna dissented without opinion. Justice Brewer did not participate in the decision.

The act was repealed in 1909 (35 *Stat*, 1155, sec. 341).

27. *Fairbank v. United States,* 181 *U. S.* 283 (1901)—

By a revenue act of 1898 Congress levied a stamp tax on bills of lading for goods destined for export (30 *Stat.* 459). The Supreme Court reversed a judgment convicting a party for refusal to pay this tax on the ground that the tax was in effect a tax on exports and hence prohibited by Art. I, Sec. 9 of the Constitution.

Justice Brewer delivered the opinion of the court.

Justices Harlan, Gray, White, and McKenna dissented. To the minority the stamp tax on a printed bill of lading was not a duty on the property itself so as to come within the inhibition of the Constitution. The majority opinion Justice Harlan believed involved a departure from canons of constitutional construction which were applied for more than a century.

28. *James v. Bowman* 190 *U. S.* 127 (1903)—

Section 5507 of the *Revised Statutes* provided for the punishment of individuals who hindered, controlled, or intimidated others from exercising the right of suffrage guaranteed by the Fifteenth Amendment (16 *Stat.* 146, 147). The Supreme Court reversed an indictment under the act on the ground that the Fifteenth Amendment related solely to action by the United States or by a state—and not to the wrongful acts of individuals. Because the act purported to regulate all elections and not merely elections of Representatives to Congress it was held beyond the authority granted by the Constitution.

Justice Brewer delivered the opinion of the court. Justices Harlan and Brown dissented without opinion. Justice McKenna took no part in the decision.

For the repeal of this section, see 35 *Stat.* 1153 (1909).

29. *Matter of Heff,* 197 *U. S.* 488 (1905)—

An act of Congress prohibiting sales of liquor to Indians (29 *Stat.* 506) was held not to apply to an Indian who had received an allotment and patent for land since another act of Congress (24 *Stat.* 388) made Indians who had received such allotments citizens of the United States and of the states in which they resided. The former act was held a police regulation and not within powers granted to the federal government.

Justice Brewer rendered the opinion of the court and Justice Harlan dissented without stating his reasons.

In *United States v. Nice* 241 *U. S.* 591 (1916) the above decision was overruled. Justice Van Devanter speaking for the court claimed that section 6 of the act of 1887 did not intend to terminate the national guardianship over the Indians at the time allotments for land were made. ''We recognize,'' he said, ''that a different construction was placed upon section 6 of the act of 1887 in the Matter of Heff, 197 U. S. 488, but after reexamining the question in the light of other provisions of the act and of many later enactments clearly reflecting what was intended by Congress, we are constrained to hold that the decision in that case is not well grounded and it is accordingly overruled.''

30. *Rassmussen v. United States*, 197 *U. S.* 516 (1905)—

Section 171 of the code for Alaska (31 *Stat.* 358) provided that in trials for misdemeanors six persons shall constitute a legal jury. In reviewing a conviction according to this procedure the provision was held void on the ground that the territory of Alaska was incorporated in the United States by the treaty of acquisition and by action of Congress and was subject to the Fifth and Sixth amendments which require a trial with a common law jury of twelve persons.

Justice White delivered the opinion of the court. Concurring opinions were given by Justices Harlan and Brown. Justice Harlan thought incorporation by Congress had nothing to do with the application of the Constitution as the acquisition of territory made its provisions apply. Justice Brown regarded the application of the provisions of the amendments to the Constitution to territories as within the control of Congress regardless of the matter of incorporation but concurred in the conclusion of the court on the ground of a provision of the treaty of cession.

31. *Hodges v. United States*, 203 *U. S.* 1 (1906)—

It was held that a United States court has no jurisdiction under the Thirteenth Amendment or sections 1977, 1979, 5508, or 5510 of the *Revised Statues*, over a charge of conspiracy made and carried out in a state to prevent Negroes because of their race from making or carrying out contracts for labor. The Thirteenth Amendment was again held not to apply to acts done by individuals and the acts of Congress intended to give the Negroes equal protection of the laws in making and enforcing contracts were held unenforceable.

Justice Brewer delivered the opinion of the court. Justice Brown concurred in the judgment.

Justices Harlan and Day dissented. Justice Harlan insisted that Congress may by appropriate legislation protect any right or privilege arising from the Constitution or laws of the United States and that on this principle the acts of Congress involved were clearly valid.

32. *The Employers' Liability Cases*, 207 *U. S.* 463 (1908)—

A federal Employers' Liability Act (34 *Stat.* 232) was held void because it purported to regulate matters belonging primarily to the states and not to Congress. The terms of the act were held not to be confined to transactions within the scope of interstate commerce. Because the illegal provisions were not separable from the remainder of the act, the entire law was invalidated.

Justice White delivered the opinion of the court. Justice Day concurred in this opinion. Justices Peckham, Brewer, and Chief Justice Fuller concurred in the result but disagreed with the majority opinion as to the views expressed relating to the power of Congress to legislate on the subject of the relations of master and servant.

Justice Moody dissenting thought the act could be interpreted without any violence to its terms so as to apply only to interstate and foreign commerce. In this opinion Justices Harlan, McKenna, and Holmes concurred.

An act passed in 1908 (35 *Stat.* 65) and applied solely to transactions in interstate commerce was held valid in Mondon v. N. Y. N. H. & H. R. R. 223 U. S. 1 (1912).

33. *Adair v. United States*, 208 *U. S.* 161 (1908)—

An act of Congress made it a criminal offense against the United States for a carrier engaged in interstate commerce to discharge an employee simply because of his membership in a labor organization (30 *Stat.* 424, sec. 10). This section was held void as repugnant to the clause of the Fifth Amendment declaring that no person shall be deprived of life, liberty or property without due process of law. The doctrine of liberty of contract applied to state acts in Lochner v. New York 198 U. S. 45 and in Allgeyer v. Louisiana 165 U. S. 578 was also held applicable to federal acts.

Justice Harlan delivered the opinion of the court. Justice Moody took no part in the decision. Justices McKenna and Holmes dissented. Justice McKenna thought that Congress after a thorough investigation of labor difficulties in the railway industry had determined on a laudable policy to improve conditions between employers and employees. And Justice Holmes believed that "it cannot be doubted that to prevent strikes, and, so far as possible, to foster its scheme of arbitration, might be deemed by Congress an important point of policy, and I think it impossible to say that Congress might not reasonably think that the provision in question would help a good deal to carry its policy along."

The act was repealed in 1913 (38 *Stat.* 108).

34. *Keller v. United States*, 213 *U. S.* 138 (1909)—

Congress made it a felony to import into the United States or to harbor any alien woman for the purpose of prostitution (34 *Stat.* 898). The Supreme Court held this provision void in so far as it was regarded as applying to one harboring a prostitute without knowledge of her alienage or in connection with her coming into the United States. The control in matters of this kind after aliens are admitted to the United States was held to belong to the states.

Justice Brewer delivered the opinion of the court. Justices Holmes, Harlan, and Moody dissented. Justice Holmes claimed that ''for the purpose of excluding those who unlawfully enter this country Congress has power to retain control over aliens long enough to make sure of the facts.'' Three years did not seem too long in the opinion of the minority.

For repeal of the above provision see 39 *Stat.* 897 (1917).

35. *United States v. Evans*, 213 *U. S.* 297 (1909)—

Section 935 of the Code of the District of Columbia (31 *Stat.* 1341) provided that a writ of error will not lie from the Court of Appeals to the Supreme Court of the District at the instance of the government to review a judgment based on a verdict of not guilty. On an appeal by the government in an indictment for murder, because of the exclusion of certain evidence it was held that there was no proper case before the court since the appellee having been freed from further prosecution by a verdict in his favor had no interest in the question to be determined and might not appear. It was held contrary to the practice of the federal courts to give advisory opinions on federal law. Section 935 was limited by this interpretation to actual cases or controversies.

Chief Justice Fuller delivered the opinion of the court.

36. *Muskrat v. United States*, 219 *U. S.* 346 (1911)—

The Indian Appropriation Act of 1907 (34 *Stat.* 1015, 1028) authorized certain Indians to bring suit in the Court of Claims to test the validity of several acts of Congress. The act permitted an appeal to the Supreme Court and the Attorney General was to defend the suits, the expenses to be paid from the Treasury. On an appeal from the Court of Claims sustaining the validity of the law the Supreme Court declined to take jurisdiction on the ground that it was not a case involving the adverse interests of claimants but merely an attempt of Congress to secure a judicial declaration of the validity of an act of Congress. There was no case involving a justiciable controversy within the authority of the court.

Justice Day delivered the opinion of the court.

37. *Coyle v. Smith*, 221 *U. S.* 559 (1906)—

Congress in the Enabling Act for the admission of Oklahoma to statehood provided that the temporary capital of the state should be at Guthrie and should not be changed to another city prior to 1913 (34 *Stat.* 267, C. 3335). An act of the state providing for the immediate removal of the capital to Oklahoma City was upheld despite the above act of Congress, on the ground that it is not within the power of Congress to impose conditions on a new state at the time of admission which would deprive a state of an attribute of power essential to its equality with the other states.

Justice Lurton delivered the opinion of the court. Justices McKenna and Holmes dissented without opinion.

38. *Choate v. Trapp*, 224 *U. S.* 665 (1912)—

Congress provided for the issuance of patents to land to Indians and stipulated that the land should be non-taxable for a specified time (30 *Stat.* 495, 507, C. 517). In 1907 Congress removed restrictions from the sale and encumbrance of lands granted under the above terms and made subject to taxation the lands from which restrictions had been removed. Oklahoma instituted proceedings to levy taxes on Indian grantees coming within the terms of these acts of Congress. The decision of the Oklahoma Supreme Court sustaining the tax proceedings was reversed on the ground that the tax exemption was a vested property right which could not be repealed under the due process of law clause of the Fifth Amendment. Indians were held to be entitled to the protection accorded by the provisions of the Constitution relating to private rights.

Justice Lamar delivered the opinion of the Court.

39. *Butts v. Merchants and Miners Transportation Co.*, 230 *U. S.* 126 (1913)—

When an issue arose as to the operation of the Civil Rights Act of 1875 in its application to vessels of the United States engaged in coastwise trade it was held that since the act was void as to its operation within the states (Civil Rights Cases 109 U. S. 3)[9] and since the provisions of the act are not separable as to their operation in such places as are under the exclusive jurisdiction of the national government, the statute was void in its entirety.

Justice Van Devanter delivered the opinion of the Court.

40. *United States v. Hvoslef*, 237 *U. S.* 1 (1915)—

The War Revenue Act of 1898 (30 *Stat.* 448, 460, C. 448) levied a stamp tax on charter parties. The levy of this tax on parties engaged exclusively in the carriage of cargo from the ports of the United States to

[9] See *supra*, 549.

foreign ports was held void as a tax on an export, and in violation of Art. I, sec. 9 of the Constitution. Cf. Fairbank v. United States 181, U. S. 283.[10] The process of exportation as well as the goods were held exempt from taxation.

Justice Hughes delivered the opinion of the Court. Justice McReynolds did not participate in the decision.

41. *Thames and Mersey Ins. Co. v. United States*, 237 *U. S.* 19 (1915)—

Following the reasoning of *United States v. Hvoslef*[11] it was held that stamp taxes on policies of marine insurance on exports are prohibited as taxes on exports by Art. I, sec. 9 of the Constitution. Hence such taxes collected under the War Revenue Act of 1898 were not legally exacted and were recoverable under the Refunding Act of 1902.

Justice Hughes delivered the opinion of the Court. Justice McReynolds did not participate in the decision.

42. *Hammer v. Dagenhart*, 247 *U. S.* 251 (1918)—

An act of Congress (39 *Stat.* 675, C. 432) prohibited transportation in interstate commerce of goods made at a factory in which, within thirty days prior to their removal therefrom, children under 14 years of age had been employed, or children from 14 to 16 years were employed more than eight hours in a day or more than six days in a week, or after the hour of 7 p.m. or before the hour of 6 a.m. The Supreme Court held this law invalid on the ground that it was an attempt to invade the state's police power over local trade and manufacture and hence it was not warranted by the authority delegated to Congress over interstate commerce.

Justice Day delivered the opinion of the Court. Justices Holmes, McKenna, Brandeis, and Clarke dissented. Justice Holmes thought the statute should have been upheld because its prohibitions applied only to the carriage of certain goods in interstate and foreign commerce which brought it clearly within one of the express powers granted to Congress. "I should have thought," he observed, "that the most conspicuous decisions of this Court had made it clear that the power to regulate commerce and other constitutional powers could not be cut down or qualified by the fact that it might interfere with the carrying out of the domestic policy of any State." But he added, "the act does not meddle with anything belonging to the States. They may regulate their internal affairs and their domestic commerce as they like. But when they seek to send their products across the state line, they are no longer within their rights."

---

10 See *supra,* 553.
11 See *supra,* 557.

43. *Eisner v. Macomber,* 252 *U. S.* 189 (1920)—

The Revenue Act of 1916 (39 *Stat.* 756, C. 463) imposed a tax on stock dividends of corporations issued from the profits accumulated since the adoption of the Sixteenth Amendment. The imposition of such a tax was held void because it did not conform to the requirement of apportionment among the states according to Art. I, sec. 2, cl. 3 and sec. 9, cl. 4 of the Constitution. A stock dividend was held not to be income within the meaning of that term as comprised in the Sixteenth Amendment.

Justice Pitney delivered the opinion of the court. Justices Holmes, Day, Brandeis, and Clarke dissented. Justice Holmes believed that the word income in the Sixteenth Amendment should be read in ''a sense most obvious to the common understanding at the time of its adoption'' and that according to this meaning the amendment clearly justified the tax. Justice Brandeis also contended that stock dividends were income within the authority granted to Congress under the Sixteenth Amendment and he claimed that the majority of the Court departed from the rule that ''the high prerogative of declaring an Act of Congress invalid should never be exercised except in a clear case.''

For the repeal of this act see 40 *Stat.* 1149, sec. 1400, 1919.

44. *Knickerbocker Ice Co. v. Stewart,* 253 *U. S.* 149 (1920)—

The Supreme Court of the United States held in Southern Pacific Co. v. Jensen 244 U. S. 205 (1917) that the New York Workmen's Compensation Law could not be applied to maritime injuries because such enforcement of state laws would destroy the uniformity in maritime matters which the Constitution intended to establish. The decision of the court was by a 5 to 4 vote. Following this decision Congress amended the Judicial Code (40 *Stat.* 395) in order to save to claimants ''the rights and remedies under the workmen's compensation law of any State.'' This amendment was held void both as an attempt to delegate the legislative power of Congress to the states and to defeat the purpose of the Constitution respecting the uniformity of the maritime law.

Justice McReynolds delivered the opinion of the Court. Justices Holmes, Pitney, Brandeis, and Clarke dissented.

The single objection to the statute that it sanctioned the application of different rules for different places the minority claimed was not prevented by the Constitution. Justice Holmes observes that, ''if my explanation, that the source [of the common law rules of liability as between master and servant at sea] is the common law of the several states, is not accepted, I can only say, I do not know how, unless by the fiat of the judges. But surely the power that imposed the liability can change it, and I suppose that Congress can do as much as the judges who introduced the rules. For we know that they were introduced and cannot have been elicited by logic alone from the mediaeval sea laws.''

45. *Evans v. Gore,* 253 *U. S.* 245 (1920)—

The Revenue Act of 1919 levied a tax upon the net income of federal judges and included in the assessment their official salaries (40 *Stat.* 1062, sec. 213). This provision was held void as contrary to Art. I, sec. 1, cl. 6, of the Constitution according to which the compensation of the judges shall not be diminished during their continuance in office. The prohibition of the Constitution was held to apply to every form of diminution of salary during a judge's term. The collection of a similar tax during the Civil War was discontinued on the ground that it was beyond the power of Congress.[12]

Justice Van Devanter delivered the opinion of the Court. Justices Holmes and Brandeis dissented. Justice Holmes found nothing in the Constitution to exonerate a judge from the ordinary duties of a citizen. A tax that applied to all other citizens seemed to him properly levied against the salaries of federal judges. The phrase of the Sixteenth Amendment that Congress might levy taxes on incomes "from whatever source derived" was thought to be an express warrant for the minority view.

46. *United States v. L. Cohen Grocery Co.,* 255 *U. S.* 81 (1921)—

The Food Control Act of 1917 as amended in 1919 (40 *Stat.* 276, C. 53, sec. 4 and 41 *Stat.* 297, C. 80 sec. 2) attached a penalty for any person to make any unjust or unreasonable charge in the handling of any of the necessaries of life. In so far as this act was construed as forbidding the exaction of an excessive price upon the sale of a commodity it was held void as in violation of the due process clause of the Fifth Amendment and the provision of the Sixth Amendment that persons accused of crime shall be adequately informed of the nature and cause of the accusation. It was claimed that the act established no ascertainable standard of guilt. The existence of a state of war was held not to suspend the application of the above provisions of the Constitution.

Justice White delivered the opinion of the Court. Justice Day took no part in the decision of the case. Justices Pitney and Brandeis concurred only in the result. The justices concurring thought the act of Congress did not condemn acts which according to the majority opinion made it invalid. The validity of the law was not in their opinion necessarily raised. Several other cases raising similar issues were disposed of in accordance with the judgment in the Cohen Grocery Co. Case; see especially Needs v. United States, 255 U. S. 109 (1921).

47. *Newberry v. United States,* 256 *U. S.* 232 (1921)—

Section 8 of the Federal Corrupt Practices Act (36 *Stat.* 822, C. 392 and 37 *Stat.* 25 C. 33) limited the amount of money which any member of

---

[12] See 13 Opinions Attorney General 161; Wayne v. United States, 26 Ct. Clms. 274 and 27 *Stat.* 306.

Congress might expend in procuring his nomination or election. This section was held unconstitutional as applied to a primary election of candidates for a seat in the Senate. Primaries were held not to be elections within the meaning of the original sec. 4, Art. I of the Constitution and the Seventeenth Amendment relating to the popular election of Senators gave the term election no new meaning.

Justice McReynolds delivered the opinion of the Court. Justice McKenna concurred in the opinion so far as it applied to the statute under consideration, which was enacted prior to the adoption of the Seventeenth Amendment. Chief Justice White and Justices Pitney, Brandeis, and Clarke, concurred in part. Chief Justice White believed that the power granted to Congress to regulate elections for members of Congress necessarily gave authority to control primary elections. He thought the indictments were bad because not warranted by the express language of the federal statute. The other justices dissenting on the main issue also regarded the term ''elections'' as sufficiently broad to cover primaries and hence deemed the provisions of the act of Congress in issue valid. The candidate himself, it was claimed, did not directly participate in the acts for which he was indicted under the federal law.

48. *United States v. Moreland*, 258 *U. S.* 433 (1922)—

An act of Congress relating to the District of Columbia made punishable by a fine or imprisonment at hard labor in a workhouse wilful neglect or refusal to provide for the support of minor children (34 *Stat.* 86, C. 1131). A prosecution by information for this offense was held invalid because imprisonment at hard labor, whether in a penitentiary or elsewhere, was considered an infamous punishment within the meaning of the Fifth Amendment, and a prosecution for a crime so punishable must be by indictment or presentment by a grand jury. The reasoning of the case Wong Wing v. United States, 163 U. S. 228[13] was followed.

Justice McKenna delivered the opinion of the Court. Justice Clarke took no part in the consideration of the case. Justices Brandeis, Holmes, and Chief Justice Taft dissented. Justice Brandeis regarded an infamous punishment as one which might involve imprisonment in a penitentiary. It was shown that the laws and the common practice of the states did not as a rule regard confinement at hard labor in a workhouse as implying infamy.

49. *Bailey v. Drexel Furniture Co.*, 259 *U. S.* 20 (1922)—

A section of the Revenue Act of 1919 (40 *Stat.* 1138 C. 18) levied a tax of 10 per cent on the net profits of any person operating a mine or factory, etc., in which children under 14 years of age were permitted to work, or children between 14 to 16 years were permitted to work more

---

[13] Cf. *supra*, 552.

than eight hours in any day, or more than six days in a week, or after 7 p.m. or before 6 a.m. This section was held void because it was designed to penalize conduct the regulation of which is reserved exclusively to the states. The law was held not to be a tax but a penalty, with the characteristics of regulation and punishment, and the case was regarded as not distinguishable from Hammer v. Dagenhart, 247 U. S. 251.[14]

Chief Justice Taft delivered the opinion of the Court. Justice Clarke dissented without opinion.

50. *Hill v. Wallace*, 259 *U. S.* 44 (1922)—

The Future Trading Act (42 *Stat.* 187, C. 86) levied a tax of 20 cents a bushel on grain involved in contracts of sale for future delivery, except when made through a member of a Board of Trade designated by the Secretary of Agriculture. This act was held void as not a proper exercise of the taxing power of Congress and not sustainable under the power to regulate interstate commerce, since sales of grain for future delivery made at Chicago between members of a board of trade are not in themselves interstate commerce. The reasoning of the Child Labor Tax Case was followed. The sections of the act were considered so interwoven as to render it impossible to hold any part valid.

Chief Justice Taft delivered the opinion of the Court. Justice Brandeis agreed that the Future Trading Act was unconstitutional but doubted whether the facts of the case warranted a consideration of the constitutional question. A similar act was held valid in Board of Trade v. Olsen, 262 U. S. 1 (1923).

51. *Lipke v. Lederer*, 259 *U. S.* 557 (1922)—

A section of the National Prohibition Act (41 *Stat.* 277, 298, C. 80, sec. 2 and 41 *Stat.* 305, 317, C. 8, sec. 35) provided that upon evidence of illegal manufacture or sale of liquor ''a tax shall be assessed against, and collected from the person in double the amount now provided by law, with an additional penalty of $500 on retail dealers and $1000 on manufacturers.'' The Supreme Court reversed a decree dismissing an injunction sought by a party upon whom a collector had assessed such a tax. The tax was held to be a penalty and not a tax and hence not enforceable by distraint of the offender's property without a fair opportunity for a hearing in accordance with the requirements of due process of law of the Fifth Amendment.

Justice McReynolds delivered the opinion of the Court. Justices Brandeis and Pitney dissented. The minority contended that the plaintiff had a full and adequate remedy at law and therefore was not entitled to raise the issue of the validity of the law in an equitable proceeding.

---

14 Cf. *supra*, 558.

52. *Keller v. Potomac Electric Power Co.*, 261 *U. S.* 428 (1923)—

Under the law of Congress creating the Public Utilities Commission of the District of Columbia, appeals from orders of the commission were permitted from the District Supreme Court to the Court of Appeals and to the Supreme Court of the United States. On such an appeal, the Court was authorized not merely to decide legal questions and questions of fact incident to the proceedings but also to amend freely valuations, rates, and regulations established by the commission and to make such an order as in its judgment the commission should have made (37 *Stat.* 938, 974, C. 150, sec. 8).

It was held by the Supreme Court that this provision gave to the court powers which were legislative or administrative and not judicial and hence beyond the authority of Congress to confer on the Court either directly or by appeal. As this section was deemed severable from the other provisions, the remainder of the act was upheld.

Chief Justice Taft delivered the opinion of the Court.

53. *Adkins v. Children's Hospital*, 261 *U. S.* 525 (1923)—

Congress enacted a Minimum Wage Law for the District of Columbia (40 *Stat.* 960, C. 174) authorizing the fixing of minimum wage standards for adult women in any occupation in the District. The standards were to be fixed by a board which was to determine an adequate wage to meet the necessary cost of living for women workers in each employment. The Supreme Court declared this law invalid as an interference with the right to contract as protected by the due process of law clause of the Fifth Amendment. The act was condemned as a price-fixing measure in private employment and as such "the· product of a naked, arbitrary exercise of power."

Justice Sutherland delivered the opinion of the Court. Justice Brandeis took no part in the decision of the case. Chief Justice Taft and Justices Sanford and Holmes dissented. Chief Justice Taft declared that "it is not the function of this Court to hold congressional acts invalid simply because they are passed to carry out economic views which the Court believes to be unwise or unsound." The Chief Justice believed that former decisions of the Court gave ample warrant for the action which Congress had taken. Justice Holmes also dissenting said: "I confess that I do not understand the principle on which the power to fix a minimum for the wages of women can be denied by those who admit the power to fix a maximum for their hours of work. . . . .

"The criterion of constitutionality is not whether we believe the law to be for the public good. We certainly cannot be prepared to deny that a reasonable man reasonably might have that belief in view of the legislation of Great Britain, Victoria and a number of the states of the Union."

54. *Washington v. Dawson & Co.*, 264 *U. S.* 219 (1924)—

The amendment to the Judicial Code (42 *Stat.* 634, C. 216, secs. 24, 25), which permitted the application of the workmen's compensation laws of the states to injuries within the admirality and maritime jurisdiction and which was held invalid in Knickerbocker Ice Co. v. Stewart, 253 U. S. 149,[15] was also held void in a case in which an attempt was made to compel an employer of stevedores to contribute to an accident fund under the provisions of a state Workmen's Compensation Act.

Justice McReynolds delivered the opinion of the Court. Justice Holmes observed that "the reasoning of Southern Pacific Co. v. Jensen and cases following it never has satisfied me and therefore I should have been glad to see a limit set to the principle." Justice Brandeis dissented. The conclusion, thought Justice Brandeis "that the state law violates the Constitution and that the consent of Congress cannot save it, is reached solely by a process of deduction," through a chain of reasoning "several links of which are, in my opinion, unfounded assumption which crumbles at the touch of reason." The legislation of Congress, intended to limit the practical effect of the decisions in the Southern Pacific Co. and the Knickerbocker Ice Co. Cases, should in his judgment be carried into effect even if necessary to overrule recent decisions of this court, "the reasons for doing so are persuasive. Our experience in attempting to apply the rule, and helpful discussions by friends of the Court, have made it clear that the rule declared is legally unsound; that it disturbs principles long established; and that if adhered to, it will make a serious addition to the class of cases which this Court is required to review."

55. *A. B. Small Co. v. Amer. Sugar Ref. Co.*, 267 *U. S.* 233 (1925)—

Section 4 of the Lever Act as amended which was held void in United States v. Cohen Grocery Co., 255 U. S. 109[16] was also held void as a test of the validity of a contract for the sale of a commodity because the standard of duty is so vague as to be no rule or standard at all. The reasoning of the Cohen Grocery Co. Case was held to apply to civil as well as to criminal proceedings.

Justice Van Devanter delivered the opinion of the Court.

56. *Trusler v. Crooks*, 269 *U. S.* 475 (1926)—

Section 3 of the Future Trading Act imposing a tax of 20 cents per bushel upon all privileges or options for contracts of purchase or sale of grain was held void as a penalty and not a tax on the authority of Hill v. Wallace, 259 U. S. 44.[17] Section 3 being "a mere feature without separate purpose, must share the invalidity of the whole."

Justice McReynolds delivered the opinion of the Court.

---

[15] Cf. *supra*, 559.   [16] Cf. *supra*, 560.   [17] Cf. *supra*, 562.

57. *Myers v. United States*, 272 *U. S.* 52 (1926)—

Section 6 of the act of Congress of 1876 (19 *Stat.* 80, 81, C. 179) providing that ''postmasters of the first, second and third classes shall be appointed and may be removed by the President by and with the advice and consent of the Senate and shall hold their offices for four years unless sooner removed or suspended according to law,'' was held void as an attempt to make the President's power of removal dependent upon the consent of the Senate. The power of removal was held incident to the power of appointment. An interpretation of the Constitution made by the First Congress and followed for seventy-three years was approved by the court.

Chief Justice Taft delivered the opinion of the Court. Justices Holmes, McReynolds, and Brandeis dissented. Justice Holmes thought that so far as the principle of the case was involved, the duty of the President to see that the laws are executed is a duty that does not go beyond the laws or require him to achieve more than Congress sees fit to leave within his power. Justice Brandeis believed that to imply a grant to the President of the uncontrollable power of removal from statutory inferior executive offices involves unnecessary and indefensible limitations upon the power of Congress to fix the tenure of inferior officers. The practice of the states and of the federal government as to the removal power was deemed contrary to the interpretation of the majority of the Court.

58. *Nichols v. Coolidge*, 274 *U. S.* 531 (1927)—

Section 402 of the Estate Tax of 1919 in so far as it required that there shall be included in the gross estate the value of property transferred by a decedent prior to its passage, merely because the conveyance was to take effect in possession or enjoyment at or after his death was held contrary to the Fifth Amendment, as an arbitrary, capricious act which amounts to confiscation.

Justice McReynolds delivered the opinion of the Court. Justices Holmes, Brandeis, Sanford, and Stone concurred in the result.

59. *Blodgett v. Holden*, 275 *U. S.* 142 (1927)—

Sections 319–324 of the Revenue Act of 1924 (43 *Stat.* 313, C. 234) interpreted so as to impose a tax on gifts fully consummated before its provisions came before Congress were deemed invalid by four members of the Court as contrary to the due process of law clause of the Fifth Amendment.

Justice McReynolds rendered an opinion in which Chief Justice Taft and Justices Van Devanter and Butler concurred. Justices Holmes, Brandeis, Sanford, and Stone thought these provisions should be construed as operating only from the date of the act and applicable only to gifts thereafter made and thus they would be clearly valid.

60. *Untermeyer v. Anderson*, 276 *U. S.* 440 (1928)—

The gift tax provisions of the Revenue Act of 1924 considered in Blodgett v. Holden, 275 U. S. 142[18] must be construed as applying to gifts made at any time during that calendar year and so far as they were applicable to bona fide gifts not made in anticipation of death, and fully consummated prior to June 2, 1924, the provisions were held arbitrary and invalid according to the due process clause of the Fifth Amendment.

Justice McReynolds delivered the opinion of the court. Justice Sanford concurred in the result. Justices Holmes, Brandeis and Stone dissented. Justice Brandeis observed: ''For more than half a century, it has been settled that a law of Congress imposing a tax may be retroactive in its operation. . . . . Except for the peculiar tax involved in Nichols v. Coolidge, 274 U. S. 531, no federal revenue measure has ever been held invalid on the score of retroactivity.'' The presumption in favor of the validity of the law should be, he thought, particularly strong, since the prohibition on Congressional power arises from the ''vague contours of the Fifth Amendment, prohibiting the depriving any person of liberty or property without due process of law.''

Two other cases deserve mention, as follows:

Grogan v. Walker & Sons, 259 *U. S.* 80 (1922) in which Justice Holmes speaking for the court refused to carry into effect sec. 3005 of the Revised Statutes, as amended and Art. XXIX of the treaty of 1871 with Great Britain (17 *Stat.* 863), so as to permit transportation in bond from Canada through the United States of whiskey intended as a beverage, destined to a foreign country, because these provisions were deemed in conflict with the express language of the Eighteenth Amendment and the National Prohibition Act (41 *Stat.* 305, 308)—

See dissent of Justices McKenna, Day, and Clarke. The minority regarded the liquor in the cases as neither in the common or legal sense an importation into the United States or an exportation from it.

Spalding & Bros. v. Edwards, 262 *U. S.* 66 (1923) in which Justice Holmes for the Court refused application of the provisions of a general revenue law to a sale of goods made in this country to a commission merchant for a foreign consignee for the sole purpose of export, as a tax on exports prohibited by Art. I, sec. 9 of the Constitution.

---

[18] Cf. *supra*, 565.

CLASSIFICATION OF ACTS DECLARED VOID

I. REFUSAL TO ACCEPT JURISDICTION CONFERRED BY CONGRESS, BECAUSE AUTHORITY GRANTED NOT WITHIN POWERS GRANTED BY CONSTITUTION OR NOT JUDICIAL IN NATURE

1. Hayburn's Case, Chandler v. The Secretary of War, and United States v. Todd, 1792–1794, see 13 Howard 52
   Refusal to pass on invalid pension claims.
2. Marbury v. Madison, 1 Cranch 137, 1803
   Authority to issue mandamus under original jurisdiction of Supreme Court denied.
3. Gordon v. United States, 2 Wall. 561, 1865
   Refusal to accept jurisdiction on appeal from Court of Claims because authority to control decisions was vested in other departments.
4. The Alicia, 7 Wall. 571, 1869
   Prize cases could not be transferred from Circuit Courts because not within grant of original jurisdiction.
5. United States v. Klein, 13 Wall. 128, 1872
   Jurisdiction denied because of attempt of Congress to restrict pardoning power of President and to prescribe rules for decisions in federal courts.
6. United States v. Evans, 213 U. S. 297, 1909
   Refusal of jurisdiction because there was no real case before court.
7. Muskrat v. United States, 219 U. S. 346, 1911
   Congress cannot refer issue to court for an advisory opinion on validity of a law.
8. Keller v. Potomac Electric Power Co., 261 U. S. 428, 1921
   Authority to revise orders and proceedings of District of Columbia Public Utilities Commission not within jurisdiction of court.

II. ACTS WHICH ENCROACHED ON THE POWERS OF THE STATES

1. United States v. Dewitt, 9 Wall. 41, 1870
   Standard for sale of petroleum oil fixed by Congress held interference with internal trade of state.
2. Collector v. Day, 11 Wall. 113, 1871
   Federal tax on salary of state judicial officer held void.

3. United States v. Railroad Co., 17 Wall. 322, 1873
   Federal tax on interest from municipal bonds held void as an interference with an agency of the state.
4. United States v. Reese, 92 U. S. 214, 1876
   Regulation of elections by Congress deemed beyond authority
   granted by Fifteenth Amendment.
5. United States v. Fox, 95 U. S. 670, 1878
   Acts not directly related to bankruptcy cannot be regulated by
   Congress under guise of bankruptcy law.
6. Trade Mark Cases, 100 U. S. 82, 1879
   Regulation of trademarks not confined to foreign and interstate
   commerce held beyond authority of Congress.
7. United States v. Harris, 106 U. S. 629, 1883
   Conspiracy to deprive persons of equal protection of laws not subject to regulation by Congress under Civil War amendments.
8. Civil Rights Cases, 109 U. S. 3, 1883
   Congress cannot require equal enjoyment of facilities of inns,
   theaters, etc., to citizens of every race and color under authority
   granted by Thirteenth and Fourteenth amendments.
9. Baldwin v. Franks, 120 U. S. 678, 1887
   Ruling of United States v. Harris applied to aliens.
10. James v. Bowman, 190 U. S. 127, 1903
    Attempt of Congress to provide for punishment of individuals for
    interfering with right of suffrage at all elections held not war-
    ranted by Fifteenth Amendment.
11. Hodges v. United States, 203 U. S. 1, 1906
    Congress has no authority to punish a conspiracy in a state to
    prevent Negroes from making or carrying out contracts of labor.
12. Employers' Liability Cases, 207 U. S. 463, 1908
    Federal Employers' Liability Act not limited to interstate and
    foreign commerce held void.
13. Keller v. United States, 213 U. S. 138, 1909
    Congress cannot control aliens for police purposes for three years
    after their entry to United States.
14. Coyle v. Smith, 221 U. S. 559, 1911
    Provision of Enabling Act for admission of a state limiting right
    to locate state capitol held void.
15. Hammer v. Dagenhart, 247, U. S. 251, 1918
    Congress cannot prohibit interstate shipments of goods produced
    by child labor.
16. Newberry v. United States, 256 U. S. 232, 1910
    Federal Corrupt Practices Act held not to apply to primary elec-
    tions for senators.

III. Encroachments Upon Individual Rights

1. *Ex parte* Garland, 4 Wall, 333, 1867
   Test oath held void as an *ex post facto* law and as an interference with pardoning power of President.

2. Reichart v. Felps, 6 Wall. 160, 1868
   Congress could not interfere with patents to land confirmed by Continental Congress in 1788.

3. The Justices v. Murray, 9 Wall. 274, 1870
   Removal of certain cases for retrial on facts and law held to violate guaranty of jury trial of Seventh Amendment.

4. Boyd v. United States, 116 U. S. 616, 1886
   Compulsory production of papers in action for forfeiture of goods for fraud held to violate guaranties of Fourth and Fifth Amendments.

5. Callan v. Wilson, 127 U. S. 540, 1888
   Trial by jury cannot be dispensed with in the courts of District of Columbia in a trial for the crime of conspiracy.

6. Counselman v. Hitchcock, 142 U. S. 547, 1892
   Self-incrimination clause of Fifth Amendment held to prohibit compulsory testimony even though a person is protected against a personal criminal action.

7. Monongahela Navigation Co. v. United States, 148 U. S. 312, 1893
   The value of a franchise to collect tolls must be included in appraisal in eminent domain proceedings in order to meet the requirements of due process of law of the Fifth Amendment.

8. Wong Wing v. United States, 163 U. S. 228, 1896
   Conviction of an alien for being unlawfully within United States on a summary hearing and sentence of imprisonment at hard labor held to violate Fifth and Sixth amendments.

9. Kirby v. United States, 174 U. S. 47, 1899
   A judgment of conviction against an embezzler cannot be made conclusive evidence of the theft in an action for receiving stolen property.

10. Matter of Heff, 197 U. S. 488, 1905
    Act of Congress prohibiting sales of liquor to Indians held void as applicable to Indians who were presumed to be citizens of the United States. Overruled by United States v. Nice, 241 U. S. 591.

11. Rassmussen v. United States, 197 U. S. 516, 1905
    Sixth Amendment held to require trial by jury in Alaska because the territory was incorporated.

12. Adair v. United States, 208 U. S. 161, 1908
    Congress cannot make it a criminal offense for an employer engaged
    in interstate commerce to dismiss an employee because of mem-
    bership in a labor organization.

13. Butts v. Merchants Trans. Co., 230 U. S. 126, 1913
    Provisions of Civil Rights Act held void in its application outside
    of the states.

14. Choate v. Trapp, 224 U. S. 665, 1912
    Tax exemption in issuance of patents to Indians held a vested
    right and not subject to repeal under due process clause of
    Fifth Amendment.

15. United States v. L. Cohen Grocery Co., 255 U. S., 81, 1921.
    Sections of Food Control Act inflicting a penalty for any person
    making an unreasonable charge for handling necessaries of life
    held void.

16. United States v. Moreland, 258 U. S. 433, 1922
    Imprisonment at hard labor in workhouse held an infamous pun-
    ishment and hence subject to limitations of Fifth Amendment.

17. Adkins v. Children's Hospital, 261 U. S. 525, 1923
    Congress cannot authorize the fixing of minimum wage standards
    for adult women in District of Columbia under requirements of
    due process of law of Fifth Amendment.

18. A. B. Small v. American Sugar Ref. Co., 267 U. S. 233, 1925
    Reasoning of Cohen Grocery Co. Case held applicable to consid-
    eration of validity of a contract for the sale of a commodity
    and applied to civil as well as to criminal proceedings.

IV. LIMITATIONS ON THE POWERS OF CONGRESS TO LEVY TAXES

1. Hepburn v. Griswold, 8 Wall. 603, 1870
   Congress denied authority to make United States notes legal tender
   in the payment of debts public and private.

2. Pollock v. Farmers Loan and Trust Co., 157 U. S. 429 and 158 U. S.
   601, 1895
   Income tax provisions of revenue act held void because not appor-
   tioned among the states as a direct tax as required by Art. 1,
   sec. 2 of the Constitution.

3. Fairbank v. United States, 181 U. S. 283, 1901
   Stamp tax on bills of lading for goods destined for export deemed
   void as tax on exports.

4. United States v. Hvoslef, 237 U. S. 1, 1915
   Stamp tax on charter parties held void as tax on exports.

5. Thames and Mersey Ins. Co. v. United States, 237 U. S. 19, 1915
   Stamp tax on marine insurance policies held void as tax on exports.

6. Eisner v. Macomber, 252 U. S. 189, 1920
   Taxation of net income on stock dividends distributed from profits
   of corporation held not authorized by Sixteenth Amendment.

7. Evans v. Gore, 253 U. S. 245, 1920
   Income tax on salaries of federal judges held void because judges'
   salaries may not be diminished while they are in office.

8. Bailey v. Drexel Furniture Co., 259 U. S. 20, 1922
   Tax of ten per cent on net profits of any person employing children
   under certain ages in a mine or factory held interference with
   exclusive authority of state.

9. Lipke v. Lederer, 259 U. S. 557, 1922
   Assessment of additional tax upon evidence of illegal manufacture
   or sale of liquor held invalid as penalty and not a tax and not
   enforceable except under requirements of due process of law of
   Fifth Amendment.

10. Hill v. Wallace, 259 U. S. 44, 1922
    Tax on contracts for sale of grain for future delivery held void as
    not within authority of Congress to tax or regulate.
    This case may also be regarded as an interference with powers
    belonging to the states.

11. Trusler v. Crooks, 269 U. S. 475, 1926
    Principle of Hill v. Wallace applied in declaring tax on future
    trading a penalty.

12. Nichols v. Coolidge, 274 U. S. 531, 1927
    Retroactive provision of Estate Tax of 1919 held void.

13. Untermeyer v. Anderson, 276 U. S. 440, 1928
    Tax on gifts made before approval of statute held invalid.

V. MISCELLANEOUS DECISIONS

1. Scott v. Sandford, 19 Howard 393, 1857
   Congress cannot prohibit the introduction of slavery in the Louisiana territory north of Missouri.

2. Knickerbocker Ice Co. v. Stewart, 253 U. S. 149, 1920
   Congress cannot adopt workmen's compensation laws of states in
   relation to maritime transactions.

3. Washington v. Dawson & Co., 264 U. S. 219, 1924

Principle of Knickerbocker Ice Co. Case held applicable in preventing enforcement of state compensation act despite act of
Congress.

4. Myers v. United States, 272 U. S. 52, 1926

Congress cannot limit authority of President to remove officers
appointed by him with the advice and consent of the Senate.

VI. ACTION BY A SINGLE HOUSE OF CONGRESS HAS BEEN DECLARED VOID
IN TWO CASES

1. Kilbourn v. Thompson, 103 U. S. 168, 1880

An order of the House of Representatives adjudging Kilbourn in
contempt for refusing to testify was held void.

2. Marshall v. Gordon, 243 U. S. 521, 1917

An order to arrest a party for writing an insulting letter to a
member of the House was held unauthorized.[19]

---

[19] For summaries of decisions declaring acts of Congress invalid, see:

Blaine F. Moore, "The Supreme Court and Unconstitutional Legislation," Col. Univ. *Stud. in Hist., Econ. and Public Law*, 54, No. 2.

Charles W. Ramseyer, "Unconstitutional Acts," *Congressional Record*,
Appendix, Feb. 11, 1925.

Charles Warren, *Congress, the Constitution and the Supreme Court*
(Boston, 1925), 273 ff.

William Marshall Bullitt, "The Supreme Court and Unconstitutional
Legislation," 10 Am. Bar Assoc. *Jour.* (June 1924) 417–425.

Robert von Moschzisker, *Judicial Review of Legislation* (Washington,
1923).

Acts of Congress Declared Unconstitutional by the Supreme Court, prepared by W. C. Gilbert, O. M. Jack, and George M. Sterritt for the Legislative Reference Service of the Library of Congress.

APPENDIX II

PROVISIONS OF WRITTEN CONSTITUTIONS
RELATING TO
REVIEW OF LEGISLATIVE ACTS BY THE COURTS
IN FOREIGN COUNTRIES
WITH EXPLANATORY NOTES AND COMMENTS

The legal customs and practices which affect judicial review of legislation, the classification of governments in relation to judicial review, and the types of judicial review in practice were briefly considered in chapter one. Supplementary information is presented herewith concerning constitutional and statutory provisions dealing with the review of legislation by the courts in foreign countries. For a number of countries the information available was so incomplete or unreliable as to render impossible any satisfactory opinions or conclusions regarding the practice of court review of legislation. Misleading impressions are so common regarding the actual results of judicial guardianship of constitutions in foreign countries that one should hesitate to form an estimate of this feature of a governmental system without a thorough study of the legal and political history of the country and of the customs, principles, and traditions which characterize the development of the national legal system.

A. GOVERNMENTS IN WHICH THE GUARDIANSHIP OF THE CONSTITUTION IS CONFERRED TO A CERTAIN DEGREE UPON THE COURTS

ARGENTINE REPUBLIC

Constitution, 1860—

Art. 100. The supreme court and the inferior courts of the nation shall try and decide all cases, not enumerated in Clause 11 of article 67, which arise under the provisions of this constitution, the laws of the nation, or treaties with foreign powers; in cases concerning ambassadors, public ministers, and foreign consuls; in cases of admiralty and maritime jurisdiction; in controversies to which the nation is a party; in cases which arise between two or more provisions, between one province and citizens of another province, between citizens of different provinces, and between a province or its citizens and a foreign state or its citizens.

From the standpoint of judicial control over legislation portions of Article 17 are also of interest, as follows:

Private property is inviolable, and no inhabitant of the nation shall be deprived of it except by judicial decision founded on law. Condemnation of property for a public purpose shall be authorized by law, and indemnification previously made.

As in the United States the authority of Argentine judges to declare acts of legislatures void is regarded as arising from the nature of a written constitution with limitations on governmental powers and individual rights guaranteed in the Constitution, rather than from any express grant of power.[1] The limitations which circumscribe this power in America were adopted by Argentine justices, namely—that the power can be exercised only on the demand of an interested party in a case brought before the court;[2] that the incompatibility between the Constitution and a law must be clear beyond a doubt, but the incompatibility may be not only with the letter but also with the spirit of the Constitution, that is, "with its real meaning when the letter is obscure or gives opportunity for diverse interpretations"; that the courts will not decide political questions, for says the Supreme Court: "it is an elemental rule of our public law, that each one of the three high powers which form the government of the nation, applies and interprets the Constitu-

---

[1] "This court is the final interpreter of the Constitution for the reason that whenever the meaning of one of its clauses is doubtful and the decision is made against the right founded on it, although the case has been decided in a court of common law, the decision is subject to review by the Supreme Court." This authority it is claimed is based on the articles of the Constitution relating to judicial authority. In the interpretation of the pertinent clauses of the constitution American authors and cases are cited. Ministerio Fiscal v. Benjamín Calvete, 1 *Fallos de la Suprema Corte de Justicia Nacional*, [cited as S. C. N.] 340, 348 (1864).

[2] In re Dr. Pérez, 2 S. C. N. 253, 258–259 (1865); see Juan A. González Calderón, *Derecho Constitucional argentino* (Buenos Aires, 1923, ed. 2) 1:435 ff. In re F. Egusquiza and C. Ayala, 4 S. C. N. 75, 95 (1861); G. H. Moores *et al.*, 30 S. C. N. 281, 283, (1886).

tion for itself when it exercises the powers that it confers upon them respectively.''[3]

As in the United States the judges are expected to decide in favor of the validity of a law unless it appears void beyond a reasonable doubt.[4] It is not their function to pass on the justice or injustice of legislative acts.[5]

Provincial (state) courts, similar to the federal courts, may pass upon the validity of national laws, subject to an appeal to the national courts.

When a law has been declared void the authorities in charge of its execution are expected to cease to execute it for it is the duty of the courts in analogous cases to conform to the decisions of the Supreme Court.[6] The Supreme Court is declared to be the

court of last instance in all controversies over which it has jurisdiction, as coming within the scope of the judicial power of the nation. Its decisions are final. No court can reverse it. It represents in the sphere of its authority the national sovereignty and it is as independent in the exercise of its authority as Congress is in its power of legislation and as the executive power in carrying out its functions. There is no recourse whatsoever from its decisions except that of revision, in a case brought before it under its original and exclusive jurisdiction.

This is the doctrine of the Constitution, the doctrine of the law and it results from the nature of things.[7]

A federal law affecting civil rights retroactively was held invalid as in violation of Article 17 of the Constitution which declares that ''private property is inviolable and no inhabitant

---

[3] J. L. Avegno v. Province of Buenos Aires, 14 S. C. N. 428, 433 (1874). J. M. Cullen v. Llerena, 53 S. C. N. 420, 431 (1893) holding that intervention in the Provinces is a political matter for the political departments of the government.

[4] Bullocq y Duanona v. Ferrocarril del Sud du B. B., 68 S. C. N. 238, 295 (1897) in which the Supreme Court reversed the decision of a lower court and held valid arts. 187 and 188 of the Commercial Code.

[5] J. Cafferena v. el Banco Argentino del Rosario de Santa Fé, 10 S. C. N. 427, 436 (1871) holding that the prohibitions against the enactment of retroactive laws or laws impairing the obligation of contracts are not in the Constitution and do not limit the legislative power and that the courts are not authorized to pass on the injustice of legislative acts.

[6] M. Videla v. V. García Aguilera, 9 S. C. N. 53 (1870) and Bustos y Ca v. J. A. Pando, *ibid.*, 294 (1871).

[7] Fisco Nacional v. M. Ocampo, 12 S. C. N. 134, 154, 155 (1872).

of the nation shall be deprived of it except by judicial decision founded on law."[8] Under this provision laws enacted to meet an emergency were held void because they seriously limited the right to use and dispose of property.[9]

Congress recognized the authority of the Supreme Court to review legislative acts when in the law organizing the national judiciary it provided that:

> The courts and national judges, while exercising their functions, are expected to apply the Constitution as supreme law, the laws that Congress may pass, the treaties with foreign nations, the laws of the provinces . . . . in the order of the preference established.

Thus a hierarchy of laws is established as follows:

1. The federal Constitution.
2. Laws of Congress sanctioned by the Constitution.
3. Treaties.
4. Constitutions and laws of the provinces.[10]

Provisions of acts of the national legislature are attacked before the Supreme Court but such acts are seldom declared void.[11]

A number of acts of the provinces levying taxes were held void as in conflict with articles 9 and 10 and 17 to 20 of the Constitution.[12] In the interpretation of these provisions of the Constitution the principle of equality before the law is required in tax procedure. As in the United States provisions of the state

---

[8] Mango v. Traha, 144 S. C. N. 219 (1925).

[9] Podesta v. Etchegorry, 145 S. C. N. 168, 172, 173 (1925).

[10] Law No. 48 (Sept. 14 1863) art. 21; González Calderón, *op. cit.*, 1:435 ff.

[11] See D'Elia v. J. Huespe, 138 S. C. N. 56 (1923); Horta v Harguindeguy, 137 S. C. N. 47 (1922); Pereyra Iraola v. Provincia de Buenos Aires, 139 S. C. N. 65 (1923).

The authority of the courts to declare a law void is confined to an authentic case presented within the scope of the courts' jurisdiction. Abstract questions of law will not be considered and decided.

[12] Cf. Ostendorf v. Cordoba, 106 S. C. N. 109 (1907); Hermanos v. Buenos Aires, 107 S. C. N. 385 (1907); in re Doña Rosa Melo de Cane, 115 S. C. N. 111 (1911); Pedro y Perdomo v. Provincia de Entre Ríos, 145 S. C. N. 334 (1925); Montial v. Provincia de Entre Ríos, 144 S. C. N. 21 (1925).

constitutions may be invalidated. Thus a provision of the constitution of Mendoza was declared void as interfering with matters of civil procedure belonging exclusively to the control of Congress.[13] To date about thirty provincial acts or parts of acts have been held void.[14]

Judicial authority it was held is authorized to pass on the validity of an assessment or a tax when it is attacked as arbitrary, oppressive, or confiscatory under the inviolability of property as guaranteed by Article 17 of the Constitution. In the application of this principle a local assessment under a law of Buenos Aires of 1907 was held void.[15]

Administrative orders and judicial decrees may also be declared void as contrary to the Constitution.[16]

The Provinces as a rule provide for the review of legislative acts by the courts.[17] This recourse prescribing judicial review of legislation has for its purpose the maintenance of an effective unity of jurisprudence and the equality of all before the law.[18] The procedure to consider the validity of ordinances is based in certain respects on the jurisdiction exercised by the courts of cassation in France, Spain, and Belgium but the recourse to determine the constitutionality of law was intended to be based on the American model.[19]

Though the American plan of judicial review was adopted in Argentine and the reasoning of American judges and commentators is frequently followed in Argentine judicial decisions there are in fact relatively few instances in which the courts have

---

[13] For information on this point as well as on the number of acts of Congress invalidated, I am indebted to Professor J. A. González Calderón.

[14] Zorraguieta y Funes v. Ferrocarril Pacífico, 146 S. C. N. 122 (1926).

[15] Pereyra Iraola v. Provincia de Buenos Aires, 138 S. C. N. 161 (1923). Procurador General J. N. Matienzo in his argument cited Cooley on Taxation and such American cases as Norwood v. Baker, 172 U. S. 269 (1898) and French v. Barber Asphalt Paving Co., 181 U. S. 324 (1901). This decision was confirmed and applied to several cases, 146 S. C. N. 36, 42, 64, 127, 204.

[16] Bourdieu v. Municipalidad de la Capital, 145 S. C. N. 307 (1925).

[17] See art. 156, sec. 6 of the constitution of the Province of Buenos Aires.

[18] Antonio Luis Gil, *Recursos de inconstitucionalidad e inaplicabilidad de ley* (Thesis, University of Buenos Aires, 1878) 14.

[19] *Ibid.*, 151 ff.

declared unconstitutional the acts either of congress or of the provincial legislatures.[29] Professor González Calderón notes that from 1863 to 1929 only two laws of Congress were definitely declared void.[21]

AUSTRALIA

The Constitution of the Commonwealth, 1900—

Article 59—The Queen may disallow any law within one year from the Governor-General's assent, and such disallowance on being made known by the Governor-General by speech or message to each of the Houses of the Parliament, or by Proclamation, shall annul the law from the day when the disallowance is so made known.

Article 60—A proposed law reserved for the Queen's pleasure shall not have any force unless and until within two years from the day on which it was presented to the Governor-General for the Queen's assent the Governor-General makes known, by speech or message to each of the Houses of the Parliament, or by Proclamation, that it has received the Queen's assent.

Article 74—No appeal shall be permitted to the Queen in Council from a decision of the High Court upon any question, howsoever arising, as to the limits *inter se* of the Constitutional powers of the Commonwealth and those of any State or States, or as to the limits *inter se* of the Constitutional powers of any two or more States, unless the High Court shall certify that the question is one which ought to be determined by Her Majesty in Council.

The High Court may so certify if satisfied that for any special reason the certificate should be granted, and thereupon an appeal shall lie to Her Majesty in Council on the question without further leave.

Except as provided in this section, this Constitution shall not impair any right which the Queen may be pleased to exercise by virtue of Her Royal prerogative to grant special leave of appeal from the High Court to

---

20 See comment of Dr. Leo S. Rowe in *The Federal System of the Argentine Republic* (Washington, 1921) 112. Dr. Rowe believes that the reluctance of the citizen to institute proceedings involving a declaration of unconstitutionality is due to Spanish customs and traditions.

21 One was the law of Congress of October 31, 1884, authorizing the opening of an avenue in the city of Buenos Aires, which was held void in so far as it authorized the condemnation of buildings and land exceeding the width necessary for the laying out of the street; cf. 33 S. C. N. 162 ff. This decision of the court was later modified so as to interpret more liberally the power of Congress to take private property for public purposes. See González Calderón, *op. cit.*, 2:180 ff. The other case resulted in the invalidation of the law of August 21, 1922, limiting the prices on contracts for leases of property, in so far as it affected contracts made prior to the passage of the act. See 137 S. C. N. 47 ff. See also 143 S. C. N. 271 declaring void an executive decree and 150 S. C. N. 150.

Her Majesty in Council. The Parliament may make laws limiting the matters in which such leave may be asked, but proposed laws containing any such limitation shall be reserved by the Governor-General for Her Majesty's pleasure.

The Commonwealth government is one of limited and enumerated powers and the parliaments of the states retain the residuary powers of government. In this respect the American rather than the Canadian plan was followed.

Declarations of individual right and the protection of liberty and property against the government such as exist in the United States are conspicuously absent from the Constitution; the individual is deemed sufficiently protected by that share in the government which the Constitution insures him.

After a prolonged controversy in which the representatives of the home government and a few of the Australian delegates aimed to establish an appeal to the Privy Council similar to that in force in Canada, section 74 was accepted by both parties and made a part of the Commonwealth Constitution.[22] The language of this section is sufficiently indefinite to leave some doubt as to the intention of the framers, but the majority of the Australian delegates accepted this wording on the belief that it gave practically final jurisdiction to the High Court on constitutional questions.

The interpretation of the section was first presented to the court when the question was raised whether the Tasmanian Stamp Act operated as an interference by way of taxation and control with a federal agency or instrumentality.[23] As a similar issue to that determined in *McCulloch* v. *Maryland* was raised, the court quoted freely from the American case and commended the opinion of Chief Justice Marshall. The doctrine of the

---

[22] For the history of the introduction and passage of this clause, consult *Quick and Garran*, especially pp. 242, 247, 724, 735, 748–50.

[23] D'Emden v. Pedder, 1 C. L. R. 91 (1904). See also Amalgamated Society of Engineers v. Adelaide Steamship Co. Ltd., 28 C. L. R. 129 (1920). In the treatment of judicial review in Australia I have made some use of my article on ''Judicial Interpretation of the Constitution Act of the Commonwealth of Australia,'' published in 30 *Harv. Law Rev.* (April 1917) 595 ff.

immunity of federal instrumentalities from taxation as formulated in the *McCulloch Case* was accepted and incorporated in the court's opinion and judgment. The intention to follow American precedents was thus expressed :

> When, therefore, under these circumstances, we find embodied in the Constitution provisions undistinguishable in substance, though varied in form, from the provisions of the Constitution of the United States which had long since been judicially interpreted by the Supreme Court of that Republic, it is not an unreasonable inference that its framers intended that like provisions should receive like interpretation.[24]

It was asserted to be the duty of the court to determine the validity of an attempted exercise of legislative power. In supporting this judgment Justice Griffith maintained :

> We are not, of course, bound by the decisions of the Supreme Court of the United States. But we all think that it would need some courage for any Judge at the present day to decline to accept the interpretation placed upon the United States Constitution by so great a Judge so long ago as 1819, and followed up to the present day by the succession of great jurists who have since adorned the Bench of the Supreme Court at Washington. So far, therefore, as the United States Constitution and the Constitution of the Commonwealth are similar, the construction put upon the former by the Supreme Court of the United States may well be regarded by us in construing the Constitution of the Commonwealth, not as an infallible guide, but as a most welcome aid and assistance.[25]

Thus the High Court definitely committed itself to the principles and the construction of constitutional law as adopted in the United States, and like the Supreme Court of the United States, assumed the rôle of guardian of the Commonwealth Constitution Act.[26]

---

24 D'Emden v. Pedder, 1 C. L. R. 113 (1904).

25 1 C. L. R. 112. In Municipal Council of Sydney v. Commonwealth of Australia, Justice O'Connor said: ''The principles laid down by Marshall, C. J., in his historic judgment in McCulloch v. Maryland . . . . are as applicable to the Australian Commonwealth Constitution as to the United States Constitution.''—1 C. L. R. 208, 239 (1904). See also Jumbunna Coal Mine v. Victorian Coal Miners' Association, 6 C. L. R. 309 (1908).

26 Cf. *Quick and Garren,* 725. Also Clark, *Australian Constitutional Law,* ed. 2, 6, wherein the author maintains that ''in regard to many provisions of the Constitution of the Commonwealth, the historic decisions of the Supreme Court of the United States which were delivered by Chief Justice

The judicial controversy which aroused the greatest interest from the standpoint of constitutional law is *Wollaston's Case,* involving an income tax act of the State of Victoria, held to apply to the salary of a Commonwealth officer.[27] By the Supreme Court of Victoria it was held that the principle laid down in *McCulloch v. Maryland,* namely, that a state of the Union has no power to impede or control any of the constitutional means to carry into effect federal constitutional powers, has no application in construing the Commonwealth Constitution.[28]

The court then referred to some recent decisions in the United States which tend to limit the principle of the *McCulloch Case* and insisted that, while the actual instrumentalities of the government of either the Union or a state cannot be taxed by a state or by the Union, there is nothing in Chief Justice Marshall's decision to prevent the taxation of the property of a person who is merely an agent of the Union or of a state. The right of disallowance of acts for Australia was then cited as evidence of an intention to give effect to a system of government fundamentally different from the American system.

On an appeal to the High Court the principle announced in the case of *D'Emden v. Pedder* was reaffirmed.[29] In rendering judgment Chief Justice Griffith said:

> They [the judges of the Supreme Court of Victoria] said that they preferred to follow the decisions of the Judicial Committee of the Privy Council upon the Constitution of Canada, suggesting that this court had indicated a disposition to show a preference for the American over the English decisions. This is, we think, a somewhat novel mode of dealing with a judgment of a court of final appeal. . . . . It is a matter of common

Marshall and his associates during the first half century of the Republic cannot fail to be followed in Australia whenever the language to be interpreted is substantially the same as that to which the irresistible reasoning of those decisions was applied.'' See Erling M. Hunt, *American Precedents in Australian Federation* (New York, 1930), chap. 5.

[27] Wollaston's Case, 28 V. L. R. 357 (1902). For a good account of this controversy, consult W. Harrison Moore, *The Constitution of the Commonwealth of Australia* (ed. 2, Melbourne, 1910), Part VII, chap. 3, on the doctrine of the immunity of instrumentalities.

[28] 28 V. L. R. 384.

[29] Deakin v. Webb, 1 C. L. R. 585 (1904).

knowledge that the framers of the Australian Constitution were familiar with the two great examples of English-speaking federations, and deliberately adopted, with regard to the distribution of powers, the model of the United States, in preference to that of the Canadian Dominion.[30]

The scheme of the Canadian Constitution, it is particularly contended, was rejected by the framers of this Constitution, and especially is this true with respect to the distribution of powers between the federal government and the states and as to section 74, which relates to the final interpretation of the Constitution.

The scheme of the Constitution plainly expressed is that for the determination of these constitutional questions this court is to be the tribunal of ultimate appeal, unless the court itself is satisfied that there is some special reason which would justify it in certifying that the question ought to be determined by the Sovereign in Council.[31] Canadian decisions were held to have no bearing on the case,[32] and the court again cited Marshall's opinion in the *McCulloch Case* with the observation that the reason of that judgment appears to be unanswerable. Continuing, Chief Justice Griffith contended:

> In my opinion the principles applicable to the granting by the Judicial Committee of special leave to appeal from this Court or from the Supreme Court of a State are not applicable in this case. Grave responsibility is cast upon this Court by the Constitution. We know historically that that responsibility was only cast upon us after long consideration and negotiation. Various proposals were made, and the establishment of the Commonwealth very nearly fell through in consequence of the differences of opinion upon the point. The final solemn determination of the English Parliament, with the assent of Australia, was that that responsibility should be cast upon the High Court. I agree with Mr. Higgins that we should be guilty of a dereliction of duty almost amounting to a breach of trust if we were to decline to accept that responsibility unless we were in a position to say in intelligible language that there was some special reason, capable of being formulated, why the Privy Council was, and why we were not, the proper ultimate judges of the question.[33]

---

[30] 1 C. L. R. 604, 606.

[31] 1 C. L. R. 621, 622.

[32] Cf. The Bank of Toronto v. Lambe, 12 A. C. 575 (1887).

[33] 1 C. L. R. 622; see also the emphatic language of Justice O'Connor, 1 C. L. R. 631.

The case did not end here, for it was soon appealed to the Privy Council, and the court of appeal for the British Empire decided to uphold the state court and thereby overruled the judgment of the High Court.[34]

Moreover, the Council denied that the Commonwealth Parliament could take away the right of appeal in this case. The contention that such an act on the part of a state is impliedly forbidden by the Constitution after the analogy of Marshall's reasoning was thus disposed of:

> The analogy fails in the very matter which is under debate. No state of the Australian Commonwealth has the power of independent legislation possessed by the states of the American Union. Every act of the Victorian Council and Assembly requires the assent of the Crown, but when it is assented to, it becomes an act of Parliament as much as any Imperial act, though the elements by which it is authorized are different. . . . . The American Union, on the other hand, has erected a tribunal which possesses jurisdiction to annul a statute upon the ground that it is unconstitutional. But in the British Constitution, though sometimes the phrase ''unconstitutional'' is used to describe a statute which, though within the legal power of the legislature to enact, is contrary to the tone and spirit of our institutions, and to condemn the statesmanship which has advised the enactment of such law, still, notwithstanding such condemnation, the statute in question is law and must be obeyed. It is obvious that there is no such analogy between the two systems of jurisprudence as the learned Chief Justice suggests.[35]

In reference to that part of the opinion which declared the United States Constitution a model for the Australian Constitution, their Lordships said they ''are not able to acquiesce in any such principle of interpretation.'' Neither of these sections (73 and 74) authorized the Commonwealth Parliament, they claimed, to take away the right of appeal in such a case as the one under consideration, nor does any other section directly give such authority.[36]

---

[34] Webb v. Outtrim (1907) A. C. 81.

[35] (1907) A. C. 88, 89.

[36] *Ibid.*, 91.

When the issue was again presented to the High Court,[37] it was held that the High Court was the ultimate arbiter upon all constitutional questions, unless it was of opinion that the question at issue in any particular case was one upon which it should submit itself to the guidance of the Privy Council, and the court was therefore not bound to follow the decision in *Webb v. Outtrim*, but should follow its own well considered decision.[38] The Chief Justice asserted:

> That the High Court was intended to be set up as an Australian tribunal to decide questions of purely Australian domestic concern without appeal or review, unless the High Court in the exercise of its own judicial functions, and upon its own judicial responsibility, forms the opinion that the question at issue is one on which it should submit itself to the guidance of the Privy Council. To treat a decision of the Privy Council as overruling its own decision on a question which it thinks ought not to be determined by the Privy Council would be to substitute the opinion of that body for its own, which would be an unworthy abandonment of the great trust reposed in it by the Constitution. It is said that such a state of things as would follow from a difference of opinion between the Judicial Committee and the High Court would be intolerable. It would not, perhaps, have been extravagant to expect that the Judicial Committee would recognize the intention of the Imperial legislature to make the opinion of the High Court final in such matters. But that is their concern, not ours. . . . . For these reasons we are of opinion that this court is in no way bound by the decision of the Judicial Committee in *Webb* v. *Outtrim*, but is bound to determine the present appeal upon its merits according to its own judgment. In other words, we think that this Court is in effect directed by the Constitution to disregard the unwritten conventional rule as to following decisions of the Judicial Committee in cases falling within sec. 74.[39]

The Privy Council accepted the situation by refusing to allow an appeal.[40] The outcome of the controversy was the passage of

---

[37] Baxter v. Commissioners of Taxation, 4 C. L. R. 1087 (1907). See also Commonwealth v. State of New South Wales, 3 C. L. R. 807 (1906), in which a transfer was declared a necessary instrumentality of the Commonwealth for the acquisition of land for public purposes and that the transfer was therefore held exempt from state taxation.

[38] 4 C. L. R. 1100.

[39] 4 C. L. R. 1117, 1118.

[40] (1908) A. C. 214.

the Commonwealth Salaries Act of 1907 which granted the states authority to impose a tax upon Commonwealth officers.[41]

Few decisions as significant as those relating to the immunity of instrumentalities from taxation have been rendered by the High Court, but the trend of constitutional interpretation is shown in some other cases. It was determined that the High Court will not decide abstract questions of constitutional law and that a complainant must show that he has personally been injured before he can have the constitutionality of a law tested.[42] The provision for the distribution of powers between the states and the Commonwealth was considered with the approval of decisions of the Supreme Court of the United States as to the distribution of powers and the insistence that a similar distribution was made in the Constitution Act.[43] In the *State Railway Servants Case* the High Court held that the inclusion of disputes relative to employment on state railways was *ultra vires* as an invasion of the exclusive powers of the state.[44] In the *Union Label Case*[45] the decision was rendered that the portion of the Trade Marks Act of 1905 establishing a workers' mark was *ultra vires* as involving the state power over domestic commerce and industry.[46]

---

[41] For the affirmance of this act, see Chaplin v. Commissioner of Taxes for South Australia, 12 C. L. R. 375 (1911).

[42] Bruce v. Commonwealth Trade Marks Label Association, 4 C. L. R. 1569 (1907). See also Attorney-General for New South Wales v. Brewery Employes Union of New South Wales, 6 C. L. R. 469 (1908).

[43] King v. Berger, 6 C. L. R. 41, 67 (1908).

[44] The Federated Amalgamated Government Railway and Tramway Service Association v. New South Wales Railway Traffic Employes Association, 4 C. L. R. 488 (1906).

[45] Attorney-General for New South Wales v. Brewery Employes Union, 6 C. L. R. 469, 491 (1908).

[46] *Ibid.*, 500, 559, 560. For other acts invalidated see Fox v. Robbins, 8 C. L. R. 115 (1909) holding a state licensing act discriminatory; Huddart Parker and Co., Ltd. v. Moorehead, 8 C. L. R. 331 (1909) setting aside sections of an Industries Preservation Act; and Australian Boot Trade Employees Federation v. Whybrow and Co., 10 C. L. R. 266 (1910) and 11 C. L. R. 311 (1910) condemning an award of the federal court of conciliation and arbitration.

When an issue arose over the Royal Commissions Act of 1902–12 the court could not come to an agreement and availed itself of the power under section 74 to refer a question of constitutional interpretation to the Privy Council. The Council held the act *ultra vires,* so far as it purported to enable a Commonwealth Royal Commission to compel answers generally to questions in relation to the intrastate sugar industry, or to order the production of documents relative thereto, or otherwise to enforce compliance by the members of the public with its requisition.[47] The Council seemed to recognize an error in its judgment in the *Webb Case* by admitting that in fashioning the Constitution of the Commonwealth of Australia the principle established by the United States was adopted in preference to that chosen by Canada.

As in the United States, the interpretation of the Constitution is not for the judiciary of the Commonwealth alone; it is part of the duty of every court throughout the Commonwealth. Although every court of competent jurisdiction is an interpreter of the Constitution, and the High Court, subject to an advisory review by the Privy Council, is the authoritative and final interpreter of the Constitution, the state parliaments enjoy a position of independence unknown to the state legislatures in the United States, or to the provincial parliaments in Canada. This arises from the fact that to the states belong the powers not granted to the Commonwealth and few prohibitions on the states are included in the Constitution. There are also no inhibitions arising from general phrases like due process of law or the impairment of the obligation of contracts. Furthermore the doctrine of implied prohibitions, although accepted by the judiciary, has been given by legislative enactment a very limited application.

The nature of judicial review of legislation in the states can best be indicated by some of the decisions in Victoria and in New South Wales. In Victoria it was decided as early as 1862 that

---

[47] Attorney-General for Commonwealth of Australia v. Colonial Sugar Refining Co., Ltd., 17 C. L. R. 644 (1913). For a criticism of the action of the Privy Council in this case, see W. J. Brown, ''The Nature of a Federal Commonwealth,'' 30 *Law Quart. Rev.* (July 1914) 301.

the Supreme Court had power to examine the validity of an act of the state parliament.[48] It was held that the courts of a colony have the power and are under obligations to decide whether an act of the Colonial legislature is in contravention of an act of the Imperial parliament and consequently not binding on the inhabitants of the colony.[49] Justices Marshall and Kent were quoted in the citation of American cases.

When the question was raised whether a power existed in a state court to grant a *mandamus* to compel a federal officer to perform duties imposed upon him by the federal parliament when the duties were to be performed within the State, Justice Owen remarked:

> There is no case analagous to this in any of the English cases that throws any light on the subject. We must go to some country where there are two such Constitutions as we have here, such as America and Canada. In America it has been decided over and over again that a mandamus will not lie in a state court to compel the performance of a duty by a Federal officer. That appears to me to be an analogous case to that now before the Court. The American decisions appeared to be based upon the principle of separate sovereignties, the Federal and the State Governments, and here the Federal Government and the State Government are two distinct entities, as distinct to my mind as if they were separated by territorial boundaries. I think that exactly the same principle must apply in dealing with the question in this State as would apply in America. For these reasons I am of opinion that we have no power to grant a mandamus to compel the Collector of Customs to perform duties imposed upon him by the Federal Parliament.[50]

In the *Royal Commissions Case* the justices, quoting Sir Edward Coke, held that the King may constitute new courts of law with the assent of Parliament, but insisted that such courts must proceed by due process of law, and administer the law, whether common law or statute law, so that the subject may know precisely how and by what law his case is to be dealt with. Consequently, a royal commission intended to inquire into a matter which was within the jurisdiction of the Court of Arbitration

---

[48] In re Dill, 1 W. & W. (L.) 171, 187 (1862).

[49] 1 W. & W. (L.) 171 (1862), and Legge 1406, 1416 (1861).

[50] *Ex parte* Goldring, 3 N. S. Wales 260, 264 (1903).

was held illegal. The theory of the separation of powers and of the independence of the courts were defended.[51]

For the states the principle had been long established that the colonists carry with them only so much of the English law as was considered applicable to their own situation—the applicability of any law being a question for judicial determination as occasion arises.

Some new light was shed on the evolution of federal relationships in Australia by the recent approval of a federal grant in aid to the states for road building and maintenance purposes.[52] On the other hand, the attempt of the states to place a sales tax on gasoline, applying it to the first sale after production or entry was thwarted on the ground that such a tax was a duty of excise.[53] It appears to be conceded that there is a federal common law in Australia.[54] And emergency powers to fix minimum prices were approved.[55]

When the Commonwealth Shipping Board entered into an agreement with the Council of Sydney to erect turbo-alternators, it was held that the Constitution gives no authority for the Commonwealth Executive to engage in business for commercial purposes. Such contracts were deemed not necessary for military and naval defense in time of peace.[56]

The query whether a Court of Inquiry established under the provisions of an act of Tasmania had authority to deal with a marine casualty was answered in the affirmative on the ground that the Commonwealth Parliament may not direct its court to

---

[51] *Ex parte* Leahy, 4 N. S. Wales 401, 425 (1904). See also Allen v. Foskett, etc., 14 N. S. Wales, S. C. R. 456 (1876) and Rex v. Smithers, 16 C. L. R. 99 (1912).

[52] Victoria v. Commonwealth, 38 C. L. R. 399 (1926).

[53] Commonwealth and Commonwealth Oil Refineries, Ltd. v. South Australia, 38 C. L. R. 408 (1926); see also John Fairfax & Sons, Ltd. and Smith's Newspapers, Ltd. v. New South Wales, 39 C. L. R. 139 (1926).

[54] Rex v. Kidman, 20 C. L. R. 425 (1915). In this case the authority to pass *ex post facto* laws was upheld.

[55] Farey v. Burvett, 21 C. L. R. 433 (1916). Three justices dissented in this case.

[56] Commonwealth v. Australian Commonwealth Shipping Board, 39 C. L. R. (1926).

deal with a collision between two vessels not engaged in interstate or foreign trade.[57] And the attempt of the Inter-State Commission to enjoin New South Wales from taking certain action under the provisions of the Wheat Acquisition Act of 1914 was held unauthorized, and in so far as the Interstate Commission Act of 1912 provided for such an injunction, the provisions were declared invalid.[58]

The principle of judicial review of the constitutionality of legislation seems to the people of Australia "a normal and inevitable feature of a federal system."[59] Familiar American principles of constitutional law are applied in Australia, such as, the constitution can only be interpreted in a cause or case,[60] the court does not annul an unconstitutional statute; it simply refuses to recognize it and determines the rights of parties as if there was no statute. The presumption is in favor of the constitutionality of a statute and the opposition must be clear.[61] Though great care was taken to avoid ambiguities in the drafting of the Constitution, nevertheless it contains phrases which are capable of a variety of interpretations, and the High Court has not hesitated to overrule earlier decisions.[62] But prohibitions and exceptions implied from matters outside of the instrument are to be kept to a minimum.[63] In the famous *Engineers Case*

---

[57] King v. Turner; *ex parte* Marine Board of Hobart, 39 C. L. R. 411 (1927).

[58] Commonwealth v. State of New South Wales, 20 C. L. R. 54 (1915).

[59] P. D. Phillips, 2 *Australian Law Jour.* (Dec. 15, 1928), 254.

[60] Attorney General for New South Wales v. Brewery Employees, 6 C. L. R. 469, 491 (1908); Attorney General for Queensland v. Attorney General for Commonwealth, 20 C. L. R. 148 (1915); in re Judiciary Act. 29 C. L. R. 257 (1921).

[61] Owners of S. S. Kalibia v. Wilson, 11 C. L. R. 689 (1910); Waterside Workers' Federation of Australia v. Commonwealth Steamship Owners' Association, 28 C. L. R. 209, 219 (1920).

[62] See Foggit, Jones & Co., Ltd. v. State of New South Wales, 21 C. L. R. 357 (1916), overruled by Duncan v. State of Queensland, 22 C. L. R. 556 (1917) and W. & A. McArthur, Ltd. v. State of Queensland, 28 C. L. R. 530 (1920).

[63] Amalgamated Society of Engineers v. Adelaide Steamship Co., Ltd. 28 C. L. R. 129 (1920).

Justice Knox indicated a change in the consideration of American precedents. ''We conceive that American authorities,'' he said,

however illustrious the tribunals may be, are not a secure basis on which to build fundamentally with respect to our own Constitution. While in secondary and subsidiary matters they may and sometimes do afford considerable light and assistance, they cannot for reasons we are about to state, be recognized as standards whereby to measure the respective rights of the Commonwealth and the States under the Australian Constitution.

Differences arising from the common sovereignty of the British Empire make it necessary to turn to English cases for guidance. The doctrine of implied prohibitions rejected in *Webb v. Outtrim,* ''though subsequently reaffirmed by three members of this court, has as often been rejected by two other members of the court, and, has never been unreservedly accepted and applied.''[64] As a result of this reasoning the *Federated Amalgamated Case* (Railway Servants Case) was reversed.

The duty of the High Court to render advisory opinions was rejected when it was held that the acts of 1903 and 1920, giving the Court jurisdiction to determine any question referred to it by the Governor General as to the validity of any enactment of Parliament and to make the determination final and conclusive, were invalid.[65]

The supremacy of the High Court in constitutional questions has been consistently maintained, only once has the Court certified a question to the Privy Council relating to the distribution of powers between the Commonwealth and the States. Attempts to appeal directly from the States to the Council have been prevented by legislation removing jurisdiction in such cases from the State Courts and requiring that appeals must go to the High Court.[66]

---

[64] 28 C. L. R. 150 ff.

[65] In re Judiciary and Navigation Acts, 29 C. L. R. 257 (1921).

[66] Sir Robert Garran, ''The Development of the Australian Constitution,'' 40 *Law Quart. Rev.* (April 1924), 201; also McCawley v. The King, 28 C. L. R. 106 (1920).

AUSTRIA

Constitution, 1920—

Art. 89, sec. 1. The courts may not inquire into the validity of any duly promulgated law.

Sec. 2. If a court has any doubt as to the applicability of a decree on the ground of conflict with the law, the proceedings must be discontinued and an application made to the Supreme Constitutional Court for the cancellation of the decree.

Art. 137. The Supreme Constitutional Court shall give judgment upon all claims against the Federation, the Provinces or the Communes which cannot be decided by the ordinary judicial procedure.

Art. 138. The Supreme Constitutional Court shall also have jurisdiction in all disputes as to competence:

(*a*) between the Courts and Administrative authorities;

(*b*) between the Supreme Administrative Court and the ordinary courts, and in particular between the Supreme Administrative Court and the Supreme Constitutional Court itself;

(*o*) between the Provinces themselves, as well as between a Province and the Federation.

Art. 139. (1) The Supreme Constitutional Court shall give judgment as to the illegality of orders issued by any Federal or Provincial authority on the motion of a court, or *ex officio* when the order presupposes a finding by the Supreme Constitutional Court, and also on the motion of the federal government in regard to the illegality of orders issued by a Provincial Government, and on the motion of a Provincial Government in regard to the illegality of orders issued by the Federal Government.

(2) Immediately upon judgment being given by the Supreme Constitutional Court, annulling an order as illegal, the competent authority shall publish notice of the annulment, which shall take effect from the day of publication.

Art. 140. (1) The Supreme Constitutional Court shall give judgment in all questions as to the unconstitutionality of laws, in the case of Provincial laws upon the motion of the Federal Government, and in the case of Federal laws upon the motion of a Provincial Government, but *ex officio* when the law presupposes a finding by the Supreme Constitutional Court.

(2) The motion mentioned in Paragraph 1 may be made at any time; the authority responsible for the motion must communicate it immediately to the Provincial Government concerned or to the Federal Government.

(3) Immediately upon the delivery of a judgment of the Supreme Constitutional Court annulling a law as unconstitutional, the Federal Chancellor or the Governor of a Province concerned shall publish notice of the

annulment, which shall take effect from the day of publication unless the Supreme Constitutional Court fixes a period for the annulment. This period may not exceed six months.

(4) The provisions of Article 89, paragraph 1, shall not apply to an inquiry into the constitutionality of laws by the Supreme Constitutional Court.

Art. 145. The Constitutional Court shall give judgment upon violations of international law in accordance with the provisions of a special federal law.

The Supreme Constitutional Court of Austria was conceived by the makers of the constitution as its central feature. It was established to secure respect for the constitution by the administrative officers and by the legislature. The court is authorized to decide only on the legality of ordinances and on the constitutionality of laws. To it is given the duty and responsibility of determining the relations between the national government and the states. By an amendment to Article 138 of the constitution in 1925 the function of the court in this respect was strengthened. The amendment provided that:

The Supreme Constitutional Court decides . . . . on the request of the federal government or a provincial government, if an act of legislation or of administration comes, according to articles 10 to 15 within the competence of the Confederation or in that of the Provinces.

The decisions are to be made along the lines similar to a case and are to secure a preventive control over the constitutionality of laws and ordinances in the reciprocal relations between the Confederation and the Provinces.

This provision adds to the legislative authority of the court. It can in this manner lay down general rules which will supplement the constitution. The axioms formulated by the court on federal relations will have the force of constitutional rules.[67]

The court is limited in its consideration of questions of constitutionality to matters raised by the national or state govern-

---

[67] Charles Eisenmann, *La justice constitutionnelle et la Haute Cour constitutionnelle d'Autriche* (Paris, 1928) 234 ff. To 1927 three such requests had been made by the governments of the Provinces.

ments or to constitutional issues which may arise in rendering its judgments.[68] In the exercise of its unquestioned power to control legislation the court has always borne in mind that it is not a political but a jurisdictional organ—designated as such to decide not what is politically or morally good or bad, but what is juridically regular or irregular.[69] The act annulled by the court disappears from the juridical order as if repealed by a subsequent act. The court can delay the time to take effect of a decision on the constitutionality of a law for not to exceed six months.[70] Laws or ordinances are regarded as effective and obligatory to the time that they are declared void.

Article 144 of the Constitution makes the Supreme Constitutional Court the guardian of individual liberties when they are guaranteed by the Constitution and are interfered with by administrative decisions. The court thus acquires a considerable portion of what is ordinarily understood as adjudication on administrative acts and procedure. It seems likely that this court will absorb the major part of *contentieux administratif*. The act impugned must involve a direct and immediate violation of the constitution.

The rights guaranteed to individuals are enumerated in the fundamental law of December 21, 1867, on the general rights of the citizen which Art. 149 of the Constitution declares a part of the federal constitutional law. Among the rights protected are: equality before the law,[71] the inviolability of property,[72] liberty of the person,[73] liberty of residence, travel and emigration,[74]

---

[68] See Constitution, 1920, art. 89 and Bundesgesetz 13 July, 1921, *Bundesgesetzblatt, 1245;* also Ludwig Adamovich, *Die Prüfung der Gesetze und Verordnungen durch den österreichischen Verfassungsgerichtshof* (Leipzig, 1923).

[69] Eisenmann, *op. cit.*, 219.

[70] *Ibid.*, 226; also M. Métall, "Die gerichtliche Prüfung von Staatsverträgen nach der österreichischen Bundesverfassung," *Zeitschrift für öffentliche Recht*, 7, 106 ff.

[71] Cf. Decision, Oct. 19, 1925, 2:449.

[72] Decision, Oct. 21, 1924, 2:335.

[73] Cf. Decision, Nov. 4, 1927, 2:184, 872.

[74] Decision, Dec. 14, 1925, 2:495.

liberty of assembly and association, freedom of opinion,[75] liberty of instruction, and liberty of conscience and religion.[76]

Under certain conditions the Supreme Court has been authorized to determine the legality of resolutions, which are not laws in the strict sense. By a decision of June 28 1921, the Court decided that a resolution of the Diet of Tyrol was void because it dealt not with an act of administration but matters which should be provided by law. Since the requirements necessary for the enactment of a statute were not complied with, the resolution was held invalid.

The court serves as a tribunal of conflicts and as a court for the trial of impeachment charges. Austrians regard the court as a successful part of their constitutional system. Its jurisdiction has been enlarged and there seems to be an increasing confidence in the impartiality of its judgments. It is the general belief in Austria that the development of jurisprudence by the special constitutional court will prove more effective than is possible under the American plan of judicial review.[77]

BOLIVIA

Constitution, 1880—

In addition to its ordinary powers and duties, the Supreme Court shall have the authority:

Art. 110, sec. 2. To take cognizance, in an individual case involving matters of pure law wherein the decision depends upon the constitutionality or unconstitutionality of laws, decrees, or any kind of resolution.

Art. 138. The authorities and tribunals shall apply this Constitution in preference to the laws, and the laws in preference to any other resolutions.

Art. 139. Laws and decrees contrary to this constitution are void.[78]

---

[75] Decisions, Mar. 18 and 23, June, 1926, 2:552, 630.

[76] Decision, May 16, 1927, 2:197.

[77] See Hans Kelsen, ''La garantie juridictionnelle de la Constitution (Justice constitutionnelle),'' 45 *Revue du Droit Public* (April-June, 1928) 197 and *Annuaire de L'Institut International de Droit Public* (129) 52 ff.

[78] Writers on the Bolivian government refer to the adoption of the American doctrine of judicial review by the Bolivian courts but few references are given to actual decisions reviewing legislative acts or declaring them void.

BRAZIL

Constitution, 1891 and 1926—

Arts. 59 and 60 as amended.

III. The Federal judges and courts shall have power to try and to judge:

(*a*) All cases in which plaintiff or defendant bases his claim or defense on a provision of the Federal Constitution;

(*b*) All suits against the Government of the Union or the National Treasury based upon provisions of the Constitution, executive laws and regulations, or contracts with the said Government.

Paragraph 1. The right of appeal to the Federal Supreme Court from the sentences of State courts of final instance shall exist:

(*a*) When there is a question as to whether the Federal laws are in force or as to their validity under the Constitution, and when a decision of the State court denies their application;

(*b*) When the validity of laws or acts of the State Government with respect to the Constitution or the Federal laws is questioned and the State court shall have decided in favor of the validity of such acts or laws.

(*c*) When two or more local courts interpret the same Federal law differently, in which case appeal may be taken by any of the said courts or by the attorney general of the Republic.[79]

The constitution of Brazil provides in Art. 59 and 60 for the jurisdiction and authority of the federal judiciary. These sections make it clear that the ultimate authority on all questions of conflict between the rights and powers of the states on the one hand and those of the federal government on the other are to be determined by the federal courts. The constitution of Brazil does not give to the federal courts the power to decide whether the federal legislature, or executive acts may or may not be applied in cases that come before them because of conflict with the constitution. It was well understood, however, that the American theory and practice of judicial review of legislation, with which Brazilian authorities on public law were familiar, were

[79] See Constitution of the Republic of the United States of Brazil, in Law and Treaty *Series,* Pan American Union, No. 5, 1927.

intended to be incorporated into the Brazilian system.[80]   Since the establishment of the Brazilian federal system it has been considered a fundamental principle of the constitution that the power to pass upon the constitutionality of acts of the national legislative or executive power resides in the courts.

Beginning with the arguments of Barbosa, familiar American principles were adopted in Brazil, as follows:

> The federal courts have the power to declare null and void legislative acts that violate the federal constitution.   This declaration, when properly invoked, is not merely a legal right of the federal courts but also an inescapable duty.   The nullity of the unconstitutional acts of the executive power, like those of the legislative, and with even more reason, is fixed by means of judicial action.   The inapplicability of the unconstitutional legislative or executive act is determined with reference to each particular case by a judgment rendered in a suit duly instituted and capable of execution as between the parties.   The violation of the individual guaranties, practiced under the guise of political functions, is not immune from the action of the courts.   These must in all cases determine whether the political power invoked as withdrawing the case from the jurisdiction of the courts includes within its limits the exercise of the power in question.[81]

The courts in the Brazilian states are also accorded the authority to declare void the acts of their legislative chambers as well as executive orders and municipal ordinances.[82]   As a rule the state constitutions follow the basic principles of the federal fundamental law.

The courts of the states pass upon constitutional questions in common with all other issues raised before them.   If a federal constitutional question is involved the case may be appealed to the federal courts which have the final word on the interpretation of the federal constitution.   If a case involves directly and exclusively a federal constitutional issue the case may be taken directly to the federal courts.   Federal courts are also authorized to try

---

[80] See Ruy Barbosa, *Os Actos Inconstitucionâes do Congresso e do Executivo ante a Justiça Federal* (Rio de Janeiro, 1893); Herman G. James, *The Constitutional System of Brazil* (Washington, 1923), 106 ff.

[81] See Barbosa, *op. cit.*, and James, *op. cit.*, 107.

[82] See Constitutions of Rio de Janeiro, 1892, art. 75, and of Amazon, 1910, art. 144.

cases involving a violation of constitutional principles by the legislative or executive acts of the municipalities.[83] The law provides a special procedure—*recurso extraordinario*—an appellate process from state courts to the Supreme Court when the validity of a federal treaty or law is concerned and the decision is against its validity, or when the validity of an act of a state is attacked as in violation of the constitution or the federal laws, and the decision is in favor of the validity of the act.[84]

Though judges and commentators set about to apply the American principles of judicial review of legislation in Brazil, the results have varied greatly from the American model. Since the details of legislation are prescribed by executive decrees, as is the custom in countries whose basic legal doctrines have been developed from the Roman and French codes, most of the acts of officials which interfere with private rights involve ordinances emanating from the executive.[85] Not many cases involve a direct conflict between the constitution and a legislative act.[86] Brazilian courts in accordance with civil law practice do not follow precedents and hence are inclined to consider each case on its merits regardless of former adjudications of the court touching similar issues. Though such a practice avoids the rigidity which characterizes much constitutional interpretation it tends to make the law uncertain even with regard to fundamental matters of constitutional law. Furthermore acts of the states do not infringe on the federal domain so frequently as they do in the United States since the fields of commercial, civil, and criminal law are under the control of the federal government.

---

[83] Pedro Lessa, *Direito Constitucional Brasileiro: Do Poder Judiciario* (Rio de Janeiro, 1915), 130 ff.

[84] Lessa, *op. cit.*, 103 ff. Lessa regards this recourse as identical with the writ of error in the federal courts of the United States. See James, *op. cit.*, 113.

[85] Cf. San Francisco S. Costa v. Procopio Oliveira and Cia, 21 Rev. Do. Sup. Trib. 283 and Luiz Rocha v. A. Herança de José Luiz Jorge, 24 Rev. Do. Sup. Trib. 134 (1920) in which decrees were held void.

[86] See União v. José Goncalves Ferraz, 7 Rev. Do. Sup. Trib. 388 (1915); also in re Electoral Appeal No. 359, 39 Rev. Do. Sup. Trib. 252 (1922).

CANADA

British North America Act, 1867—

There are no provisions relating to judicial review of legislation in the fundamental law of Canada. The following provisions relate to disallowance of acts and to the establishment of a Supreme Court for Canada:

Article 56—Where the Governor General assents to a Bill in the Queen's Name, he shall by the first convenient Opportunity send an authentic Copy of the Act to One of Her Majesty's Principal Secretaries of State, and if the Queen in Council within Two Years after Receipt thereof by the Secretary of State thinks fit to disallow the Act, such Disallowance (with a Certificate of the Secretary of State of the Day on which the Act was received by him) being signified by the Governor General, by Speech or Message to each of the Houses of the Parliament or by Proclamation, shall annul the Act from and after the Day of such Signification.

Article 57—A Bill reserved for the Signification of the Queen's Pleasure shall not have any Force unless and until, within Two Years from the Day on which it was presented to the Governor General for the Queen's Assent, the Governor General signifies, by Speech or Message to each of the Houses of the Parliament or by Proclamation, that it has received the Assent of the Queen in Council.

Article 101—The Parliament of Canada may, notwithstanding anything in this Act, from Time to Time provide for the Constitution, Maintenance, and Organization of a General Court of Appeal for Canada, and for the Establishment of any additional Courts for the better administration of the Laws of Canada.

In the courts of any one of three jurisdictions, Provincial, Dominion, and Imperial, acts of Canadian legislatures may be impeached and may be declared *ultra vires* or unconstitutional. As in the United States, courts refuse to enforce legislative acts, thereby rendering them null and void. This authority is not infrequently employed by provincial tribunals.

The courts of the provinces not only decide as to the competence of provincial legislatures to enact certain measures but also place their stamp of disapproval on Dominion acts which are regarded as beyond federal jurisdiction. This power is exercised with a greater degree of caution than in the United States, but the question of competence is raised not infrequently and the legislative department must justify to the courts its course of action as being within the scope of legislative power.[87]

A prolonged and interesting controversy arose with reference to the power of the provincial legislature to tax the salaries of Dominion officials. In an early decision the Supreme Court of Ontario, following the decision of Chief Justice Marshall in the case of *McCulloch* v. *Maryland,* approved the American doctrine of implied prohibitions and held· that the local legislature could not levy such a tax because such taxation might interfere with the powers given to the federal authorities by the British North America Act.[88] This decision was followed and approved in the provinces of New Brunswick[89] and British Columbia.[90] On an appeal to the Privy Council of a similar decision from Australia,[91] the Council reversed the Australian Court and announced the decision that the doctrine of implied prohibitions as accepted and followed in the United States could not be held to apply to the public law of the self-governing colonies.[92] When the same issue was presented to the Supreme Court of Canada the justices followed the judgment and reasoning of the Privy Council and reversed the Leprohon and other provincial decisions.[93] Thus for Canada the doctrine of implied prohibitions has been rejected.[94]

---

[87] For a summary of provincial acts held void by the courts, see my article ''Judicial Review of Legislation in Canada,'' 28 *Harv. Law Rev.* (April 1915), 570 ff. A few extracts from this article are used in the following pages with the permission of the editors of the Harvard Law Review.

[88] Leprohon v. Ottawa, 2 Ont. App. Rep. 522 (1877).

[89] *Ex parte* Owen, 20 New Bruns. Rep. 487 (1881) and *Ex parte* Burke, 34 New Bruns. Rep. 200 (1896).

[90] Regina v. Bowell, 4 Brit. Col. 498 (1896).

[91] Deakin v. Webb, 1 C. L. R. 585 (1904).

[92] Webb v. Outtrim (1907), A. C. 81.

[93] Abbott v. City of St. John, 40 Sup. Ct. Rep. 597 (1908).

[94] Cf. Deakin v. Webb, 1 C. L. R. 585 (1904) and Commissioners of Taxation v. Baxter, 4 C. L. R. 1087 (1907). See *supra,* 581 *et seq.*

Dominion acts may likewise be held *ultra vires* by provincial courts. Though seldom called upon to perform this function, there are sufficient instances to show that the lower courts do not decline when occasion arises to assert the right to refuse to enforce Dominion acts.

The Supreme Court of Canada has defended the right of the federal government in its control over commerce by prohibiting the legislature of a province from granting exclusive rights of fishing as to the open sea within a marine league of the coast.[95] On similar grounds the provincial legislature was denied power to enact legislation authorizing the construction and operation of railways in such a manner as to interfere with the physical structure or with the operation of railways subject to the jurisdiction of the Parliament of Canada.[96] An attempt on the part of the Ontario legislature to prevent appeal to the Supreme Court of the Dominion in cases where the amount in controversy is under $1000 was declared *ultra vires*.[97] At other times the provincial legislatures have not been allowed to permit the operation of lotteries[98] or to prohibit the performance of work on Sunday.[99]

There are few cases in which Dominion acts have been held invalid. Among the statutes nullified by the Supreme Court are certain provisions in so far as they attempt to confer exclusive rights of fishing in provincial waters;[100] sections of the insurance act in so far as they purport to affect companies incorporated by one of the provinces and carrying on business exclusively in such province;[101] and the provisions of the section of an act assuming to authorize references by the Governor-General in council to the judges of the Supreme Court for their

[95] Attorney-General of Brit. Col. v. Attorney-General of Canada, 15 Dom. L. Rep. 308 (1913).

[96] In re Legislation Respecting Railways, 48 S. C. R. 9 (1913).

[97] Clarkson v. Ryan, 17 S. C. R. 251 (1890).

[98] L'Assn. St. Jean Baptiste de Montreal v. Brault, 30 S. C. R. 598 (1900).

[99] In re Legislation Respecting Labor on Sunday, 35 S. C. R. 581 (1905).

[100] In re Provincial Fisheries, 26 S. C. R. 444 (1895).

[101] In re Insurance Act, 15 Dom. L. Rep. 251 (1913).

opinions in respect to matters within provincial legislative jurisdiction.[102]

The final jurisdiction in which the acts of Canadian legislatures may be invalidated is the Judicial Committee of the Privy Council. The Privy Council is the tribunal to which questions of competence may ultimately be appealed. Cases may be carried directly from the province to the Judicial Committee or may be taken in rare cases from the decision of the highest court of Canada to the Privy Council. No matter how cases reach this court it is generally conceded that the authoritative exposition of the British North America Act rests with this Imperial tribunal.[103]

Not only does the Committee check the legislative activities of the provinces, but it also sits in judgment upon the interpretation placed upon the British North America Act by the Supreme Court of Canada. That the Committee is disposed to exercise a will of its own is shown in the reversal of the highest court of the Dominion relative to the right of the executive to require answers from the justices on questions both of law and fact. Despite provincial and Dominion decisions to the contrary the Council held it not *ultra vires* for the executive government of the Dominion to request answers from the Supreme Court.[104]

The Council denied that the provincial and Dominion legislatures are organs of delegated authority, and with this the rule was affirmed that there is no sphere of liberty between the two governments. The court holds that the provincial legislature derives no authority from the government of Canada, and its status is in no way analogous to that of a municipal institution. It possesses powers, not of administration merely but of legislation in the strictest sense of that word, and within the limits assigned by section 92 of the Act of 1867, its powers are exclusive

---

[102] In re References, 43 S. C. R. 536 (1910).

[103] For early cases holding Provincial and Dominion acts invalid see 28 *Harv. Law Rev.* 575.

[104] Attorney-General for Ontario v. Attorney-General for Dom. of Can., [1912] A. C. 571; cf. Lefroy *Canada's Federal System* (Toronto, 1913) 672.

and supreme.[105] The local legislature, the Parliament of the Dominion, and the Imperial Parliament are, from the general standpoint of legislative capacity, on the same plane. Their Lordships "adhere to the view which has always been taken by the Committee, that the Federation act exhausts the whole range of legislative power and that whatever is not thereby given to the provincial legislatures rests with the Parliament."[106]

The student of judicial control in Canada is at once struck by the fact that there are some marked limitations to the exercise of control over legislation by Canadian courts, which do not restrict American justices in the exercise of similar authority.

The first among these limitations is the veto power, which the Imperial government may exercise over Dominion acts and which the Dominion government may exercise over provincial acts. While Canada is a self-governing colony and as a consequence is almost entirely free to manage her own affairs, nevertheless the Privy Council has repeatedly held that the paramount authority of the Imperial Parliament has been in no wise lessened by the Canadian constitution and that the Imperial government has regularly claimed the power to disallow any legislation which the self-governing colonies may enact.[107] In like manner the federal constitution gives the Governor-General full authority to disallow acts of the provincial legislatures, such disallowance being permitted only within two years after the passage of the act. The Imperial power of disallowance has been very rarely applied, except in regard to shipping regulations and the control over foreign affairs.[108] For the Dominion the device of a veto over provincial acts was evidently designed to avoid the bitter con-

---

105 Queen v. Burah, 3 A. C. 889, 903 (1878).

106 Bank of Toronto v. Lambe, 12 A. C. 575, 588 (1887).

107 The above provisions have been changed to a certain extent by the Statute of Westminster which repealed the Colonial Laws Validity Act of 1865 and authorized the Parliaments of the Dominions to enact laws regardless of their repugnance to the laws of England. See 12 *Journal of the Parliaments of the Empire* (October, 1931) 903.

108 For a list of subjects on which colonial acts have failed to receive the royal assent, consult 2 *Keith, Responsible Government in the Dominions* (London, 1912) 1020; among the special subjects noted are (a) copyright; (b) divorce and status; (c) immigration of colored races.

flicts waged in the United States over states' rights. The authors of the plan also conceived that this power could be used to prevent any unjust interference with private rights and property interests by means of provincial acts. In recent cases, however, the Dominion government has refused to interfere in favor of the protection of vested interests and the tenet has been announced that ''an abuse of power even so as to amount to the practical confiscation of property, or that the exercise of the power has been unwise or indiscreet,'' is no valid ground for the use of the veto power.[109]

As a result of these decisions it is confidently asserted that the veto power of the Dominion is slowly taking its place by that of the Crown and will soon disappear as a vital part of the constitution.[110] The veto power, however, remains with the general government and may be called into service at any time to check attempts to injure seriously Imperial or Dominion interests. That the power of disallowance in the Dominion may be used effectively is shown in the refusal to sanction the recent attempt of British Columbia to prohibit Asiatic immigration.[111]

A second limitation on judicial control, and one of much greater significance, is the entire absence of restrictions on the power of the legislature relative to private property and civil rights. The familiar Bill of Rights of constitutions in the United States, with the consequent fetters upon legislative authority

[109] See C. B. Labatt, ''The Scope of the Power of the Dominion Government to Disallow Provincial Statutes,'' 45 *Can. Law Jour.* (May 1909) 297 ff.; cf. also refusal to disallow the Ontario hydro-electric power legislation. ''The present interpretation of the section confines the power of disallowance to cases where there is a manifest encroachment by a Provincial legislature.'' 46 *Can. Law Jour.* (June 1926) 357. The modern theory of disallowance was announced by the Governor-General in this case: ''It is not intended by the British North America Act,'' he holds, ''that the power of disallowance shall be exercised for the purpose of annulling provincial legislation, even, though your Excellency's Ministers consider the legislation unjust or oppressive, or in conflict with recognized legal principles, so long as such legislation is within the power of the provincial legislature to enact. The legislation in question, even though confiscation of property without compensation, and so an abuse of legislative power does not fall within any of the aforesaid enumeration.''

[110] ''Democracy v. Republicanism,'' 48 *Can. Law Jour.* (April 1912) 244.

[111] For discussion of the disallowance of provincial acts, see 2 *Keith, Responsible Government in the Dominions,* 725.

and administrative procedure, is a noteworthy omission in the Canadian constitutions. Canadians take pride in the fact that all power is divided between the two governments and commend the principle that leaves no gap and that shuts off no peculiar field of non-governmental control. They frequently call attention to the fact that there is an entire "absence of any attempt to fetter the freedom of our legislatures by fundamental limitations such as abound in the United States federal and state constitutions."[112] It is customary to speak of American legislatures as confined in straight jackets.[113]

Although there are a few dicta to the contrary, the general rule appears to prevail that courts may not pronounce acts invalid because they affect private rights injuriously.[114] A statement of the principle as generally applied by the courts is given in an opinion of the Minister of Justice relative to the *Ontario Water Power Case*, in which he asserted:

> A suggestion of the abuse of power, even so as to amount to practical confiscation of property, or that the exercise of power has been unwise or indiscreet, should appeal to your Excellency's Government with no more effect than it does to the ordinary tribunals, and the remedy in such case is, in the words of Lord Herschell, an appeal to those by whom the legislature is elected.[115]

Laws interfering with the exercise of private rights are not infrequently passed, and in answer to the contention that the court should afford protection to the rights of the individual, the rule which prevails in England was affirmed, "that it does not belong to courts of justice to interpolate constitutional restrictions; their duty being to apply the law, not to make it."[116]

---

[112] "Canada's Federal System," 49 *Can. Law Jour.* (Nov. 1913) 656.

[113] 42 *Ibid.*, 463.

[114] Cf. L'Union St. Jacques v. Belisle, 20 *L. Can. Jur.* 29 (1874); Grand Junction Ry. Co. v. The Corporation of Peterborough, 8 S. C. R. 76 (1882); McGregor v. Esquimalt & N. Ry. Co. (1907) A. C. 462; Florence Mining Co. Case, 18 Ont. L. Rep. 275 (1908). For a defense of the view that the veto power of the Dominion government should be used for this purpose and for a discussion of precedents, see 45 *Can. Law Jour.* 299 ff.

[115] "The Right of Disallowance," 44 *Can. Law Jour.* (Sept 1908) 557; also 45 *Can. Law Jour.* 297.

[116] Severn v. The Queen, 2 S. C. R. 70, 103 (1878).

In theory then both federal and local acts may be impeached in any judicial tribunal and are subject to construction, as to whether or not they are *ultra vires*.[117]

To what extent appeals from Canada to the Privy Council may be limited is one of the undetermined issues of Canadian politics. In a recent case a provision of the Criminal Code in so far as it attempted to deny the right of the King in Council to determine criminal appeals from Canadian courts was held void.[118] It was then maintained that the Judicial Committee Act of 1844 relating to appeals to the Privy Council controls any Canadian legislation repugnant to it and that an Imperial Act alone could limit appeals in such cases.[119] Legal opinion in the Dominion is still inclined to favor the retention of the present

---

[117] Cf. ''British and American Constitutions Compared,'' 47 *Can. Law Jour.* (Jan. 1911) 10–11. ''An interpretation by the Parliament of Canada of the British North America Act is surely not binding on this, or on any court of justice. It is for the judicial power to decide whether the interpretation put on the Constitutional Act by either the Parliament of the Dominion or the legislatures of the Provinces is correct or not.'' From Taschereau in Valin v. Langlois, 3 S. C. R. 1, 73 (1879). This view is confirmed by the Privy Council in Citizens Ins. Co. v. Parsons, 7 A. C. 96, 108 (1881), wherein it is held to be the duty of the courts to define the limits of the respective powers of each legislature.

[118] Nadan v. The King (1926) A. C. 482. Leave to appeal was denied in this case and Viscount Cave explained: ''It has for many years past been the settled practice of the Board to refuse to act as a court of criminal appeal, and to advise His Majesty to intervene in a criminal case if and when it is shown that, by a disregard of the forms of legal process or by some violation of the principles of natural justice or otherwise substantial and grave injustice has been done.''

[119] See Ontario Act denying the right of appeal except in specified cases. *Rev. Stat.* 1914 C. 54, sec. 2.

''The English and Scotch lawyers who sat round a table in an obscure room of Whitehall to decide the nature of Canadian federalism were able to regard the issues presented to them with an air of Olympian detachment. No less than in the case of Marshall or Taney the personal mentality and political upbringing of the Judicial Committee largely determined the current of their judicial decisions. But in this personal outlook there was nothing Canadian.''—Herbert A. Smith, ''Judicial Control of Legislation in the British Empire,'' 34 *Yale Law Jour.* (Jan. 1925) 277, 283.

For the proposal that the Supreme Court of Canada be made the final court of appeal in all cases affecting private rights and that a permanent Court of Arbitration be established to determine constitutional questions and disputes between the states or provinces and the national governments and controversies concerning more than one dominion, see Judge W. E. Raney, ''The Appeal to the Privy Council,'' 8 *Can. Bar Rev.* (Oct. 1927) 607 ff.

system of appeal. The chief difficulty in the way of the abolition of the right of appeal appears to be the racial and particularistic tendencies in Quebec.[120]

The impression that the language of the British North America Act is so definite as to leave little scope for judicial legislation and that the courts are not likely to place effective checks on legislation does not seem to be borne out by the modern practice relating to judicial review in Canada. In the first place recent decisions appear to have changed the relations between the Dominion and the Provinces in one of the most important phases of federalism. Canadians usually insisted that the residue of legislation belonged to the Dominion and that the Provinces had only such powers as were expressly granted. The prevailing view was well expressed by two of the founders of the Canadian system of government. It was Macdonald's idea that the federal legislature would control "the general mass of sovereign legislation." He observed:

> We have strengthened the General Government. We have given the General Legislature all the great subjects of legislation. We have conferred on them, not only specifically and in detail, all the powers which are incident to sovereignty, but we have expressly declared that all subjects of general interest not distinctly and exclusively conferred upon the local governments and local legislatures, shall be conferred upon the General Government and Legislature. We have thus avoided that great source of weakness which has been the cause of the disruption of the United States.

Similar views were expressed by Lord Carnarvon, who said:

> The real object which we have in view is to give to the Central Government those high functions and almost sovereign powers by which general principles and uniformity of legislation may be secured in those questions that are of common import to all the provinces. . . . . I ought to point out that, just as the authority of the Central Parliament will prevail whenever it may come into conflict with the local legislatures, so the residue of legislation, if any, unprovided for in the specific classification which I have explained, will belong to the central body.

The authority granted to the central government to preserve the "peace, order, and good government" of the Dominion, in

---

[120] Berriedale Kieth, Notes on Imperial Constitutional Law, 8 *Jour. of Comp. Leg. and Int. Law* (ser. 3) 123 and 285 ff.

addition to the enumerated powers was regarded as equivalent to a grant of residue of authority to the national government. During the early years of the federation the interpretation of the constitution by the courts seemed to support this view of the distribution of powers.[121] By a gradual process of interpretation the "peace, order, and good government" clause has been restricted to reserve powers to be used only in case of war or a similar national emergency.[122] If there is a residue of power now in Canada it appears to be embraced in the general grant to the provinces of the control over property and civil rights. Referring to the change in the federal relationship of which these decisions are an indication and a forecast for the future Mr. Smith observes: "By excluding this historical evidence [the debates during the framing of the British North America Act] and considering the British North America Act without any regard to its historical setting the courts recently imposed upon us a constitution which is quite different, not only in detail but also in principle from that designed at Charlottetown and Quebec."[123] In the second place, the wavering of the courts in the interpretation of certain provisions such as those relating to prohibition, education, and direct taxation shows that no matter how much care is taken in making explicit the authority as between the nation and the states in a federal system, to a considerable degree the judges as interpreters of the terms of the constitution will participate in the determination of the policies of the country.[124]

---

[121] See Russell v. Queen, 7 A. C. 829 (1882) and Hodge v. Queen, 9 A. C. 117 (1883).

[122] In re Board of Commerce Act, 1922) 1 A. C. 191; Fort Frances Case, (1923) A. C. 695; Toronto Electric Commissioners v. Snider, (1925) A. C. 396.

[123] Herbert A. Smith, "The Residue of Power in Canada," 4 *Can. Bar Rev.* (Sept., 1926), 433.

[124] See Cotton v. The King, (1914) A. C. 176; Attorney-General for B. C. v. C. P. Ry. Co., (1927) S. C. R. 185; Rex v. Caledonian Collieries, (1928) A. C. 358; Attorney-General for Manitoba v. Attorney-General for Canada, (1925) A. C. 56; Tiny Separate School Trustees v. King, (1927) S. C. R. 637; Roman Catholic Separate School Trustees v. The King, (1928) A. C. 363.

A strange result of judicial review was the disapproval by the Judicial Committee of the Initiative and Referendum Act of Manitoba because it interfered with the powers of the Lieutenant Governor by compelling him to submit a proposed law to a body of voters totally distinct from the legislature of which he is the constitutional head. The analogy of the British Constitution on which the Canadian plan of government is founded, it was maintained, "points to the impropriety, in the absence of clear and unmistakable language of construing sec. 92 as permitting the abrogation of any power which the Crown possesses through a person who directly represents him."[125]

The right to refer doubtful questions of constitutionality to the Supreme Court for advisory opinions was made use of by the government in two recent cases. First the court was asked to give an opinion whether the Combines Investigation Act and sec. 498 of the Criminal Code were valid. This act, which provided for the investigation of alleged combines and for punishing those who render assistance in the formation or operation of the combines, was upheld despite its effect on the property and civil rights of the provinces. The control which the constitution grants the Dominion over criminal matters was considered broad enough "to enable Parliament to take notice of conduct in any field of human activity."[126]

Second, the Court was requested to give an advisory opinion relating to the legislative authority of the Dominion Parliament with respect to the permanent occupation of Provincial Crown lands, and the permanent diversion and alteration of the flow of rivers for navigation purposes in so far as the proprietary rights of the provinces are curtailed. The question arose as a result of negotiations between Canada and the United States for the building of a dam in the St. Lawrence River in order to improve navigability and incidentally to render available two million horsepower of water power. What would be the respec-

---

[125] In re the Initiative and Referendum Act, (1919) A. C. 935.

[126] Reference re Validity of the Combines Investigation Act and of sec. 498 of the Criminal Code, (1929) S. C. R. 409.

tive rights of the Dominion and the Province in relation to this Power? Claiming that the questions raised were too general and comprehensive the judges rendered an evasive opinion which sheds little light on the ultimate settlement of the issues involved.[127]

Though the legislative authority of the Dominion under the enumerated sections, such as the control over commerce and navigation, is held to carry with it "the widest discretion touching the means to be employed for the advancement of any legislative scheme or purpose," a counterpart of the Hamilton-Marshall implied power doctrine, this broad grant of power to the Dominion is deemed to be limited by the provisos that the property of the Province can only be taken by the payment of just compensation and that the sources of revenue of the Provinces must not be unduly interfered with by Dominion acts.

Cases affecting the constitution of Canada and the provinces may be taken directly on appeal from the Court of Appeal of a province to the Privy Council, though in a recent case Lord Haldane observed:

> It is desirable that topics affecting the Constitution of Canada should come before that Court [Supreme Court of Canada] before being brought to London for argument. . . . . Their Lordships . . . . attach much importance, not only to the position which belongs to the Supreme Court under the Constitution of Canada, but to the value, in the decision of important points such as those before them, of the experience and learning of the judges of that Court.[128]

CHILE

Constitution, 1925—

Art. 42. Exclusive attributes of the Senate are:

Sec. 4. To take cognizance of conflicts in jurisdiction that may arise between the political or administrative authorities and the Superior Courts of Justice.

Art. 86. The Supreme Court has direct supervision, correctional and economic, over all the tribunals of the Nation in accordance with the law determining its organization and attributes.

---

[127] Reference re Waters and Water Powers, (1929) S. C. R. 200.

[128] Re the Initiative and Referendum Act, (1919) A. C. 935.

The Supreme Court, in private cases under its cognizance, or which may have been submitted to it on appeal interposed in a cause pending before the tribunal, may declare ineffective for that case, any legal ruling as contrary to the Constitution. This appeal may be taken at any stage of the cause without suspending the proceedings.

It shall have cognizance also of disputes of competence that may arise between political or administrative authorities and the tribunals of justice not under the control of the Senate.

The constitution of Chile of 1833 placed the authority to supervise the observance of the constitution in Congress with the power to settle any questions which might arise concerning the interpretation of any articles of the constitution. When Congress was not in session this authority was delegated to an Executive Committee of seven members elected by Congress.[129] The new constitution indicates a trend in the direction of a judicial guardianship of the constitution.

COLOMBIA

Constitution, 1886

Art. 51 (Bill of Rights). The laws shall determine the responsibility to be incurred by the public functionaries of all classes who violate the rights guaranteed by this title.

Art. 76. Congress is vested with power

Sec. 1. To interpret, amend and repeal previous laws.

Art. 88. The President of the Republic shall have no power to present new objections to a bill which has been reconsidered and passed by two-thirds of the members in each house, and he shall be bound to approve it.

Art. 90. If a bill is objected to on the ground that it is unconstitutional, it shall be excepted from the provision of article 88. In this case, if the houses insist upon its passage, the bill shall be referred to the supreme court, which, within six days, shall pass upon the subject. If the decision of the court is favorable to the bill, the President shall approve it. If the decision is unfavorable, the bill shall be sent to the archives.

Art. 151. The Supreme Court shall exercise the following functions:

Sec. 4. To decide, finally, upon the validity of legislative acts which have been objected to by the government as unconstitutional.

---

129 See arts., 48, 49, 151, 155.

Sec. 5. To decide, in conformity with the law, upon the validity or nullity of departmental ordinances which have been suspended by the government, or contested before the courts by private parties, as interfering with civil rights.

Sec. 7. To take cognizance of cases of impeachment for violation of the constitution, or laws.

The Supreme Court of Colombia frequently considers the constitutionality of legislative acts and executive decrees but few are refused enforcement and hence held invalid.[130]

COSTA RICA

Constitution, 1871

Art. 17. The acts of the Legislative or Executive powers which are contrary to the Constitution, are null and void, regardless of the form in which they are issued. The acts done by those who have usurped public functions and the appointments made for any office without compliance with the requirements of the Constitution are also void.

Art. 20. Public functionaries are responsible for the violation of the Constitution and the laws. The action to accuse them is popular.

Art. 73. The following are exclusive powers of Congress.

Sec. 13. To enact, amend, interpret and repeal the laws.

Art. 132. Congress, in its first ordinary sessions, shall inquire if there has been any violation of the Constitution and whether the responsibility for the violations has been duly enforced, and for this purpose shall take the measures which seem proper.

In Costa Rica, as in the United States, the courts can declare a law void, but only with respect to the particular case and only with reference to controverted rights. The basis of the organization of the government lies in the separation of the executive, legislative and judicial powers, the independence of which is laid down in the constitution.

In accordance with the constitution, Congress has authority to enact, amend, interpret, and revoke the laws, but the judicial power is authorized to "try civil, criminal and contestable-

---

[130] See Fernando Garavito, *Jurisprudencia de la Corte Suprema de Justicia, 1886–1919*, Bogota (1915 and 1921), especially 2:1032, 1214.

administrative cases, whatsoever may be the nature thereof and the condition of the parties intervening therein; to definitely decide thereupon and to execute the sentences handed down" (art. 1, Organic Law of the Courts); and within the sphere of their powers, in order to determine each case, it is obvious that they must first decide which law is applicable.

In article 17 of the constitution lies the strongest guaranty of individual rights and of public order, as in virtue thereof no decision of the legislature can prevail against the precepts of the constitution, in the observance of which the judges find the standard for meting out the justice which gives to everyone his due. So that any legislative act, in being contrary to the constitution, loses, by this very fact thereof, all validity. The Organic Law of the Courts also prohibits the judges from giving any sanction to unconstitutional legislation. The jurisprudence of the courts of the country has been uniform in regard to ignoring in their decisions the laws deemed unconstitutional. A few cases may illustrate the practice of the Costa Rican courts.

In 1914 Congress delegated to the executive the power to legislate, authorizing the issuance of regulations which might be considered necessary in view of the circumstances created by the European conflict. This resolution delegated functions conferred upon Congress by the constitution. The President, nevertheless, issued various laws, among them one which subjected contracts to certain formalities without the fulfilment of which the recording thereof in the property register could not be effected. The registrar refused to register a deed of transfer of property in which such formalities had been omitted. The point was taken up to the Supreme Court, which decided that the law was unconstitutional and therefore inapplicable. To do so it took into account that

the unconstitutionality of the said Decree being alleged as the basis of this appeal, and that for the same reason it should not be applied by the Lower Court in order to support its decision, it becomes necessary to examine the legal value which, from the standpoint of our Constitutional Law, the aforesaid decree may possess; because the Constitution being the Supreme Law of the Republic, no other law can coexist in opposition thereto, any other regulations of the Legislative or Executive Power at variance therewith being null and void and of no effect, as established by article 17 of the Constitution itself;

The aforementioned decree, while it establishes a tax for charity more onerous than that which existed under decree of Congress of June 6, 1900, and modifies that of the said Congress dated June 13, 1902, declares absorbed therein and revoked the said Decrees, as well as any law contrary thereto; so that that administrative resolution, from its reach and importance, possesses the character of a real law, inasmuch as it goes so far as to revoke those issued previous thereto by the Legislative Power on the same matters;

It being, as established by article 73 of the Constitution, paragraph 13, the exclusive function of Congress to enact laws, interpret and revoke the same, there can be no doubt that the said Decree of November 28 opposes that constitutional article, and for the same reason cannot subsist against it, as provided by article 17 of the Constitution itself;

Article 8 of the Organic Law of Tribunals prohibits the functionaries of the judiciary from applying laws, decrees or administrative regulations which may be contrary to the Constitution; and in fulfilment of such legal provision the Court of Appeals could not properly base its decision on the said Decree in order to deny the recording of the document to which these proceedings refer.[131]

In 1920, after the downfall of the government presided over by General Tinoco, Congress issued the so-called Law of Annulments, by means of which all the acts of that government, including the contracts of civil transactions with innocent third parties, were annulled.

Such rash and undeliberated decision is contrary to the constitution inasmuch as it usurped the functions of the judicial power and interfered with rights acquired in virtue of the civil transactions of individuals with the Tinoco government.

Among the obligations of the state in favor of individuals there was one represented by a check for a considerable sum in favor of Guillermo Steinvorth against the Banco Internacional de Costa Rica. The bank, basing its action on the annulment of the acts by the above law, refused to pay Steinvorth, who resorted to the courts for the protection of his rights.

---

[131] Sentence of the Court of Cassation, March 2, 1915.

The judge before whom the case was tried abstained from applying the law, in consideration of the fact that:

In accordance with the allegations of the representative of the Bank against which claim was made, the right is impugned based on the law of July 20, 1920, which was passed over the veto on August 11 of the said year, and which declared that: ''all checks issued and all payments effected by means of checks and not by means of Government drafts drawn against the Bank of Costa Rica (Treasurer of the Government) by the Secretary of the Treasury of the Tinoco régime, are absolutely null and void and of no effect from their origin.'' From which it results that the check presented is looked upon in its last stage (certificate of validity) as a document which, even though of a private nature, bears within itself the original vitiation of nullity. Such is the argument of the defendant. In view of this new phase and the Judge being definitely called upon to declare regarding the constitutional validity of Decree No. 41 of July 20, 1920, an examination of the new points raised by the parties is imperative. The points to be determined arise as follows: (a) whether the Decree has been issued by the Congress of the Republic in the exercise of its legal functions; (b) whether, in the affirmative event, it can prevail over provisions also of a constitutional nature which are the guarantee of individual rights. In use of the powers conferred by article 8 of the Organic Law of the Courts, which also expressly prohibits the officers of justice from applying laws, decrees, regulations or other resolutions contrary to the Constitution, the point will now be examined.

Article 74 of the present Constitution determines in its various articles the powers of Congress; among the limited enumeration the authority to declare in a general way the nullity of laws, decrees, contracts, etc., is not included, nor does any similar function result from any other constitutional provision; on the contrary, the Constitution (article 16) prohibits any authority whomsoever from arrogating functions not conferred by law and expressly declares that: ''The resolutions of the Legislative or Executive Power which might be contrary to the Constitution are null and void and of no effect, whatever may be the form in which the same may be issued'' (Art. 17). From which it arises that, however much the Decree of July 20, 1920, may be based on high patriotic motives, as an express penalty of situations created by the stained régime which governed during the period comprised between January 27, 1917, and September 2, 1919, juridically it does not possess the specific efficiency which it is presented to give to it as a law of the Republic. In Costa Rica none of the powers of the State possess the faculty to decree in a general way the unconstitutionality of laws, decrees, etc. But upon the Judicial Power, by an express provision, such prerogative is incumbent in specific cases when it is a question of deciding a lawsuit. Several years ago, in a memorable discussion, a similar point having been brought up, opinions inclined that way. One of the opinions was unexpectedly contrary thereto, the same being based on the doctrines of Italian and French authors. The citation was not deemed appropriate, as it constituted a misunderstanding of the positive law, as well as by reason of its being inopportune, inasmuch as the European countries have in regard thereto regulations differing from ours. This, although a political function assigned to the Courts of Justice, called the American doctrine, through having originated from the Constitution of the United States of America, signifies a real advance, which places the Judicial Power above the condition of inferiority to which it had been relegated in the past.

America has taken a gigantic stride; it has created an independent Judicial Power; has placed between the laws of Congress and the Constitution, the Judicial Power. This latter does not possess the authority of declaring that a law is defective nor of making observations; but in private litigation it is placed between two laws, the supreme law of the country, adopted by the people as the foundation of the political structure, to which the Legislative Power is subordinate, and the law of Congress; it compares them and declares the supremacy of the former. If it finds that the law of Congress violates the Constitution it decides in favor of the latter. . . . . In exercise of the legal function cited and in the presence of article 17 of the Political Constitution, the undersigned abstains from applying in the concrete case which has been submitted to him, Decree No. 41 of July 20, 1920, which is null and void and of no effect in this concrete case, as issued by the Congress of the Republic without legal authority and inasmuch as in recanting it tends to modify, in its effects, the preexistent juridical situation, to the undervaluation of precepts which guarantee individual rights and which place private actions, which do not come into contact with public order, beyond the action of the law (articles 26–29, 38 and 50 of the Political Constitution).[132]

The First Court of Appeals also condemned the said law in the following terms:

WHEREAS: The so-called Law of Annulments of July 20, 1920, cannot legally affect the aforementioned contract for the following reasons:

1. The annulment of a commercial obligation, such as that which is the object of the present suit, must from its nature be declared in an ordinary trial with the intervention of the interested parties, and it corresponds exclusively to the Judicial Power to determine the rights arising out of a civil contract, whatsoever may be the nature thereof and the qualifications of the parties intervening in the suit (article 1 of the Organic Law

---

[132] Sentence by the Judge of the Second Civil Court of San José, Feb. 11, 1921.

of Courts); the Legislative Power, therefore, on making the said declaration of annulment has usurped functions exclusively incumbent upon the Judicial Power, the said law resulting, as a consequence thereof, inapplicable to the present case by being contrary to the provisions of articles 13 and 16 of the Constitution, which prescribe the independence of Powers and that no authority may usurp functions not conferred by law.

2. The law quoted is subsequent to the contract, the object of the lawsuit, and should it be applied in this case retroactive effect would be given thereto, against the provision of article 26 of our Constitution. Furthermore, it is not a matter of a simple law of proceedings, as the appellant pretends, but is for the concrete case a ruling on the merits thereof, because it would annul a private contract and with detriment to acquired rights.

3. The said law also proves to be inapplicable to the concrete case, for the reason that it tends to affect private actions which, according to article 50 of the Constitution, are beyond the action of the law, as long as they do not interfere with the public order or morality or do not produce damage to the detriment of third parties.

4. Property is inviolable according to the constitutional guarantee laid down in article 29, and in consequence that law cannot invalidate the check which Mr. Steinvorth acquired in virtue of a private contract.[133]

Benjamin E. Piza, holder of a promissory note signed by the Secretary of the Treasury of the Tinoco régime, filed action against the government for the collection of such obligation and the Judge of the Court of Contested Claims ordered the payment thereof, arguing with respect to the unconstitutionality of the law of July 20, 1930, as follows:

That the Executive Power having based the refusal of payment of the obligation consisting of the document presented on the fact that it does not appear that the said promissory note comes within any of the cases of exception of the nullity declared in paragraphs ''b'' and ''h'' of article 1 of the law No. 41 of July 20, 1920, it is necessary to first examine the point relative to the unconstitutionality of the said law, the declaration of which is required in the first place.

It cannot be maintained that within a régime of strict constitutional order the aforesaid law of August and the constitutional resolutions transcribed can coexist without detriment to the rights which the very principles themselves lay down, for the following reasons: (a) Because on the law declaring that the nullity of the contracts entered into between civil parties, namely the contracting State and individuals, is examined,

---

[133] Sentence of the First Court of Appeals, San José, Jan. 9, 1922.

it assumes functions which belong exclusively to the Judicial Power, inasmuch as the declaration of nullity of an obligation is the result of a civil action and article 1 of the Organic Law of the Courts provides that "it is the function of the Judicial Power to try civil, criminal and contestable-administrative cases, whatsoever may be the nature thereof and the condition of the parties intervening therein, to definitely decide thereupon and to execute the sentences handed down." If the powers into which the Government of the Republic is divided are independent among themselves and no authority may arrogate powers not conferred by law, the Legislative Power could not, without violating articles 13 and 16 of the Constitution, encroached upon the functions of the Judicial Power in making the declaration of rights of a strictly civil nature.

(*b*) Because on the enactment of the law, the contract in virtue of which was issued the document in which the obligation was set forth, had already been entered into. If the law has no retroactive effect, without the glaring violation of such principle the annulment, from their origin, of acts verified considerably prior to the enactment thereof, could not have been declared.

(*c*) Because the declaration of nullity of laws is not a function of the Legislative Power, which may enact, amend, interpret and revoke the same, but may not annul them. The enumeration with respect thereto given by the Constitution is clear and express, there is no room for any interpretation whatsoever in regard thereto.[134]

In September 1914 a law was enacted by means of which the notes of the International Bank of Costa Rica were declared legal tender for the payment of obligations contracted in gold. Teodosio Castro held a promissory note signed by Pages & Co., the payment of which had been stipulated as excluding all paper money even though a subsequent law should declare the same legal tender. Castro refused to accept the notes of the International Bank, alleging that the law, in accordance with the constitution, could have no retroactive effect and that in consequence the aforesaid decree did not affect his promissory note, which was prior thereto. The matter having been taken up to the Supreme Court, the latter supported Castro's right in the following sentence:

WHEREAS: In admitting that the decree of nineteen hundred and fourteen was a matter of issuing resolutions governing the past to the detri-

---

[134] Sentence of Aug. 29, 1922.

ment of acquired patrimonial rights, such as those alleged by the defendant in this suit, it would result that in conformity with the provisions of article 8 of the Organic Law of the Courts and article 17 of the Constitution now in effect, the Courts of Justice have had to refrain from applying that decree.[135]

Though there are not many decisions by Costa Rican courts declaring legislative acts void precedents such as the few cited indicate that the doctrine of judicial review in accordance with the American plan is accepted as a principle of the governmental system.[136]

CUBA

Constitution, 1901—

Art. 37. The laws regulating the exercise of the rights which this Constitution guarantees shall be null and void if such rights are abridged, restricted, or modified by them.

Art. 83. The Supreme Court shall have the following powers:

Sec. 4. To decide the constitutionality of the laws, decrees and regulations when a question as to their validity is raised in any controversy between parties.

Judicial review of legislation is definitely established as a feature of the Cuban system of government. By a law enacted

---

[135] Sentence of the Court of Cassation, May 16, 1920.

[136] For information regarding the practice of judicial review in Costa Rica and for the translations of the opinions quoted, I am indebted to Luis Anderson, Attorney, San José, Costa Rica. Rather unusual provisions which remained in effect only a short time in Costa Rica are found in the Constitution of 1917, as follows:

Art. 7. All orders emanating from the legislative or executive powers which are contrary to the constitution shall be null and void and without effect whatever be the form in which they may be issued. Courts of justice shall not apply them in any case. All acts of those usurping public powers or any employment given without the requirements of the constitution or in default thereof without the requirements provided by law shall also be null and void.

Art. 128. In order that the interpretation of any provision of this constitution may be considered authentic it shall be necessary that the same proceedings and formalities prescribed for their revision shall be observed.

Art. 129. Congress at its ordinary sessions shall ascertain whether this constitution has been violated and whether or not the liberty of the infractors has been enforced, and only in proper cases shall it take the necessary steps for the punishment of the guilty.

in 1903 the procedure for such review and the conditions under which review may be exercised are regulated.[137] All questions of constitutionality must be passed on exclusively by the Supreme Court. If the constitutionality of a law, decree, or regulation is raised in any judicial proceeding the judge or judges before whom the case is tried shall refrain from giving an opinion on this issue leaving to the parties the privilege of seeking a recourse of annulment before the Supreme Court. Questions of constitutionality are frequently raised before the Cuban courts. However, following the practice of other Latin-American states few legislative acts are declared void.[138]

CZECHOSLOVAKIA

Constitution 1920—

Article I, (1) Laws which are in conflict with the Constitutional Charter or with laws which may supplement or amend it are invalid.

(2) The Constitutional Charter may be altered or amended only by laws specifically designated as Constitutional Laws.

Article II, A Constitutional Court shall decide as to whether the laws of the Czechoslovak Republic and the Diet of Carpathian Ruthenia (Russinia) conform with Article I.

Article III, (1) The Constitutional Court shall consist of seven members, two of whom shall be members of and appointed by the High Court of Administration, and two shall be members of and appointed by the High Court of Justice; the remaining two members and the Chairman shall be nominated by the President of the Republic.

(2) The appointment of representatives of the above mentioned courts to the Constitutional Court, the sessions and procedure thereof, and the execution of its judgments shall be provided for by a special law.

The constitution of Czechoslovakia provides in articles 1 and 2 for a well marked distinction between constitutional laws and ordinary laws and authorizes the establishment of a Constitutional Court to consider the acts in violation of the constitution. Establishment of a special court to examine the

---

[137] Cf. Gaceta de 1° de Abril de 1903 and Angel C. Betancourt, *Recurso de Inconstitucionalidad* (Havana, 1915) 15.

[138] For a summary of opinions and judgments relating to the recourse for annulment before the Supreme Court, see Betancourt, *op. cit.*, 113 ff.

validity of legislative acts implies the principle that no other authority may pass on the validity of such acts.[139] The organization and procedure of this court have been established by special laws.   It is the duty of the court to determine whether the ordinary laws enacted by the National Assembly or by the Diet of sub-Carpathian Ruthenia are in their general effect contrary to any of the provisions of the constitutional laws. As the permanent Committee composed of 16 Deputies and 8 Senators, which acts for the Assembly while the body is not in session, has authority to make rules which have the force of law, the Constitutional Court is authorized to determine whether such rules are really urgent.

To avoid the uncertainty which may result from delay in passing on the validity of a law a provision in the organization of the court requires that an attack on the nullity of a law can be made only within three years after its promulgation.

The court can consider a question of constitutionality of a law only when an appeal comes from the Supreme Court of Justice, the Supreme Administrative Court and the Electoral Tribunal, or by the Chamber of Deputies, the Senate and the Diet of sub-Carpathian Ruthenia. The Court in its judgment is confined to the question actually presented. Few requests have been presented to consider the validity of laws.[140]

DENMARK

Constitution, 1915 and 1920—

Art. 70.   The Courts take cognizance of all matters relating to the limitation of the functions of the authorities.

---

[139] Arts. 2 and 3 of the law of Feb. 29, 1920, No. 121 and art. 2 of the law of March 9, 1920, No. 162, under which rules of procedure have been adopted by the Court. František Weyr, ''Le tribunal constitutionnel de la république tchécoslovaque,'' 1 *Bulletin de droit tchécoslovaque* (1925–26) 129, 132; also, *Recueil des lois et décrets*, No. 255, 1922.

[140] A law of Nov. 7, 1922, which authorized the government to act by means of an ordinance in a case in which action by legislation is necessary was held void as a violation of arts. 6 and 55 of the Constitution. Cf. Carré de Malberg, *Bulletin* de la societé de lég. comp. (1926) 33.

Art. 80. The right of property shall be inviolate. No person shall be forced to surrender his property, except where the common weal shall require it. Expropriation shall in each case be founded on a statute passed for the purpose, and full compensation shall be given.

It appears to be taken for granted that a limited form of judicial review of legislation is implied in the language of the constitution of Denmark. For more than forty years it is claimed, ''the right of the courts to pass upon the constitutionality of statutes has been practically unanimously accepted in theory''[141] To 1924 no law had been declared invalid by the courts.[142] In Denmark judicial review appears to have little practical significance.

DOMINICAN REPUBLIC

Constitution, 1924—

Art. 22. Attributes of the Congress are:

Sec. 23. Annually to examine all the acts of the executive power and to approve the same if in accordance with the Constitution and the laws.

Art. 40. All laws, decrees, regulations and acts contrary to the present Constitution are null for all purposes.

Art. 61. Belonging exclusively to the Supreme Court, without prejudice to other attributes conferred by law, are:

Sec. 5. To pass in original and final jurisdiction upon the constitutionality of laws, decrees, resolutions and rules whenever such may be in controversy between parties before any tribunal, the latter must in this case stay its decision upon the question until after the decision of the Supreme Court; and, in the general interest, without it being necessary that there be a judicial controversy, whenever the question of constitutionality be involved in laws, decrees, resolutions, and rules in derogation of individual rights granted by this Constitution.[143]

GERMANY

Constitution, 1919—

Article 12. So long and in so far as the Reich does not exercise its powers of legislation, such jurisdiction remains with the states. This does not apply in cases where the Reich possesses exclusive jurisdiction.

---

[141] Axel Teisen, ''Power to declare Legislation Unconstitutional in Denmark,'' 10 Am. Bar Assoc. *Jour.* (Nov. 1924) 792.

[142] See Teisen, *op. cit.,* 793–794.

[143] See Law and Treaty *Series,* Pan American Union, 1925.

The National Cabinet may object to state laws which relate to matters covered by Article 7, sub-section 13, whenever the general welfare of the Reich is affected thereby.

Article 13.   The laws of the Reich are superior to the laws of the states.

If doubt arises or a difference of opinion, whether state legislation is compatible with a law of the Reich, the proper authority of the Reich or the central authorities of the states, in accordance with the specific provisions of a national law, may have recourse to a decision of the supreme court of the Reich.[144]

Article 15.   The National Ministry shall have the right to supervise those matters in respect to which it has the power of legislation.

In so far as the national laws are to be executed by the state authorities the National Cabinet may issue general instructions. The National Cabinet has the power to send commissioners to the central authorities, and with their consent to the subordinate state authorities, in order to supervise the execution of the national laws.

It is the duty of the state cabinets, at the request of the National Cabinet, to correct any defects in the execution of national laws. In case of dispute, either the National Cabinet and that of the state may request a decision from the Supreme Court (Staatsgerichtshof), unless another court is prescribed by national law.

Article 19.   If controversies concerning the Constitution arise within a state, for the decision of which there is no competent court, or if controversies of a public nature arise between different states or between a state and the Reich, the Supreme Court of the Reich (Staatsgerichtshof) shall decide the controversy on the appeal of either of the contesting parties, unless another national court is competent. The President of the Reich executes the judgment of the Supreme Court.

Though it appears to be mainly in the realm of theory and discussion, judicial review of legislation is one of the most important subjects for public consideration in Germany. Opinions on the issue of judicial review are rather evenly divided with the preponderance of views tending to favor such review. A proposal to prohibit judicial review of legislation was defeated by one vote in the drafting committee of the convention which prepared the constitution. The whole matter was left open for interpretation by the legislative authorities and the courts as exigencies might arise.

---

[144] By law of April 8, 1920, the Staatsgerichtshof has been designated as the court competent under art. 13, sec. 2, to decide the compatibility of national and state laws.

Certain types of judicial review have always been recognized in Germany. As is customary in most European countries, decrees and ordinances conflicting with statutes might be declared void. A great deal of legislation takes the form of executive ordinances and hence is subject to judicial annulment. Since the establishment of federal government in the German Empire, state statutes conflicting with national statutes might be declared void by the courts, and the judges were supposed to have the authority to refuse to enforce an act not regularly proclaimed as a law.

Under the new constitution all these forms of review are retained with a broadening of the authority to review state enactments and at least an implication that the national courts were expected to review acts of parliament deemed contrary to the provisions of the constitution. Only the procedure in the review of state acts by the national courts and the steps to adopt judicial review of national acts can be briefly considered.

The problem of judicial review in Germany arises mainly in connection with the following questions:

1. Have the formal statutory and constitutional requirements been complied with, or is the act really a law?

2. Has the law been superseded or changed by a later law?

3. Where different jurisdictions are involved, is the law in conflict with a superior law?

With regard to the first question certain German authorities claim that the constitution authorized the President to pass on the formal constitutionality of laws in the grant of authority to promulgate laws.

This view, according to Professor Mattern, "is contrary to the fundamental conceptions of responsible government as the essential foundation of the *Rechtsstaat*." In his opinion both the President and the courts are charged with the duty of examining whether the formal requirements have been fulfilled in the enactment of a law.[145]

---

[145] Johannes Mattern, *Principles of the Constitutional Jurisprudence of the German National Republic* (Baltimore, 1928), p. 575 ff.

Judicial control over state laws may be exercised in an advisory capacity or in case of an actual conflict, and the request for an opinion can come only from national or state officers. A decision of the court is in the nature of a declaratory judgment with the force of law and is to be rendered without argument.

This form of control is distinct from the right to consider the constitutionality of a state law by the state courts or the Reichsgericht, as a supreme court—an authority which is regarded incidental to civil, criminal and administrative authority in ordinary judicial proceedings.[146]

Federal review of state acts is thus summarized by Mattern:

National control [over the states] is exercised in two ways: first, on the basis of an administrative decision by the National Cabinet, subject to judicial review by a National Supreme Court; second, on a purely judicial basis, i.e., by the judicial decision of a National Supreme Court at the request of the National or State Cabinets. In the first case we speak of administrative control or supervision with judicial review, in the second instance we speak simply of national judicial supervision. The first kind of supervision is authorized by Art. 15, the second by Arts. 13 and 19 of the National Constitution. . . . . These provisions make it clear that the recourse to the decision of a National Supreme Court, provided for in Section 2 of Article 15, as far as it applies to the question of the agreement of state law with national law, is to be had prior to the going into effect of the state law concerned, that is before the state regulation actually becomes law.[147]

By the law of April 8, 1920, the Reichsgericht has been designated as the court under the provisions of Article 13, Section 2, i.e., to decide the compatibility with national law of state legislation. The court in its decisions is not confined to actual conflicts between national and state authorities, but may pass on a mere matter of difference of opinion or doubt concerning the validity of a state law. Only national and state cabinets or ministers can request an opinion of the court and the decision has the character of a declaratory judgment with the force

---

[146] For decisions see Mattern, *op. cit.*, 257.
[147] *Ibid.*, 214, 222.

of law.[148] Exercising the authority granted under these constitutional and statutory provisions the court has invalidated a number of state laws.[149] The above proceeding is distinct from the review or *Prüfungsrecht* exercised by the state courts and the Reichsgericht as incidental to civil, criminal, and administrative proceedings in suits at law.

The issue of the right of the courts to review state acts was decided when the minister of interior of Würtenberg issued an order based on a section of the penal code to prevent public assemblies and other demonstrations in the open air. In an opinion rendered by the Reichsgericht the question was raised whether the judge is

authorized and obliged to examine into the legal validity of norms that rest expressly upon laws or ordinances having the force of law.

In the first place, the decision will be governed by any provisions (including any of customary law) of the Reich or the states, which directly or indirectly apply to the question; insofar as these are lacking, it will be necessary to fall back upon general fundamental principles, which can be deduced from the nature of the legislative or judicial power and of the functions fulfilled by these powers, as well as from their mutual relationship.

According to Section 1 of the Law on the Organization of the Courts (Gerichtsverfassungsgesetz), and Article 102 of the Constitution of the Reich, the judges are independent and subject only to the law. This signifies on the one hand the binding of the judicial power to the acts of the legislative power, and on the other hand the freedom of the judge in respect to acts of the organs of public administration, which stand in contradiction to acts of the legislative power or which encroach upon the judicial power.

---

148 *Ibid.*, 250.

149 A Bavarian School Teachers Law prohibiting employment of married women as teachers was held void, as in conflict with art. 128, sec. 2, of the national constitution. Entscheidungen des Reichsgerichts im Zivilsachen (cited RGZ.) 102:1145.

A Saxon School Law prohibiting the teaching of religion in the public schools was held to conflict with arts. 146, 149, 174 of the national constitution. *Reichsgesetz Blatt* (cited RGB) 1 (1920) 2016.

At the request of the Senate of Bremen the law of that state relating to the election of heads of schools was held void in part.

Sections of Prussian State liability laws were held void as in conflict with art. 131, sec. 1, of the national constitution. RGZ., 106:34.

According to Article 2, paragraph 1, of the constitution of the Reich of 1871, and Article 13, paragraph 1, of the constitution of the Reich of 1919, the further principle holds: "National law supersedes state law." From the nature of the Reich as a union of states, develops the consequence that the legislative power of the Reich is superior to that of the states, and that consequently also the legal norms which proceed from the lawmaking factors of the Reich (the laws of the Reich, the legal ordinances of the Reich, and the customary law of the Reich) are superior to the legal norms which proceed from the lawmaking factors of the states (the laws of the states, the legal ordinances of the states, and the customary law of the states), and the expression is derived, that legal norms of the states to which a legal norm of the Reich is opposed, lack binding power over subjects, thus also over the judge—that they are simply void.

From the two legal principles referred to, it results for the question to be discussed here, that the judge is authorized and obligated to examine into norms of state law of every kind—including those of the state constitutions and laws amending the constitutions—as to whether or not they are opposed in form or substance to a law of the Reich, to a legal ordinance of the Reich, or to a customary law of the Reich, and that if such is the case, he must refuse to apply them.[150]

Judicial review of the acts of the national parliament has been extensively discussed by German jurists and statesmen.[151] Since the Reichstag can amend the constitution by a two-thirds vote and has been granted broad legislative powers with few general limitations, judicial review of legislation would have a very limited field of operation.

It seems to have been taken for granted that some form of review of national acts would be adopted and a law to regulate procedure in such cases has been discussed at various times in the Reichstag. Some serious difficulties need to be overcome before a satisfactory procedure for the review of national acts by the courts can be formulated. In the meantime the courts have indicated that they regard the right to review national acts and to hold them void if contrary to the constitution, as one

[150] *Entscheidungen des Reichsgerichts, Strafsachen,* Bd. 56. Decided, Dec. 15, 1921. For the translation of the extracts from German cases I am indebted to Miriam E. Oatman-Blachly of Washington, D. C.

[151] For a summary of views pro and con, see Morstein Marx, *Variationen über die richterliche Zuständigkeit zur Prüfung der Rechtmässigkeit des Gesetzes* (1927).

of the normal functions belonging to the judiciary under the constitution.[152]

Though to 1930 no regularly enacted law had been declared void, the question of judicial review was considered in an opinion concerning an emergency tax ordinance and an evaluation law. The following opinion of the Reichsgericht in this case indicates an acceptance of the principle of judicial review:

It is a presupposition for the application of the provisions of the evaluation law, that no conclusive objections against the constitutionality of the law present themselves, since it was passed by a simple majority of the Reichstag. Because of the attacks made publicly against the legal validity of the evaluation law, it seems advisable, accordingly, to undertake an official examination into the constitutionality of the law.

In this connection the question immediately presents itself, whether and in how far the courts are generally authorized and obliged to examine into the legal validity of a regularly promulgated national law. Accordingly a departure must be made from the decision of the first Criminal Senate, of Dec. 15, 1921 (R. Gerichts St., Bd. 56, p. 177), that in the first place any national legal provisions, either statutory or a part of customary law, which bear directly or indirectly upon the question, must be authoritative; and that in so far as such provisions are wanting, recourse must be had to the general fundamental principles which can be derived from the nature of the legislative or judicial authority, and the practices growing out of these authorities and out of their reciprocal relationships. The constitution of the Reich has expressed in Article 102 the fundamental principle expressed in section 1 of the Law on the Organization of the Courts,[153] that the judges shall be independent and subject only to the law. The latter provision does not prevent a judge from refusing to recognize the validity of a national law or the individual provisions thereof, insofar as they stand in contradiction to other provisions that must be observed by the judge, that take precedence over them. This is the case if a law contradicts a legal principle expressed in the constitution of the Reich, and if in passing it the requirements prescribed in Article 76 of the constitution of the Reich for a constitutional amendment have not been observed. For the provisions of the constitution of the Reich can be invalidated only by a law amending the constitution, passed in the regular manner. In spite of conflicting provisions of a later national law, passed

---

[152] Carl Joachim Friedrich, "The Issue of Judicial Review in Germany," 43 *Pol. Sci. Quart.* (June 1928) 188, and Richard Thoma, "Das richterliche Prüfungsrecht," 43 *Archiv des öffentlichen Rechts* (1922) 267.

[153] Gerichtsverfassungsgesetz, Jan. 27, 1877, as revised of May 17 1898 (RGB., 1, 1898, page 371).

without observation of the requirements of Article 76, they remain, there-fore, binding upon the judge, and make it necessary for him to leave unap-plied the contradictory provisions of the later law.   Since the constitution of the Reich itself contains no provisions according to which the decision as to the constitutionality of the statutes of the Reich would be removed from the courts and transferred to another specified agency, the right and duty of the judge must be recognized, to examine into the constitutionality of statutes of the Reich.[153a]

HAITI

Constitution, 1918—

Art. 26.   Nothing shall be added to or taken away from the Constitu-tion by means of law. The letter of the Constitution shall always prevail.

Art. 99.   The Court of Cassation, in full bench, shall decide upon the constitutionality of laws. The courts shall refuse to apply all those laws which have been declared unconstitutional by the Court of Cassation. They shall not apply the decrees or regulations of the administration which are not in accordance with the law.

Art. 127.   The present Constitution and all the treaties actually in force or to be concluded hereafter, and all the laws decreed in accordance with this Constitution, or with these treaties, shall constitute the law of the country, and their relative superiority shall be determined by the order in which they are here mentioned.

The Court of Cassation has in a number of instances exer-cised the authority granted by these provisions of the Consti-tution. A case of this type arose when the Council of State acting as a legislative body (there was then no elected legislative cham-ber) passed a law denying liberty on bail to persons accused of the offense of defamation of the press, toward the President of the Republic.   Several journalists who violated the law were arrested and under the above law were refused a release on security.   They attacked the constitutionality of the law and by a decision of May 16, 1924, the Court of Cassation declared void article 21 of the law which took away the privilege of securing release on bail.   As this law was not enacted by a regular legislative assembly it seems to fall partly within the class of the declaration of the nullity of executive ordinances— a feature of judicial review which is more significant in certain Latin-American countries than the review of legislative acts.

[153a] R. G. Z., 111:320–322.

HONDURAS

Constitution, 1925—

Art. 29. Every person has the right to require protection (*amparo*) against any offense or arbitrary act of which he may be the victim, and to have made effective all the guaranties that this constitution establishes, when he may be illegally restrained from the enjoyment thereof by laws or acts of any public authority, agent or functionary.

Art. 75. The suspension or guaranties treated of in Article 73 on the State of Siege, can be decreed only by Congress, or, when not in session by the Executive Power. But the latter cannot decree suspension more than once during the period included between two legislative sessions, nor for an indefinite time, nor for more than thirty days, without convoking Congress in the same decree of suspension. In any case it must give an account to Congress of the acts performed during the suspension of guaranties.

If the executive violates any of the provisions included in this section, the person prejudiced or any other person in his name may recur to the writ of *amparo*.

Art. 92. To Congress belong the following attributes:

Sec. 5. To enact, interpret, reform and repeal the law.

Art. 96. The attributes of the permanent committee in the recess of Congress are:

Sec. 7. To receive accusations of violations of the constitution.

Art. 135. There may also be instituted directly before the Supreme Court of Justice the petition of unconstitutionality of a law referring to matters not in hearing before the tribunals, by any person who, on its being applied in a concrete case, might be prejudiced in his legitimate rights. The law will regulate the use of this remedy.[154]

IRISH FREE STATE

Constitution, 1922—

Art. 65. The judicial power of the High Court shall extend to the question of the validity of any law having regard to the provisions of the constitution. In all cases in which such matters shall come into question, the High Court alone shall exercise original jurisdiction.

Art. 66. The Supreme Court of the Irish Free State (Saorstát Eireann) shall, with such exceptions (not including cases which involve questions as to the validity of any law) and subject to such regulations as

---

[154] See Law and Treaty *Series,* Pan American Union, No. 2.

may be prescribed by law, have appellate jurisdiction from all decisions of the High Court. The decision of the Supreme Court shall in all cases be final and conclusive, and shall not be reviewed or capable of being reviewed by any other court, tribunal or authority whatsoever: Provided that nothing in this constitution shall impair the right of any person to petition His Majesty for special leave to appeal from the Supreme Court to His Majesty in Council or the right of His Majesty to grant such leave.

By article 2 of the treaty between Great Britain and the Irish Free State and article 51 of the constitution of the Irish Free State it was provided that "the law, practice and conditional usage governing the relationship of the Crown or the representative of the Crown and of the Imperial Parliament to the Dominion of Canada shall govern their relationship to the Irish Free State." As judicial review of legislation by Canadian courts with an ultimate appeal to the judicial committee of the Privy Council is a feature of Canadian constitutional law it might have been expected that the practice of judicial review of legislation would be adopted by the Irish Free State. As a matter of fact the Canadian model has not been followed with respect to the interpretation of the fundamental law.

Article 66 sanctions the right to petition the King in Council for special leave to appeal from a decision of the Supreme Court but permits limitation of appeals from the High Court to the Supreme Court except in cases involving the validity of a law. As a consequence appeals to the Privy Council may be prevented in all except constitutional cases. However, when the judicial committee of the Privy Council undertook to reverse a decision of the Supreme Court on a constitutional issue the legislature of the Irish Free State passed a law declaring the effect of the legislation involved to be that laid down by the Supreme Court.[155]

A. B. Keith refers to the attitude of the Irish Free State by which the parliament will legislate to reverse a decision which may be obtained by a litigant through an appeal to the Privy

---

[155] See Wigg v. Attorney-General of Irish Free State (1927) A. C. 674 and Irish Free State Act, No. 11, 1926.

Council from a decision of the Supreme Court of the Free State and observes:

The attitude adopted by the British government, namely, that it can take no action unless it is formally approached by the Free State government is, perhaps, the only convenient position; but it is in no wise heroic, and even a little absurd. The refusal of the Free State to recognize the appeal is clearly, as Lord Reading has stated, a breach of the treaty and of the constitution, in which the appeal was expressly inserted at the demand of the Imperial government, in order to give effect to the obligations imposed by the treaty, and, while it would have been wiser of the British government in 1926 to surrender by law the appeal, there is no doubt that the Irish attitude is a repudiation of a clear legal and moral obligation.[155a]

MEXICO

Constitution, 1917—

Art. 103. The federal tribunals shall take cognizance of:

1. All controversies arising out of the laws or acts of the authorities when the latter infringe any individual rights.

2. All controversies arising out of laws or acts of the federal authorities which limit or encroach upon the sovereignty of the states.

3. All controversies arising out of laws or acts of the state authorities which invade the sphere of the federal authorities.

Art. 105. The Supreme Court of Justice shall have exclusive jurisdiction in all controversies arising between two or more states, between the powers of government of any state as to the constitutionality of their acts, or between one or more states and the federal government, and in all cases to which the federal government may be a party.

Art. 106. The Supreme Court of Justice shall likewise have exclusive jurisdiction to determine all questions of jurisdiction between the federal tribunals, between these and those of the states, or between those of one state and those of another.

The constitution also includes detailed provisions for the issuance of the writ of *amparo*—the procedure by which constitutional guaranties are preserved and private rights upheld. (See art. 107.)

[155a] From "Notes on Imperial Constitutional Law," *Jour. of Comp. Leg. and Int. Law*, ser. 3, 12, Pt. 1 (Feb. 1930) 97; see also *ibid.*, 11, Pt. 4, 257. For recent changes in the status of the Dominions with respect to the powers of the Parliaments, see the *Statute of Westminster*, 1931.

An interesting form of judicial review of legislation has been developed in the Republic of Mexico in the writ of *amparo*, which is a common device to protect individual rights in Latin-American countries. The basis for the writ is article 101 of the constitution of 1857—a provision identical with article 103 of the constitution of 1917.

The first written constitutions in Mexico gave the legislature exclusive power to settle doubts as to the interpretation of the fundamental law. An amendment to the constitution of 1847 changed this arrangement by giving the federal judiciary authority to protect (*amparar*) all persons against unconstitutional laws, and from acts done by the legislative and executive departments of both the federal or state governments, limiting its jurisdiction always to a "specific case." The origin of this provision is traced to American law.[156] No act of Congress was passed to carry out this provision. However, the provision of this constitution was made a permanent part of Mexican law by its insertion in the constitution of 1857. The authority to grant the writ of *amparo* was granted exclusively to the federal courts—the power being regarded political in character, since the supreme court acts not merely as a court but as a branch of the national government, and protects sovereignty itself, under its duty to uphold the supremacy of the constitution. The writ is seldom used to protect the states from interferences by federal officers or to check the states from intruding upon the scope of federal authority. Very few complaints arise which involve the constitutionality of the laws themselves "whereas hundreds of cases are daily arising in which the point to be decided is whether certain facts to which the law applied were established in evidence, or whether an act done by one of the authorities violates an individual right or not."[157]

---

[156] Judge Benito Flores, "The Writ of *Amparo* Under Mexican Law," 7 Am. Bar Assoc. *Jour.* (August 1921) 388. See claim that there were precedents for the process of *amparo* in Roman law and in the Spanish law, where there are instances of the application of a process, *inhibiciones* or *procesos formales* against illegal actions of the authorities and even against the king himself. *Ibid.*, 390.

[157] Flores, *op. cit.*, 391.

The writ lies only against laws or acts done by public officers. By an act of 1869 the process may originate in a district court but the decisions of these courts must be reviewed by the supreme court. The decision applies only to the individual case, the form of the judgment being as follows:

The judicial department of the republic hereby affords support and protection to John Doe against the acts done by Richard Roe.

When an application is made in a local court for the writ of *amparo* the court must follow the federal provisions of the law and the issue is referred as soon as possible to a federal court. At the beginning of the suit the plaintiff may apply for an injunction to prevent any wrongful or illegal acts while the proceedings are under way.

The effect of the granting of a writ of *amparo* is to restore things as they were before the passage of the act.

The writ of *amparo* serves a double purpose, first, to prevent the enforcement of unconstitutional laws, either federal or state; second, to redress wrongs suffered by individuals as a result of the acts of public authorities contrary to provisions of the constitution. Under the first authority a number of laws passed by the federal legislature have been held unconstitutional. A few may be cited, as for example, the laws of December 10, 1861, of May 13 and 17, 1862, and of May 27, 1863, in which there were given to the president of the republic important powers allowing regulations of a very severe character to apply to citizens who had served the imperial government of Maximilian of Austria. As an illustration of the use of the writ against legislative acts may be noted the judgment of August 22, 1882, in which the supreme court refused to enforce a decree of the Coahuila legislature relating to the powers and authority of Catholic priests.[158] The writ was applied for a number of times by oil companies in order to protect their property from what they deemed confiscatory acts of the Mexican government.

---

[158] Cf. Fernand Bermudez, *La procédure d'amparo contre les actes et les lois contraires à la Constitution du Mexique* (Paris, 1914) 54 ff.

A recent application for the writ arose from a petition by the Mexican Petroleum Company, a California corporation, before a district judge for *amparo* to restrain the secretary of industry, commerce and labor from canceling drilling permits and enforcing the petroleum law. The company claimed a violation of constitutional guaranties, citing seven provisions of the constitution.[159] The decision of the court condemned the time limit of one year, allowed for the confirmation of the existing rights of the company and then said:

> Since the secretary of industry, commerce and labor, in violation of the principles previously expressed, cancelled the permits granted to the complainant company, relying on the lapse of the said term, without taking in consideration the unconstitutionality of the 50 year limitation, a necessary condition for confirmation, it is undisputable that the decision complained of violates in this respect the guaranties which are granted in favor of complainant by articles 14, 16 and 27 of the federal constitution.[160]

The writ of *amparo,* it was held, is not a proper proceeding to establish property rights.[161]

In effect the court held void the fifty-year limitation on petroleum concessions established by art. 14 of the Petroleum Law and the one-year period for application for confirmations. At the same time apparent approval was given to the policy of the nationalization of petroleum, since merely the procedure by which such nationalization was being accomplished was condemned.[162] The effect of this decision was that article 32 of the constitution was not retroactive so far as petroleum rights are concerned and did not apply to such rights acquired prior to May 1, 1917.[163]

---

[159] Carlos Berguido, Jr., ''The Mexican Petroleum Company's *Amparo* Case,'' 76 *Univ. of Penna. Law Rev.* (Jan. 1928) 287, 288.

[160] *Ibid.*, 293.

[161] See art. 107 of the constitution and art. 2 of the Amparo Law of 1919.

[162] See also Edward Schuster, ''The Texas Company's *Amparo* Case,'' 7 Am. Bar Assoc. *Jour.* (Nov. 1921) 583.

[163] John P. Bullington, ''The Land and Petroleum Laws of Mexico,'' 22 *Am. Jour. of Int. Law* (Jan. 1928) 52.

The writ of *amparo* partakes of the character of the writs of habeas corpus, error, and certiorari; its special purpose is to allow recourse in all cases and by all persons in the federal courts for redress against any act of authority, judicial or administrative, which is deemed in violation of the individual guaranties of the constitution.[164] Chief Justice Vallarta attempted to restrict the application of the writ of *amparo* to cases involving a violation of the constitution. After his death the federal justices sustained the jurisdiction of the court "to revise all judgments of all Mexican courts upon all matters."[165]

According to the jurisprudence established by the supreme court its decisions shall relate only to the federal constitution and other federal laws. Decisions of the court may be regarded as precedents only when seven or more of its members concur in the decision and whenever there are five judgments on the same point not reversed by other decisions. Moreover the supreme court may reverse the jurisprudence established. Under such conditions it can be readily seen that the Mexican courts cannot settle definite rules of law.[166] The supreme court apparently does not hesitate to reverse itself. In October 1921, the court declared void a law of Vera Cruz which in effect repealed an earlier law of 1912 approving a contract made by the state governor with the Eagle Oil Company for the payment of certain sums in lieu of all state taxes. The same law had been declared valid by the supreme court in a previous case.[167]

---

[164] Wheless, *Compendium of Mexican Law*, 1:515.

[165] Emilio Rabasa, *El Juicio Constitutional* (Mexico City, 1919) 222–223.

[166] Rabasa, *op. cit.*, 280.

[167] See Compañia El Aguila, *El Excelsior*, Mexico City, Oct. 20, 1921.

Amparo Law—Oct. 20, 1919. Art. 2: The *amparo* suit shall be substantiated observing the forms and procedure which this law determines, and the judgment pronounced therein shall deal only with private individuals, limiting itself to protecting them, in a special case to which the complaint refers, without making any general declaration with respect to the law or act which should give rise to it.

Art. 148: The decisions of the Supreme Court of Justice, voted by majority of seven or more of its members, constitute jurisprudence, whenever what is decided is found in five decisions not reversed by another to the contrary.

Writs of *amparo,* it is claimed, are often used by lawyers to obstruct the administration of justice.[168]

NICARAGUA

Constitution, 1911—

Art. 122. The tribunals and judges of the Republic shall apply in order of preference:

1. The constitution and constitutive laws.
2. The laws and legislative decrees.
3. The executive decrees and orders. In no case shall they apply any provision or revision made by virtue of an official communication.

Art. 123, Sec. 9. To determine the protests made against ordinances issued by municipalities and other local administrative bodies when contrary to the constitution and the laws.

Art. 63. The laws regulating the exercise of constitutional guarantees shall be void in so far as they may diminish, restrict or impair them.

Art. 85. It belongs to Congress, when convened in separate session.

1. To enact, construe, revise and repeal laws.

Art. 124. Any person injured in his rights by the application of a law in a particular case may challenge the constitutionality thereof directly before the Supreme Court of Justice, provided the law relates to matters not triable before the courts of justice.

It is the opinion of commentators on Nicaraguan law that the power of annulling or considering as non-existent an unconstitutional law is a duty which is incumbent upon the most humble judge of the nation, when he has to decide a question involving the validity of such a law. The legislature has recognized this authority by enacting in the law of July 2, 1912, that the judges are authorized to deny in a judgment the application of a law if they deem it unconstitutional, even if the law has not been attacked in the record. The authority to invalidate

---

Art. 149: The jurisprudence of the court in *amparo* suits and in those which arise over application of federal laws or treaties with the foreign powers, is binding upon the circuit magistrates, district judges and tribunals of the states, federal district and territories.

The said supreme court shall respect its own decisions. Nevertheless, it may reverse the jurisprudence established; but always expressing, in this case, the reasons for the decision. These reasons must refer to those which were taken into account in establishing the jurisprudence which is reversed. See Schuster, *op. cit.,* 583.

[168] Cf. Maurice Minchen, "The Writ of *Amparo* in Mexican Law," 1 *Mexican American* (Mexico City, June 14, 1924), 23 ff.

acts was recognized when the supreme court by direct recourse of unconstitutionality on August 8, 1918, refused to enforce the *Ley Castrillo,* enacted on April 27, 1918, relating to marriage in cases of seduction because too heavy penalties were imposed without a declaration of guilt through a jury.[169] A similar decision was rendered on October 31, 1924, invalidating an executive order of the president relating to elections.[170]

NORWAY

Constitution, 1814—

Art. 97. No law shall be given retroactive effect.

The courts of Norway have refused to apply laws which violate the constitutional principle relating to the non-retroactivity of laws.[171] They have also refused to enforce laws involving confiscation of private property as contrary to arts. 104 and 105 permitting the expropriation of private property only for public use and with complete indemnity for the loss incurred.

PANAMA

Constitution, 1904—

Art. 48. The National Assembly is prohibited from enacting laws which may diminish, restrict, or impair any of the individual rights mentioned in the present title, without a previous amendment to the Constitution, except in such cases as are provided for.

Art. 105. The Executive shall sanction every bill which, having been reconsidered, shall be passed by a two-thirds vote of the Deputies present, provided that their number be not less than that required for a quorum.

In case the Executive objects to a bill on the ground of unconstitutionality, and the National Assembly insists on its passage, the bill shall be referred to the supreme court, which shall render its judgment within six days. If the decision of the Court is in favor of the bill the Executive is required to sanction and promulgate the law; if the decision is against the bill, it shall be sent to the archives.

---

169 See *Boletin Judicial de la Gaceta, Managua,* Aug. 31, 1918.

170 La Corte Suprema de Justicia, *Sentencias* (1924).

171 See Michel H. Lie, *Domstolene og Grunloven* (Oslo, 1923); Morgenstierne, ''Das Staatsrecht des Königsreich Norwegen,'' 13 *Öffentliches Recht der Gegenwart''* (1911) 42, 73; F. Larnaude, *Bulletin de Législation comparée* (1902) 176.

PORTUGAL

Constitution, 1911—

Art. 26. It is the exclusive province of the Congress of the republic:
1. To make, interpret, suspend and revoke laws.
2. To see to the observance of the constitution and of the laws and to promote the welfare of the nation.

Art. 63. When in a case submitted for judgment either party contests the validity of a law or of an act emanating from the executive authority or from any public authority, the judicial power shall pass on its constitutional validity or its agreement with the constitution and the principles therein established.

Art. 80. Laws and decrees remain in force until they are repealed or changed by the legislative authority provided that they are not expressly or impliedly contrary to the system of government adopted by the Constitution and the principles therein established.

The idea of a fundamental law as a limit to the authority of the king was recognized in Portugal in the latter part of the seventeenth century.[172] Certain sections of the constitutions of 1822 and 1838 provided that laws contrary to the constitution should not be enforced,[173] though the courts were not regarded as authorized to refuse to enforce illegal laws or decrees. The proviso in art. 82 that the republican form of government shall not be a subject for revision is regarded as a super-constitutional principle, finding its sanction in the old doctrine of natural rights.

Art. 63 of the constitution was intended to introduce the American doctrine of judicial review in Portugal.[174]

ROUMANIA

Constitution, 1923—

Art. 36. The interpretation of the laws with the force of authority is made solely by the legislative power.

Art. 99. Any party injured by a decree or by an order signed or countersigned by a Minister which shall violate a precise reading of the

---

[172] João Maria Tello de Magalhães Collaço, *Ensaio sobre a inconstitucionalidade das leis no direito português* (Coimbra, 1915) 22 ff.

[173] *Ibid.*, 47 ff. For opinions favorable to the view that the judges ought to enforce these provisions by refusing to recognize invalid laws or orders, see *ibid.*, 54 ff.

[174] See Marnoco e Souza, *Constituição Politica da republica portuguêsa: Commentario* (Coimbra, 1913) 581–584.

Constitution or of any law, may demand of the State, in conformity with common right, money damages for the prejudice caused.

Art. 103. The Court of Appeal alone, all sections united, has the right to judge the constitutionality of laws and to declare inapplicable those which are contrary to the Constitution. A decision on the unconstitutionality of laws is limited to the case decided. The Court of Appeal shall decide, as in the past, upon conflicts of powers. The right to resort to appeal is of the constitutional order.

Art. 107. The judicial power has not the duty of reviewing acts of the Government nor those of a command of a military character.

Under the Roumanian constitution in force before the World War the courts asserted the right to review the validity of legislative acts. The court of cassation, rendering a decision in 1912 under the procedure for excess of power, approved a decision holding invalid a law of December 18, 1911, affecting the operation of the tramways of Bucarest, on the ground that the act was contrary to several provisions of the constitution. In speaking of the protection accorded by the constitution to individual rights the court observed:

That in effect these principles form a kind of a barrier for the protection of the rights of citizens and the judiciary to which is entrusted the authority of defending these rights against the attacks and interferences . . . . the courts ought to protect such rights according to the greatest guaranty possible, that is, according to the benefit of constitutional principles, for otherwise these principles would become a dead letter.

When a law contrary to the constitution is invoked in a case before a court, the judge cannot ignore the conflict and give judgment without passing on the validity of the law.

That, as in the case of a conflict between two ordinary laws, it is right and it ought to be the duty of the judge to interpret them and to decide which of the two ought to be applied, so it is just as much his duty to resolve the conflict where one of the two laws is the constitution.

In effect the constitution is different from ordinary laws, is permanent, and cannot be changed except by a special procedure defined in the constitution.

Being the basis of our social institutions its authority is above all others, being the superior and sovereign law, and consequently the judge is bound to give it preference. In so deciding the judge does not exceed his sphere and usurp the attributes of the legislative power but on the contrary he discharges a strict legal obligation, that of determining which law ought to be applied in the litigation submitted to its judgment.

Hence it was held that the court which refused to apply the contested law had not committed any excess of power.[175]

The provisions of the present constitution leave the matter to interpretation and practice whether or not the courts may exercise any effective review of legislation.

RUSSIA OR UNION OF SOVIET SOCIALIST REPUBLICS

Constitution, 1923—

Art. V, Sec. 29.   The presidium of the Central Executive Committee of the Union of Soviet Socialist Republics shall during the intervals between the sessions of the Central Executive Committee of the Union of Soviet Socialist Republics be the highest legislative, executive and administrative organ in the Union of Soviet Socialist Republics.

Sec. 30.   The presidium of the Union Central Executive Committee shall have the power to enforce the application of the Union constitution and the carrying out by all departmental authorities of all decisions of the Union Congress of Soviets and of the Union Central Executive Committee.

Art. VII, Sec. 43.   In order to firmly maintain revolutionary law throughout the territory of the Union there shall be created a Supreme Court of the Union which shall be attached to the Union Central Executive Committee.   The said Court shall have the power and jurisdiction:

(*a*) To promulgate authoritative opinions on questions concerning general Federal legislation to the constituent Republics.

(*b*) On the motion of the Attorney General of the Union the Supreme Court shall review the regulations, decisions and sentences of the Supreme Courts of the constituent Republics and appeal against them to the Central Executive Committee of the Union whenever such decisions violate the general legislation of the Union or whenever they are prejudicial to the interests of other Republics of the Union.

(*c*) To render decisions at the request of the Central Executive Committee of the Union on the constitutionality of any regulations made by the constituent Republics.

(*d*) To adjudicate all justiciable controversies between the constituent Republics.

The control of the constitutionality of laws, it is claimed, is one of the essential features of the governmental system of the

---

[175] ''L'inconstitutionalité des lois en Roumanie,'' 29 *Revue du Droit Public* (1912) 138, 365.

Soviet Union.[176] Two authorities—the presidium of the executive committee or the supreme court can exercise the authority of review of legislation. Authority to declare acts void in Russia is complicated by the fact that at least ten different organs participate in the process of legislation. As there are no special restrictions on legislation in the constitution of the union the examination of the constitutionality of acts relates primarily to the structure and power of the supreme organs of the state. The Russian theory and practice relating to review of legislation with respect to constitutionality is conditioned by the absence in Russian jurisprudence of the formal and material criteria of law, by the absence of a theory of the separation of powers, by the priority of fact over law, and by the identification of rules with principles of convenience.[177]

San Salvador

Constitution, 1886—

Art. 37. Every person has the right to ask and obtain protection from the Supreme Court of Justice or the Court of second instance, whenever any authority or private individual restrains his personal liberty or the exercise of any individual right guaranteed by the present Constitution. A special law shall regulate the manner and form of exercising this right.

Art. 39. Neither the legislative nor the executive power, nor any tribunal, authority or person whatsoever, shall have authority to abridge, alter or violate the constitutional guarantees without incurring or being subjected to the responsibilities established by law.

Art. 102. The Supreme Court has the following powers:

Sec. 11. To grant and enforce the writ of *amparo* established by article 37 of this Constitution, in the cases and in the manner provided by law.

South Africa

Constitution, 1909—

Article 65. The King may disallow any law within one year after it has been assented to by the Governor-General, and such disallowance, on being made known by the Governor-General by speech or message to

---

[176] See B. Mirkine-Guetzevich, ''Le contrôle de constitutionnalité des lois soviétiques,'' 42 *Revue du Droit Public* (Nov.–Dec. 1925) 683.

[177] 42 *Revue du Droit Public,* 693–694.

each of the Houses of Parliament or by proclamation, shall annul the law from the day when the disallowance is so made known.

Article 66. A Bill reserved for the King's pleasure shall not have any force unless and until, within one year from the day on which it was presented to the Governor-General for the King's assent, the Governor-General makes known by speech or message to each of the Houses of Parliament or by proclamation that it has received the King's assent.

Article 106. There shall be no appeal from the Supreme Court of South Africa or from any division thereof to the King in Council, but nothing herein contained shall be construed to impair any right which the King in Council may be pleased to exercise to grant special leave to appeal from the Appellate Division to the King in Council. Parliament may make laws limiting the matters in respect of which such special leave may be asked, but Bills containing any such limitation shall be reserved by the Governor-General for the signification of His Majesty's pleasure: Provided that nothing in this section shall affect any right of appeal to His Majesty in Council from any judgment given by the Appellate Division of the Supreme Court under or in virtue of the Colonial Courts of Admiralty Act, 1890.

The experience of the justices of South Africa in their attempt to declare void a legislative act shows what is likely to happen in a country imbued with the traditions and customs of the civil law. Prior to the adoption of the present constitution South Africa did not have a written fundamental law in the ordinary meaning of that term. An important statute enacted in 1858 was often referred to as the Grondwet or fundamental law. In 1897 the judges were called upon to decide whether the Grondwet was of so fundamental a character that it could not be changed by the legislature. The issue arose over the postponement of an order for public gold digging which had later been approved by a special act of the legislature. A party who had been denied the right to stake claims brought an action for damages against the government. Contending that a law can only be altered legislatively, that is by a subsequent law, and not by a mere resolution of the Volksraad, Chief Justice Kotzé adopted the reasoning of Justices Marshall, Kent, and Story and claimed that the Grondwet was a fundamental law, that it comprised a theory of the separation of powers similar to the American interpretation, and that it was the duty of the judges to refuse validity to legislative and executive action which did not conform to the provisions of the fundamental statute.[178] The chief justice summed up his opinion regarding judicial review of legislation as follows:

> The people, who have declared their independent existence in the Grondwet, and who possess the sovereign power in this Republic, have entrusted this power in various measure to the Volksraad, the Executive and the judiciary. Each of these bodies derives its authority from the Grondwet, and must regulate itself, each within its own sphere and scope, in accordance with the terms thereof. None of these powers is above or independent of the Constitution. That the Volksraad is declared to be the highest authority in the land is quite consistent with this view, for there is nothing contradictory in the fact that the highest authority in a State must conform to the terms of the Constitution, which created it, and is not at liberty to exceed the prescribed limitations. What would otherwise be the use of a Grondwet if it is not to be observed by the various departments of State, to which it has been appointed as a guide? Huber, already, has observed that the sovereign or supreme power in the State can be curtailed by fundamental laws, and he adds: "The obligation which arises from the fundamental laws is one of natural law, and renders all acts done contrary thereto null and of no effect."

> It is, moreover, within the province of the Court to consider or test a particular law by reference to the Constitution. In exercising this function the Court does not by any means raise itself above the legislature, but remains within its province, by inquiring whether what has been submitted to it is in reality a law. The Court does not take the initiative. It cannot act, and does not act, until a particular case is brought before it. If, with the view of a proper decision being arrived at, it becomes necessary, in the course of the judicial inquiry, to consider the validity of some law or other act of the legislature, it is the clear duty of the Court to exercise that function. The Court has to determine and decide upon both the facts and the law as applicable to those facts. This right and this duty belong exclusively to the Court. The proposition in Story: "No man can doubt or deny that the power to construe the Constitution is a judicial power,"[179] is irrefutable. Just as the Court has, in the case of two conflicting statutes, to determine which is of force, so, in the event of a conflict between a statute and the Constitution, the Court must not only decide upon the matter, but hold that

---

[178] Brown v. Leyds, 4 *Official Reports*, High Court, 17–54 and 14 *Cape Town Law Jour.*, 71–73; 94–109.

[179] *Constitutional Law*, sec. 376; *The Federalist*, No. 78.

the fundamental law or Constitution is supreme, and that any act or pro-ceeding of the legislature is to declare its will and intention, and in which its commands must be expressed, in order to have the force of law and bind the people, must be strictly observed. There is nothing new or strange in this doctrine. It follows from the very nature of the case—from the existence of a popular Government under a Grondwet like our own—and the general principles upon which it rests have been clearly set forth by the most approved jurists of Europe and America.

In order to sustain this reasoning it was necessary for the chief justice to reverse an earlier decision.[180] But in reversing his former opinion Chief Justice Kotzé remarked ''when upon further consideration it appears that a previous decision is not in accordance with the constitution, the court is bound to depart from such decision and follow the provisions of the Grondwet.''

Following the court's decision great indignation was expressed and the judges were severely criticized.[181] The Volks-raad reenacted the old law and condemned the judges in no uncertain terms. A resolution was adopted which required that the judges must recognize and obey the laws and all judges were required to take the following oath: ''I promise . . . . not to arrogate to myself any so-called testing-right [judicial review].'' Any judge disobeying the resolution was to be tried and dismissed from office. The present judges were to be asked if they would obey the laws and not claim the right to invali-date them. In case of a negative reply the judges were to be removed from office. The judges met and drew up a letter stat-ing that they would not exercise the right of review of legislative acts or resolutions, but requested that action be taken to place the Grondwet on such a basis that it could not be changed by special legislation. Following an interchange of views for a year between President Krüger and Chief Justice Kotzé the president peremptorily dismissed the chief justice. The dismis-sal was an arbitrary act and not in accord with the law but was approved by the legislature and the people.

---

180 McCorkindale's Executors v. Bok, Kotzé's Reports (1884) 202.

181 For a history of this case see J. W. Gordon, ''The Judicial Crisis in the Transvaal,'' 14 *Law Quart. Rev.* (Oct. 1898) 343–366.

With such a background it is not strange that the doctrine of judicial review of legislation has found small place in the South African constitution and that the courts have not ventured to seriously hamper the freedom of the legislature.

SPAIN

Constitution, 1932—

The new constitution of the Spanish Republic has the following provision:

Art. 100. When a Court of Justice shall have to apply a law which it believes contrary to the Constitution, it shall suspend proceedings and seek the advice of the Court of Constitutional Guarantees.

Art. 121. There is established, with jurisdiction over the territory of the Republic, a Court of Constitutional Guarantees which will have competence to take cognizance of,

(a) Appeals on the ground of unconstitutionality of the laws.

(b) Appeals for the protection of individual guarantees when complaint to other authorities shall have been unavailing.

(c) Conflicts of legislative competence and such other conflicts as shall arise between the State and the autonomous regions and between the latter *inter se.*

Art. 123. The following are competent to resort to the Court of Constitutional Guarantees:

1. The Ministry of Justice.
2. The judges and courts, in cases falling under Art. 100.
3. The Government of the Republic.
4. The Regions of Spain.
5. Every individual or collective person, even though it shall not have been directly affected.

URUGUAY

Constitution, 1919—

Art. 18, sec. 19. The General Assembly shall have power to settle conflicts of jurisdiction between the National Council of Administration and the President of the Republic.

Art. 119. The jurisdiction of the high court of justice shall extend to all violations of the constitution without exception.

Art. 174. All laws are declared in force and vigor with regard to all matters which are not directly or indirectly in conflict with this constitution, or with the laws passed by the legislature.

Art. 175. Whoever shall violate or render aid in the violation of the present Constitution after it has been sanctioned and published shall be known, judged, and punished as guilty of *lesée nation.*

Art. 176. The legislature shall have exclusive power to interpret or explain the present constitution, as well as to amend it in whole or in part, subject to the formalities presented in the following articles.

VENEZUELA

Constitution, 1928—

Art. 34. No federal law, or the constitution or laws of the states or municipal ordinances, shall be permitted to interfere with the guaranteed rights of the citizens; any acts of this kind shall be null, and shall be so declared by the Federal Court of Cassation.

Art. 35. Those who may administer, execute, or order carried out Decrees, Ordinances, or Resolutions that violate any of the guaranteed rights of the citizens, are guilty, and shall be punished according to the law, excepting where the measures shall be directed in the defence of the Republic or to the conservation or reestablishment of the peace, dictated by competent public officials in their official capacity, in the cases defined in the following articles.

Art. 120. The powers of the Federal Court of Cassation are:

Sec. 9*a*. To declare invalid the national or the state laws when they conflict with the Constitution of the Republic. The invalidity shall be limited to the paragraph, article or articles in which the conflict appears, except where these may be of such importance, through their connection with other párts of the act that, in the judgment of the court, its invalidity would affect the whole law.

Sec. 10. To declare the law that should prevail when the national laws are in conflict; and to declare likewise the article or articles of a law which are to govern when there shall exist conflict among them as to their application.

Sec. 11. To declare invalid those acts of the Legislature or of the Federal Executive which violate the guaranteed rights of the States or that attack their autonomy; and those acts that the Legislative Assemblies or those of the civic Municipal Bodies that violate the restrictions expressed in paragraph 3, sec. 4 of article 17, and in sec. 3 of article 18.

Sec. 12. To declare invalid the Decrees or Regulations that the Executive Power shall announce for the execution of the laws, when they shall alter the spirit, reason or meaning of them, and in general, to declare when it shall become necessary, the invalidity of all the acts to which the articles 42 and 43 of this constitution refer, whenever they emanate from a national or federal district authority, or from the high functionaries of the states.

B. GOVERNMENTS IN WHICH THE GUARDIANSHIP OF THE CONSTITUTION BELONGS PRIMARILY TO THE LEGISLATIVE OR EXECUTIVE DEPARTMENT

BELGIUM

Constitution, 1831, 1893, 1921—

Title III, Art. 28. The authoritative interpretation of laws shall belong only to the legislative power.

Belgian jurists are not in accord as to whether the courts can pass on the constitutionality of laws; the prevailing view is that they cannot. At least, any such power, if it exists at all, has been so seldom exercised as to be practically negligible. The discussion of the problem in Belgium is largely academic and not one of practice. The Belgian courts, however, as in France, exercise an extensive review of executive ordinances and administrative acts. Authority to do this is granted under Art. 107, which is as follows:

The courts and tribunals shall not apply general, provincial or local decrees or ordinances unless they are conformable to law.

The Belgian legislature has changed the constitution at various times without following the process of amendment. Such a practice has been seldom resorted to and has been in very few instances of serious import.[182] A notable violation of the constitution resulted from the law of May 9, 1919, establishing universal male suffrage and making other changes in the election laws. "The really remarkable thing," says Professor Reed, "to an American observer is the respectful adherence of the legislature to the text of the constitution in spite of the absence of any positive sanction to sustain it."[183]

[182] Paul Errera, *Sommaire du Cours de Droit Public Belge* (1921) 92 ff.
[183] Thomas H. Reed, *Government and Politics of Belgium* (Yonkers, 1924).

ENGLAND

For consideration of legislative supremacy in England consult chapter 1, pages 8 to 12.

ECUADOR

Constitution, 1906—

Art. 6. The constitution is the supreme law of the republic.

Therefore, any laws, decrees, regulations, orders, resolutions, or public acts or treaties of any kind whatsoever, shall be invalid, if they be contrary to the said constitution or if they diverge from the text thereof.

Art. 7. Congress shall have the sole power to construe the constitution in a generally binding manner, and to decide the doubts which may arise on the interpretation of one or more of the principles embodied therein.

Likewise, Congress, alone, shall have the right to declare whether or not a law or legislative decree is unconstitutional.

Art. 25. Public officials or employees who violate any of the guaranties declared in this constitution shall be responsible with their own properties, for the damages or injuries which they may cause; and the following regulations shall be observed with regard to the offenses or crimes which they may commit by violating the said guaranties:

1. They can be accused by any person whomsoever, without the necessity of bond or signature of a lawyer;

2. The penalties imposed upon the offending official or employee cannot be commuted or pardoned during the constitutional period in which the break was committed; nor subsequently, unless at least half the sentence has been served; and

3. In the case of proceedings against these crimes and offenses, as also in the case of punishment imposed upon those responsible therefor, the statute of limitations does not begin to run until after the said constitutional period.

FRANCE

Constitution 1875—

The French system of legislative supremacy was briefly considered in the first chapter along with the supremacy of parliament in England. A few additional notes and comments regarding developments relating to judicial review of legislation in France may be pertinent.

Legislative supremacy is generally approved by French statesmen and jurists. Tessier stated the prevailing doctrine of French law as follows:

The powers of the parliament in our public law being without limits, laws when they have been regularly promulgated are susceptible of no sort of recourse, even for a violation of the constitution; they constitute, therefore, in the first degree, acts of sovereignty.[184]

This doctrine of legislative supremacy was the direct result of the ideas which were current during the period of the French Revolution.[185] The revolution substituted for the absolutism of the king the absolutism of the law as voted by the representatives of the people. In the French assemblies of the revolutionary period there was a deep-seated suspicion regarding the judiciary owing to the assumption of supreme authority by the courts prior to the revolution.[186] Because of this suspicion a provision was inserted in the French constitution of 1791 that "the courts can neither interfere with the exercise of the legislative power nor suspend the execution of the laws."[187] In effect the application of Montesquieu's theory of the separation of governmental powers in France was to place the courts under the supervision and control of the legislative and executive departments.

---

[184] Responsibilité de la puissance publique (Paris, 1906) 15 ff. See famous French case in which the courts refused to hold a law regulating the press void, Sirey, *Recueil*, 33, 1:357 (1833), and F. Larnaude, "L'inconstitutionnalité des lois et le droit public francais," 126 *Revue Politique et Parliamentaire* (Jan.–March 1926), 181; also arrêt Villette, Dalloz, 1831, 1, 197 and Sirey, 1834, 1:371; arrêt Doyne et Lemaire, Dalloz, 1838, 1, 154; arrêt Alliot, Dalloz, 1863, 1, 400; arrêt Gauthier, Dalloz, 1851, 1, 142. In each case in which the court of cassation considered the validity of a law the act was held valid.

[185] André Lemaire, *Les lois fondamentales de la monarchie française d'après théoriciens de l'ancien régime* (Paris, 1907), especially chap. 4.

[186] On the conditions which resulted in limiting the authority of the courts in French law, see André Blondel, *Le contrôle juridictionnelle de la constitutionnalité des lois* (Paris, 1928) 243 ff. The declaration of the parliament of Paris of May 3, 1788 included in its provisions one which asserted "the right of the courts to verify in each province the ordinances of the king, and to order their registration only when they conform to the constitutive laws of the province as well as to fundamental laws of the state."—*Ibid.*, 138.

[187] See Title 3, chap. 5, art. 3.

Several attempts were made to set up a special court or jury to check the enactment of unconstitutional laws.[188]   These devices proved ineffective and France turned in the direction of an unrestricted legislative supremacy.

French courts have the authority to pass on the "extrinsic constitutionality of laws," that is, to determine whether the conditions required by the constitution had been followed in the enactment of a law.   Promulgation by the president is not regarded as a sufficient warrant that the formal requirements of the constitution have been fulfilled.   It is the direct control over the validity of legislative acts such as the disallowance of acts by authority of the executive or the indirect control (*l'exception d'inconstitutionnalité*), that is, the refusal of a judge to apply a law because he deems it unconstitutional, which the French refuse to accept.

M. Hauriou, a noted constitutional authority, claims that the tribunal of conflicts has recognized and exercised the power to review the validity of legislative acts.[189]

There is a distinct and well supported movement in France to have the courts of their own accord assert the authority to declare legislative acts void if in their judgment constitutional terms or principles are violated or, in case of their refusal, to amend the French constitution so as to sanction such a practice.   Some of the ablest authorities on constitutional law have for years advocated the adoption of the American doctrine or a modified form of this doctrine in France.[190]

---

[188] See proposition of Siéyès for the establishment of a constitutional jury—a special body of representatives, selected from among the members of the legislature—charged with the duty of annulling all acts deemed unconstitutional.   This constitutional jury became the Sénat conservateur of the "Constitution de l'An XIII."—Bonlay de la Maurthe, *Théorie constitutionelle de Siéyès Constitution d l'An VIII;* see also André Blondel, *op. cit.*, 170 ff.

[189] Maurice Hauriou, *Précis de droit constitutionnel* (ed. 2; Paris, 1929) 283 ff.   Most French commentators disagree with this interpretation.   See Gaston Jèze, "Le contrôle juridictionnel des lois," 41 *Revue du Droit Public* (July, Aug., Sept., 1924), 408 ff., and Jacques Leblanc, *Du pouvoir des tribunaux d'apprecier, en France, la constitutionnalité des lois* (Paris, 1924).

[190] See Léon Duguit, *Traité de droit constitutionnel* (ed. 2, Paris, 1921–25), 3:615; Maurice Hauriou, *Précis du droit constitutionnel* (Paris, 1929),

Serious objections are raised by other commentators to the adoption of judicial review of legislation in accordance with the American model.[191] Though all agree that if judicial review were adopted in France it would have relatively little influence in the shaping of public law, since the constitution contains no bill of rights or other limitations on the legislature relative to private rights which render such review effective in the United States, a few authorities claim that the bills of rights of the revolutionary constitutions are still in force in France and should be applied by the judges so as to protect individual rights and privileges. With a few exceptions, however, the courts have refused to adopt this interpretation of constitutional principles.

In countries like France with a legal system based on the ideas and principles of the Roman law as modernized in the civil codes there is less need of a judicial surveillance of legislation than in countries with public and private law based on Anglo-American principles. There is a much greater tendency in civil law jurisdictions to delegate authority to executive or administrative officers and then to exercise strict judicial control over the acts of such officers. It is customary for the French assembly to pass acts in very general terms and in mere outline and to delegate to the president and his subordinates the authority to issue ordinances to supplement its provisions and to regulate the details of its execution. The concluding

---

276 ff. H. Berthélemy, ''Les lois inconstitutionneles devant les juges,'' 133 *Revue Politique et Parliamentaire* (Nov. 1927) 183; Joseph Barthélemy, *Traité élémentaire de droit constitutionnel* (Paris, 1926); Gaston Jèze, ''Le contrôle juridictionnel des lois,'' 41 *Revue du Droit Public* (July, Aug., Sept., 1924) 408 ff. Professor Jèze believes ''it seems certain that if the review of legislation is established in France it will be without doubt in the indirect form of the *l'exception d'inconstitutionnalité*. In other words the American model will be adopted in France. The function of the courts will be not to annul irregular laws on the demands of interested parties, but to set aside upon the demand of the parties during a suit for the determination of a case a law regarded as void.''—*Ibid.*, 413.

191 Edouard Lambert, *Le gouvernment des juges et la lutte contre la législation sociale aux États-Unis* (Paris, 1921), especially chap. 11; F. Larnaude, ''L'inconstitutionnalité des lois et de droit public francais,'' 126 *Revue Politique et Parlementaire* (Jan.-March 1926), 181. See also my article, ''Some Phases of the Theory and Practice of Judicial Review of Legislation in Foreign Countries,'' 24 *Am. Pol. Sci. Rev.* (Aug. 1930), 583 ff.

clause of parliamentary enactments is that "an ordinance of public administration shall determine the measures proper for assuring the execution of the present law."

Over the authority of administrative officers in promulgating ordinances and in executing laws and administrative orders, the administrative and ordinary courts exercise extensive and effective control chiefly by remedies known as *l'exception d'illegalité* and *recours pour excès de pouvoir.*

The *l'exception d'illegalitè* is the remedy by which the ordinary courts refuse to impose fines for the violation of administrative rules or ordinances regarded as illegal. By this procedure ordinances issued by the president or on his authority may be declared illegal and the courts may pass upon the legality of nearly every administrative act for the violation of which a fine is prescribed, and illegality includes not merely nonconformity to the laws but also incompetence, vice of form, violation of the principle of equality of citizens, of personal liberty, of liberty of conscience, of inviolability of domicile, or violation of property rights.[192]

The procedure *l'exception d'illegalité* has been largely replaced by a more effective remedy before the administrative courts.[193] Since the ordinary courts were limited to a refusal to impose a fine, the ordinance remained in effect and might be enforced against those who refused to violate it. This remedy to prevent illegal action, developed by the council of state, as an administrative court, is known as *recours pour excès de pouvoir*. This authority was exercised originally against *ultra vires* ordinances of the prefects and mayors but not against the ordinances of the king. When the council of state was reorganized in 1872 express authority was granted to annul ordinances.

---

[192] James W. Garner, "French Administrative Law," 33 *Yale Law Jour.* (April 1924), 600 ff.; Reglade, "L'exception d'illegalité en France," 40 *Revue du Droit Public* (1923) 393, and Rives, *L'exception d'illegalité* (Paris, 1908).

[193] Du Chos, *Le recours pour excès de pouvoir* (1906). Dareste, *Les voies du recours contre les actes de la puissance publique* (1914). Appleton. *Les progrès récents du recours pour excès du pouvoir* (1917). Gaston Jèze, *Principes généraux de droit administratif* (ed. 3, Paris, 1925).

Originally such review was held not to apply to the ordinances of public administration issued by the president with the advice of the council of state. But decisions rendered since 1907 considerably modify this rule in that presidential ordinances are now subject to attack before the council and on several occasions have been annulled as illegal. The procedure to annul administrative acts does not apply to presidential ordinances relating to the colonies or to "acts of government," which are regarded as political in character.

In a work dealing with the recent developments in relation to the recourse for excess of power M. Alibert compares the French procedure for control of official acts through recourse in cassation before the supreme court for ordinary cases and recourse for excess of power before the administrative tribunals, with the American plan of judicial review of legislation. The three processes require that the judge examine the legality of a juridical act, i.e., a law, a judgment, or an administrative act with a rule of law or with juridical principles superior to this act.[194] Recourse for excess of power and recourse in cassation are devices by which supreme tribunals chosen as are the judges and inferior administrative officers exercise a supervisory control over these inferior officials to see that they keep within the confines of the law and do not violate principles of right and justice. In the control of the constitutionality of laws, on the contrary the judge, an officer appointed by the executive, has as one of his duties the control of the legislature. The judge surveys and checks the legislature and hence exercises political authority. Judicial review of legislation on the American plan involves frequently a consideration of the law and the facts. The court of cassation will not pass on the facts and will not decide a case involving mixed law and facts. But in an issue on excess of power before the council of state the judge considers both the law and the facts. Review of administrative acts by the French courts is largely a product of interpretation

---

[194] Raphäel Alibert, *Le contrôl juridictionnel de l'administration au moyen du recours pour excès de pouvoir* (Paris, 1926), 24.

or of what is called "jurisprudence," so also the comparison of laws by the judges with constitutional principles or with the individualistic principles of the common law is "a juridical work in the doctrinal and theoretical sense of the word." Referring to the work of the supreme court in passing on the reasonableness of laws, Alibert remarks, "it applies in this respect a social and political economy which is no longer the work of a jurist or judge but is in reality legislation."[195]

Though the American plan of review was chiefly designed to protect individual rights and the French system was worked out chiefly as an arm of the administrative régime, the tendency of the former has been to give less consideration to individual rights as such while the latter has been developing a jurisprudence which increasingly protects the rights of the individual against encroachment on his privileges and interference with his actions by public officers. In view of these tendencies in French law judicial review of legislation would add comparatively little to the protection accorded to French citizens.

GREECE

Constitution, 1927—

Art. 28. The authentic interpretation of the laws rests with the legislative powers.

Art. 127. The preservation of the constitution is committed to the patriotism of the Greeks.

Prior to the adoption of the constitutions of 1911 and 1927 the right of the courts to declare laws invalid was asserted in a number of decisions.[196] As a result of these decisions the courts of Greece are referred to as the guardians of the constitution.

GUATEMALA

Constitution, 1879—

Art. 54. The legislative power also has the following attributions:

1. To enact, interpret, amend and repeal the laws which must be observed in all branches of the administration.

---

195 Alibert, *op. cit.*, 31.
196 Cf. 1re Chambre de Aréopage, n. 145, Recueil Thémis, t. 15 (1904), 521, cited by N. Politis, in 22 *Revue du Droit Public* (1905), 481; and Cour de'Athenès, n. 1470, Thémis, t. 16 (1905–06), 169, cited by Politis, 23 *Revue du Droit Public* (1906) 795.

Art. 84. The counsellors of state are responsible for the opinion given by them in opposition to the constitution and the laws.

The constitution seems to give no authority to the courts to hold void laws which they deem contrary to the constitution.

ITALY

Constitution, 1848—

Art. 73. The interpretation of the laws in the form obligatory upon all citizens, belongs to the legislative power.

The above provisions together with the fact that the constitution makes no provision for amendment has strengthened the legislature in its practical position as the sovereign power in the Italian system. Prior to the Fascist régime, which recognizes no constitutional limitations or requirements,[197] no real distinction was recognized between fundamental law and statute law.[198]

Italian jurists frequently oppose the review of legislative acts by the courts. Thus V. Orlando, the great constitutional lawyer argued:

We do not think that judicial control of the constitutionality of laws is advisable for various reasons. In the first place, a requirement of the judicial order: an uncontestable advantage which has been secured in modern states consists of the certainty of law; it has been realized in many respects but principally in this: to know that for no legitimate reason can anyone be excused for disobedience of a law. But the theory of judicial control of legislation appears to us for this reason to be incompatible with the modern idea of law, precisely because it creates a legitimate excuse for disobedience to a law and because it leads to the distinction between valid and invalid laws; and this distinction can be made absurd or pernicious in practice.[199]

Another objection is that a large part of constitutional law is not in the written document and because too much discretion is granted to the judge in defining the rights guaranteed by the constitution.

---

[197] For some recent changes in the Italian fundamental law, consult Herbert W. Schneider, "Italy's New Syndicalist Constitution," 42 *Pol. Sci. Quart.* (June 1927), 161.

[198] On the lack of a distinction between the constituent and the legislative power in Italy, see V. E. Orlando, *Principes de droit public et constitutionnel* (Paris, 1902), 194 ff.

[199] Orlando, *op. cit.*, 387.

JAPAN

Constitution, 1889—

The constitution and political practice of Japan establish a form of executive supremacy which leaves no place for judicial review of legislation according to the American plan. Prince Ito, the chief framer of the constitution, thus describes the constitutional status of the emperor:

The sovereign power of reigning over and governing the state is inherited by the emperor from his ancestors, and by him bequeathed to his posterity. All the different legislative as well as executive [including judicial] powers of state, by means of which he reigns over the country and governs the people, are united in the Most Exalted Personage, who holds in his hands, as it were, all the ramifying threads of the political life of the country.

Though in theory the constitution provides for a separation of powers the theory is not applied in such a manner as to place the courts in an independent or semi-superior position.

PARAGUAY

Constitution, 1870—

Art. 15. The principles, guarantees, and rights recognized by the present constitution shall not be abridged or modified by any laws regulating their exercise.

Art 16. The present constitution, the laws enacted by congress in pursuance thereof, and the treaties concluded with foreign countries, shall be the supreme law of the nation.

Art. 29. All laws and decrees at variance with the provisions of the present constitution shall be inoperative and void.

Art. 103. All powers not delegated by the present constitution to the executive, shall be understood to have been denied, and reserved to Congress, which as the representative of the sovereignty of the people, is intrusted with the duty of removing any doubt which may arise in regard to the equilibrium of the three high powers of the state.[200]

PERU

Constitution, 1920—

Art. 16. Any Peruvian may institute proceedings before Congress, before the Executive Power or before any other competent authority for infringements of this constitution.

---

[200] Certain jurists claim that the courts of Paraguay have the authority to declare legislative acts void. Cf. Felix Paiva, *Estudio de Derecho Constitucional: La independencia del Poder Judicial* (Asuncion, 1915), 133–135.

Art. 69. Those entrusted with the legislative, executive and judicial power exercise the public functions, and none of them may overstep the limits prescribed by this constitution.

Art. 83. The attributes of Congress are:

Sec. 1. To enact laws, to interpret, modify and repeal existent laws.

Art. 98. The chambers, in ordinary or extraordinary sessions, are empowered to see that the guaranties and rights recognized by the constitution and the laws be observed, and to exact responsibility for violations thereof.[201]

By these provisions Congress is authorized to declare void any regulation, decree, or act of government which is contrary to the constitution.[202] Congress is also empowered to amend the constitution; the proposed amendment to be enacted by two succeeding legislatures and by a two-thirds vote in each chamber.[203]

POLAND

Constitution, 1921—

Art. 77. In the exercise of their judicial office, the judges are independent and subject only to statutes. Judicial decisions may not be changed either by the legislative power or by the executive power.

Art. 81. The courts may not inquire into the validity of duly promulgated laws.[204]

SWITZERLAND

Constitution, 1874—

Art. 113. The federal court further has jurisdiction:

1. Over conflicts of jurisdiction between federal authorities on one part and cantonal authorities on the other part.

2. Disputes between cantons, when such disputes are upon questions of public law.

3. Complaints of violation of the constitutional rights of citizens, and complaints of individuals for the violation of concordats or treaties.

Conflicts of administrative jurisdiction are reversed, and are to be settled in a manner prescribed by federal legislation.

In all the fore-mentioned cases the federal court shall apply the laws passed by the federal assembly and those resolutions of the assembly which

---

[201] Graham, H. Stuart, *The Governmental System of Peru* (Washington, 1925), 76, 77.

[202] Art. 160.

[203] See Pan American Union, Law and Treaty *Series*, No. 4, 1926.

[204] Cf. Kohl, "Die neue Verfassung der polnischen Republik," 2 *Zeitschrift für Öffentliches Recht* (1921), 433.

have a general import. It shall in like manner conform to treaties which shall have been ratified by the federal assembly.

Cantonal courts pass upon the validity of cantonal acts which are regarded as in conflict with the federal constitution, but as a rule they are not permitted to pass upon the validity of the acts of their own assemblies under the cantonal constitutions. In a few cantons the courts are authorized to review the acts of the cantonal assembly.

Recently a number of special studies have been prepared dealing with the judicial review of legislative acts in Switzerland.[205] A brief summary of comments and conclusions from the treatise of M. Solyom will indicate the nature of judicial review as it operates in Swiss law.

It is customary for continental writers to speak of the practice of reviewing legislative acts by the courts on the ground of unconstitutionality under the term *juridiction constitutionnelle*. Solyom believes that it is necessary to have a *juridiction constitutionnelle* in order to determine the order of authorities in all countries. He thinks Professor Edouard Lambert, of the University of Lyons, is incorrect in speaking of the American system of judicial control of legislation as a "government by judges." Differing from the point of view of Lambert, he accepts and follows the reasoning of Hamilton, Cooley, and Bryce. Whereas Lambert objects to the political views, conservatism, and traditionalism of judges in reviewing social legislation, Solyom finds fault with legislators for weighing constitutional matters in the political balance. Contrasting the American system with a rigid constitution only occasionally amended and with necessary adjustments to new conditions being made frequently by the judiciary with that of Switzerland, he observes:

with us on the contrary the federal constitution in forty-eight years of its existence has been amended at least twenty-five times. This corresponds very closely to the wish of the constituent legislative body and also to the

---

[205] See especially Georges Solyom, *La Juridiction Constituonnelle aux États-Unis et en Suisse: Étude sur le contrôle judiciare de l'acte législatif* (Paris, 1923).

voice of public opinion. There is, then, no occasion to fear in Switzerland that the review of legislation by the courts in federal matters could become an instrument by which the conservative forces of the nation would impose on the people a social régime established by former generations.[206]

Referring to the fact that there is no provision such as the due process clause of the Fourteenth Amendment in the Swiss constitution Solyom remarks that if such an article had been placed in the Swiss constitution it is certain that it would have been changed to prevent the abuses charged to the American courts in applying this clause. Solyom believes that the defects of the review of legislation in the United States pointed out by Lambert and certain American authors are not incident to such review in the normal *juridiction constitutionnelle* but to the peculiar belief in a rigid constitution in America among legislators and the people.

Taking up the practice of the judicial review of legislative acts in Switzerland, it is noted that the cantonal authorities do not have the right to examine cantonal laws and to hold them void as contrary to the cantonal constitutions. The federal court alone is competent to judge the constitutionality of cantonal laws and regulations.[207] With the exception of Berne and Geneva the cantons do not have the form of review of legislation which is customary in the American states.[208]

The instances in which the courts of Berne have considered the validity of legislative enactments seem to be rather rare. On the other hand, the courts of Geneva have frequently affirmed the right to examine laws and regulations in order to determine

---

[206] Solyom, *op. cit.*, 44–45.

[207] Solyom, *op. cit.*, 82–83 ff.; Affolter, *Grundzüge des schweizerischen Staatsrechts* (1904), 175. Cf. Solyom, 83 for citation in which a cantonal court speaks of a cantonal law as contrary to the federal constitution but says it can only apply the law.

[208] Solyom, *op. cit.*, pp. 83 ff. See also constitution of Uri, art. 51 and constitution of Unterwalden, art. 43. For Berne a case is cited in which a court refused to apply a law because according to a provision of the cantonal constitution, it had not been submitted to popular vote, A. T. F. 1914, 1:552 ss., and another case in which a regulation was held void as unconstitutional, A. T. F. 1915, 1:495.

whether they are in conflict either with the cantonal or the federal constitutions, and they have refused to apply such acts.[209]

Reviewing the history of article 113 of the federal constitution, which renders it practically impossible for the federal courts to annul acts of the federal assembly, Solyom finds that under the régime of the constitution of 1848 the federal political powers, namely, the assembly and the council, were the organs to determine the validity of acts both canton and federal. Under the constitution of 1874 the federal court can annul cantonal legislation, not only because it is contrary to the federal constitution, but also if contrary to federal legislation. The federal court may also interpret independently and finally the cantonal constitution.[210]

There appears to have been no real separation of powers in either the cantonal or federal governments during the eighteenth and early nineteenth centuries. As an exception the constitution of the Helvetic Republic of 1798 established a supreme court which was to act as a court of cassation, and among the duties of the latter body was mentioned the protection of the constitution. As a matter of fact, the court exercised no such function, and was really subservient to the other departments. Judicial authorities had an insecure status in Switzerland until the constitution of 1848 created a supreme court modeled after that of the United States. The court, however, was under the control of the assembly, and was not permanent in character. As a result the protection of individual rights under the constitution of 1848 was mainly in the hands of the federal assembly. The debates on the constitution of 1874 shed little light on the reason for making the assembly final in the interpretation of the constitution. The proposal to make the assembly supreme was made by Dr. Dubs, a member of the national council. Dr. Dubs claims that only in this way could the principle of the separation of powers be safeguarded.[211] The federal chambers,

---

[209] Solyom, *op. cit.*, 84, and see also a recent study by G. Werner, *Le controle judiciare a Genève* (Genève, 1914).

[210] Solyom, *op. cit.*, 86.

[211] *Ibid.*, 93.

therefore, in Switzerland are sovereign and have the right to decide whether they are remaining within the limits of the constitution.[212]

Referring to the fact that the leading criticism of the American system of judicial review of legislative acts is attributed to the examination by the judges of the reasonableness or fairness of laws, Solyom claims that several provisions of the Swiss constitution similarly require a consideration of the reasonableness or the exact purposes of the law. The sections cited principally are article 4, providing that there shall be equality of all Swiss citizens before the law, and article 31 which guarantees freedom of commerce and industry under certain restrictions. As a result of article 31, the federal courts have had to determine wherein the police regulations of the cantons interfere with the freedom of commerce and industry. Here it is contended the questions considered are mainly economic and political, and not juridical.[213] The courts have also upheld the constitutional requirement that cantonal legislation must respect the guaranty that private property shall be inviolate.[214]

An instance is cited where the letter of the constitution requiring the guaranty of the equality all citizens before the law was warped by what the judges called the spirit of the instrument so as to permit progressive taxation.

Judges of American courts pass on economic and social questions in determining the reasonableness or fairness of laws, and seemingly fill in gaps where constitutional texts or legislative acts are silent, and similar functions are performed to a limited extent by the Swiss courts. With regard to certain provisions of the constitution which have not been defined or carried into effect by appropriate legislation, Solyom says,

as in other domains where the chambers have neglected to legislate in application of the constitution, the federal tribunal has been able to create

---

212 Hoerni, *De l'état de necessité en droit public federal Suisse*, 150. Cf. Solyom, 97.

213 See cases Held c/ Neuchatel, A. T. F., 1914, 1:481; Spimler-Weber c/Conseil d'État d'Argovie, A. T. F., 1915, 1:48.

214 Cf. *Entscheidungen des Schweizerischen Bundesgerichts*, 23, Pt. II, 1001 (1897); 31, Pt. I, 645 (1905); 37, Pt. I, 503 (1911).

a jurisprudence strictly constitutional, not at all influenced by section 3, article 113, of the constitution. The judicial law thus created is certainly not inferior to parliamentary law which regulates the other domains of our public life.[215]

The federal tribunal besides does not regard it proper to say that a law is unconstitutional. If a legal provision applied by the cantonal authority is contrary to the constitution, it does not annul the legal provision itself, but merely the decision which has been made in the application of it.[216]

This practice strictly conforms to that of the American Supreme Court, safeguarding sufficiently the proper sphere of the legislature. Solyom discussed finally the interesting feature of Swiss law known as *Le régime des pleins pouvoirs,* or what is usually called the *droit de necessité* or law of necessity. Opinions seem to differ as to whether the constitution makes provision for such exercise of extraordinary powers but Swiss practice in the federation and the cantons seems to be uniform that, under the law of necessity, numerous restrictions and limitations of the constitution may be, at least temporarily, released. Solyom is of the opinion that there is an entire absence of the constitutional basis for the law of necessity other than the old doctrine of natural law. He agrees with various authors who have discussed this phase of Swiss constitutional law that certain limits and restrictions should be placed around the exercise of this extraordinary authority.

SWEDEN

The Constitution of Sweden has an unusual provision to the effect that:

No interpretation of the constitutional laws to hold good for the future shall be valid unless adopted in the manner provided for amending such laws (art. 83).

---

[215] Solyom, *op. cit.,* 112.

[216] D'Arcis c/ Glaris, A. T. F., 1922, 438.

APPENDIX III

I. Selected List of Books and Articles Dealing with Judicial Review of Legislation in the United States

BOOKS

BEARD, CHARLES A. *The Supreme Court and the Constitution.* New York, 1912.

BENSON, ALLAN L. *The Usurped Power of the Courts.* Pamphlet. New York, 1911.

BEVERIDGE, ALBERT J. *The Life of John Marshall.* Boston, 1916–19. 4 vols.

BLAND, THEODORICK. *The Opinion of Judge Bland on the Right of the Judiciary to declare an act of Assembly Unconstitutional and also, on the Constitutionality of the Act investing the County Courts with Equity Jurisdiction.* Baltimore, 1816.

BRANDIS, GOTTHARD B. *Das Recht des amerikanischen Richters, Gesetze auf ihre Verfassungsmäszigkeit zu prüfen.* Dissertation, Leipzig, 1913.

CARSON, HAMPTON L. *The Supreme Court of the United States: Its history.* Rochester. ed. 2. Philadelphia, 1902. 2 vols.

CORWIN, EDWARD S. *John Marshall and the Constitution; a chronicle of the Supreme Court.* New Haven, 1921. See bibliographical note, p. 233.
The Doctrine of Judicial Review. Princeton, 1914.

COXE, BRINTON. *An Essay on Judicial power and Unconstitutional Legislation; being a commentary on parts of the Constitution of the United States.* Philadelphia, 1893.

DAVIS, HORACE A. *The Judicial Veto.* Boston and New York, 1914.

DOUGHERTY, JOHN H. *Power of Federal Judiciary over Legislation: its origin; the power to set aside laws; boundaries of the power; judicial independence; existing evils and remedies.* New York and London, 1912.

FAGAN, HARRISON B. *Le juge créateur de droit aux États-Unis.* Thesis, Lyons, 1922.

GROAT, G. G. *Attitude of American Courts in Labor Cases.* New York, 1911.

HAINES, CHARLES GROVE. *The conflict over Judicial Powers in the United States to 1870.* New York, 1909.
The American Doctrine of Judicial Supremacy. New York, 1914.
The Revival of Natural Law Concepts. Cambridge, 1930.

HERSHEY, AMOS S. *Die Kontrole über die Gesetzgebung in den Vereinigten Staaten von Nordamerika und deren Gliedern.* Dissertation. Heidelberg, 1894.

HUGHES, CHARLES EVANS. *The Supreme Court of the United States; its foundation, methods and achievements; an interpretation.* New York, 1928.

LAMBERT, EDOUARD. *Le gouvernement des juges et la lutte contre la législation sociale aux États-Unis.* Paris, 1921.

MCLAUGHLIN, ANDREW C. *The Courts, the Constitution and Parties; studies in constitutional history and politics.* Chicago, 1912.

MEIGS, WILLIAM M. *The Relation of the Judiciary to the Constitution.* New York, 1919.

MEYER, W. G. *Vested Rights. Selected Cases and Notes on Retrospective and Arbitrary Legislation affecting vested Rights of Property.* St. Louis, 1891.

MOORE, BLAINE F. *The Supreme Court and Unconstitutional Legislation.* New York, 1913.

RANSOM, WILLIAM L. *Majority Rule and the Judiciary; an examination of current proposals for constitutional change affecting the relation of the courts to legislation.* New York, 1912.

ROE, GILBERT E. *Our Judicial Oligarchy.* New York, 1912.

RUSSELL, ELMER BEECHER. *The Review of American Colonial Legislation by the King in Council.* New York, 1913.

SHIRLEY, JOHN M. *The Dartmouth College Causes and the Supreme Court of the United States.* St. Louis, 1879.

WARREN, CHARLES. *The Supreme Court in United States History.* Boston, 1922. 3 vols.
Congress, The Constitution and the Supreme Court. Boston, 1925.

REPORTS

Report of the Committee on the Duty of Courts to Refuse to Execute Statutes in Contravention of the Fundamental Law. New York State Bar Assoc. Jan. 1915. Henry A. Forster, Chairman. *Proceedings,* 1914.

Second Report of the Committee. New York, 1916; U. S. 64 Cong. 1 sess. Senate *Doc.* 454.

RALSTON, JACKSON H. Study and Report for American Federation of Labor upon judicial control over legislatures as to constitutional questions. ed. 2. Washington, 1923.

ARTICLES

AKIN, JOHN W. "Aggressions of the federal courts." *Am. Law Rev.*, 32:669–700 (Sept.–Oct. 1898).

ANDERSON, F. M. "Contemporary opinion of the Virginia and Kentucky Resolutions." *Am. Hist. Rev.*, 5:45–63 (Oct. 1899 and Jan. 1900).

BALLANTINE, HENRY WINTHROP. "Labor legislation and the recall of the judicial veto." *Case and Comment*, 19:225–232 (Sept. 1912).

BARNETT, JAMES D. "External evidence of the constitutionality of statutes." *Am. Law Rev.*, 58:88–99 (Jan.–Feb. 1924).

"Judicial review of exceptions from the referendum." *Cal. Law Rev.*, 10:371–383 (July 1922).

BEARD, CHARLES A. "The Supreme Court: usurper or grantee?" *Pol. Sci. Quart.*, 27:1–35 (March 1912).

BIGGS, J. CRAWFORD. "The power of the judiciary over legislation." North Carolina Bar Assoc., *Proceedings*, 1915, 13.

BORAH, WILLIAM E. "The five-to-four decisions of our Supreme Court upon great constitutional questions." *Cong. Record*, 67 Cong., 4 sess., 64, no. 69; 4028–4030.

BORDWELL, PERCY. "The function of the judiciary." *Col. Law Rev.*, 7:308–336; 520–528 (May–Nov. 1907).

BOUDIN, L. B. "Government by judiciary." *Pol. Sci. Quart.*, 26:238–270 (June 1911).

BOWMAN, HAROLD M. "Congress and the Supreme Court." *Pol. Sci. Quart.*, 25:20–34 (March 1910).

BROWN, DOUGLAS W. "The proposal to give Congress the power to nullify the Constitution." *Am. Law Rev.*, 57:161–182 (March–April 1923).

BROWN, H. B. "The dissenting opinions of Mr. Justice Daniel." *Am. Law Rev.*, 21:869–900 (Nov.–Dec. 1887).

"The dissenting opinions of Mr. Justice Harlan." *Am. Law Rev.*, 46:321–352 (May–June 1912).

BURR, CHARLES H. "Unconstitutional laws and the federal judicial power." *Univ. of Penna. Law Rev.*, 60:624–642 (June 1912).

CARSON, HAMPTON L. "Judicial power and unconstitutional legislation." *Am. Law Rev.*, 34:796–810 (Dec. 1895).

"Great dissenting opinions." Am. Bar. Assoc., *Reports*, 17:273–295 (1894).

"The historic relation of judicial power to unconstitutional legislation." *Univ. of Penna. Law Rev.*, 60:687–699 (Oct. 1918).

CARTER, ORRIN N. "The courts and unconstitutional law." Illinois State Bar Assoc., *Proceedings*, 1912, 401–412.

CLARK, A. INGLIS. "The supremacy of the judiciary." *Harv. Law Rev.*, 17:1–19 (Nov. 1903).

CLARK, WALTER. "Government by judges." *Ohio Law Reporter*, 11: 485–509 (March 9, 1914).
"Back to the Constitution." *Am. Law Rev.*, 50:1–14 (Jan. 1916).

CLARKE, JOHN H. "Judicial power to declare legislation unconstitutional." Am. Bar Assoc., *Jour.*, 9:689–692 (Nov. 1923).

COLES, WALTER D. "Politics and the Supreme Court of the United States." *Am. Law Rev.*, 27:183–208 (March–April 1893).

CORWIN, EDWARD S. "The Supreme Court and unconstitutional acts of Congress." *Mich. Law Rev.*, 4:616–630 (June 1906).
"The establishment of judicial review." *Mich. Law Rev.*, 9:102–125, 283–316 (Dec. 1910 and Feb. 1911).
"The basic doctrine of American constitutional law." *Mich. Law. Rev.*, 12:247–276 (Feb. 1914).
"Marbury v. Madison and the doctrine of judicial review." *Mich. Law Rev.*, 12:538–572 (May 1914).
"Judicial Review in Action." *Univ. of Penna. Law Rev.*, 74:639–671 (May 1926).
"The progress of constitutional theory between the Declaration of Independence and the meeting of the Philadelphia Convention." *Am. Hist. Rev.*, 30:511–536 (April 1925).

CUSHMAN, R. E. "Constitutional decisions by a bare majority of the court." *Mich. Law Rev.*, 19:771–803 (June 1921).

DAVIS, ANDREW MCFARLAND. "The Case of Frost v. Leighton." *Am. Hist. Rev.*, 2:229–240 (Jan. 1897).

DAVIS, H. A. "Annulment of Legislation by the Supreme Court." *Am. Pol. Sci. Rev.*, 7:541–587 (Nov. 1913).

DODD, WALTER F. "The growth of judicial power." *Pol. Sci. Quart.*, 24:193–207 (June 1909).
"Implied powers and implied limitations." *Yale Law Jour.*, 29:137 (Dec. 1919).

DODD, WILLIAM E. "Chief Justice Marshall and Virginia." *Am. Hist. Rev.*, 12:776–787 (July 1907).

DUPRIEZ, L. "Le contrôle judiciare de la constitutionnalité des lois aux États-Unis." *Bulletin* de l'Acadamie Royale de Belgique de la Classe des Lettres, 166–189; 314–324 (1928).

ELLIOTT, CHARLES B. "The legislatures and the courts: the power to declare statutes unconstitutional." *Pol. Sci. Quar*, 5:224–258 (June 1890).

ESTERLINE, BLACKBURN. "The supreme law of the land." *Am. Law Rev.*, 40:566–579 (July–Aug. 1906).

FARRAND, MAX. "The judiciary act of 1801." *Am. Hist. Rev.*, 5:682–686 (July 1900).

"The First Hayburn Case." *Am. Hist. Rev.*, 13:281–285 (Jan. 1908).

FINKELSTEIN, MAURICE. "Judicial self-limitation." *Harv. Law Rev.*, 37:338–364 and 38:221–244 (Jan. 1924 and Dec. 1925).

FORD, JOHN. "Judicial usurpation." *Am. Federationist*, 30:306–310 (April 1923).

FREAR, JAMES A. "Seeming laws enacted by Congress." *Cong. Record*, 67 Cong., 4 sess., 64, no. 55:3140–3151 (Jan. 27, 1923).

GOODNOW, FRANK J. "Judicial interpretation of constitutional provisions." Acad. of Pol. Sci., New York, *Proceedings*, 3:49–64 (Jan. 1913).

GREEN, FREDERICK. "The judicial censorship of legislation." *Am. Law Rev.*, 47:90–110 (Jan.–Feb. 1913).

GRINNELL, F. W. "Some forgotten history about the duty of courts in dealing with unconstitutional legislation." *Am. Law Rev.*, 54:419–430 (May 1920).

GUTHRIE, WILLIAM D. "Constitutional Morality." Pennsylvania Bar Assoc. *Reports*, 18:331–364 (1912).

HADLEY, ARTHUR T. "The constitutional position of property." *The Independent*, 64:834–838 (April 16, 1908).

HAINES, CHARLES GROVE. "Judicial criticisms of legislation by courts." *Mich. Law Rev.*, 11:26–49 (Nov. 1912).

"Judicial review of Legislation in Canada." *Harv. Law Rev.*, 28:565–588 (April 1915).

"Judicial Review of Legislation in Australia." *Harv. Law Rev.*, 30:595–618 (April 1916).

"Histories of the Supreme Court of the United States written from the Federalist point of view." *Southwestern Pol. and Soc. Sci. Quart.*, 4:1–35 (June 1923).

"General observations on the effects of personal, political and economic influences in the decisions of judges." *Ill. Law Rev.*, 17:96–116 (June 1922).

"A government of laws or a government of men: judicial or legislative supremacy." Faculty Research Lecture, University of California, Los Angeles, 1929.

"Some phases of the theory and practice of judicial review of legislation in foreign countries." *Am. Pol. Sci. Rev.*, 24:583–605 (Aug. 1930).

HALLAM, O. "Judicial power to declare legislative acts void." *Am. Law Rev.*, 48:85–114, 225–273 (Jan.–March 1914).

HARRIS, LAWRENCE T. "Guardians of the Constitution." *Oregon Law Rev.*, 2:73–105 (Feb. 1923).

HAZELTINE, H. D. "Appeals from colonial courts to the King in Council." *Report* to Am. Hist. Assoc., 1894:299–350.

HIGGINS, H. B. "McCulloch v. Maryland in Australia." *Harv. Law Rev.* 18:559–571 (June 1905).

JIGGITS, LOUIS M. "The Supreme Court under fire." *Law Quart. Rev.,* 41:95–105 (Jan. 1925).

KALES, ALBERT M. "New methods in due-process cases." *Am. Pol. Sci. Rev.,* 12:241–250 (May 1918).
"The recall of judicial decisions." Ill. State Bar Assoc., *Proceedings,* 1912; 203.

LA FOLLETTE, ROBERT M. *Cong. Record,* 67 Cong., 2 sess., 62, no. 160: 9851–9856 and *Am. Federationist,* 29:469–486 (July 1922).

LA FOLLETTE PROPOSED AMENDMENT. Am. Bar Assoc., *Reports,* 1922, 47: 180–184.

LENROOT, IRVINE L. "Congress and the Constitution." *Cong. Record,* 67 Cong., 4 sess., 64, no. 67:3890–3893.

LEWIS, WILLIAM DRAPER. "A new method of constitutional amendment by popular vote." *The Annals,* 43:311–325 (Sept. 1912).

LONDON, MEYER. "Veto power of the Supreme Court." *Am. Federationist,* 30:224–231 (March 1923).

LONG, JOSEPH R. "Unconstitutional acts of Congress." *Virginia Law Rev.,* 1:417–444 (Feb. 1914).

LURTON, HORACE H. "A government of law or of men." *North Am. Rev.,* 193:9–25 (Jan 1911).

MAYNARD, FRED A. "Five to four decisions of the Supreme Court of the United States." *Central Law Jour.,* 89:206–212 (Sept. 1919). (Reprinted in *Am. Law Rev.,* 54:481–514 (July 1920).

McCLAIN, EMLIN. "Unwritten constitutions in the United States." *Harv. Law Rev.,* 15:531–540 (March 1902).

McDONOUGH, JAMES B. "The alleged usurpation of power by the federal courts." *Am. Law Rev.,* 46:45–59 (Jan.–Feb. 1912).

McLAUGHLIN, ANDREW C. "Marbury v. Madison again." Am. Bar. Assoc. *Jour.,* 14:156–159 (March 1928).

MEIGS, WILLIAM M. "The relation of the judiciary to the Constitution." *Am. Law Rev.,* 19:174–203 (March–April 1885).
"Some Recent Attacks on the American Doctrine of Judicial Power." *Am. Law Rev.,* 40:640–670 (Sept.–Oct. 1916).
"The American doctrine of judicial power and its early origin." *Am. Law Rev.,* 47:683–696 (Sept.–Oct. 1923).

MELVIN, FRANK E. "The Judicial bulwark of the Constitution." *Am. Pol. Sci. Rev.,* 8:167–203 (May 1914).

MILLER, DAVID HUNTER. ''Some early cases in the Supreme Court of the United States.'' *Virginia Law Rev.*, 8:108–120 (Dec. 1921).

MONROE, ALAN H. ''The Supreme Court and the constitution.'' *Am. Pol. Sci. Rev.*, 18:737–759 (Nov. 1924).

MOORE, B. F. ''Judicial veto and political democracy.'' *Am. Pol. Sci. Rev.*, 10:700–709 (Nov. 1916).

MOWRY, ENSMINGER. ''Political and party aspects of the national judiciary, 1789–1801.'' *Am. Hist. Mag.*, 3:83, 331, 471.

NORTON, THOMAS J. ''Supreme court's five to four decisions.'' Am. Bar. Assoc. *Jour.*, 9:417–420 (July 3, 1923).

''What damage have five to four decisions done?'' Am. Bar. Assoc. *Jour.*, 9:721–727 (Nov. 1923).

ORTON, JESSE F. ''Confusion of property with privilege: Dartmouth College case.'' *The Independent*, 67:392–397, 448–453 (Aug. 19 and 26, 1909).

OWEN, ROBERT L. ''Power of the Supreme Court.'' *Cong. Record*, 67 Cong., 4 sess., 10, no. 69:4027–4028.

''Withdrawing power from the federal courts to declare acts of Congress void.'' U. S. 64 Cong., 2 sess., Senate *Doc.* 737.

PILLSBURY, WARREN H. ''The power of the courts to declare laws unconstitutional.'' *Cal. Law Rev.*, 11:313–342 (July 1923).

PLUCKNETT, THEODORE F. J. ''Bonham's Case and Judicial Review.'' *Harv. Law Rev.*, 40:30–70 (Nov. 1926).

POPE, H. ''The fundamental law and the courts.'' *Harv. Law Rev.*, 27:45–67 (Nov. 1913).

POTTER, WILLIAM W. ''Judicial power in the United States.'' *Mich. Law Rev.*, 27:1–21; 167–190; 285–313 (Nov., Dec. 1928 and Jan. 1929).

POUND, ROSCOE. ''Liberty of contract.'' *Yale Law Jour.*, 18:454–487 (May 1909).

RALSTON, JACKSON H. ''Judicial control over legislatures as to constitutional questions.'' *Am. Law Rev.*, 54:1:38; 193–230 (Jan.–March 1920).

RICHTER, A. W. ''Legislative curb on the judiciary.'' *Jour. of Pol. Econ.* 21:281–295 (April 1913).

SARGENT, NOEL. ''American Judicial Veto.'' *Am. Law Rev.*, 51:663–710 (Sept.–Oct. 1917).

SCHLESINGER, ARTHUR MEIER. ''Colonial appeals to the Privy Council.'' *Pol. Sci. Quart.*, 28:279–297; 433–450 (June and Sept. 1912).

SCOTT, AUSTIN. ''Holmes v. Walton; the New Jersey precedent.'' *Am. Hist. Rev.*, 4:456–469 (April 1899).

SEVERANCE, C. A. ''Proposal to make Congress supreme.'' Am. Bar Assoc., *Jour.*, 8:459–464 (Aug. 1922).

SHERMAN, GORDON E. "The case of John Chandler v. The Secretary of War." *Yale Law Jour.* 14:431–451 (June 1905).

SMALLEY, HARRISON S. "Nullifying the law by judicial interpretation," *Atlantic Monthly* 107:452–464 (March 1911).

SNOW, ALPHEUS H. "The position of the judiciary in the United States." *The Annals*, 43:286–310 (Sept. 1912).

STINSON, J. WHITLA. "Marshall and the supremacy of the unwritten law." *Am. Law Rev.*, 58:856–871 (Nov.–Dec. 1924).

STONE, HARLAN F. Fifty years' work of the United States Supreme Court." Am. Bar Assoc., Jour., 14:428–436 (Aug.–Sept. 1928).

SUTHERLAND, WILLIAM A. "Politics and the Supreme Court." *Am. Law Rev.*, 48:390–402 (May–June 1914).

THAYER, JAMES B. The origin and scope of the American doctrine of constitutional law. *Harv. Law Rev.*, 7:129–156 (Oct. 1893).

TRICKETT, WILLIAM. "The great usurpation." *Am. Law Rev.*, 40:356–376 (May–June 1906).

"Judicial nullification of acts of Congress." *North Am. Rev.*, 185:848–856 (Aug. 1907).

"Judicial dispensation from Congressional statutes." *Am. Law Rev.*, 41:65–91 (Jan.–Feb. 1907).

TURNER, JESSE. "A phantom precedent." *Am. Law Rev.*, 48:321–344 (May 1914).

"Four fugitive cases from American constitutional law." *Am. Law Rev.*, 49:818–851 (Nov.–Dec. 1915).

UTTER, WILLIAM T. "Judicial review in early Ohio." *Mississippi Valley Hist. Rev.*, 14:3–38 (June 1927).

WANAMAKER, R. M. "The recall of judges." Ill. State Bar Assoc., *Proceedings*, 1912, 174.

WARREN, CHARLES. "Legislative and judicial attacks on the Supreme Court of the United States." *Am. Law Rev.*, 47:1–34; 161–189 (Jan.–Feb. and March–April 1913).

"The progressiveness of the United States Supreme Court." *Col. Law Rev.*, 13:290–313 (April 1913).

"Earliest cases of judicial review of state legislation by federal courts." *Yale Law Jour.*, 32:15–28 (Nov. 1922).

"New light on the history of the federal judiciary act of 1789." *Harv. Law Rev.*, 37:49–132 (Nov. 1923).

"The early history of the supreme court of the United States, in connection with modern attacks on the judiciary." *Mass. Law Quart.*, 8:1–23 (1923).

WATSON, DAVID K. "Power of the federal judiciary to declare legislation invalid which conflicts with the federal constitution." *Ohio Law Rep.*, 13:469–484 (Nov. 29, 1915).

WHEELER, EVERETT P. "American constitutional law as molded by Daniel Webster." New York State Bar Assoc., *Reports*, 27:170–202 (1904). "The new constitution of Ohio. Power of courts to review acts of legislatures." *Central Law Jour.*, 75:437–442 (Dec. 13, 1912).

WILSON, JOHN R. "The origin of the power of courts to declare legislative acts unconstitutional." Indiana State Bar Assoc., *Reports*, 1899: 12–62.

WOODWARD, JOHN. "The courts and the people." *Col. Law Rev.*, 7:559–572 (Dec. 1907).

II. SELECTED LIST OF ARTICLES AND TREATISES DEALING WITH REVIEW OF LEGISLATIVE ACTS BY THE COURTS IN FOREIGN COUNTRIES

ARGENTINE—

ARAYA, PERFECTO. *Comentario á la constitución de la nación argentina.* Buenos Aires, 1908–11. 2 vols.

BAS, ARTURO M. *El derecho federal argentino, nación y provincias con la síntesis de la doctrina de 1432 fallos de la suprema corte de justicia nacional, relativos a materias contenidas en las obras, y las decisiones parlamentarias aplicables á las mismas.* Buenos Aires, 1927. 2 vols.

GIL, ANTONIO LUIS. *Recursos de inconstitucionalidad e inaplicabilidad de ley.* Thesis, Buenos Aires, 1878.

GONZÁLEZ CALDERÓN, JUAN A. *El poder de declarar la inconstitucionalidad de las leyes.* Buenos Aires, 1914. *Derechio constitucional argentino.* Buenos Aires, 1923. 3 vols.

IRIGOYEN, BERNARDO DE. *Justicia nacional: apunte sobre la jurisdicción de la corte suprema.* Buenos Aires, 1903.

JOSÉ, MATIENZO NICOLÁS. *Cuestiones de derecho público Argentino.* Buenos Aires, 1924. 2 vols.

ZAVALIA, CLODOMIRO. *Jurisprudencia de la Constitución Argentina.* Buenos Aires, 1924. 2 vols. *Historia de la Corte Suprema de Justicia de la República argentina; en Relación con su modelo americano.* Buenos Aires, 1920.

AUSTRIA—

ADAMOVICH, LUDWIG. *Die Prüfung der Gesetze und Verordnungen durch den österreichischen Verfassungsgerichtshof.* Leipzig, 1923.

ADLER, FRANZ. "Verfassung und Richteramt." *Zeitschrift für Öffentliche Recht*, 10:103–122 (1930).

EISENMANN, CHARLES. *La justice constitutionnelle et la Haute Cour constitutionnelle d'Autriche.* Paris, 1928.

KELSEN, HANS. ''La garantie juridictionnelle de la Constitution (Justice constitutionnelle).'' *Revue du Droit Public*, 45:197–257 (April, May, June, 1928).

''La garantie juridictionnelle de la Constitution: rapport de M. Kelsen,'' *Annuaire de L'Institut International de Droit Public*, 1929:52–143.

LESTRADE, COMBES DE. ''Le tribunal d'Empire en Autriche.'' *Revue Politique et Parlementaire*, 1903:481–501.

MÉTALL, M. ''Die gerichtliche Prüfung von Staatsverträgen nach der österreichischen Bundesverfassung,'' Zeitschrift für Öffentliche Recht, 7:106 (1927).

BELGIUM—

BOURQUIN, M. La protection des droits individuels contre abus de pouvoir de l'autorité administrative en Belgique.

ERRERA, P. ''Das Staatsrecht des Königreichs Belgien.'' *Öffentliches Recht der Gegenwart*, 12:137. Tübingen, 1909.

FEIDER, CHARLES. ''Etude sur l'application des lois inconstitutionnelles.'' *Bulletin de l'Académie royale des sciences, des lettres et des beaux arts de Bruxelles*, 1re série, tome XVII, 2e partie 435; tome XVIII, 1re partie, 336.

PARISEL, R. *Les lois constitutionnelles.* Bruxelles, 1907.

VERHAEGEN, EUGENE. *Des lois inconstitutionnelles.* Bruxelles, 1850.

BOLIVIA—

CARRASCO, JOSÉ. *Estudios constitucionales.* La Paz, 1920. 4 vols.

LÓPEZ, MANUEL ORDÓÑEZ. *Constitución política de la república de Bolivia: leyes y disposiciones más usuales.* La Paz, 1917.

PAZ, LUIS. *Constitución política de la república de Bolivia: su texto, su historia y su comentario.* Sucre, 1912.

BRAZIL—

BARBALHO, JOÃO. *Constituição federal brasileiro: Commentarios.* Rio de Janeiro, 1902; ed. 2, 1924.

BARBOSA, RUY. *Os actos inconstituçiõnães do congresso e do executivo ante a justiça federal.* Rio de Janeiro, 1893.

JAMES, HERMAN G. *The Constitutional System of Brazil.* Washington, 1923.

LESSA, PEDRO. *Direito constituçional brasileiro: do poder judiciario.* Rio de Janeiro, 1915.

NUNES, CASTRO. *As Constituições Estaduaes do Brasil.* Rio de Janeiro, 1922. 2 vols.

Revista de direito público e de administração federal, estadual e municipal. Rio de Janeiro, 1921 to date.

COLOMBIA—

GARAVITO, A. FERNANDO. *Jurisprudencia de la Corte Suprema de Justicia.* Bogotá, 1915–1919. 2 vols.

COSTA RICA—

BÉECHE, OCTAVIO. *Estudios de derecho constitucional.* San José, 1910.

CUBA—

BETANCOURT, ANGEL C. *Recurso de inconstitucionalidad.* Havana, 1915.

CÁRDENAS Y ECHARTE, RAÚL DE. *El recurso de inconstitucionalidad.* Havana, 1912.

CZECHOSLOVAKIA—

FRANTISEK, WEYR. "Das Verfassungsrecht der tschechoslowakischen Republik." *Zeitschrift für öffentliches Recht,* vol. 2 (Wien, 1921).

"Le tribunal constitutionnel de la republique tchécoslovaque." *Bulletin de droit tchécoslovaque,* 1:129–137 (Prague, 1925–26).

FRANCE—

ANGLEYS, ALBERT. *Des garanties contre l'arbitraire du pouvoir législatif par l'intervention de l'autorité judiciare.* Thesis, Grenoble, 1924.

BARTHÉLEMY, JOSEPH. *Traité élémentaire de droit constitutionnel.* Paris, 1926.

BARTHÉLEMY, JOSEPH. "La distinction des lois constitutionnelles et des lois ordinaires sous la monarchie de Juillet—1830–1848." *Revue du Droit Public,* 26:5 (1909).

"De l'interprétation des lois par le législateur." *Revue du Droit Public,* 25:456 (1908).

BENOIST, CHARLES. "Exposé des motifs d'une proposition de loi tendant à instituer une Cour Supreme." *Doc. Par. Ch. des Deputés,* 1903:99.

BERTHÉLEMY, H. "Les lois inconstitutionnelles devant les juges." *Revue Politique et Parlementaire,* 133:183 (Nov. 1927).

"Le contrôle judiciare de la constitutionalité des lois." *Bulletin de l'Academie des sciences morales et politiques,* 64 (July–Aug. 1926).

BLONDEL, ANDRÉ. *Le contrôle juridictionnelle de la constitutionnalité des lois.* Paris, 1928.

CLAPPIER, V. "Les lois inconstitutionnelles et le pouvoir judiciare." *Gazette des tribunaux*, 18–19 (December 1902).

DESFOUGÈRES, HENRI. *Le contrôle judiciare de la constitutionnalité des lois.* Thesis, Paris, 1913.

DUGUIT, LÉON. *Traité de droit constitutionnel*, ed. 2. Paris, 1921–25. 5 vols.

GAJAC, JEAN. *De la distinction des lois constitutionnelles et des lois ordinaires.* Thesis, Bordeaux, 1903.

HAURIOU, MAURICE. *Précis de droit constitutionnel*, ed. 2. Paris, 1929.

JÈZE, GASTON. "Notions sur le contrôle des assemblées delibérantes." *Revue générale d'administration* (1895) 53:401; and 54 *ibid.*; 31 and 154.

"Le contrôle juridictionnelle des lois." *Revue du Droit Public*, 41:409 (1924).

"Notes de jurisprudence." *Revue du Droit Public*, 21:111 (1904).

"Pouvoir et devoir des tribunaux en général, et des tribunaux roumains en particulier de vérifier la constitutionnalité des lois à l'occasion des procès portés devant eux." *Revue du Droit Public*, 29:138 (1912).

LAMBERT, EDOUARD. *Le gouvernement des juges et la lutte contre la législation sociale aux États-Unis.* Paris, 1921.

LARNAUDE, F. "Étude sur les garanties judiciares qui existent dans certain pays, au profit des particuliers, contre les actes du pouvoir législatif." *Bulletin de la Société de législation comparée*, 1902:175 and 240.

"L'inconstitutionnalité des lois et le droit public français." *Revue Politique et Parlementaire*, 126:181 (Jan.–Mar. 1926).

LE BLANC, JACQUES. *Du pouvoir des tribunaux d'apprécier, en France, la constitutionnalité des lois.* Thesis, Paris, 1924.

LE BRUN, A. *L'inconstitutionalité des lois aux États-Unis.* Thesis, Paris, 1899.

LE FUR, LOUIS. "Le gouvernement des juges." *Revue du Droit Public*, 39:306 (April–June 1922).

LEMAIRE, ANDRÉ. *Les lois fondamentales de la monarchie française.* Paris, 1907.

LINAIS, RENÉ. *Le pouvoir judiciare consideré dans ses rapports avec les autres pouvoirs.* Thesis, Paris, 1917.

RIVES, A. *L'exception d'illegalité.* Paris, 1908.

SANTONI, AUGUSTE. *De la distinction des lois constitutionnelles et des lois ordinaires.* Thesis, Toulouse, 1913.

SIGNOREL, JEAN. "Du contrôle judiciare des actes du pouvoir législatif." *Revue Politique et Parlementaire*, 40:77 and 519 (1904).

WOHLGEMUTH, M. *Des droits individuel et le leur garantie judiciare.* Paris, 1906.

GERMANY—

ADAMOVICH, LUDWIG. *Die Prüfung der Gesetze und Verordnungen durch den österreichischen Verfassungsgerichtshof.* Leipzig, 1923.

BISCHOF, H. "Verfassung, Gesetz, Verordnung und richterliches Prüfungsrecht der Verfassungsmässigkeit landesherrlicher Gesetze und Verordnungen." *Zeitschrift für Civilrecht und Prosess*, n.s. 16:235 and 385 (Giessen, 1859).

BLACHLY, F. F., and OATMAN, MIRIAM E. "Judicial review of legislative acts in Germany." *Am. Pol. Sci. Rev.*, 21:113 (Feb. 1927).

FRIEDRICH, CARL JOACHIM. "The issue of judicial review in Germany." *Pol. Sci. Quart.*, 43:188 (June 1928).

GRAU, RICHARD. "Zum Gesetzentwurf über die Prüfung der Verfassungsmässigkeit von Reichsgesetzen und Reichsverordnungen." *Archiv des öffentlichen Rechts*, n.s., 11:287.

MATTERN, JOHANNES *Principles of the constitutional jurisprudence of the German National Republic.* Baltimore, 1928.

MARX, MORSTEIN. *Variationen über die richterliche Zuständigkeit zur Prüfung der Rechtmässigkeit des Gesetzes.* 1927.

For a list of important books and articles relating to judicial review in Germany, see Marx, *op. cit.*, 65 ff.

SCHACK. *Die Prüfung der Rechtmässigkeit von Gesetze und Verordnungen.* Berlin, 1918.

THEISEN. "Verfassung und Richter." *Archiv des öffentlichen Rechts*, n.s., 8:257 (1925).

THOMA, RICHARD. "Das richterliche Prüfungsrecht." *Archiv des öffentlichen Rechts*, 43:267 (1922).

HAITI—

DORSAINVIL, J. B. *Éléments de droit constitutionnel.* Paris, 1912.

JUSTIN, JOSEPH. *De l'organisation judiciaire en Haiti.* Havre, 1910.

ITALY—

HUGO, GIO BATTISTA. *Sulle leggi inconstituzionali.* Macerata, 1879.

ORLANDO, V. E. *Principii di diritto costituzionale* (ed. 4). Firenze, 1912.

MEXICO—

BERGUIDO, CARLOS, JR. "The Mexican Petroleum Company's Amparo Case." *Univ. of Penn. Law Rev.*, 76:287 (Jan. 1928).

MINCHEN, MAURICE. "The writ of Amparo in Mexican Law." *Mexican American*, 1:23 (Mexico, June 14, 1924).

Montiel y Duarte, Isidro. *Estudio sobre garantías individuales.* Mexico, 1873.

Moreno, S. *Tratado del juicio de amparo. Conforme a las sentencias de los tribunales federales.* Mexico, 1902.

Schuster, Edward. ''The Texas Company's Amparo Case.'' Am. Bar Assoc. Jour., 7:583–89 (Nov. 1921).

Vallarta, Ignacio L. *El juicio de amparo y el writ of habeas corpus; ensayo crítico — comparativo sobre esos recursos constitucionales.* Mexico, 1881.
Cuestiones constitucionales. 1879. 4 vols.

Vega, Fernando. *La nueva ley de amparo de garantías individuales: orgánica de los arts. 101 y 102 de la constitución.* San José, Mexico, 1883.

NORWAY—

Morgenstierne. ''Das Staatsrecht des Königreichs Norwegen.'' *Öffentliches Recht der Gegenwart* (1911):42, 73.

Lie, Mikael H. *Domstolene og Grunloven.* Oslo, 1923.

PARAGUAY—

Paiva, Félix. *Estudio de derecho constitucional. La independencia del poder judicial.* Asunción, 1915.

PORTUGAL—

Dos Reis, Alberto. *Organizacão judiciaria.* 1905.

Magalhães Collaço, João Maria Tello de. *Ensaio sobre a inconstitucionalidade das leis no direito português.* Coimbra, 1915.

Many, I. *Etude critique sur la constitution de la république portugaise.* Thesis, Paris, 1915.

Marnoco e Souza, José Ferriera. *Constituicão politica da republica portuguêsa.* Coimbra, 1913.

ROUMANIA—

''L'Inconstitutionalité des lois en Roumanie.'' *Revue du Droit Public,* 29:138 (1912).

RUSSIA or U. R. S. S.—

Diablo, V. ''Le contrôle de constitutionnalité de lois a l'étranger et en U. R. S. S. *Sovietskoïe Pravo,* Le droit sovietique, No. 3. Moscow, 1925.

Mirkine-Guetzévitch, A. ''Le contrôle de constitutionnalité des lois soviétiques.'' *Revue du Droit Public,* 42:682–694 (1925).

SWITZERLAND—

BEGUE, GEORGES. *Étude sur le tribunal federal suisse et specialment sur le recours pour violation de droits individuels.* Paris, 1903.

BICKEL. *Kantonales Verfassungsrecht in den Entscheidungen des Schweizerischen Bundesgerichtes.* Thesis, Zurich, 1900.

DUBS, JACOB. *Das öffentliche Recht der schweizerischen Eidgenossenschaft.* Zurich, 1878.

SCHOLLENBERGER. *Kommentar zur Bundesverfassung der schweizerischen Eidgenossenschaft.* Berlin, 1905.

SOLYOM, GEORGES. *La juridiction constitutionnelle aux États-Unis et en Suisse.* Genève, 1923.

WERNER, G. *Le contrôle judiciare à Genève.* Geneva, 1917.

URUGUAY—

GARCÍA Y SANTOS, MANUEL. *Breves consideraciones relativas a los poderes legislativo, ejecutivo y judicial.* Thesis, Montevideo, 1884.

JIMÉNEZ DE ARECHAGA, JUSTINO E. *Sobre inaplicabilidad des leyes inconstitucionales.* Extracto de la *Revista de Derecho y Ciencias Sociales.* Montevideo, 1915.

TABLE OF CASES*

---

* For citation of cases relating to judicial review of legislation in foreign countries see footnotes for each country in Appendix II.

INDEX

Abbott, E. V., cited, 510 n., 511 n.

Adair v. United States, 440, 441, 555.

Adams, Brooks, cited, 520 n.

Adams, G. B., cited, 33 n.

Adams, Henry, cited, 243 n., 244 n., 245 n., 249 n., 250 n.

Adams, John, *Works*, cited, 60 n., 61 n., 213 n., 224 n.; on the American governmental system of checks and balances, 212, 213.

Adams, John Quincy, *Memoirs*, cited, 243 n.

Adams, Samuel, *Works*, cited, 39 n., 61 n., 213 n.; favored review of legislation by courts, 140.

Addams, Jane, dissatisfaction with the judiciary, 449.

Adkins v. Children's Hospital, 563.

Agreement of the People, Cromwell's, 64, 65.

Alexander, L. H., cited, 361 n.

Alicia, the, 545.

Allen, Justice, quoted, 520 n.

Amendment of constitutions, change in process of, advocated by Progressive party, 485, 486.

American Federation of Labor, resolutions on judicial supremacy, 451, 452.

Ames, H. V., cited, 244 n., 289 n., 293 n., 306 n., 308 n., 321 n., 362 n., 469 n.

Anderson, F. M., cited, 191 n., 237 n., 240 n.

Appeals, determination of, by Privy Council, during colonial period in America, 50–59; committee on, in Congress, 124.

Argentine, judicial review in, 7 n., 573–578.

Arizona, President Taft quoted on recall section of constitution of, 498.

Austin v. Trustees of the University of Pennsylvania, 158.

Australia, judicial review in, 7 n., 578–590.

Austria, judicial review in, 8 n., 591–594.

Bailey v. Drexel Furniture Co., 561, 562.

Bakeshop law, New York, óverturned by Supreme Court, 439, 440.

Baldwin v. Franks, 550.

Baldwin v. Missouri, 448.

Baldwin, Simeon E., quoted, 260 n.

Bancroft, George, cited, 120 n.

Banning, Justice, opinion, in case of Padelford v. Savannah, 343, 344.

Barbalho, João, cited, 18 n.

Courtois du Manoir, Léon de, cited, 2 n.

Courts, superiority of, not implied in power to declare laws invalid, 139, 229; organization of federal, by judiciary acts of 1789, 144–147; Coke's theory of supremacy of common law, 222–224; attitude of state courts on judicial review, 340–342; decisions by, unfavorable to laborers, 452–455; protection of property rights by, 464–466; refusal to accept jurisdiction conferred by Congress, 567. (*See also* Judicial Supremacy.)

Coxe, Brinton, cited, 88 n., 98 n., 100 n., 105 n., 112 n., 225 n.

Coyle v. Smith, 557.

Cromwell, Oliver, attempt to establish a fundamental law in England, 64, 65.

Cruet, Jean, cited, 531 n.

Cuba, judicial review in, 8 n., 618, 619.

Culp, Mannie S., cited, 470 n., 490 n.

Cummings v. Missouri, 382–384.

Cushing, Justice, opinion in Hayburn's case, 173.

Cushman, Robert E., cited, 423 n.

Czechoslovakia, judicial review in, 8 n., 619, 620.

Dartmouth College case, 311–314.

Dash v. Van Kleeck, opinion of Justice Kent in, 404, 405.

Davie, William R., favored review of legislation by judges, 137, 140.

Davis, Andrew McFarland, cited, 56 n.

Davis, Horace A., cited, 28 n., 129 n., 132 n., 133 n., 135 n., 202 n., 462 n., 488 n., 527 n.

Dawson, Henry B., cited, 99 n., 100 n., 101 n., 102 n., 103 n., 104 n.

Denmark, judicial review in, 620, 621.

Dicey, A. V., cited, 11 n., 26 n., 496 n., 505 n., 506 n., 526 n.; on extent of judge-made law in England, 25, 26; praise of American system of judicial supremacy by, 496; on characteristics of judicial legislation, 505, 506; opinion that American courts do not control legislatures, 526, 527.

Dickerson, Oliver M., cited, 51 n.

Dickinson, John, disapproval of power of judiciary to invalidate a law, 131; opinion favorable to judicial review, 140.

Dodd, Wm. E., cited, 300 n., 301 n., 305 n., 306 n., 350 n., 351 n.

Dodd, W. F., cited, 28 n., 80 n., 149 n., 207 n., 241 n., 468 n., 488 n., 504 n.

Dominican Republic, judicial review in, 621 n.

Dos Passos, John R., cited, 445 n.

Douglas, Stephen A., debates between Lincoln and, 370–375.

Dred Scott decision, 369, 543.

AMERICAN DOCTRINE OF JUDICIAL SUPREMACY

McMaster, J. B., cited, 61 n., 105 n., 109 n., 111 n., 136 n., 142 n., 290 n.

McPherson, Edward, cited, 375 n., 376 n., 377 n.

McRee, G. J., cited, 115 n., 116 n., 117 n., 118 n., 119 n., 120 n., 214 n.

Madison, James, on council of revision, 130, 131; judicial review of legislation favored by, in Philadelphia convention, 134; Virginia Resolutions drawn up by, 190; refusal to interfere in case of Sloop Active, 291; on danger of oppression by majority rule, 214, 215; discussion of opinions of, relative to federal judiciary, 233–239; and Republican doctrines on judicial review, 236–238; on American creative spirit, 481.

Maddox, W. Rolland, cited, 474 n.

Maine, Sir Henry, cited, 24 n.; on legal fictions, 516–519.

Marbury v. Madison, 122, 163, 193–203, 542, 543; opinion of Chief Justice Marshall in, 122, 123, 140, 195–199; political aspects of Marshall's opinion in, 199–203.

Marshall, John, presentation of theory of a written constitution as the paramount law by, 193–203; judicial review of legislation favored by, 136; view of, that court can declare act void only in clear case, 228; opinion in case of Sloop Active, 290, 291; opinion in case of Cohens v. Virginia, 298–300; opinion rendered by, in McCulloch v. Maryland, 318–320; opinions rendered by, 353–357; on limitations of judicial supremacy, 228, 229; dissent in case of Ogden v. Saunders, 357; attacks of Judge Roane and Jefferson on, and replies of, 301, 306; modification of principles followed by, 335, 336; modification of doctrines of, by Chief Justice Taney, 337–341.

Martin, Luther, judicial review of legislation, favored by, 136.

Martin v. Hunter's Lessee, 294–297.

Mason, George, alarm of over lack of limitations to federal judicial power, in Constitution, 141.

Mason, Jeremiah, cited, 150 n.

Massachusetts, early constitutional case in, 120, 121.

Matter of Heff, 553, 554.

Mayflower Compact, as basis for law of colony, 65.

Meader, Lewis H., cited, 72 n., 74 n., 77 n., 79 n., 80 n., 81 n.

Meigs, W. M., cited, 58 n., 88 n., 132 n., 150 n.

Melvin, Frank E., on views of members of Philadelphia convention relating to judicial review, 133, 134.

Mercer, C. F., opponent of judicial power of invalidating laws, in Philadelphia convention, 131.

Merriam, Charles E., cited, 208 n.

Merryman, John, case of, 375–378.

Mexico, judicial review in, 8 n., 631–636.

Miller, David Hunter, cited, 178 n.

Miller, Justice, opinion on implied limitations, 414, 415.